Business Valuation

Howard E. Johnson

MBA, FCA, FCMA, CBV, CPA, CFA, ASA, CF, C.Dir.

Foreword by Ian R. Campbell, FCA, FCBV

Disclaimer

The contents of this book are for information and general guidance only. Because the specific facts relating to each company, valuation engagement and open market transaction are unique, and because income tax, legal and business situations can change, professional advice should be sought in each case.

Library and Archives Canada Cataloguing in Publication

Johnson, Howard E.[date]

      Business valuation / Howard E. Johnson.

Previously published under title: The valuation of business interests / Ian R. Campbell, Howard E. Johnson.

Includes bibliographical references and index.

Issued also in electronic format.

ISBN 978-1-55385-658-0

      1. Business enterprises--Valuation. I. Canadian Institute of Chartered Accountants II. Title.

HG4028.V3J643 2012   658.15   C2012-901398-6

© 2012
Howard E. Johnson,

Veracap Corporate Finance Limited
70 University Avenue, Suite 320
Toronto, ON
M5J 2M4
www.cvpl.com
www.veracap.com

Dedication

To my loving wife, Julie, and our four wonderful children — Veronica, Michael, Laura and Russell

Table of Contents

*Chapter 1
Valuation Terms and Principles

Chapter 2
Business and Financial Analysis

Chapter 3
Asset Valuation Methodologies 85

Chapter 4
Valuation Based on Multiples

*Chapter 5
The Capitalized Cash Flow Methodology 183

✳ Chapter 6
The Discounted Cash Flow Methodology

❋ Chapter 7
Rates of Return 277

Chapter 8
Controlling and Minority Interests

Chapter 9
Special Topics

Chapter 10
Notional Market Valuations 429

Chapter 11
Open Market Transactions 463

Foreword

Ian R. Campbell, FCA, FCBV

Business valuation as a separately recognized profession has come a very long way in Canada since The Canadian Institute of Chartered Business Valuators was incorporated in 1970. Co-founder George Ovens was then the only person in the country who held himself out to be an independent business valuation advisor. Today the Institute has more than 1,400 members and business valuation is a very broad discipline involving almost everyone with a connection to the company owners. In the public company sector, directors and executives together with their legal, accounting, banking and M&A advisors as well as investors all make their contribution; among private companies a similar range of owners, directors and their advisors play an important role. Professional business valuators, however, do most of their work for private companies, especially in the areas of litigation, damage claims, tax planning and family succession.

It is because so many people are involved in the business valuation process that wider dissemination of the fundamentals is important. *Business Valuation* with Howard Johnson's clear exposition of the technical foundation — the principles, concepts, and methodologies that underlie all business valuation exercises — provides that knowledge. Nevertheless, mastery of this technical foundation, essential as it is, is only the beginning of what anyone involved in a business valuation today needs to know to reach meaningful valuation conclusions.

The contemporary business valuator must, of course, be firmly grounded in the knowledge contained in this book. The field of study of a truly professional practitioner needs to extend far beyond what is found on these pages, however, in order for the practitioner to understand and interpret the factors that generate the numbers that go into the projections and the formulas. First, since businesses operate in the global marketplace, the valuator has to have an informed view of global macroeconomic trends. The valuator must also understand the specific economic outlook of the country, province and region in which the business operates as well as the industry operating environment and cost structures. After this far-ranging analysis, the business valuator's experience, good judgment and common sense will dictate the reliability of the valuation opinion.

In other words, business valuation is a science-based art. *Business Valuation* instructs in the "science"; it's up to you, the reader, to acquire the "art" by broadening your knowledge and improving your judgment.

Of special importance to the "art" part of business valuation is the fact that the world has changed remarkably in the recent past and continues to change apace. Important among these changes are:

- the continued development of the Internet, which now provides humanity with steadily growing volumes of instantly available information, and social and business connectivity are having, in some respects, a more profound effect on the world than the Industrial Revolution of the 18th century;

- cellular communication devices that now enable instantaneous mobile connectivity among the world's population with both good and bad outcomes;

- post-2000 growth in China and other developing countries. This short period has seen a substantial shift in manufacturing jobs away from the developed countries and ongoing change in the balance of world economic power;

- economic change that has brought escalating hardship for many in some of the developed countries — particularly after 2007 and especially in America and Europe;

- unprecedented developed-country debt burdens. The disparity between the haves and have-nots in many of these countries is much wider in 2012 than in 2000; and

- economic globalization that has overtaken the developed countries in ways that, in retrospect, ought to have been predictable, but in fact were predicted by few.

Globalization and social change continue to evolve at what seems to be an ever-increasing pace. The resultant fluid and uncertain business environment will continue for many years to come and may bring sudden, often unpredictable, changes that will have to be recognized and taken into consideration in future business valuations through continuous monitoring and assessment of both business-specific prospects and risk in the business environment prevailing at the time of the valuation.

As a result, those who render business valuation opinions today and those who rely on them ought to consider carefully:

- that such opinions are based on a combination of theory, fact, and subjectivity and are likely to be even more subjective and less certain than they have been in the past; and

- whether the valuator has the macroeconomic, industry- and sector-specific operating knowledge to render meaningful opinions.

"Best-of-breed" business valuators will:

- understand and be able to apply and explain the technicalities of business valuation set out in this book;

- monitor continuously the macroeconomic background of all business activity;

- understand the subject business's industry and have prior experience, or access to prior experience, in the sector in which the business operates;

- provide and be seen to provide independent and objective opinions.

Howard Johnson, who understands and works every day to satisfy the foregoing criteria, joined me at Toronto-based Campbell Valuation Partners Limited in 1996. By then Howard had several years' experience as a financial executive in both a multi-national and small private company. In the past 16 years he has:

- added more professional designations to his office wall than anyone else I know;

- given hundreds of valuation opinions spread over a wide range of industries;

- negotiated a large number of corporate sales on behalf of both vendors and purchasers;

- been recognized as an expert in business valuation by Canadian courts;

- written five books on business valuation, corporate mergers and acquisitions, and related subjects; and

- been a frequent speaker on both business valuation and corporate mergers and acquisitions.

This book conveys the best of Howard's intellect and experience. It will prove to be a valuable addition to your professional library. Read it carefully and retain it as a reference.

Ian R. Campbell
Toronto, Canada
April, 2012

Ian R. Campbell assisted in the creation in 1970 of The Canadian Institute of Chartered Business Valuators. The Institute awards an annual research grant in his name.

Preface

My first exposure to the field of business valuation was in the Chartered Accountancy program at McGill University in the late 1980s. I was immediately intrigued by the way it required me to take a holistic view of a business (not just the accounting side), conduct insightful analysis and apply sound judgment to formulate a credible valuation conclusion. I also enjoyed the fact that every business valuation exercise was unique and gave me an opportunity to continually learn new things that challenged my traditional thinking.

There have been many developments that have had an impact on the field of business valuation over the years, such as the increased amounts of information now available through the Internet, globalization and the speed at which technology is changing. There have also been several events that have temporarily distorted business values, such as the dot.com boom in the late 1990s and the credit crisis that came to a head in 2008. However, these developments and events have not shifted the foundations on which the economic value of a business is ultimately established, which are a combination of its future cash flow expectations and risk profile.

That is why I wrote this book: to reinforce in relatively straightforward terms the foundations of business valuation that I believe will remain the core of this important business discipline over the long term. While every valuation engagement presents a unique set of facts and circumstances, there is no substitute for the application of sound judgment and insightful analysis within a well-established framework of principles and practices. Constant attention to these principles and practices has served me well in my career, both when giving expert evidence on complex valuation matters before the courts and when negotiating the purchase or sale of a business in Canada or abroad.

Business valuation theory and the role of the business valuator have become increasingly recognized both before the courts and within the corporate community. I attribute this in large part to the efforts of the Canadian Institute of Chartered Business Valuators (CICBV), which has contributed to the development of well-founded valuation theory and better practice, created programs to provide a recognized level of professional certification and requires certified practitioners to adhere to the highest ethical standards. I also believe the demand for business valuation expertise will continue to grow, given current trends involving shareholder rights, the increasing complexity of income tax legislation and the demand from business owners, executives and boards of directors for greater diligence in corporate finance activities.

This book is divided into 11 chapters which cover both the basics of business valuation and several advanced topics:

- Chapter 1 defines common business valuation terms, including fair market value and fair value. It also sets out the underlying principles of business valuation that should be adhered to in any notional market valuation or open market transaction exercise;

- Chapter 2 covers business analysis, setting out the information normally gathered and the analysis undertaken in a business valuation engagement;

- Chapter 3 covers asset-based valuation methodologies, including the liquidation approach, used for businesses that are not a going concern. It also covers the adjusted net book value methodology, which is sometimes adopted as a test of valuation conclusions for going-concern entities and to calculate the intangible value implied by a given valuation conclusion;

- Chapter 4 sets out valuation approaches based on multiples, including the multiple of EBITDA methodology and its derivatives;

- Chapter 5 contains the capitalized cash flow methodology commonly adopted in the valuation of established businesses with relatively stable cash flows;

- Chapter 6 sets out the discounted cash flow methodology, the preferred valuation methodology where meaningful forecasts are available;

- Chapter 7 describes how rates of return, including discount rates and capitalization rates, are developed, and the related topic of capital structure;

- Chapter 8 deals with minority interests and the factors that should be considered when developing minority discounts;

- Chapter 9 includes a range a special topics, including intangible asset valuation, royalty rates, selected income tax issues and other topics that often arise in the context of valuation;

- Chapter 10 addresses common valuation engagements in a notional market context, including shareholder transactions, tax-driven valuations, matrimonial disputes, employee share ownership plans (ESOPs), purchase price allocation and fairness opinions; and

- Chapter 11 addresses business valuation in the context of an open market transaction, including the quantification of synergies and transaction structuring.

The principles and practices of business valuation as set out in this book are designed for a wide audience including: students pursuing the Chartered Business Valuator (CBV) designation; accountants, financial planners and other professionals who provide advice to their owner-managed business clients; lawyers with clients engaged in shareholder disputes, matrimonial issues, tax disputes or corporate restructuring; and business owners, executives and boards of directors who want to understand valuation in the context of performance measurement, acquisitions, divestitures, financing and other initiatives.

Whatever the reason for the valuation, I believe the principles, approaches and methodologies set out in this book will help the reader in formulating a credible and meaningful value conclusion.

Howard E. Johnson
April, 2012

About the Author

Howard E. Johnson, MBA, FCA, FCMA, CBV, CPA, CFA, ASA, CF, C.DIR.

Howard is a Managing Director at Campbell Valuation Partners Limited (CVPL) in Toronto (www.cvpl.com). Founded in 1976, CVPL is Canada's longest-established independent firm specializing in business valuation, damages quantification and related matters. Howard is also a Managing Director of CVPL's affiliate, Veracap Corporate Finance Limited (www.veracap.com), a member firm of M&A International, the world's leading affiliation of M&A advisors.

Howard has rendered valuation advice and opinions in hundreds of engagements for mid-size and large public and privately held companies, as well as government agencies and other organizations in the context of shareholder disputes, shareholder dissent and oppression remedies, income tax restructuring, tax litigation, employee share ownership plans, financial reporting, fairness opinions and other purposes. He also advises business owners and executives on acquisitions, divestitures, private equity financing and strategic value initiatives.

Howard is the author of *Building Value in Your Company* (Canadian Institute of Chartered Accountants, 2011) and *The Acquisition Value Cycle* (Carswell, 2009), editor of *Corporate Finance for Canadian Executives* (Carswell, 2007), author of *Selling Your Private Company* (Canadian Institute of Chartered Accountants, 2005), co-author of *Business Valuation* (Canadian Institute of Chartered Accountants, 2001) and a contributing editor to *Canada Valuation Service* (Carswell, periodical). He is a frequent speaker at conferences on the subjects of acquisitions, divestitures and shareholder value. In addition, Howard has served on the board of directors of public and private companies, and frequently acts as an expert witness on complex valuation matters before the courts.

Howard holds a Bachelor of Commerce degree from Concordia University (Governor General's Award, 1988), a Graduate Diploma in Public Accountancy from McGill University (Kenneth F. Byrd Prize, 1989) and a master's degree in Business Administration from McMaster University (D.M. Heddon Gold Medal, 1992). He is a Fellow of the Institute of Chartered Accountants of Ontario, a Fellow of the Society of Management Accountants of Canada and holds the designations of Chartered Accountant (Corporate Finance specialization), Certified Management Accountant, Chartered Business Valuator, Certified Public Accountant, Accredited Senior Appraiser and Chartered Director.

Howard is an avid hockey player. He currently resides in Oakville, Ontario with his wife Julie, and their four children, Veronica, Michael, Laura and Russell.

Acknowledgements

This book would not have been possible without the support of several individuals who generously provided their time and expertise, including:

- Ian R. Campbell, founder of Campbell Valuation Partners and a founding member of The Canadian Institute of Chartered Business Valuators;

- Robert H. Boulton, Director, Education and Standards at The Canadian Institute of Chartered Business Valuators;

- Jane Southren and David R. Street, Partners at Lerners, LLP in Toronto for their input on shareholder rights and remedies in Ontario, and other legal matters;

- Adrienne Woodyard, Associate Counsel at Davis, LLP in Toronto for her input on income tax matters;

- Parveen Karsan, a lawyer at Koffman Kalef, LLP in Vancouver for her input on shareholder rights and remedies in B.C.;

- Jean Lortie, Partner at McCarthy Tétrault, LLP in Montreal for his input on shareholder rights and remedies in Quebec;

- lawyers from McInnes Cooper for their input on shareholder rights and remedies in Atlantic Canada;

- Carol Jamieson, a sole legal practitioner in Lindsay, Ontario, for her input on family law matters; and

- Dennis Leung, Senior Director at Campbell Valuation Partners Limited in Toronto.

Also thanks to Sara Pender and Elvira Rago for their help with the charts and exhibits in this book.

Finally, I want to thank my editor, Douglas Adamson, Ph.D., for his sense of style and many helpful suggestions.

Glossary of
Defined Terms

Adjusted net book value

The amount by which the fair market value of the tangible assets of a business, determined on the basis of their value in continued use, exceeds the fair market value of the liabilities of the business.

Adjusted cost base

An income tax term relating to capital property, meaning the base amount from which capital gains and losses are measured. See paragraph 54(a) of the *Income Tax Act*.

Amalgamation

The joining or merging of two or more previously separate corporate entities.

Amortization

The systematic assignment of the cost of intangible assets to expense.

Appraisal

The act or process of determining the value of something. See also **Valuation**.

Appraisal remedy

See **Dissent right**.

Asset transaction

The acquisition of a business entity following the direct purchase of its tangible assets and intangible operating assets. The liabilities of the acquired business are often assumed as satisfaction of a portion of the transaction price. Contrast with **Share transaction**.

Associated corporations

Under the *Income Tax Act* two or more corporations are associated if they are owned or controlled by the same individual or group of individuals. See subsection 256 (1) of the *Act*.

Benchmark analysis

The comparison of an indicated performance measure to an expected standard or average measure.

Blockage discount

The decrease in market price resulting from the imbalance of supply and demand that occurs when market supply is increased as a result of unusual market activity. In the context of the public stock markets, the decrease in stock market trading price created by the forces of supply and demand when a block of shares larger than normal trading lots is exposed for sale at one time.

Business valuation

The act of determining the value of, or the estimated value of, a business enterprise, or an interest therein.

Canadian Controlled Private Corporation (CCPC)

A term defined in the *Income Tax Act* to mean a **Privately held company** that is not owned or controlled by non-residents of Canada. See subsection 125 (7) of the *Act*.

Capital asset pricing model (CAPM)

A theoretical comparative risk model that relates risk and return.

Capital cost allowance (CCA)

An income tax term meaning the amount of depreciation deducted by a business for income tax purposes. Capital cost allowance rates are set out in Part XI of the *Income Tax Regulations*. See also **Tax shield** and **Undepreciated capital cost**.

Capital dividend account

An account established under the *Income Tax Act* that applies to qualifying privately held corporations whereby certain amounts, including that portion of a capital gain not subject to taxation, can be distributed on a tax free basis to shareholders. See subsection 83(2) of the *Income Tax Act*.

Capital gain (loss)

The amount by which the net proceeds received upon the disposition of an asset or investment exceeds (is less than) its cost for income tax purposes.

Capital-intensive business

A business requiring significant capital investment with resultant comparatively low labour cost per unit of output relative to capital investment per unit of production.

Capitalization rate

The rate of return (usually expressed as a percentage) used to convert a point estimate of cash flow into value. The inverse of the capitalization rate is referred to as the **Multiple**. Alternately, a divisor used to convert a uniform (or constant) stream of cash flow to a capital amount or value.

Capitalized cash flow

The present value of a perpetuity determined by dividing a point estimate of cash flow (normally **Discretionary cash flow**) by a **Capitalization rate**, or multiplying cash flow by a **Multiple**.

Capital structure

The mix of debt and equity used to finance a business.

Closely held company

A corporation whose shares are neither listed for trading on a recognized stock exchange nor traded in an *Over-the-counter market*. Technically, a *Closely held corporation* has fewer than 51 shareholders excluding employees (Canada). See *Privately held company*.

Coattail provision (or *Coattail right*)

The right afforded to a minority shareholder of a business entitling them to sell with the *Controlling interest* in the business at *Ratable value*. Synonymous with *Tag-along right*.

Commercial goodwill

Intangible value in the form of brand names, proprietary technology, contracts and similar forms, which a buyer expects will be acquired as part of a transaction. Contrast with *Individual goodwill* and *Personal goodwill*.

Compulsory sale provision

The obligation of a minority shareholder to sell with the *Controlling interest* in the business at *Ratable value*. Synonymous with *Mandatory sale provision.*

Conglomerate

A business comprised of two or more distinct operating segments or divisions, each a material component of the overall operations.

Controlling interest

An equity interest in either a *Publicly held company* or a *Privately held company* that by itself carries sufficient votes to elect all (or at least a majority) of the members of the board of directors and, through them, to govern the company's business. A controlling interest can be comprised of either the outstanding voting shares that collectively represent more than 50% of the outstanding votes (*De jure control*) or, in some circumstances, 50% or less of the outstanding votes (*De facto control*).

Control premium

See *Premium for control*.

Cumulative eligible capital

An income tax pool that consists of 75% of *Eligible capital property* acquired by a corporation, which is depreciated for income tax purposes at a rate of 7% per annum on a declining balance basis.

Debt servicing costs

Annual interest and principal repayments required on interest-bearing debt obligations.

De facto control

One person beneficially owns or holds proxies for the outstanding voting shares of a corporation that collectively do not represent more than 50% of the outstanding votes, but nonetheless effectively controls the corporation, either by virtue of diffusion of ownership, or by indirect means, such as economic control or control by agreement.

De jure control

One person or group beneficially owns or holds proxies for outstanding voting shares of a corporation that collectively represent more than 50% of the outstanding votes.

Depreciated replacement cost

A term used by real estate and equipment appraisers to describe the amount determined by estimating the **Replacement cost (new)** of buildings and equipment less an amount for depreciation and obsolescence to equate the **Replacement cost (new)** to the depreciated assets being appraised.

Depreciation

The systematic assignment of the cost of tangible assets to expense.

Derivative securities

A financial instrument whose value is a function of another instrument. Examples include stock options and warrants.

Dilutive securities

A financial instrument that could cause a reduction in the **Ratable value** of the common shares of a company.

Discount for illiquidity

The amount by which the **En bloc value** of a business or **Ratable value** of an interest therein is reduced in recognition of the expectation that a ready market for the disposition of said interest does not exist. Synonymous with **Marketability discount**.

Discount for non-control

The amount by which an interest in a business is reduced from its **Ratable value** of **En bloc value** in recognition of the inability to unilaterally control the business.

Discount rate

A rate of return used to convert a monetary sum, payable or receivable in the future, into present value. Alternately, a rate of return used to convert a series of future anticipated cash flow to a present value.

Discretionary cash flow

Cash flow from operations less income taxes, **Net trade working capital** requirements and capital expenditures net of the related income **Tax shield**. Normally **Discretionary cash flow** is determined prior to **Debt servicing costs**.

Dissent right

Where provided in the incorporating statute of a company, a statutory right enabling a minority shareholder in specified circumstances to cause the corporation to purchase the minority shareholding at fair value. Synonymous with **Appraisal remedy**.

Earnout

A method of structuring a purchase and sale transaction whereby the quantum of the purchase price is established in part by the future performance of the business being acquired and a portion of the purchase price is conveyed or paid at a specified date(s) following the closing of the transaction.

EBIT

Earnings before interest and taxes.

EBITDA

Earnings before interest, taxes, **Depreciation** and **Amortization**. A measure of the operating cash flows of a business before changes in net **Working capital**.

Economic life

The period over which property may be profitably used, a product may be profitably manufactured and marketed, or a service profitably rendered.

Economies of scale

The decrease in combined operating expenses and/or increases in combined revenues that result following the merging of two or more business operations. See **Synergy** and **Post-acquisition synergies**.

Eligible capital property

Qualifying intangible property acquired by a corporation, such as **Goodwill** acquired in an **Asset transaction**. 75% of eligible capital property is added to a company's **Cumulative eligible capital** tax pool and depreciated at a rate of 7% per annum on a declining balance basis. See section 54 of the *Income Tax Act*.

Eligible dividend

A taxable dividend paid to a resident of Canada by a public company or by a *Privately held company* out of its "general rate income pool". Eligible dividends are taxed at more favourable rates than *Ineligible dividends*, given that the latter were subject to lower corporate income tax rates. See paragraph 89 (1) of the *Income Tax Act*.

En bloc value

The value of the assets or ownership interests of a business viewed as a whole.

Enterprise value

The total value of a business including both its interest-bearing debt and equity components.

Equity value

The value of a business to all shareholders.

Externally financed transaction

The purchase of a business where the funding for the acquisition is provided by the purchaser through sources external to the business being acquired.

Fair market value

The highest price available in an open and unrestricted market between informed and prudent parties, acting at arm's length and under no compulsion to act, expressed in terms of cash.

Fair value

A value term commonly used in connection with the minority shareholder *Dissent Right* and *Oppression remedy*, to describe the basis upon which the acquisition price for the minority shares is to be determined.

Family control

The circumstance where family members, who collectively own sufficient voting shares in a *Privately held company* to control it act in concert to exercise control over the economic direction and *Liquidity* of their collective investment. In Canada, the concept of family control has been put forward principally in the context of *Fair market value* determinations required for income tax purposes.

Financial leverage

The use of interest-bearing debt or other fixed-payment financial obligations in the *Capital structure* of a business.

Financial risk

The incremental risk accruing to the shareholders of a business (in addition to *Operating risk*) due to the use of *Financial leverage* in the *Capital structure* of a business.

Financial synergies

That portion of total *Post-acquisition synergies* relating to the benefits associated with a more efficient *Capital structure* or lower-cost financing.

Forced liquidation

The sale of assets (where an immediate cessation of the business and disposition of assets is assumed) on an "as is/where is" basis. In the context of equipment *Appraisal*, forced liquidation value contemplates the sale of equipment assets at auction.

Forcing out premium

See *Premium for forcible taking*.

GAAP

Generally Accepted Accounting Principles.

Going concern

A business enterprise that is both conducting operations at a given date and has every reasonable expectation of doing so for the foreseeable future after that date.

Going-concern value

The present value of all future benefits expected to accrue from ownership, where a business operation is expected to continue to operate (usually) indefinitely into the future.

Goodwill

The difference between *En bloc equity value* and the sum of the net tangible assets and *Identifiable intangible assets* (where these can be separately quantified). See also *Individual goodwill*, *Personal goodwill* and *Value to owner*.

Group control

The circumstance where a group of shareholders, who otherwise deal on an arm's length basis, collectively own sufficient voting shares in a *Privately held company* to control it, are presumed to act in concert to exercise control over the economic direction and *Liquidity* of their collective investment. In Canada, the concept of group control has been put forward principally in the context of *Fair market value* determinations required for income tax purposes.

Hindsight

The use of information that was not available at the **Valuation date**. In the context of **Notional market valuations**, the courts have found that hindsight is inadmissible, except possibly for the limited purpose of assessing the reasonableness of assumptions at the **Valuation date**.

Holding company

A company with (usually) no active business operations, owning passive investments in assets such as **Real estate**, or shares in one or more **Public company**, or **Privately held** (operating) **company**. The earnings generated by a holding company (in the form of rent or dividends, for example) are normally of less significance from a value standpoint than is the appreciating value of the underlying investments themselves.

Horizontal analysis

The process of comparing actual or projected results of a business, normally with the objective of detecting trends or anomalies.

Hurdle rate of return

See **Threshold rate of return**.

Identifiable intangible assets

In the context of a **Purchase price allocation**, the total intangible value paid in an **Open Market Transaction** is allocated among identifiable intangible assets and **Non-identifiable intangible assets**. According to **International Financial Reporting Standards (IFRSs),** an intangible asset is identifiable if it meets either the:

- contractual-legal criterion (IFRS 3.B32) — where the intangible arises from contractual or other legal rights is identifiable regardless of whether those rights are transferable or separable from the acquire or from other rights and obligations; or

- separability criterion (IFRS 3.B33) — where the intangible is separable if it is capable of being separated or divided from the entity and sold, transferred, licensed, rented or exchanged, either individually or together with a related contract, identifiable asset or liability, regardless of whether the entity intends to do so.

IFRSs

International Financial Reporting Standards.

Individual goodwill

The economic advantage that accrues to a business by virtue of its employment of a given individual who has abilities, business contacts, good name and reputation that could be, or would be, harmful to the economic well-being of the business should he or she leave the employ of the business and compete with it. In contrast with **Personal goodwill**, individual goodwill does not expire at the time of the loss of interest, retirement, or death of the individual. Rather, the business has the capacity to substitute another individual to fill the role played by said individual prior to their retirement or death. In an open market context, it is ***Non-competition agreements*** that result in individual goodwill having commercial value.

Industry-specific activity ratios

Criteria commonly used within a specific industry to gauge an element of business value. Industry specific activity ratios often are referred to as ***Rules of thumb***.

Ineligible dividend

A taxable dividend paid to a resident of Canada normally by a ***Privately held company*** out of its "low rate income pool". Ineligible dividends are taxed at less favourable rates than ***Eligible dividends***, given that the latter were subject to higher corporate income tax rates.

Initial public offering

The offering for sale of treasury-share capital. A primary offering results in the proceeds accruing to the issuer with a simultaneous dilution of the percentage ownership interest of pre-offering business owners. Synonymous with ***Primary offering***.

Insolvency

The inability of an individual or corporation to pay debt obligations as they become due.

Intangible operating synergies

That portion of total ***Post-acquisition synergies*** relating to ***Strategic advantage*** or other benefits that cannot be readily segregated and analyzed individually.

Internal rate of return (IRR)

The ***Discount rate*** that equates the present value of expected cash outflows to the present value of expected cash inflows.

Internally financed transaction

A transaction in which all or part of the outstanding shares or assets of a business are sold to a purchaser who requires the business being purchased to fund all or part of the purchase price out of funds it generates subsequent to purchase.

Intrinsic value

A ***Notional market valuation*** based on rates of return required by investors given economic and business conditions existing at the valuation date, without consideration of possible ***Post-acquisition synergies*** or ***Economies of scale*** that might accrue in differing degrees to arm's-length purchasers. Synonymous with ***Stand-alone value***.

Leverage

The relationship between interest-bearing debt and equity in a business (***Financial leverage***). Alternately, the effect of fixed charges on after-tax earnings and/or ***Discretionary cash flow*** (***Operating leverage***).

Leveraged buyout

A transaction in which an acquirer borrows against the assets of the acquired business to fund all or part of the purchase price.

Levered cost of equity

A ***Discount rate*** or ***Capitalization rate*** that reflects the cost of equity capital to a business, taking into account both ***Operating risk*** and ***Financial risk***.

Levered discretionary cash flow

Cash flow from operations less income taxes, capital investment requirements (net of the related ***Tax shield***) and incremental ***Net trade working capital*** requirements, and after consideration of ***Debt servicing costs***.

Lifetime capital gains exemption

A tax benefit available to individual Canadians who own shares of a qualifying ***Small business corporation***, whereby the first $750,000 of capital gains are not subject to taxation upon the sale of those shares.

Liquidation

The process of converting assets into cash.

Liquidation value

The net amount of money, if any, available to equity owners following a voluntary liquidation, a reorganization of a business following either a proposal to creditors or a liquidation of a business during a receivership or other proceeding under the *Bankruptcy and Insolvency Act*.

Liquidity

The ability to readily convert non-cash assets into cash for reasonably certain proceeds.

Management agreement

An agreement between two parties in which one of the parties agrees to offer either general or specific management services to the other for a specified period of time.

Mandatory sale provision

(see ***Compulsory sale provision***)

Marketability discount

See *Discount for illiquidity*.

Minority discount

The reduction from the *Pro rata value* of the *En bloc value* of the assets or ownership interests of a business as a whole to reflect the disadvantages of owning a *Minority shareholding*. A minority interest may suffer a discount for the following reasons:

- the absence of control and the resultant inability to dictate such matters as: the future direction of the corporation; the election of directors; the performance of the investment because of the inability to dictate dividend payments; or the sale of the shareholding where there are legal or contractual restrictions with respect to such a sale and a sale of all of the shares of the corporation (i.e., a *Discount for non-control*); and/or

- the inherent lack of *Liquidity* or marketability of the investment (i.e., a *Discount for illiquidity*).

Minority shareholding

Any shareholding in either a *Public company* or a *Privately held company* that does not own or control more than 50% of the outstanding voting shares of a company.

Multiple

The reciprocal of the *Capitalization rate*. In open market transactions, the multiple is usually expressed as a multiple of *EBITDA*.

Net book value

With respect to individual assets or liabilities, the capitalized cost, or otherwise determined book value, of an asset or liability less accumulated *Depreciation* or *Amortization* as it appears on the books of account of the enterprise. With respect to a business enterprise, the difference between total assets (net of *Depreciation* and *Amortization*), and total liabilities of an enterprise as they appear on the balance sheet. Depending on what is referred to, this term is synonymous with the terms book value, net worth and *Shareholders' equity*.

Net income (loss)

The amount remaining when all expenses, (including income tax), incurred and accrued during an accounting period, are deducted from all revenue received and accrued during that same period.

Net realizable value

The net proceeds obtainable upon the sale of an asset, after providing for all costs of disposition, including income taxes.

Net trade working capital

The amount by which current assets related to the principal operating activities (e.g., accounts receivable and inventories) exceed current liabilities from operating activities (e.g., accounts payable and accrued liabilities). Contrast with **Working capital**, which includes all current assets and current liabilities.

Nominal rate of return

A **Discount rate** that includes both an inflation component and a **Real rate of return**.

Non-competition agreement

An agreement between two parties in which one of the parties agrees not to compete with the other party for a specified period of time, usually within a specified geographic area and within identified parameters of product or service. See **Individual goodwill**.

Non-identifiable intangible asset

Those intangible assets that cannot be readily segregated from the operations of a business that is a going concern. Examples include deferred charges and **Goodwill**. Contrast with **Identifiable intangible asset**.

Notional market valuation

The determination of **Fair market value**, **Fair value**, or some other value in the absence of an **Open market transaction**.

Open market transaction

The purchase and sale of an asset, business, or interest therein, as negotiated between arm's length parties. Contrast with **Notional market valuation**.

Operating leverage

The use of fixed costs in the operations of the business. Contrast with **Financial leverage**.

Operating risk

The risk inherent in the operations of a business from factors such as the potential loss of key employees, major customers, competitive changes and similar exposures.

Opportunity cost

The value of benefits sacrificed in selecting a course of action among alternatives. In relation to value determination, the value of alternative investments *not* made.

Oppression remedy

Where provided in the incorporating statute of a company, a statutory right enabling a person with a *Minority shareholding* to claim the corporation has acted in a manner believed contrary to the best interest of the shareholding.

Orderly liquidation

The sale of assets under the assumption that a reasonable period of time will be used to maximize proceeds.

Over-the-counter market

The trading of securities or commodities not listed on an established stock exchange.

Partnership

A form of business organization where persons carry on a business in common with a view to profit. This term does not apply to the relationship between owners of a corporation.

Personal goodwill

The unique advantage enjoyed by a given individual that arises from his or her particular abilities, good name and reputation, and which is not transferable by contract or otherwise. The term personal goodwill can be used to describe either economic advantage, non-economic advantage, or a combination of both.

Post-acquisition synergies

The capitalized value of *Economies of scale* and/or *Strategic advantages* that a prospective buyer of a business perceives may accrue from its acquisition.

Premium for control

The amount by which the value or price of a share that forms part of a controlling interest exceeds the value or price of a share of a non-controlling interest where it is determined that the excess is attributable to the benefits associated with a *Controlling interest*.

Premium for Forcible Taking

Also referred to as a "forcing out premium" represents a premium over the *Fair value* of an equity interest awarded by the courts where a shareholder has been forced out of a company following an *Amalgamation* or other corporate restructuring.

Price

The consideration paid in an *Open market transaction* involving the purchase and sale of an asset, business or interest therein.

Price earnings multiple

The reciprocal of the ***Capitalization rate***.

Primary offering

See ***Initial public offering***.

Privately held company

Technically, an incorporated business with fewer than 51 shareholders excluding employees (Canada) that does not offer its shares to the public. For purposes of this book, a ***Privately held company*** simply is defined as one that does not offer its shares to the public. See ***Closely held corporation***.

Pro forma

A term applied to a document or statement which indicates the anticipated effects of stated assumptions or contractual commitments which have not yet been completed.

Pro rata value

See ***Ratable value***.

Proposal to creditors

A scheme for extension of time, and/or reduction or rearrangement of debt put forward to creditors by a debtor.

Public company

A company whose equity shares and/or issued debt are traded on an established stock exchange or in an ***Over-the-counter*** market. Alternately, a company that is not a ***Privately held company*** or ***Closely held company*** as defined in business corporations statutes.

Purchase price allocation

In an ***Open market transaction***, the allocation of the price paid for a business among the tangible assets acquired, ***Identifiable intangible assets*** and ***Non-identifiable intangible assets***. The standards governing purchase price allocation are established by ***Generally Accepted Accounting Principles*** (***GAAP***) or ***International Financial Reporting Standards*** (***IFRSs***).

Ratable value

That portion of the ***En bloc value*** represented by each ownership percentage. Synonymous with ***Pro rata value***.

Rate of return

An amount of income realized or expected on an investment, expressed as a percentage of that investment. See **Capitalization rate** and **Discount rate**.

Real estate

An identified parcel or tract of land including any improvements.

Real rate of return

A **Discount rate**, or **Capitalization rate**, that excludes consideration of inflation, as contrasted with a **Nominal rate of return**, which includes both an inflation component and a real rate of return.

Recaptured depreciation (Recapture)

This term is usually used in an income tax context although it is not specifically found in the *Income Tax Act*. Recaptured depreciation is measured as the excess of the proceeds of disposition of depreciable property of a prescribed class (to the extent of original cost) over the undepreciated capital cost of assets in the class. If no further assets of that class are purchased in the year, then the excess is added to income. See section 13 of the *Income Tax Act*.

Receivership

The legal status of a debtor for whom a receiver has been appointed.

Redundant asset

Any asset not required in the operations of the business and therefore not included in the **Going-concern value** of the operating assets of the business.

Refundable dividend tax on hand (RDTOH)

A tax account applicable to **Canadian Controlled Private Corporations (CCPC)** intended to create an integrated income tax system such that an individual is in the same net after-tax position regardless of whether investment income is earned directly or through a corporate entity.

Replacement cost (new)

The current cost of a similar new item having the nearest equivalent utility to the item being appraised.

Right of first offer

A right whereby the shareholder wishing to divest its interest first offers that interest to the other shareholder(s). If the other shareholder(s) choose not to accept the offer, the offering shareholder is free to divest its interest to third-party acquirers at a price and on terms no less favourable to the offering shareholder than those offered to the other shareholder(s). Contrast with **Right of first refusal**.

Right of first refusal

A right whereby a shareholder wishing to divest its interest solicits third-party offers, the highest of which is presented to the other shareholder(s) who are given the opportunity to acquire the offering shareholder's interest at the same price and on the same terms as those offered by the third party. Contrast with **Right of first offer**.

Risk-free rate of return

The prevailing rate of return on money market investments such as long-term federal government bonds, which are generally perceived as investments free of substantial credit risk. They are priced to reflect a relatively long-term holding period and, hence, aside from inflation-related purchasing power risk, put the investor in a position that in all practical respects is risk-free. These securities are fixed in income as well as in principal and, hence, generally do not offer any potential for capital growth if held to maturity.

Rollover

A tax-deferred transfer of assets among related parties.

Rules of thumb

See **Industry-specific activity ratios**.

Safe income

This term is not defined in the *Income Tax Act*, but is generally taken to mean the amount of post-1971 retained earnings in a Canadian corporation that has already been taxed and from which a tax-free dividend can be paid to shareholders.

Secondary offering

The offering of previously issued share capital for sale by the present owner.

Security analysis

The analysis of the publicly traded securities of a business based on financial models and utilizing publicly available market data.

Share exchange

A **Share transaction** whereby the consideration received is in the form of shares of the acquiring company.

Shareholder agreement

A contract between the equity holders of a corporation that defines rights, privileges and obligations.

Shareholders' equity

The aggregation of a company's paid-in capital, retained earnings, and contributed capital, appraisal and other surpluses. Alternately, the result obtained when the net book value of all liabilities of a company are subtracted from the net book value of all that company's assets. See **Net book value**.

Share transaction

The sale of a business interest through the purchase and sale of the share capital of the corporation overlying it. Contrast with **Asset transaction**.

Shotgun clause

An agreement whereby one shareholder of a corporation offers to purchase the shares of another, and the shareholder receiving the offer must either sell to the offering shareholder at the price and on the terms presented in the offer, or must acquire the shares of the offering shareholder at the same price and on the same terms as those offered.

Small business corporation

For income tax purposes a **Small business corporation** is a **Canadian Controlled Private Corporation** where 90% of the fair market value of assets are either: (i) used principally in carrying on an active business in Canada; or (ii) consist of shares or debt of one or more connected small business corporations.

Small business deduction

A reduction in the tax rate applicable to **Canadian Controlled Private Corporations** on the first $500,000 of income earned on active business carried on in Canada. The deduction must be shared among **Associated corporations**.

Sole Proprietorship

A form of business organization where one individual owns an unincorporated business.

Special-interest purchaser

A purchaser who can, or believes it can, enjoy **Post-acquisition synergies** or **Strategic advantages** by combining the acquired business interest with its own.

Squeeze-out

A corporate action taken by a controlling shareholder with 90% or more of the voting shares of the company to remove the **Minority shareholding(s)**.

Stand-alone value

The value of a business interest determined without reference to prices that might be paid by purchasers who perceive **Post-acquisition synergies**. Synonymous with **Intrinsic value**.

Strategic advantages (or benefits)

Purchaser-perceived **Post-acquisition synergies** expected to reduce risk or produce **Economies of scale** that may be realized over the long term.

Sustaining capital reinvestment

The capital outlay required each year to maintain operations at existing levels.

SWOT analysis

The process of assessing the <u>S</u>trengths, <u>W</u>eaknesses, <u>O</u>pportunities and <u>T</u>hreats of a given business.

Synergy

The effect created by **Economies of scale** or other post-acquisition benefits. The realization of increased **Discretionary cash flow** (as a result of the combination of two or more business operations over and above the aggregate **Discretionary cash flow** of the two businesses viewed separately), or reduced risk in attaining same.

Tag-along provision (right)

See **Coattail provision**.

Tangible net worth

Shareholders' equity, adjusted for the removal of intangible assets and intangible liabilities. Unlike **Adjusted net book value**, the determination of tangible net worth does not require the restatement of tangible assets and liabilities to their fair market value.

Tangible operating synergies

That portion of total **Post-acquisition synergies** related to those benefits that can be readily segregated and analyzed in isolation.

Tax shield

The present value of the anticipated tax savings that will accrue as a result of the owner of capital (depreciable) assets claiming **Capital cost allowance**.

Temporary excess assets

An asset not currently used in the operations of the business, but which does not qualify as a **Redundant asset** because it is not permanently redundant.

Threshold rate of return

A benchmark predetermined **Rate of return** (or **Discount rate**) criterion applied to a projected cash flow (generally **Discretionary cash flow**) that includes both inflation and a **Real rate of return**. **Purchaser-perceived synergies** are generally taken into account. Synonymous with **Hurdle rate of return**.

Undepreciated capital cost (UCC)

The remaining balance of depreciable capital assets used as the base for future **Capital cost allowance** claims.

Unlevered cost of equity

A **Discount rate** or **Capitalization rate** that assumes a debt-free **Capital structure**.

Unlevered discretionary cash flow

The cash flow from the operations of a business less income taxes, capital investment requirements (net of the related **Tax shield**) and incremental **Net trade working capital** requirements, but before consideration of **Debt servicing costs**.

Valuation

The act or process of determining the value of something. See **Appraisal**.

Valuation date

The specific point in time at which a value or price determination is made.

Value

A return or equivalent in goods, services, or money for something exchanged.

Value in exchange

The worth of an asset or pool of assets if sold in the open market.

Value in use (or Value in continued use)

The value of the tangible assets of an operating business viewed as a pool of assets in a specific use. Value in use is determined by reference to the contribution of that asset pool to the ongoing business.

Value to owner

The value of an asset to its owner. The term value to the owner can be used to describe either owner-perceived economic advantage, non-economic advantage or a combination of both. Viewed solely in an economic context, value to the owner may be equal to or greater than *Fair market value*. It is never less than *Fair market value*. Where value to the owner is greater than *Fair market value*, the increment over *Fair market value* is often attributable to *Personal goodwill*.

Vendor take-back

Where the vendor finances all or part of the acquisition *Price* in an *Open market transaction* by accepting non-cash consideration that defers payment (e.g., a promissory note payable or redeemable preferred shares of the acquirer).

Vertical analysis

The process of analyzing the financial statements (normally) with the purpose of understanding financial relationships and detecting anomalies.

Weighted average cost of capital (WACC)

A *Rate of return* determined as the weighted average of the after-tax cost of debt and *Levered cost of equity*. WACC assumes an ability to deduct interest expense when calculating taxable income and can be used either as a *Discount rate* (inclusive or exclusive of inflation) or a *Capitalization rate*. When applied to a stream of cash flows, the result is *Enterprise value*.

Widely held corporation

See *Public company*.

Wind-up

The process of discontinuing the operations of a corporate entity.

Working capital

The amount by which current assets exceed current liabilities. Working capital incorporates all current assets and liabilities, contrasted with *Net trade working capital* which reflects only those current assets and liabilities arising from the operations of the business.

Chapter 1

Valuation Terms
and Principles

Introduction

This book is intended to provide an in-depth understanding of the principles, concepts and methodologies employed when determining the value of a business or an equity interest therein. While the particular factors to be considered will vary in each case, the underlying discussion in this book can be broadly applied to virtually any business, whether public or private, incorporated or unincorporated.

The valuation of a given business or equity interest therein is inherently a subjective task that requires sufficient analysis and application of informed judgment in order to formulate a reasoned conclusion. Given that each situation is unique, there is no general business analysis, valuation methodology, rate of return, legal, income tax or other guidelines that can be said to apply in every circumstance. Generally it is advisable to retain qualified independent valuation professionals where a business valuation is required, supplemented by legal, tax and other advisors as necessary.

This book does not deal with public company security analysis per se. Further, although many of the underlying principles are essentially the same, there are important differences between business valuation in the context of notional valuations and open market transactions as set out in this book, and security analysis in the context of normal daily stock trades of public companies. These differences are discussed in this chapter.

For simplicity, reference is made throughout this book to the value of a "business." The value of a business is represented by the value of its share capital (or owners' equity for unincorporated entities) plus the value of its outstanding debt, which together are commonly referred to as the *enterprise value* of a business. Alternatively, the value of a business can be viewed as the value of all its net operating assets (both tangible and intangible), regardless of how they are financed. That said, in most cases, it is the determination of equity value that is of primary interest.

The typical approach to business valuation is first to determine the enterprise value of the business assuming a "normalized" capital structure. Interest-bearing debt and equivalent liabilities are deducted in order to determine the *equity value* of the business, viewed *en bloc* (i.e., 100% of the issued and outstanding shares of a corporation or all the owners' equity, in the case of an unincorporated entity). Further adjustments to equity value sometimes are required where the business has excess or deficient net operating assets (e.g., working capital) or redundant (i.e., non-operating) assets.

Where an open market transaction is not taking place, then value is determined in a notional market context. In notional market contexts the value terms most frequently adopted are fair market value and fair value. Fair market value has a generally accepted meaning, while fair value may be given different meanings depending on applicable statutes and case law. That said, in all cases, it is important to adhere to the underlying principles of business valuation in order to develop a credible value conclusion.

Importantly, where the value of a business is determined in a notional market context or crystallized as price in an open market transaction, the credibility of that value conclusion depends upon the reasonableness and internal consistency of the underlying assumptions and the proper application of appropriate valuation methodologies. Moreover, there can be, and often is, a significant difference between the value of a business determined on a "stand-alone" (or "intrinsic") basis in a notional market context, and the price at which a transaction is consummated in the open market. Valuations in the context of open market transactions are influenced by a myriad of factors, both economic and non-economic. As a consequence, any reasoned value determination must be based on a well-defined and applied theoretical foundation, in combination with the application of experience and informed judgment.

Open Market Transactions vs. Notional Market Valuations

There are two distinct circumstances where the value of a business must be determined. The first is where an open market transaction is contemplated, and *price* is negotiated between a buyer and a seller acting at arm's length. For a transaction to occur, the buyer and seller must agree on a price (and the terms of the deal) that satisfies the interests of each.

The second is where it is necessary to determine *fair market value, fair value,* or some other legislated or defined value agreed upon in the absence of open market negotiations. This can occur either in the case of a privately held business or of a public company, where it is believed that the share price (and market capitalization) is not representative of the defined value term. Such valuations are referred to as *notional market valuations*. Situations where business value determinations are required in a notional market context include:

- where transactions occur between "non-arm's length" parties as that term is defined in the *Income Tax Act* or pursuant to an income tax reorganization. Such transactions typically must be consummated at fair market value in order to satisfy the provisions of the *Income Tax Act*;

- those pursuant to provincial family law acts (generally "fair market value"), the federal *Divorce Act* and the federal and various provincial expropriations acts;

- those necessary to support the fairness of a proposed transaction pursuant to provincial securities acts (e.g., a "fairness opinion");

- the exercise by minority shareholders of appraisal and oppression remedies pursuant to federal and provincial business corporation statutes (typically "fair market value");

- those pursuant to the "value" provisions of shareholder agreements;

- the sale of shares in privately held companies to employees, including establishing employee share ownership plans; and

- business value requirements pursuant to commercial litigation and business interruption claims.

The value term most frequently encountered in notional market valuations is "fair market value." There may be important differences between fair market value and other value terms, such as "value", "fair value", or some other value term. Various definitions of value and differences between them are addressed later in this chapter. There are numerous court decisions dealing with the definition and interpretation of value terms and definitions, particularly with respect to fair market value and fair value. A list of selected Canadian court decisions by topic is set out in Appendix A.

The underlying concepts of valuation also apply when determining the price of a business in an open market transaction. However, it is important to note that there may be significant differences between fair market value (or some other value term) as determined in a notional market context and price as determined in an open market transaction. As discussed below, this difference may be attributable to factors such as:

- the negotiating skills of the buyer, seller and their respective advisors;

- the need and the desire of the buyer and seller to transact;
- the structure of the transaction (e.g., the forms of consideration);
- the amount of competition for the acquisition of a given business; and
- the possible impact of "special-interest purchasers," who may perceive certain synergies pursuant to the combination of an acquisition target with their existing operations.

This book is largely devoted to the principles and concepts adopted when determining "fair market value" or "fair value" in a notional market context. Business valuation and pricing in the context of open market transactions is covered in Chapter 11.

Value Terms

Where value is determined in a notional market context, it is important that what is meant by "value" be clearly defined. The most common definitions of value include "fair market value", "fair value", and "value to owner".

Fair Market Value

In a notional market context, the definition of fair market value generally accepted by Canadian courts has been:

> *...the highest price available in an open and unrestricted market between informed and prudent parties, acting at arm's length and under no compulsion to act, expressed in terms of cash.*

The definition postulates open market transactions that, depending on the knowledge and negotiating skills of buyer and seller, may or may not be satisfied for any particular one of those transactions. As a practical matter, in a notional market context, fair market value is quantified pursuant to what might best be described as a best-efforts basis. Such best-efforts quantifications are necessary because no information base is ever perfect, and because the degree of subjectivity in the value determination is a function of numerous factors influencing both the business being valued and the industry in which the business operates. An analysis of each of the components of fair market value follows.

Highest Price Available

The highest price available must consider that the buyer and the seller would transact only at a price and on terms deemed fair by each. Theoretically, it is necessary to identify the buyer who will pay the highest price, being the one with the greatest justifiable economic rationale to consummate the transaction. As a practical matter, a price negotiated pursuant to an open market transaction following well-researched, wide market exposure is the ultimate determinant of value at a point in time. Even then, it is not possible to be certain that all possible buyers were solicited or the highest possible price was paid. This uncertainty remains because the price paid in any open market transaction is subject to the negotiating abilities of the buyer and seller, the terms of the transaction and other factors that may be specific to that particular transaction. In addition, while certain likely buyers may have been solicited, they may not have been in a position to transact because of internal restrictions or external factors (e.g., availability of financing). As a result, even open market exposure of a business does not ensure realization of the highest possible price.

In an open market transaction, the buyer who will pay the highest price is a "special-interest purchaser", being a buyer who can afford to pay a premium over the intrinsic (i.e., stand-alone) value of a business on account of expected post-acquisition synergies that will be realized by combining the acquired business with its existing operations, subject to the seller's ability to negotiate such a premium. The anticipated synergies may be in the form of economies of scale (such as cost reductions and operating efficiencies) or perceived strategic advantages (such as cross-selling opportunities, risk reduction, enhanced market share and incremental growth opportunities). The quantification of synergies is addressed in Chapter 11. Every potential buyer can, and likely will, pay a unique price given individually perceived post-acquisition synergies. In most cases, only through negotiation with each prospective buyer can the economies of scale and strategic advantages of each be meaningfully quantified. Even then, the synergistic value that exists for the buyer may not be fully realized by the seller in the sale price because most buyers are unwilling to pay a price that confers all the synergistic value perceived in the transaction to the benefit of the seller.

In most cases, notional market valuations are conducted where no open market arm's length sale is contemplated or likely to occur. Accordingly, without testing the market or having meaningful discussions with potential buyers, the highest price available can never be ascertained in any notional market valuation with certainty.

Nonetheless, when determining fair market value in a notional market context, it is necessary to address the question of a possible premium over the intrinsic value of a business that might be paid by special-interest purchasers. However, since open market negotiations current to the date that value is established typically have not taken place, often it is difficult:

- to identify possible buyers who might be interested in acquiring a given business;

- where such possible buyers are identified, to determine which of them would be considered to be qualified buyers who have both the strategic interest in and the financial capability to effect a transaction;

- to identify the synergies each qualified buyer might enjoy;

- to quantify the identified synergies that might be realized in different degrees by each qualified buyer; and

- to assign a probability to the likelihood that the qualified buyer could be negotiated into a position of paying for some or all the possible synergies, on a cash-equivalent basis.

In a notional market context, where values are determined pursuant to business reorganizations, estate planning, family law requirements and so on, and an attempt is made to quantify an incremental amount over the intrinsic value of a business to account for possible synergies, any result derived is subjective. The degree of subjectivity is a function of the seller's knowledge of possible purchaser synergies, the obviousness of such synergies, the degree of difficulty related to the quantification of such synergies and the seller's perception of its relative negotiating position.

In a notional market context, the ability to identify special-interest purchasers varies with the characteristics of the business itself and the industry in which it competes. Further, the ability to meaningfully quantify the synergies perceived by, or available to, each possible buyer, and to determine whether a buyer could be enticed to pay for some or all such benefits varies in each case. For most large businesses, one or more special-interest purchasers generally exists. However, absent open market negotiations, it is seldom possible to reasonably quantify the post-acquisition synergies each would be willing to pay for. Accordingly, in a notional market context businesses usually are valued based on their intrinsic (or stand-alone) values (i.e., the value of the business absent consideration of possible post-acquisition synergies). Such notional market value determinations are generally qualified with regard to the inability to identify and quantify the effect on value of possible buyers who might perceive economies of scale or strategic advantage. Having said that, where there are no extenuating circumstances such as shareholder agreements that dictate or suggest value definitions that exclude consideration of special-interest purchasers, where:

- likely special-interest purchasers are readily identifiable; and
- post-acquisition synergies can be quantified in a credible manner; and
- there is a high probability that one or more special-interest purchasers would pay for some or all those benefits,

then subject to the fact-specific circumstances, notional fair market value determinations may include all or part of such assumed synergies.

Open and Unrestricted Market

The term "open market" refers to the assumption that no potential buyers are to be excluded from participation in the notional market for the business being valued. It is assumed that the business is exposed to all potential buyers with the desire and the resources to buy, notwithstanding that this rarely occurs during the course of an open market transaction. Both the buyer and seller are expected to have a deemed desire and a full facility to transact for the business in the open market at the highest price obtainable having regard to all circumstances attendant on ownership.

An "unrestricted market" refers to an assumption that any statutory, contractual, or other restrictions influencing the marketability of a business, or equity interest therein, are temporarily lifted in order to facilitate a sale in the notional market. Restrictions on ownership transfer commonly are specified in shareholder agreements and in the articles of incorporation of privately held companies, and may be found in contracts executed by the business itself. Such restrictions generally require the approval of the company's board of directors or the other shareholders. Usually these issues bear on the question of the illiquidity that often attaches to minority shareholdings of privately held businesses. As a practical matter, where all the outstanding shares of a company are sold together, such restrictions have little bearing on the price received. On the other hand, if a minority block (or in some instances a control block) of the business is valued by itself, subject to prevailing case law such restrictions on transfer and resultant illiquidity may have a significant downward influence on value. Absent the existence of a shareholder agreement that provides for liquidity to minority shareholders, the impact of restrictions on value depends on the relationships prevailing at any given point in time among shareholders.

Case law suggests that in a notional market context the assumption of an unrestricted market does not completely disregard the existence of either technical or practical restrictions on the sale or transfer of an equity interest. Rather, hypothetical buyers are assumed to assess the value of the equity interest after accounting for the prevailing restrictions. They do this by considering and, if deemed appropriate, adopting a suitable discount from the value that has otherwise been determined by subjecting the buyer to the prevailing restrictions following acquisition. It is necessary to assume that transfer approval is not withheld; however, there would be no assurance that approval for subsequent transfers would be granted. Accordingly, both technical and practical restrictions on transfer should be weighed when reaching notional value conclusions. Appropriate consideration should be given to the nature and extent of such restrictions, and the likelihood that they might prove to be an impediment to a subsequent transfer of the acquired shares.

Between Informed Parties

The phrase "between informed parties" relates to the inherent assumption that both the buyer and seller are informed with respect to all material facts important to value determination. In an open market context the seller typically is better informed with respect to its own business operations and financial outlook. Concurrently, the seller frequently either does not know, or is unable to meaningfully quantify, the buyer's perceived post-acquisition synergies, cost of capital and other tangible and intangible aspects that may influence the buyer's assessment of value. The buyer has a better idea of post-acquisition synergies than does the seller. As a result, it is not uncommon for open market transactions to be consummated at prices less than a buyer would in fact be willing to pay. On the other hand, the buyer likely will not have the same depth of information with respect to the specifics of the business being sold as will the seller. Often the buyer will not understand all the reasons (financial and other) that have motivated the seller to sell.

Canadian case law supports the assumption that information relevant to a notional market value determination had been fully and openly disclosed as of the date of valuation. In essence, all information that would or should have been available in an open market context generally should be assumed to be available on a best efforts basis in a notional market context.

The information gathering process in a notional market context in many respects parallels a buyer's due diligence process in an open market transaction where, prior to closing, a buyer gleans as much information as possible with respect to the business being acquired. Notwithstanding, neither in the notional market nor the open market are valuation decisions based on full or perfect information. Having said that, the following differences may exist between the information gathering process that occurs pursuant to a notional market value determination as contrasted to that completed pursuant to an open market transaction:

- in the open market, buyers often are provided access to important customers, suppliers, and business partners of the business being valued. Such due diligence may help them better assess the prospective post-acquisition cash flow and risk profile of the target company. However, subject to issues around confidentiality that typically preclude such communication and due diligence, that same due diligence opportunity is seldom afforded to those determining fair market value in a notional market context;

- notional market valuations sometimes are conducted where the valuation date is long past, and therefore key individuals or other information may no longer be available;

- in a notional market context, there is (theoretically) an equal information-gathering opportunity for all parties and their respective advisors. However, as a practical matter an equal information gathering (and hence information assessment) opportunity may not exist, particularly where matters are acrimonious or litigious. Accordingly, in such circumstances one group often is able to compile a greater information and knowledge base than the other;

- in the open market, people who have worked in the type of business that is being acquired generally are involved in the information-gathering process. Accordingly, they bring to bear an operational knowledge of the industry and business when requesting and analyzing information that is often greater than that of professionals. They are able to generate notional value determinations in circumstances where the professionals have comparatively little, or less, operational industry and business knowledge and experience; and

- in the open market, a large part of the cost of information gathering frequently is absorbed in the existing infrastructure of the buyer. In a notional market context, information gathering typically is expensive. Accordingly, practical cost/benefit factors come into play in the development of notional market values that may result in an incomplete information base being used to develop appropriately qualified notional market value determinations.

It follows that the achievement of a perfect and complete information base is not possible in either an open market transaction or notional market context. Accordingly, differences of opinion as to value based on somewhat different databases, analysis and conclusions inevitably result.

Between Prudent Parties

The phrase "between prudent parties" relates to the contemplation of a marketplace where both the buyer and seller exercise reasonable and appropriate diligence and care when assessing issues relevant to their respective purchase and sale decisions. A distinction can be drawn between acting without what is believed to be adequate information, which itself may be imprudent, and acting in an imprudent manner on known information.

Acting at Arm's Length

The phrase "acting at arm's length" relates to the contemplation of negotiation between parties with opposing interests, each of whom has only an economic interest in the outcome. The notion of acting at arm's length is a matter of fact. In other words, it is not necessarily the case that related parties always act on a non-arm's length basis, or that non-related parties always act on an arm's length basis.

Under No Compulsion to Act

The phrase "under no compulsion to act" relates to the contemplation of negotiation between parties where neither is forced to transact nor is constrained from acting with full choice. This is not the case in many open market transactions. For example, a seller may be compelled to transact due to health reasons. A buyer who becomes aware of this issue may attempt to take advantage of the seller's weakened negotiating position. However, the valuation of the business in a notional market context would not take the seller's circumstances into consideration.

While the notional market contemplates a circumstance where neither the buyer nor the seller is influenced pursuant to a compulsive force to buy or sell respectively, it is assumed that each is willing to buy and sell at a cash-equivalent price that is deemed to be fair.

Expressed in Terms of Cash

Open market transactions frequently are consummated in circumstances where a portion or the entire price is not in the form of cash or equivalent. Examples of non-cash consideration include shares of the acquiring corporation, promissory notes and "earnout" type arrangements. Where the subject company is publicly held, the transaction usually is consummated by way of cash or shares of the buyer at the closing date, in order to comply with securities regulations. However, where shares of the buyer are given as consideration, those shares may have a fair market value (i.e., cash-equivalent value) that is different from (typically less than) their market value, particularly where the shares of the buyer are thinly traded.

Notional market valuations are expressed on a cash-equivalent basis and assume an unequivocal transfer of the risks and rights associated with the company. The assumption of a cash-based notional market transaction avoids interpretations of value that otherwise would result from assumptions as to non-cash terms and conditions. This immediate transfer of risk from the seller to the buyer with respect to the prospective operating results of the subject business can have a material impact on what an informed and prudent buyer might be willing to pay.

Fair Market Value vs. Price

Importantly, there can be a significant difference between fair market value or other value term as defined and determined in a notional market context on the one hand, and price as established in an open market transaction on the other. If the components of fair market value are interpreted literally, at least the following differences exist between the determination of fair market value in a notional market context and price in an open market context:

Exhibit 1A
Fair Market Value vs. Price

	Fair Market Value in a Notional Market Context	Price in an Open Market Transaction
Highest Price Available	Buyers and sellers are assumed to have equal knowledge, negotiating abilities, and financial strength. Transactions are assumed to be consummated at the highest available price, but not at an unrealistically high, non-economic price.	Typically, prices are negotiated between parties with differing knowledge, negotiating abilities, and financial strength. Accordingly, transactions may or may not be consummated at the highest available prices and may be consummated at unrealistically high, non-economic prices. Further, there is no assurance that all potential buyers have been canvassed. Finally, even if canvassed, a potential buyer may be unable or unwilling to transact due to lack of interest, or financial or other constraints.

	Fair Market Value in a Notional Market Context	Price in an Open Market Transaction
Open Market	An open and unrestricted market exists in which no buyer is excluded.	Possible buyers may be excluded due to their lack of interest or inability to transact at a point in time because of other priorities, regulatory restrictions, access to financing or other reasons. Furthermore, the seller may not want to conduct a broad market search because of confidentiality concerns or for other reasons.
Unrestricted Market	Legal and contractual restrictions that prevent an unfettered sale are temporarily disregarded. However, existing restrictions are considered when formulating the value conclusion.	Legal and contractual restrictions that prevent an unfettered sale usually are enforceable. These issues typically have to do with the illiquidity that may attach to minority shareholdings.
Informed Parties	Although as a practical matter typically not realistic, it is assumed the hypothetical buyer and seller are apprised of all material information and factors relevant to the value determination at the valuation date.	The seller typically has better knowledge of its own operations, including prospective cash flows and the risk profile of the business. The buyer better understands its cost of capital, financing availability, synergy expectations, strategic initiatives and other factors that may influence the price that it is willing to pay.
Prudent Parties	The possibility of imprudent actions is not considered.	Open market price may be struck as a result of imprudent decisions by the buyer, the seller, or both.
No Compulsion to Act	Forced or compulsive acts are not considered.	Open market price may be struck as a result of forced or compulsive acts by the buyer, the seller or both.
Cash Terms	The transaction is assumed to be consummated for cash at closing.	The price paid may contain a significant amount of non-cash consideration such as promissory notes, shares of the buyer, earnouts and so on, that may have a fair market value materially different (typically lower) than its face value.

Fair Market Value in Canada vs. the U.S.

The generally accepted definition of fair market value in the United States is "*a value at which a willing seller and willing buyer, both being informed of the relevant facts about the business could reasonably conduct a transaction, neither party acting under any compulsion to do so*".

The U.S. definition does not make specific reference to "highest price available," an "open and unrestricted market," the parties being "prudent," the parties being at "arm's length" or the cash nature of the transaction. Despite the absence of these particulars, as a practical matter, there generally is no significant difference in the practice adopted for determining fair market value in the U.S. compared to Canada.

That being said, there are two other differences in the determination of fair market value between the two countries that can have an impact on the fair market value conclusion:

- in the U.S., it is generally accepted that fair market value is determined on an intrinsic (i.e., stand-alone) basis. U.S.-based literature also makes reference to "investment value", which generally is regarded as incorporating an element of post-acquisition synergies. By contrast, while fair market value in Canada usually is determined on an intrinsic basis, absent a qualification to the contrary, the impact of special-interest purchasers should be considered. This was discussed above under the caption Fair Market Value – Highest Price Available. Where: (i) special-interest purchasers can be identified; and (ii) post-acquisition synergies can be quantified in a credible manner; and (iii) it is likely that such synergies would be paid for, then the Canadian courts have sometimes held that such synergies should be considered when determining fair market value; and

- in the U.S., there tends to be more acceptance of using public company comparables when determining fair market value than in Canada. This is likely the result of guidance from the U.S. tax authorities (the Internal Revenue Service) and the larger number of U.S.-based public companies for which meaningful comparative information is often available, given the larger capital markets that exist in the U.S. compared to Canada. The application of public company comparables in valuation is addressed in Chapter 4.

Fair Value

The *Canada Business Corporations Act* and various business-corporations statutes contain what generally are termed:

- appraisal remedies. In specified circumstances these remedies enable minority shareholders to require the issuer corporation to acquire their shares at fair value; and

- oppression remedies. Pursuant to which, shareholders who believe they have been treated in a manner that is "unfairly prejudicial" can petition the courts to require the issuer corporation to be wound-up or to acquire their shares at fair value.

Fair value is not specifically defined in any of the business-corporations statutes. To date, fair value generally has been interpreted by Canadian courts to mean fair market value without the application of a discount to reflect the fact the shareholding(s) in question is a minority shareholding (i.e., a "minority discount"). In addition, as discussed below, Canadian courts have addressed other possible adjustments to fair market value otherwise determined, including post-amalgamation benefits, premiums for forcible taking and the weighing of public market trading prices where the defendant company whose shares require valuation is publicly traded. A list of selected Canadian court decisions addressing various issues that have arisen in the determination of fair value is provided in Appendix A.

Minority Discounts

A minority discount refers to a reduction from the pro-rata portion of the *en bloc* equity value afforded to a minority shareholding (i.e., 50% or less) to reflect the disadvantages related to non-control and the resultant reduction in the liquidity of the minority equity interest. A controlling shareholder generally is in a position to elect a majority of the board of directors and, by extension, to influence the strategic direction and risk profile of the business, the amount and timing of dividend payments, and the timing of the sale of the business. Furthermore, individual shareholders who control a business are able to secure personal employment and remuneration from the business, subject to corporate governance considerations.

The *en bloc* valuation of a business implicitly incorporates all these things. However, absent an agreement that provides otherwise, a minority shareholder typically does not have the ability to exercise control of the business or, in the case of a privately held company, to readily liquidate their ownership interest. Therefore, in any given fact-specific circumstance, a minority shareholding may be worth less than a ratable portion of the *en bloc* value of all the outstanding shares. Stated differently, the value of a minority shareholding may be less than the value of a control shareholding where each is expressed on a per-share basis. The quantification of minority discounts is discussed in Chapter 8.

To date, minority discounts generally have not been applied in circumstances where Canadian courts have determined fair value. Consequently, the successful exercise of an appraisal or oppression remedy may enable minority shareholders to realize liquidity and eliminate a minority discount in respect of their investment where it otherwise may not be available to them.

Post-Amalgamation Benefits

Post-amalgamation benefits such as synergies or other advantages are often expected following an amalgamation of the acquired company with the buyer's existing operations. Accordingly, where an appraisal remedy is triggered pursuant to an amalgamation, the question of whether some or all such benefits should be considered in the determination of fair value arises. Although Canadian court decisions have varied with respect to this issue, the general principles that have been applied to date by Canadian courts indicate that:

- consideration of post-amalgamation benefits is unlikely where the dissenting shareholders are not being forced out, but rather voluntarily decide to discontinue their investment in the acquired company. That is, Canadian courts generally have held that a minority shareholder cannot elect to receive a portion of the post-amalgamation benefits while foregoing the risk that such benefits might not materialize; and

- dissenting shareholders may receive some consideration for post-amalgamation benefits where specific synergies are anticipated and the dissenting shareholders are forced out of the combined firm. That is, Canadian courts generally have held that where the dissenting shareholders wanted to retain their interest in the combined firm and participate in the anticipated post-amalgamation benefits, consideration should be given to their opportunity to do so.

Premium for Forcible Taking

On occasion Canadian courts have concluded that a force-out of a minority shareholder is analogous to the interest of the minority shareholder being expropriated and have awarded the minority a "premium for forcible taking". However, the award of a premium for forcible taking has rarely been recognized by Canadian courts.

Public Equity Market Prices

Where the shares of a company are publicly traded, the relevance of the company's historical share trading prices prior to the valuation date often is an issue in the determination of fair value. In general, Canadian courts have:

- recognized that where trading was thin or sporadic, trading prices may not be, and generally are not, indicative of fair value;

- considered whether the impact of the transaction giving rise to the appraisal remedy may already be incorporated in the share price; and

- generally concluded that historical trading prices, if appropriately considered at all, in most instances should be only one factor to be considered in the determination of fair value.

Value to Owner

The term "value to owner" refers to all the economic and non-economic benefits that accrue from business ownership and increase the fair market value of the business. In this regard, the value to its owner of an equity interest in a business may be significantly greater than its fair market value (or fair value, as the case may be) for several reasons. In particular:

- the business might provide its owner with benefits not quantified as part of a fair market value determination. These might include economic benefits (e.g., employment income and generous expense accounts) and non-economic benefits (e.g., status, prestige and lifestyle). Where an owner draws remuneration from a business that does not approximate arm's length equivalents, such remuneration typically is "normalized" in the determination of fair market value. The quantification of non-economic benefits is highly subjective, and is rarely meaningful given that such benefits vary considerably because of the owner's personal value system;

- the owner might be able to cause the business to generate excess returns due to his or her non-transferable personal knowledge, abilities, contacts, and other personal characteristics, that would be lost if the owner were no longer actively involved in the business (so-called "personal goodwill" as discussed below). As subsequently discussed in this chapter, the ability to generate such excess returns that cannot be transferred to a third-party purchaser does not constitute a component of fair market value in a notional market context; and

- where a shareholder controls a corporation through ownership of voting shares and also beneficially owns redeemable (but not retractable) preference shares or another class of non-voting shares, those preference and non-voting shares may have value to the controlling shareholder beyond the price that could be realized for them in a sale to an arm's length third party to whom only the preference or non-voting shares were sold. This is because a third party may not be prepared to pay full value for an illiquid, non-controlling interest in a privately held company, particularly where control rests in the hands of one other individual.

In a notional market context, the aforementioned factors might result in the value to the owner of a business being greater than fair market value. From both a theoretical and practical standpoint, value to the owner can never be less than fair market value.

Overview of Business Valuation

Primary Approach to Value

When determining the value of a particular business, an assessment must first be made as to whether a liquidation approach or going concern approach should be the primary method of valuation. The primary method that should be adopted is the one that yields the greater net contribution to the equity owners, in order to satisfy the "highest price available" component of fair market value. This can be measured by comparing:

- the value of the business based on its ability to generate prospective cash flows and the risks attaching to realizing those cash flows; and

- the estimated net proceeds which could be attained by disposing of the underlying assets of the business and extinguishing its liabilities,

where both amounts are income tax effected in a consistent manner.

Where a business is economically viable on a stand-alone basis, a going concern approach normally yields the higher value. In some cases the going concern assumption is self-evident, whereas in others a thorough analysis must be undertaken to determine whether the business in question is viable as a going concern and hence will continue to operate. Where the operations of a business are forecast to incur continuous negative cash flow, the business may be worth more pursuant to a liquidation assumption than it is pursuant to a going concern assumption. For the most part, this book has been written on the assumption that the business being valued is a viable going concern. Liquidation-based valuation methodologies are discussed in Chapter 3.

Corporate acquirers generally are most interested in the prospective cash flows that a business may generate. Therefore, going concern values are typically based on cash flow. Common cash-flow-based valuation methodologies include the multiple of EBITDA, capitalized cash flow and discounted cash flow. Each of these approaches is discussed in this book.

The use of asset-based valuation techniques as a primary valuation methodology generally is restricted to circumstances where the business being valued has no active operations of its own, such as a holding company. In such circumstances, the most common asset-based approach is the adjusted net book value methodology (discussed in Chapter 3). Where the underlying assets of a holding company are represented by operating businesses, the value of each of those businesses is typically derived pursuant to a going concern methodology. Their respective values are then used to derive the value of the outstanding shares of the holding company. In some cases, an asset-based approach is used as a secondary method of valuation, or to calculate the amount of goodwill implied pursuant to a cash-flow-based valuation conclusion.

Exhibit 1B
Determination of Primary Valuation Approach

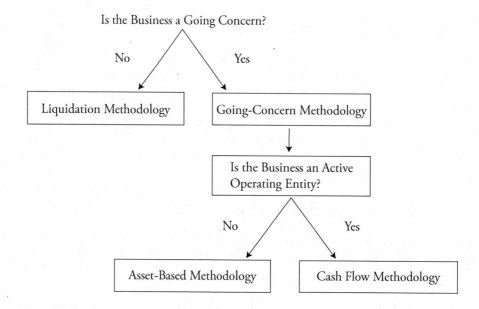

Cash Flow Valuation Methodologies

As discussed above, valuation methodologies based on cash flow are the most commonly used in business valuation. While various cash flow valuation methodologies exist, and each is unique in some way, all cash flow valuation methodologies require that:

- an assessment of the future cash flow prospects of the business be made. While there are several different measures of cash flow, the best measure typically is "discretionary cash flow", which specifically addresses all the variables that influence the economic value of a business;

- an assessment of the risk of achieving those prospective cash flows be made. Risk is expressed in terms of a rate of return (either a discount rate or capitalization rate) or valuation multiple, as the case may be, which is applied to the projected cash flows. The result of applying a rate of return or valuation multiple to prospective cash flows represents the *enterprise value* of the business. Enterprise value represents the going concern value of the underlying operations of the business, regardless of how they are financed;

- outstanding interest-bearing debt and equivalent liabilities be deducted from enterprise value in order to determine the *equity value* of the business. Equity value represents the value of 100% of the issued and outstanding share capital of a company or 100% of the owners' equity of an unincorporated entity (i.e., *en bloc* equity value); and

- an assessment be made of the underlying net assets of the business. The determination of enterprise value as noted above inherently assumes that the business has adequate net operating assets (i.e., working capital and fixed assets) in order to generate the projected cash flows upon which enterprise value is premised. Where the net operating assets of a business are believed to be greater than (less than) what is required to generate such cash flows, then an adjustment to the equity value otherwise determined is required in order to reflect that excess or deficiency. Similarly, some businesses have *redundant assets,* which are not part of their normal operations and which are not reflected in the prospective operating cash flows (and consequently the enterprise value) of the business. Accordingly, where they exist, the value of redundant assets should be reflected as a separate adjustment to equity value otherwise determined.

The basic components of a business valuation can be illustrated as follows:

Exhibit 1C
Basic Cash Flow Valuation Methodology

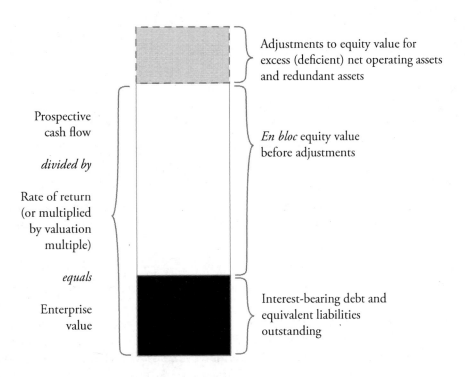

For the most part, in order to determine enterprise value in a given business valuation exercise, emphasis is placed on determining the level of prospective cash flows and the rate of return (or valuation multiple) to apply thereto. Where applicable, consideration of interest-bearing debt and equivalent liabilities, the impact of excess or deficient net operating assets and the possible existence of redundant assets should be made as separate adjustments when developing the equity value conclusion, so as not to distort the going concern value (i.e., enterprise value) of the underlying business operations.

As a simple example of a cash flow-based valuation methodology, assume that Company A generates $6 million in discretionary cash flow each year, and that a 12% rate of return is considered appropriate. Further assume that the business has $15 million of interest-bearing debt outstanding and has redundant assets of $2 million (but no excess or deficient net operating assets). The enterprise value and equity value of Company A would be determined as follows:

Exhibit 1D
Determination of *En Bloc* Equity Value for Company A

Prospective discretionary cash flows	6,000,000
Divided by: rate of return	12%
Equals: enterprise value	50,000,000
Deduct: debt outstanding	(15,000,000)
Add (deduct): excess (deficient) net operating assets	nil
Add: redundant assets	2,000,000
Equals: *en bloc* equity value	37,000,000

Importantly, the prospective cash flows and the rate of return (or valuation multiple) applied thereto are interdependent. Therefore, if the enterprise value of Company A was thought to be $50 million that figure could be derived by:

- adopting a more conservative estimate of prospective discretionary cash flows of $5 million and a lower rate of return of 10%, in order to reflect the relatively lower degree of risk in attaining that more conservative level of cash flow;

- adopting a more aggressive estimate of prospective discretionary cash flows of $7.5 million and a higher rate of return of 15%, in order to reflect the relatively higher degree of risk in attaining that more aggressive level of cash flow; or

- an infinite number of other combinations.

As noted from the examples above, the greater the risk that the discretionary cash flow projections will not be achieved, the higher should be the required rate of return. In the end, selection of these key variables must recognize their reciprocal relationship and must be based on experience and judgment that produce a value determination that is not merely arithmetic. That said, when estimating the value of a business, it generally is preferable to develop a best estimate of prospective cash flow and to adopt market-driven rates of return, without further distortion from undue optimism or conservatism.

Exhibit 1E
Relationship Between Prospective Cash Flow and Rates of Return

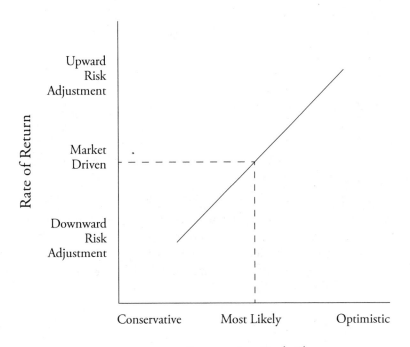

Valuation of Assets vs. Shares

The basic cash flow-based valuation methodology discussed above assumes that the shares of a business are being valued. Where the underlying assets of a business are being valued, further adjustments may be required to account for income tax considerations.

In Canada, the value of a pool of net assets that collectively comprises a business usually is greater (from the buyer's perspective) than the value of all the outstanding shares of the company that owns that net asset pool. This is because an arm's length purchaser of assets that are depreciable for income tax purposes is able to claim capital cost allowance (tax depreciation) based on the portion of the gross purchase price allocated to such depreciable assets. Where the value assigned to those depreciable assets exceeds the tax base of those assets (which is often the case), the future tax benefits to the buyer are greater than they would be had the shares been acquired.

Furthermore, to the extent that the price paid exceeds the amounts allocated to the net tangible assets of the business, the difference represents goodwill. Where the assets of a business are acquired, a buyer who pays for goodwill is entitled to increase its "eligible capital property" for income tax purposes, thus creating a future tax benefit. This benefit is not available to a buyer when it acquires the shares of a business.

As a result of these things, the price that a buyer is willing to pay for the assets of a company pursuant to an open market transaction usually is greater than what it is willing to pay for its shares. The economic impact on the buyer with respect to assets vs. shares is illustrated in Chapter 5. Furthermore, many buyers prefer to acquire assets as opposed to shares for other reasons, such as avoiding hidden liabilities (see Chapter 11). There are exceptions to the general rule that the value of underlying assets is greater than the value of outstanding shares, particularly if non-capital tax losses exist that can be utilized by the buyer to reduce income taxes otherwise payable following the transaction.

The seller, on the other hand, often experiences adverse income tax consequences where a transaction is structured as a sale of assets. A sale of assets can result in taxation both at the corporate level and at the individual shareholder level. The tax consequences of a sale of assets can be particularly burdensome to the seller if there is a significant amount of "recaptured depreciation" resulting from the value assigned to depreciable assets being greater than their tax value. On the other hand, the tax burden may be significantly mitigated where most of the purchase price is allocated to non-depreciable assets or goodwill for income tax purposes, and the seller is able to defer income tax at the personal level.

Furthermore, in Canada a sale of shares gives rise to a capital gain (or loss), and the possible use of the lifetime capital gains exemption of $750,000 per individual (in the case of a qualifying privately held company), which might result in a lower overall tax liability for the seller. Therefore, it does not necessarily follow that the higher value ascribed to a business pursuant to a sale of assets will translate into greater net proceeds to the seller. The seller should determine the after-tax proceeds that would be retained under the two alternatives. This is further explored in Chapter 11.

Unincorporated Businesses

The basic approaches to valuation are similar, whether the legal structure of the business is an incorporated entity or an unincorporated entity (such as a partnership, proprietorship, or unincorporated joint venture).

One of the deciding factors in determining whether or not to incorporate is based on taxation. That is, whether taxes should be paid at the corporate level or at the owner's level. In Canada, where taxes are paid at the corporate level, there is a second layer of taxes imposed on the shareholders (as individuals), where after-tax profits are distributed by way of dividend.

However, the value of a business is not dependent upon its legal structure. In the case of an unincorporated entity, the usual approach is to assume that the entity would be incorporated and therefore pay income tax at the applicable corporate rate. Alternatively, pre-tax cash flows can be applied against pre-tax rates of return. In any event, in the context of a notional market valuation, personal income taxes usually are not be taken into account.

By its nature, the valuation of an unincorporated entity normally is assumed to be structured as a purchase of assets. Therefore, as discussed above, there should be an adjustment on account of the future tax benefits that the purchaser will realize.

Public vs. Privately Held Companies

The valuation methodologies discussed in this book can be applied to both public companies and privately held businesses. In the case of a public company, *en bloc* valuations typically are conducted in the context of a takeover transaction, going-private transaction, dissent remedy, oppression remedy, or other circumstances. In these cases, the valuator normally has unencumbered access to non-public information and management of the public company. This is different from security analysis, as discussed in the following section.

That said, the *en bloc* valuation of the shares of a public company may be influenced by the nature and quantum of information available and the market price at which the shares trade prior to and at the valuation date.

Information Availability

Public companies are required to prepare and publicly file certain types of information, including quarterly and annual reports, management discussion and analysis (MD&A), press releases, annual information forms, management circulars, early warning reports and other documents, as required by the prevailing securities regulations. While the essence of material information contained in those filings should be captured pursuant to the valuation of any business, these documents should be specifically analyzed in a public company valuation context.

Most public companies having a meaningful market capitalization are analyzed and reported on by stock market analysts and bond rating agencies (where the company has publicly traded debt). Some analysts compile their own set of projected operating results for the company being analyzed. Where available, such reports normally should be reviewed when estimating value. However, when reviewing such reports, one should bear in mind that:

- the analyst who prepared the projections and conclusions may have done so based on less than complete information with respect to the company due to restrictions on obtaining insider information and other information that typically is obtained pursuant to a full due diligence process;

- for many industries, stock market analysts employ earnings-based valuation techniques based on actual or projected earnings per share as a principal valuation methodology. Further, the price-to-earnings multiples used generally are based on so-called comparable public companies, which often are at best only broadly comparable. Where comparable public company information is utilized, it is important to consider the degree of comparability between the subject business and the comparables adopted; and

- analysts often adopt the "capital asset pricing model" when assessing rates of return for public companies. Appropriately applied, the capital asset pricing model can be theoretically meaningful in the analysis of investments in normal-sized, public market trading lots. However, direct application of the capital asset pricing model in the rate of return determination when developing *en bloc* equity value normally is problematic. The application of the capital asset pricing model vs. the determination of rates of return in a business valuation context is discussed in Chapter 7.

Market Prices

The price at which a company's shares trade in the open market provides a point-in-time consensus of the view of stock market participants as to the value of a normal-sized trading block of shares in that company. Canadian courts generally have recognized that where a market price exists for a given company's stock, it should be accepted, weighted or rejected as meaningful when determining the *en bloc* value of the outstanding shares of a public company or the value of a specific public company shareholding. In this context, the following important things must be taken into account:

- public equity market prices typically reflect normal-sized minority trading blocks where buyers and sellers have varying amounts of information, knowledge and sophistication, and a wide range of investment time horizons. Where a public company is acquired pursuant to a take-over bid, the acquisition price per share typically exceeds the market price per share prior to the transaction. However:

  ✓ the price paid by a corporate acquirer pursuant to a take-over bid usually includes economies of scale or other anticipated post-acquisition synergies. As a result, the purchase price may not be indicative of the *en bloc* value of the outstanding shares viewed on an intrinsic basis, and

  ✓ such evidence pertains to transactions that have occurred, and should not be taken to mean that the *en bloc* value of the outstanding shares of every public company is in excess of its prevailing stock market price. The prevailing share price of many public companies is such that point-in-time analysis does not support a takeover bid in excess of their stock market price. In such instances bids are not made, and take-overs do not occur;

- where shares are thinly traded, which is often the case for small-cap and micro-cap public companies, the open market price may effectively incorporate a discount for illiquidity;

- large blocks of shares in publicly traded companies may face discounts from prevailing stock market prices when liquidated, particularly in circumstances where:

  ✓ the shares are thinly traded,

  ✓ there is little interest in the company on behalf of financial institutions, pension funds, or equity funds, and

  ✓ the public company has a comparatively small market capitalization;

- market prices can be subject to considerable volatility. Prices can fluctuate significantly in a short time frame due to news releases, market euphoria, a sudden, broad market decline, and other factors. Therefore, consideration must be given to the level of stability in the trading price of the public company's stock and the historical range in market price when assessing its comparability to current value conclusions and to the market prices of other public companies that are used as comparables; and

- the growing influence of high volume algorithmic trading can distort market prices at a given point in time. In many respects, over the past several years, the public equity markets have changed from investment markets to trading markets, a transformation that may have implications for the degree to which public market prices are reflective of fair market value.

It follows that there are important differences between the *en bloc* valuation of the outstanding shares of a public company and the price at which that company's shares trade in the open market. These differences may result in a pro-rata portion of a public company's *en bloc* value expressed as a value per share being either higher or lower (perhaps significantly so) from the prevailing trading price.

Business Valuation vs. Security Analysis

The principles and approaches set out in this book are intended for the valuation of a business *en bloc*, be it a public company, a privately held company or an unincorporated entity. The valuation of a controlling interest or a minority interest begins with the determination of an *en bloc* value for all the outstanding shares of the business, which value is then allocated among the shareholding interests. As discussed in Chapter 8, a minority discount may apply where the equity interest represents 50% or less (principally for privately held companies).

However, the valuation of a business in the context of a notional market valuation or open market transaction is not the same as security analysis. There are fundamental differences between the *en bloc* valuation of the equity in a business and the analysis of daily trading prices of public companies whose shares are listed on a stock exchange. In summary, these differences principally relate to:

- information availability;
- the degree of liquidity;
- risk and return assessment, including different investment time horizons; and
- the valuation of controlling as opposed to minority interests.

This book examines the *en bloc* valuation of business equity from a long-term investment perspective, and should not be taken to be directly applicable to the pricing of securities in a public market context. Furthermore, the analysis undertaken and methodologies adopted by stock market analysts and other public market investors generally differ to some degree from those applied by corporate acquirers. Specifically, price-to-earnings (P/E) multiples and the use of comparable companies and technical analysis play a more prominent role in security analysis than they do in business valuation.

Daily trading prices of publicly held securities and resultant rates of return implied by the public equity markets rarely can be directly applied as a principal valuation methodology in the *en bloc* valuation of a given business. Where comparative public market data is considered when determining *en bloc* value of a public company or privately held business, comparability differences must be accounted for.

Information Availability

In the public equity markets, traders generally act on a limited amount of available information. Such information normally includes quarterly and annual financial reports, Management Discussion & Analysis (MD&A), press releases, annual information forms, analysts' reports and other public documents. Investment bankers, large financial investors, and certain other individuals may be able to obtain additional information through discussions with company management and knowledgeable industry people. However, the information obtained pursuant to such inquiries seldom is of the same depth and quality as that available pursuant to an open market transaction or notional market valuation exercise. This is principally because of legislative restrictions against disclosure of inside information. This is in contrast to information availability in a business valuation context, which is intended to resemble an open due diligence process.

A corporate acquirer or a business valuator seeking to determine the *en bloc* value of the outstanding shares of a given public company or privately held business in either a notional market context or open market transaction typically has access to a greater amount and better quality of information than is available to normal-course traders of public company securities. This additional information typically includes detailed financial and operating data, details of strategic plans, long-term forecasts, and open access to management and key operating personnel. Furthermore, the information is normally subject to either implicit or explicit confidentiality agreements that prevent it from being used except in either the notional context in which the valuation is required, or in the consummation of an open market transaction.

It follows that the corporate acquirer or valuator generally is in a better position to assess the prospective cash flows and the risks and opportunities for the subject business than are stock market analysts.

Liquidity

Liquidity can be viewed as the number of potential buyers for a particular asset at any given time, and the resultant ability of a seller to convert an asset into cash at a price that is known with reasonable certainty within a very short time frame. Most widely held and actively traded public company securities offer holders of normal-sized trading lots a high degree of liquidity due to the organization and regulation of public securities markets. The equity holder typically can crystallize that value in a very short period of time (within minutes for many widely held companies) at a relatively minor cost (broker's commissions). The same degree of liquidity may not be afforded to thinly traded securities (including most of those listed on over-the-counter markets) and typically will not be available to public company shares that are escrowed or otherwise restricted as to sale pursuant to securities acts or stock exchange regulations.

A buyer acquiring a business *en bloc* accepts a different and normally greater degree of liquidity risk than does a buyer of a normal-sized trading block in an widely held public company whose shares are actively traded. This is because:

- a business purchased *en bloc* cannot be disposed of with the ease that is normally attributed to the sale of normal-sized blocks of publicly traded shares. For a business to be sold *en bloc*, the typical divestiture process may take several months or sometimes years, during which time significant events (either positive or negative) affecting the value of the business may occur;

- there is usually a degree of uncertainty regarding the ultimate price that will be fetched in an open market transaction. There are numerous reasons why the value of a business as determined in a notional market context may be significantly different from open market price. Until a business is exposed for sale, negotiations with prospective buyers are held, and the ultimate proceeds and form of consideration are known, price is uncertain;

- as a general rule, due to the relative size of the financial commitment and nature of the investment there are fewer potential buyers for a business *en bloc* than there are for normal-sized trading blocks of shares in public companies;

- given the required commitment of financial and management resources related to the purchase of a business, a buyer generally conducts more detailed due diligence than does an investor of a normal-sized block of publicly traded shares. Furthermore, in the case of a privately held company, a seller typically is required to provide indemnifications and warranties related to the financial position and underlying assets and liabilities of the business being sold, which a seller of a normal-sized trading block in a public company does not do;

- the divestiture of a business *en bloc* (particularly in the case of small and mid-sized companies) is more costly (viewed as a percentage of the sale price) than the disposition of normal-sized trading blocks in the public markets. This is because a corporate divestiture normally is a major undertaking requiring significant advisory and intermediary expenditures and management time and opportunity cost; and

- most corporate acquirers do not purchase businesses *en bloc* with the intent of selling them in the near term. Rather, a corporate acquirer typically purchases businesses *en bloc* pursuant to long-term objectives.

Risk and Return Assessment

Financial market investors can be broadly categorized into four groups:

- stock market investors, including mutual fund companies and pension funds, who typically seek a return on capital in the form of dividends and capital appreciation. Most pursue a diversified portfolio strategy, whereby the risk of losses in any particular security held is reduced pursuant to holding a diversified portfolio. As such, stock market investors typically are more focused on the performance of their portfolio as a whole rather than with gains or losses on any particular security. The prices of normal-sized trading blocks of publicly traded securities are known at any point in time. Accordingly, stock market investors can determine their return on investment on an intra-day or daily basis;

- traders, who range from individual day traders to institutional, high-volume, algorithmic, computerized trading programs. Traders typically seek to realize short-term gains through a variety of means, including technical analysis and arbitrage. They generally look to invest in securities that are actively traded, so that they can readily liquidate their positions;

- financial investors, including private equity firms, venture capital and mezzanine funds, who invest debt and equity with a pre-determined target investment horizon which generally ranges from three to seven years. Financial investors generally anticipate that their target return on invested capital will be realized pursuant to either a subsequent *en bloc* sale of the business or an initial public offering. While larger financial investors may invest in a diversified portfolio of companies, smaller financial investors often concentrate their investments within one or a few industry segments and/or geographic regions. Therefore, the degree of diversification for a financial investor typically is less than that of a stock market investor; and

- corporate acquirers who, for the most part, purchase businesses *en bloc* for their strategic value where post-acquisition returns are expected to include both the cash flow generated by the acquired company on a stand-alone basis and incremental cash flow from synergies following the business combination. Corporate acquirers typically seek to satisfy long-term financial objectives and measure returns in terms of monthly, quarterly and annual financial performance. While larger corporate acquirers may have some degree of diversification, for the most part they tend to focus on a particular industry segment (or related segments) and/or a defined geographic region. Consequently, their degree of diversification typically is less than either a stock market investor or a financial investor.

Given the differences in investment horizons, investment strategy and degree of diversification, the risk perceptions and target rates of return of the various types of investors typically will be different for a given investment opportunity.

Controlling vs. Minority Shareholdings

Trades of publicly held securities typically reflect small blocks of shares, each of which constitutes a small minority shareholding. As such, the individual (external) shareholders of a public company usually have little or no direct influence on the management of the business.

Conversely, the acquisition (or valuation) of a business *en bloc*, or of a controlling interest therein, offers the buyer the benefits of control. A controlling shareholder has the ability to elect the majority of the board of directors and, subject to possible limitations pursuant to shareholder agreements and legislative authority, to:

- establish or change the strategic direction or key operating decisions of the business, thereby altering the degree of operating risk and financial risk in the business;

- determine the quantum and timing of dividend distributions or other returns to shareholders;

- appoint themselves as management of the business; and

- decide whether to sell or wind up all or part of the business.

Although a minority shareholder is not in a position to determine any of these things, the risk associated with non-control is significantly mitigated in circumstances where the shares are freely traded in the open market. Simply put, if the individual shareholder is not satisfied with the public company's direction, management, dividend policy, and so on, and holds only a normal-sized trading block, then the shareholding can be readily sold. Absent a shareholder agreement or enforceable legal remedy that protects liquidity, this typically is not the case where the shareholder is in a minority position in a privately held company. Therefore, minority shareholders in privately held companies are often subject to a discount from pro-rata value (i.e., a minority discount) because of their inability to control the business combined with the illiquidity of their equity investment.

It is generally accepted that publicly traded securities do not trade at prices that reflect minority discounts, nor do purchasers of a controlling interest in publicly held companies necessarily pay a "premium for control." This view is supported by stock analysts' reports and other public market securities analysis, which typically does not apply a minority discount from the pro-rata value per share.

In most cases where an acquisition premium over market price is paid, the premium is based on the buyer's analysis of post-acquisition results and related synergies. Accordingly, whereas control of the subject business is necessary in order for the buyer to realize post-acquisition synergies, it is typically perceived that post-transaction synergies command the premium price and not control per se. In some cases, a premium may also reflect, in part, the elimination of a discount for illiquidity where the shares of a public company were thinly traded prior to the transaction.

Primary vs. Secondary Offerings

A factor which influences the value of a given business is whether the transaction involves existing share capital or newly issued share capital. The sale of a company's treasury shares which results in new capital being received by the company is commonly termed a *primary offering* of shares, whereas a sale of existing shares by a shareholder to another party is commonly termed a *secondary offering* of shares.

Primary Offering

In the case of a primary offering, the share sale proceeds accrue to the company that issues the treasury shares, and thus enhances the *en bloc* value of the issued shares of the company. The percentage interest held by existing shareholders is diluted by the newly issued share capital. However, the net funds raised through the sale of the newly issued share capital accrues to the company, thereby enhancing pre-issue *en bloc* equity value by the amount of the proceeds received from the offering. This higher *en bloc* equity value may arise from one or more of the following:

- a reduction in the amount of debt outstanding, where the new equity capital is used to repay debt, thereby allowing a greater portion of the enterprise value of the business to accrue to the equity holders;

- offsetting a deficiency in working capital (or other net operating assets), which had been causing a reduction in the *en bloc* equity value of the business otherwise determined;

- providing financing to undertake expansion plans which would not be possible absent the new capital; or

- held within the company as a redundant asset.

Accordingly, pursuant to a primary offering, the pro-rata value per share should remain the same.

By way of example, assume that Company B has an enterprise value of $20 million and $12 million of interest-bearing debt outstanding, resulting in an *en bloc* equity value of $8 million. The pro-rata value per common share, based one million common shares outstanding, is $8 per share. The shareholders of Company B all agree that that the business has too much financial leverage, and they seek an equity injection of $2 million that will be used to reduce outstanding debt.

Mr. Black owns 150,000 of the 1,000,000 outstanding shares. Prior to a primary (treasury) common share offering, these shares represented a 15% interest in Company B, and were valued on a ratable basis at $1.2 million (calculated as 150,000 shares @ $8 per share). Assume that a new investor purchases 200,000 treasury shares in Company B at a price of $8 per share. If this cash is used to offset outstanding debt, the following results:

Exhibit 1F
Company B
Impact of Primary Share Offering

	Before Offering	Share Proceeds	After Offering
Enterprise value	20,000,000		20,000,000
Deduct: debt outstanding	(12,000,000)	2,000,000	(10,000,000)
Equity value, *en bloc*	8,000,000	2,000,000	10,000,000
# of shares outstanding	1,000,000	250,000	1,250,000
Pro-rata value per share	$ 8.00	$ 8.00	$ 8.00
Mr. Black's position			
Number of shares held by Mr. Black	150,000		150,000
% interest held by Mr. Black	15.0%		12.0%
Pro-rata value of Mr. Black's interest	1,200,000		1,200,000

While Mr. Black continues to own 150,000 shares of Company B, following the primary share issue, his percentage interest declines from 15% to 12%. However, the value of his shareholding remains at $1.2 million (150,000 shares @ $8) on a ratable basis.

Secondary Offering

In the case of a secondary offering, the share sale proceeds accrue to the selling shareholder and as such have no effect on the *en bloc* equity value of the company; no dilution of any share interest takes place, and no funds accrue to the company.

Referring to the preceding example, assume that Company B has not identified a need for an equity injection. Accordingly, it does not intend to issue treasury shares. A new investor wishes to own equity in Company B and agrees to purchase Mr. Black's interest at $8 per share. This transaction occurs between Mr. Black and the new investor without affecting Company B. Mr. Black receives the net proceeds of the sale rather than the company. There is no dilution of any shareholding interest as no new shares are issued.

Sometimes a secondary distribution of shares is combined with a primary offering. For example, where a privately held company goes public through an initial public offering (IPO), shareholders in the privately held company may offer some of their pre-IPO shareholdings concurrently with the treasury share offering for reasons related to post-issue public market liquidity, personal liquidity, or portfolio diversification. In such circumstances, the share sale proceeds are allocated to the shareholders and the company in proportion to the shares given up by each; however, the *en bloc* equity value of the company is enhanced only to the extent of the funds accruing to it.

Components of Value

Where dealing with 100% of the outstanding shares or net assets of, or a control shareholding in, a business that is valued on the assumption that it will continue to operate as a going concern, the components that may comprise any given enterprise value are:

- the value of interest-bearing debt and equivalent liabilities, where outstanding;

- the value of all the outstanding shares, or owners' equity of the business viewed on a stand-alone basis (i.e., the *en bloc* equity value assuming the business will continue to operate as is, absent any synergies or strategic advantages that may be perceived by one or more arm's length buyers). This value component is often referred to as the "intrinsic value" of the business's equity. Intrinsic value can be comprised of two components:

    ✓ adjusted net book value, defined as the difference between the economic value of the tangible operating assets of the business (such as accounts receivable, inventories and fixed assets), and the economic value of its liabilities (see Chapter 3), and

    ✓ intangible value, which may comprise: (i) identifiable intangible assets, such as brand names, patents, copyrights, franchise agreements, trademarks, and so on; and (ii) non-identifiable intangible assets (or general "goodwill"); and

- an incremental value over intrinsic value perceived by a buyer at the time of acquisition comprised of expected post-acquisition synergies or other economic benefits not available to the business on a stand-alone basis. Common examples of synergies include incremental revenue opportunities, cost savings and overall risk reduction that the buyer expects will result from combining the acquired business with its existing operations. The quantification of synergies is unique to each potential buyer (see Chapter 11). Buyers who anticipate synergies often are referred to as "special-interest purchasers." The combination of intrinsic value and post-acquisition synergies is sometimes referred to as "strategic value," "synergistic value" or "special-interest purchaser price."

As an aside, it should be noted that in open market transactions the common name for the aggregate value of intangible assets is "goodwill." However, in the context of financial accounting, goodwill typically refers to only the non-identifiable intangible asset component. Therefore, caution is warranted to ensure that what is meant by goodwill is understood by the parties involved. In this book, unless otherwise specified, intangible value should be interpreted to mean the aggregate amount of intangible value, which may have both an identifiable and non-identifiable component.

As subsequently discussed, the enterprise value of a business is independent of how the business is financed, but the equity value of a business is net of interest-bearing debt outstanding. Accordingly, enterprise value and equity value, represented on both an intrinsic value and strategic value basis, can be illustrated as follows:

Exhibit 1G
The Components of Enterprise Value and Equity Value

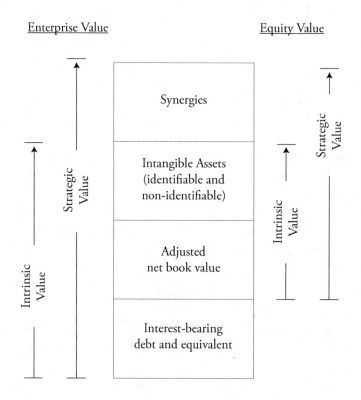

Although the adjusted net book value of a business often can be valued separately, it is usually more difficult to assess the value of a particular identifiable intangible asset. Further, the value of non-identifiable intangible assets can rarely be quantified in isolation. As a result, when reference is made to the specific amount of intangible value inherent in a business following an open market transaction, that amount is normally derived by deducting the adjusted net book value from the *en bloc* equity value of the business determined using a going concern methodology. For financial accounting purposes, the determination of residual goodwill (i.e., non-identifiable intangible value) necessitates a further deduction on account of the value of identifiable intangible assets. The valuation of intangible assets is discussed in Chapter 9.

Returning to the example introduced earlier in this chapter, recall that the *en bloc* equity value of Company A was estimated using a cash flow-based valuation methodology at $37 million. If the adjusted net book value of Company A were $10 million, then the amount of intangible value in Company A would be $27 million. If $15 million of total intangible value was assigned to identifiable intangible assets, then the non-identifiable intangible value (i.e., goodwill) would be $12 million.

Exhibit 1H
Company A
Determination of Intangible Value

Equity value, *en bloc* (from Exhibit 1D)	37,000,000
Less: adjusted net book value	(10,000,000)
Equals: Intangible value	27,000,000
Less: identifiable intangible assets	(15,000,000)
Equals: non-identifiable intangible assets	12,000,000

Furthermore, while a buyer might quantify synergies as a separate component of value when conducting its analysis, that component of value often becomes commingled with intangible value during open market negotiations, and ultimately forms part of the price paid for the shares of a business. In the absence of direct involvement with a particular open market transaction, it is rarely possible to determine how much the buyer specifically paid on account of synergies. Rather, an analysis of the purchase price usually assigns the value of synergies to intangible value.

Debt Outstanding

The amount of debt outstanding that forms part of enterprise value comprises interest-bearing debt (both long-term and short-term) as well as equivalent liabilities, such as shareholder loans, whether or not these obligations are interest bearing. Where applicable, debt obligations are restated at their economic values as opposed to their face values, an adjustment more commonly associated with longer-term debt obligations bearing an interest rate that is materially different from prevailing market rates. A similar adjustment on account of the economic value of outstanding debt is made in the adjusted net book value calculation, and hence there is internal consistency between the two calculations.

Debt outstanding does not include trade payables and other trade debts incurred in the ordinary course of business; these form part of the net operating assets of the business. Such obligations do have an impact on equity value through balance sheet adjustments that may be required where the business is believed to be operating with excess or deficient levels of working capital or other operating assets.

Adjusted Net Book Value

As noted above, adjusted net book value is calculated as the difference between the economic value of a company's tangible operating assets less the economic value of its liabilities. The starting point in calculating adjusted net book value is the shareholders' equity of the business as reported on its financial statements. The following adjustments are then made:

- tangible assets are restated to reflect their economic value as opposed to their value for financial reporting purposes. In most cases, an adjustment is not required for current assets. However, where substantial fixed assets exist, an adjustment is often warranted because the accounting values, which typically are reported at historical cost, net of depreciation and amortization, are often less than their economic value. The economic value of fixed assets is usually calculated as their replacement cost or value in use;

- intangible assets are deducted. Similarly, intangible liabilities such as deferred gains should be added back; and

- where required, liabilities are restated to reflect their economic values rather than their accounting values. In this regard, an adjustment is sometimes required for long-term debt which bears an interest rate that is materially different from prevailing market rates. The calculation of the economic value of outstanding debt should be consistent with the basis on which such obligations were calculated as described in "debt outstanding" above.

The determination of adjusted net book value is addressed in greater detail in Chapter 3.

Intangible Value

As a practical matter, determining the adjusted net book value of a business is itself a subjective task, particularly where the asset base consists of a large fixed asset component. As a result, in a notional market context, intangible value may be better viewed as a value range. Further, where intangible value is computed to be a negative amount (i.e., the *en bloc* equity value of a business as a going concern is less than adjusted net book value), it does not necessarily mean that no intangible value exists. Rather, it may indicate that certain tangible assets are not fully productive, or that the "value in use" estimates made in determining adjusted net book value are overly optimistic.

When analyzing a business with apparent intangible value, it is important to consider to what that intangible value is attributed. In this regard, intangible value can be broadly characterized as commercial goodwill, individual goodwill or personal goodwill.

Commercial Goodwill

Commercial goodwill accrues to a business by virtue of its brand names, proprietary product and service offerings, customer base, advantageous location, and other features that are not dependent upon, or particular to, individual employees of the business. Many of these items constitute identifiable intangible assets, which are often valued separately for financial reporting purposes or other reasons. The valuation of identifiable intangible assets is discussed in Chapter 9.

Commercial goodwill is transferable to a buyer upon the sale of the business. Therefore, where commercial goodwill exists, it is reflected in *en bloc* business value.

Individual Goodwill

Individual goodwill accrues to a business by virtue of its employment of one or more individuals who have the abilities, business contacts, good name and reputation that could be, or would be, harmful to the economic well-being of the business should those individuals leave the employ of the business and compete with it. However, at the time of retirement or death of said individuals, individual goodwill does not expire in so far as the business is concerned where:

- the business has the capacity to substitute other people to fill the role played by those individuals who cease to be employed by the business; and

- those individuals who cease to be employed by the business are precluded from competing with it (assuming an enforceable non-competition agreement).

In an open market context, it is non-competition agreements that result in individual goodwill having commercial value. A non-competition agreement typically is considered to be an identifiable intangible asset since it is represented by a contract.

In a notional market context, it generally is assumed that the buyer and seller will execute a mutually satisfactory non-competition agreement upon the sale of the business. Therefore, individual goodwill is typically included as a component of fair market value. That said, the risks attaching to such individual goodwill must be duly considered in the value determination.

Personal Goodwill

Personal goodwill is goodwill that accrues to a specific person. It arises from his or her personal characteristics and attributes as evidenced by particular abilities, physical characteristics, good name and reputation. Such personal characteristics are not transferable by contract or otherwise. While the benefits of personal goodwill may be reflected in the operating results of the business, such personal goodwill expires at the time the person who enjoys it is no longer involved in the business for any reason, including loss of interest, retirement, disability or death.

In an open market transaction, little, if any, portion of the purchase price is paid on account of personal goodwill. In some cases, personal goodwill is paid for under the terms of a post-transaction management contract that ensures the continued involvement of the person having personal goodwill, so that the related benefits continue to accrue to the business. However, in most cases, the payment terms on that contract require both the continued active involvement of the individual in question and the attainment of agreed post-transaction results. Hence, the risk attaching to personal goodwill remains with the seller.

Given that buyers normally will not pay for personal goodwill in the form of cash or equivalent at closing, it typically is not included when determining fair market value in a notional market context.

Principles of Business Valuation

The following principles are the foundation of valuation theory. As a general rule, they are applicable in both a notional market context and in open market transactions. These principles are founded in a combination of economic theory, common sense, open market reality, and generally through court decisions. The principles are:

- value is specific to a point in time;

- the value of a business is independent of how it is financed;

- value is principally a function of prospective cash flow;

- the market dictates the required rate of return;

- value is influenced by liquidity;

- the value of a business based on a cash flow valuation methodology is influenced by its underlying net tangible operating assets;

- commercial value and non-commercial value are distinct concepts; and

- absent liquidity in the public markets or an agreement among shareholders to the contrary, non-controlling interests are worth less on a per-share basis than controlling interests.

Value Specific to a Point in Time

Value is determined at a specific point in time. It is a function of facts known and expectations made only at that point in time. By way of simple example, prices of normal-sized trading lots of public company shares typically fluctuate daily. Businesses themselves are constantly in a state of flux as a result of changes in product lines, management, financing arrangements, market conditions, general and business-specific economic conditions, industry and competitive conditions, and other factors. Such changes may be dictated by things within the control of management or be imposed by circumstances external to the business over which management has little or no control. Under any circumstance, internal and external changes that affect the prospects of the business typically lead to changes in value. Hence, value is time-specific.

Commensurate with the notion of time-specific value, it generally is accepted in notional market valuations and a fact in open market transactions, that hindsight or retrospective information (i.e., related to events occurring subsequent to the valuation date) should not be considered. Since, when negotiating an open market transaction, neither the buyer nor the seller has the benefit of knowledge of future events, they can only use informed judgment to hypothesize such events. Canadian courts generally have excluded hindsight evidence when determining value in a notional market context, except in limited circumstances where hindsight has been permitted solely for the purpose of determining whether or not subsequent actual events were consistent with the assumptions made and conclusions reached at the relevant valuation date. In this latter regard, where projections were prepared prior to the valuation date and utilized in the value determination, Canadian courts sometimes have permitted the limited use of hindsight when reviewing those financial projections. Thus in a notional market context, hindsight is simply a factor that may be considered in post-valuation date evidence, not in the actual value determination.

Value of a Business Independent of Financing Method

In both a notional market valuation context and in open market transactions, the enterprise value of a business (i.e., the going concern value of the underlying business operations) typically is determined assuming a "normalized" capital structure. Therefore, the cash flows are determined before consideration of debt servicing costs (i.e., interest expense and changes in debt principal). The ability of a business to utilize debt in its capital structure is reflected in the rate of return or valuation multiple applied to those cash flows, which may be different (perhaps materially) from the amount of debt financing the business actually employs. The actual amount of debt outstanding is deducted from enterprise value in order to determine the *en bloc* equity value of the business. Therefore, the enterprise value of a business is independent of how the business is financed. However, equity value is affected by the actual amount of interest-bearing debt (and equivalent liabilities) outstanding.

While this general rule holds in a notional market context, it may not always be so in open market transactions. For example, businesses that operate with excessive amounts of financial leverage can experience challenges caused by banking covenants and cash flow constraints, which may result in the deferral of required expenditures (such as capital expenditures required to sustain or grow the operations), which in turn can have a negative impact on enterprise value. Furthermore, a business that finds itself in serious financial difficulty due to excessive financial leverage may see an erosion in enterprise value due to the loss of confidence by its:

- suppliers, who may place the company on tighter payment terms, thereby constraining working capital required for growth; and

- customers, who may choose not to purchase from a business that might not survive, and therefore not be in a position to honour its warranty commitments.

While in a notional market context it is assumed that a seller is not compelled to transact due to excessive debt levels, in open market negotiations, the existence of excessive debt may place the seller at a disadvantage.

In addition, in some open market transactions, particularly those involving the buyout of existing shareholders by other shareholders or management (i.e., a management buyout), a portion of the purchase price is financed by the prospective cash flow that will be generated from the business following the closing date. The need to allocate cash to service the debt incurred in such circumstances means that less cash is available to finance the growth of the business and, in some cases, may even impair the ability of the business to reinvest in ongoing capital requirements. These factors can have an impact on the price that is negotiated pursuant to such transactions. The issue of "internal vs. external financing" is addressed in Chapter 10.

Value Principally a Function of Prospective Cash Flow

Value principally varies directly with the ability of a business to generate prospective cash flow, except in unusual circumstances where liquidation would result in a higher value.

Cash flow, and not accounting earnings, is the principal determinant of economic value. While accounting earnings are important, there can be many differences between accounting profit and cash flow. Accounting profit is influenced by a myriad of factors, including the accounting policies that a business adopts for such things as inventory costing, depreciation, amortization and leases. Ultimately, cash flow is required in order to reinvest in a business and to provide a return to its owners in the form of dividends, remuneration above market rates or other means. In the open market, buyers typically are most interested in the cash flow generating capabilities of a business when assessing value. While buyers usually consider the underlying operating assets of a business when making their value determinations (as discussed below), cash flow remains the primary determinant of business value in most cases.

There are many different definitions of cash flow. As discussed in Chapter 5, discretionary cash flow usually is the preferred basis to measure business value because it captures all the key variables that influence economic value, including cash flow from operations, income taxes thereon, working capital requirements, and capital investment requirements net of the related income tax shield. Importantly, in open market transactions, buyers usually assess acquisition candidates on the basis of their apparent ability to generate post-acquisition discretionary cash flow, even though they may negotiate all or in part by reference to some other measure of cash flow, such as EBITDA (earnings before interest, taxes, depreciation and amortization).

In this regard, the key is *future* discretionary cash flow. Historical operating results are only meaningful to the extent that they provide insight into prospective results. It is necessary to carefully analyze and understand the significant factors that gave rise to those historical results to determine whether such factors—both internal to the business and therefore to some large degree controllable, and external to the business and therefore generally less controllable—are likely to continue in the manner consistent with their historical behaviour patterns. Forecasting prospective results is by any measure a difficult and subjective task. However, the better the historical data base the greater the ability to identify and assess assumptions that underlie the forecast.

Market Dictates Required Rate of Return

While market rates of return are constantly in a state of flux, they provide important benchmarks at any given point in time, and over the long term influence rates of return sought by investors. At any given point in time, market forces work to dictate prescribed rates of return to be applied in the determination of the value of a business. These market forces include:

- general economic conditions, particularly short-term and long-term borrowing rates, which influence both the acquisition and divestiture activity level and the rates of return investors require. Given that the acquisition of a business generally is viewed by a buyer as a long-term investment, anticipated long-term borrowing rates tend to influence required rates of return on invested capital;

- the market's view of an industry in general, including its risks, growth prospects, competitive landscape, regulatory environment, potential for consolidation and other variables that impact businesses operating within that industry. These variables are reflected to some degree in the implied valuation multiples based on the trading prices of shares of public companies operating within that industry (although the valuation multiples for a particular company can be significantly influenced by company-specific factors as well); and

- company-specific risk factors, including the market's view of the risks and growth prospects that are unique to the business being valued.

As discussed earlier in this chapter, the prospective cash flows of a business and the rate of return applied to those cash flows are interdependent in a business valuation context. All other things being equal, the greater the risk of realizing the prospective cash flows, the higher the required rate of return. The value of a business cannot be altered by changing either the prospective cash flows or the rates of return applied thereto in isolation from one another.

Risk is measured in terms of volatility (i.e., the likelihood that actual results will be different from expectations, and the degree of variability). By way of example, if there is a 50/50 chance of making $10 or losing $10, that proposition is considered less risky than having a 50/50 chance of making $1,000 or losing $1,000. Even though the average expected payoff is the same, the magnitude of the downside has to be considered in addition to the odds of it happening. Stated another way, given a choice between two possible investments with the same average cash flow expectations, an investor will pay more for the investment with the lower risk profile.

As a practical matter, buyers generally are more concerned with downside risk than with pure variability against an average number. Downside risk is usually viewed as the likelihood that the cash flow generated by a business will fall short of expectations, thereby eroding its value.

Value Influenced by Liquidity

As a general rule the greater the liquidity of a business (or an equity interest therein), defined in terms of the number of prospective buyers at a given point in time, the greater the value of the business (or equity interest).

Liquidity refers to the ability to convert a non-cash asset into a known amount of cash within a relatively short time frame. The ability to do this is a function of prevailing economic and industry conditions, as well as the attractiveness of a business to would-be buyers. When financing is relatively inexpensive and easily available, it increases the number of potential buyers in the market and the price that they can pay for acquisition targets, thereby increasing the number of transactions and the prices paid for companies in general.

All other things being equal, greater liquidity decreases risk, which in turn leads to higher value. This is commonly observed in the public equity markets where shares of widely held and actively traded public companies often trade at higher multiples of historical earnings when contrasted with shares of thinly traded public companies operating within the same industry.

When a business is sold in an open market transaction, the seller usually maximizes the selling price by widely marketing the business for sale, as opposed to approaching only one or a few possibly interested parties (although this is not always the case). By soliciting numerous prospective buyers, the price fetched for the business is likely to be greater where:

- one or more prospective buyers are identified that might enjoy significant post-acquisition synergies; and

- given more than one interested party, the seller typically is in an improved negotiating position.

In both a notional market valuation and open market transaction context, it is important to identify whether or not one or more special-interest purchasers exist. In theory, absent consideration of speculators who might buy to immediately resell:

- if there is only one buyer with a special interest in acquiring a business, that buyer will pay only a nominal amount more than buyers without such special acquisition interest (so long as they are aware that they are the only buyer). Having said that, where only one special-interest purchaser exists, as a practical matter open market negotiations with that buyer may result in price concessions related to perceived synergies due to the negotiating skill of the seller, scarcity of acquisition opportunities available to the buyer, and other factors; and

- where there are two or more special-interest purchasers, buyers without such special interests may be excluded from the market by economic conditions beyond their control. This would be the case where buyers with special interests bid the price up, thereby creating a market in which only they participate. In this regard, special-interest purchasers sometimes can include financial investors who have access to significant amounts of financial leverage (i.e., debt) at reasonable rates, which can be used to magnify their equity returns.

Value Influenced by Underlying Net Tangible Operating Assets

As noted above, cash flow usually is the primary determinant of business value. However, as a general statement, all other things being equal, the existence of higher net tangible operating assets (normally represented by the adjusted net book value of the business) lends support to a higher value based on a cash flow methodology than would otherwise be the case. This principle finds conceptual support on the following bases:

- businesses that operate in industries characterized by significant capital requirements often pose a barrier to entry for new participants. All other things being equal, it follows that the higher the cost of industry entry, the lower the probability of new competition, and the lower the buyer's required rate of return at the time of acquisition;

- the greater the tangible assets of a business, the more likely debt financing is available. The buyer's cost of capital is thus lowered and therefore its required rate of return;

- on the date a business is acquired, the net tangible operating assets have an underlying liquidation value. In theory, the greater the liquidation value, the lower the downside risk to the buyer, and hence the lower the buyer's required rate of return at the time of acquisition. However, absent unusual circumstances, buyers acquiring what they believe to be a going concern typically do not weight liquidation value heavily, if at all, when pricing an acquisition; and

- in an open market transaction, buyers usually assess the amount of intangible value (or goodwill) that is implied by a certain purchase price, and normally perceive the intangible assets to be of greater risk than the net tangible assets that are being acquired. Higher net tangible assets lead to lower intangible value for a given *en bloc* value conclusion, which lowers perceived risk and in turn increases value. While somewhat of a circular calculation, it goes to show the relationship between business value determined pursuant to a cash flow approach and the underlying net tangible operating assets of a business.

Setting aside the possible influence of liquidation values, in theory, at the date of acquisition or valuation of a business that is a going concern, the prospective cash flow of that business can be thought of as having two layers:

- a first layer, being a return at an appropriate rate on the net tangible operating assets of a business (e.g., accounts receivable, inventories and fixed assets less operating liabilities such as accounts payable, accrued liabilities and deferred revenues, but excluding interest-bearing debt and equivalents); and

- a second layer, to the extent there is incremental cash flow over and above that required to service the first layer, being a return at an appropriate rate on the intangible assets, calculated as the difference between the aggregate value of the business and the net tangible operating assets. The theoretical required rate of return applied to this second layer would be higher than that applied to the first layer, since the risk attaching to the second layer is theoretically greater than the risk attaching to the first.

The following example will serve to illustrate this point. Companies C and D are competitors in the same industry. Both companies generate discretionary cash flow of $2 million, and are otherwise identical in all respects except that Company C's net tangible operating assets are $6 million, whereas the net tangible operating assets of Company D are $2 million. Neither company has interest-bearing debt outstanding or redundant assets. Therefore enterprise value and equity value are the same.

Assume that Company C and D are each valued as a going concern, and that the required rates of return to be applied to the discretionary cash flows are taken to be 15% on net tangible operating assets, and 20% on intangible assets. It follows that given the perceived rates of return, the enterprise value of Companies C and D would be calculated as follows:

Exhibit 1I
Tangible Assets vs. Intangible Value

	ref.	Company C	Company D
Discretionary cash flow	A	2,000,000	2,000,000
Net Tangible Operating Assets	B	6,000,000	2,000,000
Return on net tangible operating assets	C	15%	15%
Cash flow related to net tangible operating assets	D = (BxC)	900,000	300,000
Discretionary cash flow related to intangible assets	E = (A-D)	1,100,000	1,700,000
Return on intangible assets	F	20%	20%
Value related to intangible assets	G = (E / F)	5,500,000	8,500,000
Enterprise value (and equity value)	H = (B+G)	11,500,000	10,500,000
Implied combined rate of return	I = (A / H)	17.4%	19.0%

In this example, Companies C and D are both assumed to have an identical discretionary cash flow, that is, $2 million. The one composite rate of return that would have to be adopted to determine the enterprise value (and equity value, given the debt-free balance sheet) of Company C to be $11.5 million is 17.4%. The one composite rate of return that would have to be adopted to determine the enterprise value of Company D to be $10.5 million is 19.0%.

As a practical matter, there may be reasons that when viewing Companies C and D on a going concern basis the fact that their underlying net tangible operating asset values are different may not result in their respective enterprise values being different, particularly where the determination of net tangible operating assets involves a high degree of subjectivity (e.g., where there are significant fixed assets having an economic value that is materially different from their accounting value). At the same time, a review of underlying net tangible operating assets, especially where value is being determined for smaller businesses, may assist in sounder risk analysis and hence result in better-based value conclusions. The higher level of net tangible operating assets in Company C may also indicate that there is excess working capital or redundant assets that should be reflected in the overall value conclusions.

In theory the greater the difference between enterprise value and net tangible operating assets, the more such difference should be considered when finally determining enterprise value. The same comparison could be made between *en bloc* equity value and adjusted net book value, where the component of interest-bearing debt included in each of these variables is calculated on a consistent basis. In the end, the significance (if any) of comparisons of imputed enterprise value with net tangible operating assets (or equity value against adjusted net book value) is fact specific, and must be based on experience and informed judgment.

Commercial and Non-Commercial Value — Distinct Concepts

Where the value of a business is based on its prospective cash flows, it may have two distinct components: (i) commercial (or transferable) value; and (ii) non-commercial (or value-to-owner) value.

The prospective cash flows of a business may be generated, on the one hand, irrespective of the involvement of specific individuals or, on the other, all or in part directly as a result of the non-transferable talents or specific characteristics or abilities of certain individuals. Where prospective cash flows accrue:

- irrespective of the involvement of specific individuals, value generally may be said to be commercial, or transferable; and

- all or in part directly as a result of the non-transferable characteristics or abilities of specific individuals, value generally may be said to be non-commercial in nature. In such circumstances, all or part of value determined pursuant to a valuation methodology employing prospective cash flows may represent "value to owner" that is not commercially transferable. While this concept is not difficult to articulate, often it is very difficult to quantify. This is particularly so when it is commingled with apparent value consolidated in an open market transaction pursuant to post-acquisition management contracts and non-competition agreements. As discussed earlier in this chapter, Canadian courts generally have adopted the position that fair market value in a notional market context does not encompass personal goodwill since it does not include a component of commercial value.

For example, assume Company E is in the creative design business, and that all the outstanding shares of Company E are owned by one person, Mr. Everest. Further assume that:

- whereas Company E employs eight other people, it is dependent on Mr. Everest to generate virtually all sales; and

- with few exceptions, Company E's revenues are of a project-based, non-repetitive nature.

An extremely creative person, Mr. Everest also is highly independent. Business accrues to Company E as a result of his personal contacts, his reputation for creativity, his selling abilities, and his high level of personal time commitment. Mr. Everest generates a much higher personal income each year from Company E than he could earn elsewhere in an employee capacity.

Even if Mr. Everest was agreeable to signing a long-term management and non-competition agreement in conjunction with the sale of his Company E shares, absent unusual circumstances it is unlikely a buyer would pay a higher cash purchase price at closing than the net tangible assets of Company E (and possibly the value of newly awarded projects). Goodwill in the form of contingent consideration may be paid, but the economic value (i.e., net present value) of that consideration would be less (perhaps significantly) than its face value. This is because the business of Company E essentially is a function of Mr. Everest's interest in, and ongoing involvement with, Company E. Accordingly, so long as Mr. Everest:

- continues to have the same degree of interest in operating the business of Company E as he has had in the past; and

- does not die or become disabled such that he is unable to continue to operate Company E,

then the outstanding shares of Company E have a value to Mr. Everest that exceeds the commercial value of those same shares.

Controlling vs. Minority Interests

Absent a shareholder agreement or other agreement or legislation that dictates otherwise, the value of a controlling interest in a privately held business may have a greater value per share than does a minority interest in that same business when each is viewed in isolation. As previously discussed, discounts from pro-rata value typically do not apply to public companies where the shares can be freely traded. This is because in most public companies, no one individual or group has a controlling interest, and because a disenchanted shareholder can readily liquidate their shares if they do not agree with the decisions of the board of directors. The advantage of such liquidity typically is not available for minority shareholders of privately held companies.

In either a notional or open market context it is important to distinguish between the determination of the *en bloc* value of the outstanding shares of a company and the determination of the value of an individual shareholding that comprises less than all those outstanding shares. Individual shareholdings essentially fall into two classes, those that control and those that do not. A controlling interest can be represented by either an individual shareholding, a combination of shareholdings of different outstanding share classes beneficially owned by the same owner which together constitute control, or a grouping of shareholdings each of which by itself would not constitute a control position. Simply stated, a controlling interest is one that carries sufficient votes to be able to elect at least a majority of the members of the board of directors and, through them, to govern the business. All other individual shareholdings typically are referred to as minority interests.

Agreements among shareholders can fetter the ability of a controlling interest to unilaterally control business operations, business strategy, and to dictate either a return on investment or the timing of a sale. Absent such agreements or court intervention, the owner of a controlling interest typically can dictate the timing of an offer to sell their shareholding. As previously discussed, the essential reason that a minority interest viewed in isolation may have less value per share than does a controlling interest has to do with the minority shareholder's inability to be guaranteed influence over business strategy, business operations, and the timing and quantum of return on investment. When determining the value of a minority interest in either a notional market valuation or open market transaction context, subject, in the case of notional valuations, to overriding case law, these factors often result in discounts from what otherwise would be the per-share value of the shareholding. Broadly, such discounts are referred to as "minority discounts" – see Chapter 8.

Commensurate with this principle is the notion that the sum of the values of the individual shareholdings that comprise the entire business may be less than the value of total ownership viewed *en bloc*. Where all the outstanding shares of a business are sold in the open market, an appropriate portion of the sale proceeds is typically allocated to each share class. Each shareholder typically then receives their pro-rata portion of the aggregate sale proceeds allocated to the class of shares of which their shareholding comprises a part.

When dealing with business interests in an open market context, the value of a control shareholding is seldom viewed in isolation. This is because most often when controlling interests are sold, all the outstanding shares are sold, or there is a contractual commitment on the part of the buyer ultimately to buy them all. Further, where value is determined for a controlling interest in a notional market context, it is typically perceived to be equal to a pro-rata portion of the *en bloc* value of all the outstanding participating shares of the company that it controls. Rarely in a notional market context is a controlling interest afforded a value in excess of the pro-rata value. In essence, this is because:

- there are legislative fetters governing the behaviour of controlling shareholders that preclude them, in theory and generally in practice, from economically abusing minority shareholders;

- although the controlling shareholder can dictate the quantum and timing of return on investment by causing dividends to be declared and paid, such dividends are shared pro-rata with all other shareholders of a particular share class; and

- in the event of an open market sale of all the outstanding shares, it is assumed each shareholder will receive their pro rata share of that portion of the proceeds attributed to each outstanding share class.

Where controlling and minority interests are valued in isolation from one another and are accorded different values per share, again in the case of notional valuations (subject to prevailing case law) it follows that it would be an unusual circumstance where the aggregation of those separate values was equal to the *en bloc* value of all the outstanding shares.

Consider the following example. Company F has one class of shares outstanding. The *en bloc* value of its outstanding shares is $10 million. There are two shareholders, one owns 60% of the outstanding shares, and the other 40%. Where the two shareholdings are valued independent of one another, it is determined that the 60% shareholding has a value of $6 million ($10,000,000 × 60%), and that the 40% shareholding has a value of $2.8 million, reflecting a minority discount of 30% ($10,000,000 × 40% = $4 million less a minority discount of 30% = $2.8 million). The sum of the parts valued separately is $8.8 million, being $1.2 million less than the *en bloc* value of the outstanding shares.

Minority discounts are both subjective and fact-specific. They can vary significantly, from nil to 40% or more from pro-rata value, depending on the circumstances. One of the key elements to consider is the provisions of a shareholder agreement, which establishes the rights, privileges and obligations of both the minority shareholders and the controlling shareholders of a company. Shareholder agreements are discussed in Chapter 8.

Summary

There are many circumstances where it may be necessary to determine the value of a business, including both notional market valuations and open market transactions. Fair market value or fair value generally is the value term adopted in a notional market context. These concepts are distinct from value to owner, which may reflect economic and non-economic benefits, including personal goodwill, generally not incorporated as an element of either fair market value or fair value. In addition, value as determined in a notional market context may be different from price as negotiated pursuant to an open market transaction.

The first step in the valuation of a business is to determine whether or not it is a going concern. If not, a liquidation-based approach should be adopted. In most cases, the business is assumed to be viable as a going concern, and is valued based on its ability to generate prospective cash flows and the perceived risks relating thereto. The most common approach to business valuation involves determining the enterprise value of the business then deducting interest-bearing debt (and equivalent liabilities), in order to determine equity value, *en bloc*. Where required, equity value is further adjusted to reflect excess or deficient net operating assets (e.g., working capital and fixed assets) and the value of redundant assets.

The *en bloc* equity value of a business can be viewed as comprising its adjusted net book value, intangible value (which may include both identifiable intangible assets and non-identifiable intangible assets) and, where special-interest purchasers are considered, post-acquisition synergies.

The underlying principles of business valuation generally apply in both a notional market valuation and open market transaction context. That being said, every notional market valuation and every open market pricing exercise is unique, and in each case the relevant facts must be considered in order to form a credible value conclusion.

Chapter 2

Business and Financial Analysis

Introduction

In order to develop a credible value conclusion, whether pursuant to a notional market valuation exercise or in an open market transaction context, it is important to have a sound understanding of the business being valued, the industry in which it operates and the relevant prevailing macroeconomic factors. While it is not possible to have complete and perfect information due to constraints relating to timing, cost and other factors, it is important to ensure an adequate understanding of the key economic drivers underlying both the historical and prospective operating results of the business.

One of the first issues that business analysis should establish is whether the business being valued is viable as a going concern, or whether it would be worth more if its assets were liquidated. If a liquidation approach is appropriate, then the balance of the analysis should focus on establishing a value for the individual assets to be sold (see Chapter 3). Assuming that the going concern assumption is valid (which usually is the case), then the analysis should focus on the three principal variables that influence the value of a business, being:

- the amount and timing of prospective cash flows (generally discretionary cash flows) that the business is expected to generate;

- the level of risk perceived referable to realizing those cash flows, which influences the rate of return or valuation multiple adopted; and

- the underlying assets required to generate those prospective cash flows. Analysis of these assets includes working capital requirements, capital expenditures, and establishes whether redundant assets exist.

The information-gathering process and analysis should be conducted in a manner that will provide insight into, and an objective assessment of, these key variables. The balance of this chapter has been written assuming that the business being valued is viable as a going concern.

In a notional market valuation exercise, the breadth and depth of analysis will depend on the size and complexity of the organization, as well as the type of report that has been commissioned (i.e., a calculation valuation report, an estimate valuation report, or a comprehensive valuation report) (see Chapter 10). The extent of the analysis conducted in an open market transaction normally depends on the relative size of the target company compared to the buyer, the buyer's ability to mitigate risk pursuant to deal structuring (as discussed in Chapter 11) and the similarity of the operations of the buyer and the seller. In this regard, open market transactions normally are conducted among companies operating in the same or similar industry. Therefore, the buyer usually has the benefit of existing operating knowledge. This generally is not the case in a notional market valuation where the person(s) determining value may not have industry-specific operating experience. This may require the valuator to place greater reliance on management or, if appropriate, to seek industry expertise from independent sources.

Sources of Information

The initial steps in determining the value of a business are to identify the purpose for which the valuation is required, to identify the shares or assets to be valued and to assemble an information base. Where the valuation is being conducted in a notional market context, it also is necessary to know whether the determination of value is to be made as at a current date or at some prior date. Where a notional valuation is to be made at a prior date, care must be taken to focus and rely only on information available at that time.

The information base can be viewed as comprising three interrelated components:

- facts contained in the documents and records of the business;

- facts, opinions, and observations obtained from discussions and correspondence with the owners and management of the business. If believed useful and appropriate, facts, opinions and observations can also be obtained from external parties, such as industry experts, advisors to the business, real estate appraisers, equipment appraisers, environmental engineers, and other parties with specific knowledge sets; and

- published information concerning the industry such as trends and developments, recent transactions, public market participants and relevant economic indicators.

A useful strategy for accumulating an information base is to assemble and review financial and other documents of the business and general industry information prior to conducting in-depth interviews with management and others. A list of information normally obtained pursuant to a business analysis is discussed below.

General checklists or questionnaires (where used in the information-gathering process) should not be taken to be all-inclusive summaries of required information. Every business has its own unique characteristics. A generic document cannot contemplate all the peculiarities of all industries and business situations. In the end, the terms of reference specific to a given valuation exercise, experience and judgment are required to determine an appropriate scope of review and analysis.

Documents and Records of the Business

Every business is unique in terms of the nature and extent of its management information systems. It is important to assess how the required information can be gathered in an efficient manner without compromising the integrity of the business analysis process. The following sets out a list of documents normally requested, although it is not meant to be all-inclusive. The list should be modified as necessary based on the specifics of the business and the nature of the valuation mandate.

General Corporate Information

- incorporation documents, bylaws and amendments. These should include a summary of the share structure of the business, including number and class of shares authorized, issued and outstanding, and the characteristics of each class of shares;

- a listing of shareholders (including their respective ownership interests) and the relationships, familial or otherwise, among them;

- a corporate organizational chart denoting subsidiaries and investments in other entities;

- minutes of meetings of shareholders, directors and relevant board committees;

- business plans, marketing plans and related qualitative analyses;

- product and service brochures, and other marketing materials;

- public filings (where the business is public) such as annual reports, the annual information form, management circular, material change reports, press releases and other documents;

- stock analysts' research reports covering the business (where it is public) and the industry in which it operates;

- recent independent valuation reports or asset appraisal reports;

- names of auditors, legal counsel, and other outside advisors;

- information contained in a company's website;

- details of offers previously received for the business, including letters of intent and related correspondence; and

- details (including price, terms and conditions) of past share ownership transfers, and how value was established.

Contractual Documents

- shareholder agreements and other contracts affecting business ownership;

- stock option agreements, documentation related to employee share ownership plans (ESOPs) and similar agreements;

- a summary of significant lease contracts for property and equipment, indicating material terms and conditions;

- franchise agreements and licences;

- patents and copyrights;

- a summary of significant customer and supplier contracts;

- a summary of any agency or distributor agreements;

- special permits or licences required by the business and related terms;

- a summary of the terms of collective bargaining agreements;

- pension plan documentation and actuarial valuations;

- a summary of insurance coverage, such as the insured values of fixed assets and life insurance policies on the lives of key managers and business owners, including the cash surrender value of those policies, where applicable;

- legal claims, including the statement of claim, statement of defense and counter-claims;

- documentation supporting recent acquisitions or divestitures of operating divisions; and

- other contracts important to business continuity.

Financial Information

- financial statements (preferably reviewed or audited) for the past several years (normally five years);

- detailed internal financial statements for the same periods where these contain necessary additional detail. This would include divisional financial statements where the business operates one or more subsidiaries or divisions;

- monthly financial statements, generally for the past 24 to 36 months, to assess recent trends and the seasonality of business operations;

- interim financial statements and supporting trial balance, where applicable;

- a schedule of historical transactions between the business, its shareholders and other related parties, and an explanation of how the prices were established;

- a schedule of unusual or non-recurring transactions for the past several years, with supporting explanations;

- a schedule of discretionary expenditures not required in the operations of the business for the past several years, with supporting explanations;

- a listing of redundant assets in the business and their estimated market values;

- projections, including details of underlying assumptions and accompanying narrative;

- capital budgets, including details of underlying assumptions and accompanying narrative;

- federal and provincial corporate income tax returns and supporting schedules for the most recent fiscal years (normally 3 to 5 years);

- analyses of historical and projected sales and profit margins by major product and service offering, major customer, geographic region, distribution channel and other relevant metrics;

- financial filings made to regulatory and other bodies; and

- banking agreements and terms of any outstanding debt obligations, including banking covenants.

Operational Information

- management's assessment of the principal strengths and weaknesses of the business and the major opportunities and threats that it faces (SWOT analysis);

- an employee organizational chart, setting out key individuals, their responsibilities, tenure and successor;

- a summary of key employee data, such as number of employees, turnover levels and relevant qualifications;

- a list of major customers and an analysis of sales by customer for the past several years (normally 3 to 5 years);

- a breakdown of sales by product and service offerings, geographic region and other relevant parameters, for the past several years (normally 3 to 5 years);

- a summary of major inputs and suppliers and an analysis of purchases by major supplier for the past several years (normally 3 to 5 years);

- an explanation of the unique technology, proprietary processes and other competitive advantages of the business, including whether those advantages are sustainable over the longer term and transferable to a third-party buyer;

- research and development initiatives, including the timing and expected revenues from new product and service introductions;

- a summary of operating facilities, including their location, production or service volumes, age, size and capacity, and whether the facilities are leased or owned;

- a summary of distribution channels and distribution-related assets such as fleet;

- flowcharts or diagrams of significant operating processes;

- a copy of any environmental assessments, management consulting, market research or engineering studies completed for the business in recent years (normally 2 to 3 years);

- a copy of valuations or property or equipment appraisals completed in the past several years (normally 5 years); and

- a summary of historical and prospective key performance indicators (units produced, number of service calls, and so on) and operational indicators considered important by management in running the affairs of the business.

Discussions with Management and Other Parties

An analysis of the information collected should generally be incorporated into discussions with management, owners and other parties regarding the historical, current, and anticipated future operating results of the business. This is necessary to ensure that the views and opinions of management are supported by the facts, and that the facts are correctly interpreted. The inability to interview key management personnel would usually pose a limitation on the review, render any value determination subject to qualification and, as a result, make it less reliable than it otherwise would be. Where a notional valuation is being conducted for a prior period, it may be helpful to have discussions with past employees who can provide insights relevant to the time period involved.

When conducting interviews with the owners and managers of a business, each likely will bring his or her own biases and objectives to the discussion. Accordingly, the interests of those individuals in the outcome of the value determination, whether direct or indirect, must be understood.

Depending on the size and complexity of the business, consideration should be given to interviewing one or more managers from each key operating area, including business strategy, sales and marketing, operations and finance. The reliance placed on such discussions will vary with the managers' knowledge of the business and the industry, their length of service, possible biases, and other relevant considerations. Where believed necessary and if possible, key information obtained from inside sources should be externally confirmed. In addition, where a notional valuation is being conducted pursuant to a shareholder buyout, shareholder dispute or litigation, it usually is beneficial to have discussions with representatives of opposing parties and to understand the reasons underlying the differences in their respective points of view.

Outside parties can be a useful resource in understanding the business, particularly where those parties bring an unbiased view. Outside parties can comprise different groups, such as:

- real estate and equipment appraisers who provided an estimate of the values for the underlying assets of the business at or near the valuation date;

- advisors to the business, such as external legal counsel, auditors, management consultants and others who are engaged by management for their particular expertise; and

- industry experts or technical experts (e.g., software engineers or environmental experts) who are engaged directly by the valuator in order to provide an objective view of the business, the industry or specific technical matters.

Industry and Economic Information

In any valuation exercise, it is important to understand the key elements underlying the industry in which the business operates and all relevant economic data. This usually entails gathering the following information:

- a listing of key competitors, whether they are public or private, their product and service offerings, and their estimated size;

- annual and quarterly reports, press releases and other filings for publicly traded companies in the same industry and recent filings of public-offering documents and prospectuses for companies in the same industry;

- information regarding recent transactions involving businesses in the same industry, including the price paid, terms of payment and implied valuation multiples, to the extent that such information is publicly disclosed;

- information from industry or trade associations, or independent industry statistics regarding industry size, growth rates, identifiable market segments, and so on;

- relevant published information concerning the industry, the business and its competitors derived from sources such as Internet searches, newspaper articles, and trade journals;

- a summary of any significant industry-specific regulations, including recent and proposed amendments thereto and the potential impact on companies operating within the industry;

- research reports regarding the industry or various participants prepared by financial analysts, economists or other external parties;

- a listing of key industry and economic indicators tracked by management and how that information is used; and

- general economic indicators that influence the business environment at the valuation date, such as borrowing rates, unemployment rates, projected GDP growth, and so on.

Analysis of Business Operations

A thorough and objective assessment of the operations of the business is important in order to understand the reasons for historical and prospective operating results. While each business is unique, the analysis usually can be categorized as follows:

- general background information;
- sales and marketing;
- management and employees; and
- production, distribution and service delivery.

General Background Information

In addition to reviewing the information noted above under the caption "General Business Information," the background of the business usually requires discussions with business owners (where they are active in the company) and senior management. An analysis of general background information normally includes:

- an understanding of the history of the business and significant developments that have shaped the business over time. This is important when assessing the relevance of historical information. For example, where the business has acquired a major division or significant production capacity has been added in recent years, financial results prior to that period likely will not be indicative of post-valuation-date expectations;

- the nature and general structure of the business, including product and service offerings, customer base, markets served, location of facilities, and so on. This will help in establishing the type of information that needs to be assessed, and whether the valuation should be conducted on a consolidated basis, or whether there are individual business segments that should be valued separately;

- the long-range strategic plans for the business and their key variables and assumptions. These include specific goals, risks and significant trends or developments that have an overarching impact on the risk profile and growth prospects of the business;

- the key operating indicators employed in managing the business. These should include an understanding as to why the operating indicators are considered important, and how they compare to those of competitors or industry guidelines, where such comparatives are available;

- a discussion regarding the major competitors to the business, the scope of their operations, relative size and market share, their major strengths and weaknesses, significant developments among those companies, and how the subject business effectively competes;

- whether there have been any recent transactions involving industry participants and what senior management believes is the underlying reason and potential impact from those transactions. Such discussion can assist in identifying the most likely buyers for the business and the synergies that might result; and

- where there are major issues such as a significant outstanding legal claim or environmental issues facing the business, these should be addressed, along with the likely outcome and expected costs. It may be necessary to discuss these matters with legal counsel or other outside experts (e.g., environmental experts) to ensure a sufficient understanding of the issue.

Sales and Marketing

It is important to have an understanding of the key sales and marketing aspects of a business, as these will drive future revenues and profitability. A sales and marketing review normally includes an examination of business strategy and an assessment of whether cash flow projections are reasonable and consistent based on the business's sales plans and production capacity. Marketing strategy and plans may address the following areas:

- the products and services offered by the business and the degree to which they are proprietary or differentiated from the competition;

- a breakdown of sales by major product and service line should be completed along with associated costs and contribution margin;

- an assessment as to where various principal products and services are in their respective life cycles (introduction, maturity or decline) and plans for new product and service introductions and product line rationalization. New products and services can be classified as to whether they represent extensions of existing offerings or new offerings altogether. There usually is a greater degree of risk associated with the latter. It generally is insightful from the point of view of risk assessment to analyze the percentage of future revenues expected to be derived from new products or services;

- research and development (R&D) initiatives, including the importance of R&D activities to the business, the history of success with new products and pending new product introductions, and the timing and expected results from new introductions (including launching costs);

- the primary and secondary target markets, including market segments the business focuses on, and principal demographic, geographic and other relevant characteristics. Where practical, the rate of growth of each market segment should be established, along with major trends and developments. To the extent that a business expects to grow faster than the market in general, it must focus on taking market share away from its competitors, a challenge that can entail additional risk;

- an assessment of complementary and substitute products and services, including relevant trends and developments;

- the customer base, including such things as the number of customers, the portion of revenues generated through repeat business, customer churn, customer concentration, whether there are significant long-term customer contracts or purchase commitments, and so on;

- how major accounts are managed and the degree to which customer retention relies on certain individual employees;

- key decision metrics for customers which may include such things as price, product and service quality, availability, after-sales service and other factors. It is also necessary to understand how the business ranks in terms of these customer decision drivers;

- the selling cycle for gaining new customers and whether there are certain thresholds, criteria or processes that the business must achieve in order to secure new customers;

- an analysis of customer satisfaction surveys, the reasons underlying customer retention and the risk that major customers might leave to deal with competitors;

- order backlog, quotes, prospects, and management's assessment of the likelihood of being awarded new contracts;

- the sales force and distribution channels, including whether intermediaries are used and, if so, the contractual relationship with, and commitments to, those parties, the number of distribution locations, and so on;

- the compensation structure (e.g., base salary vs. commissions) for the sales team, sales agents and other parties involved in the selling process;

- the pricing structure, including price sensitivity, volatility, discounts and rebates;

- the methods of advertising, including reliance on general media, direct marketing and promotional tools, emarketing and digital media, and any meaningful trend relationships between advertising expenditures and revenues; and

- an analysis of market research reports and research studies involving the business, its product and service categories or the industry in general.

Management and Employees

Management and employees are an integral part of any organization. The quality of the management team can have a significant impact on the risk profile and growth prospects of a business. Therefore, it is important to understand the following:

- key individual managers and their areas of responsibility, experience, age, tenure with the company and level of authority. An understanding should also be obtained as to how key operating and financial decisions are made;

- assessing whether there are key employees whose knowledge, abilities or business contacts are essential to the future prosperity of the business, and whether it could be particularly damaging to the business if they were hired by a competitor. In some cases, key employees possess "personal goodwill" (see Chapter 1) which would be lost in the event that the individual were no longer employed by the business;

- whether one or more successors exist for key individuals within the organization, or whether their replacement would need to be found externally. Lack of management succession can make a company a less attractive acquisition target;

- the composition of the workforce, including the extent to which part-time or contract labour is used and can be reduced in slower periods, thereby mitigating downward risk to some degree;

- the availability of the labour pool in general, including whether specific skills, knowledge or experience is required;

- the basis of remuneration, including the degree to which management and employees are compensated on a variable basis, and related performance criteria. While variable-rate pay can somewhat mitigate risk (through a lower fixed-cost infrastructure), it can also contribute to unexpected decisions or results, given that a person's behaviour is influenced by their remuneration;

- the turnover rate of employees and the reasons for departure (i.e., terminations vs. departure for higher pay or improved working conditions);

- the company's benefit plans, including pensions and post-employment benefit obligations; and

- the relationship between employees and management, particularly where the workforce is unionized. In that case, it is important to have an understanding of the key elements of the collective bargaining agreement and an assessment of the likelihood of business disruption due to a strike or other labour action.

Production, Distribution and Service Delivery

The analysis of a business's production, distribution and service delivery usually involves a tour of the facilities and discussions with the key individuals involved in those operations. Specific considerations typically include:

- for manufacturers, the source and reliability of raw material supply and an analysis of key suppliers. Particular attention should be given to the issue of supplier dependence and whether alternative sources of supply exist. The terms of any significant contracts or commitments that exist with any suppliers should be assessed. Historical and projected fluctuations in the prices of key inputs are important;

- production and operating capacity and the cost to increase capacity. A business that is operating at or near its practical operating capacity normally will have to incur fixed "step costs" to increase capacity, if it is planning revenue growth. Similarly, the labour component of operations (e.g., servicing, delivery, etc.) should be assessed for scalability;

- the distribution systems used by the business, including the composition of the fleet, warehousing requirements and logistics. Where external brokers or agents are used, it is important to understand the terms of the agreements with those parties;

- the age, condition and expected life of production and service equipment. A review of these factors will assist in estimating sustaining capital requirements and in assessing whether near-term equipment upgrades are necessary for technological or other reasons. An analysis of prior years' repairs and maintenance expenses often is helpful in this regard;

- the use of technology and the susceptibility to technological changes in production, operations and other areas;

- the identification of existing or potential environmental liabilities, including estimated clean-up costs. Where the nature of the business is such that environmental liabilities might be significant, legal and engineering expertise in environmental matters may be required;

- the degree to which the operations are capital or labour intensive, whether or not the labour force is unionized, the terms of any collective agreement(s), and the history of labour relations;

- quality control procedures, and whether or not the business conforms to quality standards such as ISO 9000; and

- where the business is subject to government regulation, an understanding of the salient requirements and confirmation that the business is in compliance.

Financial Analysis

A detailed analysis of historical and projected financial statements is a critical element of any value determination. The objective of the analysis is to understand the future prospects of the business in terms of cash flows expectations, the risks attached to achieving them and the capital requirements of the business (i.e., working capital and capital expenditures).

While financial analysis usually involves an assessment of the audited or reviewed financial statements of a company, it should also incorporate an analysis of internal (management) financial statements, which normally provides additional details. A review of the trial balance may also be required, where the internal financial statements are not sufficiently detailed.

Historical Operating Results

An analysis of historical operating results should be undertaken to understand past performance as a starting point in the assessment of prospective operating results. In this regard, where the operations of the business or the dynamics of the industry have changed significantly over the review period, historical operating results may not be indicative of prospective financial performance. Significant change may result from the acquisition or divestiture of an operating division, fundamental change in the competitive landscape or the strategic direction of the business, significant changes in production capacity, and other developments. It is also important to understand the prevailing economic and industry conditions that may have influenced those results at the time (e.g., foreign exchange rates, recessionary periods, etc.).

Forecast Operating Results

A thorough and objective assessment of available business plans and forecasts is an essential component of business analysis. The objective is to reach a conclusion as to their overall reasonableness and credibility. Where business plans and forecasts are available, they usually form the starting point in determining prospective discretionary cash flows which in turn are utilized as one component in determining the value of the business (see Chapters 5 and 6). When reviewing business plans and forecasts, the following things typically should be considered and addressed:

- the business plan and forecast preparation process. In some organizations, the forecasting process is well established, with input from employees knowledgeable about the operations, and whose forecasts pass through a series of reviews and approvals. Conversely, other organizations develop only cursory top-line revenue and expense forecasts with little underlying analysis or support;

- the level of detail employed in forecast preparation. A forecast that is prepared on a line-by-line basis with careful consideration as to what drives each income and expense item typically is more credible than a forecast based on the philosophy of "last year plus X%." In many cases, where longer-term forecasts are compiled, the first-year forecast is prepared in detail, with subsequent-year forecasts being less detailed;

- the individuals involved in preparing the forecast and the reason it was prepared. This is important for two reasons. First, the level of knowledge and experience of those preparing the forecast will influence its credibility. Second, in many cases the persons preparing the forecast have some degree of bias. For example, a forecast prepared by the owners of a business to secure bank financing may present an optimistic view of the business. Conversely, a forecast prepared by management that will be used to establish targets for their performance reviews and bonuses likely will reflect a more conservative scenario. Forecasts prepared in contemplation of the sale of a business tend to be optimistic. If follows that it is important to recognize bias in the forecast and to make adjustments, as necessary, either to the forecast itself or to the rates of return applied to the forecast;

- the accuracy of historical forecasts. A comparison of historical forecasts to actual operating results and analysis of the reasons for variations between them may assist in assessing the credibility of prospective forecasts; and

- the underlying assumptions upon which the forecasts were prepared. When reviewing these assumptions, it is important to assess whether they are reasonable based on the then prevailing business, industry and economic conditions, and whether the assumptions have been applied to the forecasts on an internally consistent basis.

Analysis by Division or Entity

Where financial statements are prepared on a consolidated basis, it is important to assess whether that represents the most appropriate basis to conduct the valuation. Where the business has more than one operating division or subsidiary, analysis of divisional income statements, cash flow statements, and balance sheets (where available) generally is required to determine whether the organization should be valued on a combined basis or on a divisional basis.

Where each division or subsidiary represents a component of an integrated group, preparing the valuation on a consolidated basis may be most appropriate. However, where certain divisions or subsidiaries can operate on a stand-alone basis, and those entities have a risk profile that is materially different than the other related businesses, then it may be appropriate to separate the valuation analysis into its component parts.

The Tax Position of the Business

Financial analysis should include an assessment of the tax status of the business. Specifically:

- the historical and prospective income tax rates applicable to the business, and whether the business is associated with any other companies for income tax purposes;

- whether the business qualifies for reduced tax rates or credits such as the small business deduction, manufacturing and processing profits deduction, scientific research and experimental development (SRED) tax credits and investment tax credits, and other incentives;

- whether there are net capital or non-capital losses available, or other tax-loss pools, including expiry dates and restrictions on use;

- the balance in any undepreciated capital cost allowance and eligible capital expenditure tax pools;

- a review of historical income tax returns and pending income tax returns (where available); and

- for privately held companies, whether there is a balance in the refundable dividend tax on hand account or capital dividend account.

Given that income tax rates and regulations have changed significantly over time, and continue to do so, it is important to ensure the rates adopted are those that prevailed (or were expected to prevail) at the valuation date. Various income tax matters are addressed in Chapter 9.

Balance Sheet Analysis

Financial analysis should include an assessment of the historical and current balance sheets. Specifically, this analysis should include consideration of:

- historical working capital requirements and how key working capital items (e.g., accounts receivable, inventories, accounts payable and accrued liabilities) vary in relation to sales. It is also important to assess whether any working capital deficiency (or surplus) exists at the valuation date and the seasonality of working capital requirements. This may require a review of monthly or quarterly financial results;

- historical capital asset additions and the reasons therefore (e.g., to replace old equipment, to accommodate sales growth or technological advancements);

- the business's current capital structure, being the blend of debt and equity used in financing the business, and whether that represents an appropriate mix given the nature of the business and industry in which it competes. Capital structure is an important consideration in the derivation of appropriate discount and capitalization rates, a subject addressed in Chapter 7; and

- whether any redundant assets exist. A redundant asset is defined as one that is not required to generate the prospective operating cash flows of the business. Identification and treatment of redundant assets is addressed later in this chapter.

While historical balance sheets typically are readily available, forecast balance sheets are often not prepared, even where an income statement has been forecast. However, it generally is worthwhile to prepare the corresponding balance sheets to ensure that all components of value have been properly considered, including changes in working capital and fixed asset balances. Furthermore, forecast balance sheets may provide important insights as to whether banking covenants will be at risk.

Working Capital

For most businesses, there usually is a range of working capital that should be maintained to appropriately support its operations. Where actual working capital is above this range, a portion may represent a surplus, or may provide incremental borrowing capacity. Conversely, where actual net working capital is below this range, a deficiency may be indicated which must be remedied by an infusion of capital or by liquidating redundant non-current assets.

In an open market transaction, the buyer and seller typically will negotiate a working capital target or range at the closing date. In the case of a privately held company, there usually is a price adjustment clause where working capital delivered at closing is above or below the agreed target. Accordingly, in a notional market context, the same principle should apply. Determining an appropriate range of working capital requires analysis and judgment.

Failure to analyze working capital means a buyer could reap a windfall due to a temporary excess or have to inject capital to compensate for a deficiency. Furthermore, in the case of a seasonal business, short-term debt and non-cash working capital usually are correlated to some degree (e.g., high levels of accounts receivable normally are financed by increasing the operating line of credit). Given that debt is deducted from enterprise value in order to determine the equity value of the business, it is important to assess whether working capital is high or low. Excess (deficient) working capital is added to (deducted from) enterprise value in the determination of equity value.

The analysis of working capital should not be limited to an annual basis. Rather, it is important to understand the degree of seasonality of the business and where the valuation date lands during that cycle. This normally entails examining working capital on a monthly or quarterly basis for the past 24 or 36 months.

The working capital of a business can be segregated into four components:

- net trade working capital;
- cash on hand;
- short-term debt; and
- redundant assets of a current nature.

Net Trade Working Capital

Net trade working capital items are non-cash current assets and current liabilities which arise from a business's normal ongoing operating activities. Trade working capital assets generally include accounts receivable, inventories and prepaid expenses. Trade working capital liabilities generally include accounts payable, taxes payable, accruals and, in some cases, short-term reserves (e.g., warranties) and deferred revenues. Net trade working capital represents the amount by which trade current assets exceed trade current liabilities. For most companies, over the long run, variations in net trade working capital tend to correlate with changes in revenues. Net trade working capital excludes cash, short-term interest-bearing debt (and equivalent liabilities) and redundant assets.

The assessment of net trade working capital requirements of a particular business is important not only from the standpoint of assessing whether an excess or deficiency exists, but also in the determination of discretionary cash flows pursuant to a capitalized cash flow methodology and discounted cash flow methodology (as discussed in Chapters 5 and 6, respectively). An assessment of a business's net trade working capital requirements typically includes the computation and comparison of key operating ratios over time. Common working capital ratios include:

- the current ratio;
- the quick ratio;
- days sales in accounts receivable;
- days purchases in accounts payable;
- inventory turnover; and
- average net trade working capital as a percentage of revenues.

These ratios are discussed later in this chapter. In addition, if available and meaningful, the net trade working capital of a business and related ratios can be compared with companies in the same industry or with industry statistics in general.

Although an analysis of these and other operating statistics may indicate that a business is becoming more or less efficient over time or is more or less efficient than its competitors, it does not necessarily mean that a surplus or deficiency in working capital exists. For example, where:

- accounts receivable are comparatively high, it may be due to a poor collection record or inadequate allowance for doubtful accounts or seasonality issues;

- inventories are comparatively high, it could indicate an obsolescence problem, poor inventory management practices or the impact of seasonality; and

- accounts payable are comparatively low, the business may have credit problems and suppliers are demanding cash on delivery, or the business may be taking advantage of supplier discounts for early payment. In the latter case, the impact of supplier discounts should appropriately be reflected in the determination of prospective cash flows.

In some cases, management may state that excess net trade working capital exists at the valuation date because of plans to better manage inventories, receivables, and other working capital accounts that will reduce trade working capital levels in the future. Caution should be exercised in adding any such perceived excesses to equity value. As a practical matter, management expectations as to the amount of working capital that can be freed up pursuant to more efficient operating practices often are overstated. Incremental value from excess net trade working capital should only be considered when the benefits of realization are very likely based on both reasonable expectations and a sound strategy for achieving the result.

Cash on Hand

It is customary to add cash on hand to the enterprise value of a business at the valuation date or to apply that cash on hand as an offset to outstanding interest-bearing debt. This assumes that cash is redundant, and can be withdrawn from the business without impairing its operations. But this assumption does not always hold true.

Most businesses require a cash balance on hand (or available line of credit) in order to meet their current obligations as they come due. In particular, where net trade working capital is negative, a business requires cash to compensate for the difference. An appropriate amount or range of estimated operating cash requirements normally should be estimated based on consideration of:

- net trade working capital, both in absolute dollars and expressed as a percentage of sales. The sum of the operating cash balance plus the net trade working capital requirements should be at a level that allows the business to maintain its operations. Where net trade working capital is low or negative, a notional cash injection may be required to compensate for the perceived shortfall;

- the nature of the business. For example, service businesses whose expenses primarily consist of labour costs may require an operating cash balance to satisfy payroll;

- the composition of current liabilities. For example, current liabilities might include deferred revenues which will be brought into income in the normal course of business as opposed to requiring a cash outflow;

- ratio analysis, particularly the quick ratio, number of days sales in accounts receivable, and number of days purchases in accounts payable, as discussed below; and

- operating cash balances and balance sheet relationships of comparable businesses. Although the cash needs of each business are unique, an analysis of companies in the same industry may provide insight with respect to an appropriate operating cash balance for the business being valued.

Excess (Deficient) Working Capital

The sum of net trade working capital and operating cash balances should be within what is considered to be an appropriate range of working capital for the business. Where actual working capital is greater than or less than this range, it may indicate a surplus or deficiency, respectively. However, before concluding that a redundancy or deficiency exists, the following things should be considered:

- whether there are any debt covenants specifying minimum working capital requirements;
- the reason(s) for the apparent excess or deficiency. For example, sometimes the working capital requirements of a business will increase due to collection issues or to accommodate recent revenue growth; and
- whether the excess or deficiency is temporary due to the seasonal nature of the business or for other reasons.

When valuing a business pursuant to a discounted cash flow methodology (Chapter 6), changes in working capital may already be incorporated in the projected discretionary cash flows. Where this has been done, excess (or deficient) working capital likely already has been accounted for, and should not be double-counted pursuant to an adjustment to *en bloc* equity value of the business otherwise determined. That said, where excess or deficient working capital exists at the valuation date, it is usually preferable to account for that surplus or deficiency as a separate adjustment to equity value rather than incorporating the adjustment into prospective cash flows.

Non-Current Assets

Non-current assets include capital assets and other long-term assets, such as intangibles and long-term investments. An analysis of capital assets is important in order to assess the level of capital investment required to generate revenues and cash flows, and annual capital expenditure requirements. This is aided through a review of the notes to the financial statements and supporting documents, which normally provide a breakdown of fixed assets by category. The conversion to International Financial Reporting Standards (IFRSs) in Canada may result in greater disclosure and changes to the classifications of capital asset balances.

Intangible assets include those having a legal substance (e.g., franchises, licences, patents, etc.) and those created by accounting policies. For example, where a business acquires another entity, the purchase price must be allocated among the net tangible and intangible assets acquired, where the latter might include identifiable intangible assets such as customer contracts or brand names, as well as non-identifiable intangible assets such as general goodwill. Intangible assets having a legal substance provide the business certain rights or protections that, in themselves, normally have an intrinsic value. The value of such intangibles might be different (normally greater) than their accounting value. The valuation of intangible assets is discussed in Chapter 9.

Other long-term assets can comprise a variety of accounts, and might include long-term investments, loans and advances to affiliates, and similar assets of a non-current nature. Each of these other long-term assets should be assessed to determine whether they represent an integral part of the business's operations, or whether they represent redundant assets (see discussion below). Where the long-term asset is an investment in another entity, then the basis of that relationship must be understood as well as transactions between the business and the other entity. Such assets may represent a separate component of equity value where not otherwise accounted for in the enterprise value of the business.

Financing

It is important to understand the existing capital structure of the business and thus the extent to which the business is financed by debt as opposed to equity. In this regard, debt financing refers to:

- long-term interest-bearing debt such as term debt, capital leases and similar obligations;

- short-term interest-bearing debt such as bank operating loans;

- equivalent liabilities, such as loans and advances from shareholders and related parties, whether or not such obligations are interest-bearing. Equivalent liabilities also include one-time payments that a prospective buyer would need to make following a notional or open market transaction, such as bonuses to shareholders; and

- preferred shares that have a redeemable or retractable characteristic. Preferred shares normally are viewed as debt, particularly where they can be retracted by the holder. While the redemption of redeemable preferred shares is subject to a company's board of directors, they normally are viewed as debt as well. This is because most valuation exercises focus on the value of common equity. While preferred shares normally are valued at their retraction or redemption amount, there sometimes are exceptions to this rule. The valuation of preferred shares is addressed in Chapter 9.

Recall that the approach normally adopted when valuing a business is to first determine enterprise value and then to deduct interest-bearing debt and equivalent liabilities to derive equity value (subject to possible further adjustments for redundant assets and excess or deficient working capital or other operating assets). Therefore, while debt financing does not impact the value of a business, it has a direct impact on the value of the equity interest therein.

As explained in Chapter 7, the use of debt financing introduces financial risk into an organization, which impacts the required rate of return. However, the capital structure in existence at the valuation date might not represent a normalized capital structure for the organization.

Other Long-Term Liabilities

Other long-term liabilities include accounts such as long-term deferred revenues, warranties, future income taxes, leasehold inducements and loss provisions of a long-term nature (e.g., environmental reserves). It does not include long-term debt and equivalent liabilities, which constitute financing and are discussed in the following section.

Other long-term liabilities may represent obligations that should be separately adjusted for as part of the determination of *en bloc* equity value. Specifically:

- intangible liabilities such as unamortized leasehold inducements and the unamortized premium on bonds do not represent financial liabilities and are not deducted from enterprise value;

- future income taxes (formerly deferred income taxes) also are not adjusted for directly. However, an adjustment for the tax base of the assets is conducted pursuant to the capitalized cash flow methodology and the discounted cash flow methodology, as discussed in Chapters 5 and 6, respectively;

- long-term liabilities such as warranties and deferred revenues should be analyzed in conjunction with working capital. This is because such liabilities typically are associated with the realization of current assets. For example, where a company invoices for services to be rendered over a two-year period, a portion of the revenues will be recognized in the following fiscal year thus giving rise to long-term deferred revenues. The offsetting accounting entry is a current asset such as cash or accounts receivable. Therefore, the long-term liability is associated with the current asset; and

- provisions for long-term liabilities may include such things as a reserve for pending lawsuits, environmental liabilities, and so on. Such obligations normally are deducted (subject to adjustment, as applicable) when determining the equity value of the business.

Redundant Assets

Redundant assets are defined as tangible and identifiable intangible assets (such as brand names, patents and licences) that are not required by a business to generate the cash flows as projected. Redundant assets do not include excess trade working capital which is adjusted for separately, as discussed above.

Where redundant assets exist, their net realizable value is added to the equity value of the business as determined using a cash flow-based valuation methodology. The determination of the net realizable value of redundant assets is addressed in Chapter 4. Therefore, the net realizable value of redundant assets directly increases the equity value of a business otherwise determined.

The principal reasons for identifying and segregating redundant assets are that redundant assets may not contribute cash flow to the business, or may contribute cash flow that has a significantly different risk profile from the cash flow generated by the operating assets of the business. In such circumstances cash flow-based valuation techniques would not attribute appropriate economic value to these assets, even though these assets might have a realizable value in and of themselves.

It could be argued that the different risk levels related to redundant assets could be factored into the overall rate of return or valuation multiple in the determination of enterprise value, and that this would result in full value being attributed to all the assets of the business. However, the selection of a rate of return or valuation multiple is sufficiently complex and subjective without incorporating further subjectivity into them. Furthermore, the inclusion of redundant assets can distort the derived valuation multiple, which sometimes is used as a comparator for the purpose of assessing the reasonableness of a valuation conclusion.

From a notional market valuation standpoint, the identification and segregation of redundant assets is important in order to satisfy the "highest price available" requirement of fair market value. In open market transactions, the identification of redundant assets normally will allow a seller to realize a higher overall price. No prudent seller would sell a business without either first extracting redundant assets from the business or, alternatively, adding the net realizable value of redundant assets to the equity value of the business. Extracting redundant assets from the business prior to sale is normally preferable in an open market transaction because a buyer usually does not want the redundant assets, and hence either may discount their value for the nuisance factor and liquidation risks related to acquiring them or not fully recognize their value as loan collateral.

Identifying Redundant Assets

The identification and segregation of redundant assets requires a detailed review of the balance sheet (and trial balance, where additional details are required) in conjunction with an understanding of the business's operations, prospects, and the industry in which it operates. Examples of redundant assets include marketable securities, vacant land, unused operating licences, and other assets that are not required in the normal ongoing operations of the business.

To qualify as a redundant asset, three criteria must be met:

- the redundant asset must represent an asset in excess of the current and prospective operating requirements of a business. That is, the asset must not contribute to the operating cash flow projections of the business (or, alternatively, the cash flow contributed from redundant assets must be removed);

- redundant assets are characterized by the degree of permanence of their redundancy, and accordingly excludes those assets that are temporarily idle or underutilized, but are expected to be utilized appropriately in the near to medium term. For example a business may own vacant land required in the near term for expansion. To the extent the benefits of the expansion program have been integrated into the determination of enterprise value, the excess land would not be redundant. However, such assets may have incremental value as a "temporary excess asset" (see Chapter 5); and

- there must be an ability to liquidate the redundant asset or utilize it in the business to generate incremental value to the business owners beyond what otherwise is the equity value of the business. This might be achieved by:

  - ✓ liquidating the asset and paying a dividend to the owners without affecting either the risk or return attached to the underlying business operations,

  - ✓ transferring the asset to another business or withdrawing the asset pursuant to a taxable or tax-free distribution, without affecting either the risk or return attached to the underlying business operations,

  - ✓ liquidating the asset and reinvesting the proceeds in the business, thereby generating growth in excess of what has otherwise been forecast,

  - ✓ using proceeds from the sale of the asset to reduce the level of debt in the business, resulting in a greater proportion of enterprise value flowing through to equity value, or

  - ✓ selling the shares or the underlying assets of the business at a price that satisfies the seller includes equivalent value for the redundant asset.

Redundant asset adjustments affect both projected cash flows and rate of return assessments. In order to avoid double counting, prospective cash flow must be adjusted to account for the notional removal of redundant assets. That is, where an asset has been assessed as redundant, any income generated from that asset (e.g., dividends on portfolio investments) must be removed from the cash flow stream being capitalized or discounted in the determination of enterprise value.

Redundant assets can be found either in working capital accounts or non-current accounts. Identification of redundant assets normally follows from:

- an analysis of the balance sheet at the valuation date. In this regard, it is important to have an understanding of the composition of balance sheet accounts, since redundant assets sometimes are combined with other assets for financial statement presentation purposes. For example:

  ✓ accounts receivable may include non-trade receivables such as loans to directors, shareholders and affiliated companies,

  ✓ inventories may include an obsolete component which has not been factored into projected cash flows, and which can be readily sold, and

  ✓ prepaid expenses and other current assets may include items which are not required in the ongoing operations of the business, and which have not been segregated for financial statement presentation purposes;

- inquiries of management, who should be aware of redundant assets;

- ratio analysis. As discussed later in this chapter, ratio analysis is a tool used to detect trends and anomalies in key operating ratios over time and in comparison with industry norms. Importantly, a ratio suggesting that an asset account is high relative to the norms of the business and the industry does not necessarily mean that a redundant asset exists. Further investigation and analysis must be undertaken; and

- developing a thorough understanding of the nature of the business, including its plans and key economic drivers. In so doing, it is important to address the issue of whether the business is subject to seasonal or longer-term cyclical trends. Although a particular asset may be temporarily underutilized, if it eventually is required to enable the business to meet its cash flow projections, that asset likely is not redundant.

Non-current assets typically include fixed assets, long-term receivables and investments, intangible assets, and other assets that will not be realized by a business within one year. Redundant assets may exist within these accounts, and may include:

- long-term loans to affiliated and related businesses, shareholders, directors or other parties that arose outside the normal course of business;

- long-term investments, such as an equity investment in another business. As noted above, the relationship between a subsidiary or investment and other entities within the corporate group needs to be understood, in order to assess whether it is an integral component of the valuation, or should be assessed as a separate component of value;

- redundant fixed assets, including holdings of vacant land, rental property, and excess equipment. Again, it is important to ensure that these items are not temporarily idle and awaiting the implementation of a planned expansion program to be put into use; and

- unutilized or underutilized licences, franchises, copyrights and patents.

Sometimes redundant fixed assets are not obvious. For example, a business may own land and buildings worth more in the open market than the value they contribute to enterprise value functioning as operating assets. A manufacturer owning premises in the downtown core of a major city might maximize value by entering into a sale-leaseback arrangement for the property. In such a case, redundancy would exist to the extent that the market value of the property exceeds the present value of the lease cost savings (after-tax). This is discussed in Chapter 4.

Redundant Assets and Risk Assessment

When assessing the components of a business's going concern value, care must be taken to recognize and properly deal with redundant assets. This is because it is foremost the business's operations that are being valued. Where ratios and multiples are being calculated based on inferred valuation conclusions, those calculations should exclude redundant assets. For example, the ratio of enterprise value to revenues, enterprise value to EBITDA and equity value to earnings should exclude the impact of redundant assets in both the numerator and the denominator.

Consider the following example. Company G generates EBITDA of $2 million per annum from its operations, and has an enterprise value of $10 million. At the valuation date, Company G owns vacant land that is worth $3 million. The vacant land is used as a parking lot and generates net cash flow of $100,000 per year. A comparison of how the implied multiples of enterprise value to EBITDA would be calculated, with the inclusion and the exclusion of redundant assets, is illustrated in Exhibit 2A:

Exhibit 2A
Company G
Valuation Multiples and Redundant Assets

	Including Redundant Assets	Excluding Redundant Assets
Cash Flow from Operations (EBITDA)	2,000,000	2,000,000
Net cash flow from redundant assets	100,000	n/a
Total cash flow (EBITDA)	2,100,000	2,000,000
Enterprise value – core operations	10,000,000	10,000,000
Value of redundant assets	3,000,000	n/a
Total value (Enterprise Value)	13,000,000	10,000,000
Enterprise value to EBITDA	6.2x	5.0x

As evidenced from Exhibit 2A above, the inclusion of redundant assets in both the enterprise value and the EBITDA stream of Company G results in the multiple of enterprise value to EBITDA being overstated. This is because the income generated from the vacant land does not reflect the underlying economic value of that asset.

Since a significantly different (normally lower) risk profile generally attaches to redundant assets (in this case vacant land), comparisons should refer only to the operating assets of the business. In this example, it is the primary operations of Company G that are being valued. Accordingly, where implied multiples and ratios are calculated for comparative or testing purposes, the impact of redundant assets should be segregated.

Balance Sheet Segregation

A useful exercise that assists in understanding the composition of the net assets of a business is called balance sheet segregation. This entails segregating the balance sheet at the valuation date into four components:

- net tangible operating assets. These include net trade working capital, capital assets and other long-term assets that are part of the primary operations of the business. It may include some or all of cash on hand, where required to support the business operations (e.g., to offset a deficiency in net trade working capital). Net tangible operating assets also include long-term liabilities such as long-term deferred revenues, long-term warranties, reserves and similar obligations. They do not include interest-bearing debt and equivalents, nor any intangible assets or liabilities. Net tangible operating assets represent the net capital investment required to generate the revenues and operating cash flows of the business. This segregation also helps in assessing the adequacy of net trade working capital;

- intangible assets and liabilities. Intangible assets can include those having a legal substance (e.g., franchises, licences, etc.) as well as other intangible assets, such as deferred costs, customer lists and goodwill. Any identifiable intangible assets considered redundant are categorized separately, as noted below. Intangible liabilities might include deferred lease inducement costs and the unamortized premium on the issuance of bonds. The purpose of segregating intangible assets and liabilities is to permit the aggregate economic value of these intangibles to be assessed in the calculation of intangible value when using a cash flow-based valuation methodology;

- financing. As noted above, financing includes both short-term and long-term interest-bearing debt, as well as equivalent obligations such as loans and advances from shareholders. Cash and equivalents normally are classified as an offset to financing. However, some or all the cash on hand may appropriately be classified with net tangible operating assets (as noted above), to offset a deficiency in net trade working capital. The segregation of financing helps in assessing the operating value of the business, independent of how it is financed. It also helps in assessing whether cash on hand can be applied against debt, or whether it should be classified as an operating asset; and

- redundant assets, including those that are included in current accounts, long-term accounts and redundant intangibles. The segregation of redundant assets helps to ensure that the operations of the business are not distorted by the inclusion of non-operating assets.

The balance sheet segregation exercise is conducted based on the book value of assets and liabilities. This may be different from their economic values, particularly for non-current assets and non-current liabilities. The determination of the economic value of assets and liabilities which form part of the adjusted net book value calculation is addressed in Chapter 3.

An example of a balance sheet segregation exercise for Company H is illustrated below:

Exhibit 2B
Company H
Balance Sheet Segregation

	As Stated	Segregated Net Tangible Operating Assets	Intangibles	Financing	Redundant Assets
Current Assets					
Cash	1,100,000			1,100,000	
Accounts receivable	2,200,000	2,200,000			
Inventories	1,800,000	1,800,000			
Shareholder advances	500,000				500,000
Prepaid expenses	300,000	300,000			
Total current assets	5,900,000	4,300,000		1,100,000	500,000
Fixed assets (net)	2,700,000	2,700,000			
Goodwill	1,400,000		1,400,000		
Total Assets	10,000,000	7,000,000	1,400,000	1,100,000	500,000
Current Liabilities					
Current portion of term debt	300,000			300,000	
Accounts payable and accruals	2,100,000	2,100,000			
Deferred revenues	800,000	800,000			
Income taxes payable	400,000	400,000			
Total current liabilities	3,600,000	3,300,000		300,000	
Long-term debt	2,500,000			2,500,000	
Future income taxes	600,000	600,000			
Deferred lease inducement	400,000		400,000		
Total liabilities	7,100,000	3,900,000	400,000	2,800,000	
Equity					
Share capital	100,000				
Retained earnings	2,800,000				
Total equity	2,900,000	3,100,000	1,000,000	(1,700,000)	500,000
Total liabilities and equity	10,000,000	7,000,000	1,400,000	1,100,000	500,000

Pursuant to the previous example, the segregation of Company H's balance sheet reveals the following:

- the company has net tangible operating assets of $3.1 million. This amount can be compared to the enterprise value of the business determined by using a cash flow-based methodology, to assess the reasonableness of the enterprise value conclusion. The net tangible operating assets of $3.1 million are comprised of $1.0 million in net trade working capital and $2.7 million of capital assets, less $600,000 in future income taxes. The next step would be to assess whether the $1.0 million of net trade working capital was adequate, or whether a portion of the cash on hand should be classified as net tangible operating assets as opposed to an offset to financing;

- there is $1.0 million of intangibles, comprised of goodwill of $1.4 million less deferred leasehold inducements of $400,000. The segregation of intangibles helps to ensure that any analysis is not distorted by their inclusion;

- there is $1.7 million of net debt outstanding, comprised of interest-bearing debt of $2.8 million less $1.1 million in cash. This assumes that cash outstanding can be applied against outstanding debt. As noted above, it may be appropriate to reclassify a portion (or all) of the cash on hand to net tangible operating assets, if net trade working capital is deemed to be insufficient to support the business. The net amount of financing is deducted from the enterprise value of the business in determining equity value; and

- Company H has redundant assets of $500,000 represented by advances to shareholders. The segregation of redundant assets helps to ensure that the operating values of the business are not distorted by their inclusion.

Income Statement Analysis

Historical and Current Results

An analysis of historical and current income statements should focus on the following:

- the nature of the business's revenue and expense streams. Where long-term contracts and supplier and customer relationships exist, the associated revenues and expenses generally are more predictable as contrasted to, for example, businesses that generate revenues through a competitive bidding process on each project undertaken;

- significant trends and anomalies in the historical and prospective operating results. It is important to understand why the historical operating results were achieved in light of the industry conditions and the economic environment prevailing at the time. This will help in assessing the degree to which historical operating results are reflective of future expectations;

- whether unusual or non-recurring items (revenues or expenses) may be included in historical operating results. Because the objective is to assess the quantum and quality of prospective cash flows, such items should be segregated. Common examples include one-time expenses associated with new product line introductions, product recalls, reorganization (and related severance expense) and moving costs. Importantly, just because an income or expense item was reported as an unusual item in the financial statements does not necessarily mean it should be assumed to be non-recurring when assessing prospective cash flows. This often requires a review of detailed financial results;

- discretionary expenditures. For privately held companies in particular, the business owners often expense items through the business that are not required to generate revenues and which would not be incurred by an arm's length buyer. Common examples include personal travel costs, life insurance premiums and club dues. The identification of these items normally requires a thorough review of detailed financial results. Importantly, items that appear to be discretionary on the surface may not be so in fact. For example, while donations normally are considered discretionary, the discontinuance of donations could have negative repercussions on the goodwill of the business;

- non-arms length transactions, which might include remuneration to the business owners or their family members, rental payments to premises owned by related persons, or transactions between businesses under common control. Where non-arms length transactions are material and are conducted at other than market rates, they should be adjusted to reflect market rates;

- where the business generates revenues or incurs expenses in a foreign currency, the impact of foreign currency fluctuations on revenues and profitability should be understood. For example, the significant rise of the Canadian dollar against the U.S. dollar from around 2002 to 2007 distorted the financial results of many importers and exporters during that period; and

- historical operating ratios, such as revenue per employee, capacity utilization and gross profit per unit of output. Such ratios can help in assessing the reasonableness of forecast operating results.

Income statement analysis should also incorporate revenues and profitability by division, by product or service group, major customer, geographic area, distribution channel and other metrics that are believed to be important in understanding the risks and growth prospects inherent in the business.

With respect to expenses, an assessment should be conducted of major expense categories and the degree to which operating expenses are fixed or variable. Higher fixed operating costs provide greater upside potential when revenues grow, but also entail a higher degree of risk, since they cannot be readily reduced in the case of a revenue shortfall.

Forecast Operating Results

An analysis of forecast operating results often sets the foundation for valuation. Therefore, scrutiny and skepticism are important. It is not uncommon for projected income statement results to be optimistic. Failure to recognize and compensate for undue optimism would result in an overstated valuation conclusion. Specific elements that should be incorporated in a review of prospective operating results include the following:

- the basis of revenue projections. Ideally, revenue projections should be completed by major product or service offering, by major customer, geographic region and other relevant metrics. While such levels of detail are onerous to prepare, and inherently subjective, it can provide some insight as to the likelihood that the projections can be achieved. For example, where revenue projections are highly dependent on new product and service introductions, gaining new customers and entering new geographic territories, such projections normally would entail a higher degree of risk;

- a comparison of the rate of revenue growth in the business against the growth rate in the market. Where revenues are expected to growth at a faster rate than the market in general, it requires the business to increase its market share or to expand into new markets or new product or service offerings, which generally entails an element of higher risk;

- key assumptions with respect to product and service pricing, and the sensitivity of pricing decisions to sales volumes and prospective profit margins;

- profit margin levels, including gross profit and operating profit. The expectation that margins will increase over the forecast period may indicate that insufficient consideration has been afforded to the costs associated with growth, such as headcount additions and incremental operating expenses;

- operating ratios such as revenues per employee, capacity utilization, profit per unit of output, and other relevant metrics. Comparing such forecast operating ratios to historical operating results can provide some insight into the plausibility of forecast assumptions; and

- financial ratios, as discussed later in this chapter, which also provide insight into the plausibility of the assumptions underlying the forecast.

Sensitivity analysis and break-even analysis may be helpful in understanding the risks inherent in the projected operating results. These normally require the segregation of operating costs into their variable and fixed components, and determining the key variables such as sales, gross margin, and so on that result in significant cash flow and earnings variations.

Cash Flow Statements

Historical cash flow statements represent cash earnings and changes to historical balance sheet accounts. While formal cash flow statements normally are available for historical and current periods, they often are not explicitly prepared as part of the forecasting exercise. However, important cash flow items (capital expenditures and changes to working capital) normally are considered as components of a forecasting exercise. In this regard particular consideration should be afforded to:

- the capital investment requirements to meet forecasted operating results. Where material, these should be segregated into sustaining capital and growth capital. Capital requirements should take into account the condition of existing equipment, current and prospective capacity levels, the impact of technological change, and other factors that necessarily influence business investment; and

- incremental working capital required in order to support the growth prospects of the business. In most cases, higher revenues result in higher levels of accounts receivable and inventories, which may be offset to some extent by increases in accounts payable and deferred revenues. The net increase, if any, represents a net cash outflow for the business that should be considered as part of the valuation.

Ratio Analysis

Ratio analysis frequently is used in both notional market valuations and open market transactions to assist in understanding important trends and relationships for the business being valued, and to help in detecting issues that should be further investigated during the course of the valuation assignment. In particular, ratio analysis assists in the assessment of a business's liquidity, the identification of redundant assets, and the development and understanding of historical and prospective revenue and expense relationships.

Ratios calculated from a business's financial statements for only one year generally are of limited value. However, they take on meaning when compared with other ratios either internally (with a series of similar ratios of the same business over a period), or externally (with comparable ratios of meaningfully similar companies, or with meaningful industry benchmarks). Where believed useful in a particular analysis, ratios should be calculated for the period corresponding to the historical analysis (generally five years). If the operating cycle of the company is longer than five years, then it may be appropriate to review ratios for a longer period of time.

The nature and extent of ratio analysis conducted depends on the fact-specific situation. However, the computation of a myriad of financial ratios and other ratios should not be taken to provide an all-encompassing view of a particular business. Furthermore, a comparison of financial ratios to other companies and industry statistics in general can be distorted due to factors such as seasonality and differences in accounting policies. Therefore, while ratio analysis can be useful, it must be combined with careful interpretation of the economic, industry and business-specific factors affecting each component and ratio.

Ratios commonly used in business analysis can be categorized as follows:

- liquidity ratios, which measure short-term solvency;

- financial leverage ratios, which are used to assess financial risk;

- profitability ratios, which measure expense control and shareholder returns;

- efficiency ratios, which measure business productivity;

- return on investment ratios, which measure the adequacy of historical and prospective economic returns to the capital providers of a business;

- operating ratios that measure financial performance against a non-financial metric; and

- common-size financial statements.

Liquidity Ratios

Liquidity ratios are a measure of the short-term financial strength of the business and generally focus on:

- the ability of the business to meet its short-term obligations as they come due;

- the general degree of risk associated with the types of assets held by the business;

- the possible existence of excess or deficient working capital or redundant assets; and

- the ability of the business to withstand short-term fluctuations in cash flow.

Commonly used measures for assessing short-term liquidity are the: (i) current ratio; and (ii) quick ratio.

$$\text{Current Ratio} = \frac{\text{Current Assets}}{\text{Current Liabilities}}$$

Sometimes referred to as the working capital ratio, the current ratio indicates the extent to which short-term creditors' claims are covered by assets expected to be converted to cash in the normal operating cycle of the business (usually one year). When compared to the current ratio of prior periods and industry averages, the short-term strength of the operations can be assessed and, if apparently stronger than normal in the industry, may be an indicator of excess (deficient) working capital, which in turn, serves to increase (decrease) equity value. Alternatively, if a company's current ratio is consistently high relative to industry norms (e.g., due to excessive overdue accounts receivable or inventory levels), this ratio may indicate financial mismanagement. Care must be taken to analyze the composition of the current assets, having regard to the quality of each asset in terms of its convertibility into cash during the normal operating cycle of a business. A variation of the current ratio is to use only trade current assets in the numerator and trade current liabilities in the denominator, in order to assess the adequacy of net trade working capital.

$$\text{Quick Ratio} \quad = \quad \frac{\text{Cash \& Equivalents + Accounts Receivable}}{\text{Current Liabilities}}$$

This ratio, when used in conjunction with the current ratio, assists in the assessment of short-term strength, and may reveal current asset-composition differences from industry averages. The relative strength or weakness of liquidity in the business and the existence of excess (deficient) working capital or redundant assets may be determined through interperiod comparisons or industry average comparisons.

Financial Leverage Ratios

Financial leverage ratios measure the degree to which the business is financed by debt as opposed to equity. The use of debt within the capital structure of a business introduces financial risk which, as explained in Chapter 7, impacts the rate of return. Financial leverage ratios are commonly employed in the determination of a normalized capital structure for a business. They are also often used by lending institutions when establishing loan covenants. Common financial leverage ratios include the: (i) debt serviceability ratio; (ii) debt to equity ratio; (iii) debt to total capital ratio; and (iv) interest coverage ratio.

$$\text{Debt Serviceability} \quad = \quad \frac{\text{Total interest-bearing debt}}{\text{EBITDA}}$$

The debt serviceability ratio provides an indication of the number of years the business would need to generate cash flow from operations (normally defined as EBITDA – earnings before interest, taxes, depreciation and amortization) in order to settle its outstanding obligations. The numerator includes all sources of interest-bearing debt, both short-term and long-term. The denominator is sometimes modified to reflect any ongoing capital expenditures required to sustain the operations of the business.

$$\text{Debt to Equity} \quad = \quad \frac{\text{Total interest-bearing debt}}{\text{Shareholders' equity}}$$

The debt to equity ratio is a macro indicator of the degree to which a business is financed by debt as opposed to equity. A variation of this ratio commonly found in banking and loan agreements is the use of tangible net worth in the denominator in order to remove the impact of any intangibles recorded for accounting purposes. Tangible net worth usually is calculated as the shareholders' equity of the company, excluding intangible assets and intangible liabilities. Unlike adjusted net book value, tangible net worth adopts the accounting values of assets and liabilities, as opposed to their economic values. Loan agreements referring to shareholders' equity or tangible net worth will often allow for the reclassification of shareholder loans and advances from affiliated companies as equity, subject to those obligations being subordinated to senior debt financing.

$$\text{Debt to Total Capital} = \frac{\text{Total interest-bearing debt}}{\text{Enterprise Value}}$$

The debt to total capital ratio is a variation of the debt to equity ratio, where enterprise value is used as the denominator, expressed using market values. This calculation is commonly used when comparing the debt capacity of the subject business to publicly traded companies, where market valuations are readily available.

$$\text{Interest Coverage} = \frac{\text{Earnings Before Interest and Taxes (EBIT)}}{\text{Interest Charges}}$$

The interest coverage ratio is used as a measurement of safety or risk in a business financed by debt and helps assess long-term solvency from an income statement rather than from a balance sheet perspective. Interest coverage helps to measure the extent that a business's operating income can decline before the business may be unable to meet its financial (interest expense) obligations.

Efficiency Ratios

Efficiency ratios may be used to assess asset productivity, and sometimes assist in detecting uneconomic management practices or redundant assets within a business. Commonly used efficiency ratios include: (i) average days sales in accounts receivable; (ii) inventory turnover; (iii) net trade working capital to sales; (iv) average days purchases in accounts payable; and (v) total asset turnover.

$$\text{Average Days Sales in Accounts Receivable} = \frac{\text{Average Accounts Receivable}}{\text{Revenues}} \times 365$$

This ratio reflects the efficiency of management in collecting accounts receivable, particularly when measured against the company's credit terms and industry averages. The denominator, revenues, should reflect sales on credit, excluding cash sales. Business, industry, and economic conditions must be evaluated in order to assess control over collections versus a restrictive element in sales growth due to tight credit policies.

$$\text{Inventory Turnover} = \frac{\text{Cost of Goods Sold}}{\text{Average Inventory}}$$

This ratio indicates how often during an accounting cycle the inventory available for sale is sold. Generally a high turnover ratio would suggest reduced risk since relatively large sums of money are not tied up in inventories, and management appears efficient in its inventory control. However, a high inventory turnover ratio must also be considered for its effects on inventory shortages and possible resultant lost sales or production problems. A low turnover may indicate obsolete or slow-moving inventories.

$$\text{Net Trade Working Capital to Revenues} \quad = \quad \frac{\text{Net Trade Working Capital}}{\text{Revenues}}$$

The ratio of net trade working capital to revenues assists in measuring the amount of net trade working capital that a business requires in order to support existing and prospective revenue levels. Recall from the discussion earlier in this chapter that net trade working capital normally consists of accounts receivable plus inventories and prepaid expenses, less accounts payable, accrued liabilities, deferred revenues and income taxes payable. In many businesses, as revenues grow, a portion of the cash flow must be used to finance increases in net trade working capital requirements, and hence is not discretionary cash flow.

$$\text{Average Days Sales in Accounts Payable} \quad = \quad \frac{\text{Average Accounts Payable}}{\text{Cost of Goods Sold} + \text{Operating Costs}} \times 365$$

The average days purchases in accounts payable measures the length of time it takes for a business to settle its trade obligations. The denominator should exclude non-cash expenses (such as depreciation and amortization) as well as expenses that do not factor into accounts payable (such as payroll that is paid on a regular basis). However, it should include other costs, such as capital expenditures in order to be consistent with the accounts payable numerator. This ratio can be compared to the trade credit terms advanced by suppliers. As a general rule, businesses will try to stretch out the payment of accounts payable in order to take advantage of trade financing. However, lengthening the payment period might indicate that a business is having cash flow difficulties. This, in turn, could negatively impact the business's reputation with suppliers, thereby increasing the risk that key inputs may not be readily available, or that suppliers may insist on cash-on-delivery terms. In some cases, the average days purchases in accounts payable will be low where the business can take advantage of early payment discounts. The impact of such discounts should be reflected in the cash flow of the business.

$$\text{Asset Turnover} \quad = \quad \frac{\text{Revenues}}{\text{Average Total Assets}}$$

The asset turnover ratio measures the ability of a business to generate revenues using its existing asset base. A higher ratio implies greater efficiency. As is the case with other financial ratios, the asset turnover ratio is sensitive to the accounting policy choices of a business. In particular, accounting policies affecting depreciation, asset capitalization, and operating vs. capital leases can have a significant impact on the calculated asset turnover. Therefore, care must be taken in comparing the asset turnover ratio to industry averages or other benchmarks. Total assets should exclude redundant assets, so that the measure reflects operating efficiency. Variations of this ratio include deducting current trade liabilities from average total assets, or adopting average net tangible operating assets as the denominator (i.e., excluding intangibles). The calculation of net tangible operating assets was illustrated as part of the balance sheet segregation exercise earlier in this chapter.

Profitability Ratios

Profitability ratios help in assessing what portion of revenues is retained by the business at some level. As such, profitability ratios focus on the income statement of a business. Common profitability ratios include: (i) gross profit margin; (ii) EBITDA margin; and (iii) net profit margin.

$$\text{Gross Profit Margin} \quad = \quad \frac{\text{Gross Profit}}{\text{Revenues}}$$

Gross profit margin is useful in determining the relationship between direct costs (and other costs classified with cost of goods sold) and selling prices over a period of time. When compared to industry averages and in light of changing business conditions, it may give some insight into the effectiveness of management in coping with change or indicate that pricing pressure exists. The relationship of each component of cost of goods sold to revenues will also assist in the analysis of the changes in the gross profit margin ratio. That is, it may become apparent that one or more of direct labour, materials, or overhead has had a significant effect on the gross profit margin. If the information is available, an attempt should be made to assess gross profit margins by product or service line, geographic area, division, or such other basis as may be appropriate in order to better assess the risks and returns comprising the business results. A variation of this ratio is the contribution margin to revenues, where the contribution margin is calculated as revenues less all variable costs (including production costs, selling costs and other costs that vary in direct proportion to volume sold).

$$\text{EBITDA Margin} \quad = \quad \frac{\text{EBITDA}}{\text{Revenues}}$$

EBITDA (earnings before interest, taxes, depreciation, and amortization) is a measure of cash flow from the operations of a business, before working capital, capital investment, and income taxes. It therefore avoids distortions due to the classification of expense items for financial accounting purposes. EBITDA levels are a popular reference point both in notional market valuations and in open market transactions. Variations of this ratio include [EBITDA less capital expenditures] to revenues, and EBIT (earnings before interest and taxes) to revenues. In calculating this ratio, it is common to normalize historical operating results to remove the impact of unusual and non-recurring items, as well as discretionary expenditures and distortions caused by non-arm's length transactions.

$$\text{Net Profit Margin} \quad = \quad \frac{\text{Net Profit}}{\text{Revenues}}$$

When compared to industry averages, the net profit margin ratio may assist in measuring management's ability to operate successfully from an equity holder's perspective. The net profit measure is determined after income taxes. The risk inherent in falling selling prices or increases in costs may be more readily understood when considered in relation to this ratio. The net profit margin ratio should be compared with the gross profit margin and EBITDA margin, and their trends analyzed over time. As with the calculation of EBITDA, it is common to normalize the net profit margin calculation to remove the impact of unusual and non-recurring items, as well as discretionary expenditures and distortions caused by non-arm's length transactions.

Return on Investment

Ratios that focus on return on investment are those that help measure whether a business is generating income at levels that produce an adequate return given the resources that are employed by it. Return on investment ratios principally focus on: (i) return on assets; and (ii) return on equity (or return on invested capital).

$$\text{Return on Assets} \quad = \quad \frac{\text{EBIT}}{\text{Average Total Assets}}$$

The return on assets ratio measures the ability of a business's asset base to generate income. The income measure normally used is earnings before interest and taxes (or EBIT), so that the measure of profitability is not distorted by how those assets are financed. EBIT is a pre-tax return. A variation of this ratio is to use [EBIT x (1 − tax rate)] in the numerator to generate an unlevered (i.e., pre-debt) net income measure. Alternatively, unlevered discretionary cash flow sometimes is used in the numerator in lieu of after-tax EBIT. Another common variation is to use net assets in the denominator, being total assets less current trade liabilities. This ratio is more meaningful where the impact of redundant assets has been removed from both EBIT and the asset base.

$$\text{Return on Equity} \quad = \quad \frac{\text{Net Income}}{\text{Shareholders' Equity}}$$

Return on equity determines the rate of return on the owners' investment in the business and may be compared with industry averages (recognizing important differences in accounting policies and other differences that might exist). Shareholders' equity sometimes is measured at market rates (i.e., *en bloc* equity value) rather than based on historical accounting data. The ability of a business to generate a return on equity is a function of its operating profitability, financial leverage, and operating efficiency. Accordingly, in what commonly is referred to as the Dupont Formula, the return on equity can be derived as follows:

Return on Equity = Net Profit Margin × Asset Turnover × Assets to Shareholders' Equity

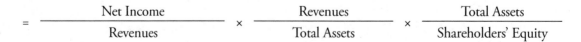

$$= \quad \frac{\text{Net Income}}{\text{Revenues}} \quad \times \quad \frac{\text{Revenues}}{\text{Total Assets}} \quad \times \quad \frac{\text{Total Assets}}{\text{Shareholders' Equity}}$$

Operating Ratios

Operating ratios measure a financial performance indicator (usually revenues or gross profit) against a non-financial metric. Common examples include revenues or gross profit per employee, revenues or gross profit per ton of output and revenue per subscriber. Operating ratios can be helpful in gauging the efficiency of historical performance and in assessing the plausibility of financial projections. For example, financial projections that show revenues per employee are expected to increase significantly over historical levels may indicate an unsupportable assumption with respect to headcount additions in order to achieve the prospective results.

In some cases, operating ratios can be compared to industry benchmarks. This is more commonly the case where the business produces a commodity product. In other cases, operating ratios act as a "rule of thumb" in valuation and may be expressed in terms such as "price per subscriber." Where industry-specific measures are available, they generally should be considered both in measuring operating performance and valuation conclusions. However, any comparison is subject to the caveat that no two businesses are identical. Furthermore, industry benchmarks may fall within a wide range, and they tend to change over time.

Common-Size Financial Statements

Common-size financial statements are those that express each account group as a percentage of the total. For the income statement, this entails expressing each line item as a percentage of revenues. Similarly, each balance sheet line item is expressed as a percentage of total assets. Common-size financial statements prepared over time can provide insight into segregating fixed and variable costs and can assist in identifying unusual or non-recurring expenditures. Common-size financial statements also may be helpful when comparing businesses of different size, and may provide insight into questions such as normal expense ratios, working capital requirements, capital structure and fixed asset additions.

Difficulties Inherent in Financial Analysis

When undertaking financial analysis, it is not sufficient to calculate a myriad of ratios, trends and other indicators; rather, it is important to select those indicators that are meaningful in the circumstances, calculate them correctly and in context, and interpret them appropriately. Analysis of financial information typically encounters difficulties including:

- subjectivity employed in the application of underlying Generally Accepted Accounting Principles and changes due to the conversion to International Financial Reporting Standards (IFRSs). For example, alternate methods of calculating depreciation on the same or similar assets, alternate bases of valuing both tangible and intangible assets, and the manner in which lease commitments are classified for financial accounting purposes (i.e., either operating leases or capital leases) all are subject to some element of subjectivity;

- the extent of judgment and estimates adopted when preparing financial statements. For example, the estimation of an allowance for doubtful accounts or provision for inventory obsolescence;

- understanding the economic and industry conditions that were prevailing at the time the financial results were generated. This is particularly problematic where the valuation date is several years in the past;

- the fact that the balance sheet typically is neither a reflection of the current worth of the underlying capital assets of a business nor of the net equity of the business. Balance sheet items usually are stated at historical cost, inherently distorting the comparison of a particular business to an industry average. This is more of an issue for capital intensive businesses; and

- annual financial statements may be too summarized and aggregated. That is, they may represent a consolidation of different operating entities and hence reflective of different risks inherent in those different operating entities. Further, annual financial statements often do not provide sufficient detail to permit the analysis of operating results generally on more than an overview basis. Detailed internal-management financial statements should be requested in order to carry out the necessary review.

Industry Analysis

A comprehensive review of the industry in which the business competes is important when identifying its growth prospects and risks. Industry analysis normally should include an assessment of the market for the products or services, the competitive environment, and other factors that affect all businesses that operate within a given industry.

Industry Overview

An industry overview can be helpful both in understanding the nature of the operations of a business and in assessing from a macro perspective the reasonableness of, and risk related to, its projections. In general terms, the following things should be reviewed:

- the industry in terms of market size, maturity, fragmentation, major changes or developments, and perceived growth potential of distinct market segments;
- the market for the products and services offered, including possible substitute and complementary products, important trends, and recent developments or new product and service introductions;
- the importance of technology and the apparent speed and impact of technological change on industry participants;
- key success factors. Most industries have one or more key economic drivers that companies within the industry must consider in order to be competitive. Common industry drivers include price, product and service quality, product features and delivery time;
- the ability of the industry as a whole to control pricing and cost structure, and to pass along price increases to customers;
- the degree to which the industry is impacted by macro economic trends, such as outsourcing, globalization and other developments;
- social attitudes toward the industry;
- demographic changes that will have an impact on the industry; and
- government policies and regulations with respect to the industry and recent or pending changes thereto.

Competitive Environment

An important element of industry analysis is the assessment of the competitive landscape, including recent and pending changes. Subject to the availability of meaningful information, the businesses of principal competitors should be reviewed to the extent practical, including their comparative size (typically measured by revenue and employee base), comparative product and service offerings, estimated market share, known strengths and weaknesses, production capability, geographic coverage, and other relevant metrics. The ease of entry of new competitors and the threat of competition from other industries (e.g., substitute products) also should be considered.

For competitors that are public companies, copies of their most recent annual reports and other regulatory filings should be obtained and analyzed. Where industry or stock market analysts report on public company competitors, consideration should be given to obtaining copies of their most recent research reports. Other filings, such as prospectuses, annual information forms, management circulars and press releases can provide additional meaningful insights.

Consideration generally should be given to completing a comparative analysis of key operating ratios, financial ratios and pertinent statistics for the business with those of competitors where relevant and detailed segmented competitor information can be obtained. In this regard, publicly available composite industry ratio and operating data generally is not particularly useful other than as broad guidelines. There usually are significant limitations to the generation of meaningful, directly comparative analysis.

Information available with respect to recent industry open market transactions should be reviewed. In some cases it may be possible to interview industry representatives and analysts with respect to industry value criteria and acquisition practices. However, in the absence of direct involvement with a particular industry transaction it generally is difficult, if not impossible, to draw well founded conclusions and to relate the value of a particular business to one or more open market transactions in a meaningful way.

Finally, the stock market performance of public companies operating in the industry can provide some insights into valuation. This is particularly the case where the public companies represent reasonable comparables to the subject business; where several such public companies exist, distortions and anomalies from any particular company can be removed from the data. While the valuation multiples implied in the public equity markets can provide some insight into the valuation of the subject business, the limitations on the application of stock market multiples in business valuation must be recognized, as discussed in Chapter 4. That said, trends in the median valuation multiples within the industry can sometimes provide insight into the relative attractiveness and market expectations of an industry over time.

Economic Analysis

Economic analysis focuses on the relevant historical and prospective economic factors and credit market conditions that affect the business community as a whole, and on those specific historical and prospective economic factors that bear directly on the business being analyzed. It incorporates both trend analysis as well as the economic conditions at a specific point in time. Where historical performance is being used as an indicator of anticipated future results, the economic conditions under which historical results were achieved must be reviewed in order to assist in predicting prospective results. It also is helpful to review the impact of past economic conditions on the business in order to assess management's ability to cope through changing economic cycles.

The amount of economic information obtained and the depth of review conducted depends on the degree to which such factors influence the business being valued. Examples of the type of economic information that normally are reviewed include historical and prospective:

- interest rates, such as long-term government bond yields, long-term investment-grade corporate bond yields, and other securities that are believed to be relevant;

- borrowing rates, such as the bank prime rate and mortgage rates;

- macroeconomic indicators such as unemployment rates, general wage levels, price index and gross domestic product (GDP) levels, and import/export tariffs;

- economic factors specifically related to the business under review. For example, housing starts and vacancy rates would be relevant for builders and developers;

- foreign exchange rates;

- if applicable, historical and prospective price trends in commodities associated with the sales or cost of sales of the business; and

- changes in government fiscal policies.

Where management actively tracks certain economic indicators, that data should be collected, and the relationship between each economic indicator and the operating performance of the business understood.

SWOT Analysis

After obtaining, organizing and analyzing data regarding the prevailing economic environment, the industry and the business, and following discussions with management and other relevant parties, conclusions should be drawn with respect to the business's strengths, weaknesses, opportunities and threats (i.e., a "SWOT" analysis).

The strengths and weaknesses components of the SWOT analysis largely relate to the business itself. They arise from the business's particular advantages or disadvantages in several areas including management, product and service offerings, customer base, market position, operating practices, and so on. The opportunities and threats components of the SWOT analysis largely relate to the industry in which the business operates, as well as prevailing and prospective economic conditions. Opportunities and threats may arise from competitive or market developments, changing industry regulation, economic conditions and other external factors.

An objective and comprehensive SWOT analysis generally is important in the assessment of risk attaching to achievement of prospective cash flows. The SWOT analysis typically forms an important component in the determination of appropriate rates of return, as discussed in Chapter 7.

Common Deficiencies in Business and Financial Analysis

A properly conducted business and financial analysis requires both thoroughness and skepticism to understand the basis for historical results and to assess the plausibility of forecast results. Some of the more common deficiencies in this analysis are as follows:

- not testing the reasonableness of forecast operating results against operating metrics, such as revenues per employee, capacity utilization, market share and other relevant indicators;

- not relating the operating results of a particular period with the prevailing economic and industry conditions at that time (e.g., competition, exchange rates and market demand);

- failing to assess the net trade working capital requirements of the business adequately, and to understand the impact of seasonality;

- failure to recognize and properly segregate redundant assets; and

- failing to use or interpret ratios properly or to recognize the limitations in ratio analysis.

These deficiencies can result in a valuation conclusion that is unreasonable or, in some cases, misleading.

Summary

Whether a business is being valued pursuant to a notional market valuation or an open market transaction, detailed analysis of the business itself, the industry in which it operates and prevailing economic factors must be completed. A comprehensive and objective assessment of the quantitative and qualitative elements of the business and its environment is important in order to assess prospective cash flows, the risks attaching thereto and the capital requirements of the business.

Business analysis should consider relevant background information, sales and marketing initiatives, management and employees, and production, distribution and service delivery. The nature and extent of the information-gathering process should be tailored as appropriate in each specific instance.

The objective of financial analysis is to understand the reasons for historical operating results, the forecast cash flows and the likelihood they will be achieved. Financial analysis is aided by segregating the balance sheet into its component parts of net tangible operating assets, intangible assets, financing and redundant assets. Ratio analysis, trend analysis, and common-size financial statements sometimes can also be helpful, so long as the caveats of such analyses are recognized.

Chapter 3

Asset Valuation Methodologies

Introduction

As noted in Chapter 1, where a business is not a going concern, a liquidation approach is the primary valuation methodology. The liquidation approach involves estimating the net proceeds that would be generated by selling the assets on an individual basis and settling the outstanding liabilities following either an orderly or a forced liquidation.

Where the business is believed to be a going concern, then a cash flow-based valuation methodology is normally adopted, such as the capitalized cash flow methodology (Chapter 5) or the discounted cash flow methodology (Chapter 6). However, as noted in Chapter 1 – Principles of Business Valuation, the underlying assets of a business will have an influence on the value conclusion determined using a cash flow methodology because the:

- amount of assets required in order to operate a business successfully within a particular industry segment has an impact on the ease of entry for new competitors, which influences business risk and hence the rate of return to apply against cash flows;

- nature and quantum of assets owned by a business are factors that are considered in the assessment of its ability to raise debt financing, which in turn influences the rate of return; and

- amount of intangible value (goodwill) in a business is derived by deducting adjusted net book value from the *en bloc* equity value determined using a cash flow-based methodology. As a general rule, the greater the relative amount of intangible assets, the greater the perceived risk, and hence the higher the required rate of return.

In addition, in some circumstances (more commonly in the case of capital-intensive businesses), the economic value of the underlying net tangible assets may be greater than the equity value of the business based on its ability to generate cash flows. Such a case might suggest that a business has underutilized assets that can be liquidated separately or that the rate of return adopted in the cash flow valuation is overstated. In any case, it is important to consider the economic value of the underlying assets used within the business.

In a notional market context, the shareholders' equity at the valuation date as reported on the financial statements should usually be adjusted to reflect the economic value of the underlying tangible assets and liabilities of the business. The result derived is commonly referred to as the *adjusted net book value* of the business. The difference between *en bloc* equity value determined pursuant to a cash flow (or earnings) based valuation methodology and adjusted net book value represents the intangible value implied in the valuation conclusion. Where a business has substantial non-current assets, adjusted net book value estimates may be subject to wide variation depending on the assumptions adopted and any analysis of the economic values of the individual underlying assets.

Occasionally adjusted net book value is used as a primary basis of determining business value. As a practical matter, the use of the adjusted net book value methodology as the principal determinant of value is generally restricted to holding companies whose value is derived from a collection of individual assets. The valuation of holding companies is discussed in Chapter 9.

In open market transactions the buyer and seller typically weight the current market values of underlying adjusted net book value and/or net tangible assets (i.e., tangible assets less liabilities) when negotiating the price of the outstanding shares or assets of a business. While buyers typically place more emphasis on prospective cash flows, they also consider the underlying assets required to generate that cash flow.

Furthermore, buyers (most notably public companies) are wary of the amount of intangible value acquired in a transaction, since the amortization of intangibles impacts post-acquisition earnings per share.

Liquidation Value

Where it has been determined that a business is not viable as a going concern, it is valued on a liquidation basis. Liquidation value may also be appropriate in the unusual circumstance where the expected liquidation proceeds attributable to the equity owners exceed the *en bloc* value of the equity determined on a going concern basis.

Liquidation value is calculated as the net amount, if any, available to the equity owners on the liquidation of all assets and settlement of all liabilities. Liquidation value can be established under a voluntary liquidation that assumes favourable circumstances for the business owners, or under a forced liquidation that assumes the business is forced into receivership by its creditors. As a practical matter, where a business is not viable as a going concern, the value of the net assets frequently leaves no residual accruing to the equity owners.

Approaches to Determining Liquidation Value

The assumptions on which a liquidation value calculation is premised can have a significant impact on the conclusion. In this regard, two principal determinations must be made:

- whether the business is subject to a forced or voluntary liquidation; and

- the time frame of the liquidation. That is, whether an immediate liquidation or an extended liquidation period is assumed.

From a conceptual standpoint, liquidation value can be computed according to one of four scenarios as follows:

Exhibit 3A
Liquidation Value Scenarios

	Immediate liquidation	Extended liquidation
Forced liquidation	Scenario 1	Scenario 2
Voluntary liquidation	Scenario 3	Scenario 4

The assumption of either a forced or voluntary liquidation is normally dictated by prevailing circumstances. A failed or failing business will typically be valued using a forced liquidation assumption whereas a business being dissolved by its owners with no undue external influence to do so will be valued pursuant to a voluntary liquidation assumption. This is sometimes the case for smaller businesses that may be difficult to sell (e.g., a single location retail operation).

As a rule, a receiver controls a forced liquidation after secured creditors have petitioned the business into bankruptcy. In Canada, the creditor payment process is governed by the *Bankruptcy and Insolvency Act*. Where a business has petitioned the court for protection under the *Companies' Creditors Arrangement Act* (CCAA) while it works out a restructuring plan, a liquidation approach may or may not be appropriate. A successful restructuring plan requires the approval of a company's creditors. Presumably, such approval indicates that the creditors anticipate recovering a greater portion of the monies owed to them by allowing the business to continue operating rather than if the company were to be liquidated. As a result, a company under CCAA protection appropriately may be valued using a discounted cash flow methodology (see Chapter 6). In these circumstances there may or may not be residual value accruing to the equity holders.

In a voluntary liquidation, the equity owners effectively control the liquidation process and seek to maximize their after-tax net proceeds on dissolution of the business. A voluntary liquidation generally occurs under relatively favourable circumstances, generally with the expectation that some residual value will accrue to the equity holders. Presumably, the business's owners have determined that the net after-tax proceeds from a voluntary liquidation will be greater than the net proceeds from a sale of the shares or assets. Residual value to the equity owners might also be anticipated in a court-ordered wind-up.

Both a forced and orderly liquidation can occur quickly or over an extended period of time. Given the time value of money, the risk of adverse market developments during the liquidation period and that liquidation over a period of time necessitates continuity of some overhead expenses, an immediate liquidation may yield greater net proceeds than liquidation over time. The determination of whether an immediate or extended liquidation assumption is appropriate should be based on which is expected to generate greater proceeds net of all disposition costs, costs during the liquidation period and income taxes, and having regard to the time value of money.

When a receiver liquidates a business, the choice of an immediate or extended liquidation time frame depends to a large extent on the nature of the underlying assets. It is not possible to generalize as to the time required to complete a liquidation process. Certain smaller, simpler businesses may be liquidated within a few months whereas others may require a year or more. The time needed for a liquidation depends on many things, including the condition of the business and its records, whether any portion of the business can be sold as a going concern, whether the owners are cooperative in the liquidation process, the type of assets being sold, and other factors. A voluntary liquidation scenario is more likely to take place over an extended time period, particularly where the business owners are involved in the wind-down of the operations.

Liquidation Value Methodology

Overview

The mechanics of the liquidation value methodology are as follows:

- the balance sheet is adjusted to restate assets to their respective current net realizable values, being the amount that individual assets could be expected to bring (i.e., value in exchange) at the valuation date, net of disposition costs;

- liabilities are deducted from the estimated net proceeds expected from the sale of the assets. Most liabilities are valued at their face value, although adjustments may be required for items such as long-term debt and future income taxes;

- liquidation costs are deducted to derive the net proceeds before income taxes; and

- corporate income taxes are deducted based on the net proceeds expected from the sale of the assets measured against their respective tax base. Corporate income tax calculations must take into account liquidation costs and the existing values in any tax pools at the valuation date. The net assets remaining (if any) after payment of liquidation costs, corporate income taxes, and all liabilities are referred to as "proceeds available for distribution" (i.e., net liquidation proceeds at the corporate level).

Where the business is incorporated and owned by one or more individual shareholders and the determination of net proceeds available to shareholders is required, then personal income taxes are deducted to derive liquidation value at the owner level. Personal income taxes take into account the nature of the amounts being distributed and the components of the refundable income tax system, where applicable.

Each of these components is discussed in greater detail below. When preparing an estimate of liquidation value, it is important to be consistent in the application the underlying assumptions of either forced or orderly liquidation and an immediate or extended time period.

The Valuation of Assets

All tangible assets and identifiable intangible assets (e.g., patents and licensing agreements) where separately saleable are valued at their net realizable values. Net realizable value is defined as the estimated proceeds such assets are expected to bring, net of disposition costs, based on their value in exchange (as contrasted with their value in continued use).

It is not possible to generalize either as to the likely net realizable value of the various types of assets held by operating businesses or the likely overall costs of liquidation. Common bases of net realizable value estimation and issues that should be considered are as follows:

- marketable securities, in the case of normal-sized trading blocks of actively traded shares, are valued at their present market values. When valuing marketable securities, disposition costs must be considered. If the business owns a large block of shares in a public company, a block premium or discount may be appropriate (see Chapter 8);

- accounts receivable are estimated at the greater of the expected net proceeds derived from factoring the entire receivables portfolio or the amount that might reasonably be collected over the liquidation period. The profile of the customers owing money to the business often establishes the likelihood of accounts being collected following public disclosure of liquidation. Where there are numerous small accounts, a lower recovery rate may be more likely than if there are only a few large outstanding accounts. Creditors owing relatively small amounts will sometimes withhold payment assuming the receiver will not pursue small accounts. An added degree of complexity exists where there are long-term holdbacks. In these circumstances, it is normally appropriate to discount the net amount expected to be received after consideration of the likely quantum of charge-back costs to the business;

- raw material inventory valuations are based on the composition of the inventory and whether, on a category-by-category basis:
  - ✓ suppliers will buy back the materials and if so, at what price,
  - ✓ a sale at auction or through some other means is more likely, or
  - ✓ all or part of the raw materials are so specialized that they will realize only scrap value, and what scrap value is;

- work-in-progress inventory must be assessed in terms of whether greater proceeds will be realized if the inventory is sold on an as-is basis, or if completion of the manufacturing process and sale as finished goods will yield a greater net recovery. Consideration must be given to the cost of completion, which would include:
  - ✓ the cost and availability of any additional direct materials to be added,
  - ✓ the direct and indirect labour costs required to finish the inventory,
  - ✓ the overhead cost that would be incurred in maintaining production during the completion period, and
  - ✓ selling and administrative costs to be incurred during the completion process.

Where a failed business is being liquidated and that failure is attributable to product problems, it is unlikely that finishing work in progress will maximize recovery. However, in the circumstances of a favourable liquidation, it is usual to assume the work in progress is worth at least book value;

- finished goods inventory generally should be considered in conjunction with the treatment of work in progress. Where it is assumed that work in progress will be completed, the sale of the finished goods inventory must include the additional product to be produced. Where finished goods are assumed to be sold immediately, it is necessary to establish whether higher proceeds will be realized by selling the entire lot to a jobber or liquidator or by selling to existing customers, possibly at a discounted price;

- prepaid expenses may be comprised of deposits for utilities and other services, and various amounts that have been paid for services not yet received, such as insurance premiums, property and business taxes, and similar assets. Prepaid expenses should be analyzed item by item to determine whether any portion of each amount should be refunded in cash if the business were to cease;

- furniture and fixtures are normally valued based on the estimated net proceeds they would likely bring if sold *en bloc* to a used furniture wholesaler or jobber. Frequently, net realizable value is less than net book value, particularly where the furniture is relatively new and has not been significantly depreciated;

- leasehold improvements are, as a practical matter, generally of no value. A liquidation calculation normally assumes the premises occupied by the business will be vacated in the near term. This is because leasehold improvements generally cannot be separated from the premises and sold individually.

Leasehold improvements may have indirect value if they enable the business to sublet its leased premises sooner or at more favourable rates, thereby reducing any penalty suffered upon lease termination;

- machinery and equipment are valued at their value in exchange assuming piecemeal sale, or sale of groups of related assets. Such sales require consideration of the estimated quantum of gross proceeds, the commissions and fees involved in the sale, any expenses in preparing the equipment for sale, and any transportation costs not paid for by the purchasers. For certain of these assets, there may be a significant difference between value in use, replacement cost and value in exchange (as discussed later in this chapter);

- real estate assets such as the land and building are valued at their market values less disposition costs including legal fees and commissions. In addition, the likely timing of the sale should be considered, and the net proceeds discounted accordingly. Real estate valuation is addressed later in this chapter;

- identifiable intangible assets such as patents, franchise agreements, licences and royalty agreements are valued at the estimated net proceeds such assets would realize in the open market if sold individually. In a liquidation-value context, these assets often have minimal or no value. For example, where a business is party to a licensing or franchising agreement, there usually are restrictions on the transfer of those rights. Further, most such agreements contain provisions terminating them automatically on the insolvency of one of the parties. Patents, copyrights or intellectual property may have specific value that can be transferred to a third party. The valuation of identifiable intangible assets is addressed in Chapter 9;

- non-identifiable intangible assets such as deferred charges, capitalized product development costs and goodwill are assigned a nil value since such assets are not commercially viable in and of themselves; and

- for those businesses with defined benefit pension plans, the market value of the pension assets sometimes exceeds the actuarial present value of the pension liabilities. Whether such a pension surplus belongs to the business or the employees is a legal issue and may vary depending on the circumstances. If the amount of the pension surplus is significant, legal advice should be obtained as to what portion, if any, can be recovered by the business. The book value of any deferred pension assets represents a non-identifiable intangible and should be assigned a nil value. Where the defined-benefit pension plan is in a deficit position, it should normally be assumed that any shortfall will have to be funded. It may be necessary to obtain an actuarial valuation at the time of liquidation to determine the quantum of pension surplus or deficiency, if any. Post-employment benefit obligations other than pensions (e.g., extended medical coverage after retirement) should also be considered.

The Valuation of Liabilities

Liabilities are usually stated at their accounting values except for certain long-term liabilities where the economic value may be materially different due to market rates of interest or where adjustments to reserve accounts are considered appropriate. Specifically:

- current liabilities are usually valued at their respective face values. The quantification of income taxes payable (if any) should be considered in light of the net tax liability or refund the business likely will realize as a result of the liquidation;

- long-term liabilities, which may include notes payable, bonds, debentures, and the current portions thereof, should be analyzed individually and valued at their estimated present values. Penalties for early retirement should be reflected, where appropriate. Any premium (or discount) which arose on the initial sale of long-term debt and which has an unamortized value represents a non-identifiable intangible liability (asset) and should be assigned a nil value;

- deferred revenues may exist for accounting purposes where a business invoices or collects money from customers prior to revenue being earned. Where such amounts represent deposits from customers and the goods or services are not to be provided because of the liquidation, the deferred revenues represent a liability and should be deducted when determining liquidation value. However, in circumstances of a liquidation where the business is expected to fulfill its order backlog and other commitments, the portion of the deferred revenues that will be earned should not be included as a liability;

- lease obligations should be valued at their face amounts, with consideration given to any penalties for discontinuance. Penalties for both operating and capital leases must be considered;

- future income tax credits (or debits) are assigned a nil value since the tax consequences of the liquidation will be determined separately;

- where intangible liabilities exist (e.g., deferred lease inducement costs), they are assigned a nil value;

- reserve accounts are often established for product warranties, self-insurance, environmental liabilities, and other potential liabilities. Where reserve accounts exist, they should be scrutinized carefully to determine the quantum of legitimate liabilities that exist and to assess the sufficiency of the reserve. This is particularly the case where the business is being liquidated and product liability issues are not adequately covered by insurance. Since reserve accounts are usually not allowed for Canadian income tax purposes until a liability is actually incurred, the expected settlement of such liabilities should also include consideration of any associated tax deductibility;

- contingent liabilities may exist where the business is party to a legal action or other matter where the outcome may not be known for some time. Where contingent liabilities exist, a reasonable estimate should be made regarding the likely outcome and its timing. The existence of contingent liabilities is usually disclosed in a business's financial statements or in the notes, but not always. Consideration should be afforded to contingent liabilities that may not be disclosed such as environmental and other obligations. Where the business engages in any activity that may be hazardous to the environment, there might be an obligation for cleanup or restoration before the business vacates the premises. Such costs should be accounted for in the determination of liquidation value. The advice of legal counsel and other experts may be required where significant contingent liabilities are involved; and

- the business may be party to financing arrangements or other obligations such as debt swap arrangements, debt securitization agreements, forward currency exchange contracts and other arrangements. Therefore, it is important to review the financial statements and notes carefully to assess whether such assets and liabilities do in fact exist and, if they do, what should be the value and appropriate treatment of each.

Liquidation Costs

The quantification of liquidation costs is dependant on whether a forced liquidation or voluntary liquidation is assumed. Under a voluntary liquidation, the owners' control of the liquidation process normally reduces the fees and costs associated with the dissolution of the business. A forced liquidation necessitates additional expenses such as the cost of a trustee-receiver and may not have the cooperation of the business owners. Liquidation costs frequently include the following:

- receiver, legal, accounting and other professional fees that can be significant, even in a relatively small and simple liquidation. The quantum of professional fees should be related to the overall time-frame assumption, to the assumptions made as to the collection of receivables, the means of dealing with other assets and other relevant considerations;

- termination benefits and payment of vacation pay to discontinued employees, which may or may not have been accrued in the financial statements. When estimating employee termination costs, it is necessary to consider the time frame over which the employees would be terminated, and to quantify the business's legal and contractual obligations as to severance, vacation pay and related costs such as outplacement services. This typically involves reviewing each individual's employment history to establish remuneration levels, tenure and contractual obligations other than the applicable labour legislation;

- shutdown costs related to the termination of active operations. These may include equipment cleaning and safety procedures prior to storage. Care should be taken to ensure double-counting of costs does not occur with disposal costs calculated as part of the net realizable value estimates for the equipment;

- outstanding commitments that must be satisfied. These may include minimum purchases from suppliers, forward sales contracts, and other commitments. Where an immediate liquidation is assumed and it is likely the business will not satisfy its commitments, a provision for any penalties or damages must be accounted for where applicable. In addition, where premises are leased, the leases should be reviewed to determine what early discharge penalties apply, as well as costs of removing signs, partitions and other alterations made to any buildings. Capital and other leases should be reviewed to establish responsibility for the costs of returning these items to the lessor plus any applicable penalties;

- it is necessary to conceptualize the entire wind-down process, to estimate the period of time required and to estimate the level of overhead costs to be incurred at each stage of the wind-up. The estimate of overhead costs must consider whether an immediate or extended liquidation is assumed. An analysis of overhead costs is needed to understand the nature of each expense as to whether it is fixed or variable, and whether contractual obligations impose any penalties for termination. It is also necessary to consider whether any overhead cost savings are possible during the liquidation period; and

- miscellaneous liquidation costs should be accounted for. These may include expenses such as the placement of newspaper notices, notification of affected parties, and other wind-up-related costs.

Corporate Income Taxes

When determining the net amount available for distribution to owners, income taxes and recoveries on the disposition of the assets and liabilities must be accounted for. These include:

- capital gains or losses which may arise on the disposition of marketable securities;

- losses (gains) incurred where the estimated net proceeds of accounts receivable are less than (greater than) their net book values;

- losses incurred on inventories where they are disposed of at amounts less than their tax base. Alternatively, where an extended liquidation is assumed and inventories are expected to be completed and sold at amounts in excess of their tax base, the income taxes on any resultant taxable income should be considered;

- the value of prepaid expenses written off usually gives rise to a tax deduction;

- the estimated net proceeds of fixed asset dispositions (excluding land) must be compared with the cost base of the assets and the undepreciated capital cost. Where the net proceeds exceed the original cost, a capital gain will result. Recapture or a terminal loss will result where the net proceeds are greater than or less than the undepreciated capital cost of the asset pool, respectively. The disposition of land normally will give rise to either a capital gain or a capital loss;

- the disposition of identifiable intangible assets may also give rise to a capital gain, recapture or a terminal loss, depending on circumstances, where such assets were recorded for tax purposes;

- where goodwill (eligible capital property) exists for tax purposes, a terminal loss will result where goodwill has no value in a liquidation scenario. Other non-identifiable intangibles (such as deferred charges) must be analyzed on an individual basis. Where cost deferrals have no cost base for tax purposes, no tax consequences will arise;

- reserves and contingencies are generally not allowable for Canadian income tax purposes until a liability is actually incurred. Therefore, the amount paid in respect of contingencies or from reserve funds generally gives rise to a tax deduction; and

- liquidation costs will give rise to an income tax deduction.

Several other considerations should be taken into account when estimating the amount of corporate income tax on liquidation. For example:

- where a net capital loss and/or non-capital loss arises on the disposition of the net assets of the business, consideration must be given to whether those net losses have any value. Since the business is being discontinued, capital losses may be of no value, except to the extent that they can be used to offset capital gains arising on liquidation. Non-capital losses can be carried back three years (and forward for between seven and 20 years, depending on when the loss was incurred. However, such a carry-forward is usually irrelevant in a liquidation scenario). Therefore, the quantum of previous income taxes paid which can be recovered through the carry-back of non-capital losses must be determined; and

- any existing income tax losses (i.e., losses which existed before the process of liquidating the business) must be considered, including the type of loss (e.g., capital losses, non-capital losses and allowable business investment loss) and whether some or all of said losses can be utilized to reduce the income taxes otherwise payable on the disposition of the business' net assets.

Personal Income Taxes

Where a business is liquidated pursuant to a court order or some other order arising out of an insolvency proceeding, the net proceeds from the disposition of its underlying assets are typically less than its outstanding liabilities. Accordingly, in a forced liquidation, there is seldom any residual accruing to the equity holders after settlement of debts. However, in a voluntary liquidation the owners sometimes expect they will receive a portion of the net proceeds, and thus create personal income tax considerations.

Whether or not personal income taxes are taken into account depends on the purpose of the liquidation value calculation. Where net proceeds to owners are being determined, then personal taxes are relevant. However, liquidation value does not take into account personal taxes where such value is being compared to the going concern value of a business, which is also computed before consideration of personal income tax.

For an unincorporated business, personal income taxes that arise on liquidation may be taken into account in the liquidation calculation depending on its purpose. Where the business is an unincorporated entity, the net proceeds available to its owner(s) (being the adjusted equity less liquidation costs) constitute business income in the hands of the individual taxpayer and is taxed at the individual's marginal tax rate.

Where the business being liquidated is incorporated and the shareholder is a corporate entity, then:

- the subsidiary can normally be wound up into the parent on a tax-deferred basis where the parent owns at least 90% of the subsidiary's shares; or

- dividends can normally be paid from the subsidiary to the corporate shareholder on a tax-free basis.

Therefore, from the standpoint of a corporate shareholder, no further income tax implications need to be considered.

Where the business being liquidated is a corporation with individual shareholders, the net proceeds, if any, available to those individual shareholders in a liquidation or wind-up generally comprise the following:

- a return of paid-up capital, which is tax free;

- a capital dividend account, which is only available to privately held companies. The capital dividend account represents that portion of capital gains which are not taxable (presently 50% in Canada) and certain other items, such as life insurance proceeds. Capital dividends are distributed to shareholders on a tax-free basis;

- for companies incorporated prior to 1972, there may be a balance available in the pre-1972 contributed surplus on hand (CSOH) account. The pre-1972 CSOH is the accumulation of the capital gains net of losses that had been realized to December 31, 1971, plus those gains (net of losses) which existed at December 31, 1971, but have only been realized subsequent to that date. Pre-1972 CSOH is only available on the wind-up of a company; and

- the balance, which represents a taxable dividend, and is eligible for the dividend tax credit at the personal shareholder level. In the case of a Canadian-controlled private corporation (CCPC), any taxable dividend should be assessed to determine the impact on the refundable dividend tax on hand (RDTOH).

The cash available for distribution less the paid-up capital and taxable dividend represents the adjusted proceeds of distribution, which generally are equal to the amount of paid-up capital and pre-1972 CSOH, if any. Where the adjusted proceeds of distribution are greater or less than the individual's adjusted cost base for the shares, a capital gain or loss will arise. The tax consequences to the individual shareholder of the gain or loss must be considered in the determination of the net proceeds.

The determination of the deemed taxable dividend and capital gain or loss on liquidation are as follows:

Exhibit 3B
Determination of Deemed Taxable Dividend

Funds available for distribution (including RDTOH)

Less:	paid-up capital
Equals:	deemed dividend on wind-up
Less:	pre-1972 CSOH (if any)
Equals:	taxable dividend
Less:	capital dividend account (if any)
Equals:	deemed taxable dividend

Exhibit 3C
Determination of Capital Gain or Loss

Funds available for distribution (including RDTOH)

Less:	deemed dividend on wind-up (per Exhibit 3B)
Equals:	adjusted proceeds for distribution
Less:	adjusted cost base of shares
Equals:	capital gain (loss)

Liquidation Value Calculation Example

Company I is a machine shop. The sole shareholder is Mr. Irwin, who has operated the business since its inception. Due to failing health, he has decided wind up Company I immediately following its December 31, 2011, year-end.

Company I's balance sheet at December 31, 2011, along with the tax base of the assets and their estimated market values is as follows:

Exhibit 3D
Company I
Balance Sheet
At December 31, 2011

	Net book value	Original cost	Undepreciated capital cost	Estimated market value
Current assets				
Cash	73,000			73,000
Marketable securities	124,000	124,000		188,000
Accounts receivable	150,000	150,000		150,000
Inventories	125,000	125,000		110,000
Prepaid expenses	20,000	20,000		10,000
Total current assets	492,000			
Fixed assets				
Land	146,000	146,000		250,000
Building	234,000	440,000	234,000	500,000
Production equipment	168,000	393,000	92,000	175,000
Furniture & other	48,000	79,000	36,000	20,000
Total fixed assets	596,000			
Total assets	1,088,000			
Liabilities				
Accounts payable	102,000			
Accrued liabilities	16,000			
Future income taxes	19,000			
Total liabilities	137,000			
Equity				
Capital stock	1,000			
Retained earnings	950,000			
Total shareholder equity	951,000			
Total liabilities and equity	1,088,000			

Other information related to Company I and to Mr. Irwin is as follows:

- Company I pays income tax at a rate of 15% on the first $500,000 of active business income and 28% on active business income in excess of that amount. Non-active business income is subject to income tax at a rate of 46.67%, which includes 26.67% of additional refundable tax;

- Mr. Irwin's effective marginal personal income tax rates are 46% for employment income, 32% for dividend income, and an effective rate of 23% for capital gains (which recognizes that capital gains are only 50% taxable);

- as a Canadian-controlled private corporation, Company I is eligible for dividend refunds at a rate of 26.67%. Company I has no balance in its refundable dividend tax on hand account or capital dividend account at December 31, 2011;

- sales commissions equal to 5% of gross proceeds are payable on the disposition of all fixed assets. There are no other disposition costs; and

- when winding up the corporation, Mr. Irwin expects to incur $25,000 in overhead costs during the wind-up period and $40,000 in professional fees and other costs to dissolve the corporation.

Solution:

The after-tax proceeds available for distribution are determined as follows:

Exhibit 3E
Company I
Estimated Proceeds Available for Distribution at December 31, 2011

	Estimated market value	Disposition costs	Net realizable value	Business income (loss)	Taxable capital gain	Capital dividend account	RDTOH
Current Assets							
Cash	73,000		73,000				
Marketable securities	188,000		188,000		32,000	32,000	8,534
Accounts receivable	150,000		150,000				
Inventories	110,000		110,000	(15,000)			
Prepaid expenses	10,000		10,000	(10,000)			
Fixed Assets							
Land	250,000	(12,500)	237,500		45,750	45,750	12,202
Building	500,000	(25,000)	475,000	206,000	17,500	17,500	4,667
Production equipment	175,000	(8,750)	166,250	74,250			
Furniture & other	20,000	(1,000)	19,000	(17,000)			
Total net proceeds			1,428,750	238,250	95,250	95,250	25,403
Deduct:							
Current liabilities			102,000				
Accrued liabilities			16,000				
Future Income Taxes							
Adjusted equity			1,310,750				
Liquidation costs:							
Overhead costs		25,000					
Professional fees		40,000					
Net liquidation costs			65,000				
Net proceeds before taxes			1,245,750				
Corporate income taxes:							
First $500,000 business income	15%	35,738					
Excess business income	28%						
Taxable capital gains	46.67%	44,453					
Liquidation costs	15%	(9,750)					
Refundable dividend tax	(above)	(25,403)					
Net corporate tax			45,038				
Proceeds available for distribution			1,200,713				

Assets are estimated at their net realizable value. For fixed assets, 5% of the market value is deducted for disposition costs. The total net proceeds of all assets amount to $1,428,750.

Accounts payable and accrued liabilities are deducted from the total net proceeds at their respective face values to yield an adjusted equity amount of $1,310,750. Future income taxes are assigned a nil value since the income tax consequences arising on the disposition of the assets will be considered separately.

Liquidation costs of $65,000 are deducted, including overhead costs of $25,000 and professional fees of $40,000. This results in net proceeds before income taxes of $1,245,750.

Income taxes at the corporate level are then deducted. The income taxes are estimated at $45,038, as follows:

- net active business income is estimated at $238,250, which is comprised of the following:
  - ✓ losses of $15,000 and $10,000 are expected on the disposition of inventories and prepaid expenses respectively, being the difference between their estimated market values and tax cost,
  - ✓ the building will generate recapture of $206,000, being the difference between its original cost of $440,000 (which is less than market value) and its undepreciated capital cost of $234,000,
  - ✓ the production equipment will generate recapture of $74,250, being the difference between its net realizable value of $166,250 (which is less than original cost) and its undepreciated capital cost of $92,000, and
  - ✓ a terminal loss of $17,000 is realized on the disposition of the furniture, which represents the amount by which its undepreciated capital cost of $36,000 exceeds its net realizable value of $19,000;

- active business income of $238,250 is below the $500,000 small business threshold. Therefore, the applicable tax rate is 15%, resulting in $35,738 of taxes;

- capital gains are realized on the disposition of marketable securities, land and the building, being the excess of the net realizable value over the original cost of these assets. One half of the capital gains ($95,250 in aggregate) is classified as taxable, while the other 50% (also $95,250 in aggregate) is allocated to the capital dividend account. Taxable capital gains are subject to income taxes at a rate of 46.67%, including the refundable tax component, which amounts to taxes thereon of $44,453;

- liquidation costs of $65,000 are deductible at a rate of 15% ($9,750 in total) since pretax income on dissolution was below the small business threshold (specifically, $238,250, as noted above); and

- there is refundable dividend tax (RDTOH) on the amount of taxable capital gains at a rate of 26.67%, or $25,403 in total. This reduces the amount of corporate taxes otherwise payable. It should be noted that the dividend refund accrues at a rate of 33 1/3% of deemed dividends, to a maximum of the balance in the RDTOH account. The refundable dividend tax calculation must take into account the total deemed dividend amount. In this case, the amount of deemed dividend (discussed below) is sufficient to provide for full recovery of RDTOH.

The net proceeds available for distribution are $1,200,713. Upon the wind-up of Company I, Mr. Irwin will be subject to personal income taxes calculated as follows:

Exhibit 3F
Personal Income Tax Calculation for Mr. Irwin at December 31, 2011

Tax on Deemed Dividend

Proceeds available for distribution (Exhibit 3E)		1,200,713
Less: paid-up capital		(1,000)
Deemed dividend on wind-up		1,199,713
Less: capital dividend account (Exhibit 3E)		(95,250)
Deemed taxable dividend		1,104,463
Tax on deemed taxable dividend	32%	353,428

Tax on Capital Gain (loss)

Proceeds available for distribution (Exhibit 3E)		1,200,713
Less: deemed dividend on wind-up (above)		(1,199,713)
Adjusted proceeds of disposition		1,000
Less: adjusted cost base of the shares		(1,000)
Capital gain (loss)		0
Tax on capital gain at effective rate	23%	
Total personal taxes on wind-up		353,428
Proceeds available for distribution (Exhibit 3E)		1,200,713
Net proceeds to Mr. Irwin		847,285

Mr. Irwin receives a deemed taxable dividend of $1,104,463 on the wind-up. This is determined as the proceeds available for distribution of $1,200,713 less the paid-up capital of $1,000 and the balance of the capital dividend account of $95,250. The return of paid-up capital and capital dividends are paid to Mr. Irwin tax free. Because the adjusted cost base of Mr. Irwin's shares ($1,000) is equal to the paid-up capital amount, there is no resulting capital gain or loss.

The amount of income tax on the deemed dividend equates to $353,428 given that Mr. Irwin's tax rate in dividends of 32%. (As an aside, these are considered ineligible dividends, given that they are paid from income that was subject to the small-business deduction). The proceeds available for distribution of $1,200,713 less personal income taxes result in the net proceeds retained by Mr. Irwin of $847,285.

Adjusted Net Book Value

Overview

Traditionally, financial statements prepared under Generally Accepted Accounting Principles have adopted historical cost as the basis of measurement. As a result, equity as stated in financial statements may be considerably different from equity based on the current market values of the underlying net assets of the business. International Financial Reporting Standards (IFRSs) allows companies to restate the value of their assets and thus could militate against such discrepancies. However, many businesses may choose not to adopt that policy.

The adjusted net book value methodology (sometimes referred to as tangible asset backing) is used:

- where a holding company is being valued. Holding companies usually have no active operations of their own, but rather may hold various assets such as the shares of operating companies, real estate, marketable securities and other passive assets. Holding companies are further discussed in Chapter 9;

- where intangible value is being calculated. The *en bloc* equity value of a business, determined pursuant to a cash flow-based methodology, less the adjusted net book value represents the total intangible value. The determination of intangible value is used by some buyers as a risk measurement tool, given that intangible assets generally are viewed as having a higher level of risk than tangible assets. In other cases, the total intangible value is segregated between identifiable intangible assets and non-identifiable intangible assets (e.g., goodwill) pursuant to a purchase price allocation (as discussed in Chapter 10); and

- as a test of the value conclusions developed pursuant to a cash flow-based valuation methodology. Where the adjusted net book value is greater than the *en bloc* equity value of a business determined pursuant to a cash flow-based approach, it might suggest that the rates of return adopted in the cash flow approach were too high, or that the business has underutilized assets that should be sold off. If the difference is significantly greater than expected between the *en bloc* equity value (determined using a cash flow-based methodology) and the adjusted net book value, the rate of return adopted in the cash flow-based approach might have been understated, and thus will fail to adequately reflect the risks inherent in intangible assets.

In some limited circumstances the adjusted net book value is used as the primary methodology for establishing the *en bloc* equity value of a business. This might occur where it is believed that:

- no commercial goodwill exists in the business, and

- a buyer likely would acquire the business based on its underlying asset values, as opposed to the ability of the business to generate prospective cash flow. That said, cash flow-based valuation methodologies are usually preferred.

Adjusted net book value is not the same as tangible net worth. Tangible net worth is calculated as shareholders' equity less the book value of intangible assets. However, no adjustment is made to reflect the economic value of assets and liabilities. Consequently, there tends to be a larger difference between adjusted net book value and tangible net worth for capital-intensive businesses vs. those that are not capital-intensive. Tangible net worth sometimes is referenced in the context of a banking covenant, such as a maximum debt to tangible net worth ratio (see Chapter 2).

The adjusted net book value methodology involves making the following adjustments to shareholders equity as reported on a company's financial statements:

- adding (deducting) the amount by which the economic value of each tangible asset exceeds (is less than) its accounting value. In the case of current assets, no adjustment generally is required. However, an adjustment may be required on account of fixed assets, particularly where the business owns significant real estate, machinery and equipment and other capital assets;

- deducting the book value of intangible assets;

- adding the tax shield relating to intangible assets that have a tax base;

- adding the economic value of other tax pools;

- deducting (adding) the amount by which the economic value of the business's liabilities exceeds (is less than) their respective book values. No adjustment generally is required for current liabilities. However, an adjustment may be required for long-term liabilities such as interest-bearing debts that have a stated interest rate materially different from prevailing market rates. Adjustments may also be required where the business has other long-term liabilities such as loss provisions, or where intangible liabilities exist (e.g., deferred lease inducement costs);

- adding (deducting) the book value of future income tax liabilities (assets); and

- deducting (adding) the amount by which the economic value of future income tax obligations is greater than (less than) the book value of future income tax liabilities. In this regard, the economic value of future income tax obligations should reflect the present value of the capital cost allowance tax shield not available to a purchaser of shares (as contrasted to that available to a purchaser of the underlying net assets of the business) where fixed assets have been adjusted to reflect their market values.

Schematically, the calculation of adjusted net book value is as follows:

Exhibit 3G
Adjusted Net Book Value Methodology

	Shareholders equity per the financial statements
Add:	economic value of tangible assets
Deduct:	net book value of tangible assets
Deduct:	net book value of intangible assets
Add:	tax shield on intangible assets
Add:	economic value of other tax pools
Add:	book value of liabilities
Deduct:	economic value of liabilities
Add (deduct):	book value of future income tax liabilities (assets)
Deduct:	economic value of future income tax obligations
Equals:	adjusted Net Book Value

Tangible Assets

Asset values in an adjusted net book value calculation are premised on a going concern assumption. That is, their values are determined based on their net contribution to the business assuming continued use as opposed to value in exchange (except for highly marketable assets, such as marketable securities and certain real estate). The essential difference between value in use and value in exchange in this context is that value in use reflects the net cash inflows accruing from asset utilization and includes all installation and start-up costs. In the context of adjusted net book value, value in use is never less than value in exchange. Furthermore, unlike the liquidation approach discussed above, there is no deduction for disposition costs given the assumption that the assets of the business will continue to be utilized as opposed to being sold (except where they represent redundant assets).

Current Assets

Adjustments on account of current assets normally are not required, except where:

- marketable securities are included in current assets and their book value is greater or less than their aggregate current market value;

- book value represents a significant overstatement or understatement of the going concern value of accounts receivable or inventories; and

- the book value of other current assets (such as advances to related parties, notes receivable, and so on) are materially different from their market values when considered in terms of payment and collectability.

Fixed Assets

When determining the going concern value of fixed assets such as land, building, machinery and equipment, it may be necessary to obtain the opinions of real estate and equipment appraisers. In a notional market context these assets typically are valued as follows:

- market value for land and building where these assets are readily salable. In cases of special-use property, depreciated replacement cost normally is adopted as the appropriate measure. Real estate valuation is discussed later in this chapter;

- the greater of depreciated replacement cost or value in use for machinery, production equipment, fleet and other equipment employed in the business. Equipment valuation is discussed later in this chapter; and

- depreciated replacement cost for other fixed assets such as furniture and fixtures, leasehold improvements and office equipment. As a practical matter, where these assets are not significant, their net book value for accounting purposes normally is adopted as a proxy for depreciated replacement cost.

Intangible Assets

Where a business accounts for intangible assets such as goodwill, deferred charges, and so on, that are not separately identifiable from the business itself, such intangibles are assigned a nil value for the purpose of calculating adjusted net book value.

Where a business has identifiable intangible assets such as royalty agreements, patents and licences, these may have a distinct value that can be measured in isolation. The valuation of identifiable intangible assets is addressed in Chapter 9.

Where adjusted net book value is adopted to measure the total intangible value implied in the *en bloc* equity value of a business as determined pursuant to a cash flow valuation approach, then identifiable intangible assets do not form part of the adjusted net book value calculation. Rather, the total intangible value that is implied by the value conclusion may subsequently be allocated between identifiable intangible assets and non-identifiable intangible assets (i.e., goodwill) for purposes such as purchase price allocation. However, the value of intangible assets may be indirectly included in adjusted net book value in the case of a holding company whose holdings include the shares of operating businesses.

In some cases, the intangible asset may have a basis for income tax purposes. Common examples include franchises and goodwill (where acquired pursuant to a purchase of assets), which qualifies as eligible capital property and is added to the cumulative eligible capital (CEC) tax pool. An acquirer of shares would enjoy the tax benefits associated with the ability to claim capital cost allowance on these tax pools on the basis prescribed in the *Income Tax Regulations*. At present in Canada, 75% of the purchase price for eligible capital property is added to the CEC pool, which can be depreciated for income tax purposes at a rate of 7% per annum on a declining balance basis. Therefore, where a company has a residual balance in its

CEC pool, the adjusted net book value should be increased to reflect the present value of such tax benefits, calculated as follows:

Formula 3.1
Present Value of Tax Shield on Cumulative Eligible Capital Tax Pool

$$\frac{CEC \times D \times T}{(K + D)}$$

Where:

CEC = the balance remaining in the cumulative eligible capital tax pool at the valuation date

D = the tax depreciation rate on eligible capital property (currently 7%)

T = the marginal tax rate

K = the company's cost of capital, which should be expressed as the nominal weighted average cost of capital (see Chapter 7)

For example, assume that a Company J has a remaining CEC balance of $2 million, an income tax rate of 30% and a cost of capital of 12%. It follows that the present value of the remaining tax shield on the CEC balance would be calculated as follows:

$$\frac{\$2,000,000 \times .07 \times .30}{(.12 + .07)} \quad = \quad \$221,053$$

Tax Pools

In some cases, a business will have non-capital loss carry-forwards or other tax pools such as balances in its Scientific Research and Experimental Development (SRED) accounts that can be used to reduce prospective income taxes. The economic value of these tax benefits normally is considered in the determination of adjusted net book value. When calculating the economic value of available tax pools, consideration must be given to the expected timing of utilization, restrictions on use, the possible expiry of these tax pools and the prospective income tax rate that will be in effect when they are used. The determination of the benefits of existing tax pools is addressed in Chapter 5.

Liabilities

Current liabilities generally are taken at their face value. Where the business has deferred revenues, they represent obligations to provide future goods or services. Assuming that the business is a going concern, such deferred revenues normally will be earned in due course. Accordingly, deferred revenue accounts usually are not adjusted where the goods and services have not yet been provided.

Adjustments may be required in the case of long-term liabilities. For example, where the stated interest rate on long-term debt is materially different from prevailing rates, then the economic value of the liability will be different from its net book value. For example, assume that Company J has an outstanding long-term loan with a face value of $10 million and a stated interest rate of 7%, with principal and interest repayable in equal annual installments over the next 5 years. The prevailing market interest rate for a similar loan has declined to 5%. The economic value (i.e., net present value) of the loan would be calculated as follows:

Exhibit 3H
Company J
Economic Value of Loan

	Year				
	1	2	3	4	5
Opening Balance	10,000,000	8,261,093	6,400,463	4,409,588	2,279,352
Total payment	2,438,907	2,438,907	2,438,907	2,438,907	2,438,907
Interest at 7%	700,000	578,277	448,032	308,671	159,555
Principal Repayment	1,738,907	1,860,630	1,990,875	2,130,236	2,279,352
Closing balance	8,261,093	6,400,463	4,409,588	2,279,352	0
Total payment (above)	2,438,907	2,438,907	2,438,907	2,438,907	2,438,907
Discount factor at 5%	0.952	0.907	0.864	0.823	0.784
Present value	2,322,769	2,212,160	2,106,820	2,006,495	1,910,947
Net present value	10,559,191				

The net present value of $10,559,191 represents the economic value of the loan, which should be used in lieu of its book value when calculated adjusted net book value.

Deferred pension liabilities may exist where there is defined-benefit pension plan for employees. The deferred liability represents a non-identifiable intangible which should be assigned a nil value. However, adjusted net book value should be increased (decreased) by the tax-effected excess (deficiency) of the market value of the pension fund assets over the estimated present value of the actuarial liabilities of the pension plan. This information is normally disclosed in the notes to the financial statements. Pursuant to a going concern assumption, a pension surplus represents the approximate present value of the pension contribution savings. The net surplus (deficiency) should be tax-effected where contributions to a pension plan are deductible for income tax purposes. In addition, the business may offer its former employees other post-employment benefits which should also be considered in determining the completeness of its liabilities.

Future Income Taxes

Future income taxes arise due to timing differences between the recognition of income and expenses for financial reporting purposes and for income tax purposes. A future income tax liability implies that a business has deducted expenses for income tax purposes before the expense has been recognized for financial reporting purposes. A common example of this is the difference between capital cost allowance (CCA) and accounting depreciation, whereby most assets are depreciated at a faster rate for tax purposes than they are for accounting purposes, thereby giving rise to a future income tax liability.

Apart from classification between current liabilities (or current assets) and long-term liabilities (or long-term assets), the calculation of future income taxes does not take into account the expected timing of reversal. Therefore, while the economic value of future income tax liabilities (assets) classified as current liabilities (assets) usually is not materially different from the book value amount, the same generally cannot be said about long-term future income tax liabilities (assets). Therefore, in the determination of adjusted net book value:

- the book value of long-term future income tax liabilities should be added back, and the economic value of future income tax liabilities should be deducted; or

- the book value of long-term future income tax assets should be deducted and the economic value of future income tax assets should be added.

The economic value of future income tax liabilities (assets) should be based on the difference between the tax base of the applicable assets and the basis by which they have been valued in the determination of adjusted net book value. Specifically, where assets such as equipment and real property have been restated to their economic values (as opposed to their book values), there is an inherent assumption that the buyer of such assets would benefit from being able to claim CCA at the stepped-up cost. However, where the buyer purchases the shares of a company, then the existing tax bases of the underlying assets flow through to the buyer. It follows that where shares are valued, when determining adjusted net book value an adjustment may be necessary to reflect the value of the capital cost allowance tax shield inherent in fixed asset appraisals that would not be available to an acquirer of shares.

Capital Cost Allowance Formulas

Where assets are acquired directly, then the buyer is able to claim CCA, normally on a declining-balance basis, at a rate based on the class of assets as prescribed in the *Income Tax Regulations*. The present value of the tax shield available is calculated as follows:

Formula 3.2
Present Value of CCA Tax Shield on Newly Acquired Assets
Depreciated on a Declining Balance Basis

$$\frac{C \times D \times T}{(K + D)} \times \frac{(1 + 0.5 \times K)}{(1 + K)}$$

Where:

C = the cost of the asset (i.e., its economic value as determined for the purpose of calculating adjusted net book value)

D = the depreciation rate (CCA rate) for income tax purposes, based on the rate prescribed for the class in which the asset falls under the Canadian *Income Tax Regulations*

T = the marginal income tax rate at which CCA is deducted

K = the cost of capital. The cost of capital should be the nominal weighted average cost of capital (see Chapter 7).

Formula 3.2 assumes that the newly acquired asset is subject to the half-year rule (i.e., that only 50% of the CCA otherwise allowable can be claimed in the year that the asset is acquired). While the half-year rule applies to most asset classes, there are some exceptions. Where the half-year rule is not applicable, the expression $[(1 + 0.5 \times K) / (1 + K)]$ can be eliminated.

Conversely, where the shares of a company are acquired, and the existing tax pools flow through, then the formula to determine the present value of the tax shield (on a class-by-class basis) is as follows:

Formula 3.3
Present Value of CCA Tax Shield on the Existing Tax Pools

$$\frac{UCC \times D \times T}{(K + D)}$$

Where:

UCC = the undepreciated capital cost balance of the asset class

D = the depreciation rate (CCA rate) for income tax purposes, based on the rate prescribed for the class in which the asset falls under the *Income Tax Regulations*

T = the marginal income tax rate at which CCA is deducted

K = the cost of capital (specifically, the nominal weighted average cost of capital)

It should be noted that the half-year rule does not apply in the above formula.

Certain asset classes are depreciated for income tax purposes on a straight-line basis. Where this is the case, the formula applicable to newly acquired assets is as follows:

Formula 3.4
Present Value of CCA Tax Shield on Newly Acquired Assets Depreciated on a Straight Line Basis

$$C / N \times T \times PVIFA_{K, N} \times [(1 + 0.5 \times K) / (1 + K)]$$

Where:

C = the cost of the asset

N = the number of years over which CCA is claimed

T = the marginal tax rate at which CCA is deducted

$PVIFA_{K, N}$ = the present value interest factor of an annuity for N years at a given cost of capital (K)

Again, the above formula assumes the application of the half-year rule.

Where shares are acquired, the formula for determining the present value of the residual tax shield on assets depreciated on a straight line basis is as follows:

Formula 3.5
Present Value of the Remaining CCA Tax Shield on Assets Depreciated on a Straight Line Basis where Shares are Acquired

$$C \,/\, N \times T \times PVIFA_{K,N}$$

Where:

C = the cost of the asset

N = the number of years over which CCA is claimed

T = the marginal tax rate at which CCA is deducted

$PVIFA_{K,N}$ = the present value interest factor of an annuity for N years (being the remaining life) at a given cost of capital (K)

Capital cost allowance formulas are further discussed in Chapter 5.

Foregone Tax Shield Example

Assume that a Company J owns equipment with a book value of $5 million, an undepreciated capital cost of $3 million and an economic value (depreciated replacement cost) of $8 million. The equipment qualifies for CCA at a rate of 30%. Company J pays income tax at a rate of 25% and has a nominal cost of capital of 15%. The value of the foregone tax shield would be calculated as follows:

Exhibit 3I
Company J
Calculation of Foregone Tax Shield

PV of CCA Shield on Acquisition of Assets

Formula 3.2:

$$\frac{C \times D \times T}{(K + D)} \times \frac{(1 + 0.5\,K)}{(1 + K)}$$

Where:

C = Economic Value	8,000,000
D = CCA Rate	30%
T = Tax Rate	25%
K = Cost of Capital	15%

PV of CCA shield on asset purchase: 1,246,377

PV of Existing UCC Shield

Formula 3.3:

$$\frac{UCC \times D \times T}{(K + D)}$$

Where:

UCC =	3,000,000
D = CCA Rate	30%
T = Tax Rate	25%
K = Cost of Capital	15%

PV of existing UCC shield on share purchase: 500,000

Foregone Tax Shield   746,377

Note that the book value of the equipment does not factor into the above calculation.

Example of the Adjusted Net Book Value Methodology

Assumed Facts

Company K is a construction and roadwork contractor. Company K's balance sheet for its most recent fiscal year ending October 31, 2011 is as follows:

Exhibit 3J
Company K
Balance Sheet at October 31, 2011

Current assets	
Accounts Receivable	6,924,000
Inventories	650,000
Prepaid expenses	228,000
	7,802,000
Construction Equipment	4,530,000
Other fixed assets	308,000
Goodwill	1,880,000
Total Assets	14,520,000
Current liabilities	
Bank operating loan	3,200,000
Accounts payable and accruals	1,455,000
Current portion of term debt	650,000
	5,305,000
Future income taxes	711,000
Long-term debt	3,350,000
Total liabilities	9,366,000
Shareholder Equity	5,154,000
Total liabilities and Equity	14,520,000

Additional information related to Company K's assets and liabilities is as follows:

- the market value of current assets and current liabilities approximates their respective book values;

- the construction equipment has an estimated economic value of $7.2 million, based on its depreciated replacement cost. The UCC base of the construction equipment is $2.5 million. The CCA rate applicable for construction equipment is 30%;

- other fixed assets include furniture and fixtures, office equipment and leasehold improvements. The economic value of these assets is not materially different from their net book value, which approximates the UCC base of these assets;

- goodwill arose on the purchase of the assets of another company several years ago. The cumulative eligible capital balance relating to goodwill is $900,000;

- future income taxes entirely relate to the timing difference between CCA and accounting depreciation for the fixed assets;

- the long-term debt has a stated coupon rate of 6% and five years remaining. The current market rate of interest has increased to 8%; and

- Company K has an income tax rate of 28% and a cost of capital of 17%.

Given these facts, the adjusted net book value for Company K would be calculated as follows:

Exhibit 3K
Company K
Adjusted Net Book Value at October 31, 2011

Shareholder equity per financial statements		5,154,000
Add: Economic value of construction equipment		7,200,000
Deduct: net book value of construction equipment		(4,530,000)
Deduct: net book value of goodwill		(1,880,000)
Add: PV of cumulative eligible capital tax shield		73,500
Add: future income tax liability balance		711,000
Deduct: PV of forgone tax shield, determined as:		
PV of tax shield under share purchase	446,809	
Less: PV of tax shield under asset purchase	(1,193,322)	
		(746,514)
Add: book value of long-term debt (including current portion)		4,000,000
Deduct: economic value of long term debt		
Annual payments based on 6%, 5 years:	949,586	
PVIFA, 8%, 5 years	3.993	
		(3,791,420)
Adjusted net book value		6,190,566

The starting point in the above solution is the shareholder equity as reported on Company K's balance sheet. The following adjustments are then made:

- the economic value of the construction equipment is added and the net book value thereof is deducted. It was assumed that the book value of other fixed assets approximated their economic value, so no adjustment was required in that regard. Similarly, no adjustments were required in respect of current assets or current liabilities in this case;

- the net book value of goodwill is deducted because it is a non-identifiable intangible asset. However, since there is an associated tax balance of $900,000 (cumulative eligible capital), the present value of the tax shield was added, as such a benefit would accrue to a buyer of Company K's shares. The present value of the remaining cumulative eligible capital balance was determined as follows:

$$\frac{\$900,000 \times .07 \times .28}{(.17 + .07)} = \$73,500$$

- the future income tax liability balance of $711,000 was added back. A deduction was made for the fact that a buyer of the shares would not be eligible to claim CCA on the economic value of the construction equipment, but rather based on its UCC balance. The present value of the foregone CCA tax shield is calculated as $746,514, being the difference between the:

Present value of the tax shield based on the existing UCC balance (Formula 3.3):

$$\frac{\$2,500,000 \times .30 \times .28}{(.17 + .30)} = \$446,809$$

and the present value of the tax shield based on the economic value of the construction equipment (which is subject to the half-year rule) (Formula 3.2):

$$\frac{\$7,200,000 \times .30 \times .28}{(.17 + .30)} \times \frac{(1 + .5 \times .17)}{(1 + .17)} = \$1,193,322$$

The book value of the long-term debt of $4 million is added back (including the current portion) and the economic value of the long-term debt is deducted, being $3,791,420, based on the prevailing interest rate of 8%.

The resultant adjusted net book value is $6,190,566. This amount would be compared to the *en bloc* equity value for Company K, determined pursuant to a cash flow-based methodology, to determine the amount of intangible value included in the equity value conclusion.

Real Estate Valuation

Real estate values are commonly required in order to develop adjusted net book value and liquidation value. In addition, as discussed in Chapter 4, where a business owns the real estate that houses its operations, and that real estate is commercially saleable, then the value of that real estate should normally be viewed as a type of redundant asset, and ascribed a value that is separate from the business operations.

The determination of the going concern value of real estate is usually satisfied through an estimate of either market value or value in use. The Appraisal Institute of Canada defines market value as:

> ... The most probable price, as of a specified date, in cash, or in terms equivalent to cash, or in other precisely revealed terms, for which the specified property rights should sell after reasonable exposure in a competitive market under all conditions requisite to a fair sale, with the buyer and seller each acting prudently, knowledgeably, and for self-interest, and assuming that neither is under undue duress.[1]

Implicit in this definition is the assumption of a sale and passing of title at the valuation date under conditions whereby:

- the buyer and seller are typically (i.e., not unusually) motivated;
- the buyer and seller both are well informed, well advised and acting in their respective best interests;
- the property has been exposed to the market for a reasonable time; and
- payment is made in cash or cash equivalent.

The valuation of real estate assets often requires the assistance of a qualified real estate appraiser. When accredited real estate appraisers estimate the market value of real estate in a notional market context in respect of income-producing property, they typically adopt a cash flow-based methodology, assuming market-based rental income and standard vacancy rates. The value conclusions reached using the cash flow-based methodology are normally tested with reference to recent open market transactions involving similar properties and, in some cases, an estimate of depreciated replacement cost.

Market value is typically determined using the highest and best use of the property, and on the assumption that the property is free and clear of all encumbrances and possible encumbrances, including unidentified contingent environmental liabilities. Where there are known environmental liabilities, these either are considered in the value determination or the value determination is qualified in that regard.

In the determination of adjusted net book value, the value of real estate generally is taken to mean the greater of market value (i.e., value in exchange) or depreciated replacement cost. Where such real estate has special characteristics and is an important part in the operations of the business, a going concern value measure may involve an estimate of value in use. For example, a business that manufactures hazardous materials might be required to ensure that its manufacturing facilities conform to applicable standards set for explosion-proofing, and may incur significant costs to upgrade those facilities to those standards. Such improvements would have value to the hazardous materials manufacturer, but not to a manufacturer of non-hazardous products.

---

1   Appraisal Institute of Canada. *Canadian Uniform Standards of Professional Appraisal Practice.* (Ottawa: Appraisal Institute of Canada, 2012), Standard 12.16.1, p. 52.

Value in use is generally determined using a cash flow-based valuation methodology. As a practical matter, it often is difficult to segregate the cash flows associated with a special-use property from those of the business as a whole. As a result, depreciated replacement cost often is adopted as the appropriate measure of value for special-use properties.

Where the business being valued is not a going concern, market value is normally adopted as the appropriate measure of real estate value. Market value also is used where the real estate is regarded as a redundant asset pursuant to a cash flow-based methodology.

The three methodologies that are commonly employed when determining the value of real property are the:

- cash flow methodology (often referred to as the "income approach" by real estate appraisers);
- direct comparison methodology; and
- depreciated replacement cost methodology.

Varying valuation estimates can result from the application of each methodology. In practice, real estate appraisers often use all three methodologies concurrently and compare, and sometimes blend, the results when reaching notional real estate value conclusions. The nature of the property and purpose of the valuation should govern the selection of the approach(es) to be relied upon. As a general rule, for income-producing properties (or those that could be income producing) the cash flow methodology is preferred. On the other hand, the depreciated replacement cost methodology may be appropriate to develop the going concern value of a special-use property utilized in the operation of a viable ongoing business. The direct comparison methodology is useful as a primary methodology for non-income-producing properties where there is significant commonality of property characteristics and numerous transactions (such as single family dwellings). However, in the valuation of commercial and industrial properties the direct comparison methodology typically is best used to test values determined pursuant to the cash flow methodology, and to a lesser extent the depreciated replacement cost methodology.

In determining the market value of real estate, it is assumed that the buyer would be able to claim CCA at the appraised value. However, as noted above, where adjusted net book value is determined pursuant to a valuation of shares, then an adjustment is required with respect to the foregone tax shield, given that a buyer of shares will claim CCA based on the existing tax pools of the company.

Cash Flow Methodology

When the cash flow methodology is used to develop the market value of real estate, value is determined as the present value of all future expected net cash flows. The two principal methods employed in the valuation of income-producing real estate are the capitalized cash flow methodology and the discounted cash flow methodology. The basic elements of these two approaches are similar to the capitalized cash flow methodology and the discounted cash flow methodology adopted in business valuation, as discussed in Chapters 5 and 6, respectively. However, real estate industry practice generally has been to value income-producing real estate on a pre-tax basis, where pre-tax cash flows are subjected to pre-tax discount rates and capitalization rates.

When estimating the quantum of pre-tax cash flows to capitalize (or discount) for an income-producing property, the following things should be considered:

- historic operating results, including non-recurring and unusual revenues and expenses;

- the physical condition and general attractiveness of the property. This includes consideration of the amount of sustaining capital reinvestment, lease inducements, and whether any one-time improvements are required. An estimate of sustaining capital normally is deducted when determining cash flow;

- the composition of the tenant base. For retail, industrial and office premises, this includes the type of tenants, their financial stability, the duration and terms of the lease, and expected turnover rates. For residential properties, considerations may include the demographics of the tenant base (age, income, marital status), tenant turnover, and other relevant factors;

- expected vacancy rates; and

- prospective property management fees.

When determining appropriate discount rates or capitalization rates for an income-producing property, the following things should be considered:

- the ability to finance the property with debt, and to what degree;

- the rates of return imputed based on recent sales of what are believed to be comparable properties;

- the age, location and physical condition of the property;

- relevant legal considerations (e.g., rent control and zoning);

- the stability of prospective cash flows; and

- general and local economic conditions at the valuation date.

Income Approach Example

Company L owns a 200-unit, one-and-two-bedroom apartment complex. The property enjoys an attractive location and a stable tenant base. The building is 15 years old. Its electrical, heating, ventilating and air conditioning systems have been kept up to date and are well maintained, as are the building structure, lobbies, elevators and common areas. Roof repair is expected to have a net cost $500,000. Other facts are:

- the average rental rate is $1,000 per month;

- the 5% historical vacancy rate is expected to continue;

- operating expenses are approximately $1 million per annum;

- annual required refurbishments (e.g., painting, appliances and repairs) average $500 per unit;

- a management fee of 4% of gross income is considered appropriate; and

- a capitalization rate of 8% is considered appropriate for this type of property.

Based on the foregoing, the market value of Company L's property would be estimated at $13,110,000 as follows:

Exhibit 3L
Company L's Property
Estimate of Market Value

Gross potential income	200 suites @ $1,000 per month	2,400,000
Less: vacancy allowance	5% of gross potential income	120,000
Effective gross income		2,280,000
Operating expenses	Fixed	1,000,000
Refurbishments	200 suites @ $500 per year	100,000
Management fee	4% of effective gross income	91,200
Net operating income		1,088,800
Capitalization rate		8%
Capitalized value		13,610,000
Less: roof repair costs		500,000
Estimated market value		13,110,000

The starting point in the above calculation is the calculation of gross potential income, assuming full occupancy at $1,000 per month. A vacancy allowance of 5% is deducted to generate effective gross income of $2,280,000.

Expenses are then deducted, which consist of operating expenses of $1 million, refurbishments at $500 per unit per year, and the management fee at 4% of effective gross income (i.e., net of the vacancy allowance). The result is net operating income of $1,088,800.

Dividing the net operating income by the capitalization rate of 8% yields a capitalized value of $13,610,000. The cost of roof repairs is deducted from the capitalized value to derive the market value of $13,110,000. Note that the roof repairs represent a one-time cost, and therefore are not divided by the capitalization rate, which inherently assumes that the indicated net operating income will be generated on an annual basis.

The capitalized cash flow methodology used above is similar to that used in business valuation, except that in the context of business valuation, additional adjustments are made on account of income taxes, working capital and sustaining capital requirements. The capitalized cash flow approach in the context of business valuation is discussed in Chapter 5.

Direct Comparison Methodology

The direct comparison methodology involves comparing sales and listings of properties believed similar enough to the property being valued to make comparisons meaningful. The principal difficulties encountered in this approach are identifying properties that in fact are comparable in a meaningful way, assessing the degree of their respective comparability, and adjusting for the differences, if any. The basic elements of comparison that normally are relevant in direct comparison analysis include:

- size, age and physical condition;
- location;
- use (e.g., zoning);
- conditions of sale (e.g., whether special motivation exists). However, absent direct involvement in the sale, these things typically are not known;
- market conditions at the time the sale was made;
- environmental issues, if any; and
- whether there were any special financing terms that may have distorted the stated purchase price. For example, if a favourable-rate mortgage was transferred with the property, then the stated purchase price of the property may be inflated to reflect the financial gains from the interest rate savings.

The advantages of the direct sales comparison methodology are that it is easily understood and it is an approach accepted by many courts. Depending on the specific property being valued, to varying degrees it may reflect actual market behaviour. However, it can be difficult to find meaningful comparables for certain types of properties or for properties in remote areas. Furthermore, absent direct involvement in the transaction, the motivation of each party and their relative negotiating positions, which may have influenced the purchase price, cannot be known.

The direct comparison methodology may be of assistance when valuing properties and vacant land in larger urban centres where there is an active market and numerous transactions involving similar properties. With respect to income-producing properties, the direct comparison methodology often is useful as a test of the value conclusions derived using a cash flow-based methodology, and may assist in identifying relevant considerations not readily apparent.

The direct comparison methodology generally is less useful when determining the value of special-use properties and properties located in areas where few comparables are available. Where there are special-interest purchasers for a subject property, the applicability of the direct comparison methodology generally is limited.

Depreciated Replacement Cost Methodology

Depreciation theory referable to buildings and other improvements is founded on the general concept that there is a loss or decrease in the present value of improvements with the passage of time. In this sense, it is different from the accounting concept of depreciation which allocates costs rather than estimating value. The three main depreciation categories are:

- physical deterioration, which is a reduction in utility resulting from an impairment of physical conditions (i.e., wear and tear);

- economic obsolescence, which is the loss in the value in use of a property arising from factors external to the property, such as economic forces or environment changes, which affect market supply/demand relationships; and

- functional (or technological) obsolescence, which is the loss in value brought about by such factors as inefficiency, inadequacy, and other changes that affect the property, or the ability of a structure to adequately perform its function. Functional obsolescence may result from structural deficiencies, or overbuilding that a buyer or owner would not be justified in replacing, adding, or removing.

The depreciated replacement cost methodology is comprised of four steps:

- the value of the site (i.e., the land) is estimated as though vacant. This normally is conducted pursuant to the direct comparison methodology (discussed above);

- an estimate is made of the cost of replacing the building and site improvements (e.g., sewer system, paving, fencing, and so on) with a new identical building and site improvements;

- a depreciation factor is deducted from the replacement cost of the new identical building and site improvements to reflect the current condition and status of the building and site improvements on the subject property. In this regard, the depreciation factor is normally comprised of physical deterioration, economic obsolescence, and functional obsolescence, as discussed above; and

- the estimated vacant-site value is added to the estimated depreciated replacement cost of the property to derive depreciated replacement cost.

Application of the depreciated replacement cost methodology can be problematic. Because costs constantly change, building cost estimates may not be accurate. Physical, economic and functional depreciation estimates are based to a considerable degree on judgment. Due to building age and quality of estimates, depreciation cannot be precisely measured, especially as buildings get older. Finally, as a practical matter there may be circumstances where the depreciated replacement cost approach may not adequately reflect market conditions. Accordingly, an estimate of depreciated replacement cost may require the assistance of qualified experts in real estate, construction and engineering.

The depreciated replacement cost methodology is most commonly used in the valuation of special-use properties, where the cash flow approach and the direct comparison approach are not practical. In some cases, depreciated replacement cost is used as a test of the value conclusions developed pursuant to a cash flow-based methodology. Where depreciated replacement cost is significantly greater than market value derived using a cash flow approach, it might suggest that:

- there are components of value that were not considered in the cash flow approach that should be reconsidered;

- the estimates of replacement cost were overstated, or conversely that the depreciation factors were understated; or

- changes in the economic environment since the property was built have resulted in the income-producing capability of the property being less than the level that would have to be justified to replace the subject property.

Apportionment Between Land and Building

When the property being valued includes both land and building (or some other physical structure) because the building portion is eligible for CCA and the land portion is not, it generally is necessary to apportion the aggregate property value between the two components. The allocation of aggregate property value between land and building necessarily involves analysis and judgement. In general, the allocation should be determined based on considerations including:

- recent sales of comparable vacant land in the area;

- alternate uses available for the land, based on its size, zoning and prospective or possible zoning;

- the estimated depreciated replacement cost of the facilities, excluding the land component; and

- insured values, where it is believed the property and insurance risk managers have objectively valued the building component for insurance purposes.

Where both the buyer and seller are taxable entities, the buyer generally seeks to have a greater portion of value assigned to the building component in order to claim higher CCA. On the other hand, the seller generally seeks a greater apportionment to the land component in order to convert recaptured depreciation to capital gains, thereby reducing income taxes that otherwise would be payable.

Equipment Valuation

An independent assessment of equipment values is often required in the development of liquidation value or adjusted net book value. Equipment valuation can also assist in estimating capital expenditure requirements when developing the value of a business using a cash flow-based valuation methodology. Equipment value estimates often are aided by the assistance of a professional equipment appraiser.

Equipment Values in a Liquidation Context

Where liquidation value is being developed, the equipment is valued based on its "value in exchange" based on the estimated proceeds that could be expected from the sale of the assets at auction, either on an individual basis or as a group of related assets. In developing liquidation value, it is assumed that:

- the assets are sold on an assembled "as is, where is" basis;

- the assets are removed for offsite use;

- sales are completed within a short time period (normally 3 to 12 months) from the valuation date; and

- market conditions will remain relatively constant during the liquidation period.

Where the assets are not in working order, they may have to be sold at their salvage value (where certain parts can be salvaged) and/or at scrap value, based on their material components.

Liquidation value can be further categorized as either a forced liquidation or an orderly liquidation, as discussed earlier in this chapter. A forced liquidation generally occurs pursuant to a court order (or some other order) issued on the insolvency of a business, and is overseen by a trustee. An orderly liquidation is normally presumed to take place under more favourable circumstances such as the voluntary wind-up and dissolution of a business. It is generally assumed that the net proceeds generated on an orderly liquidation will exceed those of a forced liquidation, although this is not always the case.

When determining liquidation value, equipment appraisers normally consider:

- prospective market prices for similar used equipment;
- continuing operating costs, including overhead costs that may be incurred during the liquidation period;
- brokers' and dealers' fees that will arise on the sale of the assets; and
- the costs to remove, dismantle and transport the assets that will be incurred by the seller.

In addition, liquidation value normally takes into account corporate income tax consequences (including recapture, capital gains and terminal losses) that will arise on disposition of the assets.

Equipment Values in a Going-Concern Context

The various bases for valuing equipment in connection with the determination of adjusted net book value, or the going concern assumption in general, include: (i) replacement cost new; (ii) depreciated replacement cost; and (iii) value in use.

Replacement Cost New

For off-the-shelf assets, replacement cost new is the cost of an equivalent new asset of similar capacity, utility and current technology as available from manufacturers, suppliers and distributors, on a lowest available price basis, plus installation costs.

For custom-built assets, replacement cost new is the current cost to replace similar or reasonably similar assets of equivalent utility, as obtained from custom designers and cost engineers or as established utilizing quantitative valuation procedures, plus installation costs.

Similar to the development of replacement cost in real estate, estimating the cost to replace equipment can be subjective because of changing cost estimates. Replacement cost estimates can be particularly problematic for older pieces of equipment, or where significant technological advances have occurred since the time that the equipment was first constructed.

Depreciated Replacement Cost

Depreciated replacement cost is defined as replacement cost new, less an allowance for accumulated depreciation. The depreciation allowance takes into account physical deterioration, functional obsolescence and economic obsolescence, based on a comparison of the asset with new like units. As in the case of real estate valuation, the estimate of depreciation is subjective. In addition, any estimate of depreciation should be internally consistent with the assumptions underlying the development of replacement cost new, with respect to production capacity, technical capabilities and other factors.

Value in Use

An estimate of value in use is normally restricted to special-use equipment essential to the ongoing business operations. Value in use is usually determined as the present value of discretionary cash flows expected to accrue from use of the equipment. In the context of equipment valuation, discretionary cash flows are defined as cash flows from operations, less required refurbishment costs and income taxes. As a practical matter, it is frequently difficult to segregate discretionary cash flows that accrue from the use of specific special-use equipment from the aggregate discretionary cash flows of a business. Furthermore, the determination of value in use pursuant to a cash flow-based methodology makes certain assumptions regarding operating capacity. Where the equipment runs below that capacity level, the valuation result can be distorted.

In theory, value in use should not exceed the replacement cost new of identical (or substantially similar) equipment. This is because no prudent buyer would pay more for a piece of existing equipment than it would cost to acquire and install a new piece of identical equipment. Where value in use exceeds replacement cost new, it may be because the discretionary cash flow projections used to calculate value in use contain an element of value from other aspects of the business (e.g., the brand name on the products produced using the equipment).

Summary of Valuation Methods

The various equipment valuation methodologies can be summarized as follows:

Exhibit 3M
Approaches to Equipment Valuation

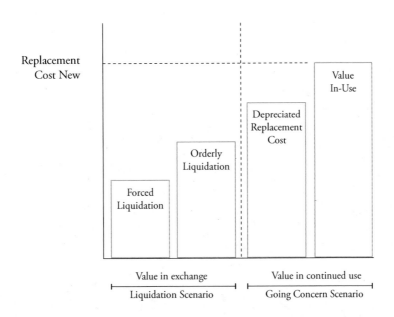

Common Issues with Asset Valuation Methodologies

Some of the most common issues encountered when preparing a liquidation value calculation are:

- ensuring all costs related to liquidation and wind-up have been adequately accounted for. This is particularly the case where an orderly liquidation scenario is assumed, and operating costs are expected to continue for some period of time; and

- the calculation of income taxes on wind-up, including both corporate income taxes and, where applicable, personal income taxes. Tax calculations can be complex, and may require the assistance of a tax specialist.

With respect to the adjusted net book value methodology, some of the more common issues include:

- estimating the economic value of fixed assets, particularly real property that is not readily saleable (such as special-use property) and equipment, where an estimate of replacement cost new, depreciated replacement cost or value in use are required. Such estimates inherently are subjective. Furthermore, it is difficult to segregate cash flows associated with a specific piece of equipment or special-use real estate from cash flows accruing to the business as a whole; and

- in some cases, adjusted net book value is adopted as a primary valuation methodology. However, depending on the nature of the business, this may not be appropriate. A value conclusion premised on the adjusted net book value methodology inherently assumes that no commercial goodwill exists, and that the cash flows of the business are adequate to support the replacement cost and value in use values ascribed to the fixed assets.

Buyers typically place more emphasis on the prospective cash flows from a business as opposed to its underlying net assets. Consequently, adjusted net book value is more commonly used to calculate the intangible value implied in an equity value conclusion developed using a cash flow-based valuation methodology.

Summary

Where a business is believed not to be a going concern, its value is premised on the net proceeds that would accrue upon the liquidation of its underlying assets and the settlement of its outstanding liabilities. Liquidation values can be developed under the assumption of either a forced liquidation or an orderly liquidation. Liquidation values should take into account disposition and wind-up costs, as well as income taxes at the corporate level to develop proceeds available for distribution. Where personal income taxes are deducted, the result is net proceeds available to the business owners.

The adjusted net book value methodology consists of adjusting the shareholders' equity of the business, as stated for accounting purposes, to reflect the economic values of the business's underlying assets and liabilities. In this regard, assets and liabilities are valued based on their value in use (or market value, if greater), and adjustments are made where appropriate for income taxes where the shares of the business are being valued. Intangible assets are assigned a nil value. Therefore, deducting the adjusted net book value from *en bloc* equity value determined using a cash flow-based methodology results in the total intangible value implied by the equity value conclusion.

The importance attaching to the underlying net assets and adjusted net book value of a business vis-à-vis the valuation conclusion varies in each case. Corporate acquirers typically place greater emphasis on the prospective cash flows that a business is expected to generate as opposed to the value in use of its underlying net assets. Accordingly, the application of the adjusted net book value methodology as a principal valuation methodology normally is restricted to non-operating businesses (such as holding companies). Where believed to be meaningful, the adjusted net book value methodology sometimes serves as a check on the valuation conclusions developed pursuant to a cash flow-based methodology.

Chapter 4

Valuation Based on Multiples

Introduction

In many cases, the value of a business is estimated by applying a valuation multiple to some measure of its earnings or cash flow. The most popular approach in this regard is the multiple of EBITDA (earnings before interest, taxes, depreciation and amortization) methodology. Other approaches include a multiple of EBIT (earnings before interest and taxes), a multiple of EBITDA less capex (i.e., capital expenditures) and a multiple of after-tax cash flow or earnings.

The starting point in each of these is normalized EBITDA, which is typically based on an analysis of historical and current operating results, adjusted for transactions with non-arm's length parties, unusual and non-recurring items, discretionary expenditures and income or costs associated with redundant assets. Valuation multiples for a given business are influenced by a myriad of factors, including its customer base, management team, growth expectations, industry transactions and other variables.

Other approaches based on valuation multiples include the multiple of revenue or multiple of some operating metric (e.g., units produced or number of customers), sometimes referred to as "rules of thumb".

The application of valuations based on multiples is fraught with caveats. Accordingly, such approaches are normally better suited to develop a preliminary indication of value and as a test of value conclusions determined based on other methodologies such as a discounted cash flow methodology (discussed in Chapter 6). However, valuation multiples, particularly multiples of EBITDA, are often referenced by buyers and sellers when negotiating an open market transaction.

The Multiple of EBITDA Methodology

Overview

The mechanics of the multiple of EBITDA methodology are relatively straightforward. A valuation multiple is applied to *normalized EBITDA* to determine the *enterprise value* of the business. Recall that enterprise value represents the total operating value of a business, regardless of how it is financed. Outstanding interest-bearing debt and equivalent liabilities (net of excess cash on hand) are then deducted to determine equity value. In some cases, adjustments are made to the equity value that has been otherwise determined because of redundant assets, prospective one-time adjustments (e.g., one-time income, operating expenses or capital expenditures), or excess or deficient net operating assets (e.g., working capital) at the valuation date.

Exhibit 4A
Multiple of EBITDA Methodology

Normalized EBITDA

Multiplied by:	EBITDA multiple
Equals:	enterprise value
Deduct:	interest-bearing debt and equivalents (net of excess cash)
Add:	redundant assets
Add (deduct):	one-time adjustments
Add (deduct):	excess (deficient) net operating assets
Equals:	equity value

It follows that the key variables to be considered are: (i) normalized EBITDA; (ii) the EBITDA multiple; (iii) the amount of interest-bearing debt and equivalents outstanding (net of excess cash on hand); and (iv) adjustments that may be required on account of redundant assets, prospective one-time items or excess (deficient) net operating assets.

Normalized EBITDA

EBITDA reflects the operating cash flow of a business before consideration of financing, income taxes or capital expenditure requirements. As such, it is not a holistic measure of cash flow. However, EBITDA is a common reference point in business valuation, open market transactions and executive compensation plans.

Note that the starting point in the multiple of EBITDA methodology is *normalized* EBITDA, which typically is based on the historical or current operating results of a business. However, since valuation looks to the future, it may be necessary to adjust historical or current operating results to remove the impact of revenues and costs that an arm's length buyer would not be expected to incur, which may include:

- unusual and non-recurring revenues and expenses;
- discretionary expenditures;
- non-arm's length income or costs above or below market rates; and
- income or costs relating to redundant assets.

Making normalization adjustments can be a subjective exercise.

Normalized EBITDA represents the amount of operating cash flow the business is expected to generate year over year. The multiple of EBITDA methodology assumes either a:

- constant or average level of EBITDA is generated each year in perpetuity; or
- base level of EBITDA that grows at a consistent rate in perpetuity, where growth is incorporated in the valuation multiple adopted.

Because absolute consistency is not part of this assumption, normalized EBITDA represents the point estimate (or range) reflective of average operating cash flow expectations. As a result, the multiple of EBITDA methodology does not account for timing differences that may result from average but uneven future cash flows.

The first step in calculating normalized EBITDA is to assess which periods to include in the normalization calculation which itself may include historical, current or future operating results. A reasoned estimate of normalized EBITDA requires an understanding of prevailing and prospective relevant economic, industry and business factors, as well as a thorough and objective assessment of the current, historical and prospective financial position and operating results of the business. Specific considerations for each time period (historical, current and future) are discussed below.

For each time period selected, the following calculation should be made in order to calculate normalized EBITDA:

Exhibit 4B
Normalized EBITDA Calculation for a Given Period

	Income before taxes as reported
Add:	interest expense
Add:	depreciation and amortization expense
Add (deduct):	other non-cash expenses (income)
Equals:	actual EBITDA
Add (deduct):	normalization adjustments
Equals:	normalized EBITDA

The starting point in determining normalized EBITDA for a given period is income before taxes as reported on the income statement. Interest expense is added back because the enterprise value of a business is independent of how it is financed. Financing does impact equity value, however, by way of deducting interest-bearing debt outstanding from enterprise value. Therefore, in the first instance, it is necessary to set aside financing and deal with the operating value (i.e., enterprise value) of a business.

Depreciation and amortization expense is also added back because it represents a non-cash charge. This includes depreciation on fixed assets, the amortization of intangible assets and other sources of amortization (e.g., the amortization of a pension surplus or deficiency where the business offers a defined-benefit pension plan for its employees). In addition, other non-cash expenses (income) should be added back (deducted). Examples of other non-cash expenses (income) include losses (gains) on the disposal of fixed assets that are recorded on the income statement for financial accounting purposes. To ensure depreciation and amortization and other non-cash charges are fully accounted for, these items should be sourced from the cash flow statement.

Adding back interest, depreciation and amortization and other non-cash items to pre-tax income quantifies the actual EBITDA for the business.

Normalization Adjustments

Adjustments to reported operating results for a given period are commonly required to reflect unusual and non-recurring items, as well as non-arms length transactions that were not consummated on commercial terms. The objective in business valuation is to estimate future earnings or cash flow (or, in this case, EBITDA) as it would be viewed from the perspective of an arm's length buyer acting rationally (excluding the impact of synergies or other post-acquisition advantages where the business is being valued on a stand-alone basis). Therefore, adjustments to historical and current operating results may be necessary in order to accomplish this.

Examples of the most common normalization adjustments include the following:

- owners of privately held businesses frequently draw compensation and benefits disproportionate to the time and effort they expend in the business. Similarly, business owners may pay excessive remuneration to related parties such as their spouse or children (even if their involvement in the business is negligible). This is often done for income tax purposes. Excessive drawings from the business are a form of return on investment. On the other hand, inappropriately low drawings contribute to profit overstatement. When determining fair market value, economic compensation for services performed must be segregated from return on investment. Accordingly, EBITDA should be adjusted up or down to reflect market-rate salaries for business owners and related parties. Sources of data for normalized remuneration include such things as industry salary surveys and remuneration paid to executives of public companies that are reasonably comparable to the subject business. When relying on such sources of industry data, it is important to consider the degree of comparability in terms of industry segment, company size, geographic location and other important variables. In some cases, an independent consulting firm may be engaged to estimate market-rate remuneration;

- where a business deals on a non-arm's length basis with other companies or individuals, it often is difficult to ascertain whether costs and revenues are reflective of arm's length amounts. Where non-arm's length transactions are being consummated at non-commercial rates, appropriate adjustments to EBITDA are necessary. An example of non-arm's length transactions is rental payments, where the facilities in which the business operates are owned by related parties, or where the subject business purchases or sells goods or services to related parties;

- in some cases (more often in privately held companies), owners incur discretionary expenses such as personal trips that are expensed through the business but are not part of the business's operations. To the extent that discretionary expenses within a business can be identified, they should be added back to income, since they reflect a return on capital as opposed to an economic cost (much like remuneration levels that are above market rates). However, it is important to ensure that such expenses are truly discretionary, and that their discontinuance will not impair the operations or risk profile of the business over the long term. For example, while donations might be viewed as discretionary expenses, most companies will incur some donations in order to maintain a positive reputation with their community and employees;

- unusual or non-recurring items. To the extent that a business incurred expenses or generated income in the past that is of an unusual or non-recurring nature, that expense (income) should be added back (deducted) on the grounds that it is not expected to occur in the future. Examples of unusual and non-recurring items include:

  - ✓ new product lines, or capacity or other operating changes. EBITDA might have to be adjusted upward to eliminate non-recurring start-up costs,

    ✓ a product recall. The associated costs would normally be added back to historical operating results, assuming that such recalls were infrequent,

    ✓ a large property tax refund in a particular period. That income should be deducted from historical results. However, it may be appropriate to increase EBITDA in other years to which that property tax refund applies (i.e., in those periods where the property taxes were overstated),

    ✓ moving costs and related expenses associated with relocating its facilities. These costs should be added back, and

    ✓ a restructuring. The associated costs (e.g., severance and related expenses) would be added back to reported results.

- When making adjustments on account of unusual items and non-recurring items, consideration must be given to whether said items are expected to recur. For example, a business may experience periodic labour disputes and classify the related cost as an unusual item. However, if labour disputes are expected to recur with some degree of regularity, then an allowance should be made for such costs either in the estimation of normalized EBITDA, or alternatively in the valuation multiple adopted; and

- income and expenses relating to redundant assets. As discussed in Chapter 2, redundant assets are those that are not required in the ongoing operations of a business (e.g., vacant land). Because the value of redundant assets is added to enterprise value in order to determine the equity value of the business, it is assumed the income and expense streams associated with redundant assets will terminate. Accordingly, any income or expenses attributed to those redundant assets should be removed from reported operating results so as to avoid double counting.

When considering normalization adjustments, it is important to be aware of the classification of income and expense items. For example, "other income and expense" line items may include non-recurring revenues and expenses, normal operating items and income or expenses relating to redundant assets. Therefore, a thorough analysis of the financial statements and supporting documentation is essential when determining whether or not adjustments are necessary.

Historical Operating Results

In virtually all circumstances, historical operating results should be analyzed to help assess both general and specific business trends and management's ability to adapt to change. Normalized historical operating results frequently form an effective base from which to project future operating results.

When adopting historical results to estimate normalized EBITDA, there should be reasonable assurance that said historical results are likely to indicate maintainable future results. However, where significant changes have occurred in past years, historical results may not be indicative of future operating cash flows. This may be the case where there have been:

- major changes in the industry (e.g., a substantial change in the competitive landscape or a dramatic shift in consumer behaviour); or

- significant changes in the business's principal operations such as the addition or disposal of a division, major changes in management personnel or business strategy, increased operating capacity, and so on.

Normalized EBITDA should be calculated for each historical period considered relevant to future operating results.

Finally, it may be appropriate to adjust historical (normalized) EBITDA for the effects of inflation. This can be done using a measure such as the Consumer Price Index, the GDP deflator or other relevant inflation indicator. As a practical matter, an adjustment for inflation is often not made, given the relatively subdued levels of inflation experienced in recent years. However, an adjustment for inflation may become more relevant in the event that inflationary pressures increase, or where the subject business operates in a high inflation environment. Inflation may also be a factor where a notional valuation is being conducted at a valuation date that fell during or shortly after a high inflationary period.

Historical results may also be impacted by fluctuations in foreign exchange rates or commodity prices. Where this is the case, it may be appropriate to adjust historical results. Caution is warranted, however, as the impact of such adjustments cannot be made in isolation. For example, many Canadian manufacturers experienced elevated revenues and income when the Canadian dollar was trading at a significant discount to the U.S. dollar (e.g., 1994 to 2003). While it may be possible to adjust for the impact of a stronger Canadian dollar, it is not possible to know what actions management would have taken had the business actually been subject to a stronger Canadian dollar.

Current Operating Results

An evaluation of current (annual or trailing 12 months) operating results is essential. This includes not only the income statement, but also the balance sheet and statement of cash flows. It is important to understand the drivers behind the current operating results, which results are sometimes accepted as the most appropriate measure of normalized EBITDA. This is particularly the case where meaningful financial projections are not available and the business has:

- recently changed its product or service offerings;
- experienced a material change in operating cash flow which is expected to continue; or
- experienced a constant upward trend in cash flow which is expected to continue after the valuation date.

Care must be taken to ensure that current operating results are representative of what are anticipated to be future cash flows. Analysis must ensure adequate consideration has been given to cyclicality, results of most recent months, short-term product line changes, and other factors. As is the case with historical operating results, adjustments to current operating results may be necessary to derive a normalized EBITDA amount.

Prospective Operating Results

Many businesses prepare annual budgets that represent management's best estimate or target financial results for the next fiscal year. In some cases, management also prepares longer-term forecasts beyond the next fiscal year (usually three to five years). During the ensuing fiscal year, management often re-forecasts monthly or quarterly for the balance of that fiscal year.

The selection of normalized EBITDA levels typically is aided by thoughtfully developed financial projections. The use of forecast cash flows in large measure is a refinement of current cash flow. In most cases, normalized EBITDA calculations do not take into account more than one year's forecast (i.e., next year's budget or current-year forecast). However, where meaningful long-term projections are available, they may influence the valuation multiple. Specifically, where the longer-term projections indicate:

- significant fluctuation in cash flow, that suggests increased risk which, in turn, has a downward influence on the valuation multiple; and

- expected growth, that has an upward influence on the valuation multiple.

As a practical matter, where longer-term meaningful projections are available, it is usually appropriate to employ a discounted cash flow methodology, as discussed in Chapter 6. However, the multiple of EBITDA methodology may be used as a test of those value conclusions.

Regardless of whether historical cash flows are believed to provide a reliable indication of future expectations, a review of prior-year management forecasts measured against comparative-year historical operating results is often useful. A review of prior years' forecasts and business plans, coupled with the assumptions that underlie them, can provide valuable insight into management's forecasting abilities. It may also highlight unusual risks or opportunities that have been anticipated in the past, and generally may assist in assessing the probability of achieving current forecasts.

When assessing forecast or budgeted EBITDA, care must be taken to ensure that expected operating cash flows are plausible, and that the assumptions underlying the forecasts have been consistently applied. For example, an assumption of significantly increasing sales without a provision for required increases in manufacturing capacity, increased overheads, changes in gross margins, or market demand and competitive reaction would result in a meaningless arithmetical exercise.

Weighting Normalized Results

A key issue to address is which period(s) should be considered when calculating normalized EBITDA and, for each period adopted, how it should be weighted. Where current results or forecast results (where they exist) viewed in isolation are not appropriate as a guide to prospective cash flows, an averaging (trend) analysis of historical, current, and forecast results may be warranted. These methods are simply aids to the exercise of informed judgment which results in the selection of normalized EBITDA.

The weighting of normalized operating results depends on the nature of the business and the industry in which it operates. Historical and current operating results are only meaningful to the extent they reflect future expectations. In this regard:

- if a business operates in a cyclical industry, it may be appropriate to consider the average operating results over an economic cycle, rather than applying the valuation multiple to a high point or low point in the cycle;

- if a business has recently undergone significant changes to its operations (e.g., bought or sold a division, entered a new market or experienced major changes in its product line), then the operating results prior to those changes may not be reflective of future results; and

- if a business has grown significantly over the last few years, then its most recent operating results or current year forecast may be the best indicator of future results.

A simple average of the adjusted EBITDA calculations for historical, current and forecast periods may be appropriate where adjusted cash flow from operations has been relatively stable and a future change in the cash flow generation pattern is unlikely. For a simple average of adjusted EBITDA to be a fair reflection of future cash flow, industry conditions, operating capacities, and overall business operations must all be generally consistent over the review period and must be expected to remain so beyond the valuation date.

The review period must reflect an appropriate number of years' operations, and prospects for the business must be reflected in historical or adjusted historical activity.

Another technique sometimes utilized to develop normalized EBITDA entails adopting a weighted average of adjusted historical, current and projected results. The EBITDA for each relevant period is multiplied by a weighting factor. The sum of the results is then divided by the sum of the weighting factors to derive a weighted average. A weighted-average-adjusted EBITDA may be appropriate where cash flows have been inconsistent from year to year, but have shown an overall upward or downward trend.

For example, assume the normalized EBITDA results for a business were as follows:

Fiscal Year	Normalized EBITDA
2009	($6,000,000)
2010	$9,000,000
2011	$6,000,000

Further assume that an analysis of the business, the industry in which it operates and economic factors revealed that an appropriate weighting of the years would be 3/2/1 for 2011, 2010 and 2009, respectively. In that case, the weighted average would be calculated as follows:

$$\frac{[1 \times (\$6,000,000)] + [2 \times \$9,000,000] + [3 \times \$6,000,000]}{[1 + 2 + 3]} = \$5,000,000$$

The weighting factors adopted are a matter of judgment, reflecting the overall rate of earnings growth or decline and future expectations. Again, for a weighted average result to be meaningful, the nature of the operations of the business must be consistent over the period reviewed, and it must be expected that future operations will not be materially affected by the changing business environment, technological change, operating capacity changes within the business, or other factors.

As a practical matter, buyers in an open market transaction often place the greatest emphasis on the most recent operating results of the target company (normally the latest fiscal year or trailing twelve months). They reflect the risk and growth prospects of that EBITDA level in the selection of the valuation multiple. Whatever basis is used, it is important that the normalized EBITDA adopted and the valuation multiple be viewed in conjunction and not in isolation.

Other Considerations

When estimating normalized EBITDA, it is sometimes necessary to look beyond adjustments normally encountered. Such considerations include circumstances where:

- distinct divisions or subsidiaries operate under one corporate umbrella. Difficult issues may arise in the valuation of one division within a business viewed in isolation because it may not be possible to allocate all costs by specific division or subsidiary. Common overhead costs, including management costs, are often allocated arbitrarily. Further, there may be economies of scale reflected in consolidated earnings due to the integration of operations. For example, divisional management charges are generally less if several divisions enjoy common centralized management than is the case where each division is autonomous. Similarly, if two divisions manufacture complementary goods that can be sold by the same sales force, selling costs per unit are typically less than if each division operates separately. This economy of scale issue tends to be magnified where fixed costs are high and excess capacity exists. In such circumstances, any increase in capacity utilization often results in large incremental profits if the original level of fixed costs is maintained. Such factors need to be considered where one division is valued in isolation from the others;

- a business consists of different divisions or subsidiaries that could be sold or operated in isolation. Where the risk attaching to the cash flows of each differs, it is necessary to estimate normalized EBITDA for each division or subsidiary. Where such risk variations occur, depending upon other variables such as perceived risk profiles and prospective growth rates, different valuation multiples are typically assigned to the estimated EBITDA of each division or subsidiary to reflect such differences;

- the operations of a business are situated in facilities that are owned by the business. As discussed later in this chapter, it is often appropriate to view real estate as an asset separate from the business because of its different (usually lower) risk profile. Where this is the case, normalized EBITDA should be reduced by a market-based rent for the property. This adjustment effectively reduces the operating value of the business, but reallocates value to the real estate component; and

- there is clear evidence of buyers who perceive post-acquisition synergies. It may be important to consider the incremental EBITDA said buyers may be able to generate. It is usually appropriate to segregate such incremental EBITDA and apply a lower multiple to reflect its higher risk of not being realized (or, alternatively, to estimate the probability of incremental EBITDA being realized, quantify it and apply a market-driven EBITDA multiple) given the uncertainty of successfully negotiating a price that incorporates an element of the prospective synergies. This is in contrast to the presumed lower risk related to the generation of EBITDA expected from the business viewed on a stand-alone basis.

Finally, it is usually useful to perform an analysis of the sensitivity of the estimated normalized EBITDA to variations in each of the key economic drivers. This provides a measure of the degree to which cash flows are at risk. The impact of an optimistic scenario, a pessimistic scenario, and a most-likely-case prospective cash flow scenario then can be considered when selecting an appropriate valuation multiple.

The EBITDA Multiple

An EBITDA multiple is the inverse of a rate of return on capital before consideration of income taxes and capital expenditure requirements. For example, if the rate of return is 20%, the equivalent EBITDA multiple would be calculated as 1/20% = 5x. Multiplying normalized EBITDA by the EBITDA multiple results in the enterprise value of the business.

The EBITDA multiple reflects the risk that the normalized EBITDA adopted will not be maintained at the indicated level or that the prospects for future growth will not materialize. The principal factors that should be considered when developing valuation multiples are discussed later in this chapter.

The EBITDA multiple must reflect the fact that the cash flow base (i.e., EBITDA) is before depreciation (capital spending) and income taxes. Therefore, these factors must be taken into account when selecting the appropriate multiple.

To avoid double-counting and to ensure internal consistency, the EBITDA multiple cannot be viewed in isolation of the EBITDA base against which it is applied. Therefore, if a particular risk is reflected in the determination of normalized EBITDA, that same risk should not be reflected in the valuation multiple. Likewise, if growth has been factored into the normalized EBITDA base (e.g., where budgets or forecasts have been incorporated in the EBITDA estimate), the EBITDA multiple should not double-count that growth.

The discussion in Chapter 1 regarding internal consistency applies equally to the selection of valuation multiples. For example, if a business is expected to generate normalized EBITDA in the range of $10 million to $12 million, and a multiple of 5x to 6x EBITDA is considered appropriate, then the higher multiple should be applied against the lower EBITDA to reflect the lower degree of risk in generating that level of income, and vice versa. In effect, the enterprise value is the same:

Exhibit 4C
Enterprise Value and Valuation Multiples

	Low	High
Normalized EBITDA	$10 million	$12 million
EBITDA Multiple	6×	5×
Enterprise Value	$60 million	$60 million

For a given business, the relationship between normalized EBITDA and the EBITDA multiple can be graphically depicted as follows:

Exhibit 4D
Relationship Between Normalized EBITDA and the EBITDA Multiple

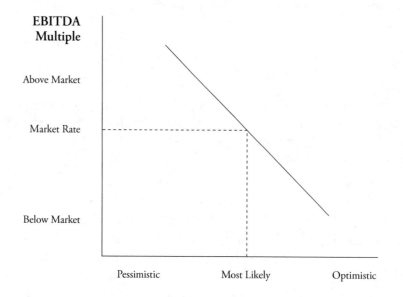

That having been said, it is usually preferable to adopt a best estimate of normalized EBITDA applied to EBITDA multiples that reflect market-driven rates of return, rather than trying to adjust the EBITDA multiple to compensate for overly aggressive or overly conservative normalized EBITDA estimates.

Interest-Bearing Debt and Equivalents

Multiplying normalized EBITDA by the EBITDA multiple represents the enterprise value of the business (i.e., total value of the business's operations) regardless of how it is financed. Outstanding interest-bearing debt and equivalent obligations are deducted from enterprise value to determine equity value. Interest-bearing debt and equivalent obligations may be short term or long term. In addition, cash on hand is usually netted against interest-bearing debt outstanding, subject to the operating requirements of the business. In effect, the amount of interest-bearing debt and equivalents outstanding (net of excess cash on hand) can be taken from the balance sheet segregation exercise presented in Chapter 2.

Short-Term Interest-Bearing Debt

Most businesses have a short-term operating credit facility with a financial institution that they draw on principally to finance current assets such as accounts receivable and inventory. Such debts normally bear interest at the prime lending rate plus a premium, depending on the risk profile of the business (as perceived by the lending institution) and the terms of the loan. Short-term debts can also include the portion of a term loan coming due within the next fiscal year.

Depending on the nature of the business, the amount of a bank operating line may fluctuate significantly during the year. This is particularly the case for businesses whose operations are seasonal, such that periods of high levels of accounts receivable and inventory are financed to a large extent by a higher than normal bank operating line. Consequently, the argument is sometimes made that a short-term operating loan should not be deducted from enterprise value or, alternatively, that an average amount outstanding during the course of the year represents a better measure. However, in order to ensure internal consistency, it is better to:

a)   deduct the actual amount of short-term interest-bearing debt outstanding at the valuation date; and

b)   where applicable, to make a separate adjustment for current assets (e.g., accounts receivable and inventory) that are greater than, or less than, normal levels.

This approach helps to ensure that adequate consideration is afforded to the normal working capital levels of the business being valued. In many cases, at a given point in time, higher (lower) levels of a bank operating loan will roughly be offset by excess (deficient) net trade working capital. This approach is consistent with most open market transactions involving privately held businesses, whereby a post-acquisition "true-up" is made on account of interest-bearing debt and working capital outstanding against an agreed target level at the transaction closing date.

In addition, it is necessary to determine (after a detailed assessment of the financial statements and accompanying notes, or otherwise) whether there are any other debt obligations that should properly be included as part of either short-term or long-term interest-bearing debt. Such amounts might include guarantees by other companies that may be called by the lender or securitized inventories or accounts receivable.

Long-Term Interest-Bearing Debt

Long-term interest-bearing debt commonly includes term debt, mortgages payable, bonds payable, capital lease obligations, and similar obligations. In most cases, the value of long-term interest-bearing debt is taken to be its face value. However, where the rate of interest is not reflective of market rates prevailing at the valuation date given the risks and characteristics of the debt, it may be appropriate to determine the market value of the debt obligation and deduct that amount (as contrasted with the face amount of the long-term debt) from enterprise value. This approach is consistent with the calculation of adjusted net book value as discussed in Chapter 3.

Recall that the market value (or economic value) of debt is determined as the present value of the cash flow obligations (given the coupon rate and principal repayments on the debt) discounted at the prevailing market rate of interest for similar outstanding debt instruments of companies with a comparable risk profile.

For example, assume that Company M has a $20 million subordinated loan with three years remaining. The loan bears interest at a stated rate of 15%, payable annually. Interest payments are due semi-annually (i.e., $1.5 million every six months) while the entire principal is repayable at the end of the three-year term. The prevailing market rate of interest on similar debt has declined to 12%. Accordingly, the economic value of the subordinated loan obligation would be determined as follows:

Exhibit 4E
Company M
Economic Value of Subordinated Loan

Year	Interest at 15%	Principal Repayment	Total Payments	PV factor at 12%	Present Value
0.5	1,500,000		1,500,000	0.945	1,417,367
1.0	1,500,000		1,500,000	0.893	1,339,286
1.5	1,500,000		1,500,000	0.844	1,265,506
2.0	1,500,000		1,500,000	0.797	1,195,791
2.5	1,500,000		1,500,000	0.753	1,129,916
3.0	1,500,000	20,000,000	21,500,000	0.712	15,303,275

Total Net Present Value (Economic Value)   21,651,141

Interest-Bearing Debt Equivalents

The liabilities of a business (particularly a privately held business) sometimes include non-interest-bearing loans and advances from shareholders, directors, affiliated organizations, governments, and other parties. These may be classified for financial statement presentation purposes as being either short -term or long-term.

Interest-bearing debt equivalents should be deducted from enterprise value since they represent a source of non-operational financing and a one-time cash outflow. As a practical matter, in an open market transaction, advances from shareholders are usually either repaid when the shares of the business are sold or (infrequently) left in place on commercial terms. In either case, such advances represent a financial obligation that diminishes what otherwise would be equity value.

Normally, accrued bonuses payable to owner-managers at the valuation date also represent a form of non-interest-bearing debt, and should be deducted accordingly since, in most cases, a selling shareholder to whom the business owes a bonus will insist on receiving it either at or following the transaction closing date. Similar to other interest-bearing debt equivalents, the bonus causes a near-term cash outflow or creates the need to obtain external funds.

Interest-bearing debt equivalents do not include ordinary-course operating liabilities such as accounts payable, accrued liabilities, deferred revenues, warranties and similar liabilities. While such debts must be settled as well, they provide an ongoing source of trade financing for a business in the ordinary course of its operations. However, those liabilities should be considered when assessing the adequacy of working capital within a business. Therefore, regardless of whether a liability is classified as "financing" or "operating," in theory it should have the same net result on the equity value of the business. The balance sheet segregation exercise discussed in Chapter 2 can assist in classifying liabilities and in assessing the adequacy of a business's working capital position.

Preference Shares

Where the value of the common shares of a company is being determined, it is necessary to deduct the value of the preferred shares since they rank ahead of the common. In most cases, preferred shares are redeemable and/or retractable, and hence their value is set at their redemption or retraction price. However, preferred shares are sometimes ascribed a different value, depending on their features, cross-ownership with common shares and other attributes. The valuation of preferred shares is addressed in Chapter 9.

Pension Plans

Some companies have a defined-benefit pension plan for their employees. Every three years (or even more frequently) the pension plan will undergo an actuarial valuation, whereby the net assets of the plan will be compared to the present value of the plan's future liabilities.

The accounting rules for pension surpluses and deficiencies are complex, and the financial reporting standards have changed over the years. Therefore, the pension surplus or deficiency as reported on a company's balance sheet may be significantly different from its economic value. For the purpose of valuation, the economic value of the pension plan deficiency should be deducted from enterprise value, as is the case with other interest-bearing debt obligations. However, the amount of the deficiency should be reduced by the income tax savings that will be realized on the contributions to compensate for such deficiency. Likewise, the economic value of a pension surplus (net of tax) should be added to enterprise value, on the grounds that it represents a reduction in future cash outflows.

Note that pension adjustments are only required in respect of defined-benefit pension plans. In a defined-contribution pension plan, the amount of pension expense is based on the cash contribution and no surplus or deficiency arises.

Excess Cash on Hand

Where a business has cash on hand, it is customary to apply it against interest-bearing debt outstanding. Alternatively, where cash on hand exceeds interest-bearing debt and equivalents outstanding, it is customary to add that excess cash balance to enterprise value, as is done with a redundant asset.

However, the treatment of cash as an offset to debt or as a redundant asset is not always warranted. Where a business has both cash and short-term interest-bearing debt (or similar obligations), the cash can usually be applied against that debt, given that it would not change the working capital balance of the business, since both the asset and the liability are classified as short-term. However, where the cash could be applied against long-term debt, then an assessment must be made as to whether doing so would reduce working capital below the level required to maintain operations. If so, then the cash required for working capital purposes should not be applied against long-term debt.

Similarly, where cash on hand exceeds the total amount of debt outstanding (both short-term and long-term), then an assessment must be made to ensure the withdrawal of excess cash will not cause the working capital of the business to be insufficient to support operations.

It may be appropriate to segregate cash between an "operating" component and a "financing" component. The balance sheet segregation exercise, as illustrated in Chapter 2, can help to ensure that cash balances, debt and working capital are considered in a holistic and internally consistent manner.

Redundant Assets

Recall from Chapter 2 that redundant assets are those not required in the ongoing operations of a business. In a notional market context, the value of redundant assets is added to enterprise value to determine equity value. In open market transactions, redundant assets are typically removed from the business prior to closing because most buyers have no interest in acquiring redundant assets.

The value ascribed to redundant assets is typically based on their respective net realizable values. In this context, net realizable value is generally taken to mean the market value of the redundant assets based on their value in exchange rather than value in continued use. In some cases market values may be readily available (e.g., marketable securities), whereas in other cases, estimates must be made (e.g., vacant land). Where redundant assets are not readily liquid, it may be appropriate to consider the uncertainty with respect to the timing of their sale when developing their net realizable value. As previously discussed, any income or costs associated with redundant assets should be removed when determining normalized EBITDA in order to avoid double-counting.

Disposition Costs and Taxes

Depending on the circumstances and assumptions, disposition costs and income taxes that will be incurred on the disposition of redundant assets are deducted when determining the net realizable value of redundant assets. Disposition costs should reflect all costs incurred to convert the redundant asset to cash. These costs may include commissions on the disposition of marketable securities or real estate properties, legal and consulting fees on the disposition of non-productive patents, and similar costs.

Where corporate income taxes may arise on gains realized on the notional or actual disposition of redundant assets, it is important that the tax rate applied reflect the nature of the income. For example, recapture of undepreciated capital cost (i.e., tax depreciation) on the sale of a redundant building will give rise to business income taxed at operating income tax rates, whereas a capital gain on the disposition of capital property is taxed at the lower capital gains tax rate. If a capital loss is incurred, and no capital gains are available against which to apply it, the value of the capital loss may be nominal if it is unlikely to be utilized in the foreseeable future. Selected income tax issues are discussed further in Chapter 9.

In notional market valuations the net realizable value of redundant assets is typically determined at the corporate level and not at the shareholder level. This ensures internal consistency with business valuation, where the value of a business is determined before consideration of taxes payable by the shareholders on dividends and before the sale of the business.

In an open market transaction, it is usually advisable for the seller to remove any redundant asset(s) from the business prior to sale. Doing so often simplifies the transaction, and reduces the purchase price to the buyer. However, on occasion in open market transactions, redundant assets may not be extracted prior to a sale of shares. Where this occurs, the seller typically considers the net cash available after paying income tax on the distribution of the net proceeds from the sale of the redundant asset to be the minimum acceptable price for that part of the total transaction price. Such a seller would then reject a share price which included redundant assets that would not generate after-tax proceeds at least equivalent to the redundant asset component of the share sale.

Conversely, where redundant assets are not extracted by the seller prior to sale, a buyer might pay a price for the shares that reflects the full market value of the redundant asset if the buyer had a use for the asset that was not contemplated by the seller. For example, the buyer might be able to use vacant land for the expansion of its own business that the seller could not use effectively. It follows that in an open market context, a share price that included a retained redundant asset component would normally reflect an amount ranging:

- from the low end: the net realizable value of the redundant asset, net of the full amount of disposition costs and income taxes incurred at the corporate level; and
- to the high end: the market value of the redundant asset before any disposition costs or income taxes.

As a result, when estimating the value of redundant assets as a component of *en bloc* equity value in a notional market context, depending on their nature, it may be appropriate to discount disposition costs and income taxes on their assumed notional disposition to reflect the fact that in an open market transaction:

- most redundant assets can be extracted from the business on a tax-deferred basis prior to a sale of shares, and the sale of those redundant assets can be deferred to a later date; or

- the buyer and seller may agree on a price for redundant assets included in the transaction that is between their net realizable value and their market value. The buyer can then hold the redundant assets, dispose of them, or employ them (or the net proceeds generated from them) in its other operations.

It follows that in a notional market valuation, there are three alternatives:

- no amount is deducted for disposition costs and income taxes. This assumes that the redundant assets are held in perpetuity. Such an approach assumes that a third-party buyer would pay the full market value for the redundant asset;

- the full amount of disposition costs and income taxes is deducted. This is the most conservative assumption because it assumes the redundant asset is liquidated immediately; or

- a discounted amount of disposition costs and income tax are deducted. This approach assumes the redundant asset will be disposed of at some point in the future, but will retain its value in real terms (i.e., adjusted for inflation). The degree to which disposition costs and income taxes are deducted depends on the assumption as to the length of time the asset will be held. In notional market valuations, it is not uncommon to discount disposition costs and income taxes by 50%.

Real Estate

Where a business owns the real estate that houses its operations, that real estate is usually regarded as a redundant asset for valuation purposes because of the differing risk levels attaching to real property as opposed to operating a business. Therefore, the EBITDA of the business is reduced by a market rent amount which in turn reduces the enterprise value of the operating company. The market value of the real estate is then viewed as a redundant asset.

By way of example, assume that Company N generates normalized EBITDA of $5 million and that a valuation multiple of 5x is considered appropriate. Company N operates out of facilities owned by the company. If Company N did not own its facilities, it would pay market rent of $800,000 per year. The market value of the building is estimated at $8 million. A comparison of the enterprise value of Company N, based on how the real estate is treated, is as follows:

Exhibit 4F
Company N
The Impact of Real Estate in Valuation

	Real Estate Not Segregated	Real Estate Segregated
Normalized EBITDA	5,000,000	5,000,000
Less: market rent	n/a	(800,000)
Adjusted EBITDA	5,000,000	4,200,000
EBITDA multiple	5.0x	5.0x
Enterprise value	25,000,000	21,000,000
Add: market value of real estate	n/a	8,000,000
Total	25,000,000	29,000,000

As indicated from the example above, the segregation of real estate derives a higher equity value for Company N than would otherwise be the case. This is because the EBITDA multiple applicable to the real estate is 10x (being the $8 million market value of the property divided by the market rent of $800,000), as contrasted with a multiple of 5x for the operations of the business. This analysis assumes the EBITDA multiple for the operations of the business is not affected by the segregation of real estate, which might not always be the case. As subsequently discussed, the valuation multiple should be influenced by the ability of the buyer to finance the business with debt as opposed to equity. A greater debt capacity of the business should afford a higher multiple. Therefore, where real estate assets are treated as an operating asset and can be used to secure debt, the EBITDA multiple may be higher than the EBITDA multiple that would otherwise be applied to the operating cash flow of the business where real estate was treated as a redundant asset.

An important consideration when treating real estate as a redundant asset is the amount of taxes and disposition costs that should be taken into account. In many cases involving open market transactions, where the seller is willing to retain the property and sell the operations, the seller transfers the real property into a separate holding company on a tax-deferred basis. The property can then be rented to the new owner of the business or to another third party. Therefore, taxes and disposition costs may be deferred for a long period. In other cases, the buyer or seller enters into a sale-leaseback with a financial institution in respect of the property thereby immediately triggering disposition costs and income taxes. Therefore, the facts of each specific situation must be assessed to determine the amount of disposition costs and income taxes that should be deducted, if at all.

In some cases a range of real estate values is developed based on different assumptions regarding income taxes and disposition costs.

The decision of whether to segregate real estate is a matter of judgment, but usually should consider the following factors:

- the nature of the property. Where the real estate is an attractive asset and readily marketable as a stand-alone asset, it is more likely to be segregated (e.g., a quality office property);

- the age and condition of the property. Properties that are newer and in relatively good condition are more likely to be segregated than those that are older and run down;

- the location of the property. Where the property is located in a major urban centre with an active market, it is more likely to be segregated than property located in a remote area where the demand may be limited;

- the likelihood a financial institution or other group would have an interest in entering into a sale-lease-back for the property;

- the buyer's intentions pursuant to an open market transaction (i.e., whether the buyer intends to acquire the property with the operations of the business, lease the property from the seller or move the operations of the business to another facility); and

- the materiality of the property. The more significant the property is to the overall value conclusion, the more likely real estate should be segregated.

While in theory a real estate asset should normally be viewed as a separate asset, as a practical matter, where a major manufacturing concern is being valued and the operations are housed within a manufacturing plant, most buyers in open market transactions will include the real estate as part of the overall operating business. However, the buyer should consider whether the business has higher debt capacity due to the underlying real estate. Where a greater proportion of debt financing can be used, the cost of capital is lower and the value of the operations increases. Therefore, in most cases where real estate is not segregated, its value will be recognized indirectly (at least in part).

Temporary Excess Assets

In some cases, a business has assets that are not immediately required in its ongoing operations but which cannot be withdrawn due to seasonal fluctuations, bank covenants, expansion plans, and other reasons. These temporary excess assets do not qualify as redundant, nor do they represent excess net operating assets that can be added to enterprise value. However, they may still contribute to the equity value of the business beyond what otherwise would be the case.

Where temporary excess assets generate income (e.g., interest, dividends or rental income), that income stream should be segregated from operating cash flows and valued separately. It is appropriate to apply a lower rate of return to that income stream where the risk pertaining to it is lower than the risk attributable to the business's operations. The discounted value of the after-tax income stream for the period the temporary excess asset is available should be added to the enterprise value of the business's operations. The value of temporary excess assets based on the income they generate should not exceed their market value.

Temporary excess assets sometimes do not generate income. For example, a seasonal business might make interest-free loans to affiliated companies during times where surplus funds are available. Where non-income-generating temporary excess assets are significant, consideration should be given to assuming that such funds are invested at a risk-free rate of return during the time they are available and capitalizing that income stream – concurrently assuring no double-counting of value occurs.

One-Time Adjustments

Prospective One-Time Expenses (Income)

Applying a valuation multiple to a normalized EBITDA base assumes that such EBITDA will remain relatively stable or increase at a constant rate over the long term. However, in some cases, a company may expect to incur a one-time cost or benefit in the near term. Examples include prospective income from a one-time gain (e.g., the pending receipt of insurance proceeds), non-recurring operating expenses (e.g., the cost to clean up contaminated land) or the use of non-capital income tax loss carry-forwards.

Where prospective revenues or expenses are non-recurring, they are not multiplied by a valuation multiple. Rather, their impact should be reflected through a one-time addition to (or deduction from) enterprise value. The adjustment should be net of income taxes that would be incurred (saved) as a result of the income (expense).

One-Time Capital Expenditures

Valuations based on a multiple of EBITDA (and similar approaches) inherently assume (either in the earnings base or in the multiple adopted) a normalized level of capital expenditures in order to sustain the operations of the business. However, in some cases, the business will require higher (or lower) than normal capital spending in the near term. Where this is the case, the difference between expected capital spending and normalized capital spending should be shown as a one-time adjustment.

Similar to one-time expenses (income) discussed above, the adjustment on account of one-time capital expenditures should be net of the income tax impact. The calculation of the present value of the capital cost allowance tax shield on capital expenditures was discussed in Chapter 3.

Contingent Liabilities

In some cases, the company being valued has a contingent liability outstanding at the valuation date. Examples of contingent liabilities include lawsuits, environmental issues and pending product recalls. In an open market transaction involving privately held companies, it is common for contingent liabilities to be covered by the seller's representations and warranties and for a portion of the purchase price to be held back pending the outcome of the matter. However, in a notional market context, the determination of fair market value requires that the contingent liability be quantified as part of the value conclusion.

The fair market value of a contingent liability is normally established by applying a probability factor to the estimated liability amount, based on the likelihood it will materialize. This may require legal advice or the assistance of specialists such as environmental experts. Where the settlement of the contingent liability would be tax deductible, then the net amount should be tax-effected. Furthermore, the estimated probable amount should be discounted to present value if it is expected to be incurred at a future date.

Net Operating Assets

Adjustments to equity value may also be made on account of excess or deficient net operating assets (e.g., working capital) at the valuation date. In both notional market valuations and open market transactions, it is necessary to consider whether the subject business has adequate net operating assets to support the indicated level of normalized EBITDA. In doing so, consideration must be given to historical and prospective relationships among net operating assets, revenues and EBITDA, as discussed in Chapter 2. A deficiency is deducted from enterprise value, whereas a surplus results in an upward adjustment.

Working Capital

At any given point in time, working capital levels may be above or below normalized amounts. This can be caused by seasonality, the timing of accounts receivable collections, the timing of payment of accounts payable and other reasons. Ratios for assisting in the assessment of normal working capital levels were addressed in Chapter 2. In open market transactions involving privately held companies, an adjustment to the purchase price is normally made where working capital is above or below agreed target levels.

Higher than normal levels of trade working capital are often financed by short-term interest-bearing debts, such as bank operating loans. Therefore, to deduct said short-term debt without consideration of the offsetting assets would understate the equity value conclusion. Similarly, the assessment of whether a business has excess cash on hand at a given point in time requires an assessment of the adequacy of other working capital accounts.

Other Long-Term Assets and Liabilities

In some cases, a business owns tangible operating assets that are classified as long-term (other than fixed assets) such as prepaid contracts that extend beyond one year. A business may also have operating liabilities such as warranties, deferred revenues or reserves that are classified as long-term.

As with working capital, an assessment should be made as to whether these long-term operating assets and long-term operating liabilities represent a surplus or deficiency at the valuation date that should be adjusted for when determining equity value. For example, a long-term reserve might represent a prospective one-time expense that should be adjusted for as noted above.

In some cases, it may be appropriate to view certain long-term operating liabilities such as long-term deferred revenues, as an extension of the working capital analysis. The offsetting entry to long-term deferred revenues is typically a current asset such as cash or accounts receivable. Therefore, to recognize the current asset without consideration of the related liability could result in missing a component of value.

Example of the Multiple of EBITDA Methodology

Background Information

Company O is a distributor of electrical supplies used by professional contractors. The company's historical operating results are set out below. Company O does not prepare any formal budgets or projections.

Exhibit 4G
Company O
Historical Income Statements

	Fiscal Years Ending December 31				
	2007	**2008**	**2009**	**2010**	**2011**
Revenues	10,624,310	11,228,301	9,168,450	10,459,113	10,860,784
Cost of goods sold	6,741,338	7,065,145	6,067,684	7,173,110	6,941,338
Gross profit	3,882,972	4,163,156	3,100,766	3,286,003	3,919,446
	36.5%	37.1%	33.8%	31.4%	36.1%
Salaries and benefits	1,270,196	1,288,130	1,319,288	1,336,712	1,357,861
Shareholder bonuses	600,000	750,000			400,000
Advertising	480,221	497,311	450,200	486,554	495,086
Professional fees	79,767	83,211	79,359	85,244	154,750
Other expenses	870,021	889,824	892,968	820,870	881,900
Depreciation	116,626	109,480	107,266	137,532	131,574
Interest expense	175,927	169,724	166,972	188,815	159,107
Other income	(85,000)	(85,000)	(85,000)	(85,000)	(85,000)
Total expenses	3,507,758	3,702,679	2,931,052	2,970,727	3,495,278
Income before taxes	375,214	460,477	169,714	315,275	424,169
Income taxes	71,216	83,577	29,955	53,187	68,418
Net income	303,999	376,901	139,760	262,088	355,750

Other relevant facts relating to Company O are as follows:

- the company's operations are subject to economic cycles. Consequently, the company experienced strong operating results in 2007 and 2008, followed by a significant decline in 2009. Revenues and profitability recovered in fiscal 2010 and 2011;

- the owner of the company, who serves as president, pays himself a market-rate annual remuneration which is included in salaries and benefits. At the end of each year, the owner declares himself a bonus, depending on operating results, in order to reduce pretax income below the small business threshold of $500,000;

- the company experienced a significantly lower gross profit margin in fiscal 2010 due to an inventory write-down of $400,000 included with cost of sales. The write-down for inventory should have been recognized evenly from 2007 through to 2010;

- professional fees were higher than usual in 2011 by $70,000 due to a non-recurring legal issue relating to a former employee;

- the company owns the facilities that house its operations. A portion of the premises are rented to a third party for $85,000 per year and recorded as other income. The market-rate rent for the portion occupied by Company O is $120,000 per year. The market value of the property is $2 million, allocated 75% to the building and the balance to the land. The property has an undepreciated capital cost of $700,000. The original cost of the property was $2 million for the building and $300,000 for the land. Disposition costs are estimated at 3% and the company has a marginal income tax rate of 30% (on income in excess of the small business rate);

- the company has outstanding debt of $3 million consisting of an operating loan and mortgage payable, and also owes the owner $400,000 on account of accrued but unpaid bonuses at December 31, 2011. There are no redundant assets (apart from the property) and no prospective one-time items. Working capital is at normal levels; and

- given the nature of the company's operations, a reasonable EBITDA multiple is estimated in the range of 4.0× to 4.5×.

Solution

The first step in the multiple of EBITDA methodology is to estimate normalized EBITDA. Since no budgets or projections exist, the estimate is made by reference to normalized historical financial results. Beginning with pretax income for each of the last five fiscal years, the following adjustments are made:

- depreciation is added back;

- interest expense is added back since the multiple of EBITDA develops an enterprise value which is independent of the basis by which the company is financed;

- shareholder bonuses are added back given that they represent remuneration in excess of market rates;

- non-recurring legal costs of $70,000 in fiscal 2011 are added back, based on the assumption that they will not be incurred in future years;

- the inventory adjustment serves to redistribute the $400,000 write-down in fiscal 2010 equally to the four-year period from 2007 through 2010 at $100,000 per year (which serves to increase fiscal 2010 income by a net amount of $300,000);

- other income is deducted since it represents income from the company's real estate which is a redundant asset; and

- market rent of $120,000 is deducted on the assumption the company rents its facility rather than owns it.

Judgment is required in selecting the range of normalized EBITDA. In this case, the low end of the range ($800,000) represents the average of the normalized results from fiscal 2007 through 2011, in order to reflect the cyclicality of Company O's operations. The high end of the range ($980,000) is based on the operating results for fiscal 2011, as buyers in the open market commonly reference a company's most recent operating results.

Exhibit 4H
Company O
Normalized EBITDA

	Fiscal Years Ending December 31				
	2007	2008	2009	2010	2011
Pretax income as reported	375,214	460,477	169,714	315,275	424,169
Add (deduct)					
Depreciation	116,626	109,480	107,266	137,532	131,574
Interest expense	175,927	169,724	166,972	188,815	159,107
Shareholder bonuses	600,000	750,000			400,000
Non-recurring legal costs					70,000
Inventory adjustment	(100,000)	(100,000)	(100,000)	300,000	
Other income	(85,000)	(85,000)	(85,000)	(85,000)	(85,000)
Market rent	(120,000)	(120,000)	(120,000)	(120,000)	(120,000)
Normalized EBITDA	962,767	1,184,681	138,951	736,623	979,850

Selected Range of Normalized EBITDA

Low (average fiscal 2007 - 2011)	800,000
High (fiscal 2011)	980,000

The next step is to determine enterprise value and, subsequently, equity value. Enterprise value is determined by applying the indicated EBITDA multiples of 4.0x to 4.5x to normalized EBITDA. The higher multiple is applied to the lower normalized EBITDA base in order to reflect the lesser degree of risk in normalized EBITDA at that level. The resultant enterprise value falls in the range of $3,600,000 to $3,920,000.

Equity value is determined by deducting interest-bearing debt of $3 million, deducting the bonus owing to the shareholder of $400,000, and adding the net realizable value of the real estate of $1,842,875 (see Exhibit 4J). In this case, no adjustment is necessary for one-time items or working capital. The resultant fair market value of the equity of Company O falls in the range of $2,040,000 to $2,360,000.

Exhibit 4I
Company O
Determination of Fair Market Value

	Low	High
Normalized EBITDA (Exhibit 4H)	800,000	980,000
EBITDA multiple	4.5×	4.0×
Enterprise value	3,600,000	3,920,000
Less: interest-bearing debt	(3,000,000)	(3,000,000)
Less: shareholder bonuses outstanding	(400,000)	(400,000)
Add: redundant assets (real estate) (Exhibit 4J)	1,842,875	1,842,875
Add (deduct): one-time adjustments		
Add (deduct): working capital surplus (deficiency)		
Equals: equity value (en bloc)	2,042,875	2,362,875
Rounded	2,040,000	2,360,000

The net realizable value of the redundant real estate requires a separate calculation. The market value of the property is $2 million. However, disposition costs and income taxes need to be addressed. In this case, a deduction was made for 50% of the disposition costs and income taxes on the assumption that sale of the real estate would be deferred to some future date.

The gross amount of disposition costs was estimated at $60,000, being 3% of the market value of the property. Income taxes were estimated based on the amount of recapture and capital gains that would arise on the sale of the property, as illustrated in Exhibit 4J. Refundable taxes were not factored into the calculation on the assumption that an adequate dividend would be paid to recover that amount (see Chapter 9). As an alternative, a range of real estate values may be appropriate.

Exhibit 4J
Company O
Net Realizable Value of Real Estate

	Market Value	Disposition Costs (3%)	Cost Base	UCC	Capital Gain	Recapture
Land	500,000	15,000	300,000	n/a	185,000	
Building	1,500,000	45,000	2,000,000	700,000		755,000
Taxable portion (50%)					92,500	
Income tax rate					30%	30%
Total	2,000,000	60,000			27,750	226,500
Total disposition costs and taxes						314,250
Probability factor						50%
Probabilized amount	157,125					157,125
Net realizable value	1,842,875					

Limitations of the Multiple of EBITDA Methodology

Despite its widespread popularity, the multiple of EBITDA methodology has some significant limitations. Most notably, the normalized EBITDA base ignores capital expenditure requirements and income taxes, which must somehow be reflected in the valuation multiple. This can make the application of the multiple of EBITDA methodology particularly problematic in capital-intensive industries. Furthermore, depending on the accounting standards adopted by a particular business, certain costs may be capitalized and amortized over a period of time, rather than being expensed in the period in which they are incurred (e.g., product development costs). Where such expenditures are not somehow accounted for in the multiple of EBITDA methodology, the resultant value conclusion can be distorted.

In addition, because the EBITDA multiple is applied to a point estimate or range of normalized EBITDA, there is the inherent assumption that said point estimate or range will continue in perpetuity or will grow at a constant rate. In reality, this is seldom the case, as most businesses go through periods of differing growth rates and may be impacted by cyclicality.

As a result, sophisticated investors normally adopt more comprehensive valuation models (such as the discounted cash flow methodology, discussed in Chapter 6) when estimating the value of a business. However, buyers and investors will often convert the valuation results derived by using those more comprehensive methodologies into a multiple of EBITDA equivalent when referring to value or when negotiating the purchase or sale of a business.

As discussed below, the determination of EBITDA multiples is subjective and reflects numerous commingled variables. There are also difficulties in identifying comparable public companies for the purpose of developing EBITDA multiples. Even where information is available, it is seldom possible to fully adjust for items that should be factored into a normalized EBITDA calculation.

Further, as discussed below, any comparative analysis based on EBITDA multiples observed from industry transactions can be distorted due to factors such as the impact of synergies, the terms of the deal, the negotiating position of the buyer and seller, and a myriad of other factors.

Other Methodologies Based on Valuation Multiples

Multiple of EBIT Methodology

The multiple of earnings before interest and taxes (EBIT) methodology is similar to the multiple of EBITDA methodology, except that the earnings base adopted is net of depreciation and amortization expense. Accordingly, the multiple of EBIT methodology attempts to compensate for one of the major deficiencies in the multiple of EBITDA methodology – ignoring capital spending. The mechanics of the multiple of EBIT methodology are as follows:

Exhibit 4K
Multiple of EBIT Methodology

	Normalized EBIT
Multiplied by:	EBIT multiple
Equals:	enterprise value
Deduct:	interest-bearing debt and equivalents (net of excess cash)
Add:	redundant assets
Add (deduct):	one-time adjustments
Add (deduct):	excess (deficient) net operating assets
Equals:	equity value

The determination of normalized EBIT is similar to the determination of normalized EBITDA as discussed above, except that depreciation and amortization are not added back in the determination of normalized EBIT.

EBIT is sometimes used as a proxy for cash flow before income taxes and financing. Its validity as a proxy depends on whether depreciation and amortization expense for accounting purposes approximates the sustaining capital expenditure requirements of the business. If so, then normalized EBIT may have some merit as a cash flow proxy (before tax).

Since capital expenditure requirements are reflected in the EBIT base, the EBIT multiple does not have to account for that factor. Therefore, the EBIT multiple for a given business is greater than its corresponding EBITDA multiple.

When adopting the multiple of EBIT methodology, it is important to understand the sources of depreciation and amortization. Depreciation relates to fixed assets, which typically need to be replaced at some point. Therefore, the difference between depreciation and capital spending is, to some extent, a timing issue. The same is not necessarily true for amortization expense. For example, where amortization expense relates to identifiable intangible assets acquired through the acquisition of another business, then those assets will not be replaced per se. Accordingly, it may be necessary to modify the multiple of EBIT methodology such that amortization expense is added back to the EBIT base, but depreciation expense is deducted.

The Multiple of EBITDA Less Capex Methodology

The multiple of EBITDA less capex methodology also explicitly considers capital expenditure (i.e., "capex") requirements. It is preferable to the multiple of EBIT methodology where ongoing capital expenditure requirements do not reflect historical depreciation and amortization expense for accounting purposes (e.g., where amortization relates to identifiable intangible assets acquired in a corporate acquisition). In addition, the multiple of EBITDA less capex methodology may be more suited for companies that operate in capital-intensive industries.

The mechanics of the multiple of EBITDA less capex methodology are as follows:

Exhibit 4L
Multiple of EBITDA Less Capex Methodology

	Normalized EBITDA
Deduct:	sustaining capital expenditures
Equals:	normalized EBITDA less capex
Multiplied by:	EBITDA less capex multiple
Equals:	enterprise value
Deduct:	interest-bearing debt and equivalents (net of excess cash)
Add:	redundant assets
Add (deduct):	one-time adjustments
Add (deduct):	excess (deficient) net operating assets
Equals:	equity value

Sustaining capital expenditures should reflect the average annual capital spending required to maintain the business's normalized EBITDA at the level indicated. This may or may not be different from depreciation and amortization expense for accounting purposes. It is important that there be internal consistency between the level of normalized EBITDA adopted and the assumptions with respect to sustaining capital expenditures.

Sustaining capital expenditures may also be quite different from actual capital spending in a given year. In many cases, a company's capital expenditure requirements are lumpy, as major spending initiatives take place in some years and not others. The sustaining capital expenditure estimate deducted in this methodology should reflect a prospective long-term average amount in order to generate the indicated normalized EBITDA. A thorough analysis of capital spending requirements necessitates an objective assessment of the nature and condition of a business's fixed assets and its capital needs over the longer term. The determination of sustaining capital expenditures is discussed in greater depth in Chapter 5.

Since sustaining capital expenditure requirements are reflected in the earnings base adopted (i.e., EBITDA less capex), the valuation multiple does not have to account for that factor. Therefore, the EBITDA less capex multiple for a given business is greater than its corresponding EBITDA multiple.

Multiple of After-Tax Cash Flow Methodology

The multiple of after-tax cash flow methodology considers both capital spending requirements and income taxes. It is similar in many respects to the capitalized cash flow methodology discussed in Chapter 5. The mechanics of the multiple of after-tax cash flow methodology are as follows:

Exhibit 4M
Multiple of After-Tax Cash Flow Methodology

	Normalized EBIT
Deduct:	cash income taxes
Equals:	normalized after-tax income
Add:	depreciation and amortization
Deduct:	sustaining capital expenditures
Equals:	normalized after-tax cash flow
Multiplied by:	after-tax cash flow multiple
Equals:	enterprise value
Deduct:	interest-bearing debt and equivalents (net of excess cash)
Add:	redundant assets
Add (deduct):	one-time adjustments
Add (deduct):	excess (deficient) net operating assets
Equals:	equity value

The starting point in this calculation is normalized EBIT determined on a basis consistent with the explanation set out in this chapter. Cash income taxes are deducted from that amount. The determination of cash income taxes is typically based on prevailing income tax rates. This approach assumes that EBIT approximates pre-tax income for tax purposes (excluding consideration of financing costs). Accordingly, it ignores timing differences that result in future income tax accounting.

The multiple of after-tax cash flow methodology recognizes that sustaining capital expenditures may be different than depreciation and amortization. Therefore, historical depreciation and amortization are added back and sustaining capital expenditures are deducted. In making this adjustment, it is important to ensure that the amount of depreciation and amortization added back is consistent with the amount embedded in the normalized EBIT base adopted.

The after-tax cash flow multiple should reflect the fact that capital expenditures and income taxes have been taken into account. Therefore, the after-tax cash flow multiple applicable to a particular business will be higher than other corresponding multiples based on EBITDA, EBIT, or EBITDA less capex.

Multiple of Revenue Methodology

On occasion, the value of a business is expressed as a multiple of its historical or current (e.g., last-12-months or current-year forecast) revenues. While revenues may be far removed from profit or cash flow, this methodology is sometimes used to develop a broad indication as to value. The mechanics of the multiple of revenue methodology are as follows:

Exhibit 4N
Multiple of Revenue Methodology

	Revenue base
Multiplied by:	revenue multiple
Equals:	enterprise value
Deduct:	interest-bearing debt and equivalents (net of excess cash)
Add:	redundant assets
Add (deduct):	one-time adjustments
Add (deduct):	excess (deficient) net operating assets
Equals:	equity value

A multiple of revenue approach is sometimes used when assessing the value of an early stage company or one that is experiencing operating losses (or is not yet generating normalized levels of cash flow). The assumption is that over the long term the business will generate positive cash flow and be a going concern. However, this is not always the case.

While attractive due to its simplicity, the multiple of revenue approach has significant shortcomings. First, higher revenues do not necessarily translate into higher cash flow or, by extension, higher value. Second, revenue multiples are based on broad generalizations that may not hold in specific circumstances. It follows that the multiple of revenue methodology may be useful as a preliminary indication of value or as a rough test of valuation conclusions derived from other methodologies, but is seldom valid as a primary approach. That being said, in many cases reported industry transactions provide only sufficient information to determine the multiple of revenue that was paid. Therefore, the multiple of revenue methodology may have some (albeit generally limited) use as a comparator against industry transactions.

Rules of Thumb

On occasion, the value of a business is determined based on a "rule of thumb". Rules of thumb are industry-specific determinants that normally relate value to a given operating measure. Examples include value per subscriber in the publishing industry, value per ton produced in steel manufacturing, or value per assets under management in the mutual fund industry. Multiplying an operating metric by the rule of thumb multiple derives the enterprise value of the business. As with each of the methodologies outlined above, adjustments are made for interest-bearing debt, redundant assets, one-time items and excess or deficient net operating assets in order to determine the equity value of the business.

As in the case of the multiple of revenues approach, rules of thumb are attractive because of their simplicity. However, they make broad generalizations about operating metrics that may not hold for a given business. For example, a rule of thumb based on the number of subscribers may assume that a business should generate a given level of revenues and cash flow for each subscriber. However, differences in size, geographic area and other product and service offerings may distort the results for any particular business.

In addition, rules of thumb are commonly premised on average transaction multiples that evolve over time. Accordingly, they may not be applicable at a certain point in time and may reflect an element of expected post-acquisition synergies. Implied valuation multiples based on rules of thumb may also be distorted due to the terms of a transaction. This may be inconsistent with a valuation conducted on a cash-equivalent, stand-alone basis.

The Determination of Valuation Multiples

Valuation multiples are subjective. They are influenced at any given point in time and to varying degrees by a myriad of factors including:

- company-specific factors;
- industry, economic and capital market conditions;
- comparable public companies;
- industry transactions; and
- transactions involving the subject business.

Ultimately, the valuation multiple(s) selected should reflect a synthesis of factors that have been assessed in an objective, comprehensive and internally consistent manner. Furthermore, in an open market transaction, valuation multiples are influenced by the terms of the transaction and the relative negotiating positions of the parties.

When establishing a valuation multiple for a given business, it is important to ensure internal consistency between the valuation multiple and the earnings base against which it is being applied. For example, after-tax multiples have to be applied to after-tax cash flows, and pretax multiples (e.g., multiples of EBIT and EBITDA) must be applied to those respective pretax measures. Ideally, this should result in the same value conclusion in each case. However, some differences usually arise.

Consider the example of Company P. The company generates $10 million in normalized EBITDA on $100 million in revenues. The company has recorded $2.5 million of depreciation and amortization expense. Sustaining capital requirements are estimated at $2.75 million. Company P pays cash income taxes at a rate of 30%. If a reasonable estimate of the enterprise value of Company P is $50 million, that figure can be derived through a multiple of 0.5× revenues, 5× EBITDA, 6.7× EBIT or 10× after-tax cash flow.

Exhibit 40
Company P
Internal Consistency in Valuation Multiples

	Operating Results	Valuation Multiple	Rate of Return	Enterprise Value
Revenues	100,000,000	0.5×	n/a	50,000,000
Operating expenses	90,000,000			
Normalized EBITDA	10,000,000	5.0×	20%	50,000,000
Depreciation and amortization	2,500,000			
Normalized EBIT	7,500,000	6.7×	15%	50,000,000
Income taxes	2,250,000			
After-tax income	5,250,000			
Add back: deprec. and amort.	2,500,000			
Deduct: sustaining capex	2,750,000			
After-tax cash flow	5,000,000	10.0×	10%	50,000,000

As discussed above, to ensure internal consistency and to avoid double-counting, the valuation multiple and the earnings base against which it is applied must be viewed as interrelated, and cannot be viewed in isolation. For example, if the risk of an employee strike has been accounted for by reducing the cash flow or earnings base, then it is not appropriate to incorporate that same risk factor in the valuation multiple adopted.

Company-Specific Factors

Valuation multiples reflect the expectations as to future earnings or cash flow, given the risk profile and growth prospects of a particular business. The more common company-specific considerations are set out below. Some of these factors overlap so that, while it is important to be thorough, it also is important to avoid double-counting. It should also be noted that these are broad generalizations, and their application to any particular business must be carefully considered. For a given level of earnings or cash flow, a business's strengths and opportunities will serve to increase its valuation multiple, while its weaknesses and threats will serve to reduce the multiple.

Nature of Product and Service Offerings

Businesses that have developed some uniqueness or differential advantage in their product or service offerings enjoy higher valuation multiples. This may come in the form of proprietary technology, an established brand name or other advantages that are difficult for competitors to replicate easily. These factors sometimes are referred to as "barriers to entry". By contrast, businesses with "me too" type product and service offerings that are easier to replicate tend to have lower multiples. Such businesses tend to be more susceptible to greater price competition and consequently to profit margin erosion.

Competitive Advantage

A competitive advantage can be attributed to a variety of things such as a strong distribution network, strategic location, proprietary production equipment or other factors. For a competitive advantage to translate into a higher valuation multiple, it must provide the business with a differential advantage and help it to generate economic returns superior to those of its competitors. Furthermore, it is important to assess whether the competitive advantage is sustainable over the long term. Sustainability may require continuous investment in advertising, R&D, capital spending and so on. It is also important to ensure the competitive advantage is transferable and does not rely on the skills or knowledge of a particular individual (e.g., personal goodwill, as discussed in Chapter 1).

Revenue Stability and Diversification

A business's customer base can have a significant impact on the appropriate valuation multiple. Specifically, valuation multiples are higher for businesses that have developed a diverse base of repeat customers as opposed to companies that are dependent on a handful of customers or have little in the way of repeat business. In particular, companies that enjoy a loyal customer base or who have created "barriers to exit" for their customers often enjoy a premium multiple.

Management Team

The knowledge and abilities of a business's management and employees are a major consideration for most businesses. In some cases, employees may have specialized skills or knowledge that may be difficult to replace. Skilled employees can create a barrier to entry for competitors or be an attractive asset for a strategic buyer thereby increasing the valuation multiple.

Likewise, the breadth and depth of a company's management team can significantly impact its valuation multiple. Where a good management succession plan is not in place, the valuation multiple may be lower. In cases where the business owner and family members are actively involved in a company, that factor can have negative implications on that business's risk profile if strong successors cannot be readily identified. Similarly, businesses dependent on the owner or a handful of key employees generally experience a lower valuation multiple.

Supply Risk

Companies are subject to supply risk where they are exposed to supplier concentration, or where key raw materials might not otherwise be available because of general market shortages. Supply risk can also stem from fluctuating raw materials prices, a common problem for companies whose production inputs include commodities.

Supply risk should not be viewed solely from the standpoint of raw materials; rather, it should encompass all inputs required to operate the subject business, including utilities, machinery, spare parts and other requirements. Shortages in labour supply would also fall into this category. Businesses exposed to supply risk or supplier concentration will experience a reduction in their valuation multiple.

Company Size

In many cases, smaller companies within a given industry receive lower valuation multiples than their larger counterparts. This is particularly the case where a small company has a limited market presence and relies on a handful of customers or employees. As a practical matter, in open market transactions, smaller companies usually generate less interest among prospective buyers thereby reducing liquidity and, hence, value. If these factors are already reflected in the valuation multiple, then it is important not to double-count their impact because of a size discount.

Historical Operating Results

Where a business has a history of relatively stable or improving operating performance, that record has a positive influence on valuation multiples. Conversely, businesses that have experienced considerable volatility in their operating results or are exhibiting a declining trend in revenues and profitability tend to experience lower multiples.

Growth Expectations

Where the earnings or cash flow of a business is expected to grow significantly, such growth will be reflected in the valuation multiple because valuation is forward-looking, and driven by future cash flow. By way of example, if the EBITDA for a business is expected to grow by 20% in the coming year from $5 million to $6 million, then a multiple of 6x historical EBITDA translates into a multiple of 5x forward EBITDA. The enterprise value in both cases is $30 million.

Exhibit 4P
Valuation Multiples and Growth

	This Year	Next Year
Normalized EBITDA	$5 million	$6 million
EBITDA multiple	6x	5x
Enterprise value	$30 million	$30 million

The degree to which growth should be reflected in the valuation multiple must be considered in conjunction with the factors used to establish normalized EBITDA. Where normalized EBITDA is determined by way of reference to budgets or projections, then an element of growth may already be provided for in the earnings base, and it would not be appropriate to double-count that growth in the valuation multiple.

One of the challenges to factoring a growth element into the valuation multiple is that there are other factors that influence value. For example, growing companies often require additional capital spending and working capital in order to accommodate growth. Therefore, any adjustment to the valuation multiple on account of growth must take the cost of growth into account.

Capital Expenditure Requirements

When adopting a multiple of EBITDA methodology (or multiple of revenue), the valuation multiple must take into account the capital expenditure requirements of the subject business, since capital spending is not reflected in the EBITDA (or revenue) base. Companies with low capital expenditure requirements tend to fetch higher valuation multiples. This is because a greater proportion of EBITDA will contribute to discretionary cash flow (the ultimate determinant of economic value), rather than having to be re-invested into the business in order to maintain its operations. Because capital expenditure requirements can distort the EBITDA multiple, the multiple of EBITDA methodology may be less reliable in capital-intensive business as contrasted with businesses that are less capital intensive (e.g., service-type businesses).

Debt Capacity

The greater the ability of a business to finance its operations with debt rather than equity, the higher its valuation multiple. This is because the cost of debt financing is lower than the cost of equity financing, and the use of debt serves to reduce the business's overall cost of capital. Recall that a valuation multiple is the inverse of a rate of return (or cost of capital).

The debt capacity of a business is influenced by the level and stability of its cash flow (required to service interest and principal repayments) and the amount and quality of its underlying assets. The estimation of the debt capacity for a given business is discussed in Chapter 7.

Income Tax Rates

When applying a valuation multiple to a measure of pre-tax earnings or cash flow (such as revenue, EBIT, EBITDA or EBITDA less capex), the valuation multiple should consider the rate at which earnings will be taxed. Higher income taxes reduce the amount of discretionary cash flow for a given level of pre-tax earnings and should lead to a lower valuation multiple.

Industry, Economic and Capital Market Conditions

Industry Conditions

Many industries go through cycles. Where the industry in which the subject business operates is undergoing a period of consolidation, valuation multiples tend to be higher than would otherwise be the case because of the number of buyers actively seeking acquisition targets (i.e., greater liquidity). By contrast, where a particular industry is experiencing widespread challenges and many companies are being acquired for low values (or going into receivership), the valuation multiples for all participants within that industry face downward pressure.

Competitive Landscape

The nature and extent of competition within an industry will impact the valuation multiple. Where competition is intense and driven by price, the valuation multiple tends to be lower. Companies operating in an industry characterized by large, well-financed competitors may be subject to a lower valuation multiple if they are unable to compete effectively against those larger entities. Conversely, a fragmented industry may be viewed as opportunistic, if a particular business can distinguish itself within a particular niche.

The ease with which new competitors can enter the industry also influences valuation multiples. Industries characterized by high barriers to entry (e.g., capital requirements, government licences, and so on) tend to enjoy higher multiples than those where competitors can enter with little capital investment or other requirements.

An assessment of the competitive landscape should also include complementary products and substitute products. For example, where substitute products are gaining in popularity, valuation multiples could be depressed for businesses unable to convert to those substitutes.

Economic Conditions

As a general rule, valuation multiples tend to be higher during buoyant economic times than in more depressed economic times because the financial markets generally perceive that most companies will be able to grow more readily when economic conditions are favourable, and because there tends to be more transaction activity (and hence greater liquidity) during good economic times.

Capital Market Conditions

Where the capital markets are such that both debt and equity financing are readily available on attractive terms, that factor tends to have a positive influence on corporate acquisition activity (due to greater liquidity), which in turn increases valuation multiples. Access to lower-cost capital serves to increase the valuation multiple.

Public Equity Market Multiples

At any given moment in the trading day, stock market indices reflect public expectations for both the economy as a whole and specific industry sectors in particular. Valuation multiples of public companies that operate in the same industry as the subject business are often used as reference points when determining appropriate valuation multiples. The use of public equity market multiples is sometimes referred to as the "comparable companies" approach to valuation. However, what is really being compared is the valuation multiple.

While enterprise value to EBITDA and EBIT are the most common bases of comparison, other bases include:

- equity value to net income, net book value or net tangible assets;
- enterprise value to revenues; and
- for certain industries, operating ratios such as enterprise value per ton of capacity, value per customer or some other performance or value indicator commonly used by acquirers or analysts in those industries.

The analysis of somewhat comparable public companies and industry transactions (discussed below) generally forms part of a notional market valuation or open market pricing exercise. However, as a general rule, only in limited circumstances can comparative analysis be applied as a primary approach to develop a meaningful valuation conclusion in a particular situation. The use of comparables is usually restricted to providing a general understanding of the risk-reward parameters of a given industry, and as a test of valuation conclusions derived using other valuation methodologies.

As discussed in Chapter 1, there are fundamental differences between public equity market multiples and the multiples applicable to a particular privately held or public company viewed *en bloc*. These differences exist because of generally greater liquidity in the public markets and the availability of information. Consequently, even where applied as tests of values otherwise derived, the comparison can be distorted. In addition, valuation multiples based on equity value measures can be distorted by differing capital structures. That being said, public equity market multiples may provide some general guidance with respect to the relative magnitude of the multiples within a given industry and overall trends in those multiples.

Where comparative data is used, it is not uncommon to compare the subject business with average ratios or multiples calculated from the group of comparables. The use of a simple average may lead to inappropriate conclusions, particularly where there is a large variance in the performance indicators of the individual comparables. Therefore, it is common to adopt a median or adjusted average of companies considered comparable. However, careful analysis is required as to which companies should be included as comparable and to recognize important differences that exist. Prior to finalizing a benchmark based on some sort of average it is important to analyze the data and, if possible, to adjust it for any outliers or anomalies.

Whether or not companies assessed as comparable are used explicitly in a particular valuation, stock price levels in the public equity markets and their impact on the perceived values of companies in the same industry should usually be considered because trends in the public equity markets reflect both general economic and industry-specific conditions at particular periods of time. Specific public company data may assist in the valuation process where meaningful comparables can be identified.

The use of comparative company data in notional market valuations has been more common in the United States than in Canada. This may be due in part to IRS Revenue Ruling 59-60, which is regarded as an important guideline for valuing privately held companies for U.S. income tax purposes. This Revenue Ruling suggests that a measure of value can be found in the prices at which stocks of companies engaged in the same or in a similar line of business are selling in a free and open securities market. In addition, for most industries, there are normally fewer Canadian companies whose shares are publicly traded to provide information that can be considered meaningful.

In some cases, data from U.S. (or other country) sources may be used when conducting comparative analysis with respect to Canadian businesses. However, where used, it is important to recognize that there are often material differences that may impair the usefulness of such analysis. For example:

- U.S. public companies tend to be considerably larger than their Canadian counterparts. As a result, they may enjoy greater economies of scale and other benefits associated with greater size;

- depending on the industry, business, or products and services offered, there may be important differences based on markets covered due to the size of those markets, competitors, demographics, logistics, and other factors;

- securities traded in U.S. public markets tend to be more liquid and active than those traded in Canadian public markets. This may bear on comparability where "small-cap" and "micro-cap" stocks are adopted for comparison purposes;

- there may be important differences regarding the laws and regulations surrounding the products or services the business offers;

- income tax rates are different in Canada than in the U.S.; and

- accounting policies in the U.S. are different from those in Canada. For example, many U.S. companies use LIFO (last-in first-out) for inventory valuation because it is accepted for tax purposes in that country. By comparison, few Canadian companies use LIFO. The conversion to IFRSs in Canada may further complicate any meaningful comparison.

Adjusting for some of these differences in a meaningful way is difficult, and often impossible. This supports the proposition that comparative analysis should seldom be used as a primary valuation methodology.

Where used to test value conclusions otherwise determined, comparative valuation multiples derived from public market proxies seldom, if ever, can be appropriately adjusted for one-time items, excess or deficient net operating assets, and redundant assets. Since these things will (or should) have been adjusted for pursuant to the application of one or more primary valuation methodologies, comparisons based on valuation multiples may consequently be flawed.

Furthermore, it is important to recognize that reported public company valuation multiples are based on historical operating results, where the earnings base can be distorted (e.g., due to non-recurring expenses that might not be readily identifiable). Therefore, it is helpful to test the reported profit margins of comparable companies against the subject business to assess the degree of comparability.

For example, assume that a public company has an indicated enterprise value of $100 million. Further assume that the normalized EBITDA for the company is $15 million, implying an EBITDA multiple of approximately 7x. Assume the company incurred a one-time cost of $5 million, thereby reducing its reported EBITDA to $10 million. The implied EBITDA multiple would increase to 10x (calculated as

$100 million enterprise value divided by $10 million EBITDA). Failure to recognize and appropriately adjust for the one-time cost would cause any comparison based on EBITDA multiples to be distorted.

Identifying Comparable Companies

Comparative analysis is usually based on companies in the same industry, under the assumption that all firms within a given industry segment are faced with common risks and opportunities. In order to be considered as a meaningful comparable, the selected company should be in the same business and undertake the same business functions as the subject business. For example, while a manufacturer and a distributor may operate in the same industry, they are fundamentally different businesses. When selecting companies that are comparable, consideration should be given to factors such as:

- company size. Size should be assessed in terms of revenues, net assets, operating capacity, market share, number of employees, and other relevant measures. Larger companies tend to enjoy a greater degree of market presence, management depth, financial stability, financing options and economies of scale. These factors influence operating performance and, importantly, rates of return required by prospective buyers. As a result, companies of significantly different size may not be meaningfully comparable;

- the nature of the products or services offered. Comparative analysis presumes that companies exist whose products and services are very similar to the business being valued, and that the mix of these business activities is similar enough to be comparable both as to the percentage of business by product and service offering and level of profitability by product and service. As a practical matter, the greater the diversification within an individual business, the less likely a meaningful comparable company can be found. Further, where a company that might be comparable has operations in more than one industry segment, the amount of information publicly available for any particular segment is often insufficient to form any basis of meaningful comparison;

- the degree of vertical integration. A vertically integrated business normally has different risk-return parameters compared with one that purchases its inputs or sells its outputs to an unrelated business. A vertically integrated company may face less risk in its supply stream, and may enjoy economies of scale not available to a business that is not vertically integrated;

- geographic coverage and market characteristics. For most businesses, the markets covered have a bearing on the degree of comparability because of differences in customer base, logistics, cost to service a particular market, local competition, tax rates and other factors. In particular, there may be significant differences between the dynamics of domestic markets as compared with international markets;

- level of net tangible assets and sustaining capital. Comparability can be distorted due to the quantum and age of a company's fixed assets and near-term capital spending requirements. This is particularly the case for companies that operate in capital-intensive industries;

- profitability and operating measurements. These measures commonly include:
  - ✓ profitability ratios such as gross profit or operating profit (e.g., EBITDA and EBIT) expressed as a percentage of sales,
  - ✓ turnover ratios such as revenues to total assets,
  - ✓ capital expenditures to revenues. In this regard, consideration should be afforded to important differences between companies that lease equipment pursuant to an operating lease as opposed to purchasing outright or entering into a capital lease,

   ✓   liquidity ratios such as the current ratio and working capital to revenues, and

   ✓   leverage ratios such as long-term debt to invested capital.

   While ratio analysis provides an indication of risk levels that influence comparability, the ratios are affected by the use of different accounting policies;

- historical growth in earnings or cash flow. Businesses with a demonstrated history of strong growth normally enjoy a relatively higher valuation multiple. Where the comparables have not demonstrated similar growth patterns, they may not be meaningfully comparable. Consideration should also be afforded to cyclicality and the relative stability in historical earnings or growth; and

- strategic direction and focus. Although two companies may appear to have been similar in the past, a change in the strategic direction of either will affect comparability. A change in strategic direction can arise because of new opportunities, management change, a major acquisition or divestiture, and other reasons. All of these variables influence the degree of risk and, as a result, required rates of return. Such information often can be gauged by reviewing the Management Discussion & Analysis (MD&A) portion of a public company's annual report.

No two companies are exactly alike and judgment must be exercised when determining whether a basis for meaningful comparison exists. As a practical matter, sufficient information is usually not available (even for public companies) to reach an informed conclusion as to the degree of comparability between two businesses. As a result, comparative analysis is rarely used as a primary valuation methodology, but rather is used to test value conclusions otherwise determined. Further, even where applied as a test methodology, such tests may not be meaningful.

Having said that, some industries lend themselves better to comparative analysis than others. Subject to availability of meaningful detailed information, in theory:

- a greater degree of comparability may be possible in commodity-type industries than may be possible in industries with a high degree of propriety in their products and services;

- industries that are better defined in terms of the products and services they offer or markets they serve provide a better basis for comparison than those that do not; and

- industries having a large number of publicly traded companies can facilitate identifying more meaningful comparables and removing outliers.

Where a public company has been identified as possibly being comparable to the subject business, it is necessary to assess the degree of comparability and any adjustments that may be required to improve comparability. In this regard, sources of information commonly include:

- the annual and quarterly financial statements;

- the annual report and quarterly report, including the Management Discussion & Analysis (MD&A);

- various statutory filings, including the annual information form and management circular;

- prospectuses and other public offering documents; and

- analysts' reports.

When comparable companies have been identified, adjustments to their stated financial results may be appropriate to enhance comparability. Such differences may include those arising from accounting policies, income tax rates, capital structure, and other variables. However, it is often difficult to make such adjustments and, in practice, such adjustments are frequently not made. Furthermore, in most cases, the detailed data required to make these adjustments (such as the impact of accounting policies or analysis of forecasts) is not available. Where the difference(s) could be significant, the absence of this data further militates against meaningful comparability.

Benchmark Analysis

Financial and operational data of somewhat comparable public companies is sometimes used to assess how the performance of the subject business compares to normal or industry-standard measures. The applications of benchmark analysis may include:

- determining a normalized capital structure. A review of the debt to equity (i.e., market capitalization) or debt to total capital ratios of comparable companies may assist in formulating a meaningful conclusion as to the amount of debt that would be considered normal for the subject business. As discussed in Chapter 7, a normalized capital structure is a key input in the determination of rates of return. However, it is important to note that capital structures may vary considerably among businesses within a particular industry, and a simple average of comparables may not provide a sound basis for a conclusion;

- evaluating the adequacy of net trade working capital. Where net trade working capital of the subject business is significantly greater than industry norms, it may indicate the existence of a redundant asset that should be segregated for valuation purposes (such as non-trade receivables being grouped with trade accounts receivable). Alternatively, it could indicate inefficiencies in the subject business. Conversely, where net trade working capital is below industry norms, it might suggest that a capital injection is required (i.e., a net operating asset deficiency which is deducted from enterprise value). When applying comparative analysis to assess net trade working capital, it is important to recognize the possible impact due to differences in accounting policies, as well as to consider the impact of seasonality where comparisons are made based on year-end financial results and comparables have different fiscal year-ends; and

- assessing the relative strengths and weaknesses of the subject business and the reasonableness of its projected operating results. When comparing ratios of the subject business to those of similar businesses in the same industry, comparative advantages or disadvantages of the subject business may become evident. For example, where the inventory turnover of the subject business is slower than industry norms (adjusted for the impact of different accounting policies where necessary and possible), inventory management difficulties may be indicated or it may become evident the business has obsolete or slow-moving items in its inventory. In addition, where operating ratios are computed for forecast data, comparable analysis can help in assessing the probability of those results being realized. For example, where sales per employee are expected to rise well above industry norms, analysis may suggest sufficient headcount additions have not been factored into the projections. While such analysis by itself would rarely provide conclusive evidence, it may assist in identifying areas for further investigation.

Benchmarking data can also be found in some reports, such as those produced by Statistics Canada and other entities. However, in many cases such data is based on an aggregation of many companies operating within an industry, and the average result may not be applicable to the subject business. In other cases, where the average is computed based on a limited number of entities, the average result can be distorted by one or more outliers.

Public Company Analysts' Reports

When the subject business itself is a public company, it may be followed by one or more stock analysts who will periodically write reports and buy-sell-hold recommendations. In many cases, stock analysts measure a particular business against its industry peers. A review of stock analysts' reports for a particular company can sometimes provide meaningful insight into the status and outlook for the company and the industry in which it operates.

Even for privately held companies, a review of analysts' reports for comparable public companies may provide meaningful insight into trends, developments and risk factors that influence all companies within a given industry, and which therefore should be considered when developing the valuation multiple for the subject business.

Initial Public Offerings

Initial public offerings (IPOs) occur when a company whose shares were previously privately held elects to offer its securities to the public for the first time. The underwriters typically bring the IPO to market at a share price high enough to raise the funds needed by their corporate client on the least number of shares, yet not so high as to discourage institutional and retail investors from fully subscribing the issue. Further, the price of many IPOs may be distorted by aggressive promotion by underwriters, securities dealers and the company itself. These factors can militate against comparability.

IPO offering memoranda often contain useful industry and company data that has up to this time been unavailable. Risk factors, competition, growth potential, customer base, and many other important elements are typically identified and discussed. This information not only helps in assessing comparability, but can also help in a general sense by identifying important factors that should be considered when deriving value for the subject business.

Buyer's or Seller's Stock Price

Where the shares of a company trade in the public equity markets, the implicit public equity multiples may indicate minimum rates of return that public equity participants expect on prospective acquisitions by the company. Further, as a practical matter, public company buyers are reluctant to consummate a transaction that will likely result in an erosion of consolidated earnings per share that might depress their own share price.

From the standpoint of the seller whose shares are publicly traded, the public equity markets provide an indication as to the relative and absolute degree of risk perceived for the business. In the case of a takeover bid, the price at which the seller's shares traded up to the date of the takeover offer represents a benchmark against which the company's management and its shareholders will evaluate the offer. Furthermore, as noted in Chapter 1, in some cases Canadian courts have concluded that the price at which a company's shares trade should be taken into account in determining value (see Appendix A).

However, even when using the buyer's or seller's own stock prices and implied valuation multiples, the previously noted caveats of using public market data still apply. In particular, public equity market participants usually are not aware of detailed long-term forecasts that can have a significant influence on valuation conclusions. In addition, the prices at which a company's shares trade in the open market are usually representative of normal-sized trading lots that may enjoy greater immediate liquidity as compared to an *en bloc* or controlling interest in a business. Conversely, in the case of small-cap and micro-cap public companies, the absence of liquidity may place downward pressure on the share price and the resultant multiples.

Limitations of Public Equity Market Multiples

The use of comparable public market multiples is popular among stock market analysts preparing research reports and stock recommendations. These analysts tend to identify a public company's peer group of publicly traded companies and assess why the stock being analyzed should trade at a higher or lower multiple of earnings (or some other measure) than its peers. Public equity market data may lend itself relatively well to that purpose. However, as noted in Chapter 1, there are numerous fundamental differences between the public equity markets and the market for all outstanding shares, net operating assets, or control of a public company or privately held business. In particular:

- public market participants have a wide range of time-horizon objectives (from a few minutes to many years), whereas buyers of a controlling interest in either a public or privately held company tend to be long-term holders;

- stock prices can fluctuate erratically within a short time period based on investor sentiment and the market reaction to economic, political and other developments. In general, value in a notional market sense tends to be less volatile;

- there may be significant differences in the degree of liquidity. Normal-sized trading blocks of shares of a widely held public company enjoy a high level of liquidity, particularly in comparison to a thinly traded stock or a large block of shares that the market may not be able or willing to absorb readily. The liquidity of a controlling interest in a public company or privately held business can vary considerably depending on the nature of the industry and the company itself;

- stock market transactions are usually based on available information that does not include important strategic and other insider information not publicly disclosed. Typically, a greater amount of pertinent data is available where *en bloc* value is determined (e.g., detailed operating plans, access to management, and other non-public information) in the course of detailed due diligence reviews. Such additional information usually has a significant bearing on risk assessment, business prospects and required rates of return; and

- an open market transaction is often characterized by lengthy negotiations between sophisticated parties, which negotiations generally influence price. This is not the case in a stock market transaction where parties seldom directly interact and, in the case of normal-sized trading lots, rarely have a significant impact on price.

The application of stock market data is rarely useful in the valuation of small, privately held businesses, and can often lead to inappropriate conclusions. Data based on comparables may be of some use in the valuation of public companies and larger privately held businesses where meaningful comparables can be identified. Even where this is the case, the application of public equity market data is usually limited, at best, to providing an understanding of the risk-reward dynamics of a given industry, and in assessing value conclusions derived by using other valuation methodologies.

In addition, differences between public and privately held companies may relate to the fact that public companies generally are:

- larger, often significantly so, than businesses that are privately held. Size provides public companies with greater market presence, customer diversification, management depth and other important factors that influence the risk profile of the business;

- directed by management groups that emphasize accounting earnings because of the influence earnings have on the share price. In contrast, management of privately held companies tend to focus principally on cash flow and relate earnings principally to income tax liability and satisfaction of banking covenants;

- predisposed to develop a corporate income tax strategy without consideration for the private tax planning of shareholders. Owners of privately held businesses frequently gear income tax planning on a composite personal/corporate basis, with the prime consideration being to minimize income tax at a personal level. Therefore, as compared with public companies, privately held businesses may pursue more conservative accounting policies; and

- capable of accessing a larger number of funding sources with larger amounts of capital available than are privately held businesses. As a result, companies whose shares are publicly traded often have a lower cost of capital than do privately held businesses.

Consequently, it is not uncommon for privately held companies to be valued at a multiple below that of somewhat comparable public companies. Therefore, public equity market multiples may be more meaningful for large privately held companies where an initial public offering is a real alternative means of financing, or where the company being valued is itself public.

Industry Transactions

Valuation multiples are influenced by transactions involving other companies within the subject business's industry. Despite the caveats associated with reliance on industry transaction multiples, they usually should be considered when estimating the value of the subject business. However, the degree to which they represent a meaningful comparison depends on the nature of the subject business and the amount of information available with respect to industry transactions. Sometimes within an industry group there will be enough recent transactions and information about them that useful data is available.

It usually is beneficial to identify and analyze recent transactions where the acquired company is perceived to be comparable in a meaningful way. The identification and analysis of such transactions may provide insight as to the:

- relative degree of liquidity in a given industry. Where there have been numerous transactions within a given industry and it is believed the industry is going through a consolidation phase, liquidity may be enhanced at that point in time which, all other things equal, may have an upward influence on valuation multiples;

- perceived risks and rates of return of corporate acquirers. Depending on the parties involved, there may be sufficient information available with respect to transactions to enable some understanding of the valuation parameters employed in them;

- most likely buyers and post-acquisition synergies that might be expected. This can be particularly informative in open market transactions, as discussed in Chapter 11. Furthermore, in notional market valuations, it usually is appropriate to consider whether special-interest purchasers exist and the synergies they might be able to realize. That being said, the quantification of post-acquisition synergies available to a specific buyer is usually difficult to assess, and the ability to get the buyer to pay for some or all of that benefit is questionable; and

- price-range competitors might bid for a business.

Furthermore, in an open market context, the multiples observed from somewhat comparable industry transactions influence the expectations and relative negotiating positions of the buyer and seller.

Although data derived from an analysis of transactions involving comparable companies may provide such insights, the direct application of the implied valuation multiples to any particular notional value determination is rarely possible because:

- normally sufficient information is not available to fully understand the valuation dynamics of the business acquired. The missing pieces often include the segregation of non-evident redundant assets, undisclosed liabilities, long-range plans, and so on. The level of disclosure in open market transactions is usually insufficient to formulate concrete conclusions regarding rates of return that can be directly applied to a given business. The quantity and quality of disclosure is particularly restricted where both the buyer and the seller are privately held;

- each open market transaction is unique. In the end the price and consideration paid are a function of the relative knowledge and negotiating position of the buyer and the seller, as well as the amount of competition for the acquired business; and

- an open market transaction price normally is comprised (either implicitly or explicitly) of the perceived intrinsic value of the acquired business plus, in varying degrees, synergies perceived by the purchaser. Therefore, even where sufficient information exists to compute earnings and cash flow multiples in an acquisition, in the absence of direct involvement with the buyer, it is unusual that the underlying value components can be meaningfully analyzed. Even where information is available that enables some quantification of the synergies paid for, there is no assurance that such synergies were *fully* paid for.

The application of open market transaction multiples is further complicated where all or part of the consideration paid involves a non-cash component such as shares of the buyer, promissory notes, or earnout-type arrangements, which may inflate the observed valuation multiple. Where non-cash consideration is involved, a cash-equivalent price should be estimated for purposes of comparison. In many cases, insufficient detail regarding the fair market value of the non-cash components is available or determinable. Further, where open market transactions are stale-dated, important changes in industry, business, and economic factors during the interim period must be considered.

Where the business acquired was publicly held prior to the transaction, the following additional things generally should be considered:

- the transaction price per share is influenced by the market price of the target company's shares prior to the takeover bid. In the acquisition of a public company, premiums above market trading prices are the norm, often in the order of 30% to 40%. As noted in Chapter 1, such premiums typically are paid on account of fact-specific synergies and not the elimination of a minority discount embedded in public company share prices (although in the case of thinly traded shares, a portion of the premium may be on account of the elimination of a discount for illiquidity). Furthermore, as a practical matter, a bid at (or below) the prevailing market price typically does not succeed. In addition, the magnitude of takeover premiums varies significantly, particularly for small-cap and micro-cap public companies whose shares are thinly traded prior to the takeover. However, in the absence of direct knowledge of the transaction, it is usually not possible to determine what portion of the premium, if any, is attributable to anticipated post-acquisition synergies vs. the buyer's perception that the stock price was less than the intrinsic value of the shares on a pro-rata basis;

- the price paid may be influenced by competitive bidding once the offer has been publicly disclosed;

- there may be some run-up in the price of the target's share price in the days or weeks immediately preceding the takeover transaction (due to speculation, inappropriately applied insider knowledge, and other reasons); and

- in an unsolicited public market takeover bid, the bidder seldom has free access to non-public information with respect to the target company prior to making the bid. Rather, the bidder is forced to rely on publicly available information, plus whatever other information is available.

Sources of information which may provide quantitative data (in cases where the buyer is a public company) include:

- annual reports and accompanying audited annual financial statements, which disclose the acquisition activity undertaken by a public corporate acquirer. Disclosure requirements in Canada generally include the price paid, form of consideration, net assets acquired and intangibles acquired;

- statutory filings. For example, smaller Canadian public companies that undertake an acquisition that surpasses certain size thresholds are required to file a Business Acquisition Report shortly after the transaction; and

- news releases often provide some, albeit limited, information regarding acquisition activity involving both public and medium-to-large privately held companies.

Each open market transaction involves a unique set of circumstances and buyer and seller motivations. Accordingly, in the absence of active participation in an industry transaction, it is seldom possible to obtain the detail necessary to draw firm conclusions regarding the factors from which the implicit multiples were derived. As a result, the use of data derived from an analysis of comparable industry transactions is usually limited to evaluating the reasonableness of a value determination derived using other valuation methodologies.

In some cases, industry transaction multiples can be misleading since they are calculated using reported results, as opposed to normalized earnings, which are usually not known to anyone other than the parties directly involved in the transaction. For example, a $50-million acquisition based on reported EBITDA of $7 million would suggest a multiple of about 7× EBITDA was paid for that company. However, it may be the case that the target company had $3 million of non-recurring expenses that, when adjusted for, resulted in normalized EBITDA of $10 million, and a "true" multiple of 5× EBITDA. However, this fact would not be known to a third-party observer.

Acquisitions of Minority Interests in Comparable Businesses

Privately Held Businesses

For the most part, there is a general lack of knowledge of transactions in which minority shareholdings in privately held businesses are bought and sold in arm's length transactions. Unlike stock market trades, details of transactions involving equity interests in privately held businesses are not documented or compiled in any manner that permits them to be meaningfully researched and analyzed. More important than simply identifying comparable private market transactions, the required understanding of the background and motivations behind those transactions is also usually missing.

Public Companies

Minority interest sales involving public companies typically involve normal-sized lots of freely trading shares, as previously discussed. However, public companies will sometimes offer an investor (usually a financial institution or fund management company) treasury shares in a private placement. Further, large holdings of shares in public companies trade in negotiated blocks. Private placements or block trades normally involve significantly more shares than are normally traded on the open markets in board lots of 100 or 1,000 shares (depending on price), and may, in limited circumstances, influence control of the company. Pursuant to the terms of the private placement and prevailing securities laws, the investor is usually prohibited from trading the acquired shares for a period of time. As a result, the degree of liquidity may be less than that of normal-sized trading lots in public equity market transactions. Even where not restricted, liquidity may become an issue if the block of shares is sufficiently large that it cannot be readily absorbed in the market place. All these things may have implications for comparability in a particular value determination.

When using private placement information it is necessary to understand the terms of the private placement such as the time period, restrictions on transfer, and other relevant considerations. In addition, it is important to note that the buyer in a private placement is typically investing money in the company itself as opposed to purchasing an interest held by a third party (i.e., a primary offering vs. a secondary offering, as discussed in Chapter 1). This distinction should be considered in any comparative analysis.

Transactions Involving the Subject Business

Acquisition of Control of the Subject Business

Occasionally 100% or control of the subject business may have been acquired in the months or years leading up to the valuation date. Where this is the case, details of the transaction should be analyzed to determine what the buyer perceived to be the risks and growth potential of the business. When assessing comparability, such analysis must take into account changes during the interim period in:

- the economic environment, including changes to prevailing rates of return (e.g., the risk-free rate);
- the industry in which the business operates. Following the transaction, there may have been significant developments regarding the competitive environment, advancements in technology, and so on; and

- the business itself. This might include changes in size, levels of profitability, products or services offered, and other factors. In particular, following an acquisition, a business may experience changes in its management team and business strategy that would make any comparison less valid.

It is also important to understand the terms of the transaction. To the extent the transaction involved non-cash consideration, a comparison to a current cash-equivalent value becomes more problematic.

Where possible and practical, it is helpful to speak with those involved in the prior transaction in order to understand:

- from the buyer's perspective, the expected synergies, normalization adjustments and anticipated operating results. To the extent the synergies that were paid for can be segregated, they assist in reconciling the price paid with the current intrinsic value of the business; and

- from the seller's perspective, the number of parties that were interested in the company and alternative offers that were received.

Acquisitions of Minority Interests in the Subject Business

Where there have been recent transactions involving minority shareholdings in a privately held business, information from those transactions may aid in the determination of value of a minority shareholding or control shareholding in the same business. In such circumstances, the following things should be considered:

- the basis on which prior prices were established. In particular, whether there were any contractual agreements governing the basis upon which the transactions were effected, particularly whether there was a shareholder agreement that addressed how value was to be established (including whether a minority discount was applied);

- the parties transacting, whether they were acting at arm's length, and what their motivations were when transacting;

- the percentage interest represented by the minority shareholding(s) acquired;

- how informed the buyer was as to the existing financial position of the business and its prospective operating results at the time;

- the terms of the transaction. Where the transaction involved non-cash consideration, that factor makes any comparison more problematic;

- whether the transaction was funded by company funds or external funds, and whether there was an element of company-sponsored financial assistance present in any of the transactions. The issue of internal vs. external financing is discussed in Chapter 10; and

- changes that have occurred in the economy, the industry, and the prospects for the business between the dates of prior transactions and the valuation date.

Where such things are capable of analysis, it may be possible to adjust prior sales of minority shareholdings, thereby assisting in the determination of the current value of a given minority shareholding. When comparing a previous transaction involving the purchase of a minority interest to a current transaction involving a controlling interest (or vice-versa), it may be appropriate to adjust for the add-back (or deduction) of a minority discount, where such discount was embedded in the minority sale price – see Chapter 8.

Acquisitions Undertaken by the Subject Business

Where the subject business has acquired other businesses, these transactions should be analyzed. In particular, such transactions might provide an indication as to the target rates of return of, and level of synergies anticipated by, the subject business. As in all cases, care is necessary when evaluating such transactions, particularly with respect to the degree of comparability between the buyer and seller. In particular, in comparison to the buyer, the seller might:

- be considerably smaller in size and not enjoy the same economies of scale;

- be subject to a different degree of operating risk;

- have one or more key employees who may or may not be retained under the terms of a management contract, or are subject to a non-competition agreement; and

- participate in different markets, with different product and service offerings, and so on.

In addition, the buyer may have succeeded in its acquisition bid because it overpaid. In circumstances where that is the case, it is not appropriate to apply the same multiples when determining the *en bloc* value of the buyer's business.

Adjusting for Non-Cash Consideration

The definition of fair market value assumes a cash price paid in full at the valuation date. In an open market transaction, such payment terms rarely take place, except where a public company is being acquired for cash (where securities laws typically require payment in full at closing, either in the form of cash or shares of the buyer). The acquisition of privately held companies may involve various other forms of consideration, including holdbacks, promissory notes, share exchanges and earnouts. Deal structuring is addressed in Chapter 11.

Where industry transactions or transactions involving the subject company are adopted as a benchmark for testing the reasonableness of a valuation conclusion, and that transaction includes non-cash consideration, then it is necessary to convert that non-cash consideration into a cash-equivalent in order to better assess comparability. This assumes that adequate information regarding the forms and terms of payment are disclosed so that meaningful adjustments can be made.

Holdbacks

Holdbacks are commonly used to protect a buyer against the risk that the balance sheet acquired contains certain unrealizable assets (e.g., non-collectible accounts receivable) or hidden liabilities. Holding back a portion of the purchase price also provides a buyer with an added level of comfort regarding representations and warranties made by the seller. Where the holdback is on account of working capital, debt levels and other balance sheet targets, no adjustment to the stated purchase price is required. This is because, in a notional market valuation, it is typically assumed that the balance sheet of the subject company at the valuation date is fairly stated in accordance with GAAP (or IFRSs). While the holdback may only be collected by the seller after several months, a year, or more (and may not be interest-bearing), the risk of collection is usually low (barring accounting adjustments or breached representations and warranties) and the holdback portion of the purchase price is usually not significant (e.g., 10% of the aggregate purchase price). Consequently, any adjustment on account of risk and the time value of money is usually immaterial.

The exception occurs where the holdback is being used because of an outstanding contingent liability, such as a legal claim or environmental issue, at the valuation date. In such cases, it is usually necessary to assign a probability factor to the potential liability in order to generate a cash-equivalent amount. Advice from legal counsel or other specialists (e.g., environmental engineers) may be required in order to determine a reasonable probability factor.

Promissory Notes

Promissory notes (or vendor take-backs) are sometimes used where the buyer does not have sufficient cash available to consummate the transaction. The structure of a promissory note can vary significantly in terms of the number of years over which payment will be made (one to five years is not uncommon), applicable interest rate (which can range from nil to subordinated debt interest rate levels) and security granted by the buyer and conditions for payment (if any). Promissory notes (principal and interest payments) should be discounted to their present value amount to reflect the time value of money and the risk of non-collection. In many cases, the risk is significant given that such notes are subordinated to other obligations of the buyer, and the buyer may not be able to offer a strong covenant.

Share Exchanges

Where a share-for-share exchange takes place, the value of the shares received as consideration must be established. In cases where the buyer is a privately held company, this may require an independent valuation of the buyer's equity. Furthermore, the seller may be subject to a minority discount where they become a minority shareholder in the combined entity following the transaction, depending on the terms of the shareholder agreement and other factors, as discussed in Chapter 8. However, it is unusual for a seller to accept the shares of a privately held company as consideration, given the issues involved.

Where the buyer is a public company, the market price for the shares is readily determinable. However, the market value of the shares received as consideration may *not* be reflective of their fair market value. This is particularly the case where:

- the shares of the buyer are thinly traded;

- the seller becomes the holder of a significant block of shares, which may warrant a block premium or discount; and

- trading restrictions that reduce the liquidity of the shares may be imposed on the seller for a period of time following the transaction.

Earnouts

Where the transaction includes an earnout component, the estimation of its cash-equivalent value can be both subjective and complex. In an earnout, the seller receives further consideration for achieving agreed target performance measures. The structure of an earnout agreement can vary widely, in terms of duration, performance targets, minimum or maximum amounts, and other parameters. In calculating the cash-equivalent value of an earnout, consideration should be afforded to the:

- likelihood that the earnout target(s) will be attained, having regard to the:
    - ✓ performance targets established, given the historical operating results of the business and prevailing industry conditions,
    - ✓ ability of the seller to influence the achievement of performance targets, given the nature and extent of their continued involvement in the business following the closing date,
    - ✓ duration of the earnout. As a general rule, the likelihood of achieving earnout targets diminishes over time due to unforeseen issues that may arise, and
    - ✓ structure of the earnout. Many earnouts as structured with "cliffs" such that a minimum performance level is required prior to any earnout entitlement. On the other end, while in some cases earnouts do not have a ceiling on the payout amount, it is more common in Canada to impose an upper limit on the earnout for income tax purposes (see Chapter 11). In other cases, earnouts are cumulative, so that if the performance target is missed in a particular year, the seller is afforded the opportunity to recover that amount by over-achieving the performance target in a subsequent year;
- time value of money, particularly where the earnout extends over several years; and
- possibility that, even if the targets are attained, the earnout payment is not collected due to the weak financial condition of the buyer or other factors.

Given the degree of uncertainty normally attaching to an earnout payment, the cash-equivalent amount is often estimated by assigning a probability factor to the earnout payments, and then discounting the estimated probable amount by a discount rate that reflects: (i) the time value of money; and (ii) the risk of non-collection even if the earnout target has been achieved (based on the quality of the buyer's covenant).

For example, assume the seller of Company Q is entitled to receive an earnout of $1 million per year for each of the next three years based on achieving revenue growth of not less than 10% per year. Further assume that, given the historical operating results of Company Q, prevailing industry conditions and other factors, the likelihood of achieving the earnout target is estimated at 75% in year 1, 50% in year 2 and 25% in year 3. Given the time value of money and the buyer's covenant, a discount rate of 10% is considered appropriate. Based on these assumptions, the cash-equivalent value of the earnout for Company Q would be estimated as follows:

Exhibit 4Q
Company Q
Cash-Equivalent Earnout Value

	Year 1	Year 2	Year 3	Total
Potential earnout	1,000,000	1,000,000	1,000,000	3,000,000
Probability factor	75%	50%	25%	
Estimated probable amount	750,000	500,000	250,000	
Discounted at 10%	681,818	413,223	187,829	**1,282,870**

Other Forms of Consideration

There can be numerous other forms of consideration embedded in a particular transaction, including royalty payments, management or consulting fees in excess of market rates, and other economic incentives. Estimating the cash-equivalent amount of these deferred and conditional payments helps to provide a more meaningful comparison to cash-equivalent fair market value. However, estimating the cash-equivalent value is inherently subjective, and the level of detail required to make such calculations is often not adequately disclosed.

Common Deficiencies in the Multiple of EBITDA and Related Methodologies

While valuations based on multiples are popular, these approaches are subject to issues in their application and the interpretation of results. Some of the more common deficiencies encountered in valuations based on multiples are as follows:

- internal inconsistency between the valuation multiple and the earnings base against which it is applied. In particular, growth and risk sometimes are double-counted as a result of their inclusion in both normalized EBITDA and the valuation multiple;

- failing to adjust the value conclusion for a working capital surplus or deficiency, which is normally attributable to inadequate analysis regarding normal working capital levels;

- placing too much emphasis on comparable public companies that are only of limited comparability. It is not uncommon for a valuation report to set out a lengthy list of public companies purported to be "comparable" to the subject (privately held) company simply because they operate in the same industry. As noted above, important differences usually exist between any two companies in terms of size, product and service offerings, market coverage, and other factors, such that the validity of each so-called "comparable" can be brought into question. Furthermore, the multiples adopted from a list of "comparables" often represent an average or median figure. In many cases, public company multiples in a given industry fall within a wide range because of the fact-specific circumstances of each business. An average figure based on a wide range of results may not be meaningful;

- over-reliance on industry transactions. The multiples observed in industry transactions can be distorted by factors such as the earnings base of the acquired company prior to the transaction, the terms of payment, expected synergies and a variety of other factors which typically are not adequately enough disclosed to permit a meaningful adjustment to be made; and

- application of a so-called "control premium". In some cases, a notional valuation performed according to the comparable public companies methodology includes an adjustment for a control premium. Such an adjustment is normally made on the assumption that public company shares trade at prices that reflect "a minority discount" and that an adjustment is necessary in order to eliminate the inherent minority discount embedded in the trading price (see also Chapter 8). It is generally accepted that shares of widely held public companies do not trade at prices that reflect a minority discount, as evidenced by the usual approach to public market securities valuation taken by stock analysts and other public equity market participants. That being said, the premium paid for small-cap and micro-cap public companies may represent to some extent the elimination of an illiquidity discount where the shares were thinly traded prior to the transaction.

Summary

The multiple of EBITDA methodology (and similar methodologies) is attractive due to its relative simplicity. Valuation multiples also serve as popular reference points when negotiating an open market transaction. However, the usual application of these methodologies is in the context of a test of the valuation conclusions derived from other (more sophisticated) valuation methodologies.

The primary components of these methodologies are normalized EBITDA and the valuation multiple. Normalized EBITDA should reflect the buyer's expectations of maintainable earnings levels going forward. The valuation multiple is influenced by a myriad of factors that impact the risk profile and growth prospects of the business. Multiplying normalized EBITDA by a valuation multiple represents the enterprise value of the business. Interest-bearing debt and equivalents (net of excess cash) is deducted to determine the equity value of the business. Where applicable, further adjustments to the equity value are made on account of redundant items, one-time items and excess or deficient net operating assets.

As a test of the valuation multiple, reference is sometimes made to comparable public companies and industry transactions. However, such comparisons can be problematic given that no two businesses are exactly alike and, in the case of industry transactions, because of the normally limited amount of disclosure involving important elements such as the terms of the deal, expected synergies and other factors.

Chapter 5

The Capitalized Cash Flow Methodology

Introduction

The capitalized cash flow (CCF) methodology is a common approach to business valuation. To some degree, it is a refinement of the multiple of after-tax cash flow methodology presented in Chapter 4.

The CCF methodology involves dividing normalized discretionary cash flow by a capitalization rate to develop capitalized cash flow. Discretionary cash flow represents the cash flow available as a return on investment to the providers of capital. Discretionary cash flow can be withdrawn from the business without impairing prospective operating results or, alternatively, can be reinvested in the business to generate growth and incremental financial returns. Discretionary cash flow is calculated as normalized EBITDA (earnings before interest, taxes, depreciation and amortization) less income taxes, sustaining capital expenditures (net of the related tax shield) and incremental net trade working capital requirements, where applicable. The capitalization rate represents the rate of return given the risk profile of the business, as well as prevailing industry, economic and credit market conditions. The capitalization rate is expressed net of a long-term growth rate that may include inflationary growth as well as an element of real growth.

The present value of the tax shield on existing assets is added to the capitalized cash flow to determine the enterprise value of the business. The equity value of the business is determined by deducting interest-bearing debt and equivalents, and adjusting for redundant assets, prospective one-time items and excess or deficient net operating assets (e.g., working capital), where applicable.

The CCF methodology can be used as a stand-alone valuation methodology or as the "terminal value" component of the discounted cash flow methodology (discussed in Chapter 6). Importantly, the CCF methodology assumes discretionary cash flows will be relatively stable in perpetuity or will grow at a fairly constant (generally low) rate over the long term.

A variation of the CCF methodology is the capitalized earnings methodology, which generally is a more simplified approach to valuation. Because of these simplifications and its emphasis on accounting income rather than cash flows, the capitalized earnings methodology tends to be less accepted. However, it is sometimes used where simplified assumptions are valid or as a secondary approach to valuation.

Mechanics of the Capitalized Cash Flow Methodology

Overview

The mechanics of the CCF methodology are as follows:

- an estimate (or range) of normalized discretionary cash flow is developed;
- the normalized discretionary cash flow is divided by a capitalization rate to develop capitalized cash flow;
- the present value of the tax shield on existing tax pools is added to capitalized cash flow in order to determine the enterprise value of the business;
- interest-bearing debt and equivalent liabilities (net of excess cash) are deducted from enterprise value in order to determine the equity value of the business, *en bloc*; and
- where applicable, further adjustments are made to *en bloc* equity value on account of redundant assets, prospective one-time items, or excess or deficient net operating assets at the valuation date.

Exhibit 5A
Mechanics of the Capitalized Cash Flow Methodology

	Normalized discretionary cash flow
Divided by:	capitalization rate
Equals:	vapitalized cash flow
Add:	present value of existing tax pools
Equals:	enterprise value
Deduct:	interest-bearing debt and equivalents (net of excess cash)
Add:	redundant assets
Add (deduct):	one-time adjustments
Add (deduct):	excess (deficient) net operating assets
Equals:	equity value

The methodology set out above assumes the shares of a business are being valued. Where the assets of a business are being valued further adjustments are necessary. These adjustments are addressed under the caption "Assets vs. Shares", below.

Importantly, the CCF methodology assumes discretionary cash flow will be relatively stable in perpetuity or will grow at a fairly constant (generally low) rate over the long term. As such, its application is generally appropriate in circumstances:

- of mature businesses with relatively consistent discretionary cash flow;

- of businesses where average discretionary cash flow through a business cycle can be reasonably estimated;

- when forecasts are not available or are not believed meaningful. Estimated prospective cash flow must then be developed based on an analysis of historical and current operating results; and

- when the terminal value component in a discounted cash flow methodology is determined at the time discretionary cash flows are expected to be relatively stable. As will be discussed in Chapter 6, the discounted cash flow methodology is typically the preferred approach to valuation. Pursuant to this methodology, discretionary cash flows are forecast for a period of time (generally three to five years) and discounted back to their present value. The value of the cash flows beyond the forecast period (the terminal value) is usually developed using a capitalized cash flow methodology, and likewise discounted to present value. Terminal value typically represents a significant portion of the total value developed following the discounted cash flow methodology.

Normalized Discretionary Cash Flow

Discretionary cash flow (sometimes referred to as "free cash flow") refers to the amount of cash that can be withdrawn from the business as a return on capital or retained to generate growth that has not otherwise been accounted for. Importantly, the withdrawal of discretionary cash flow cannot impair the ability of a business to generate the indicated operating results adopted for the purpose of calculating capitalized cash flow.

Discretionary cash flow normally is determined as follows:

Exhibit 5B
Discretionary Cash Flow

	Normalized EBITDA
Deduct:	cash income taxes on EBITDA
Deduct:	sustaining capital expenditures
Add:	present value of the tax shield on sustaining capital expenditures
Deduct:	incremental net trade working capital requirements
Equals:	normalized discretionary cash flow

The calculation of discretionary cash flow above is determined on an "unlevered" basis (i.e., before consideration of debt servicing costs). The (unlevered) discretionary cash flow is applied against a capitalization rate that represents a weighted average cost of capital (WACC) in order to derive the enterprise value of the business (after accounting for the present value of existing tax pools). The ability of a business to use debt financing is reflected in the WACC capitalization rate (see Chapter 7).

Therefore, discretionary cash flow as set out in Exhibit 5B above represents the return to all providers of capital in a business (both debt and equity). A portion of the unlevered discretionary cash flow will be required to make interest payments (net of the related income tax deduction) and to repay debt principal outstanding. Once the holders of the business's interest-bearing debt and equivalents have been satisfied, the remaining discretionary cash flow represents the amount of free cash that can be:

- withdrawn by the owners (through dividends, excess remuneration or other distributions) without impairing the prospective operating results of a business, thereby generating a return on their equity investment;

- reinvested in the business, thereby creating incremental discretionary cash flow in excess of the amount indicated;

- applied against the interest-bearing debt of a business, thereby enhancing the equity component of its enterprise value;

- retained in the business as a redundant asset, which would increase the *en bloc* equity value of the business; or

- a combination of these things.

It is possible to determine discretionary cash flow on a levered basis (i.e., net of after-tax interest payments and changes in debt principal outstanding). The levered discretionary cash flow is then divided by a capitalization rate that reflects a levered return on equity. The difference between the levered approach and the unlevered approach is discussed later in this chapter. However, the levered approach tends to be more complex due to the iterative calculations involved. In theory, both the unlevered approach and the levered approach should result in the same *en bloc* equity value for the business.

Normalized EBITDA

Estimated normalized EBITDA is based on an analysis of current, historical and (where available) budgeted or forecast operating results, and consideration of company, industry and economic factors believed to impact the prospective cash flow generating ability of the business. These are the same considerations discussed in Chapter 4 pursuant to the multiple of EBITDA methodology.

Normalized EBITDA represents a point estimate (or range) that is expected to remain relatively stable on a prospective basis. It may also represent an estimated average amount over an earnings cycle. Where EBITDA is expected to grow at a constant rate over the long term, that growth is reflected in the capitalization rate (discussed below).

In theory, where normalized EBITDA is developed based on historical or current operating results, it should be increased by the growth factor embedded in the capitalization rate. This is because the capitalization rate is based on the assumption that cash flows begin one year forward. For example, assuming that following an analysis of historical and current operating results the normalized EBITDA was estimated at $5 million and the capitalization rate incorporated a long-term growth assumption of 2%, then normalized EBITDA should be increased to $5.1 million (calculated as $5 million × 1.02). However, in practice, this adjustment is often not made.

Income Taxes

Income taxes are deducted from normalized EBITDA to determine estimated normalized after-tax cash flow from operations (before consideration of capital spending). The tax rate normally utilized should be the effective corporate cash tax rate on active business income. Where EBITDA does not approximate taxable income before consideration of capital cost allowance (CCA) (the term used in the *Income Tax Act* for depreciation and amortization allowed for income tax purposes), a more detailed income tax calculation may be required. In particular, estimated normalized EBITDA may include certain items that are not fully deductible for income tax purposes (such as meals and entertainment expenses), or where there is a timing difference between an expense for financial accounting purposes and an allowable deduction for income tax purposes (such as warranty reserves).

It is important that income tax rate considerations be consistent with the level and composition of estimated normalized EBITDA. For example where:

- some or all of the normalized EBITDA may be eligible for the small business deduction (discussed below), it may be appropriate to reflect that benefit, depending on the purpose of the valuation;

- normalized EBITDA incorporates research and development expenditures believed to be eligible for Scientific Research and Experimental Development (SRED) credits, the net benefit of such credits should be considered;

- normalized EBITDA is generated in more than one province, then a blended provincial tax rate should be adopted. The provincial allocation is based on an average of two measures: (i) revenues generated by province; and (ii) gross wages paid by province; and

- a portion of normalized EBITDA will be generated outside Canada, then consideration must be given to the income tax rate and regulations in those other countries. In addition, consideration should be afforded to the tax consequences associated with repatriating the cash flows generated in other countries.

Income tax rates are always subject to changes in government fiscal policies and political developments. Where appropriate, the capitalization rate adopted should reflect the risk of changes to taxation policies that would impact the estimated normalized discretionary cash flow of a business, where such changes were not otherwise quantified as part of the capitalized cash flow methodology.

The Small Business Deduction

A deduction in computing tax payable is available to a Canadian-controlled private corporation (CCPC) that earns active business income. A CCPC is a private corporation resident in Canada that is not controlled directly or indirectly by one or more non-residents or public corporations. An active business is any business other than the provision of services by an "incorporated employee" or a business of earning income from property such as rents, interest or dividends, except in either case, where the corporation employs more than five full-time employees in the business. Qualifying corporations are entitled to a tax credit which effectively reduces the federal tax rate on the first $500,000 of active business income in any year (in addition to lower provincial rates). Special rules require the small business deduction to be shared among a group of associated corporations and to be "clawed back" in the case of larger, otherwise eligible corporations. The small business rate and small business threshold have changed significantly over the past several years, and the rules vary by province. Therefore, any valuation conducted at a prior date must reflect the then prevailing tax laws.

In the context of a business valuation, the issue sometimes arises whether or not to include the benefit of the small business deduction in calculating the discretionary cash flow of a company that normally qualifies for that deduction.

In a notional market valuation the small business deduction may be factored into the discretionary cash flow calculations where fair market value is determined on a stand-alone or intrinsic basis, assuming the business is expected to be eligible. The small business deduction is normally not taken into account where fair market value includes a component of post-acquisition synergies, given that the buyer would likely not enjoy such a benefit.

In an open market context, where a small business is being acquired by an individual and the company is expected to continue to qualify for the small business deduction, the deduction is normally taken into account. Conversely, in the case of mid-size and larger businesses, where the buyer will likely be another corporation, the small business deduction is normally not considered if the combined taxable income of the buyer is expected to exceed the small business limit.

In any case, there must be internal consistency between the assumed level of normalized EBITDA and the use of the small business deduction. For example, many business owners will declare bonuses to themselves and related parties in order to reduce the pretax income of their corporation to the small business threshold and only pay corporate tax at the small business rate. However, when EBITDA is normalized to reflect market-rate remuneration for non-arm's length parties, it may be the case that normalized EBITDA is at a level where there is a "claw back" of the small business deduction, and hence corporate income taxes are payable at the full corporate rate.

Scientific Research and Experimental Development (SRED) Tax Credits

In general, expenditures on scientific research and experimental development are deductible in computing income, providing the expenditures are made in Canada and the research and development are carried out in Canada. The Canada Revenue Agency's administrative guidelines for what constitutes scientific research and experimental development are complex. Various provinces also have incentives for qualifying research and development (R&D) expenditures.

A business that incurs qualifying R&D expenditures may claim an investment tax credit to reduce tax otherwise payable. The tax credit is refundable for a CCPC with taxable income which does not exceed its business limit for purposes of the small business deduction for the year. The federal investment tax credit rate is generally 20% (declining to 15% in 2014). An enhanced 35% SRED credit is available for eligible CCPC's on the first $3 million of annual expenditures. Certain provinces have initiated similar incentives. SRED tax credits are included in computing income in the year in which they are received, which in effect makes the receipt of SRED credits a taxable benefit to the corporation. Unutilized SRED credits can be carried forward indefinitely and applied against future taxable income.

In valuing a company, whether or not SRED tax credits should be taken into account in computing discretionary cash flow is sometimes at issue. Where the EBITDA expected to be generated includes an amount in respect of R&D activities, and it is likely that those R&D activities will qualify for SRED tax credits, such benefit should normally be taken into account. It should be noted, however, that not all expenses that a business classifies as R&D may qualify for SRED credits. Therefore, R&D expenditures to be made should be analyzed to assess the likelihood they will qualify for SRED. Furthermore, it is important to ensure discretionary cash flow accounts for the fact that SRED credits are included with taxable income when received.

By way of example, assume that normalized EBITDA for Company R is estimated at $5 million, which is net of $1 million in annual R&D expenses. Further assume that Company R is subject to a corporate income tax rate of 30% and that all its R&D expenses qualify for federal SRED credits (ignoring any provincial credits). The calculation of the income tax provision for Company R would be as follows:

Exhibit 5C
Company R
Calculation of Income Tax Provision with SRED Credits

Basic Taxes		
Maintainable EBITDA	5,000,000	
Taxes at 30%		1,500,000
Deduct: SRED credit		
Qualifying R&D expenditures	1,000,000	
Federal SRED credit at 20%		(200,000)
Add: taxes on SRED credit received		
$200,000 × 30%		60,000
Net income taxes on EBITDA		1,360,000

Prospective Tax Rate Changes

Another factor to consider is whether to adopt prevailing or prospective income tax rates, where changes have been announced. While in theory prospective tax rates are more appropriate, consideration should be afforded to the following:

- if prospective tax rate changes have not been passed into law, then there is greater risk that they may not materialize; and

- if prospective tax rate changes are expected to be implemented over the course of several years, then the use of a constant tax rate will distort the economic result.

Therefore, it may be preferable to adopt the current tax rate to calculate normalized discretionary cash flow and to calculate the impact of prospective changes to income tax rates as a separate adjustment to capitalized cash flow. Where appropriate, the adjustment can be subject to a probability factor to reflect the risk that such changes may not materialize. Where discretionary cash flow incorporates prospective tax rate reductions, the capitalization rate should reflect the risk that said reductions will not materialize, or that a buyer may not be willing to pay for prospective tax rate reductions.

As a practical matter, in an open market transaction, many buyers are reluctant to pay for the benefit of a reduction in corporate income tax rates that have not yet materialized. Whether such benefits are paid for normally is subject to the relative negotiating positions of the parties involved.

Sustaining Capital Reinvestment

Sustaining capital reinvestment represents the estimated level of fixed asset expenditures that a business expects to incur each year, on average, in order to support the estimated normalized EBITDA over the long-term. Developing a reasonable estimate of sustaining capital reinvestment is a subjective task but generally should incorporate an analysis of the following:

- historical fixed asset additions. This requires an analysis not only of the absolute amount of spending, but also an understanding of the reason for the spending. For example, to the extent the capital expenditures were incurred in order to accommodate growth, such expenditures would not be considered as sustaining. The separation of historical capital spending into growth capital and replacement (sustaining) capital is often difficult, since capital expenditures frequently incorporate a component of each. Furthermore, to the extent that capital expenditures were made in order to generate operating efficiencies required in order to maintain the competitive position of the business, these would be considered sustaining in nature. In other words, sustaining capital reinvestment is the annual capital cost over and above normal repair and maintenance costs required to remain competitive and not erode estimated normalized EBITDA;

- where sustaining capital expenditures are estimated based on an analysis of historical spending during a period of high inflation, the impact of inflation on the replacement cost of assets should be considered;

- budgets or projections of capital expenditure amounts. In this regard, it is important to understand the underlying assumptions used to develop such budgets or projections, and management's expectations of the operating results from such spending;

- the age, nature and condition of the capital assets used by the business. For example, if the fixed assets are old, it may be the case that prospective capital expenditures will exceed recent historical amounts;

- the estimated replacement cost of fixed assets. This analysis is sometimes aided by an independent equipment appraiser;

- the impact of technological change. It is sometimes the case that the cost of replacing technology-based machinery and equipment declines over time. Further, the replacement of old technology with new technology sometimes leads to incremental benefits in terms of operating efficiencies, production capacity, product quality and so on. To the extent such benefits can reasonably be expected to materialize, they should be reflected in normalized EBITDA or alternatively in the capitalization rate adopted. However, caution is warranted. In many cases, such benefits are eroded by competitive pressures where the new technology becomes the industry standard. As noted above, to the extent that capital additions are required for the business to remain competitive in the face of new technological developments, the non-growth portion of such expenditures should be considered sustaining;

- whether the equipment utilized by a business may change, or may be expected to change (e.g., due to a change in a company's strategy);

- the estimated useful life of fixed assets by category. For example, if the average useful life of the office equipment owned by a business is estimated at five years, then it may be reasonable to expect average capital expenditures on office equipment will approximate 20% of the gross amount. In most cases, all depreciable fixed assets will have to be replaced over time;

- the amount recorded for depreciation. While the amounts recorded for depreciation and capital expenditures may differ in any given year, that difference is attributable to timing; these amounts will, however, reconcile over the long term. In this regard, International Financial Reporting Standards attempt to segregate fixed assets based on their nature and useful life, more than was the case with Generally Accepted Accounting Principles. Therefore, depreciation for accounting purposes may become a better measure of sustaining capital expenditures in the future;

- past and prospective repair and maintenance expense. In this regard, privately held businesses (which tend to be driven by income tax minimization as opposed to earnings-per-share maximization) tend to expense what a public company (whose managers are driven in part to report higher earnings) might capitalize. Furthermore, increased repair and maintenance spending may be indicative of aging equipment that will need to be replaced in the near term;

- capital expenditure levels of public companies that are believed to be meaningfully comparable to the subject business. Caution is warranted, however, in that such analysis can be distorted for various reasons such as differences in product and service offerings, capitalization policies, growth initiatives and other factors; and

- industry developments vis-à-vis capital spending. Where competitors are undertaking aggressive capital expansion programs, the business being valued may have to increase capital spending to maintain its market share and generate prospective EBITDA at the levels estimated. To the extent that a business must expend capital in order to maintain its competitive position, such spending would be considered sustaining capital.

It is usually beneficial to have a tour of the operating facilities of a business in order to visually assess the condition of fixed assets and to have discussions with management regarding both sustaining and growth capital investment. Where appropriate, equipment appraisers, equipment manufacturers, engineers or other experts should advise on existing equipment with reference to both the company's present technology and to the historic, current, and prospective rates of change in the technology used in the company's industry.

The estimate of sustaining capital reinvestment is usually stated as a constant level of expected annual fixed asset additions. Where this is the case, it should exclude any near-term one-time upgrades or additions that may be required by the business. For example, where the business will be undertaking a one-time plant expansion project in order to expand its operations and generate the projected levels of EBITDA, capitalized discretionary cash flows should reflect the impact of that investment. While the one-time expansion cost should be segregated and deducted as a one-time adjustment to enterprise value, the estimate of sustaining capital should take into account that the one-time addition will likely have to be replaced over time.

As in the determination of normalized EBITDA, in theory sustaining capital reinvestment estimated on the basis of historical and current expenditure levels should be increased to reflect the long-term growth rate assumptions embedded in the capitalization rate. Where the capitalization rate incorporates an element of long-term growth, further analysis of sustaining capital expenditures should be undertaken to determine what level of expenditures will be required to support that assumption. For example, if a business has facilities operating near capacity, then an assumption of long-term real growth may necessitate capital expansion in the coming years. The cost of expansion would normally be recorded as a one-time adjustment. However, as noted above, that expansion may result in increased sustaining capital expenditure requirements over the long term. As is the case in any valuation methodology, it is important to ensure internal consistency.

Tax Shield on Sustaining Capital

The tax shield on sustaining capital represents the sum of the present values of anticipated tax savings which will accrue as a result of the business claiming capital cost allowance. Under the *Income Tax Act*, depreciation and amortization in any fiscal period is determined by:

- adding the cost of capital assets acquired in a taxation year to the previous taxation year-end balance of an asset class specified by the Income Tax Regulations; and

- calculating CCA on the balance existing in that class at the rates prescribed in the Income Tax Regulations (which are organized by fixed asset class).

Accordingly, the final determination of sustaining capital reinvestment should consider the benefit of income tax savings arising from the future CCA tax shield that will result from sustaining capital reinvestment expenditures.

As discussed in Chapter 3, where the Income Tax Regulations prescribe that CCA is to be determined on a declining balance basis (which is usually the case), the determination of the present value of the CCA tax shield can be calculated pursuant to the following formula (which is the same as Formula 3.2 and repeated here for expediency):

Formula 5.1
Present Value of the CCA Tax Shield on Newly Acquired Assets Calculated on a Declining Balance Basis Incorporating the Half-Year Rule

$$\frac{C \times D \times T}{(K + D)} \times \frac{[(1 + (0.5 \times K)]}{(1 + K)}$$

where:

C = the cost of the asset. That is, the adjusted cost base for income tax purposes, including all costs capitalized for tax purposes, including transportation, installation, and other qualifying expenses;

D = the CCA rate applicable to a class of assets, as prescribed in the Income Tax Regulations;

T = the marginal income tax rate at which capital cost allowance would reduce taxable income, having regard to estimated normalized EBITDA; and

K = the cost of capital. Pursuant to the above formula, the cost of capital should be the nominal weighted average cost of capital (see Chapter 7).

The above formula incorporates the "half-year rule" whereby only 50% of the eligible CCA can be deducted in the year of acquisition. This rule is applicable to most capital asset additions in Canada. Where the half-year rule is not applicable, the formula can be simplified by removing the second part of the equation (i.e., $[(1 + 0.5 \times K) / (1 + K)]$).

As noted in Chapter 3, certain capital assets are eligible for CCA calculated on a straight-line basis. Examples include leasehold improvements. Where this is the case, the annual calculation of CCA is determined as follows (note that this formula is the same as Formula 3.4, and reproduced here for expediency):

Formula 5.2
Present Value of the CCA Tax Shield for Newly Acquired Assets Calculated on a Straight Line Basis Incorporating the Half-Year Rule

$$C / N \times T \times PVIFA_{K, N} \qquad \times \qquad [(1 + 0.5 \times K) / (1+ K)]$$

Where:

C = the cost of the asset

N = the number of years over which CCA is claimed

T = the marginal tax rate at which CCA is deducted

$PVIFA_{K, N}$ = the present value interest factor of an annuity for N years at a given cost of capital (K)

K = the cost of capital. Pursuant to the above formula, the cost of capital should be the nominal weighted average cost of capital (see Chapter 7)

The above formula takes into account the half-year rule. Where the half-year rule is not applicable (for example, on Class 14 assets such as licences), the equation can be simplified by removing the last part $[(1 + 0.5 \times K) / (1 + K)]$.

The cost of capital (K) adopted in the calculations of the CCA tax shield noted above should represent the weighted average cost of capital (WACC) discount rate determined on a nominal basis (i.e., including inflation) because:

- it is consistent with the capital structure of the business, which is the basis by which capital additions will be financed over the long term; and

- the annual tax deduction is calculated on a cost base that is being continuously eroded in real dollars due to inflation.

The WACC discount rate typically is different from the capitalization rate adopted in the CCF methodology. As explained in Chapter 7, the discount rate represents the cost of capital for a business, given its risk profile, as well as industry, economic and credit market conditions. The capitalization rate is derived by deducting long-term growth (which may consist of both nominal growth and real growth) from the discount rate. In order to be consistent with the determination of sustaining capital expenditures, however, the growth component should not be factored into the tax shield calculation.

Generally, the estimate of sustaining capital reinvestment includes various types of assets which, according to the Income Tax Regulations, are eligible for CCA at differing rates. While sometimes a blended CCA rate is adopted where annual sustaining capital reinvestment is significant or CCA rates on the additions differ significantly, consideration should be given to segregating the assets into groups with similar CCA rates when calculating the CCA tax shield.

If a portion of the capital asset additions will be incurred in other countries, then a different calculation of the tax shield benefit may be appropriate. For example, in the U.S., capital asset additions are often eligible for tax depreciation calculated using the Modified Accelerated Cost Recovery System (MACRS), which is similar to a "double-declining balance" basis of depreciation. Where the tax shield attributable to other countries is significant, then the calculation should be segregated as such.

Incremental Net Trade Working Capital

Where the capitalization rate adopted in the capitalized cash flow methodology incorporates an element of long-term growth (because of inflation and, in some cases, an element of real growth), consideration should be given to the incremental net trade working capital required to support that growth.

In most cases, a company experiencing growth in revenues and EBITDA will require additional net trade working capital. As explained in Chapter 2, net trade working capital generally includes current assets such as accounts receivable and inventories net of current liabilities such as accounts payable and accruals.

For example, revenue growth typically results in higher accounts receivable (although not always in the same proportion). An increase in accounts receivable represents a cash outflow for the business (as evidenced on the statement of cash flows). To the extent that cash must be used to support higher levels of accounts receivable (and other current trade assets), net of increases in accounts payable (and other current trade liabilities), that cash is not available as a return on capital and must be deducted from the determination of discretionary cash flow.

Estimating the incremental net trade working capital requirements should take into account the following factors:

- the historical, current and prospective relationship between net trade working capital and revenues;
- ratios involving key net trade working capital accounts such as days sales in accounts receivable, inventory turnover, days purchases in account payable and trends therein. These ratios were discussed in Chapter 2;
- the company's policies and practices with respect to key net trade working capital accounts, such as customer credit terms and inventory management;
- the impact of seasonality on net trade working capital accounts; and
- economic, industry and business developments that could impact future working capital requirements for the business.

Where the historical ratio of net trade working capital to revenues has remained relatively stable, and is expected to do so in the future, it is common to estimate the annual incremental net trade working capital requirements by applying the long-term growth rate in revenues to the net trade working capital balance at the valuation date.

For example, assume that Company S has net trade working capital of $2 million, and is expected to generate annual after-tax cash flows from operations of $1 million (before consideration of capital spending or working capital requirements) on revenues of $20 million. Based on general economic, industry and business analysis, the appropriate capitalization rate is estimated at 15%, which incorporates a long-term growth component of 3% per annum. Annual sustaining capital reinvestment is estimated at $160,000, net of the associated CCA tax shield. Assuming that the ratio of net trade working capital to sales will remain constant, it should further be assumed that Company S will require a 3% annual increase in its net trade working capital to support the underlying long-term growth assumption. This amounts to $60,000 (calculated as $2 million net trade working capital at the valuation date × 3% growth rate). Therefore, Company S's discretionary cash flow and capitalized cash flow would be determined as follows:

Exhibit 5D
Company S
Capitalized Cash Flow

After-tax operating cash flow	1,000,000
Less: sustaining capital reinvestment (net of related tax shield)	(160,000)
Less: annual incremental net trade working capital requirements	(60,000)
Estimated discretionary cash flow	780,000
Capitalization rate	15%
Capitalized cash flow	5,200,000

The above example illustrates the impact of long-term (perpetual) growth on annual net trade working capital requirements. However, in some cases a business may have a working capital surplus or deficiency at the valuation date. Where the working capital adjustment is a one-time occurrence, it should not be capitalized. Rather, the adjustment should be made following the determination of the enterprise value of the business (as noted in Exhibit 5A). Because working capital calculations are expressed on an after-tax basis, no further tax adjustment is required.

Capitalization Rates

The capitalization rate represents the rate of return on capital required by the market, given economic and industry conditions and in consideration of company-specific factors. Where normalized discretionary cash flows have been determined before interest expense (i.e., on an unlevered basis, as is the convention in the CCF methodology), the capitalization rate represents a weighted average cost of capital (WACC).

The WACC capitalization rate is based on what is believed to be a normalized capital structure (i.e., mix of debt and equity) for the business, regardless of the extent to which debt financing is actually used. Therefore, financial leverage and the associated risks are incorporated in the rate of return as opposed to the cash flow.

The capitalization rate is derived by deducting long-term perpetual growth from a discount rate. The long-term growth rate is normally comprised of the long-term inflation rate and, in some cases, long-term real growth (i.e., growth in excess of inflation). By way of example, if the discount rate is estimated at 15%, inflation at 2% and long-term real growth at 1%, then the capitalization rate is estimated at 12% (calculated as 15% less 2% inflationary growth less 1% real growth). This approach assumes discretionary cash flow will increase in perpetuity at the long-term growth rate.

The determination of discount rates and capitalization rates is subjective and complex. However, it should be based on:

- important underlying principles of business valuation such as the risk- return tradeoff, as discussed in Chapter 1;

- a thorough and objective assessment of prevailing industry, economic and credit market conditions and company-specific factors, similar to those underlying the determination of appropriate valuation multiples as set out in Chapter 4;

- ensuring internal consistency between the capitalization rate and the basis by which estimated discretionary cash flows were developed; and

- consideration of the achievability of the long-term growth rate embedded in the capitalization rate adopted.

The derivation of discount rates and capitalization rates is addressed in detail in Chapter 7. Dividing the estimated normalized discretionary cash flow by the capitalization rate results in the capitalized cash flow of the business.

Present Value of Existing Tax Pools

Recall that the present value of the income tax shield on sustaining capital reinvestment was deducted from the cost of sustaining capital expenditures when determining normalized discretionary cash flow. This adjustment accounts for the tax benefits associated with prospective capital expenditures. However, at the valuation date, most businesses have some amount of undepreciated capital cost (UCC) because of historical capital spending. In some cases, a business may also have a remaining balance in its cumulative eligible capital (CEC) accounts having regard to the acquisition of eligible capital property (ECP). Further, some businesses have unused income tax losses and other tax pools at the valuation date. The future benefits associated with the remaining balances in these income tax accounts should be accounted for separately. Adding the present value of the existing tax pools to capitalized cash flow results in the enterprise value of the business.

The discussion in this section is applicable where the outstanding shares of a business are being valued, and not the net assets. The reason for this is that, where assets are acquired, the existing tax pools do not flow to the buyer. Rather, in Canada an acquirer of assets is able to claim capital cost allowance on the "stepped up" value of the assets acquired, subject to the half-year rule where applicable. Furthermore, income tax loss carry-forwards do not flow through to a buyer on a purchase of assets. Rather, such losses remain with the seller, who normally can apply them against income created after a sale of assets. The subject of assets vs. shares is addressed later in this chapter.

The calculations set out below represent Canadian legislation. Where residual income tax pools reside in other countries, a different calculation may be required.

Undepreciated Capital Cost (UCC)

At any given point in time, businesses usually have a UCC balance on hand referable to their existing depreciable asset base. These UCC balances (by income tax asset class) typically can be determined by reference to the UCC schedule included in the income tax returns of the business for its latest fiscal year, combined with capital additions made since the end of its latest fiscal year. Pursuant to the Income Tax Regulations, each asset class is depreciated for income tax purposes at prescribed rates.

As illustrated in Chapter 3, for income tax asset classes that prescribe a declining balance methodology for determining CCA, the appropriate tax shield formula is as follows (note that this is the same as Formula 3.3, and repeated here for expediency):

Formula 5.3
Present Value of the Existing UCC Tax Shield
Calculated on a Declining Balance Basis

$$\frac{UCC \times D \times T}{(K + D)}$$

Where:

UCC = the undepreciated capital cost balance of the asset class

D = the depreciation rate (CCA rate) for income tax purposes, based on the rate prescribed for the class into which the asset falls according to the Income Tax Regulations

T = the marginal income tax rate at which CCA is deducted

K = the cost of capital (specifically, the nominal weighted average cost of capital)

This formula reflects the fact that there is no half-year rule on existing UCC balances. Where significant capital additions have been made after the previous fiscal year-end up to the valuation date and included in the UCC balance for purposes of the foregoing calculation, an adjustment may be required to take into account the half-year rule on those acquisitions. Under that rule, in the year capital assets are acquired only 50% of what otherwise would be the UCC on those capital additions is allowed for income tax purposes (see Formula 5.1).

Also as noted in Chapter 3, some classes of assets (e.g., Class 13 and 14) are eligible for CCA on a straight-line basis. The present value of the remaining CCA tax shield on these classes is determined as follows (note that this formula is the same as Formula 3.5, and repeated here for expediency):

Formula 5.4
Present Value of the Existing UCC Tax Shield Calculated on a Straight Line Basis

$$C \:/\: N \times T \times PVIFA_{K,N}$$

Where:

C = the cost of the asset

N = the number of years over which CCA is claimed

T = the marginal tax rate at which CCA is deducted

$PVIFA_{K,N}$ = the present value interest factor of an annuity for N years (being the remaining life for income tax purposes) at the nominal weighted average cost of capital (K)

As is the case for calculating the present value of the tax shield on sustaining capital expenditures, the cost of capital (K) used in the UCC calculations is the nominal weighted average cost of capital (i.e., the discount rate) and not the capitalization rate, which incorporates an element of long-term growth. The nominal rate is used because the future tax benefits are calculated in nominal dollars, which will erode in real terms over time.

Eligible Capital Property

As discussed in Chapter 3, where a business acquires an asset that qualifies as eligible capital property, it serves to increase the company's cumulative eligible capital (CEC) tax pool for income tax purposes. CEC can arise where goodwill is acquired from another business pursuant to an asset purchase (subject to a 75% inclusion rate), and where there have been incorporation costs or transactions other than the acquisition of goodwill that have resulted in an incremental CEC balance. Where a CEC balance exists, the present value of the related tax shield should be added to the value of the capitalized discretionary cash flows. The formula to apply for calculating the present value of the tax shield on existing CEC is as follows (note that this formula is the same as Formula 3.1, and is reproduced here for expediency):

Formula 5.5
Present Value of the Existing CEC Tax Shield

$$\frac{CEC \times D \times T}{(K + D)}$$

Where:

CEC = the balance remaining in the cumulative eligible capital tax pool at the valuation date

D = the tax depreciation rate on eligible capital property, which is currently (2012) 7%

T = the marginal tax rate

K = the company's cost of capital, which should be expressed as the nominal weighted average cost of capital (see Chapter 7)

Income Tax Loss Carry-Forwards

The benefit of income tax loss carry-forwards can be an important consideration in the determination of value. While the rules have changed over the years, at the time of writing (2012), non-capital losses can be carried back three years and forward twenty years, while net capital losses can be carried back three years and forward indefinitely. However, there are restrictions on the deductibility of loss carry-forwards where there has been a change in control of a corporation.

The *Income Tax Act* provides that net capital losses realized before the change in control are not deductible in computing taxable income or subsequent taxation years and cannot be carried back to years prior to the change in control. In addition, to the extent that the adjusted cost base of any capital property (other than depreciable property) exceeds the fair market value of such capital property, the adjusted cost base of the property will be reduced to fair market value and the reduction considered a capital loss of the taxation year immediately prior to the change in control. If there is a change of control, a company may elect to have disposed of any capital property in the year prior to the change and to have realized proceeds of disposition in excess of the adjusted cost base of that property up to fair market value. This has the effect of triggering capital gains to utilize the capital losses triggered on the change of control and step up the cost base of these assets.

Net capital losses include allowable business investment losses which have not been utilized within the maximum carry-forward period. On a change of control, such losses expire at the end of the carry-forward period and are not included in net capital losses.

Non-capital losses can only be carried forward or back to the extent of the corporation's income from the business in which the losses arose, and where the business of the corporation in which the losses arose, was carried on continuously since the change of control for profit or with reasonable expectation of profit. In addition, where the undepreciated capital cost of a class of depreciable property exceeds the total of: (i) the fair market value of that class at the date of the change of control; and (ii) the amount of CCA taken or terminal loss allowed in respect of that class for the taxation year ending on the acquisition of control, the undepreciated capital cost is deemed to be reduced to fair market value and the difference treated as capital cost allowance claimed for the year immediately preceding the change in control. There are similar provisions under which the excess of the CEC balance over its fair market value becomes a non-capital loss of the prior year. Non-capital losses from a business, therefore, can be carried backward or forward on a change of control and only under certain circumstances. Non-capital losses arising from losses on property and allowable business investment losses cannot be carried forward or back under any circumstances after a change in control. Importantly, a change in control will trigger a deemed year-end which must be considered in relation to the expiry dates of the losses.

The present value of available income tax loss carry-forwards should be added to capitalized cash flow. These losses represent incremental value pursuant to the fact that income taxes are deducted when deriving normalized discretionary cash flow. When applying income tax loss carry-forwards in the valuation of the shares of a business, consideration must be given to:

- whether the tax loss carry-forward is a capital, non-capital, or allowable business investment loss carry-forward. Generally, net capital losses are not considered as part of the business's value because capital loss carry-forwards can be applied only against capital gains; normalized discretionary cash flow rarely includes capital gains against which capital losses can be utilized. Moreover, in Canada net capital loss carry-forwards expire upon a change of control of the business. However, capital losses may have value where they can be applied to reduce a capital gain arising on an assumed disposition of redundant assets prior to a change in control, or where the circumstances of the valuation assume no change in control;

- the amount of the tax loss and the time over which it will likely be utilized. For example, in circumstances where a company has non-capital loss carry-forwards of $5 million and normalized pretax income is estimated at $1.25 million, the aggregate loss carry-forward would take approximately four years to be absorbed. In such circumstances its value should be discounted to present value to account for this timing difference. Normalized pretax income should take into account the indicated levels of normalized EBITDA as well as interest expense (based on the assumed debt structure) and capital cost allowance (based on the existing UCC balances and prospective capital expenditures);

- the date(s) the losses expire for income tax purposes. Any portion of the losses that cannot be used before expiry generally is of no value; and

- the appropriate income tax rate to apply. For example, where a business is eligible for the small business deduction, consideration may be given to maximizing the present value of non-capital loss carry-forwards by applying them against taxable income only in excess of the small business limit in any fiscal period. Residual non-capital loss carry-forwards would then be carried forward to ensuing fiscal periods. This then becomes a timing issue in loss carry-forward utilization.

An issue that sometimes arises is whether a buyer would pay for non-capital losses existing at the valuation date. In many cases involving open market transactions, buyers are reluctant to pay for such losses in full given that:

- the buyer may view its ability to utilize the losses as a form of synergy, which may or may not be paid for, depending on the negotiating positions of the buyer and seller and the terms of the deal; and

- there is an element of uncertainty as to when (and if) the non-capital losses will be utilized.

Accordingly, in a notional market context, it may be appropriate to discount the value of the non-capital losses otherwise determined.

Other Income Tax Pools

Some Canadian companies have additional income tax pools available such as unused investment tax credits, SRED tax credits and remaining resource exploration pools. Where they exist, each should be analyzed to determine:

- whether there are restrictions on utilization following transfer to an arm's length buyer;

- the likelihood and timing of their utilization; and

- whether any pool expires, and if so when.

Where appropriate, the present value of the benefit from these tax pools should be added to the capitalized cash flow of the business. Further, consideration should be given to the risk in the utilization of these tax pools and the likelihood that they would be paid for.

Deriving Equity Value

Adding the present value of the existing tax pools to capitalized cash flow results in the enterprise value of the business. As discussed in Chapter 4, *en bloc* equity value is determined by making the following adjustments to enterprise value:

- deducting interest-bearing debt and equivalent liabilities, net of excess cash on hand. As discussed in Chapter 2, some or all of the cash on hand at the valuation date may be required to support the on-going operations of the business and therefore would not be applied against outstanding debt;

- adding redundant assets, net of disposition costs and corporate income taxes where appropriate;

- adding or deducting prospective one-time items. Examples include prospective one-time costs or income and contingent liabilities (e.g., legal claims). These adjustments should be tax-effected, as applicable. Where an item is of a one-time nature, it should be adjusted for separately rather than capitalized. Prospective one-time items could also include prospective capital expenditures not accounted for in the estimation of sustaining capital spending (net of the related CCA tax shield). Where the one-time item is subject to uncertainty or will occur several years in the future (e.g., a contingent liability), that fact should be recognized by applying a probability factor or discount rate to the one-time item as appropriate; and

- adding (deducting) surplus (deficient) net operating assets at the valuation date. This includes excess or deficient net trade working capital compared to normalized levels as well as excess or deficient long-term operating assets or liabilities, where applicable.

Example of the Capitalized Cash Flow Methodology

Background Information

Company T is a privately held Canadian manufacturer of healthy snack foods sold in supermarkets and other food retailers under its branded name as well as private label offerings. The company is wholly owned by a single shareholder.

Company T began operations in the late 1990s and experienced strong organic growth through to 2009, given the strengthening trend toward healthier eating. In early 2010, Company T acquired the operations of a competitor, Company U, for $5 million, consisting of $3 million for equipment and $2 million for goodwill. The acquisition was a purchase of assets, financed through a long-term loan of $3 million and available cash of $2 million. Company T's cumulative eligible capital (CEC) account was credited for 75% of the goodwill acquired in the transaction. One-time costs associated with the acquisition were $300,000.

Company T's operating results for the past five fiscal years (2007 through 2011 actual) and its budget for fiscal 2012 are provided below. The company is expecting fiscal 2012 to be its strongest year ever, based on some new product introductions as well as reduced manufacturing costs attributable to new equipment acquired in 2011.

Exhibit 5E
Company T
Balance Sheets at December 31

	Actual					Budget
	2007	2008	2009	2010	2011	2012
Current Assets						
Cash					102,222	1,210,108
Accounts receivable	3,059,556	3,304,869	4,313,909	6,041,489	6,541,586	7,200,000
Inventory	2,392,195	3,148,387	3,627,322	4,529,599	4,957,951	5,500,000
Prepaid expenses	134,171	183,694	153,110	216,205	247,611	250,000
	5,585,922	6,636,949	8,094,341	10,787,293	11,849,370	14,160,108
Fixed Assets (net)	2,514,468	2,529,349	2,567,435	5,376,605	5,355,804	5,030,002
Goodwill				2,000,000	2,000,000	2,000,000
Due from related party					250,000	250,000
Total assets	8,100,390	9,166,299	10,661,776	18,163,898	19,455,174	21,440,110
Current liabilities						
Bank indebtedness	815,640	1,712,844	1,148,644	1,671,346		
Accounts payable and accrued liabilities	3,190,620	3,042,306	3,832,468	5,013,727	5,913,260	6,500,000
Income taxes payable	288,400	384,680	111,175	270,854	172,380	200,000
Current portion of long- term debt				288,776	316,112	352,800
	4,294,660	5,139,830	5,092,288	7,244,703	6,401,752	7,052,800
Long-term debt				2,684,300	2,395,524	2,079,412
Total liabilities	4,294,660	5,139,830	5,092,288	9,929,003	8,797,276	9,132,212
Shareholder equity						
Share capital	10,000	10,000	10,000	10,000	10,000	10,000
Retained earnings	3,795,730	4,016,469	5,559,488	8,224,895	10,647,898	12,297,898
	3,805,730	4,026,469	5,569,488	8,234,895	10,657,898	12,307,898
Total liabilities and equity	8,100,390	9,166,299	10,661,776	18,163,898	19,455,174	21,440,110

Exhibit 5F
Company T
Statements of Income and Retained Earnings
Fiscal Years Ending December 31

	Actual					Budget
	2007	2008	2009	2010	2011	2012
Net Sales	36,844,440	40,267,474	46,335,735	67,322,886	71,654,011	77,000,000
Cost of goods sold	30,587,519	34,109,345	38,756,060	56,237,513	59,953,182	63,700,000
Gross profit	6,256,921	6,158,129	7,579,675	11,085,373	11,700,829	13,300,000
Operating expenses	3,342,816	4,318,673	4,880,837	6,991,679	7,399,981	8,000,000
Interest expense	69,188	127,540	101,257	355,540	208,604	150,000
Foreign exchange loss (gain)	7,426	(68,151)	371,128	(253,684)	(116,906)	
Income before taxes	2,837,491	1,780,066	2,226,453	3,991,839	4,209,149	5,150,000
Income taxes	930,747	559,328	683,433	1,326,432	1,286,146	1,500,000
Net income	1,906,744	1,220,738	1,543,020	2,665,407	2,923,003	3,650,000
Opening retained earnings	1,888,987	3,795,730	4,016,469	5,559,488	8,224,895	10,647,898
Dividends		(1,000,000)			(500,000)	(2,000,000)
Closing retained earnings	3,795,730	4,016,469	5,559,488	8,224,895	10,647,898	12,297,898

Exhibit 5G
Company T
Cash Flow Statements at December 31

	Actual					Budget
	2007	2008	2009	2010	2011	2012
Net income for the period	1,906,744	1,220,738	1,543,020	2,665,407	2,923,003	3,650,000
Items not involving cash						
Depreciation and amortization	267,602	283,974	299,009	559,193	587,864	552,717
Loss (gain) on disposal of capital assets				(32,211)	18,464	
	2,174,346	1,504,712	1,842,029	3,192,388	3,529,331	4,202,717
Changes in non-cash working capital						
Accounts receivable	(147,803)	(245,313)	(1,009,041)	(1,727,580)	(500,097)	(658,414)
Inventory	(251,644)	(756,192)	(478,935)	(902,277)	(428,352)	(542,049)
Prepaid expenses	29,276	(49,523)	30,584	(63,095)	(31,406)	(2,389)
Accounts payable	(59,424)	(148,314)	790,163	1,181,259	899,533	586,740
Income taxes	279,051	96,280	(273,505)	159,679	(98,474)	27,620
	(150,543)	(1,103,062)	(940,734)	(1,352,014)	(158,796)	(588,492)
Cash Flow from Operations	2,023,803	401,651	901,295	1,840,374	3,370,535	3,614,225
Purchase of capital assets	(190,899)	(298,855)	(337,094)	(3,381,752)	(663,925)	(226,916)
Disposition of capital assets				45,600	78,399	
Purchase of goodwill				(2,000,000)		
Advances to related parties					(250,000)	
Cash Flow from Investing	(190,899)	(298,855)	(337,094)	(5,336,152)	(835,526)	(226,916)
Proceeds from long-term debt				3,000,000		
Repayment of long-term debt				(26,924)	(261,440)	(279,424)
Dividends paid		(1,000,000)			(500,000)	(2,000,000)
Cash flow from financing		(1,000,000)		2,973,076	(761,440)	(2,279,424)
Total change in cash flow	1,832,904	(897,205)	564,201	(522,702)	1,773,569	1,107,885
Net cash – beginning of year		(815,640)	(1,712,845)	(1,148,644)	(1,671,346)	102,223
Net cash – end of year	(815,640)	(1,712,845)	(1,148,644)	(1,671,346)	102,223	1,210,108

Other relevant facts regarding Company T are as follows:

- the company operates out of a leased facility now at 80% capacity;

- most of the company's revenues are generated through a few major Canadian retailers, although the company sells some of its products to U.S. customers. In addition, some of the company's raw materials are sourced from the U.S.;

- the business has minimal seasonality. Its net trade working capital accounts have remained fairly stable in relative terms and are expected to remain so;

- annual capital expenditures required in order to sustain the operations of Company T at their current level are estimated at $600,000. The average CCA rate on assets acquired is 30%;

- the sole shareholder holds the position of president of the company and is paid a salary and benefits that approximate market-rate remuneration. While other family members are not active in the business, the shareholder pays his spouse and children $150,000 per year for income splitting purposes;

- during 2011, the company advanced $250,000 to one of the shareholder's children to help her start a new business;

- at December 31, 2011, the company had a balance in its undepreciated capital cost pools of $4 million, with an average CCA rate of 25%, and a balance in its cumulative eligible capital account of $1.3 million;

- the company has a long-standing environmental issue. Following discussions with government authorities, the company has agreed to clean up the issue in fiscal 2012 at a cost of $400,000. This cost has been including in the company's 2012 budget under operating expenses;

- the company's corporate income tax rate has been declining over the years, and now stands at 28%; and

- based on an analysis of Company T's operations and growth prospects, as well as the industry dynamics and prevailing economic and credit market conditions, appropriate capitalization rates are believed to be in the range of 12% to 13%, representing weighted average cost of capital discount rates of 15% to 16%, less long-term growth of 3%.

Valuation Determination

As a first step, the balance sheet at the valuation date (December 31, 2011) should be segregated, as illustrated in Chapter 2. This analysis helps to establish the following:

- the sufficiency of net trade working capital, which should be assessed in connection with other tests such as various working capital ratios and seasonality. In this case, the balance sheet segregation exercise helps to support the plausibility of the assumption that no excess or deficient net trade working capital exists at the valuation date;

- that it is reasonable to apply the cash on hand against interest-bearing debt outstanding; and

- the redundant assets are comprised of a loan to related parties of $250,000.

Exhibit 5H
Company T
Balance Sheet Segregation at December 31, 2011

	Balances	Net Tangible Operating Assets	Intangible Assets	Financing	Redundant Assets
Current Assets					
Cash	102,222			102,222	
Accounts receivable	6,541,586	6,541,586			
Inventory	4,957,951	4,957,951			
Prepaid expenses	247,611	247,611			
	11,849,370	11,747,148		102,222	
Fixed Assets (net)	5,355,804	5,355,804			
Goodwill	2,000,000		2,000,000		
Due from Related Party	250,000				250,000
Total assets	19,455,174	17,102,952	2,000,000	102,222	250,000
Current liabilities					
Bank indebtedness					
Accounts payable and accrued liabilities	5,913,260	5,913,260			
Income taxes payable	172,380	172,380			
Current portion of long term debt	316,112			316,112	
	6,401,752	6,085,640		316,112	
Long term debt	2,395,524			2,395,524	
Total Liabilities	8,797,276	6,085,640		2,711,636	
Shareholders' equity					
Share capital	10,000	10,000			
Retained earnings	10,647,898	11,007,312	2,000,000	(2,609,414)	250,000
	10,657,898	11,017,312	2,000,000	(2,609,414)	250,000
Total liabilities and equity	19,455,174	17,102,952	2,000,000	102,222	250,000
Net trade working capital		5,661,508			

The next step is to normalize historical and budgeted operating results. In this regard, starting with pretax income, the following adjustments are made:

- depreciation and amortization are added back, because they are non-cash charges;

- similarly, the loss (gain) on the sale of fixed assets is added (deducted) as these also represent non-cash items;

- interest expense is added back, given that enterprise value is being determined;

- remuneration to related parties (the spouse and children of the shareholder) of $150,000 is added back, given that these individuals are not actively involved in the business;

- the expenses relating to the acquisition of another company in 2010 for $300,000 are added back, given that they are a non-recurring item; and

- the prospective clean-up costs of $400,000 in 2012 are added back because they are also a one-time item included in the 2012 federal budget.

No adjustment was made for foreign exchange gains and losses. This is because Company T's foreign exchange gains and losses relate to its normal operating activities (as opposed to financing or non-operating activities), and are based on the assumption that exchange rates have remained relatively stable in recent years and are expected to remain so.

The results of the adjusted EBITDA are shown below. As evidenced from this analysis, Company T's operating results prior to 2010 are significantly less than those in 2010 through to the 2012 budget. This is primarily due to the company's recent growth and its acquisition of another business in early 2010.

Following from the foregoing, and based on the analysis conducted, the normalized EBITDA is estimated in the range of $5.2 million to $5.8 million. The low end of the range approximates the average results for fiscal 2010 and 2011 actual. As a practical matter, many buyers tend to place the greatest weight on recent historical results. The high end of the range approximates the average of fiscal 2011 actual and the 2012 budget. Assuming that a budget is meaningful, it is normally taken into consideration when developing normalized EBITDA. In this case, however, it was assumed that a buyer would only place a weight of 50% on the budget, given the uncertainty of attaining the implied growth in revenues and profitability.

Exhibit 5I
Company T
Determination of Normalized EBITDA
Fiscal Years Ending December 31

	Actual					Budget
	2007	2008	2009	2010	2011	2012
Pretax income as reported	2,837,491	1,780,066	2,226,453	3,991,839	4,209,149	5,150,000
Adjustments						
Depreciation and amortization	267,602	283,974	299,009	559,193	587,864	552,717
Loss (gain) on sale of fixed assets				(32,211)	18,464	
Interest expense	69,188	127,540	101,257	355,540	208,604	150,000
Related party remuneration	150,000	150,000	150,000	150,000	150,000	150,000
Acquisition related costs				300,000		
Environmental clean-up						400,000
Normalized EBITDA	3,324,281	2,341,581	2,776,719	5,324,360	5,174,081	6,402,717
% of revenues	9.0%	5.8%	6.0%	7.9%	7.2%	8.3%
Selected range of Normalized EBITDA (rounded)						
Low - Average of Fiscal 2010 and 2011					5,200,000	
High - Average of Fiscal 2011 and 2012 (budget)						5,800,000

The next step in the analysis is the determination of enterprise value. In this regard, the estimated normalized EBITDA of $5.2 million to $5.8 million is adjusted as follows:

- income taxes are deducted at the cash tax rate of 28%;

- sustaining capital expenditures of $600,000 are deducted;

- the tax shield on sustaining capital expenditures is added back, using Formula 5.1. The mechanics of the calculation, at the low end, are as follows:

$$\frac{[\text{annual capex } \$600{,}000] \times [\text{CCA rate } 30\%] \times [\text{tax rate } 28\%]}{[\text{cost of capital } 15\%] + [\text{CCA rate } 30\%]} \times \frac{(1 + 0.5 \times 15\%)}{(1 + 15\%)} \quad [\text{half-year rule}]$$

= $104,696

Note that the cost of capital adopted (15%) represents the weighted average cost of capital before the 3% growth factor. The high end of the calculation uses the same formula, except that the cost of capital is 16% (instead of 15%), which reduces the present value of the tax shield; and

- incremental net trade working capital requirements of $169,845 are deducted. This amount is determined by applying the long-term growth rate of 3% (embedded in the capitalization rate) to the net trade working capital at December 31, 2011, of $5,661,508 (which can be derived from the "operating" column of the balance sheet segregation exercise, in Exhibit 5H). The existing net trade working capital balance is the appropriate base in this case, given the assumption that no surplus or deficiency in working capital existed at the valuation date. This calculation implies that Company T will require an additional $169,845 in net trade working capital each year in order to support its long-term growth rate of 3%.

The resultant discretionary cash flow falls in the range of $3,078,850 to $3,508,164. These figures are divided by the indicated capitalization rate of 12% and 13%, respectively. Note that the lower discretionary cash flow is applied against the lower capitalization rate to reflect the lesser degree of risk in maintaining that figure, and vice versa. The resultant capitalized cash flow falls in the range of $25,657,087 to $26,985,875.

In order to derive enterprise value, the capitalized cash flow needs to be adjusted for the following:

- the present value of the existing UCC shield. This is derived using Formula 5.5. The calculation at the low end is:

$$\frac{[\text{UCC } \$4,000,000] \times [\text{avg. CCA rate } 25\%] \times [\text{tax rate } 28\%]}{[\text{cost of capital } 15\%] + [\text{avg. CCA rate } 25\%]} = \$700,000$$

Recall that the half-year rule does not apply in the case of the existing UCC shield. As before, the cost of capital of 15% represents the weighted average cost of capital discount rate, before the growth factor. The calculation of the present value of the UCC shield at the high end of the range is the same, except that a cost of capital of 16% is used, thereby reducing the present value of the benefit; and

- the present value of the CEC tax shield, which arose on the acquisition of the assets of Company U in 2010. The calculation at the low end, based on Formula 5.5 is as follows:

$$\frac{[\text{CEC } \$1,300,000] \times [\text{CEC rate } 7\%] \times [\text{tax } 28\%]}{[\text{cost of capital } 15\%] + [\text{CEC rate } 7\%]} = \$115,818$$

The prescribed rate for amortizing the CEC tax shield is 7%. As before, the cost of capital represents the weighted average cost of capital discount rate, which is 15% at the low end and 16% at the high end.

The resultant enterprise value of Company T at December 31, 2011, falls in the range of $26.5 million to $27.8 million (rounded).

As a test of the enterprise value conclusions, the implied multiple of enterprise value to trailing normalized EBITDA for fiscal 2011 of 5.1x to 5.4x respectively could be compared to the EBITDA multiples of publicly traded companies and industry transactions, assuming that meaningful comparables can be identified. The caveats associated with such a comparison should be duly considered. As discussed in Chapter 4, these caveats include:

- the differences between the implied multiples of public companies and those of privately held companies, for reasons such as size, liquidity, information availability, etc.; and

- the possible impact of synergies, transaction structuring, relative negotiating position and other factors that could distort the multiples implied from open market transactions.

Exhibit 5J
Company T
Determination of Enterprise Value at December 31, 2011

	Low	High
Normalized EBITDA	5,200,000	5,800,000
Deduct: income taxes at 28%	(1,456,000)	(1,624,000)
Deduct: sustaining capital expenditures	(600,000)	(600,000)
Add: tax shield on sustaining capex	104,696	102,009
Deduct: incremental working capital requirements	(169,845)	(169,845)
Equals: normalized discretionary cash flow	3,078,850	3,508,164
Divided by: capitalization rate	12.0%	13.0%
Equals: capitalized cash flow	25,657,087	26,985,875
Add: present value of existing UCC tax shield	700,000	682,927
Add: present value of existing CEC shield	115,818	110,783
Equals: enterprise value	26,472,905	27,779,584
Rounded	26,500,000	27,800,000
Multiple of trailing normalized EBITDA		
Normalized EBITDA for fiscal 2011 (Exhibit 5I)	5,174,081	5,174,081
Enterprise value to EBITDA	5.1×	5.4×

The final step is the calculation of *en bloc* equity value. Commencing with the enterprise value above, the following adjustments are made:

- interest-bearing debt and equivalents are deducted. This amount is comprised of the term debt, including the short-term portion. The cash on hand is applied against the outstanding debt on the basis that it can be used to service the current obligation without impairing working capital, as illustrated in the balance sheet segregation exercise (Exhibit 5H);

- redundant assets are added, which in this case represent the advance to a related party of $250,000;

- the company needs to incur one-time clean up costs of $400,000 in 2012 because of its environmental issue. Since this is a non-recurring item, it is not included with discretionary cash flow. However it has to be adjusted for separately, net of the related tax shield of $112,000; and

- no adjustment is required for excess or deficient working capital (or other net operating assets), assuming that the balance falls within a normalized range at the valuation date.

The resultant *en bloc* equity value of Company T at the valuation date falls in the range of $23.8 million to $25.2 million.

As a further test of the equity value conclusions, the *en bloc* equity value could be compared to adjusted book value. The economic value of Company T's fixed assets and liabilities was not provided in this case. However, assuming that tangible net worth can be used as a proxy for adjusted net book value, that amount is $8,657,898 (calculated as the difference between shareholders' equity of $10,657,898 and goodwill of $2 million as recorded on the balance sheet relating to the acquisition of Company U). This implies intangible value in the range of $15.1 million to $16.5 million (rounded).

Exhibit 5K
Company T
Determination of Equity Value at December 31, 2011

	Low	High
Enterprise Value (Exhibit 5J)	26,500,000	27,800,000
Deduct: interest bearing debt and equivalents		
Term debt (including current portion)	(2,711,636)	(2,711,636)
Add: excess cash on hand	102,222	102,222
Add: redundant assets		
Loans to related party	250,000	250,000
Deduct: one-time adjustments		
Environmental clean-up	(400,000)	(400,000)
Add: tax shield thereon (at 28%)	112,000	112,000
Add (deduct): working capital surplus (deficiency)		
Equals: *en bloc* equity value	23,852,586	25,152,586
Rounded	$23,800,000	$25,200,000
Implied intangible value		
Adjusted net book value (tangible net worth)	8,657,898	8,657,898
Intangible value (rounded)	15,100,000	16,500,000

The Capitalized Cash Flow Methodology vs.
the Multiple of After-Tax Cash Flow Methodology

The multiple of after-tax cash flow methodology was discussed in Chapter 4. While that approach is substantially similar to the capitalized cash flow methodology, there are some important differences which can be illustrated through a comparison of the mechanics:

Exhibit 5L
Comparison of Methodologies

Capitalized Cash Flow Methodology	Multiple of After-Tax Cash Flow Methodology
Normalized EBITDA	Normalized EBITDA
	Deduct: depreciation and amortization
	Equals: normalized EBIT
Deduct: income taxes	Deduct: income taxes
	Equals: after-tax income
	Add: depreciation and amortization
Deduct: sustaining capital reinvestment	Deduct: sustaining capital reinvestment
Add: present value of tax shield on capex	
Deduct: incremental working capital required	
Equals: discretionary cash flow	Equals: after-tax cash flow
Divided by: capitalization rate	Multiplied by: after-tax valuation multiple
Equals: capitalized cash flow	
Add: present value of existing tax pools	
Equals: enterprise value	Equals: enterprise value

The adjustments below enterprise value for interest-bearing debt and equivalents (net of excess cash), redundant assets, one-time items and excess or deficient net operating assets are the same in each case. However, as evidenced from Exhibit 5L, the two methodologies differ in how enterprise value is derived, primarily through their treatment of:

- taxation. The multiple of after-tax cash flow methodology assumes that accounting depreciation and amortization approximate capital cost allowance for tax purposes, whereas the capitalized cash flow methodology incorporates more a more detailed analysis of existing tax pools and prospective tax pools based on sustaining capital expenditures;

- working capital. In its traditional form, the multiple of after-tax cash flow methodology does not account for incremental net trade working capital requirements in order to support long-term growth expectations, whereas the capitalized cash flow methodology does; and

- rates of return. The multiple of after-tax cash flow methodology adopts an after-tax valuation multiple, whereas the capitalized cash flow methodology adopts an after-tax capitalization rate. In theory, the two measures should be identical, given that the valuation multiple is the inverse of the capitalization rate. However, the two measures tend to be developed on a different basis. As a general rule, valuation multiples tend to be influenced to a larger degree by comparable public companies and industry transactions (as explained in Chapter 4), whereas capitalization rates tend to be developed based on a build-up approach (as discussed in Chapter 7).

While in theory the two approaches should arrive at the same value conclusions, as a practical matter this does not occur. In most cases, the capitalized cash flow methodology is preferred over the multiple of after-tax cash flow methodology due to the additional considerations that it incorporates.

Common Deficiencies in the Application of the Capitalized Cash Flow Methodology

Some of the more common deficiencies in the application of the capitalized cash flow methodology are as follows:

- misapplication in rapidly growing businesses. The capitalized cash flow methodology is best suited for businesses that exhibit relatively stable cash flow, such as mature companies. It is not well suited for companies where near-term growth is expected to be significant. Rather, the discounted cash flow methodology (discussed in Chapter 6) should be adopted in such situations. Attempting to incorporate a high growth rate into the capitalization rate adopted using the capitalized cash flow methodology can result in a misleading (usually overstated) valuation conclusion since it assumes the high rate of growth will continue in perpetuity;

- in the case of cyclical businesses, misapplication of the capitalized cash flow methodology sometimes arises where the computed average cash flow does not represent a complete industry cycle. Rather, placing greater weight on more recent results can lead to an overstatement or understatement of normalized cash flows depending on whether the calculation is made when the business is at a high point (overstatement) or low point (understatement) in its cycle. Attempting to compensate for cyclicality by adjusting the capitalization rate is a subjective exercise that can result in a misleading conclusion;

- working capital. One of the most common oversights is the omission of a deduction for incremental net trade working capital requirements from discretionary cash flow. Where the capitalization rate incorporates a long-term growth assumption, consideration must be afforded to the incremental net trade working capital required to support that growth. The magnitude of the impact depends on the level of net trade working capital in the business and the assumed rate of growth. Where one or both of these items is significant, the valuation conclusion could be materially distorted;

- sustaining capital expenditures. In some cases, insufficient analysis is conducted to determine the amount of sustaining capital required over the long term. This is particularly the case where a business has gone through a period of low capital spending prior to the valuation date, and that period is adopted as the baseline for estimating capital expenditure requirements over the long term. In most cases, all depreciable assets will have to be replaced at some point in order to sustain the indicated level of normalized EBITDA over the long term; and

- the long-term growth rate. It is important to recognize that the long-term growth rate embedded in the capitalization rate inherently assumes that a business can generate a return on capital in excess of its cost of capital in perpetuity. This can be an unfounded assumption given the competitive pressures in most industries. The determination of capitalization rates and common deficiencies in that regard are further addressed in Chapter 7.

Assets vs. Shares

The capitalized cash flow methodology as presented above assumes that the outstanding shares of a business are being valued. When the assets of a business are being valued, some modifications must be made to this methodology to recognize that in Canada:

- a buyer is entitled to claim capital cost allowance on the "stepped up" values assigned to the depreciable assets acquired in an arm's length transaction, subject to the half-year rule. However, the buyer does not receive the flow-through of existing tax pools, including undepreciated capital cost, cumulative eligible capital, any non-capital loss carry-forwards and other existing tax pools at the valuation date; and

- to the extent that the purchase price exceeds the amounts allocated to the net tangible assets acquired, that excess is attributable to eligible capital property and deductible for Canadian income tax purposes. At the time of writing (2012), 75% of eligible capital property is added to the CEC tax pool and deductible at a rate of 7% computed on a declining balance basis. The half-year rule is not applicable. The calculation of the present value of the tax shield on eligible capital property was provided in Formula 5.5 above.

The difference between the *en bloc* fair market of share equity vs. underlying net assets can be reconciled as follows:

Exhibit 5M
Assets vs. Shares

	En bloc fair market value of the shares
Deduct:	present value of existing tax pools (including UCC, loss carry-forward, etc.)
Add:	present value of the tax shield based on the purchase price of acquired assets
Equals:	fair market value of the net assets before consideration of the present value of the tax shield on eligible capital property
Add:	present value of the tax shield arising from eligible capital property
Equals:	*en bloc* fair market value of net assets

When determining the *en bloc* fair market value of equity pursuant to a purchase of assets, two specific issues arise:

- in a purchase of assets the buyer and seller normally agree on an allocation of the total value among tangible and intangible assets. When determining notional fair market value in the absence of actual negotiations, the determination of goodwill as a residual value necessitates a determination of the market value of the underlying net tangible assets and intangible assets that are recognized separately for income tax purposes (e.g., franchise agreements). Book values may not be indicative of market values for many assets, particularly non-current assets. Estimates of asset values are normally completed in the determination of adjusted net book value, as discussed in Chapter 3; and

- given the tax deductibility of eligible capital property (i.e., goodwill), the determination of notional fair market value of the assets becomes a circular calculation since a greater *en bloc* fair market value leads to a greater notional eligible capital property amount which in turn generates a greater CEC tax shield. That greater tax shield in turn leads to higher fair market value, and so on.

This circular calculation can be solved by grossing up the value of the goodwill (before consideration of the eligible capital property) by a CEC tax shield factor, determined as follows:

Formula 5.6
Cumulative Eligible Capital Tax Shield Factor Pursuant to a Purchase of Assets

$$1 - \frac{75\% \times D \times T}{(K + D)}$$

Where:

   T = the marginal income tax rate

   D = the applicable tax depreciation rate on eligible capital property (currently 7%)

   K = the cost of capital (expressed as a nominal weighted average cost of capital)

For example, if Company V has a tax rate of 30% and a cost of capital of 12%, then the CEC tax shield factor is:

$$1 - \frac{75\% \times 7\% \times 30\%}{(12\% + 7\%)} = .9171$$

Therefore, if the fair market value of the goodwill of Company V is estimated at $1 million prior to consideration of deduction for eligible capital property, then the fair market value of the goodwill inclusive of the eligible capital property will be calculated as follows:

Value before consideration of eligible capital property tax shield	$1,000,000
Divided by: CEC tax shield factor	0.9171
Equals: value inclusive of the eligible capital property tax shield	$1,090,394

The resultant present value of the CEC tax shield is $90,394, the difference between the two amounts.

Because of the tax advantages that accrue to a buyer of net assets where non-capital loss carry-forwards do not exist, the *en bloc* fair market value of underlying assets is typically greater than the fair market value of the shares.

However, that might not translate into a net benefit from the seller's perspective. As discussed in Chapter 11, a seller of shares typically pays income tax at a capital gains rate. However, where assets are sold, the seller could be subjected to recaptured depreciation as well as income tax on the sale of goodwill.

A second layer of taxation is incurred when the money is withdrawn from the company in the form of a taxable dividend. Depending on the circumstances, the difference in taxes to a seller between a share sale and an asset sale could be significant. This issue is examined in Chapter 11.

Example

Returning to the example of Company T above, assume that the depreciated replacement cost of its fixed assets was estimated at $8 million in aggregate, as contrasted with the UCC balance of $4 million. The average CCA rate on Company T's assets is 25%. Further assume that the economic values of all other assets and liabilities approximate their net book values. Also recall that Company T had a cost of capital in the range of 15% to 16% and a tax rate of 28%. A buyer acquiring the assets of Company T (as opposed to the shares) would make the following calculation:

Exhibit 5N
Company T
Fair Market Value of the Assets
Buyer's Perspective

	Low	High
Fair market value of the shares (Exhibit 5K)	23,800,000	25,200,000
Deduct: present value of existing tax pools		
UCC tax shield (Exhibit 5J)	(700,000)	(682,927)
CEC tax shield (Exhibit 5J)	(115,818)	(110,783)
Add: present value of the tax shield on acquired assets	1,308,696	1,271,657
Equals: fair market value of assets before		
consideration of tax shield on eligible capital property	24,292,877	25,677,947
Add: present value of the CEC tax shield (Exhibit 5O)	930,173	981,538
Equals: fair market value of assets	25,223,050	26,659,485
Premium over price of shares	1,423,050	1,459,485

The present value of the tax shield on the acquired assets is calculated using Formula 5.1, which at the low end of the range is as follows:

$$\frac{[\text{asset value } \$8,000,000] \times [\text{CCA rate } 25\%] \times [\text{tax rate } 28\%]}{[\text{cost of capital } 15\%] + [\text{CCA rate } 25\%]} \times \frac{(1 + 0.5 \times 15\%)}{(1 + 15\%)} \quad [\text{half-year rule}]$$

= $1,308,696

The calculation at the high end of the range is similar, except that the cost of capital is 16%, rather than 15%, thereby slightly reducing the present value of the tax shield.

Calculating the present value of the eligible capital property tax shield requires some additional effort. First, it is necessary to determine the adjusted net book value of the underlying assets prior to consideration of any tax impact. This amount is represented by the net book value of Company T of $10,657,898 at December 31, 2011, (Exhibit 5E) less goodwill for accounting purposes of $2 million. The economic value of the fixed assets of $8 million now replaces the net book value of the fixed assets of $5,355,804. Note that there is no need to adjust for the present value of the tax shield foregone since this calculation is being made pursuant to a purchase of assets rather than shares.

The adjusted net book value is deducted from the fair market value of the assets before consideration of the tax shield in order to derive goodwill before consideration of the gross-up. The CEC tax shield factor is determined using Formula 5.6, as follows (at the low end of the range):

$$1 - \frac{[75\% \text{ inclusion rate}] \times [7\% \text{ CEC rate}] \times [28\% \text{ tax rate}]}{[15\% \text{ cost of capital}] + [7\% \text{ CEC rate}]} = .9332$$

The calculation at the high end of the range is similar, except that a 16% cost of capital is used.

Deducting the pre-grossed-up amount from the grossed-up amount results in the present value of the tax shield on eligible capital property.

Exhibit 5O
Company T
Present Value of CEC Tax Shield

	Adjusted Net Book Value	Low	High
Fair market value of assets before consideration of tax shield on eligible capital property (Exhibit 5N)		24,292,877	25,677,947
Net book value at Dec. 31, 2011 per balance sheet (Exhibit 5E)	10,657,898		
Less: goodwill on balance sheet (Exhibit 5E)	(2,000,000)		
Add: economic value of fixed assets	8,000,000		
Less: net book value of fixed assets (Exhibit 5E)	(5,355,804)		
Adjusted net book value		11,302,095	11,302,095
Goodwill before consideration of gross-up (A)		12,990,783	14,375,853
CEC tax shield factor		0.9332	0.9361
Total value of goodwill (B)		13,920,956	15,357,390
Present value of the eligible capital property tax shield (B–A)		930,173	981,538

As noted in Exhibit 5N above, a buyer might be willing to pay approximately $2.2 million more for the assets of Company T than for the shares. However, from the seller's perspective, additional taxes would be paid within the corporation on account of:

- recaptured depreciation, to the extent the amount paid for depreciable assets is greater than the UCC balance, up to the original cost of the assets;

- capital gains, to the extent the amount paid for capital assets is greater than their cost base, and where the price paid for depreciable assets exceeds their original cost; and

- goodwill, 50% of which is taxable. The balance forms part of the capital dividend account (for privately held companies) and can be paid out to the shareholders on a tax-free basis.

Furthermore, where the shareholder is an individual, they will incur additional taxes on dividends received from the corporation (other than capital dividends).

The calculation of the taxes payable by Company T on an asset sale and the resultant net proceeds is calculated below. This calculation assumes that the $8 million paid for the fixed assets is less than their original cost and, therefore, the entire premium over the UCC base represents recaptured depreciation.

Exhibit 5P
Company T
Assets vs. Shares
Seller's Perspective

	Low	High	Low	High
Purchase price of assets (Exhibit 5N)			25,223,050	26,659,485
Less: income taxes on recapture				
Economic value of fixed assets	8,000,000	8,000,000		
Less: UCC	(4,000,000)	(4,000,000)		
Equals: recapture	4,000,000	4,000,000		
Income taxes at 28%			(1,120,000)	(1,120,000)
Less: income taxes on goodwill				
Goodwill acquired (Exhibit 5O)	13,920,956	15,357,390		
Taxable portion (50%)	6,960,478	7,678,695		
Income taxes at 28%			(1,948,934)	(2,150,035)
Equals: net proceeds remaining in Company T			22,154,117	23,389,450
Fair market value pursuant to a sale of shares (Exhibit 5K)			23,800,000	25,200,000
Difference (rounded)			(1,600,000)	(1,800,000)

The net proceeds remaining in Company T are approximately $1.6 million to $1.8 million less than the price that would be paid for the shares. Furthermore, there may be less favourable personal tax consequences to the seller, depending on how and when the net proceeds are extracted from the company. The issue of assets vs. shares in the context of an open market transaction is further addressed in Chapter 11.

The Capitalized Earnings Methodology

The capitalized earnings methodology is similar in many respects to the capitalized cash flow methodology, except that after-tax net income is used rather than discretionary cash flow. Given that cash flow rather than accounting earnings is typically a key value driver from the perspective of a corporate acquirer, the application of the capitalized earnings methodology is generally limited to circumstances where a business has relatively stable accounting earnings that approximate discretionary cash flows. Accounting earnings therefore serve as a reasonable proxy for cash flow. This is more commonly the case in less capital-intensive businesses.

Accounting earnings and discretionary cash flows of a business may differ significantly, particularly where:

- sustaining capital reinvestment does not approximate accounting depreciation;

- accounting policies include significant accruals, reserves, and cost deferrals for warranties, development costs, pension expenses, and the like;

- depreciation and amortization for accounting purposes differ significantly from capital cost allowance for income tax purposes; and

- there are changes over time in a business's working capital requirements as a result of the levels of operating activity.

Notwithstanding the foregoing, an earnings-based approach may provide insight into the reasonableness of a valuation conclusion determined using a cash flow-based approach. In addition:

- given that the price/earnings multiple remains a popular indicator in public market valuations, public company acquirers normally will consider the post-acquisition impact on their consolidated earnings per share when making an acquisition;

- use of an earnings-based approach has historically been accepted by the courts, although recent court decisions increasingly have emphasized a discounted cash flow methodology (see Appendix A); and

- earnings-based valuations are generally less complex than those based on cash flows and in some cases can serve to provide a rough estimate of value.

Components of the Capitalized Earnings Methodology

In its traditional form, the mechanics of the capitalized earnings methodology are as follows:

Exhibit 5Q
Capitalized Earnings Methodology

Normalized earnings before interest and taxes (EBIT)

Less:	income taxes
Equals:	net income
Divided by:	capitalization rate
Equals:	enterprise value
Deduct:	interest-bearing debt and equivalents (net of excess cash)
Add:	redundant assets
Add (deduct):	one-time adjustments
Add (deduct):	excess (deficient) net operating assets
Equals:	equity value

The starting point in the calculation is to estimate normalized EBIT in a similar manner to the multiple of EBIT methodology discussed in Chapter 4. When interpreting actual and projected operating results, it is important to understand the accounting policies adopted, and to ensure they have been consistently applied.

Income taxes are then deducted to derive net income (before interest expense). The capitalized earnings methodology assumes that EBIT approximates pre-tax cash flow before interest expense. Net income is divided by the capitalization rate to determine enterprise value. As with other methodologies, equity value is derived by:

- deducting interest-bearing debt and equivalents outstanding (net of excess cash on hand);
- adding the net realizable value of redundant assets;
- adding or deducting prospective one-time items; and
- adding (deducting) any excess (deficient) net operating assets at the valuation date.

The Capitalized Cash Flow Methodology vs. the Capitalized Earnings Methodology

A comparison of the capitalized cash flow approach with the capitalized earnings approach reveals the following:

- the capitalized cash flow methodology specifically addresses the tax shield on capital cost allowance, whereas the capitalized earnings methodology assumes depreciation and amortization expense approximates capital cost allowance;

- the capitalized cash flow methodology specifically addresses sustaining capital expenditures, whereas the capitalized earnings methodology assumes sustaining capital approximates depreciation and amortization expense; and

- the capitalized cash flow methodology deducts incremental net trade working capital required to support long-term growth in the determination of discretionary cash flow, whereas incremental net trade working capital requirements are not factored into the capitalized earnings methodology.

The capitalized cash flow methodology tends to require more rigour in its analysis, and emphasizes cash flow, which is a better determinant of value when contrasted with accounting earnings. Consequently, the capitalized cash flow methodology is preferred.

Example of the Capitalized Earnings Methodology

Returning to the example of Company T, recall that normalized EBITDA was estimated in the range of $5.2 million to $5.8 million. Depreciation and amortization are deducted from this amount using the same basis adopted in the determination of normalized EBITDA (i.e., an average of fiscal 2010 and 2011 at the low end, and an average of fiscal 2011 and 2012 at the high end). This ensures internal consistency. The resultant normalized EBIT falls in the range of approximately $4.6 million to $5.2 million. Deducting income taxes at 28% results in normalized net income in the range of approximately $3.3 million to $3.8 million (Exhibit 5R).

Normalized net income is divided into the capitalization rates of 12% to 13% to derive an enterprise value in the range of approximately $27.8 million to $29.0 million. As before, adjustments are made to:

- deduct interest-bearing debt and equivalents (net of excess cash);

- add redundant assets (the loan to related parties);

- deduct the cost of the prospective one-time environmental clean-up, net of taxes; and

- no adjustments are required on account of working capital (or other net operating assets).

The resultant *en bloc* equity value falls in the range of $25.1 million to $26.4 million.

Exhibit 5R
Company T
Determination of Fair Market Value
Capitalized Earnings Methodology at December 31, 2011

	Low	High
Normalized EBITDA (Exhibit 5I)	5,200,000	5,800,000
Less: depreciation and amortization	(573,528)	(570,290)
Equals: normalized EBIT	4,626,472	5,229,710
Deduct: income taxes at 28%	(1,295,412)	(1,464,319)
Equals: net income	3,331,060	3,765,391
Divided by: capitalization rate	12.0%	13.0%
Equals: enterprise value	27,758,829	28,964,545
Deduct: interest-bearing debt and equivalents		
Term debt (including current portion)	(2,711,636)	(2,711,636)
Add: excess cash on hand	102,222	102,222
Add: redundant assets		
Advances to related party	250,000	250,000
Deduct: one-time adjustments		
Environmental clean-up	(400,000)	(400,000)
Add: tax shield thereon (at 28%)	112,000	112,000
Add (deduct): working capital surplus (deficiency)		
Equals: *en bloc* equity value	25,111,415	26,317,131
Rounded	25,100,000	26,400,000

The *en bloc* equity value conclusion in the range of $25.1 million to $26.4 million derived using the capitalized earnings methodology is slightly greater than the conclusion in the range of $23.8 million to $25.2 million derived by the capitalized cash flow methodology (Exhibit 5K). This difference is primarily due to the following:

- the capitalized earnings methodology assumes depreciation approximates sustaining capital expenditures. However, the deduction for depreciation and amortization of approximately $570,000 is less than sustaining capital expenditures of $600,000; and

- the capitalized earnings methodology does not account for incremental net trade working capital requirements to support growth, which represent a deduction of approximately $170,000 per annum under the capitalized cash flow methodology (Exhibit 5J).

Therefore, in this case, the results derived pursuant to the capitalized earnings methodology may overstate the fair market value of the shares of Company T. However, the capitalized earnings methodology does serve to support the reasonableness of the conclusions derived with the capitalized cash flow methodology.

Levered Approach to the Capitalized Earnings Methodology

A variation of the capitalized earnings methodology (and capitalized cash flow methodology) is to calculate earnings on a levered basis. Pursuant to this approach, interest expense is deducted from normalized EBIT to derive pretax income. (Interest expense is based on a normalized amount of debt outstanding at the valuation date.) Taxes are deducted from pretax income (which incorporates the tax deductibility of interest expense) to derive after-tax earnings which are then divided into a capitalization rate. Since interest expense is deducted from the earnings base, the capitalization rate represents a levered cost of equity. The result is equity value. Equity value is then adjusted for redundant assets, prospective one-time items and excess or deficient net operating assets. Pursuant to the equity value approach, no deduction is made for interest-bearing debt and equivalents. Rather, a financing adjustment is made to the extent that a normalized amount of debt outstanding differs from the actual amount of debt outstanding. A comparison of the unlevered approach and the levered approach is as follows:

Exhibit 5S
Unlevered Approach vs. Levered Approach

Unlevered Approach	Levered Approach
Normalized EBIT	Normalized EBIT
	Deduct: normalized interest expense
	Equals: pretax income
Deduct: income taxes	Deduct: income taxes
Equals: normalized net income (unlevered)	Equals: normalized net income (levered)
Divided by: capitalization rate (weighted average cost of capital)	Divided by: capitalization rate (levered cost of equity)
Equals: enterprise value	Equals: equity value (before adjustments)
Deduct: interest-bearing debt and equivalents	Add (deduct): financing adjustment
Add: redundant assets	Add: redundant assets
Add (deduct): one-time adjustments	Add (deduct): one-time adjustments
Add (deduct): excess (deficient) net operating assets	Add (deduct): excess (deficient) net operating assets
Equals: equity value (*en bloc*)	Equals: equity value (*en bloc*)

In theory, the levered approach and the unlevered approach should result in the same conclusions, if applied on an internally consistent basis with respect to normalized debt levels and capitalization rates. This concept is demonstrated in Chapter 7.

As a practical matter, when the levered approach has been adopted, it is often based on prevailing interest expense levels. While this avoids the necessity of making a financing adjustment, it assumes the existing capital structure of the business represents a normalized level of debt and equity, which may not be accurate.

The Dual Capitalization Methodology

The dual capitalization methodology is a variation of the capitalized cash flow methodology. It recognizes that different risks may attach to the net tangible operating assets of a business than may attach to the value of the business represented by intangible value (or goodwill). In comparison with more conventional valuation methodologies, the dual capitalization methodology requires additional subjective estimates and is highly theoretical. As such, it is infrequently used in practice. Where it is adopted, it is usually applied as a test of the value determined by other going concern methodologies.

While the dual capitalization methodology is seldom used in the valuation of a business *en bloc*, a variation of the dual capitalization methodology, referred to as the excess earnings method, is sometimes adopted for the purpose of establishing the value of an intangible asset, as discussed in Chapter 9.

The dual capitalization methodology involves segregating the enterprise value of a business into two components:

- the value attributable to the return a business generates on its net tangible operating assets; and
- the value attributed to the ability of the business to generate returns in excess of appropriate levels of return on its net tangible operating assets.

Based on the presumption that risk attaching to intangible value is higher than the risk attaching to tangible assets, capitalization rates attributed to returns on the former are taken to be higher than those attributed to returns on the latter. Accordingly, the dual capitalization methodology requires an estimate of two capitalization rates. The first (lower) capitalization rate is applied to cash flow presumed derived from net tangible operating assets, and the second (higher) capitalization rate is applied to cash flow presumed derived from intangible assets (or goodwill).

By its nature, the dual capitalization methodology is a hybrid asset and cash flow (or earnings) valuation methodology. Discretionary cash flow selection and capitalization rate determination requires the same considerations in the dual capitalization methodology as in the capitalized cash flow methodology. As with other going concern valuation methodologies, equity value is derived by deducting interest-bearing debt and equivalents (net of excess cash), adding redundant assets, and adjusting for prospective one-time items and any excess or deficient net operating assets.

As an example of the dual capitalization methodology, assume Company W operates a chain of grocery stores and generates $3 million of annual discretionary cash flow. Company W has net tangible operating assets $16 million. Adopting a capitalization rate of 15%, the enterprise value of Company W is estimated at $20 million.

Assuming appropriate capitalization rates on net tangible operating assets and intangible assets to be 12% and 20% respectively, the enterprise value of Company W would be estimated pursuant to the dual capitalization methodology as follows:

Exhibit 5T
Company W
Determination of Enterprise Value
Based on the Dual Capitalization Methodology

Discretionary cash flow		3,000,000
Less: return on net tangible operating assets		
Net tangible operating assets	16,000,000	
Return thereon at	12%	
		(1,920,000)
Return on intangible assets		1,080,000
Capitalized at		20%
Intangible value		5,400,000
Add: net tangible operating assets		16,000,000
Enterprise value		21,400,000

The discretionary cash flow stream associated with Company W's net tangible operating assets is 12% of $16 million, or $1,920,000. Therefore, of the $3 million annual discretionary cash flow generated by Company W, $1,080,000 is attributable to intangible value. Since intangible value typically faces greater risk than net tangible operating assets, the rate of return for intangible assets should be greater than the rate of return for net tangible operating assets, in this case 20%. The capitalized value of Company W's intangible value ($5.4 million) is added to the net tangible operating assets of $16 million to develop an estimated enterprise value for Company W of $21.4 million. The value derived using the dual capitalization methodology is higher than the $20 million derived pursuant to the capitalized cash flow approach. Therefore, consideration should be given to revisiting the capitalization rates adopted in each case, to ensure that no components of value have been understated or overstated.

A higher value produced by the dual capitalization methodology may indicate insufficient emphasis was placed on underlying tangible asset values when a using single capitalization rate. Conversely, a lower value using the dual capitalization methodology may indicate insufficient recognition of a comparatively high implied intangible value when a single capitalization rate was used.

A second application of the dual capitalization methodology as a test method is to use it to force out the implied rate of return on intangible value inherent in the initial value determination. This is done by determining an appropriate rate of return on net tangible operating assets, and then determining the imputed rate of return on the implied intangible value component of the initial value determination. This imputed rate of return is then assessed for reasonableness on a stand-alone basis and as compared to the selected return on net tangible operating assets.

In the example of Company W above, the enterprise value was estimated at $20 million using the capitalized cash flow methodology. This suggests intangible value of $4 million (calculated as $20 million less $16 million of net tangible operating assets). Given the return on intangible assets of $1,080,000 as indicated in Exhibit 5T, the implied rate of return on intangible value is 27% (calculated as $1,080,000 / $4 million of intangible value). The reasonableness of the implied rate of return of 27% on intangible value must be assessed both relative to the 12% return required on net tangible operating assets and to the 15% composite return required as the selection of a single capitalization rate. If there had been an expectation that the rate of return on intangible value should have been 20%, the composite capitalization rate (and hence the value determination) would require reconsideration.

The foregoing describes the dual capitalization methodology as a variation of the capitalized cash flow methodology. The dual capitalization methodology also has equal applicability as a variation of the capitalized earnings methodology, where accounting earnings form the capitalization base.

To summarize, the dual capitalization methodology can assist in the assessment of the overall value conclusion determined using a single capitalization technique. In addition, it serves as a reminder of the integration of the various value components. However, it is not widely used in the valuation of a business *en bloc*, and rarely is appropriate as a primary valuation methodology. That said, a variation of the dual capitalization methodology (termed the excess earnings approach) is sometimes adopted for the valuation of intangible assets, as discussed in Chapter 9.

Summary

The capitalized cash flow methodology has applications both as a stand-alone valuation methodology and as the terminal value component of the discounted cash flow methodology. In both cases, it assumes relative stability in the level of cash flow. The capitalized cash flow methodology is premised on estimating normalized discretionary cash flows, normally defined as EBITDA, less income taxes, sustaining capital reinvestment (net of the related CCA tax shield) and incremental net trade working capital requirements. Discretionary cash flows are normally determined on an unlevered basis (i.e., before debt servicing costs comprised of interest expense net of tax and changes in debt principal outstanding). Accordingly, the capitalization rate reflects a weighted average cost of capital. Dividing the normalized discretionary cash flow by the capitalization rate derives the capitalized cash flow. Adding the present value of existing tax pools results in the enterprise value of the business. Equity value is determined by deducting interest-bearing debt and equivalents (net of excess cash), adding the net realizable value of redundant assets, adding (deducting) one-time adjustments and adding (deducting) any excess (deficient) net operating assets (e.g., working capital) at the valuation date.

Where the assets of a business are being valued, the fair market value of the shares is adjusted to deduct the present value of existing tax pools and to add the present value of the tax shield based on the cost of the capital assets acquired and the present value of the eligible capital property tax shield on the acquisition of goodwill.

The capitalized earnings methodology is to some extent a simplified version of the capitalized cash flow methodology. However, its application is usually limited to businesses that are less capital intensive and possibly as a test of the value conclusions derived pursuant to cash flow-based valuation approaches. Similarly, the dual capitalization methodology is sometimes adopted as a test of valuation conclusions, but rarely as a primary valuation methodology.

Chapter 6

The Discounted Cash Flow Methodology

Introduction

The discounted cash flow (DCF) methodology is commonly seen as the most theoretically sound valuation methodology because it forces detailed analysis of key forecast and valuation variables and hence facilitates an understanding of important external and internal business drivers, revenue and expense behaviour and business risks. Accordingly, where meaningful financial projections are available, the DCF methodology should usually be adopted, either by itself or in conjunction with other valuation methodologies. In open market transactions, sophisticated buyers and investors normally adopt the DCF methodology when evaluating an acquisition target.

The DCF methodology involves projecting the discretionary cash flows for a period of time (normally three to five years) then discounting them at an appropriate rate of return given the risk profile of the business, industry factors and prevailing economic and credit market conditions. The relevant forecast period depends on factors such as the term of prevailing contracts, expansion plans, cyclicality and other factors. Importantly, the forecast discretionary cash flow must reflect the capital expenditures and incremental net trade working capital required to meet these forecast operating results. A terminal value is then developed to capture the value of the business beyond the forecast period, which value also is discounted to its present value amount. The present value of existing tax pools is added to determine the enterprise value of the business. Equity value is determined by deducting interest-bearing debt and equivalents, adding the net realizable value of redundant assets, adding (deducting) any excess (deficient) net operating assets at the valuation date and adjusting for other items that have not otherwise been accounted for in the cash flow forecast.

The validity of the value determinations developed from the application of the DCF methodology, as with all other business valuation methodologies, is dependent upon the objectivity, quality of analysis, thought process, experience and judgment of those completing the analysis. Integral to a meaningful DCF valuation is a reasonable and internally consistent financial forecast. In this regard, it is important that discretionary cash flows are neither overly aggressive nor overly conservative, all assumptions are applied consistently within the DCF model, and the discount rates (i.e., rates of return) used are reasonable and internally consistent within the DCF model.

Analyzing Forecasts

Prior to adopting the DCF methodology, it is essential to ensure that forecast operating results are both realistic and developed in an internally consistent manner; otherwise, the DCF methodology becomes a meaningless mathematical exercise that may even result in misleading conclusions. Ideally, the forecast operating results should include a complete set of financial statements (income statement, balance sheet and cash flow statement) and underlying assumptions with supporting rationale. When analyzing the forecast, consideration should be given to the following:

- who prepared the forecast and for what purpose;
- the time period of the forecast;
- the level of detail in the forecast;
- the key variables and underlying economic drivers;
- underlying assumptions and internal consistency;

- whether inflation has been built into the forecast; and
- what reasonableness tests have been used to assess the plausibility of the forecast results.

Who Prepared the Forecast and for What Purpose?

It is important to determine who prepared the forecast, the extent of their experience, biases they may have had or that may have been imposed upon them when developing the forecast, and the process they adopted when developing, reviewing and finalizing the forecast. Ideally, those involved will be the same people who developed prior years' forecasts, the forecasting accuracy of which can be used as one benchmark to assess the probability of achievement of the most recent forecast.

The quantity and quality of input received from various disciplines within the organization (e.g., divisional management, sales and marketing, manufacturing, human resources, and so on) are important considerations in forecast analysis. Some management groups have a formal strategic planning process while others are less rigorous when preparing forecasts. Where a forecast goes through a detailed review and approval process by several levels in an organization (including board approval) it will likely better reflect management's consensus expectations for the business than otherwise would be the case.

The Forecast Period

Long-term forecasts are typically prepared for a three to five year period, with a five-year period being common in long-term strategic planning. In both the preparation and evaluation of long-range forecasts, each successive forecast year is subject to an ever increasing degree of uncertainty. It should be noted however that, in the DCF methodology, any year for which financial results are not specifically projected will fall into the terminal value component discussed below.

Because uncertainty increases with the number of years forecast and is exacerbated by a rapidly changing economic and business environment, a cash flow forecast period may be as short as one year (i.e., next fiscal year's budget) or as long as 10 years. Where the forecast period is only one year, then the capitalized cash flow methodology is normally adopted (see Chapter 5). Depending on the circumstances, the reliability of forecast cash flow may diminish significantly beyond a short time frame. Business prospects beyond the forecast period are then a component of the terminal value in the DCF methodology.

The determination of the length of the forecast period stems from the circumstances of the business. The forecast period may be dictated by the finite, or term-certain, nature of the business, such as for:

- single project ventures, where value would relate to the cash flow to be derived over the term of the project;
- business ventures limited in life to the remaining term of a contract or agreement where there is no right of renewal, or where relocation is not feasible following the remaining term of a premises lease; and
- resource extraction businesses, where the depletion of a non-renewable resource is expected to occur over a predicable time period without replacement.

However, most businesses are presumed to have an infinite life. Therefore, the forecast period for each will depend on specific circumstances. In general, the forecast period should be sufficiently long to consider:

- the likely reactions of the business to known or prospective economic, technological and industry changes, including the likely effects on discretionary cash flow of planned expansion, product line changes, or changes in the competitive environment. For example, if a capital expansion program is planned over the next four years, and it takes three years after the capital expenditure period to fully realize the benefits of the expansion, then it would be appropriate to extend the forecast period to seven years;

- the reliability and likely effect of trends affecting cash flow. The forecast period should include anticipated revenue growth reflecting market maturation during the forecast period and the effects of a changing cost-of-sales structure or other cost components;

- where the business has historically been, and prospectively is expected to be, subject to cyclicality, the forecast period should be sufficiently long to demonstrate cash flow trends during an entire business cycle. The forecast utilized in the terminal value calculation should reflect what are expected to be trend operating results; and

- the prospective synergies anticipated to be derived from an acquisition where the forecast is being prepared in connection with an open market transaction (as contrasted with a notional market valuation conducted on a stand-alone basis). Some expected synergies, such as administrative efficiencies, may be realized quickly. Conversely, other expected synergies such as benefits from facility and product integration and rationalization may take longer to materialize, if they are realized at all.

Level of Detail in the Forecast

Many businesses prepare detailed budgets in respect of their next fiscal year and high-level projections for the ensuing two to four years. The usefulness of forecasts that have not adequately considered the key underlying variables may be suspect. While a forecast may or may not prove to be accurate in hindsight, it is the rigour of the analysis underlying a forecast and the adoption of reasonable and internally consistent assumptions that dictate whether the forecast is credible and can be adopted as a basis for determining value.

It is usually helpful where revenues can be forecast by product and service offering, major customer, geographic region and other relevant parameters. While such an exercise may be difficult and somewhat subjective, it helps in assessing the reasonableness and internal consistency of the projections and the risk profile of the business. For example:

- where new product and service introductions are expected to represent a significant component of future revenue, additional investment is normally required in sales and marketing, and R&D. Such an analysis also helps in assessing the life cycle of the product and service offerings;

- where new customers will be required in order to generate revenue, competitive pricing and competitive reactions could influence the risk profile of the business; and

- where the forecast contemplates geographic expansion, additional transportation costs, foreign exchange fluctuations, political risks and other factors may have to be considered.

A similar level of analysis should be conducted for operating costs. Ideally, such costs would be segregated into fixed costs, variable costs and step costs (i.e., costs that increase upon attaining certain capacity limitations). This separation helps in conducting sensitivity analysis on the forecast assumptions. Details of capital expenditures are also important including, where possible, the division of prospective capital expenditure requirements between sustaining capital and growth capital.

A forecast should include a full set of financial statements (income statement, balance sheet and cash flow statement) to ensure completeness and internal consistency in the forecast assumptions. From a business management perspective, the more time and effort expended on preparing a forecast, the more useful the forecasting exercise.

Key Variables and Economic Drivers

Every industry and business has a set of economic drivers that collectively influence business risk at a given point in time. Key drivers normally have a direct impact on revenues, operating costs and capital employed. When reviewing financial forecasts particular attention should be devoted to these important variables. As a general guideline, such a review would include consideration of revenues, operating costs and capital investment.

With respect to revenues, the following items should be considered:

- assumptions regarding current and future selling prices. It is often helpful to review historic trends to determine when and why price changes have occurred and their impact on revenues (i.e., as an assessment of price elasticity). Where significant increases in unit selling prices are anticipated, the effect on forecast revenues should be clearly explained;

- sales volume. An assessment should be made as to whether growth (or decline) in sales volume is due to industry growth or changes in market share. Further, the underlying reasons for growth, be they product line extensions, new products and services, geographic expansion and so on, require analysis. The source(s) of anticipated growth may directly impact risk inherent in the projections. As a general rule, increases in market share are more difficult to realize;

- current and future foreign exchange rates, where goods and services are sold in other currencies. Changes in foreign exchange rates can also impact the degree to which a business's goods and services are competitive in the global market place and, by extension, may impact sales volumes; and

- reasonableness of projected returns. It is not uncommon for long-term projections to be aggressive in the expectation that planned expenditures will generate exceptional returns. Consideration should be given to whether those returns are reasonable in light of economic and industry projections, and anticipated competitive reaction.

With respect to operating costs, the following should be considered:

- the cost structure and the degree of operating leverage (i.e., the degree to which operating expenditures are fixed as opposed to variable). Cost structure relates both to cost of sales and other cash operating costs (i.e., excluding depreciation and amortization) and any interest expense associated with financing. The greater the comparative fixed cost component as a percentage of total cost, the greater the sensitivity of the operating results to revenue change and vice versa;

- where revenue growth is anticipated, an assessment should be made as to which costs will increase and to what degree. Many businesses incur step costs when certain capacity limitations are met (i.e., a significant increase in costs in order to accommodate higher sales volumes). For example, where revenue growth is expected, the number of sales staff may have to be increased because each sales person is limited as to the number of customer accounts they can effectively handle. Determining where step costs may be incurred requires an understanding of where capacity limitations exist in all aspects of a business's operations, including sales and marketing, production, distribution, management and administration, and other areas; and

- whether one-time costs will be incurred with respect to new product line introductions, facilities start-up costs, and so on.

With respect to capital investment requirements, the following should be considered:

- capital expenditures representing sustaining capital and growth capital requirements. Recall that sustaining capital includes expenditures required in order to maintain a competitive market position. Growth capital represents incremental spending to accommodate higher sales volumes, incremental operating efficiency or other benefits that serve to increase profitability;

- working capital to meet growth expectations. Revenue growth usually necessitates increased net trade working capital requirements. To the extent cash has to be used to finance accounts receivable, inventories or other working capital accounts, it is not available for distribution to owner(s) or for reinvestment in the business. Accordingly, it must be deducted when determining discretionary cash flow; and

- the projections must be assessed in light of the business's production, distribution and service delivery capacities. Specifically, the practical operating capacity of the plant facilities, production equipment, service vehicles and other resources must be considered to determine whether capacity constraints exist. Where capacity additions are required, they should be accounted for in the capital expenditure projections.

Underlying Assumptions

Forecasts are premised on assumptions regarding revenues, cost behaviour, capital requirements, and other variables. Thorough, objective analysis of those assumptions is important. In particular, it is important that assumptions be: (i) complete; (ii) reasonable; and (iii) internally consistent.

Completeness refers to ensuring that the forecast assumptions encompass all key variables believed to impact prospective discretionary cash flows. All sources of revenues, operating costs, fixed asset additions and working capital requirements should be accounted for. Completeness also addresses whether all materially relevant factors, including the variables that influence economic trends, market growth, competitive behaviour, and so on, have been considered.

Reasonableness means the underlying assumptions should be plausible given the past operating performance of the business, and current and prospective industry and economic conditions. It is not unusual for assumptions to be based on overly optimistic expectations that downplay the risks involved. Therefore, forecasts should be reviewed with some skepticism.

An internal consistency review should be completed to assess the validity of the forecast as a whole. It should address issues such as:

- whether forecast marketing and selling expense increases are consistent with increased revenue forecasts;

- whether existing and planned production and service capacities are consistent with increased revenue forecasts; and

- whether forecast labour, equipment and other production and distribution costs are consistent with forecast capacity increases.

There must be internal consistency with respect to the type of operating costs (e.g., variable, fixed and step costs) and assumptions regarding sales volumes. Similarly, capital expenditure requirements must be consistent with revenue assumptions.

Inclusion (Exclusion) of Inflation

It is important to consider whether inflation has been incorporated in the forecast and, if it has, the basis on which it has been included since discount rates applied to forecast cash flows can be either nominal rates of return which include an inflation component (the more commonly used rate), or are real rates, which do not. As a result, if a forecast that does not include an inflation component is discounted by a nominal rate of return, the resultant value determination will be understated (i.e., the discount rate will be overstated by the inflation component included in it). Conversely, if a forecast that includes an inflation component is discounted by a real rate of return, the resultant value determination will be overstated (i.e., the discount rate will be understated by the inflation component excluded from it).

Regardless of whether inflation has been included in forecasts, it is important to consider the relative inflationary impact of cost and revenue components. For example:

- businesses that operate in highly price-sensitive industries may have difficulty passing on cost increases to customers. Where this is the case, the forecast should contemplate that the business may experience an erosion of its profit margin in real terms;

- where a business's key manufacturing input is a commodity (e.g., steel, wheat or oil) the near-term and long-term selling price and raw material cost-trend forecasts (in either real or nominal terms consistent with the inclusion or exclusion of inflation in the forecast) of the commodity should be considered;

- where a business has long-term fixed price contracts with either suppliers or customers, the forecast should be consistent with those terms;

- certain expenses such as rent are fixed for a period of time. Expense increases upon contract renewal or over time should be reflected in the forecast; and

- for those businesses with collective bargaining agreements, the terms of the agreement should be considered when forecasting labour costs.

It follows that the growth rates employed in forecasting revenue and expense streams may be different. Accordingly, it is important that there be internal consistency in forecast revenues and expenses on the one hand, and in the risk (and hence discount rate) assessment on the other.

Reasonableness Tests

It can be helpful to employ certain tests to aid in assessing the reasonableness of a forecast. These tests assess various operating metrics implied by the forecast, which themselves can then be compared to past business and industry performance metrics, where meaningful comparables can be found. Reasonableness tests will vary depending on the nature of the business, but may include the following:

- capacity utilization, measured in terms of sales volumes, hours worked, distribution capabilities and other relevant parameters. Where sales volumes are expected to exceed available capacity, capital expenditures may be required to accommodate expansion. When assessing capacity, it is important to consider seasonality;

- revenue per employee. Where revenue per employee is expected to increase significantly, and even exceed industry norms, adequate consideration might not have been given to the higher headcount that will be required to support growth;

- revenues per subscriber, per ton produced or some other operating metric, as a test of the reasonableness of pricing assumptions;

- market share. Where a business expects to grow its market share, it may face challenges from competitors in terms of price competition which may erode profit margins. As a practical matter, in many industries it is difficult for management to reasonably estimate market share, given that reliable industry statistics with respect to market size and market growth rates are not readily available;

- operating costs and margins (e.g., gross margin, EBITDA margin). It is not unusual for a forecast to assume that fixed costs can be leveraged as sales volumes increase, thereby causing profit margins to expand. Where profit margins are expected to exceed industry norms, further consideration should be given to step costs that might be required to accommodate volume growth. In addition, as a practical matter, most fixed costs only remain fixed within a certain range of sales volumes (e.g., rent expense). Consequently, higher sales volumes ultimately lead to higher fixed costs. Finally, it is axiomatic that high profit margins attract competition which reduces the return on capital that businesses operating within a certain industry can reasonably expect to generate over the long term;

- financial ratios such as the current ratio, quick ratio, asset turnover, and others, as discussed in Chapter 2. The expectation that such ratios will deviate significantly from historical levels or industry norms may indicate that certain underlying assumptions are not realistic; and

- working capital as a percentage of revenues. As previously noted, the ideal forecast should include a full set of financial statements, including income statements, balance sheets and cash flow statements. In some cases, adequate consideration is not afforded to the growth needed in accounts receivable, inventories and other working capital accounts to accommodate growth. In other cases, an assumption is made that working capital accounts will grow at a slower rate than revenues because of assumed efficiencies in accounts receivable collection, inventory management and so on. Such assumptions are often optimistic and can significantly understate the cash required to accommodate growth.

Adjusting for Unreasonable Forecasts

A forecast thought to be unreasonably optimistic or pessimistic can be dealt with by:

- revising the forecasts to levels believed reasonable so as to develop forecasts that then can be discounted by unadjusted market-driven rates of return;

- increasing or decreasing the rates of return to reflect the high or low levels of cash flow included in the forecasts; or

- applying a probability factor to forecast revenues, expenses or cash flow in order to develop forecasts that then can be discounted by unadjusted market-driven rates of return.

As noted throughout this book, there is a direct connection between the cash flow projections and the rates of return applied to them. As a result, a determination of appropriate rates of return requires a thorough and unbiased assessment of the forecasts themselves.

That said, it is preferable for management to develop their best estimate of future operating results, to be satisfied as to the reasonableness and internal consistency of the underlying assumptions and to adopt market-driven rates of return. These elements must be in place first because discount rates and capitalization rates are sufficiently subjective without the further complication of having to adjust those rates of return for excessive optimism or pessimism in the estimates and assumptions supporting the forecast.

Components of the Discounted Cash Flow Methodology

The mechanics of the DCF methodology are as follows:

- discretionary cash flows are determined for each year of the forecast period (generally three to five years);

- a terminal value is developed at the end of the forecast period, usually based on a capitalized cash flow methodology;

- the forecast discretionary cash flows and the terminal value are discounted to their present value amounts based on a discount rate;

- the present value of existing tax pools is added to determine the enterprise value of the business;

- interest-bearing debts and equivalent liabilities are deducted from enterprise value to determine the equity value of the business; and

- where applicable, further adjustments are made to equity value on account of redundant assets, excess or deficient net operating assets (e.g., working capital) at the valuation date and other items that have not otherwise been accounted for in the forecast cash flows.

Note that no separate adjustment is required for prospective one-time revenues, expenses or capital expenditures, since such items are typically captured as a component of the forecast discretionary cash flows. However, a separate adjustment on account of contingent liabilities may be made, where such costs cannot reasonably be predicted in the cash flow forecast. A graphical depiction of the DCF methodology is provided in Exhibit 6A.

Exhibit 6A
Graphical Depiction of the Discounted Cash Flow Methodology

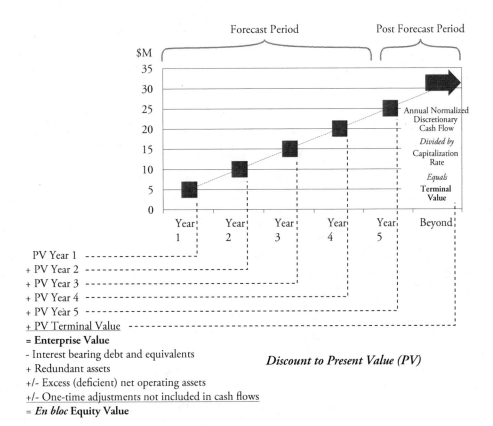

The value conclusion derived using the approach illustrated above represents the *en bloc* value of the shares of a company. Where the underlying assets of a business are being valued, further adjustments are required because of the tax base of the assets and other tax pools (where they exist), as discussed under in section "Assets vs. Shares" in Chapter 5.

Forecasting Discretionary Cash Flows

Discretionary cash flows are determined for each year of the forecast period. Discretionary cash flows are determined as follows:

Exhibit 6B
Determination of Forecast Discretionary Cash Flows

	Forecast EBITDA
Deduct:	income taxes
Deduct:	capital expenditure requirements
Add:	the present value of the tax shield on capital expenditures
Deduct (add):	increases (decreases) in net trade working capital
Equals:	forecast discretionary cash flows

As is the case with the capitalized cash flow methodology, the discretionary cash flows in the DCF methodology typically are determined on an unlevered basis (i.e., before consideration of interest expense and changes in debt principal outstanding).

Forecast EBITDA

EBITDA should be projected for each year of the forecast period and, in the final year, for the purpose of determining terminal value. Importantly, any prospective one-time benefits or costs should be reflected in the EBITDA projections in the year they are expected to be realized or incurred. Forecast EBITDA should be determinable for each year of the forecast period by adjusting the forecast income statement as follows:

Exhibit 6C
Determination of Forecast EBITDA

	Pre-tax income
Add:	interest expense
Add:	depreciation and amortization
Add (deduct):	other non-cash expenses (income)
Deduct (add):	income (costs) pertaining to redundant assets
Add or deduct:	adjustments on account of non-arm's length and discretionary items
Equals:	forecast EBITDA

As with other valuation methodologies, interest expense is added back where the approach is based on the determination of enterprise value (i.e., an unlevered approach) and consequently the use of debt financing is embedded in the rates of return.

Depreciation and amortization are added back because they are non-cash charges. Similarly, an adjustment is made for other non-cash items such as the loss or gain on the sale of capital assets, where such things are embedded in the forecasts.

Any income or costs pertaining to redundant assets are removed from the forecast EBITDA stream in order to avoid double counting, since the net realizable value of redundant assets is accounted for separately. As discussed in Chapter 4, where the business owns real estate that is treated as a redundant asset, an adjustment should be made for market-based rent expense.

In some cases, the forecast will contain costs or revenues arising from transactions with related parties. Where this is the case, an adjustment may be required if such transactions are not consummated at market rates (e.g., salaries to the business owner and family members). Similarly, where discretionary expenditures are embedded in the forecast, it is usual to remove such costs when determining forecast EBITDA, since they represent a form of return on capital. As noted in Chapter 4, discretionary expenditures do not include those that would be detrimental to the business if they were discontinued.

Note that adjustments are not usually made on account of unusual or non-recurring items embedded in the forecast because, if such items are expected to occur, they should be accounted for in the appropriate period. Consequently, there is no need to adjust the equity value otherwise determined for prospective one-time items, as was the case in the capitalized cash flow methodology (Chapter 5).

The exception to this general rule occurs where the prospective one-time item has a different risk level from the other components of forecast EBITDA. For example, if the outcome of an outstanding lawsuit cannot reasonably be estimated, it may be preferable to show the impact of a range of possible outcomes as an adjustment to enterprise value, rather than speculate as to when and on what terms a final determination will occur. The adjustment would be tax-effected where applicable.

Income Taxes

The cash tax rate (i.e., the effective tax rate for the operations of the business) should be applied against forecast EBITDA without consideration for future income tax accounting. Where the business operates in more than one jurisdiction, the cash tax rate should represent the blended rate. This may require some additional calculations where the business operates in several provinces or other countries.

Where the tax rate is expected to change, it may be appropriate to reflect the anticipated impact in the period in which the change is expected to come into effect. However, as a general comment, tax rates change with changes in the political party in power, government policies and other factors. Therefore, it is not uncommon to adopt the prevailing cash tax rate and to reflect the risk of favourable or adverse changes to this tax rate as a component of the rates of return applied to the discretionary cash flows.

Where the business is expected to incur research and development expenses that qualify for SRED credits, the benefit of those credits should be reflected in the discretionary cash flow projections. As discussed in Chapter 5, SRED credits at the federal level in Canada generally are calculated at a rate of 20% of qualifying R&D expenditures (declining to 15% in 2014). There may also be provincial R&D tax credits to consider. Unused credits can be carried forward indefinitely and applied against future taxable income. In addition, Canadian Controlled Private Corporations are eligible to receive a refund of SRED credits, even if their taxable income is negative. Any SRED credits received in a particular year are included in income and are subject to taxation at the effective corporate income tax rate.

Where a business has existing or prospective tax losses, they require separate consideration. Net capital losses are not normally factored into discretionary cash flow, except in the unusual case where capital gains are a component of forecast cash flow. However, net capital losses may have value in other circumstances and, as such, require separate consideration (as discussed in Chapter 5).

Where the business has existing non-capital losses at the valuation date, or where a non-capital loss is projected during the forecast period, consideration should be given to the timing of the income tax recovery. Non-capital losses (the rules for which in Canada have changed over the years, but at the time of writing [2012] can be carried forward twenty years and back three years from the year incurred) are applied against taxes otherwise payable during the forecast year in which they first can be absorbed. The timing of forecast recovery of non-capital losses depends in part on whether those losses can be carried back to recover previous years' taxes paid. If the aggregate taxable income in the three years preceding the loss year is sufficient to enable a full immediate recovery by carrying a loss back, the operating cash flow loss should be reduced in the year the income tax loss arises. Where aggregate taxable income in the preceding three years is less than the current-year loss, a portion of the related tax recovery should be reflected in future years as appropriate.

When determining the amount of non-capital losses that can be absorbed in any given year, consideration also should be given to the capital cost allowance (CCA) projected through both the tax shield on existing UCC and on prospective fixed asset additions. That is, EBITDA in any given year should be reduced by the amount of CCA for that year to determine the amount of non-capital losses that can be utilized. Where annual CCA is significant, an adjustment to the timing of income tax recovery may be necessary. However, in Canada, a business can elect not to claim CCA in a particular year (or to claim less than the allowable amount) in favour of utilizing tax losses that would otherwise expire.

Additionally, where pre-tax operating cash flows have been determined on an unlevered basis (i.e., before interest expense) consideration should be given to what the prospective annual interest expense will be, based on normalized debt levels. This analysis may result in a reduction of the amount of the non-capital losses otherwise recoverable in a given year. Note that the interest expense deducted should be based on a normalized debt level, consistent with the assumed capital structure for the business, as discussed in Chapter 7.

Where the business is a Canadian controlled private corporation and qualifies for the small business deduction, then consideration should also be afforded to when the non-capital losses will be utilized in order to maximize their value (i.e., against taxable income in excess of the small business limit).

In summary, where non-capital losses exist, it is usually necessary to calculate forecast taxable income and then forecast the timing of their utilization.

By way of example, assume that Company X operates in a cyclical industry. It has non-capital losses of $8 million at December 31, 2011, which expire in 2015. Management of Company X has forecast EBITDA as follows:

Exhibit 6D
Company X
EBITDA Forecast

	Fiscal Year Ending December 31						
	2012	2013	2014	2015	2016	2017	2018
EBITDA	6,000,000	10,000,000	4,000,000	(5,000,000)	2,000,000	7,000,000	12,000,000

Other information regarding Company X is as follows:

- capital cost allowance is relatively stable at $2 million per year;
- interest expense on normalized debt levels is $1 million per year; and
- Company X does not qualify for the small business deduction. Its effective cash income tax rate is 30%.

Based on the foregoing, the timing of non-capital tax loss utilization would be as follows:

Exhibit 6E
Company X
Utilization of Non-Capital Losses

	Fiscal Year Ending December 31						
	2012	2013	2014	2015	2016	2017	2018
Forecast EBITDA	6,000,000	10,000,000	4,000,000	(5,000,000)	2,000,000	7,000,000	12,000,000
Deduct: CCA	(2,000,000)	(2,000,000)	(2,000,000)	(2,000,000)	(2,000,000)	(2,000,000)	(2,000,000)
Deduct: interest expense	(1,000,000)	(1,000,000)	(1,000,000)	(1,000,000)	(1,000,000)	(1,000,000)	(1,000,000)
Equals: pre-tax income	3,000,000	7,000,000	1,000,000	(8,000,000)	(1,000,000)	4,000,000	9,000,000
Non-capital loss carry-forward used	(3,000,000)	(5,000,000)				(4,000,000)	(2,000,000)
Non-capital loss carried back				(3,000,000)			
Taxable income		2,000,000	1,000,000	(3,000,000)			7,000,000
Taxes payable (recoverable) at 30%		600,000	300,000	(900,000)			2,100,000
Non-capital losses available at							
Beginning of year	8,000,000	5,000,000			5,000,000	6,000,000	2,000,000
End of year	5,000,000			5,000,000	6,000,000	2,000,000	

The existing non-capital loss of $8 million is applied against net earnings in fiscal 2012 up to the maximum of $3 million. The balance of $5 million is carried forward to fiscal 2013. The loss of $8 million forecast for fiscal 2015 is not fully recoverable in that year. Taxes can be recovered only to the extent of taxes paid in the previous three years. In this case, the tax recovery is calculated as $900,000 determined by multiplying the tax rate of 30% by the aggregate taxable income in the previous three years of $3 million (after applying the tax losses). The remaining $5 million is carried forward. The $1 million loss forecast for fiscal 2016 is not recoverable in that year because the previous three years have no taxable income after the application of the loss forecast for fiscal 2015. The unused losses from fiscal 2015 and 2016 are carried forward to fiscal 2017 up to the taxable income in that year. The remaining $2 million is carried over to fiscal 2018 and applied in that year.

In this example, it is assumed that Company X claims CCA prior to the application of income tax losses. As noted above, businesses in Canada can elect to claim less than the full amount of CCA in favour of utilizing tax losses. However, where non-capital losses are not expected to expire before utilization, it is usually advantageous to claim the full amount of the CCA tax shield each year.

Capital Expenditures

The timing and quantum of capital expenditures is particularly relevant when applying the discounted cash flow methodology. Again, there must be internal consistency between the cash flow projection and the capital investment required to achieve it. In any given forecast year, capital investment should consider:

- the required amount of sustaining capital reinvestment, (i.e., the annual fixed asset additions required to maintain operations at the level projected each year). This calculation should take into account changes in technology, industry developments, and other relevant considerations necessary for the business to maintain its competitive position (as discussed in Chapter 5). As operating cash flows are projected to increase, there may be an associated increase in the level of sustaining capital reinvestment required to maintain forecast cash flows; and

- the incremental capital investment required for planned capacity additions or efficiencies to generate incremental forecast revenues and operating cash flows. This amount may include new machinery and equipment for expansion (growth in revenues), for operating efficiencies (reduction in costs), or both.

Where incremental capital expenditures are forecast to increase revenues or to realize operating efficiencies, the forecast period should be of sufficient length to fully reflect the benefits attributable to the capital expenditure, thereby ensuring both capital expenditures and resultant cash flows are properly integrated.

Tax Shield

The present value of the CCA tax shield should be determined for each year of the forecast period based on the corresponding capital expenditures. The formulae for calculating the tax shield were provided in Chapter 5. Formula 5.1 is applicable for most tax shield calculations since most capital asset additions in Canada are depreciated for tax purposes on a declining balance basis and subject to the half-year rule.

Net Trade Working Capital Requirements

Recall from Chapter 3 that most businesses require a net trade working capital balance in order to sustain their operations.

Further, net trade working capital balances are normally correlated with changes in operating activity, such as revenue levels. Net trade working capital is determined as the difference between trade current assets (such as accounts receivable, inventories and prepaid expenses) and trade current liabilities (such as accounts payable, accrued liabilities, taxes payable and deferred revenue). Where a business requires a cash balance to support its operations, the required cash amount is also considered a trade current asset.

Net trade working capital does not include:

- short-term interest-bearing debt (e.g., bank operating facilities) and current non-interest-bearing equivalents (e.g., advances from related parties);

- non-operating assets, such as advances to shareholders, non-trade receivables, and similar items. These items are normally dealt with as redundant assets which are segregated and valued separately;

- future income tax balances included in current assets or current liabilities because future income taxes do not relate to cash flow from operations; and

- excess cash balances. Changes in cash (and interest-bearing debt) normally represent discretionary cash flow that is subject to discounting. Therefore, in many cases the entire change in net cash (cash less interest-bearing debt) is considered discretionary. To the extent that some or all of that cash is not discretionary (i.e., where the business requires an operating cash balance), it should not form part of discretionary cash flow and should be included with trade current assets, as noted above.

The balance sheet segregation exercise presented in Chapter 2 can help to ensure internal consistency with respect to the inclusion of net trade working capital accounts, and a reasonable starting point for measuring working capital growth.

A forecast revenue increase generally necessitates a corresponding increase in net trade working capital, which, in turn, must be financed by cash (or increased borrowing). Consequently, an increase (decrease) in net trade working capital during the forecast period is deducted (added) when determining discretionary cash flow for a given year.

Where income and cash flow forecasts are compiled, corresponding balance sheets may or may not be prepared. Where balance sheets have been prepared for the forecast period, the change in net trade working capital can be computed. However, it is important to determine whether the assumptions underlying prospective working capital requirements are reasonable. In some cases, net trade working capital is actually projected to *decrease* on the expectation of reducing days sales outstanding in accounts receivable, higher inventory turnover or more favourable credit terms from suppliers. Where such assumptions are made, they should be closely scrutinized to determine whether they are well founded. If not, adjustments may be necessary.

Where projected balance sheets do not accompany cash flow projections, an estimate of net trade working capital requirements should be made. This can usually be done after analysis of historic relationships among revenues, operating results, current assets and current liabilities. As discussed in Chapter 2, it may be appropriate to calculate historic ratios such as:

- the current ratio and quick ratio;

- net trade working capital as a percentage of revenues;

- days sales in accounts receivable;

- inventory turnover; and

- days purchases in accounts payable.

If these ratios are consistent and are expected to remain so, they can be used to assist in estimating net trade working capital requirements. Where appropriate, the ratio of net trade working capital to revenues can be used to estimate the changes in net trade working capital resulting from a change in revenues.

In some cases, a business has a working capital surplus or deficiency at the valuation date which is expected to be rectified in the first year of the forecast period. If the impact of adjusting for the surplus or deficiency is incorporated in the forecast discretionary cash flow, it can distort the enterprise value of the business. Therefore, it is usually preferable for the discretionary cash flows to reflect normal-course changes in net trade working capital related to the operating activity of the business, based on the assumption of a normalized balance sheet at the valuation date. Where appropriate, a separate adjustment should be made when determining the equity value of the business to account for the difference between the actual net trade working capital balance sheet at the valuation date (which may reflect a working capital surplus or deficiency) and the assumed normalized balance sheet. This approach is consistent with most open market transactions, in which the purchase price is subject to adjustment where working capital is above or below an agreed threshold level. Similarly, where net trade working capital levels are higher or lower than normal because of seasonality, the excess or deficiency should be adjusted in order to be internally consistent with the deduction for interest-bearing debt and equivalents (which normally fluctuate in conjunction with the net trade working capital accounts).

To understand the calculation of net trade working capital, assume Company Y has compiled a three-year financial projection which includes the following working capital balances:

Exhibit 6F
Company Y
Projected Working Capital
Fiscal Years Ending December 31

	Actual	Forecast		
	2011	2012	2013	2014
Cash			303,000	898,000
Accounts receivable	1,830,000	2,013,000	2,214,000	2,386,000
Loan to affiliated company	300,000	250,000	200,000	150,000
Inventories	775,000	853,000	938,000	1,032,000
Future income taxes	135,000	146,000	156,000	164,000
Prepaid expenses	80,000	80,000	80,000	80,000
Total current assets	3,120,000	3,342,000	3,891,000	4,710,000
Bank loan	360,000	145,000		
Accounts payable & accruals	2,262,000	1,421,000	1,564,000	1,720,000
Taxes payable	261,000	287,000	316,000	347,000
Warranty provision	450,000	485,000	520,000	545,000
Current portion of long-term debt	150,000	158,000	169,000	180,000
Total current liabilities	3,483,000	2,496,000	2,569,000	2,792,000
Net working capital	(363,000)	846,000	1,322,000	1,918,000
Current ratio	0.90	1.34	1.51	1.69
Revenues	7,500,000	8,000,000	8,500,000	9,000,000

Other relevant information includes the following:

- at December 31, 2011, Company Y had a working capital deficiency of $1 million which was reflected in overstated accounts payable; and

- Company Y does not require an operating cash balance.

Based on the foregoing, Company Y's net trade working capital requirements are determined as follows:

Exhibit 6G
Company Y
Net Trade Working Capital Requirements
Fiscal Years Ending December 31

	Actual	Forecast		
	2011	2012	2013	2014
Trade Working Capital Assets				
Accounts receivable	1,830,000	2,013,000	2,214,000	2,386,000
Inventories	775,000	853,000	938,000	1,032,000
Prepaid expenses	80,000	80,000	80,000	80,000
	2,685,000	2,946,000	3,232,000	3,498,000
Trade Working Capital Liabilities				
Accounts payable and accruals	2,262,000	1,421,000	1,564,000	1,720,000
Taxes payable	261,000	287,000	316,000	347,000
Warranty reserve	450,000	485,000	520,000	545,000
	2,973,000	2,193,000	2,400,000	2,612,000
Net trade working capital	(288,000)	753,000	832,000	886,000
Deficiency at the valuation date	1,000,000			
Adjusted net trade working capital	712,000	753,000	832,000	886,000
Increase (decrease) in net trade w/c	n/a	41,000	79,000	54,000
Net trade w/c as a percentage of revenue	9.5%	9.4%	9.8%	9.8%

Trade current assets include accounts receivable, inventories and prepaid expenses. In this case, since no operating cash balance is required, changes in cash are captured as a component of discretionary cash flow. The loan to the affiliated company is assumed to be a redundant asset, and is valued separately. Changes in the future income tax asset are not part of operating cash flows.

Trade current liabilities include accounts payable and accruals, taxes payable and warranties. The bank loan and current portion of long-term debt are part of Company Y's capital structure, which is factored into the discount rate (as discussed in Chapter 7).

Given that Company Y has a working capital deficiency of $1 million at the valuation date, an adjustment is made to normalize the balance sheet by that amount. Consequently, the net change in net trade working capital is not distorted by that deficiency. Rather, a separate adjustment is made when determining Company Y's equity value in order to account for the working capital deficiency. The annual increase in net trade working capital is deducted when determining discretionary cash flow in each of the corresponding forecast years.

As a test of the reasonableness of the working capital projections, net trade working capital is calculated as a percentage of revenues. Given that the ratio of net trade working capital to revenues remains fairly stable (in the range of 9.4% to 9.8%), it provides some comfort as to the reasonableness of the forecast net trade working capital amounts in aggregate.

Terminal Value

The terminal value represents the value of a business beyond the forecast period. Most businesses are not perceived to have a finite life. However, where they do, they nonetheless may have residual value including net working capital, fixed assets, and other miscellaneous assets. When calculating the net residual proceeds of a business with a finite life, an orderly liquidation approach normally is adopted. Recall from Chapter 3 that, pursuant to an orderly liquidation approach, all assets are valued at their net realizable value and all wind-up costs are taken into account. Income taxes are determined at the corporate level. The expected net residual proceeds are then discounted to present value.

Where a business is expected to continue as a going concern for an indefinite period (which is usually the case), the terminal value represents the value of discretionary cash flows expected to be generated from the end of the forecast period to perpetuity. In a discounted cash flow valuation methodology, terminal value is normally determined using the capitalized cash flow methodology as follows:

Exhibit 6H

	Normalized EBITDA beyond the forecast period
Deduct:	cash income taxes
Deduct:	sustaining capital reinvestment
Add:	present value of the tax shield on sustaining capital
Deduct:	incremental net trade working capital requirements
Equals:	discretionary cash flow
Divided by:	capitalization rate
Equals:	capitalized cash flow (terminal value)

As a practical matter, the present value of the terminal value often accounts for the largest portion of enterprise value in a DCF calculation. Accordingly, well-founded analysis is important in the development of the key terminal value calculation components. It is often beneficial to perform sensitivity analysis on the terminal value components to better assess the underlying risks.

The terminal value should be determined at a point where discretionary cash flows are expected to remain relatively stable or to grow at a modest rate over the long term. Where this is not the case, the forecast period should be extended to a point where relative stability is expected to begin.

In some cases, the terminal value is determined pursuant to a different methodology such as a multiple of EBITDA. This approach tends to be more common among investment bankers and private equity firms, where a "liquidity event" (such as an initial public offering or *en bloc* sale of the business) is assumed to occur at some point in the future.

Normalized EBITDA

Normalized EBITDA beyond the forecast period is based on an analysis of historic and forecast EBITDA. If EBITDA has demonstrated a growth trend throughout the forecast period and growth is expected to continue, normalized EBITDA in the terminal value period is usually based on the last-year EBITDA (as projected in the forecast) increased by the growth factor embedded in the capitalization rate. For example, if EBITDA in the last year of the forecast is projected to be $5 million, and the long-term growth rate incorporated in the capitalization rate is 3%, then normalized EBITDA in the terminal value could be $5,150,000 (calculated as $5,000,000 × 1.03).

Caution is warranted, however. Normalized EBITDA in the terminal value period should reflect an average or sustainable level over the long term. Therefore, where a business operates in a cyclical industry, normalized EBITDA in the terminal value period should be based on an estimate of the mid-point for the cycle and not at a high point or low point. In the case of a cyclical industry, the forecast period should be extended, where necessary, so that the last year of the forecast will correspond with the mid-point of the cycle. This will help to avoid distortions caused by fluctuations in capital spending and working capital between the last year of the forecast period and the terminal value calculation.

Since the terminal value is often the most significant component of the value conclusion derived by using the DCF methodology, an overstated or understated normalized EBITDA calculation can materially affect the value conclusion. Therefore, normalized EBITDA in the terminal value period is often calculated as a range in order to reflect the inherent uncertainty involved.

Income Taxes

Income taxes are deducted from EBITDA at the appropriate cash tax rate to yield net operating (after-tax) cash flows before consideration of interest expense. As before, the cash tax rate should reflect an effective average, based on the jurisdictions in which the business operates. Where the business is expected to conduct ongoing R&D activities that qualify for SRED credits, then the impact of those SRED credits should be reflected in the discretionary cash flow calculation either as a reduction of taxes payable or as an "other income" item. Recall that SRED tax credits are included with taxable income when received. For example, assume that Company Z has normalized EBITDA of $5 million which is net of $1 million of qualifying R&D expenses. If the applicable tax rate is 30% and the SRED tax credit is 20%, then normalized after-tax income during in the terminal value period can be calculated in one of two ways, as follows:

Exhibit 6I
Company Z
Impact of SRED Credits on Cash Flow

	Tax Reduction Basis	Incremental EBITDA Basis
Normalized EBITDA before SRED credits (net of $1 million in qualifying R&D)	5,000,000	5,000,000
Other income - SRED credits received		200,000
Normalized EBITDA including SRED credits	5,000,000	5,200,000
Deduct: income taxes at 30%	(1,500,000)	(1,560,000)
Add: SRED credit (20% x $1 million qualifying R&D)	200,000	
Deduct: income tax on SRED credit received	(60,000)	
Net income tax	(1,360,000)	(1,560,000)
Net operating cash flow	3,640,000	3,640,000

In some cases, SRED credits received are included in normalized EBITDA or revenues (the "incremental EBITDA basis" in Exhibit 6I). While the resultant net operating cash flow is the same as the "tax reduction basis", including SRED credits in EBITDA can serve to artificially decrease the implied multiple of enterprise value to EBITDA. To the extent that such a measure is relied upon as a test of reasonableness, it could distort the analysis. Therefore, it is preferable to adopt the tax reduction basis with respect to SRED credits in order to avoid such distortions.

Sustaining Capital Reinvestment

Sustaining capital reinvestment in the terminal value period must be carefully considered. If the forecast has assumed growth then, in most cases, sustaining capital in the terminal value will be greater than sustaining capital during the forecast period. For most businesses, all capital assets must be replaced at some point; sustaining capital expenditures must contemplate this fact. Consequently, sustaining capital expenditures in the terminal value period may be considerably different from capital expenditures during the forecast period. Where the forecast contemplates the business will expend significant capital during the forecast period which will be followed by a period of significantly lower capital spending, the forecast period should be extended to include the complete capital expenditure cycle. Extending the forecast period makes the calculation of sustaining capital in the terminal value easier than adjusting for timing differences.

In addition, where normalized EBITDA during the terminal value period has been increased on account of the long-term growth rate incorporated in the capitalization rate, then to ensure internal consistency, such long-term growth should also be considered when determining sustaining capital.

Tax Shield on Sustaining Capital Expenditures

The present value of the tax shield on sustaining capital expenditures should be calculated based on the formulas presented in Chapter 5. Since most capital expenditures in Canada are depreciated for income tax purposes on a declining balance basis and subject to the half-year rule, Formula 5.1 will likely be used. In determining the tax shield on sustaining capital expenditures, it is important to remember the following:

- the CCA rate should reflect the weighted average of the rates at which sustaining capital expenditures will be eligible;
- the tax rate adopted should be consistent with the tax rate assumption in the terminal value calculation; and
- the cost of capital should be the nominal discount rate and not the capitalization rate.

Incremental Net Trade Working Capital

As noted in Chapter 5, over the long term most businesses require incremental net trade working capital (e.g., accounts receivable and inventories, net of accounts payable and accruals) in order to support growth. Accordingly, when establishing the discretionary cash flow to be used in the terminal value calculation, there should be a deduction because of the growth in net trade working capital consistent with the growth rate embedded in the capitalization rate.

A meaningful adjustment on account of net trade working capital also requires a reasonable starting point. Where forecast balance sheets have been prepared based on realistic working capital assumptions, then the net trade working capital indicated on the balance sheet for the last year of the forecast period would normally be the starting point. However, adjustments may be required where the business is cyclical, and the last year of the forecast period does not correspond with the normalized EBITDA adopted for the purpose of determining terminal value. As noted above, ideally the forecast period should be extended to a mid-point in the cycle in order to avoid any distortion in the discretionary cash flow figure on account of working capital.

Where forecast balance sheets have not been prepared, it is necessary to estimate what the net trade working capital would be at the end of the forecast period in order to generate a starting point. This can be done with the assistance of the financial ratios discussed in Chapter 2.

Capitalization Rate

Normalized EBITDA less income taxes, sustaining capital reinvestment (net of the related tax shield) and incremental net trade working capital requirements represent the normalized discretionary cash flow in the terminal value period. The discretionary cash flow is then divided by a capitalization rate to derive capitalized cash flow, as in the capitalized cash flow methodology discussed in Chapter 5.

The capitalization rates adopted must consider the risk inherent in the level of normalized discretionary cash flow adopted in the terminal value determination. The capitalization rate is usually based on the discount rate (discussed below) less a long-term growth factor. The long-term growth factor is normally comprised of inflationary growth and, in some cases, a modest amount of real growth. As noted above, the terminal value calculation should be made at a point where the operations of a business are expected to remain relatively stable or grow at a modest rate. If strong growth is expected to continue, then the forecast period should be extended, until relative stability is achieved.

If long-term real growth is assumed, then it is important to ensure that such an assumption is realistic in light of business, industry and economic conditions (e.g., capacity limitations, competitive reaction, and so on). Capitalization rates are addressed in detail in Chapter 7.

Discount Rate

The annual forecast discretionary cash flows and the terminal value are discounted to their present value. The present value factor for a particular year is determined as follows:

Formula 6.1
Present Value Factor

$$1 / (1+K)^N$$

Where:

K = the discount rate (normally expressed as a weighted average cost of capital)

N = the number of years forward

For example, the present value factor for a discount rate of 15% over two years is determined as:

$$1/ (1 + .15)^2 = 0.7561$$

When discounting the annual discretionary cash flows, it is common to assume the cash flows accrue relatively evenly throughout the year. Therefore, the present value factor adopted is based on the midpoint of the following year, based on the following formula:

Formula 6.2
Present Value Factor – Mid-Year

$$1 / (1 + K)^{N-1/2}$$

In the above example, if the cash flows were assumed to occur mid-year on average, then the present value factor applied in the second year (based on a discount rate of 15%) would be determined as follows:

$$1 / (1 + .15)^{1.5} = 0.8109$$

It should also be noted that, when discounting the terminal value, the present value factor should be the same as that used in the last year of the forecast period since the capitalization of an income stream assumes the cash flows are generated one year forward.

Where discretionary cash flows are determined on an unlevered basis (i.e., before consideration of interest expense and changes in debt principal) then the discount rate reflects the weighted average cost of capital for the business. As explained in Chapter 7, weighted average cost of capital is based on the mix of debt and equity financing considered "normal" for the business. Hence, pursuant to the DCF methodology, the ability to use debt financing is incorporated in the discount rate as opposed to the cash flows.

Given that normalized debt levels are assumed, the implications of financial risk arising from an existing over-levered or under-levered financial structure are effectively disregarded. Accordingly, when determining fair market value in a notional market context it is assumed that:

- a buyer is able to ensure that following the transaction, the acquired business will operate with what is believed to be a normalized amount of debt; and

- in circumstances of existing excess financial leverage, the seller is not disadvantaged in negotiations.

These assumptions are consistent with that portion of the fair market value definition which prescribes that fair market value is to be determined on the assumption that neither the buyer nor the seller is under compulsion to transact. In an open market transaction where a buyer believes a target business is over-levered and, as a result, it has a negotiating advantage, the buyer will normally consider this in its offer. As a practical matter, the ability of a buyer to exploit such perceived negotiating advantage depends on, among other things, the prospective number of buyers interested in the target business and the alternatives available to seller.

The discount rate is also influenced by the risk of attaining the forecast cash flows, given the risk profile of the business as well as prevailing and prospective industry and economic conditions. As previously noted, there is a direct relation between the discount rate and the forecast cash flows against which the discount rate is applied.

The discount rate adopted must be determined on a basis internally consistent with the basis used to determine the cash flows. That is, where:

- inflation has been incorporated into the determination of discretionary cash flows throughout the forecast period, the discount rate selected to be applied to the those forecast cash flows should reflect a nominal rate (i.e., inclusive of inflation). Conversely, where inflation has not been incorporated into the determination of discretionary cash flows throughout the forecast period, the discount rate selected to be applied to those forecast cash flows should reflect a real rate (i.e., exclusive of inflation); and

- the tax rate incorporated in the discount rate (as illustrated in Chapter 7) must be consistent with the tax rate incorporated in the forecast discretionary cash flows.

In some cases, a business has two or more distinct cash flow streams, each of which is subject to different risks. For example, a segment of the business might generate cash flows based on low-risk contractual-type activities whereas another segment might generate cash flows from activities that are more volatile. In such circumstances either:

- the discretionary cash flows should be segregated by business segment and appropriate risk-adjusted rates of return applied to each; or

- a blended rate of return should be applied to aggregate discretionary cash flows to account for the different risk profiles of the different revenue streams.

The decision as to which approach to use rests on whether the segments can be sold as separate entities (in which case separate cash flows and separate rates of return should be adopted), or whether the segments are intertwined such that their segregation would be impractical (in which case a blended discount rate should be used against aggregate cash flows).

Present Value of Existing Tax Pools

The approach set out above accounts for the tax shield on capital expenditures both during the forecast period and in the terminal value. Therefore, a separate adjustment is required for the present value of the remaining tax shield on existing assets (i.e., undepreciated capital cost [UCC]). The formulae were presented in Chapter 5. In particular, Formula 5.3 would be most commonly adopted.

Another approach is to account for the tax shield on existing capital assets throughout the forecast period as a reduction to taxes otherwise payable. Where this approach is adopted, it is necessary to estimate the residual balance at the end of the forecast period and to calculate the present value of the residual tax shield at that time. This amount would be added to the terminal value and therefore discounted to its present value amount.

For example, assume that A1 Limited has a UCC balance at December 31, 2011, of $20 million and that substantially all of its assets are subject to CCA at a rate of 30%. Further assume that A1 has an income tax rate of 25% and a cost of capital (discount rate) of 12%. If A1 Limited has prepared a five-year forecast, then the tax calculations in respect of UCC on the existing asset base would be as follows:

Exhibit 6J
A1 Limited
Tax Shield on Existing Capital Asset Base
Fiscal Years Ending December 31

	Actual	Forecast					Terminal
	2011	2012	2013	2014	2015	2016	Value
Opening UCC balance		20,000,000	14,000,000	9,800,000	6,860,000	4,802,000	
CCA at 30%		6,000,000	4,200,000	2,940,000	2,058,000	1,440,600	
Ending UCC balance	20,000,000	14,000,000	9,800,000	6,860,000	4,802,000	3,361,400	
Tax savings at 25%		1,500,000	1,050,000	735,000	514,500	360,150	
Residual (calculated using Formula 5.3)							600,250
Discounted at 12%		1,339,286	837,054	523,158	326,974	204,359	340,598
Present value of tax shield	3,571,429						

The present value of the tax shield derived pursuant to the approach above is the same as what would be determined by applying Formula 5.3 to the UCC balance of $20 million at December 31, 2011. Specifically:

$$\frac{[\text{UCC of } \$20,000,000] \times [\text{CCA rate of } 30\%] \times [\text{tax rate of } 25\%]}{[\text{cost of capital of } 12\%] + [\text{CCA rate of } 30\%]} = \$3,571,429$$

The benefits of making the annual CCA calculation as illustrate in Exhibit 6J are as follows:

- its better reflection of the unlevered cash flows for each year in the forecast period may be preferable from the standpoint of managing cash flow and assessing debt servicing capacity;

- by including the residual tax shield in the terminal value calculation, the terminal value reflects the estimated enterprise value of the business at that time, as opposed to its capitalized cash flow which does not. This may assist in assessing the reasonableness of implied valuation multiples in the terminal value period; and

- it provides a better indication of the timing of tax loss utilization, where such losses exist (subject to consideration of interest expense). In some cases, CCA claims may be deferred in favour of utilizing tax losses that might otherwise expire.

Unlike the capitalized cash flow methodology, the discounted cash flow methodology does not normally consider existing non-capital tax losses and SRED pools separately as a possible addition to value otherwise determined. The reason for this is that such losses are normally reflected as a reduction of the cash income taxes otherwise payable in the cash flow forecast of the year in which they can be utilized. Any non-capital income tax losses (and other tax shields) not accounted for as part of discretionary cash flows should be included in the separate tax shield calculation.

The present value of tax shield is added to the present value of the annual discretionary cash flows during the forecast period and to the present value of the terminal value to determine the enterprise value of the business.

Interest-Bearing Debt and Equivalents

Since enterprise value reflects the aggregate of the debt and equity components of a business, the amount of interest-bearing debt outstanding at the valuation date must be deducted from enterprise value to determine the equity value. As discussed in Chapter 4, interest-bearing debt outstanding includes short-term and long-term interest-bearing debt, and equivalents such as interest free loans. Where a business has cash on hand, an assessment must be made as to whether that cash can be applied against outstanding debt. The balance sheet segregation exercise (Chapter 2) can assist in this determination.

Redundant Assets

As with other valuation methodologies, the discounted cash flow valuation methodology assumes the realization of redundant assets at the valuation date; their estimated net realizable value is added to enterprise value. As noted above, any income or expense stream associated with redundant assets should be removed from projected EBITDA.

As discussed in Chapter 4, when determining the net realizable value of redundant assets, disposition costs and income taxes are often discounted in recognition of tax deferral opportunities.

It is important to ensure the redundant assets will not be required to meet cash flow forecasts. For example, while a business may have vacant land at the valuation date, if that land will be required in order to accommodate forecast growth, it would not be considered redundant. Consequently, any income or expense stream associated with that operating asset should be incorporated in the forecast discretionary cash flows (or separately accounted for as a temporary excess asset, as discussed in Chapter 5).

Excess or Deficient Net Operating Assets

Changes in net trade working capital are reflected in the annual discretionary cash flow calculations. However, in some cases, the business will have a working capital surplus or deficiency at the valuation date. It is preferable to record that excess or deficiency as a separate adjustment to enterprise value rather than incorporate it into the first year of the forecast period. The former approach is consistent with most open market transactions, which are premised on the business having an adequate level of working capital at the closing date, failing which an adjustment is made to the purchase price. Furthermore, if the excess or deficiency is reflected in the first year of the cash flow, then:

- it can significantly change the enterprise value conclusion, which in turn can distort any comparative analysis against valuation multiples based on EBITDA or other measures; and

- discounting the one-time adjustment to working capital can inappropriately reduce the impact of the excess or deficiency, the magnitude of which will depend on the discount rate adopted.

Where an adjustment is made for a working capital excess or deficiency, it is important to ensure internal consistency with the notional net trade working capital at the valuation date and any ensuing annual changes. Similar consideration should be given to long-term operating assets and liabilities (e.g., the adequacy of long-term warranty reserves).

Example of the Discounted Cash Flow Methodology

B2 Limited manufactures production control software and equipment. The company has recently developed a new product line that it believes will lead to significant gains in both revenues and profitability. In order to launch its new product line, B2 needs to acquire equipment worth $5 million. Given that the company is almost at its limit in its lending facilities, B2 has approached a subordinated debt lender to finance the expenditures. As part of its conditions, the prospective lender has requested a valuation of the company.

B2 Limited has prepared the following five-year financial projections for the lender:

Exhibit 6K
B2 Limited
Forecast Income Statements
Fiscal Years Ending December 31
($000)

	Actual	Forecast				
	2011	2012	2013	2014	2015	2016
Revenues	38,472	45,000	60,000	70,000	80,000	90,000
Cost of goods sold	23,665	27,000	36,000	42,000	48,000	54,000
Gross profit	14,807	18,000	24,000	28,000	32,000	36,000
Selling and administration	12,915	15,000	20,000	22,500	25,000	28,000
R&D expenditures	1,500	500	500	500	500	500
R&D tax credit received	(80)	(300)	(100)	(100)	(100)	(100)
Equity earnings in C3 Ltd.	(36)	(50)	(50)	(50)	(50)	(50)
Interest expense	288	1,003	728	562	300	150
Income before taxes	220	1,847	2,922	4,588	6,350	7,500
Income taxes	59	499	789	1,239	1,715	2,025
Net income	161	1,348	2,133	3,349	4,636	5,475

Exhibit 6L
B2 Limited
Forecast Balance Sheets at December 31
($000)

	Actual	Forecast				
	2011	2012	2013	2014	2015	2016
Current assets						
Cash				64	2,150	5,055
Accounts receivable	6,257	7,397	9,863	11,507	13,151	14,795
Tax credits receivable	300	100	100	100	100	100
Inventory	1,142	1,350	1,800	2,100	2,400	2,700
Prepaid expenses	150	150	150	150	150	150
	7,849	8,997	11,913	13,921	17,950	22,800
Capital assets	12,753	17,753	18,253	18,753	20,253	21,753
Accumulated depreciation	(8,773)	(10,393)	(12,296)	(13,847)	(15,261)	(16,697)
	3,980	7,360	5,958	4,906	4,992	5,056
Investment in C3	595	645	695	745	795	845
Total assets	12,424	17,002	18,566	19,572	23,737	28,701
Current liabilities						
Bank indebtedness	4,222	2,126	1,866			
Accounts payable and accrued liabilities	1,560	1,849	2,466	2,877	3,288	3,699
Income taxes payable	87	125	197	310	429	506
Current portion of long-term debt		1,000	1,000	1,000	1,000	1,000
	5,869	5,100	5,529	4,186	4,716	5,205
Loans from shareholders	2,000	2,000	2,000	2,000	2,000	2,000
Long-term debt		4,000	3,000	2,000	1,000	
Total liabilities	7,869	11,100	10,529	8,186	7,716	7,205
Shareholders' equity						
Share capital	1,000	1,000	1,000	1,000	1,000	1,000
Retained earnings	3,555	4,903	7,036	10,386	15,021	20,496
	4,555	5,903	8,036	11,386	16,021	21,496
Total liabilities and equity	12,424	17,003	18,566	19,572	23,738	28,701

Exhibit 6M
B2 Limited
Forecast Cash Flow Statements
Fiscal Years Ending December 31
($000)

	Actual	Forecast				
	2011	2012	2013	2014	2015	2016
Net income for the period	161	1,348	2,133	3,349	4,636	5,475
Items not involving cash						
Depreciation and amortization	1,226	1,620	1,903	1,552	1,414	1,435
Income from equity investment	(36)	(50)	(50)	(50)	(50)	(50)
	1,351	2,918	3,986	4,851	5,999	6,860
Changes in non-cash working capital						
Accounts receivable	(554)	(1,140)	(2,466)	(1,644)	(1,644)	(1,644)
Tax credits receivable	45	200				
Inventory	(111)	(208)	(450)	(300)	(300)	(300)
Prepaid expenses	(14)					
Accounts payable	102	289	616	411	411	411
Income taxes	7	38	73	112	119	78
	(525)	(821)	(2,227)	(1,420)	(1,414)	(1,455)
Cash flow from operations	826	2,097	1,759	3,431	4,585	5,405
Investment in capital assets	(966)	(5,000)	(500)	(500)	(1,500)	(1,500)
Investment in C3 Ltd.						
Cash flow from investing	(966)	(5,000)	(500)	(500)	(1,500)	(1,500)
Advances from (to) shareholders						
Proceeds from long-term debt		5,000				
Repayment of long-term debt			(1,000)	(1,000)	(1,000)	(1,000)
Cash flow from financing		5,000	(1,000)	(1,000)	(1,000)	(1,000)
Total change in cash flow	(140)	2,097	259	1,931	2,085	2,905
Cash (bank debt)–beginning of year	(4,082)	(4,222)	(2,126)	(1,866)	64	2,150
Cash (bank debt)–end of year	(4,222)	(2,126)	(1,866)	64	2,150	5,055

Other information regarding B2 Limited and its financial projections are as follows:

- revenues are expected to increase from approximately $38 million in 2011 to $45 million in 2012 and double to $90 million by 2016;

- the gross margin is expected to remain relatively stable at 40%, while operating costs will decline slightly as a percentage of revenues;

- the company's net trade working capital at December 31, 2011, approximates normalized levels. The ratios for working capital accounts are expected to remain relatively stable throughout the forecast period;

- the UCC of the company's existing assets is $3.5 million with an average CCA rate of 25%;

- the company is financed by a bank loan of $4,222,000 at December 31, 2011, which is near the company's financing limit of $4.5 million. The shareholders have loaned $2 million to the company to support its operations. Further, the shareholders have agreed the company will not repay their loans until the subordinated debt is repaid in full;

- the company recently spent considerable amounts on R&D to develop its new product line. The company is eligible for SRED tax credits at a rate of 20%. Beginning in 2012, ongoing R&D expenditures will revert to historical norms of $500,000 per year;

- the company pays income taxes at a rate of 27% but does not qualify as a CCPC. As a privately held company, B2 has elected not to account for future income taxes;

- the subordinated loan that the company is seeking is for a five-year term, bearing interest at 15% per annum, with principal repayment of $1 million annually;

- in 2009, B2 Limited acquired a 25% interest in C3 Ltd. for $500,000. C3 is a privately held company owned by a relative of B2's majority shareholder. C3's operations are unrelated to those of B2. B2's investment in C3 is accounted for using the equity method. The fair market value of the investment in C3 approximates the net book value. Income taxes on disposition would not be material;

- the company will use the proceeds of the subordinated debt to acquire equipment worth $5 million in 2012. Capital spending will be limited to $500,000 per year in each of 2013 and 2014. Thereafter, the company expects to invest about $1.5 million per year in order to maintain its competitive position over the long term. Capital additions have an average CCA rate of 30%;

- the operations of the company are expected to stabilize beyond 2016 and experience long-term growth at a rate of 3%; and

- following an analysis of the company, the industry in which it operates, current and prospective economic and credit market conditions and the risks inherent in the forecast, a discount rate of 20% is believed to be appropriate.

Value Determination

The first step in the determination of the fair market value of B2's shares is to estimate the forecast discretionary cash flows of the company for 2012 through 2016, as follows:

- forecast EBITDA is estimated by starting with pretax income and adding back interest expense and depreciation and amortization, and deducting the equity income on the investment in C3;

- income taxes are deducted from forecast EBITDA at a rate of 27%;

- capital expenditures are deducted based on forecast cash flow statements. The present value of the tax shield on capital expenditures is determined using Formula 5.1 and is based on a CCA rate of 30%, tax rate of 27% and a cost of capital of 20%; and

- changes in net trade working capital are taken from the forecast cash flow statements.

Next to be determined is the terminal value which represents the present value of the discretionary cash flows beyond fiscal 2016. The terminal value is determined as follows:

- normalized EBITDA is estimated at $9,306,000, representing 3% growth over the 2016 level, a rate consistent with the long-term growth rate;

- income taxes are deducted at a rate of 27%;

- sustaining capital expenditures are deducted at $1,545,000, representing a 3% growth rate over the 2016 level of $1.5 million. The present value of the tax shield on sustaining capital expenditures is calculated using Formula 5.1, based on an average CCA rate of 30%, tax rate of 27% and a cost of capital of 20% (being the discount rate, *not* the capitalization rate);

- the annual increase in net trade working capital of $406,000 is based on the projected balance at December 31, 2016, of $13,540,000 (calculated as accounts receivable plus tax credits receivable, inventory and prepaid expenses, less accounts payable and accruals and taxes payable), multiplied by the long-term growth rate of 3%; and

- the normalized discretionary cash flow of $5,114,000 is divided by the capitalization rate of 17%, (i.e., the 20% discount rate less the 3% long-term growth rate). The resultant terminal value is $30,081,000 ($5,114,000 / 17% = $30,081,000).

The annual discretionary cash flow and the terminal value are discounted to their present value amounts using a discount rate of 20% based on mid-year discounting. Therefore, the terminal value component is discounted based on 4.5 years ($30,081,000 / $(1 + .20)^{4.5}$ = $13,243,000).

The present value of the tax shield on existing capital assets is added, based on Formula 5.3, is determined as follows:

$$\frac{[\text{UCC base } \$3,500,000] \times [\text{average CCA rate } 25\%] \times [\text{tax rate } 27\%]}{[\text{cost of capital } 20\%] + [\text{average CCA rate } 25\%]} = \$525,000$$

The resultant enterprise value is $18,573,000. The following adjustments are then made:

- interest-bearing debt and equivalents of $6,222,000 are deducted, comprised of the bank loan of $4,222,000 and loans from shareholders of $2 million;

- the net realizable value of the investment in C3 is added, estimated $595,000; and

- no adjustment is required on account of excess or deficient working capital (or other net operating assets), given that working capital levels at the valuation date of December 31, 2011, are considered to be at normalized levels.

The resultant *en bloc* equity value for B2 Limited is $12,946,000.

Exhibit 6N
B2 Limited
Discounted Cash Flow
Fiscal Years Ending December 31
($000)

		Forecast					Terminal
		2012	2013	2014	2015	2016	Value
Income before taxes		1,847	2,922	4,588	6,350	7,500	
Add (deduct)							
Interest expense		1,003	728	562	300	150	
Depreciation and amortization		1,620	1,903	1,552	1,414	1,435	
Income from equity investment		(50)	(50)	(50)	(50)	(50)	
EBITDA		4,420	5,503	6,652	8,014	9,035	9,306
Income taxes	27%	(1,193)	(1,486)	(1,796)	(2,164)	(2,440)	(2,513)
Capital expenditures		(5,000)	(500)	(500)	(1,500)	(1,500)	(1,545)
Tax shield on capital expenditures	30%	878	88	88	263	263	271
Change in net trade working capital		(821)	(2,227)	(1,420)	(1,414)	(1,455)	(406)
Discretionary cash flow		(1,717)	1,378	3,023	3,199	3,904	5,114
Long-term growth rate	3%						
Capitalization rate	17%						
Terminal value							30,081
Discounted at	20%	(1,568)	1,048	1,917	1,690	1,719	13,242
Present value of forecast cash flows		4,806					
Present value of terminal value		13,242					
Present value of existing tax shield		525					
Enterprise value		18,573					
Deduct: debt outstanding		(6,222)					
Add: redundant assets		595					
Add (deduct): excess (deficient) net operating assets							
En bloc equity value		12,946					

As a test of the reasonableness of the valuation conclusion, the implied multiple of enterprise value to normalized trailing (2011) EBITDA and forward (2012) EBITDA are calculated. In this regard, normalized trailing EBITDA is calculated as pretax income adjusted for the following:

- interest expense is added back;

- depreciation and amortization are added back;

- income from the equity investment in C3 is deducted;

- actual R&D expense is added back, given that it is in excess of normalized levels in 2011;

- the SRED credits received are deducted assuming that a buyer would view SRED credits as a reduction in taxes, as opposed to operating income; and

- normalized R&D expense of $500,000 is deducted.

The resultant normalized trailing EBITDA is $2,618,000 and normalized forward EBITDA is $4,120,000. Based on an enterprise value of $18,573,000, the implied multiple of enterprise value to EBITDA is 7.1x for trailing (2011) EBITDA and 4.5x for forward (2012) EBITDA. The large swing is due to the difference in the EBITDA base, given the expected benefits from the new equipment. These multiples can be compared to those in the public equity markets and industry transactions to assess their reasonableness, subject to the caveats of such comparisons noted in Chapter 4.

Exhibit 6O
B2 Limited
Test of Valuation Conclusion
Implied Multiple of EBITDA
($000)

	Actual 2011	Forecast 2012
Pretax income as reported	220	1,847
Add (deduct)		
Interest expense	288	1,003
Depreciation and amortization	1,226	1,620
Income from equity investment	(36)	(50)
Actual R&D expense	1,500	500
R&D tax credit	(80)	(300)
Normalized R&D expense	(500)	(500)
Normalized EBITDA	2,618	4,120
Enterprise value (Exhibit 6N)	18,573	18,573
Multiple of enterprise value to EBITDA	7.1x	4.5x

Sensitivity Analysis

It is often useful to conduct sensitivity analysis on the forecast and the valuation inputs. Frequently several scenarios may be prepared reflecting pessimistic, most likely and optimistic assumptions with respect to key economic drivers. These sensitivity tests can assist in developing a meaningful forecast and in assessing the risk inherent in the business. As a general rule, the greater the sensitivity of the valuation conclusion to changes in assumptions, the greater the risk profile of the business. Therefore, sensitivity analysis can lead to a more informed basis for establishing the discount and capitalization rates and the overall valuation conclusions.

With respect to forecast assumptions, while each case is fact unique, the following items are commonly addressed:

- unit sales, including the rate of sales growth and market share;
- pricing of goods or services sold;
- the impact of foreign exchange, where a significant portion of the business's sales or purchases are made in foreign currencies;
- production costs, including raw materials prices, labour, overheads and overall gross profit margins;
- operating costs, such as sales and distribution, general and administrative expenses, R&D costs, etc.;
- tax rates;
- capital expenditure requirements; and
- net trade working capital requirements.

In the case of B2 Limited, the following analysis could be conducted to assess the degree of sensitivity of the enterprise value conclusions to key assumptions:

Exhibit 6P
B2 Limited
Sensitivity Analysis — Key Assumptions
Impact on Enterprise Value Conclusions
($000)

	Enterprise Value	% Change From Base Case
Base case	18,573	n/a
Revenues 1% lower than forecast	17,346	-7%
Gross margin 1% lower than forecast	15,117	-19%
Selling and admin. costs 1% higher than forecast	17,510	-6%
R&D costs 10% higher than forecast	18,380	-1%
Tax rate 1% higher than forecast	18,229	-2%
Capital spending 10% higher than forecast	18,134	-2%
Working capital requirements 10% higher than forecast	18,393	-1%

Based on this analysis, it becomes evident that, in the case of B2 Limited, the valuation conclusions are most sensitive to changes in the assumptions regarding cost of goods sold and the resultant gross margin.

As noted throughout this book, discount rates and capitalization rates are inherently subjective. Therefore, it is common practice to use a range of possible rates or to create a matrix that illustrates the sensitivity of the enterprise value to a relatively minor change in the discount rate and long-term growth rate (which influences the capitalization rate).

In the case of B2 Limited, this test could be performed by adopting a discount rate in the range of 18% to 22% (given the 20% point estimate) and a long-term growth rate in the range of 1% to 5% (given the 3% point estimate).

Exhibit 6Q
B2 Limited
Sensitivity Analysis — Rates of Return
Enterprise Value Conclusions
($000)

		Long-Term Growth Rate				
		1%	2%	3%	4%	5%
Discount Rate	18%	19,971	20,864	21,876	23,032	24,366
	19%	18,493	19,257	20,116	21,090	22,204
	20%	17,180	17,838	**18,573**	19,401	20,339
	21%	16,006	16,577	17,211	17,919	18,717
	22%	14,952	15,449	15,999	16,610	17,293

This matrix serves to illustrate that, while the enterprise value conclusion was approximately $18.6 million, it would not be unreasonable to adopt a range of approximately $17 million to $20 million.

Start-Up and High-Growth Businesses

Start-up and high-growth businesses are defined as those that do not have a long operating history. They may be pre-revenue or generating revenues significantly below future expectations. Common examples include companies operating in the biopharmaceutical industry and leading edge technology, but such businesses can be found in any sector. It is common for start-up and high-growth businesses to demonstrate a shortfall in discretionary cash flow in the near term. Given these circumstances, these businesses normally are valued using a DCF methodology.

In most cases, value determinations are necessarily more subjective in start-up and high-growth businesses because of the absence of quality historical data and the uncertainty regarding the assumptions underlying the projections. Accordingly, the valuation of such businesses is discussed here to focus on the assessment of the reasonableness of their forecast cash flows and the determination of appropriate rates of return to apply to those forecast cash flows.

Forecast Discretionary Cash Flows

Long-term cash flow forecasts are fundamental to the valuation of start-up and high-growth businesses. As a practical matter, such forecasts often reflect an overly optimistic outlook for the business because of:

• management's incentive to present the business in a positive light in order to obtain financing;

• the failure to account for all costs associated with revenue growth; and

- insufficient recognition of the risks associated with a start-up or high-growth ventures that are attributable to factors such as being by-passed in technology, increased competition from larger and better financed competitors and overreliance on one or a few key personnel.

As with any business, assessing the reasonableness of the cash flow forecasts necessitates an understanding of the business itself and the industry in which it operates. A careful, objective analysis of the assumptions underlying the projections is essential. In particular, emphasis should be placed on the reasonableness of:

- the business plan that normally accompanies the revenue and cash flow forecast. Business plans set out important details regarding the business, including its target market, competition, management team, strategic advantages, strengths and weaknesses, and so on;

- revenue forecasts. Normally revenues should be analyzed by product or service offering, customer, territory and other relevant parameters in order to determine precisely what the driving forces are behind anticipated revenue growth. Both quantity and pricing assumptions should be set out; and

- cost forecasts. In particular, costs should be analyzed in the context of consistency with revenue assumptions and completeness. With respect to completeness, consideration should be given to step costs, capital spending requirements, net trade working capital requirements, and all other cash outlays required to generate forecast revenues.

In many cases, it will be appropriate to temper the projected cash flows by some probability factor or otherwise adjust the projections in recognition of the uncertainty of the unknowable future. In most cases, the probability factor applied will be greater for long-term vs. short-term projections given that uncertainty will increase over time. Finally, as a practical matter, where a start-up or high-growth business is valued using a DCF methodology, virtually all of the *en bloc* value is attributed to the terminal value component. Therefore, the assumptions used to develop the terminal value must be carefully considered.

Rates of Return

The risks associated with achieving forecasts are generally perceived to be greater in start-up or high-growth businesses than is the case with mature businesses. As a result, the rates of return utilized in valuing start-up or high-growth businesses are normally much greater than those utilized in the case of mature businesses. In the context of start-up or high-growth businesses rates of return on equity often match those sought by venture capitalists, which are commonly in the range of 30% to 40% or greater.

Because rates of return and the prospective cash flows to which they are applied are related, care must be exercised to appropriately reflect the degree of risk attached to the forecasts in the rates of return adopted. Just as adopting overly aggressive forecasts and applying an inappropriately high rate of return would understate value, so too would adopting overly optimistic forecasts and applying an inappropriately low rate of return serve to overstate value.

As discussed in Chapter 7, the capital structure decision is an important part of the discount rate and capitalization rate determination. In the context of a start-up or high-growth business, the ability to use financial leverage is often severely limited because of the inability of such businesses to finance operations conventionally through senior debt. Many traditional lenders are wary of start-up and high-growth companies because of the degree of subjectivity required when assessing forecast risk, potential near term cash flow volatility, and what is often an absence of underlying tangible assets. As a result, it may be appropriate to assume that little or no conventional debt financing is reflective of a normalized capital structure.

The Value Conclusion

As with all notional market valuations and open market transactions, the conclusion reached for a start-up or high-growth business must be objectively assessed for overall reasonableness. Because the level of subjectivity in value determinations related to start-up and high-growth businesses is normally greater than it is in the case of mature businesses, it may be beneficial to consider the following when concluding on value:

- ratios of enterprise value to historical and future (generally one-year forward) revenues, EBITDA and EBIT, subject to the caveats of such comparisons, as discussed in Chapter 4. As a practical matter, such ratios are often meaningless due to operating losses or very low income levels at the valuation date;

- rules of thumb. In some start-up and high-growth businesses, rules of thumb are used as a guide to value. For example, for certain technology businesses rules of thumb based on a multiple of revenues are sometimes cited. A rule of thumb in isolation will rarely provide an appropriate base for a well-founded value conclusion; and

- cost of reproduction. For start-up companies in particular, a buyer may have the option of acquiring an existing business or starting a new one. A cost of reproduction analysis also may help identify those components that are not readily replaceable (e.g., proprietary technology) that might properly influence value.

In the end, the value conclusion derived for any business must comprise a carefully considered synthesis of the specific economic, industry and business facts that affect each.

The DCF Methodology vs. the Capitalized Cash Flow Methodology

The DCF methodology in many respects is an extension of the capitalized cash flow methodology discussed in Chapter 5. In essence, the capitalized cash flow methodology assumes that revenues, profitability and discretionary cash flow will increase each year at the growth rate embedded in the capitalization rate. By contrast, the DCF methodology is premised on an annual forecast, normally for a period of three to five years, followed by the terminal value, which typically is based on the capitalized cash flow methodology. In theory, the DCF methodology and the capitalized cash flow methodology should result in the same value conclusion for a business that is growing at a constant rate over the near term and the long term. However, in most cases, the growth rate or other assumptions embedded in the DCF methodology do not assume such linearity.

The requirement for an annual forecast means that the DCF methodology generally necessitates more rigour in terms of vetting the forecast operating results for reasonableness. Furthermore, pursuant to the DCF methodology, consideration must be afforded to the specific year in which revenues will be generated and costs will be incurred, including operating costs, capital expenditures and incremental net trade working capital. The capitalized cash flow methodology uses an average, and therefore dismisses timing issues, except to the extent that an adjustment is made to enterprise value on account of prospective one-time items.

As a practical matter, the capitalized cash flow methodology is based on normalizing current and historical operating results on the assumption that such historical results (when normalized) are representative of the future. By comparison, the DCF methodology is premised on forecast operating results and no normalization is necessary (except to the extent that remuneration and transactions with related parties do not reflect market rates). Since value is future oriented, the DCF methodology is generally the preferred approach, assuming that a meaningful forecast exists or can be created.

In addition, the DCF methodology generally encompasses the following:

- varying growth rates and/or cyclicality reflected in the near-term projections;

- the requirement to consider both sustaining capital expenditures and incremental capital expenditures to support growth initiatives;

- the requirement to analyze incremental net trade working capital that will be required to support growth initiatives; and

- no need to adjust for prospective one-time items separately, since such items should be reflected in a particular forecast period. However, one-time items may be adjusted for separately in the DCF methodology when they involve a significantly different level of uncertainty (e.g., an outstanding legal claim).

In summary, the capitalized cash flow methodology often serves as a good test of the valuation conclusions derived pursuant to the DCF methodology because it allows a forecast-driven valuation to be assessed against a valuation based on normalized historical results.

The DCF Methodology vs. Valuations Based on Multiples

Compared to valuations based on multiples, which are normally influenced to some extent by comparable public equity market data and industry transactions, the DCF methodology is a preferable approach to business valuation for at least the following reasons:

- multiples drawn from comparable equity market valuations are dependent on the existence of meaningful comparables for the subject company being valued. In any event, directly comparable companies are rare. The DCF methodology is dependent (in part) on the selection of an appropriate discount rate (normally a weighted average cost of capital) which is typically based on commonly recognized benchmark rates of return for corporate acquirers, adjusted as appropriate for the risks and prospects of the target company;

- valuation multiples based on earnings levels such as EBIT and net income are subject to the application of GAAP or IFRSs. The DCF methodology, in contrast, utilizes forecast discretionary cash flows, which are not subject to accounting policies;

- valuation multiples observed from industry transactions are often skewed by numerous variables such as the terms of the deal, the relative negotiating positions of the parties, perceived synergies, and other factors that may not be known to a party not involved in the transaction. By comparison, the DCF methodology assumes the buyer and seller are adequately informed as to all material facts influencing the business and the industry in which it operates;

- comparative valuation multiples are typically derived using the value conclusion as the numerator over historical reported results as the denominator. Such reported historical results may not reflect normalized results or prospective expectations, which would in turn impact the derived valuation multiple;

- stock market prices (and implied valuation multiples) generally represent transaction prices of shares with a high degree of liquidity. Corporate acquirers, in contrast, generally have long-term investment time horizons, typically making the DCF methodology their valuation methodology of choice;

- valuations based on public equity market data rely on publicly available information, as contrasted with reliance on undisclosed (to the public) fact-specific information known to management of the comparables. By comparison, buyers normally complete detailed due diligence prior to closing a transaction. Through that process they develop their valuation models based on detailed information that is not all publicly available – both their own proprietary information and information related to the target company. As a result, the DCF methodology forces detailed analysis of, and conclusions related to, fact-specific variables, something the comparative methodology does not do as specifically, if at all;

- comparative public market analysis depends on market multiples to reflect forecast revenue growth, gross margins, operating costs, income taxes, profit growth, capital expenditures, working capital requirements, and so on. In contrast, the DCF methodology segregates, analyzes and utilizes a multiple-year forecast of all of these things determined on a fact-specific basis; and

- valuations based on comparative public market analysis typically do not segregate redundant assets from operating assets. These two asset categories typically face different risks and are dealt with separately by the DCF methodology.

Common Deficiencies in DCF Valuations

While the DCF methodology is conceptually sound, the conclusions derived from its application can be misleading for various reasons, including the following:

- the reasonableness of the forecast. Fundamental to a credible value conclusion are financial projections that are founded on reasonable, internally consistent assumptions. In some cases, the value conclusions are derived from projections premised on aggressive sales growth assumptions or cost savings that are not realistically attainable. An objective assessment of the forecast requires an understanding of the business itself and the industry in which it operates;

- inadequate consideration of costs. While the revenue growth set out in the forecast might be plausible, the costs associated with achieving that growth are sometimes not adequately considered. For example, revenue growth often necessitates additional capital spending or other fixed costs to support expansion. A common oversight in financial forecasts is the failure to consider the incremental investment required in terms of net trade working capital to finance growth in revenues. Another common, flawed assumption is the ability of a business to leverage its fixed cost structure. Most fixed costs eventually increase with higher sales volumes. The use of reasonableness tests can help in identifying assumptions that might not be supportable;

- the terminal value calculation. In most DCF valuations, the terminal value represents the largest component of the enterprise value conclusion. However, the terminal value calculation is sometimes premised on assumptions of normalized discretionary cash flows and growth rates (embedded in the capitalization rate) that may not be sustainable over the long term; and

- technical errors. Because DCF calculations are sometimes complex, they are generally more prone to include technical valuation errors as opposed to other valuation methodologies. One of the more common technical errors is the inconsistency between the discount rate adopted and the process by which the projected cash flows have been developed. For example, where inflation is included in the cash flow projections, inflation should also be included in the discount rate, and vice-versa.

Summary

The DCF methodology is the preferred valuation methodology, both in theory and practice. The in-depth analysis and forecasts that accompany a DCF methodology usually contribute to a more comprehensive understanding of the risks and opportunities faced by a business, and hence to a more supportable value conclusion.

Forecast discretionary cash flows are discounted to their present value. The terminal value component captures the value of the business beyond the forecast period and is discounted to its present value amount. The present value of tax pools not accounted for in the forecast or terminal value are added in order to determine the enterprise value of the business. Interest-bearing debt and equivalents (net of excess cash) are deducted, and adjustments are made for redundant assets, excess or deficient net operating assets (e.g., working capital) and other items not otherwise accounted for, to derive the equity value of the business.

A meaningful value conclusion must ensure the forecast adopted is both reasonable and internally consistent. Particular attention should be paid to implied operating ratios (e.g., market share, profit margins, etc.) as well as to the assumptions regarding incremental capital expenditures and working capital requirements. Given that, in most cases, the terminal value represents the most significant component of the value conclusion, careful consideration must also be afforded to the determination of normalized discretionary cash flow and to the long-term growth rate beyond the forecast period.

Chapter 7

Rates of Return

Introduction

Developing rates of return (i.e., discount rates and capitalization rates) is a subjective exercise. There is no definitive correct method. However, the rates of return adopted in a capitalized cash flow or discounted cash flow methodology should represent a highly plausible synthesis of factors that have been objectively and thoroughly considered. This synthesis should include important factors influencing the business itself, the industry in which it operates and the economic and credit market conditions prevailing at the valuation date. In addition, there must be internal consistency between the rates of return and the cash flows to which they are applied.

In valuation parlance, rates of return are normally expressed as a cost of capital. The starting point in assessing the cost of capital for a given business is the determination of an unlevered cost of equity, (i.e., a discount rate or capitalization rate that assumes a debt-free capital structure). The unlevered cost of equity is a function of operating risk (as distinct from financial risk) given the nature of the business, the industry in which it competes, and prevailing economic and credit market conditions.

The next step is to determine the degree to which the total capital requirements of a business should be financed by debt as opposed to equity in normal circumstances (i.e., a "normalized" capital structure). Where some level of debt financing is assumed, the unlevered cost of equity is adjusted to reflect the introduction of "financial risk" into the business. Financial risk is incremental to operating risk and arises because debt holders have a claim on the cash flows and assets of a business ahead of equity holders. The rate of return is then either expressed as a:

- weighted average cost of capital, where cash flows are determined on an unlevered basis (i.e., before debt servicing costs — the usual approach); or

- levered cost of equity where discretionary cash flows are determined net of debt servicing costs (i.e., interest expense and changes in debt principal).

Regardless of whether an unlevered approach or a levered approach is used, the cost of equity, viewed either in isolation or as a component of the weighted average cost of capital, should be the levered cost of equity. Stated differently, the cost of equity should reflect the risk associated with financial leverage (debt) in the business. It is axiomatic that the greater the amount of debt in the capital structure, the greater the financial risk and, all other things being equal, the higher the cost of equity.

Discount Rates vs. Capitalization Rates

The terms discount rate and capitalization rate are related, but they are not interchangeable. A discount rate refers to the rate of return that a rational, prudent investor requires in order to put capital at risk in expectation of realizing a future stream of cash flows from a business, given current and anticipated economic, industry and business conditions.

A discount rate is the rate of return used in a discounted cash flow methodology to convert a series of forecast discretionary cash flows to a present value (see Chapter 6). The discount rate is a function of the perceived risk that the business being valued will not achieve the levels of discretionary cash flows projected, as contrasted to the return on a benchmark "risk-free" stream of cash flows (i.e., the yield to maturity on long-term federal government debt).

A capitalization rate is the rate of return used to convert a point estimate of maintainable discretionary cash flow to present value. The capitalization rate is derived by deducting a long-term growth rate from the discount rate. Accordingly, there is an assumption the indicated cash flow will continue to increase at that growth rate in perpetuity. Depending on company-specific and industry-specific circumstances, the growth factor is normally comprised of expected long-term inflation and, in some circumstances, may include an incremental real rate of growth or other adjustments. A capitalization rate is applied to an assumed perpetual discretionary cash flow in the capitalized cash flow methodology or in the terminal value portion of a discounted cash flow valuation methodology. The inverse of the capitalization rate represents a valuation multiple (i.e., a multiple of discretionary cash flow).

The discount rate is the rate of return required on the investment, whereas the capitalization rate is the required rate of return less a long-term growth factor. The capitalization rate will only equal the discount rate when long-term growth (including consideration of inflation) is expected to be non-existent and where no other adjustments are required. Therefore, the discount rate should be determined first. Adjustments to the discount rate for long-term growth and other factors (where applicable) are then made to determine the capitalization rate.

Where discretionary cash flows are determined before debt servicing costs (which is normally the case) rates of return are expressed as a weighted average cost of capital (WACC). Therefore, the ability of a business to use debt in its capital structure and the risks associated with that debt are incorporated in the discount rate or the capitalization rate, as applicable. A weighted average cost of capital is a function of the relative mix of debt and equity and the appropriate returns on each.

Conversely, where discretionary cash flows are determined net of debt servicing costs (a less common approach), the rates of return are expressed as a "levered" return on equity in order to derive equity value. The levered return on equity reflects the risks of using debt in the capital structure. A levered return on equity is the rate of return required by equity holders, given both the operating and financial risks of the business. As discussed in this chapter, assuming internal consistency, either the unlevered (WACC) approach or the levered (i.e., levered return on equity) approach should generate the same equity value conclusion.

Regardless of whether a weighted average cost of capital or a levered return on equity is adopted, an assessment of capital structure is an important determinant in discount rate and capitalization rate selection.

Throughout this book, unless otherwise specified, discretionary cash flows are determined on an unlevered basis (i.e., before consideration of debt servicing costs). By extension, the rates of return (i.e., discount rates and capitalization rates) are expressed as a WACC.

Principles of Rate of Return Determination

While the development of rates of return is subjective, it is important to adhere to the following principles:

- discretionary cash flows are the appropriate income stream to be discounted or capitalized;
- there must be internal consistency between the derivation of the rate of return and the cash flows to which it is applied;
- the tradeoff between risk and return should be considered in the derivation of a rate of return;
- the rate of return should reflect both operating risk and financial risk; and
- the discount rate or capitalization rate should consider relevant market rates of return.

Discretionary Cash Flows

Discretionary cash flows are the appropriate income stream against which to apply a discount or capitalization rate. As discussed in Chapter 5, discretionary cash flow is the amount of cash available to the capital-providers of a business after considering income taxes, capital spending (net of the related income tax shield) incremental net trade working capital and other costs that must be incurred to generate (or maintain) projected operating cash flows.

Discretionary cash flows are preferred to accounting earnings because earnings determined pursuant to Generally Accepted Accounting Principles (GAAP) or International Financial Reporting Standards (IFRSs) are subject to policy choices. In addition, accounting income can be smoothed according to the choice of depreciation and amortization policy, whereas discretionary cash flows must reflect the timing of a particular income or expense item. Recall from Chapter 1 the underlying principle that valuation is based on cash flows.

Internal Consistency

There must be internal consistency between the derivation of the rate of return and the cash flow stream to which it is applied. For example:

- where cash flows are forecast on a pre-tax basis (a less common approach) the rate of return should also be determined on a pre-tax basis. That being said, discretionary (after-tax) cash flows and after-tax rates of return usually are preferred;
- where discretionary cash flows are determined on an unlevered basis, the rate of return should represent a weighted average cost of capital. Conversely, where debt servicing costs (comprised of interest expense net of the related tax shield and changes in debt principal outstanding) are deducted when deriving discretionary cash flows, the rate of return adopted should represent a levered return on equity. The derivation and application of unlevered vs. levered rates of return is addressed later in this chapter; and
- the rate of inflation included in the discount rate should be consistent with the rate of inflation incorporated in the forecast cash flows. Where inflation has been excluded from forecast cash flows, it should also be excluded from the discount rate. A capitalization rate typically represents a real rate of return (i.e., net of inflation).

Risk-Return Tradeoff

The direct relation between perceived risk levels and required rates of return is commonly referred to as the "risk-return tradeoff." This is one of the fundamental principles of business valuation, as discussed in Chapter 1. In simple terms, all other things being equal, the greater the risk of achieving the discretionary cash flow projections, the higher should be the rate of return and vice versa. The discount rate or capitalization rate and the cash flows to which they are applied are interdependent. That said, as noted in Chapter 6, it is preferable to develop best-estimate cash flow projections and to adopt market-driven rates of return, rather than try to adjust the rate of return to an overly aggressive or overly conservative forecast.

Operating Risk and Financial Risk

The risks faced by any business can be broadly categorized as operating risk and financial risk. In the context of rate of return determination, operating risk represents the risk that projected discretionary cash flows (before debt servicing costs) will not materialize due to factors such as loss of customers, obsolete products, competitive pressures and so forth. Financial risk is the incremental risk assumed by equity holders resulting from the use of debt (financial leverage) since debt holders rank ahead of equity holders in their claim on the cash flows and assets of a business.

Regardless of whether the rate of return is expressed as a WACC or a levered cost of equity, consideration must be given to both operating risk and financial risk: each should be segregated and addressed sequentially. The first step is to determine a discount rate based on the assumption of a debt-free capital structure. Financial risk (or "financial leverage") is then introduced. In most cases, financial risk is based on what is believed to be a normalized capital structure for the business. As a result, the capital structure decision becomes a component of the rate of return derivation.

Market Rates of Return

Required rates of return are influenced by prevailing general market rates of return and any anticipated changes. Accordingly, when adopting what are believed to be appropriate rates of return, consideration should be given to prevailing and prospective economic factors and credit market conditions, including the risk-free rate of return, inflation rates, stock and money market conditions and the availability of capital.

Although market returns fluctuate on a daily basis, investor expectations are typically influenced by long-term historic returns experienced in public financial markets, measured both in absolute terms and in relation to returns on risk-free investments. This is not to suggest that discount rates and capitalization rates solely reflect stock market returns, but rather that investors normally consider alternative investment opportunities and the comparative risks related thereto in their rate of return calculations.

The Theory of Cost of Capital

Cost of capital refers to the rate of return required by the providers of capital, given the risks they perceive in the business and its industry, as well as prevailing economic and credit market conditions. There are two basic forms of capital: debt and equity. In this chapter debt refers to senior debt, which has a first claim on the cash flows and underlying assets of a business. Equity refers to common share equity. While there is a myriad of other forms of financing (e.g., subordinated debt, preferred shares and so on) they are essentially instruments that make possible useful variations in the basic debt vs. equity (i.e., borrowing vs. ownership) balance/tradeoff. Valuation considerations involving other forms of capital are addressed in Chapter 9.

Debt financing is attractive because the cost of debt financing is typically less than the cost of equity financing. Furthermore, interest expense is usually tax deductible, which makes debt financing even more compelling.

Modern finance theory postulates that the value of a levered firm (i.e., a business that uses debt in its capital structure) is equal to the value of an unlevered firm plus the tax deductibility of interest-bearing debt. Mathematically this is expressed as follows:

Formula 7.1
The Value of a Levered Firm

$$V_L = V_U + T \times D$$

where:

V_L = the value of a levered firm;

V_U = the value of an unlevered firm;

T = the marginal corporate income tax rate; and

D = the market value of interest-bearing debt.

For example, assume that D1 Limited generates annual cash flows of $2 million before consideration of interest and taxes. D1 has $10 million in net operating assets, comprised of net trade working capital and fixed assets. The company is subject to an effective tax rate of 25%. If D1 Limited were financed entirely through equity (say, 1 million shares at $10 per share), the return on equity and return on total capital would be 15%:

Exhibit 7A
D1 Limited
Rates of Return with a Debt-Free Capital Structure
($000)

	Cash Flow		Capital	Rate of Return
Cash flow before interest and taxes	2,000			
Less: interest expense		Debt		n/a
Cash flow before taxes	2,000			
Less: income taxes at 25%	(500)			
Discretionary cash flow	1,500	Equity	10,000	15.0%
Total net cash flow	1,500	Total capital	10,000	15.0%

(Discretionary cash flow plus
  interest expense net of tax savings)

In this case, the $10 million represents both D1's enterprise value and its equity value since there is no interest-bearing debt.

Now assume that D1 can finance $4 million of its net asset requirements with interest-bearing debt at an interest rate of 7%. The remaining $6 million is financed through equity (600,000 shares at $10).

If interest expense were not deductible for income tax purposes, the company's return on equity would increase from 15% to 20.3%. However, the return on total capital remains unchanged at 15% (based on discretionary cash flow plus interest expense).

Exhibit 7B
D1 Limited
Rates of Return with Financial Leverage
Non-Deductible Interest Expense
($000)

	Cash Flow		Capital	Rate of Return
Cash flow before interest and taxes	2,000			
Less: income taxes at 25%	(500)			
Less: interest expense (not tax deductible)	(280)	Debt	4,000	7.0%
Discretionary cash flow	1,220	Equity	6,000	20.3%
Total net cash flow	1,500	Total capital	10,000	15.0%
(Discretionary cash flow plus interest expense)				

Therefore, in circumstances where interest expense is not tax deductible, there is no impact on the value of D1's equity (on a per share basis), since the higher rate of return on equity only serves to compensate for the increased financial risk associated with using debt. Hence the return on total capital remains unchanged at 15%. Therefore, the (levered) value of D1's equity remains at $6 million ($10 per share), and the enterprise value of D1 remains at $10 million (comprised of $6 million in equity and $4 million in debt).

However, interest expense is usually deductible for income tax purposes. This serves to increase the rate of return on equity from 20.3% to 21.5%. The cash flow to equity holders increases from $1,220,000 to $1,290,000. The difference of $70,000 represents the tax shield on interest expense (calculated as $280,000 x 25%).

Exhibit 7C
D1 Limited
Rates of Return with Financial Leverage
Interest Expense is Tax Deductible
($000)

	Cash Flow		Capital	Rate of Return
Cash flow before interest and taxes	2,000			
Less: interest expense ($4 million at 7%)	(280)	Debt	4,000	7.0%
Cash flow before taxes	1,720			
Income taxes at 25%	(430)			
Discretionary cash flow	1,290	Equity	6,000	21.5%
Total net cash flow	1,500	Total capital	10,000	15.0%
(Discretionary cash flow plus interest expense net of tax savings)				

The tax-deductibility of interest expense causes the return on equity (21.5%) to be greater than the required rates of return (20.3% from Exhibit 7B). The result is that the value of D1's equity increases. Stated another way, from the viewpoint of D1's shareholders, the claim by the debt holders against the net operating assets of the company has effectively been reduced because the interest paid to the debt holders is tax deductible. Consequently, the value of D1's equity increases to $7 million.

Exhibit 7D
D1 Limited
Impact of Financial Leverage
($000)

Total net assets	10,000
Deduct: interest-bearing debt	(4,000)
Add: tax saving on debt at 25%	1,000
Value of equity	7,000

Given the increase in the value of D1's equity, the company's enterprise value has increased to $11 million, comprised of $7 million in equity and $4 million in debt. This result agrees with Formula 7.1 presented earlier:

$$V_L = V_U + T \times D$$
$$= \$10 \text{ million} + 25\% \times \$4 \text{ million}$$
$$= \$11 \text{ million}$$

In this example, the cost of equity is reduced to 18.4% from 20.3%. D1 Limited's return on total capital (i.e., its weighted average cost of capital) can be calculated as total net cash flow of $1,500,000 divided by the enterprise value of $11 million to yield 13.6%. Alternatively, the company's enterprise value could be determined by dividing the unlevered discretionary cash flow of $1,500,000 by the WACC of 13.6%, which equates to $11 million.

Exhibit 7E
D1 Limited
Rates of Return with Financial Leverage
Adjusted for Benefits of Financial Leverage
($000)

	Cash Flow		Capital	Rate of Return
Cash flow before interest and taxes	2,000			
Less: interest expense ($4 million at 7%)	(280)	Debt	4,000	7.0%
Cash flow before taxes	1,720			
Income taxes at 25%	(430)			
Discretionary cash flow	1,290	Equity	7,000	18.4%
Total net cash flow	1,500	Total capital	11,000	13.6%

(Discretionary cash flow plus
  interest expense net of tax savings)

Note that the total net cash flow remains at $1,500,000 in each of the above exhibits because the capital structure of a business does not impact operating cash flows; it simply dictates the allocation of those cash flows between debt holders and equity holders.

To summarize, given the tax-deductibility of interest expense, the *actual* rate of return to D1's equity holders has increased from 15% to 20.5%. At the same time, the company's *cost* of equity has declined to 18.4% because the level of financial risk is reduced as a consequence of the tax-deductibility of interest expense. As a result, the value of D1's equity increases from $6 million to $7 million, or from $10 to $11.67 ($7 million / 600,000 shares) on a per share basis.

The levered cost of equity can be determined pursuant to the following formula:

Formula 7.2
Levered Cost of Equity

$$K_{LE} = K_{UE} + (K_{UE} - K_{DP}) \times (D/E) \times (1\text{-}T)$$

Where:

K_{LE} = the levered cost of equity;

K_{UE} = the unlevered cost of equity;

K_{DP} = the cost of debt (pre-tax);

D/E = the ratio of interest-bearing debt to equity; and

T = the marginal income tax rate.

In the example of D1 Limited, the levered cost of equity is determined as follows:

$$K_{LE} = K_{UE} + (K_{UE} - K_{DP}) \times (D/E) \times (1\text{-}T)$$
$$= 15\% + (15\% - 7\%) \times (\$4 \text{ million} / \$7 \text{ million}) \times (1\text{-}25\%)$$
$$= 18.4\%$$

Note that the equity value (E) in the above equation is $7 million, based on its market value.

A strict interpretation of the preceding formula suggests that for a given unlevered cost of equity (K_{UE}), the levered cost of equity (K_{LE}) decreases as interest rates (K_{DP}) increase and, by extension, that the cost of debt (K_{DP}) has no impact on WACC. However, this is not the case in practice. As interest rates rise, businesses tend to employ less debt financing, thereby reducing the degree of financial leverage and increasing WACC. In addition, the unlevered cost of equity may increase with an increase in the cost of debt in circumstances where the:

- nominal cost of debt increases because of inflationary factors. Where the nominal interest rate increases, the nominal unlevered cost of equity should (in theory) increase by the same amount. As a result, interest and inflation rates over the long term have a direct impact on WACC calculations; or

- real cost of debt increases as a result of higher risk to the operating cash flows of the business (e.g., the volatility of unlevered discretionary cash flows). Where operating risk increases, it should also be reflected in the unlevered cost of equity, and by extension, WACC.

However, an issue arises where the real cost of debt increases because of the use of excessive amounts of debt in the business's capital structure (i.e., excessive financial risk). In this case, the unlevered cost of equity would not increase, assuming no change in the operating risk of the business. However, the incremental financial risk should be reflected in the levered cost of equity and WACC. The example below will serve to illustrate.

Assume that for D1 Limited in the previous example, the rate of interest increased from 7% to 9% because the company's debt holders believed the amount of debt utilized by D1 was excessive. Further assume that, because there was no change in the operating risk of the business, the unlevered cost of equity for D1 remained at 15%. A strict application of Formula 7.2 would result in the levered return on equity decreasing from 18.4% (computed above) to 17.6%:

$$K_{LE} = K_{UE} + (K_{UE} - K_{DP}) \times (D/E) \times (1\text{-}T)$$

$$= 15\% + (15\% \text{-} 9\%) \times (\$4 \text{ million} / \$7 \text{ million}) \times (1 - 25\%)$$

$$= 17.6\%$$

Based on this calculation, the financial risk component of the levered cost of equity would decline from 3.4% (18.4% less 15%) to 2.6% (17.6% less 15%), despite the increase in financial risk created by the higher real rate of interest. Clearly, this is counter-intuitive. The financial risk component of the levered cost of equity should be at least as high, and likely higher, with an increase in the real rate of interest due to incremental financial risk. Therefore, under these circumstances, the strict application of the conventional formulas for the levered cost of equity and WACC would be inappropriate.

Because, as a practical matter, the cost of both debt and equity financing escalate until financing is unavailable at reasonable rates, the equation for the value of a firm can be expressed as follows:

Formula 7.3
The Value of a Levered Firm with Excessive Debt

$$V_L = V_U + [T \times D] - C$$

Where:

C = bankruptcy costs, and is generally represented by a step function.

Therefore, where appropriate, an estimate should be made to reflect the incremental financial risk component in the levered cost of equity and WACC of a business that utilizes what is believed to be excessive financial leverage, unless an assumption is made that the buyer has the ability to refinance the business following the transaction. In a notional market context, it is typically assumed that a seller is not under compulsion to act because of excessive debt levels. Furthermore, normalized debt levels are typically based on the capacity of a business to accommodate senior debt financing as opposed to higher-risk forms of debt. However, in an open market transaction, excessive debt may influence the negotiating positions of the parties and the ultimate price and terms for the business.

In the end the capital structure decision becomes a tradeoff between financing through debt to increase equity value and financing through equity to reduce the risk of insolvency. In practice, it is rarely possible to determine precisely an optimal mix of debt and equity. Most businesses operate within a target range believed appropriate.

Limitations to the Theory of Cost of Capital

The theory of cost of capital presented above is premised on the assumption that the operating risks of a business are independent of its financial risks. This may not always be the case. For example, a business that employs excessive amounts of financial leverage may:

- risk losing customers who fear the business will become insolvent and be unable to honour its warranty obligations. The resultant prospective decrease in revenues, or relative increase in the uncertainty of revenues, would increase operating risk;

- be placed on cash-on-delivery (COD) terms by its suppliers, thereby necessitating an increase in net trade working capital requirements;

- have to forego required operating expenditures or capital spending in favour of debt servicing costs (principal repayment and interest expense), thereby placing its prospective operating cash flows at greater risk; and

- have to forego growth opportunities because of its inability to raise capital at reasonable rates to finance opportunities.

In each case, the prospective unlevered discretionary cash flows of the business would either decline or become more volatile, and create a lower enterprise value of the business on an unlevered basis. Consequently, a key assumption underlying the theory of capital structure presented above would not hold, in which case strict application of the theory would not be valid.

Also on the topic of excessive financial risk, recall from Chapter 1 that the definition of fair market value in a notional market context assumes that a seller is not disadvantaged in its negotiations, nor is the seller presumed to be under any compulsion to act as a result of its existing capital structure This is not necessarily the case in an open market transaction where the buyer may try to exploit the seller's excessive financial leverage in its negotiations.

Weighted Average Cost of Capital

Where discretionary cash flows have been determined on an unlevered basis (i.e., before debt servicing costs—the usual approach), the discount rate or capitalization rate adopted in the valuation methodology should reflect a weighted average cost of capital (WACC). WACC is a finance concept that reflects what is believed to be an appropriate fact-specific blend of debt and equity financing and their respective costs. The traditional formula for determining WACC is as follows:

Formula 7.4
Weighted Average Cost of Capital (Traditional Formula)

$$\text{WACC} = (K_D \times W_D) + (K_{LE} \times W_E)$$

where:

K_D = the cost of debt after-tax;

W_D = the relative weight of debt, (i.e., the ratio of: [interest-bearing debt] to [interest-bearing debt plus equity]);

K_{LE} = the levered cost of equity; and

W_E = the relative weight of equity (i.e., the ratio of: [equity] to [interest-bearing debt plus equity]).

The relative weight of debt and equity are normally determined by reference to their market values, not their book values. Although the business's cost of capital will change over time, its cost of capital or that of its industry is usually relatively stable from period to period, absent some dramatic structural reason that dictates change.

The determination of the cost of each of the WACC components follows. The issue of appropriate relative weights for each of the components, which is the essence of the capital structure decision, is addressed later in this chapter.

The Cost of Debt

The cost of debt that should be used in the WACC calculation is the after-tax cost of interest expense on senior debt. The appropriate tax rate is the marginal rate at which interest will be deducted for corporate income tax purposes. Importantly, the derivation of WACC assumes interest expense is tax deductible. The cost of interest should be calculated at current market rates based on a normalized level of senior debt financing. In this regard, the appropriate measure of senior debt financing is long-term debt, consistent with the long-term nature of a corporate investment decision.

The cost of long-term debt is not always readily evident. For larger companies, an indication of the cost of long-term debt may be reflected in a recent or prospective private or public placement, or by comparison to the yield on long-term corporate bonds of companies of similar size and business risk. For smaller companies, particularly those that are privately held, direct comparables are usually not available. In such cases, the existing or prospective senior term-debt arrangements the company has with its banks or other lenders may provide some guidance. Alternatively, the cost of debt could be developed based on prevailing long-term government bond yields plus a premium based on debt reporting services such as Dominion Bond Rating Service (DBRS), Standard & Poors (S&P) or other sources. The premium adopted would be based on the perceived riskiness of the business and the industry in which it operates.

When assessing the rate of return on long-term debt, it is important to note that it is the current or prevailing rate which is being evaluated; rates on existing long-term debt may not be indicative of current rates. Further, it is important that the long-term debt rate be based on pure debt instruments. Stated differently, debt which includes conversion features, bonus interest, and similar equity characteristics likely does not bear a stated interest rate which, viewed in isolation, is reflective of the return sought by a prudent arm's length lender whose only return will be interest income and principal repayment.

In theory, debt issue costs such as arrangement fees, legal fees and other expenses should be considered in the determination of the effective cost of long-term debt. These costs are sometimes significant. For example, if a company issues $10 million of long-term bonds at 7% and issue costs are 3% of the gross proceeds, the effective cost of the debt would be 7.22%, determined as follows:

Formula 7.5
Effective Cost of Debt (Pre-Tax)

Annual interest payment / (face value of debt – issue costs)

= $700,000 / ($10,000,000 - $300,000)

= 7.22%

However, in practice, issue costs are usually not factored into the cost of debt calculation. Furthermore, it should be noted that the above calculation represents the pre-tax cost of debt. The result would have to be multiplied by (1 – tax rate) to determine the after-tax cost of debt.

The Cost of Equity

As a general rule the cost of equity refers to the cost of common share equity. A detailed discussion of the derivation of the cost of equity is discussed later in this chapter.

The cost of equity incorporated in the WACC calculation (or adopted as a cost of equity applied against cash flows determined net of debt servicing costs) should be the levered cost of equity (i.e., the cost of equity given both the operating risks of the business and the financial risks introduced by using financial leverage).

Generally, the appropriate unlevered cost of equity is determined first, and that rate is then adjusted in accordance with Formula 7.2 to account for financial risk attributable to the amount of financial leverage deemed appropriate.

WACC Calculation Example

E1 Limited has an unlevered cost of equity of 12%, based on its operating risks. The company can raise long-term debt at a cost of 6%. A normalized capital structure is believed to be in the order of one-third debt and two-thirds equity. The applicable income tax rate is 30%. Given these facts, E1's WACC would be determined using Formula 7.4 as follows:

$$WACC = (K_D \times W_D) + (K_{LE} \times W_E)$$

Where: the after-tax cost of debt (K_D) is determined as:

[pre-tax cost of debt of 6%] x [1 – tax rate of 30%] = 4.2%:

The levered cost of equity (K_{LE}) is determined using Formula 7.2:

$$K_{LE} = K_{UE} + (K_U – K_{DP}) \times (D/E) \times (1\text{-}T)$$

$$K_{LE} = 12\% + (12\% \text{ - } 6\%) \times (33.3 / 66.7) \times (1 – 30\%)$$

$$K_{LE} = 14.1\%$$

The relative weight of debt (W_D) and equity (W_E) is 33.3% to 66.7%. Therefore, the WACC for E1 Limited is 10.8%:

$$WACC = (4.2\% \text{ x } 33.3\%) + (14.1\% \times 66.7\%)$$
$$= 10.8\%$$

Note that the 10.8% WACC determined above represents the discount rate for E1, to be applied against unlevered discretionary cash flows (before debt servicing costs).

Alternative WACC Formula

Rather than determining the levered cost of equity and then applying the costs of debt and levered equity against their relative weights, WACC can be derived by the following alternative formula:

Formula 7.6
Alternative WACC Calculation

$$WACC = K_{UE} \times (1 – T \text{ x } D)$$

where:

K_{UE} = the unlevered cost of equity;

T = the marginal income tax rate; and

D = the ratio of interest-bearing debt to the sum of interest-bearing debt plus equity (i.e., enterprise value), based on market weightings

Note that the alternative WACC formula uses the ratio of debt to enterprise value (debt plus equity), whereas the levered cost of equity calculation (Formula 7.2) uses the ratio of debt to equity.

Applying Formula 7.6 to the facts provided for E1 Limited derives the same WACC of 10.8%

$$WACC = 12\% \times [(1 – (30\% \times 33.3\%)]$$
$$= 10.8\%$$

The alternative formula gives effect to the cost of both debt and levered equity through the interaction of the unlevered cost of equity (K_{UE}) and the ratio of debt to total capital (D), where both are based on market weightings.

While the cost of debt is not specifically addressed in the alternative formula, it is effectively embedded in it since interest expense and the unlevered cost of equity (K_{UE}) are influenced by the same factors. Specifically, both measures are influenced by a real rate of return (given the operating risks of the business) and inflationary factors. Therefore, where the relevant factors are viewed on a consistent basis, the net effect is that the cost of debt is cancelled out.

The benefits of using the alternative formula are that:

- it does not require a separate conversion of the unlevered cost of equity to the levered cost of equity; and

- importantly, it helps to ensure internal consistency in the derivation of the components of the cost of capital (i.e., the cost of debt, the unlevered cost of equity and financial risk).

It follows that the formula for the derivation of the cost of capital for any given business can be viewed as having two components:

- the unlevered cost of equity (K_{UE}); and

- the ratio of debt to enterprise value (D), the essence of the capital structure decision.

Determining the Unlevered Cost of Equity

As previously noted, a discount rate is the rate of return used in the discounted cash flow methodology to convert a series of forecast discretionary cash flows to present value. The derivation of an appropriate discount rate or range of discount rates necessitates thorough analysis of the business being valued, the industry in which it operates, and economic and credit market conditions that influence rates of return in general. Discount rates are point-in-time specific.

The starting point in discount rate determination is the estimation of an appropriate unlevered cost of equity. The unlevered cost of equity reflects the risks attached to achieving the projected discretionary cash flows before consideration of debt servicing costs (i.e., unlevered discretionary cash flows). It follows that the unlevered cost of equity should reflect the degree of operating risk attached to the business and hence to any projection of its unlevered discretionary cash flows.

Assuming a long-term investment horizon, the unlevered cost of equity employed when determining enterprise value at a specific point in time is typically determined by building up the following factors (the "build-up approach"):

- the prevailing long-term risk-free rate of return, which is taken from the yield to maturity on long-term federal government bonds;

- a public equity market risk premium, which is generally taken to be equal to the historic long-term premium generated by common equity in the public markets over average risk-free rates of return that prevailed during the same period (typically calculated on a geometric basis);

- adjustments for industry-specific risks and opportunities where it is believed such factors are not adequately reflected in the equity risk premium adopted;

- adjustments for company-specific risk factors and opportunities that have not otherwise been taken into account; and

- in some cases, other adjustments for factors such as liquidity considerations, abnormal market conditions or assumptions embedded in the forecast cash flows.

Exhibit 7F
Determination of the Unlevered Cost of Equity
Build-Up Approach

Risk-free rate of return

Add: public equity market risk premium

industry-specific risk factors

company-specific risk factors

other adjustments (where required)

Equals: unlevered cost of equity

Risk-Free Rate of Return

Time specific, market-dictated, risk-free rates of return are important reference points in the determination of cost of capital because at any given point in time liquid investments are available that offer virtual certainty as to timing and quantum of stated cash flow returns. It follows that a risk premium must explicitly or implicitly accrue either where risk attaches to the realization of prospective cash flow or is attributable to a lesser degree of liquidity.

The risk-free rate used normally is taken to be the prevailing yield to maturity on long-term federal government bonds. This is consistent both with the long-term investment horizon normally attaching to *en bloc* equity investments and with the determination of a normalized capital structure. The risk-free rate is a nominal rate, incorporating both an inflation component and a real rate of return. Over the past fifty years, the major variant in the nominal composite risk-free rate has been the inflation rate, in circumstances where the pre-tax real return component generally has fluctuated between approximately 1% and 4%. As discussed below, when adopting pre-tax risk-free market rates of return as the base for determining the unlevered cost of equity, the inflation component of the risk-free rate must be either integrated or eliminated.

When taken as the yield to maturity on government bonds, the risk-free rate represents a pre-tax rate of return. However the risk-free rate is usually not adjusted for the impact of corporate income taxes. Where a corporate acquirer invests in a risk-free debt instrument, the income on that investment is subject to corporate tax, thereby reducing the resultant discretionary cash flows. However, in the context of both notional market valuations and open market transactions, buyers can be viewed as intermediaries between public equity market participants (e.g., individual investors, equity funds, pension funds and other investors) and the target company. Public equity market investors typically assess their returns before personal income taxes. Therefore, public equity market investors typically compare the gross rate of return on risk-free debt instruments to the expected gross pre-tax returns from dividends and capital gains accruing from equity investments. In order to be successful in their role as intermediaries, buyers must earn average long-term rates of return on acquisition targets that are greater than or equal to the average long-term rate of return required by public equity market investors. Failure to do so results in a decline in the value of the buyer's equity per share. While not all buyers are public companies, the same theory extends to privately held businesses where individual investors are placing capital at risk (either directly or through a financial vehicle such as a pension fund) and therefore assess comparative economic returns.

Public Equity Market Risk Premium

The public equity market risk premium represents the historical return that public equity market investors have realized for placing capital in equity investments as opposed to risk-free securities. This premium is usually quantified with reference to long-term stock market rates of return (which includes dividends and capital appreciation) in excess of the yield to maturity on long-term federal government bonds.

In the United States, a common source of stock market returns is the publication *Ibbotson SBBI Classic Yearbook Stocks, Bonds, Bills, and Inflation*, published annually by Morningstar Inc. of Chicago. The 2011 *SBBI Classic Yearbook* suggests the equity risk premium from 1926 through 2010 (large company stock total returns minus long-term government bond income returns) was approximately 4.4% on a geometric average basis. In theory, the geometric average is preferable to the simple average in the context of business valuation because the geometric average measures expected returns assuming a long-term holding period.

In Canada, a source of historic stock and money market returns can be found in the *Report on Canadian Economic Statistics* published annually by the Canadian Institute of Actuaries. That publication suggests that the long-term equity risk premium in Canada (from 1923 to 2010) was approximately 3.9%, calculated on a geometric basis.

As a general rule, stock market returns cannot be directly applied when deriving an appropriate discount rate for purposes of determining the *en bloc* value of the business. In particular, aggregate stock market data largely reflects returns from relatively small lots of highly liquid shareholdings in a diversified portfolio. Therefore, when using public equity market data as a proxy to assist in establishing the unlevered cost of equity, the following things should be kept in mind:

- the rates of return in the public equity markets reflect a composite return on a wide range of industries. Therefore, adjustments may be required where the industry in which the subject business operates is perceived to be of significantly different risk than the market as a whole;

- company-specific risk factors, sometimes referred to as unsystematic risk. Modern corporate finance theory assumes that unsystematic risk is eliminated where a diversified portfolio is held;

- the comparatively lower degree of liquidity in an *en bloc* equity investment in the particular business as contrasted with public equity investments;

- market rates of return incorporate the impact of financial leverage by measuring returns on common equity. (It is not practical to segregate the financial leverage component of the market risk premium.) As a result, if a discount rate or capitalization rate derived using public market data is subsequently adjusted for financial leverage, then some double-counting of financial leverage may occur; and

- because of differences in individual and corporate taxation rates, prevailing corporate law, and other factors affecting the composite returns in public equity markets, rates of return derived from public equity markets in the United States and other countries may not, without adjustment, reflect appropriate risk-premium adjustments in Canada.

Some authors and practitioners have suggested that public equity market returns, being prices established from trading in normal-sized minority-interest shareholdings, incorporate a "minority discount." Accordingly, those individuals have suggested that, when determining the *en bloc* equity value of a business, a downward adjustment should be applied to a public equity market risk premium (resulting in a higher equity value) to reflect the benefits associated with control; or, alternatively, that the implied public equity valuation multiples be increased on account of a so-called "premium for control." However, it is generally accepted that highly liquid shares of public companies do not experience a minority discount since an investor has full control over whether to retain or dispose of the investment.

The notion that a minority discount does not apply to freely traded shares is further demonstrated in that no such discount is normally applied by stock analysts. However, in cases where a public company's shares are illiquid, that factor should be taken into account.

As a result, in most cases, it follows that where *en bloc* equity value is being determined, no adjustment should be made to the public equity market risk premium (or implied valuation multiples) to account for a so-called "premium for control." The concept of, and reasons for, discounts from *en bloc* value in the context of minority shareholders in privately held companies is discussed in Chapter 8.

Industry-Specific Risk Factors

Industry-specific (or external) risk factors address primarily the risks faced by all companies in a particular industry. The public equity market risk premium discussed above normally reflects a composite rate of return, and may not reflect the particular risks and opportunities of a given industry. Accordingly, an adjustment may be required to increase or decrease the unlevered cost of equity, depending on whether the industry is more or less risky than the level of risk implied in public equity market rates of return.

Where applicable, an adjustment for industry-specific risks is necessarily subjective. Having said that, it normally should consider:

- industry susceptibility to general economic conditions. Certain industries are more susceptible than others to fluctuations in the economy. For example, steel producers tend to experience greater cyclicality in their business than do food and drug producers;

- the regulatory or political environment. Where an industry is subject to government intervention and controls that are expected to continue at the same or increased levels, rates of return tend to be higher than otherwise would be the case. The exception to this is where government regulation effectively grants an exclusive or protective licence to operate. In such circumstances, the resultant market protection generally contributes to comparatively reduced operating risk and therefore a lower required rate of return than otherwise would be the case;

- the degree to which the industry is affected by social trends, such as health consciousness, environmental awareness, etc.;

- the degree to which the industry is affected by demographic trends such as age, income, education, etc.;

- financial market psychology. At various times, certain industries may go through glamour periods, an example being the technology industry in the late 1990s where investments in internet related businesses were being made at imputed near-term rates of return that were difficult, if not impossible, to rationalize in traditional economic terms;

- the competitive structure, including industry ease of entry. Capital-intensive industries are sometimes viewed as having a barrier to entry for new competitors. It is axiomatic that unusually high rates of return and profitability attract competition. This, in combination with considerations related to market share, cost structure, required capital investment, and existing competition's comparative positions with respect to these and other things, all influence the rate of return selection. Where industry entry is costly, difficult, or regulated, existing businesses tend to be at less risk and therefore require rates of return lower than would otherwise be the case. The converse is also true;

- sources, prices, and price trends of key inputs where they are subject to volatility (e.g., the price of oil to the airline industry);

- industry rationalization. Historically, significant transaction activity in a given industry has resulted in point-in-time downward adjustments to expected rates of return within those industries. The primary reason for this relates to the fact that there are a finite number of available viable acquisition targets. Acquisition interest on the part of more than one buyer typically results in a higher ultimate price being paid for a business than would otherwise be the case. Moreover, industry consolidation generally results in a greater degree of liquidity, which in turn has an upward influence on price;

- the current and future impact on an industry of changes in regional, provincial, national and international trading patterns, manufacturing costs, transportation costs, and similar factors;

- the current and future impact of continually escalating technological change on an industry; and

- the projected industry growth rate. Businesses participating in growing industries are more likely to experience near-term growth in discretionary cash flows than are businesses participating in mature or declining industries where growth depends to a large extent on increasing market share which for them is usually more costly and riskier.

When making adjustments for industry-specific risks, it is important to avoid double-counting. Stated differently, many of the critical risk factors may already be considered in the cash flow forecast. For example, where a business is subject to environmental regulation, related capital and maintenance compliance costs will typically be included in a cash flow forecast and hence need not be further considered as a separate adjustment for industry-specific risk. However, the direction of the regulatory process may indicate that, although the business is currently in compliance, without incurring additional future costs, business continuity may be at risk. These future costs, not being quantifiable, cannot be accounted for in the cash flow forecast. Accordingly, this incremental risk must be accounted for by increasing what would otherwise be the unlevered cost of equity.

Company-Specific Risk Factors

Company-specific (or internal) risk factors are those peculiar to a business that are not accounted for in an assessment of industry risk factors. An upward or downward adjustment in the unlevered cost of equity may be required where a business faces more or less risk than does its industry in general, where the cash flow projections do not adequately reflect the specific risks or opportunities of the business being valued. Identifying the critical factors influencing the direction, opportunities and potential of a business is essential to the determination of an appropriate unlevered cost of equity. Each such factor, viewed separately, may have either a positive or a negative impact; a melding of these positives and negatives will contribute to the selection of an appropriate rate of return.

The adjustment for company-specific risk (sometimes referred to as "unsystematic risk") in the derivation of the unlevered cost of equity (and by extension the discount rate) is one of the fundamental differences between public market securities analysis and the derivation of discount rates pursuant to business valuation. As a general rule, analysts of publicly traded securities do not adjust for company-specific risks on the assumption that the investor holds a diversified portfolio of publicly traded securities and, consequently, in theory, the changes in the market value of any particular investment because of non-systematic (i.e., non market-related) factors has little bearing on the overall portfolio return. However, most corporate buyers do not view *en bloc* equity investments as one component of a portfolio, and therefore will normally adjust for company-specific risk factors where they believe that these are not otherwise adequately accounted for. Further, and as a practical matter, the perceived risk of an *en bloc* equity investment to a corporate buyer is normally relatively greater compared to the purchase of a normal-sized trading lot of securities, from the standpoint of the holder of a diversified portfolio. This is so from the standpoint of the impact a failed acquisition has on the buyer's consolidated earnings, the potential longer-term consequences to the buyer's business and the personal implications to the business managers responsible for the investment decision.

When determining an appropriate rate of return, company-specific risk factors that should be considered normally include:

- product and service offerings. Where the company's products and services are differentiated, protected by patent or copyright, or have brand name recognition, a lower rate of return would generally be expected than if no such benefits existed;

- the degree of diversification in both product and service offerings, and geographic coverage. As a general rule, the wider the product and service offering and the wider the geographic coverage, the lower will be the required rate of return;

- life cycles of the product offerings. Where product life cycles are short and continuing investment in research and development is required, there is additional risk that a business's competitive position may erode, perhaps quickly, if such investments are diminished or stopped;

- competitive advantage. Where a company has developed a competitive advantage that is both sustainable and transferable to a new owner, that fact tends to reduce the required rate of return sought by investors;

- customer stability and concentration. In general, where a business is dependent on a few customers, required rates of return are higher than where a business has many customers and little or no customer dependence. Further, where the business has a pattern of repeat business, that tends to reduce risk and hence reduce the required rate of return;

- management depth, including consideration of whether there is dependence on specific managers or other key personnel for business continuity. In general, greater management depth and continuity implies lower risk. Where business continuity is dependent on the personal involvement of one or more individuals, as a general rule risk is greater and required rates of return are higher than they would be otherwise. A certain amount of management dependence is a factor common to many privately held companies. The important distinction to be made is that between dependence on management ability and dependence on existing management's personal contacts (i.e., personal goodwill, as discussed in Chapter 1);

- ability to cope with and react to change. Where the management has demonstrated an ability to cope successfully with changing economic, industry, business, social and other conditions, a lower rate of return would be selected than if the business had not demonstrated this ability;

- supplier dependence. Where the business is dependent on one or a few suppliers for key materials or other inputs, that factor increases risk;

- labour force. Labour availability combined with historic and prospective labour relations affect risk assessment. In this regard, rates of return adopted for labour-intensive businesses tend to be higher than those adopted for capital-intensive businesses;

- the size of the business, both in absolute terms and in relation to other businesses in the industry. Smaller businesses normally have less market influence, less customer awareness, more restricted access to capital, less management depth, greater customer dependence, and so on. Each of these factors affects the risk to varying degrees. Where the rate of return is adjusted for one or more of these factors separately, those factors should not be considered again in any composite risk adjustment made on account of size;

- historic operating results and projections. Lower rates of return are adopted where historical results have remained relatively stable or demonstrated consistent growth, as opposed to historical earnings that have been erratic; and

- cost structure. A business that incorporates a high degree of fixed costs in its operating cost structure is subject to a higher degree of risk than a business that employs a cost structure with a high proportion of variable costs. The reason for this is that, by definition, fixed costs cannot readily be reduced or eliminated in the event of a downturn in operating performance, or it may not be practical to do so.

These company-specific risk factors are similar to those discussed in the derivation of valuation multiples in Chapter 4. As is the case with industry-specific risk factors, the unlevered cost of equity is not adjusted where company-specific risk factors have already been quantified in the discretionary cash flow forecast.

In some cases, an equity risk premium adopted from a service such as SBBI is taken as the return attributable to mid-cap or small-cap companies. For example, the 2011 *SBBI Classic Yearbook* indicates the following equity risk premiums (calculated as the difference between total returns within the stock category less the income return on long-term government bonds, on a geometric basis):

Exhibit 7G
SBBI Equity Risk Premiums
Geometric Average Basis

Category	Market Cap (U.S. $millions)	Equity Risk Premium
Large company stocks	over $6,794	4.8%
Mid-cap stocks	$1,777 to $6,794	5.9%
Low-cap stocks	$478 to $1,776	6.4%
Micro-cap stocks	$1 to $477	7.2%

Additional breakdowns are provided within each of these categories. Caution must be exercised in using any risk premiums reported in sources such as SBBI. One must first understand how they were derived in order to apply them in an appropriate and internally consistent manner, subject to further adjustments as required.

The rates of return for mid-cap and small-cap companies are premised on the lower degree of liquidity inherent in the shares of those businesses, as well as risks more commonly attributable to smaller businesses (e.g., greater customer concentration and less management depth). Therefore, where such data from SBBI is adopted in estimating appropriate rates of return, it is important not to double-count the embedded factors after a separate adjustment.

Other Adjustments to the Unlevered Cost of Equity

In some cases, adjustments to the unlevered cost of equity should be made for other factors such as:

- liquidity considerations;
- abnormal market conditions;
- inflationary assumptions in the forecast cash flows;
- aggressive or conservative forecast cash flows; and
- synergies embedded in the forecast cash flows.

Liquidity Considerations

As previously discussed, the market for businesses sold *en bloc* (or a controlling interest) is subject to fundamentally different drivers than is the market for normal-sized trading blocks in freely tradable shares of public companies. The public equity markets entail a certain degree of risk. Stock prices change every day and can sometimes be highly volatile. However, in most cases at any given point in time a public equity market participant dealing in normal-sized trading lots can readily convert public company shareholdings into cash at the prevailing market price with minimal cost. Absent unusual circumstances, even public equity market investors who claim to be in for the long term almost always have the option of liquidating their positions if they so choose.

As a general rule, the greater the length of time required to market and sell an asset, the greater is the illiquidity attached to it. The divestiture of a business *en bloc* or divestiture of a controlling interest may take several months or even years to complete, during which time significant events may occur that affect the value of the business. The ultimate proceeds that a seller may realize are much less certain than are proceeds generated from the sale of freely tradable shares in a public company. Further, the costs involved in the disposition of a business can be significant (including intermediary fees, legal fees and other costs) as a percentage of the ultimate sale proceeds.

Because of the reduced liquidity, rates of return for privately held businesses are usually greater than those implied in the share prices of widely held public companies operating in the same industry. Hence public equity market returns may require an upward adjustment to account for this added degree of risk. That being said, in most cases a separate adjustment for liquidity risk is not made because such risk is usually incorporated in the company-specific risk factors already accounted for. For example, a risk premium calculated because of a company's relatively small size usually reflects the fact that the business is less appealing to a broad range of prospective buyers. Consequently, a further adjustment on account of illiquidity for that same business may constitute double-counting.

The rates of return ultimately adopted using any valuation methodology should reflect the demand for the business *en bloc* at a given point in time, which itself is influenced by company-specific factors, industry conditions and prevailing economic and credit market conditions. Recall from Chapter 1 that liquidity is dictated by the number of prospective buyers for a business or equity interest at a given point in time. Where the rates of return determined by the build-up approach discussed above do not adequately reflect the degree of liquidity in the business, then a separate adjustment on account of liquidity should be made.

Quantifying the "premium for illiquidity" for any given *en bloc* equity investment is necessarily a subjective exercise. However, where it is believed that an adjustment for incremental *en bloc* illiquidity differences is appropriate, the following factors should be considered:

- the nominal risk-free rate and public equity market risk premium at a given point in time, and their historical and prospective near-term volatility;

- expected long-term economic and credit market trends and developments;

- the known or stated objectives of likely identifiable buyers;

- the current and prospective status of the industry vis-à-vis buyer interest, consolidation activity, number of competitors, degree of vertical and horizontal integration, and so on;

- the size of the business. Larger companies frequently have a greater number of potentially interested buyers because of the quantum of assets, market presence and other factors, than do many small privately held companies. Again, if the risks associated with business size have been previously adjusted for, they should not be double-counted; and

- the ongoing cash flow generated from the business, which will typically accrue to the benefit of the seller while awaiting a liquidity event. Greater levels of ongoing discretionary cash flow serve to reduce liquidity risk.

Abnormal Market Conditions

The prevailing conditions and projected trends in the economy and financial markets influence rates of return at any given point in time. In some cases, the financial markets may experience short-term anomalies that can distort the rate of return determined using a build-up approach. Examples include the credit crisis of 2008 or major geo-political events.

As a general rule buyers do not adjust their threshold rates of return for short-term fluctuations in the economy or financial markets. However, adjustments may be considered appropriate where changes in the economy or financial markets are expected to prevail over the medium-to-long term, or near-term changes are expected to reverse. In theory, adjustments to the rate of return for evaluating *en bloc* equity investments should be made only where the rate of return is deemed not reflective of expected long-term changes in general economic and credit market conditions. However, it is also important to look beyond a short-term adjustment such as the credit crisis of 2008 that created a weakened market for corporate acquisitions. Importantly, an adjustment to the rate of return would not likely be made where cash flow projections are thought to adequately account for these factors.

Inflationary Assumptions in the Forecast Cash Flows

The build-up approach for determining the unlevered cost of equity set out above begins with the risk-free rate, which is the yield to maturity on long-term federal government bonds. Prices of such securities are expressed in nominal dollars and include an estimated long-term inflation rate and a real rate of return.

In most cases, financial forecasts are prepared in nominal dollars. As such they include an estimated rate of inflation. So long as the inflation rate embedded in the forecast cash flows approximates the inflation rate embedded in the risk-free rate, no further adjustments for inflation are necessary. However, where the forecast cash flows are prepared in real dollar terms (i.e., net of inflation) or they contain inflationary projections that are materially different from those embedded in the risk-free rate, then the rate of return should be adjusted accordingly, in order to ensure internal consistency with respect to inflationary expectations. Discounting real-dollar cash flows by a nominal rate of return results in an understatement of value.

In theory, the inflation adjustment should be made on a geometric as opposed to a linear basis. For example, if the nominal discount rate is 15% and inflation is 3%, the real rate of return (or capitalization rate before further adjustments) is not 12%, but rather 11.65%. The applicable formula is:

Formula 7.7
Inflation Adjustment

$$[(1 + \text{nominal discount rate}) / (1 + \text{inflation rate})] - 1$$

As a practical matter, the calculation normally is made on a linear basis for simplicity (e.g., 15% - 3% = 12%). The difference between the geometric and linear adjustment increases as the rate of inflation increases.

Aggressive or Conservative Cash Flow Forecasts

As previously discussed, an appropriate rate of return selection is based on a risk-reward tradeoff or, stated differently, is a function of an appropriate relation between the rate of return and the cash flow to which it is applied. All other things being equal, an aggressive cash flow forecast should be subject to a higher rate of return and a conservative cash flow forecast should be subject to a lower rate of return. It bears repeating that it is important not to double-count rate of return adjustments made in respect of market, industry and company-specific risk factors, and those specifically reflected in forecast cash flows. The degree to which a forecast is aggressive or conservative is a matter of judgment having regard to:

- the general economic and industry-specific outlook;
- the nature of the industry and the business;
- the assumptions used in the forecast regarding sales growth, cost savings, competitive developments, and so on; and
- the purpose for which the forecast was prepared, including consideration of the knowledge, experience and potential bias of those individuals who prepared it, the time and extent of analysis incorporated in it, and various other considerations influencing its credibility (see Chapter 6).

Generally, where the cash flow forecast is believed optimistic or pessimistic, it should be adjusted to reflect what is believed to be a reasonable projection. This can be accomplished by:

- applying a probability factor to either the revenue projection or other forecast variable(s) and recalculating the discretionary cash flow, or applying the probability factor to the discretionary cash flow forecast itself, based on the perceived likelihood of achievement; or

- directly adjusting those revenue and expense items believed to be outside a reasonable range.

The projected probable or normalized discretionary cash flow would then be discounted at appropriate unadjusted "market-dictated" rates of return.

It is preferable to adjust the forecast and apply market-driven discount rates rather than attempt to adjust the discount rate itself. The reason for this is that the cash flow forecast reflects specific variables that can be analyzed individually when determining whether adjustments are required. As a result, adjusting the cash flow forecast is a less subjective exercise than making an adjustment to the discount rate. However, where a forecast believed to be aggressive or conservative is not given an estimated probability or normalized, it is necessary to reflect the risk in achieving the forecast through an upward or downward adjustment to the discount rate to compensate for the undue optimism or conservatism, respectively.

Synergies in the Forecast Cash Flows

Where the fair market value of a business is being determined for notional market purposes, the cash flow forecast typically is prepared on a stand-alone basis, excluding the impact of synergies that might be perceived by one or more possible buyers. However, in some cases, consideration of synergies might be included within the forecast cash flows. Similarly, where the value is being determined in the course of a contemplated transaction, the buyer will sometimes incorporate synergies into its analysis.

As discussed in Chapter 11, the realization of post-acquisition synergies is less certain than the cash flows of the business operating on a stand-alone basis. In some cases, synergies are subjected to a probability factor in order to reflect the risk they will not materialize. Where this is the case, no further adjustment to the unlevered cost of equity is required.

However, where the probability of synergies has not been estimated, an upward adjustment to the unlevered cost of equity is required to reflect the risk of their realization, in a manner similar to aggressive cash flow forecasts as noted above.

Capital Structure

Capital Structure in Theory and Practice

Once the unlevered cost of equity has been determined, a normalized debt to total capital ratio is applied to determine the WACC discount rate (as in Formula 7.6). The use of debt (financial leverage) serves to reduce the cost of capital and increase the enterprise value of a business. The issue to be addressed is how much debt should be employed in a particular business. This is the essence of the capital structure decision.

In theory there is an optimal capital structure for every business, being the mix of debt and equity that minimizes its cost of capital. As evidenced by Formula 7.1, all other things being equal, an unlevered firm can increase its enterprise value by employing debt in place of equity. As the percentage of debt in the capital structure increases, the cost of capital decreases, which in turn has the effect of increasing enterprise value.

Exhibit 7H illustrates this concept. As financial leverage increases, the cost of both debt and equity increase because of the increase in financial risk. At comparatively low levels of financial leverage, the cost of debt increases minimally as leverage increases. As a result, substituting debt for equity initially leads to a lower WACC. The savings resulting from substituting a lower cost source of funds (i.e., debt for equity) more than offsets the increase in the cost of equity capital. The cost of debt begins to increase more dramatically as financial risk increases (e.g., as a company exceeds its capacity to accommodate senior debt and must rely increasingly on high-rate subordinated debt financing). The levered cost of equity increases exponentially with financial risk levels. Beyond some point, which determines the point of the optimal capital structure in Exhibit 7H, the increase in the cost of debt and equity capital more than offsets the savings resulting from substituting debt for equity. In theory, by adopting the optimal capital structure, WACC is minimized and enterprise value is maximized.

Exhibit 7H
Cost of Capital

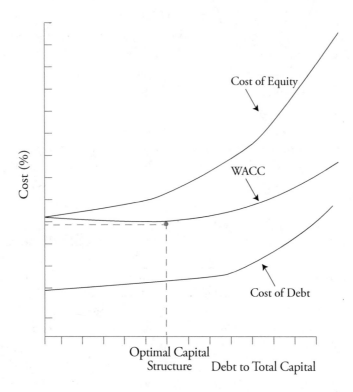

From a shareholder's point of view, an optimal capital structure results in maximizing the price per share. Additional debt beyond the point of an optimal capital structure causes the incremental increase in the cost of equity to exceed the incremental benefit of using additional debt, thereby eroding shareholder value. Stated differently, common share prices begin to decline when the present value of the expected tax advantages of incremental debt are no longer attractive enough to compensate investors for the additional financial risk associated with that debt.

Although in theory the optimal capital structure can be found by balancing the tax-shield benefits of leverage against the financial distress and agency costs of leverage, in practice there are no set formulas or methodologies for determining the optimal capital structure for a particular business. Empirical evidence shows capital structures vary widely among businesses, even those operating in the same industry. It follows that informed judgment is a major component in capital structure decisions.

In a notional market valuation, it is assumed the enterprise value of the business is not influenced by the way in which the business is financed (as set out in the "Principles of Business Valuation" section of Chapter 1). As previously discussed, modern capital structure theory assumes that the operating risks of a business are distinct from its financial risks. Therefore, the impact of the debt/equity mix is reflected in the allocation of enterprise value among the providers of capital to the business, first to the holders of interest-bearing debt (and equivalents), with the residual accruing to the equity holders.

The definition of fair market value assumes a sufficient number of potential buyers are interested in acquiring a business and, in addition, the seller is not disadvantaged in negotiations by employing levels of debt higher or lower than those perceived as normal by the market. Stated another way, it would be usual to assume that although a business may be under-levered or over-levered, prospective buyers value the business (on a stand-alone basis) on what they believe to be a normalized capital structure.

In open market transactions, a buyer will consider its ability to finance an acquisition with debt as opposed to equity. The ability of a buyer to raise financing on attractive terms will lower its cost of capital and may influence investment decisions. Therefore, a buyer's debt capacity has an influence on the price they are prepared to pay for an acquisition target. In open market transactions, there may be a significant difference between the debt financing capacity of the buyer and the seller, particularly where the buyer is a large enterprise with the ability to raise debt on attractive terms.

Whether or not the buyer reflects its lower cost of capital (effectively a synergy) in its offer price is a function of the relative negotiating positions of the parties. Where a buyer believes a target business is over-levered and, as a result, the buyer thinks it has a negotiating advantage that can be exploited against the seller, the buyer will normally consider this in its pricing decision. Furthermore, where a non-controlling interest is being acquired, the buyer will usually consider the existing capital structure in its pricing decision since it cannot unilaterally control the capital structure decision following the transaction.

Whether or not debt exists as a component of the capital structure of a target company at the valuation date, the market will reflect the capacity of the business to finance with debt. It follows that in the context of a notional market valuation or open market transaction, it is necessary to consider whether the existing capital structure is "normal" or "appropriate" based on the nature of the business being valued and the industry in which it competes. This task is necessarily subjective. However, where the debt to equity ratio appears to be outside a reasonable range, adjustments should be made to normalize the level of debt financing and financial risk. In an open market transaction, the buyer can then decide whether it wants to modify its offer based on its ability (or inability) to raise debt financing, and to consider other matters such as the terms of the deal and the relative negotiating positions of the parties. These factors are discussed in Chapter 11.

Estimating a Normalized Capital Structure

Estimating a normalized capital structure represents a trade-off between senior debt and common share equity. While debt and equity financing can assume other forms such as subordinated debt, convertible debt, participating debt or preferred shares, each of these financial instruments is a variation of senior debt financing or common share equity financing or a combination of the two. Other forms of financing and their implications on valuation are discussed in Chapter 9.

The amount of debt used in privately held businesses is often a reflection of the personal preferences and personal financial position of the owner(s). Therefore, there may be a wide gap between the amount of debt utilized and that considered normal, given the nature of the business and the industry in which it operates. On the other hand, public companies are more likely to employ a capital structure management believes to be appropriate (although this is not always the case). Notwithstanding, notional adjustments to a public company's capital structure may be required where the company:

- is conservatively financed, both in absolute terms and in relation to other companies in its industry. This sometimes occurs where the public company is closely controlled and as a result is not at risk of being acquired; or

- employs excessive debt financing such that leverage is beyond what can reasonably be regarded as acceptable given the nature of the business and the industry.

When determining an appropriate amount of debt for both privately held and public companies, it should be recognized that companies normally do not borrow to the maximum of their debt financing ability. Management groups typically prefer to be in a position where they can choose to borrow or pay off debt instead of being compelled to borrow or pay off debt. Excessive debt can also have negative implications for a business that has to forego capital spending or growth initiatives in favour of debt servicing. Consequently, managers generally use less debt than would maximize the near-term value of their business because they want to maintain borrowing flexibility, thereby maximizing long-term value. Moreover, because debt and equity offerings are usually executed in blocks and not small increments, businesses normally operate within a range of debt to equity ratios.

The determination of the weighted average cost of capital demonstrates a convex as opposed to linear relationship (see Exhibit 7H). Therefore, minor deviations from the "optimum" amount of debt generally have little impact on either the determination of the weighted average cost of capital or resultant enterprise value.

By way of example, recall that the estimated WACC for E1 Limited was 10.8%, based on an unlevered return on equity of 12%, a debt to total capital ratio of 33.3% and a tax rate of 30%. Had the normalized debt capacity for E1 been estimated at 40% (rather than 33.3%), then the WACC discount rate would have declined to 10.6% (using Formula 7.6):

$$\text{WACC} = 12\% \times [(1 - (30\% \times 40\%)]$$
$$= 10.6\%$$

This would not have a significant impact on the enterprise value of the business. Therefore, an effort should be made to get within a reasonable range of debt and equity financing, rather than a specific point estimate. That said, estimating a normalized capital structure for a business is a subjective exercise that requires consideration of a wide range of factors.

The literature on capital structure is extensive and sometimes contradictory. In the end, the capital structure decision is one that involves thorough analysis and judgment. When estimating a normalized capital structure for a firm, the following quantitative and qualitative factors should be taken into account:

Quantitative Factors

- the quantum of underlying tangible assets that can be used as security. Among other things, senior debt lenders are interested in the level of security of their investment. In general, the greater the quantum of underlying tangible assets, the greater the debt capacity of the business. Where substantial tangible assets exist, only in unusual circumstances would potential buyers conclude that an assumption of no debt is appropriate. That said, where a business owns real estate, the determination of debt capacity should assess the debt capacity of the real estate on a basis consistent with how the real estate is treated for valuation purposes (i.e., an operating asset vs. a redundant asset);

- the nature of the underlying assets. In particular, traditional lenders normally lend against specific assets (based on the quality of the assets) according to pre-set formulas such as:
  - ✓ up to 75% (or possibly higher) of quality accounts receivable under 90 days;
  - ✓ up to 50% of book value of inventories, although this can vary widely depending on their age and composition;
  - ✓ up to 75% of the appraised value of real estate assets; and
  - ✓ up to 60% of the appraised value of other fixed assets, which again varies depending on their nature (i.e., salability if they need to be seized as security);
- the estimated level of maintainable cash flows and potential variability thereof. Businesses with volatile cash flows, and hence substantive inherent risk, normally employ less debt than those whose cash flows are less volatile. Since cash flow is required to service interest expense and principal repayments, lenders will assess the debt capacity of a business with ratios such as: (i) total funded debt to EBITDA; (ii) debt to tangible net worth; and (iii) interest coverage. These ratios were addressed in Chapter 2;
- banking covenants that focus on balance sheet strength, such as the current ratio, the quick ratio and debt to equity (see Chapter 2);
- the degree of operating leverage measured by the relationship between fixed and variable operating costs. Businesses with higher operating leverage generally experience greater relative fluctuations in cash flow due to changes in revenue than do businesses that incorporate a greater variable component in their operating cost structure. As a result, they normally employ less debt than do those with relatively lower fixed operating costs;
- the amount of leverage employed by public companies believed reasonably comparable in terms of size and business risk. Where believed useful, a review of comparable public company financial information should address key debt ratios employed by those companies (e.g., debt to equity, debt to EBITDA, times interest earned and debt serviceability) and reports from security analysts pertaining to those companies should be read, when possible; and
- where the business being valued is a public company, additional information may be available to assist in determining an appropriate capital structure. This may include debt rating agency reviews or stock analysts' reports.

Qualitative Factors

- the nature of the industry. Businesses in non-cyclical industries generally employ proportionately more debt than do those that are highly susceptible to economic cycles;
- the effective marginal income tax rate paid by the business. The greater the tax rate, the greater the benefit of using tax-deductible debt financing. Concurrently, it is necessary to consider the ability of the business to fully utilize the interest tax shield;
- the prevailing and prospective pre-tax cost of debt. The lower the cost of debt, the more attractive it is as a financing source;
- the near-term and long-term strategies of the business. A business with aggressive expansion plans will employ proportionately more equity because of the greater risks attached to achieving growth and,

hence, the generally greater difficulty in obtaining debt at reasonable rates. Traditional lenders tend to prefer stable, slow-to-moderate-growth businesses since lenders do not share in the returns from aggressive growth plans, and may find their security eroded if the plans fail;

- the stage of the life cycle of the business. Businesses in early or growth phases tend to employ proportionately more equity in their capital structures compared with stable or mature companies where a higher portion of debt is more common; and

- existing banking agreements, which provide an indication as to current maximum borrowing capacity, security, rates, debt covenants, and other pertinent measures.

Capital Structure Estimation Example

F1 Limited is a manufacturer of heavy equipment. F1 has always been conservatively financed. Its balance sheet at December 31, 2011 is as follows:

Exhibit 7I
F1 Limited
Balance Sheet at December 31, 2011
($000)

Cash	23
Accounts receivable	1,656
Inventory	1,165
Prepaid expenses	66
Total current assets	2,910
Land and Building (net)	256
Production equipment (net)	652
Office furniture & equipment (net)	97
Net fixed assets	1,005
Total assets	3,915
Accounts payable & accruals	1,200
Taxes payable	64
Total current liabilities	1,264
Share capital	10
Retained earnings	2,641
Total shareholders' equity	2,651
Total liabilities & equity	3,915

The heavy equipment industry is cyclical and fluctuates with the level of capital spending in the economy. F1's financial performance over the last five years is summarized below. The company has not prepared any budgets or forecasts.

Exhibit 7J
F1 Limited
Statement of Income and Cash Flows
Fiscal Years Ending December 31
($000)

	2007	2008	2009	2010	2011
Revenues	14,262	16,163	10,619	10,450	12,780
Cost of goods sold	11,632	12,873	9,012	8,911	10,719
Gross profit	2,630	3,290	1,607	1,539	2,061
	18%	*20%*	*15%*	*15%*	*16%*
Operating costs	1,491	1,542	1,149	1,115	1,280
Income before taxes	1,139	1,748	458	424	781
Income taxes	320	510	148	132	237
Net income	819	1,238	310	292	544
EBITDA	1,320	1,936	594	581	950
Cash flows:					
Net income per above	819	1,238	310	292	544
Depreciation	181	188	136	157	169
Capital investment	(266)	(204)	(158)	(123)	(180)
Change in non-cash working capital	(238)	(423)	220	21	(291)
Net cash flow	496	799	508	347	242

Analysis reveals that:

- accounts receivable are 80% current (under 90 days) and 20% holdback for performance (i.e., over 90 days);

- inventories primarily include supplies and work in progress;

- the depreciated replacement cost of the equipment is estimated at $800,000;

- the current market value of the property (land and building) is $600,000. Because the building has been customized and is located in a rural area, it has been regarded as an operating asset as opposed to a redundant asset for valuation purposes;

- there are no unusual expenses. The company has always paid its active employees, including its shareholders market rates of compensation. Dividends were paid out in years of strong earnings;

- a commercial bank has indicated it will lend up to 75% against current accounts receivable, 33% against the book value of inventories, 50% against the depreciated replacement cost of equipment, and 75% against the market value of real estate;

- long-term debt rates for the company are 7%; and

- an analysis of market conditions indicates that the company could finance its operations up to the following levels:

Debt to EBITDA: 2.5×

Debt to tangible net worth: 1×

Interest coverage: 5×

Debt Capacity Estimation

From a quantitative standpoint, when estimating a normalized capital structure for F1, consideration should be given to:

- the company's debt capacity based on its underlying tangible assets; and

- the company's ability to service its debt through cash flow generation.

Using this information, an estimate of F1's borrowing capacity could be derived from analysis of underlying tangible assets, comparable ratios and interest coverage as follows:

Exhibit 7K
F1 Limited
Estimated Debt Capacity at December 31, 2011
($000)

Based on Asset Values:	Book Value	Market Value	Maximum	Borrowing Capacity
Accounts receivable	1,656	1,656	75% x 80%	994
Inventory	1,165	1,165	33%	384
Total short-term assets				1,378
Land and building	256	600	75%	450
Production equipment	652	800	50%	400
Total long-term assets				850
Borrowing capacity based on tangible assets				2,228

Based on Cash Flows:			
Debt to EBITDA			
EBITDA	950		
Multiple	2.5×		
Debt capacity (a)		2,375	
Debt to tangible net worth			
Equity	2,651		
Multiple	1.0×		
Debt capacity (b)		2,651	
Interest coverage ratio			
EBIT	781		
Coverage ratio	5.0×		
Maximum interest	156		
Interest rate	7%		
Debt capacity (c)		2,231	
Debt capacity based on cash flows - least of (a), (b), (c)			2,231

F1's debt capacity based on its underlying tangible assets is up to $2,228,000, given the ratios provided above. The debt capacity based on cash flows is $2,231,000, based on the least of the amounts that can be supported pursuant to the three tests provided.

Based on this analysis, the company might conclude that a normalized level of debt to employ in the business is approximately $1.5 million. While less than the maximum that might be available, it provides some cushion against unforeseen events, particularly given the cyclical nature of F1's operating results.

In addition to the quantitative analysis above, management of F1 should consider important qualitative factors such as the:

- company's near-term and long-term business plans and related spending initiatives;
- seasonality of the business; and
- general business strength and weaknesses (e.g., customer dependence, management depth, competitive positioning, and so on).

As a test of the reasonableness of F1's debt capacity, consideration should also be afforded to the implied debt to enterprise value ratio for the business. This can become somewhat of an iterative calculation, since higher debt levels reduce the cost of capital, which in turn increases the enterprise value of the business.

For example, if we assume that the enterprise value of F1 is $4 million, then $1.5 million of debt capacity implies a debt to enterprise value ratio of 37.5%. This ratio should be compared to industry norms, where meaningful data is available.

Threshold Rates of Return

Some businesses establish "threshold rates of return" or "hurdle rates" when assessing capital investment proposals and corporate acquisitions. Threshold rates of return may be expressed as an unlevered cost of equity, a levered cost of equity or a weighted average cost of capital.

Threshold rates of return are usually relatively static over a period of time and tend not to change with minor changes in prevailing market interest rates. They may be influenced over the long term by alternative investment returns, corporate income tax rates, public equity market trends and economic developments. Accordingly, they tend to be adjusted as circumstances both internal and external to the business change.

Threshold rates of return normally reflect a company's long-term cost of capital estimates and as such reflect the long-term risk-free rate, public equity market risk premium and industry-specific risk factors. Where they are expressed as a levered cost of equity or a WACC, the threshold rates of return have embedded the company's long-term targeted capital structure. As such, for any particular valuation exercise, adjustments to the threshold rates of return may need to be adjusted for:

- company-specific risk factors that apply to the target company;
- abnormal market conditions;
- strategically important considerations unique to the target company;
- differences in capital structure between the corporation and the acquisition target, where the acquisition target is being valued on an intrinsic basis; and
- other factors as required, in order to ensure internal consistency with the cash flows against which the rates are applied (e.g., forecasts prepared in real terms or those based on optimistic assumptions).

When adopting a threshold rate of return as a starting point, it is important to understand what it represents (e.g., a levered cost of equity or a WACC) and the underlying assumptions in its determination with respect to inflation, capital structure and other considerations. Failure to do so could create inconsistencies between the discount rate and the cash flows against which it is applied, with the result that the value conclusion would be misleading.

Capitalization Rate Determination

A capitalization rate is applied in the capitalized cash flow methodology and the terminal value component of the discounted cash flow methodology. As previously discussed, a capitalization rate is derived by deducting a growth rate from the discount rate. The growth rate contains an inflation factor and may incorporate an additional adjustment for real growth. Finally, where a capitalization rate is used to develop the terminal value component in a discounted cash flow calculation, a further adjustment for company-specific and time-specific risk may be necessary to convert a discount rate to a capitalization rate.

The relation between discount rates and capitalization rates can be summarized follows:

Exhibit 7L
Capitalization Rate Determination

	WACC discount rate
Deduct:	inflation
	real growth (where applicable)
Add / deduct:	terminal value adjustments (where applicable)
Equals:	WACC capitalization rate

The approach illustrated assumes the starting point is a discount rate expressed as a WACC, which typically is the case. Where the discount rate is expressed as a levered cost of equity, that would be the appropriate starting point.

Inflation Adjustment

Where the discretionary cash flow is determined net of inflation, the capitalization rate must also be expressed net of inflation (i.e., in real terms). In such circumstances inflation should be deducted from the nominal discount rate (typically expressed as a WACC). Where the discount rate is already stated net of inflation, no further inflation adjustment is necessary.

Using a real capitalization rate inherently assumes discretionary cash flows will continue to grow at the rate of inflation to perpetuity. The business will thus be able to pass along inflationary cost increases to its customers over the long term. This assumption may not hold for certain industries that are expected to experience long-term erosion in their profit margins. Therefore, a deduction for inflation should not be viewed as a mechanical adjustment, but rather should only be made after due consideration has been given to the ability of the business to realize such long-term growth.

Real Growth

The real growth rate does not include growth due to inflation, but rather growth due to sustained annual increases in real discretionary cash flows. Where real growth in after-tax cash flows from operations is anticipated, perpetual annual increases in both net trade working capital and growth-related capital expenditures are normally required to support the long-term real growth assumption. Accordingly, such costs should be incorporated in the determination of discretionary cash flows.

It is important to recognize that an adjustment for real growth assumes the business will generate a return on its invested capital in excess of its cost of capital. This may not be a valid assumption given that, for most industries, over the longer term, competitive pressures serve to reduce the ability for any particular business to earn a premium return on its capital. Accordingly, in most cases, an adjustment on account of real growth is relatively low (e.g., 1% to 2%), if made at all. Further, in theory the adjustment for real growth (where applicable), like the adjustment for inflation, should be made on a geometric basis, although a linear basis is usually adopted.

As the rate of growth embedded in the capitalization rate increases, the resultant enterprise value conclusion increases exponentially to a point where the implied value may not be realistic. For example, consider the case of G1 Limited, which generates annual discretionary cash flows of $5 million. Assume the nominal WACC discount rate for G1 is 12%. As the expected long-term growth rate increases, the capitalized cash flow for the company increases significantly:

Exhibit 7M
Impact of Real Growth

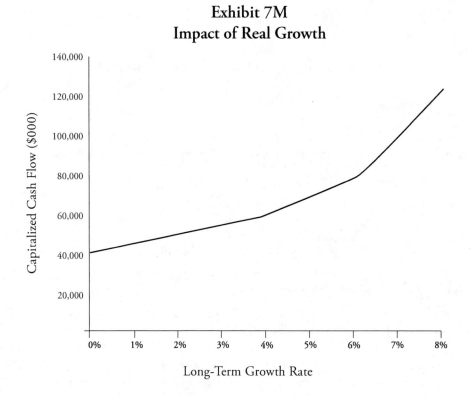

It is important to assess the reasonableness of real growth projections in light of the nature of the industry and of the business itself. The real rate of growth in discretionary cash flow may be greater than the real rate of growth in revenue if certain fixed costs can be leveraged over the long run. However, over the long term virtually all fixed costs will have to increase to accommodate higher revenues. As noted above, if a business cannot be reasonably expected to pass on inflationary costs to its customers over the long term (for example, where the business is in the decline stage of its product life cycle), it may be necessary to build a "real decline" into the rate of return (as contrasted with a real growth rate).

The prospect of a business sustaining high rates of real growth over the long term is unrealistic. Where a relatively high rate of real growth is expected in the near term, a discounted cash flow methodology should be adopted, with the forecast period extended to a point where modest long-term growth rates can be assumed. The reason for this is that the discounted cash flow methodology considers all pertinent factors relevant to the achievement of growth, and enables a more informed assessment of whether such a growth is sustainable beyond the forecast period.

To reiterate: while a business may expect to grow its revenues and profitability over the long term, that growth does not translate into incremental value (i.e., real growth) unless the return on invested capital exceeds the cost of capital over the long term.

Terminal Value Risk Adjustment

Pursuant to the discounted cash flow methodology, forecast discretionary cash flows are discounted for a given number of years (normally three to five), and maintainable discretionary cash flows are estimated at the end of the forecast period for the purpose of determining terminal value. Those maintainable discretionary cash flows may have a significantly different (typically higher) risk profile compared with forecast-period discretionary cash flows. This may be the case where, for example:

- the industry in which the business operates is going through a period of rapid change, and the discretionary cash flows maintainable beyond the forecast period are highly unpredictable;

- the business has a licence, patent, or some other strategic advantage that expires beyond the forecast period and might not be renewed; and

- the business is particularly sensitive to a political or regulatory environment that is subject to sudden change (e.g., because of an election or pending industry deregulation scheduled to come into force at some point in the future).

In such circumstances, the capitalization rate should be increased to recognize the greater uncertainty associated with the maintainable discretionary cash flow to which the rate is applied. In theory, such an adjustment should be applied to the unlevered cost of equity component of the capitalization rate where the change in risk relates to the operating cash flows of the business. An adjustment for financial leverage would then be applied. However, as a practical matter, where a terminal value risk adjustment is made, it more commonly is applied to the WACC capitalization rate otherwise determined.

Reconciling Capitalization Rates and Valuation Multiples

Recall from Chapter 4 that a valuation multiple is the inverse of a capitalization rate, not the discount rate. Furthermore, valuation multiples are normally expressed on a pre-tax basis, usually either as a multiple of EBIT or a multiple of EBITDA.

Valuation multiples normally are determined following an assessment of the business itself, industry and economic conditions, comparable public companies and comparable transactions (where meaningful information can be found). However, as a test of reasonableness of the capitalization rate derived using the approach outlined above, it can be compared to the imputed valuation multiple.

For example, assume that the WACC capitalization rate for H1 Limited is estimated at 13%, and that the company is subject to a tax rate of 28%. Further assume that depreciation and amortization expense typically run at around 20% of EBITDA. It follows that the implied valuation multiples for H1 would be determined as follows:

Exhibit 7O
H1 Limited
Determination of Valuation Multiples

Capitalization rate	13%
Implied multiple of discretionary cash flow (inverse of capitalization rate)	7.7×
Implied multiple of EBIT (multiply by 1 - tax rate of 28%)	5.5×
Implied multiple of EBITDA (multiply by 1 - depreciation as a % of EBITDA of 20%)	4.4×

The analysis above assumes that discretionary cash flows approximate EBIT less income taxes and, by extension, assumes that: (i) sustaining capital expenditures approximate depreciation and amortization expense; (ii) depreciation and amortization expense approximate capital cost allowance for income tax purposes; and (iii) there are no annual incremental net trade working capital requirements. Where these assumptions do not hold, further adjustments are necessary to reconcile the capitalization rates and valuation multiples. However, this reconciliation exercise is meant as a test of reasonableness more than as a means of arriving at a precise figure.

Discount and Capitalization Rate Example

J1 Limited manufactures parts for the automotive industry. J1 is contemplating the acquisition of K1 Limited, a small automotive parts manufacturer whose products are complementary to those of J1. K1 management has compiled the following unlevered discretionary cash flow projection for its business ($000's):

Exhibit 7P
K1 Limited
Discretionary Cash Flow Projections
Fiscal Years Ending December 31
($000)

	2012	2013	2014	2015	2016
Discretionary Cash Flow	1,200	1,400	1,600	1,800	2,000

Management of J1 is considering what discount and capitalization rates are appropriate to apply to this series of discretionary cash flows. Other relevant information follows:

- the prevailing yield to maturity on long-term government bonds is approximately 4%;

- the long-term public equity market risk premium is 5%;

- K1 relies on two customers for a significant percentage of its business. Furthermore, the business does not have significant management depth. The company is also susceptible to economic cycles, which have not been accounted for in the cash flow forecast. For these reasons, management believes that a company-specific risk premium of 12% is appropriate;

- the design patents on some of K1's product will expire in five years. Management believes this factor justifies an additional 3% risk adjustment in the terminal value;

- a normal debt to total capital ratio is estimated at 30%;

- the existing UCC tax shield is $6 million, with a blended average CCA rate of 35%;

- K1 pays cash income taxes at a rate of 27%;

- after five years, K1 is expected to grow at the long-term inflation rate of 2% without any real growth; and

- cash flows are expected to accrue mid-year.

Solution

Given the above scenario, as a first step, the unlevered cost of equity for K1 is determined as follows:

Risk-free rate	4%
Public equity market risk premium	5%
Company-specific risk	12%
Other adjustments (assume n/a)	0%
Unlevered cost of equity	21%

Next, the nominal WACC discount rate is determined pursuant to Formula 7.6, as follows:

$$K_{UE} \times (1 - T \times D)$$
$$21\% \times (1 - 27\% \times 30\%)$$
$$= 20\%$$

The capitalization rate is derived by deducting the long-term growth rate of 2% from the nominal WACC discount rate because of inflation. As noted above, no real growth has been assumed. However, a further 3% risk adjustment is required for patent expiry. The resultant capitalization rate is 21% (calculated as 20% - 2% + 3%).

Applying these discount rates and capitalization rates to the forecast discretionary cash flows results in an enterprise value of $10,314,000.

Exhibit 7Q
K1 Limited
Enterprise Value Determination
Based on the Discounted Cash Flow Methodology
($000)

	2012	2013	2014	2015	2016	Terminal
Discretionary Cash Flow	1,200	1,400	1,600	1,800	2,000	2,040
Capitalized at						21.0%
Capitalized cash flow						9,714
Discounted at 20%						
Discount factor (mid-year)	0.913	0.761	0.634	0.528	0.440	0.440
Discounted cash flow	1,095	1,065	1,014	951	880	4,277
Present value of discounted cash flows	9,283					
Present value of existing tax shield	1,031					
Enterprise value	10,314					

In developing this enterprise value conclusion, the following should be noted:

- for the purpose of determining the terminal value, the discretionary cash flow is increased by 2% over the 2016 level, consistent with the long-term growth rate assumption embedded in the capitalization rate;

- the present value of the existing UCC tax shield is calculated using Formula 5.4, as follows:

$$\frac{[\text{UCC of \$6 million}] \times [\text{CCA rate of 35\%}] \times [\text{tax rate of 27\%}]}{[\text{WACC discount rate of 20\%}] + [\text{CCA rate of 35\%}]}$$

$$= \$1,031,000$$

- mid-year discounting has been assumed.

It is important to remember that discount rates and capitalization rates are subjective. Therefore, sensitivity analysis should be conducted to measure the degree of sensitivity value conclusions have to changes in key assumptions, including:

- assumptions in the forecast discretionary cash flow;

- the company-specific risk premium of 12% (and the resultant discount rate of 20%);

- the long-term growth rate of 2%; and

- the terminal value risk adjustment of 3%.

An example of such sensitivity analysis was illustrated in Chapter 6.

Levered Cost of Equity Discount Rates

Where forecast discretionary cash flows are determined on an unlevered basis (i.e., excluding debt servicing costs — the usual approach), the unlevered cost of equity is converted to a WACC discount rate based on Formula 7.6. The resultant discounted cash flows represent the enterprise value of the business, from which interest-bearing debt is deducted to derive equity value (subject to possible other adjustments for redundant assets, one-time items and excess or deficient net operating assets). This methodology is commonly referred to as the "enterprise value approach" (or the "unlevered approach").

Where discretionary cash flows are determined on a levered basis (after interest expense, net of the related income tax shield, and changes in debt principal outstanding), the unlevered cost of equity should be increased by an appropriate financial risk factor to determine the levered cost of equity (Formula 7.2). The discounted (or capitalized) cash flows then represent the *en bloc* equity value of the business. In this methodology (commonly referred to as the "equity value approach" or the "levered approach"), if an adjustment is made to the notional amount of outstanding debt in the determination of an appropriate capital structure, a corresponding financing adjustment must be made to the *en bloc* equity value otherwise determined. Where the equity value approach is adopted, then the enterprise value is determined by adding the outstanding interest-bearing debt to the equity value conclusion.

Therefore, in the equity value approach:

- discretionary cash flows are reduced by interest expense, net of the related tax shield. The amount of interest expense deducted is based on current market rates and a normalized level of debt, which may be different from the amount of debt actually outstanding;

- changes in debt principal (to reflect an ongoing normalized capital structure) are factored into discretionary cash flow;

- the capitalization rate adopted then reflects a levered cost of equity as contrasted with a WACC. Again, the levered cost of equity is based on a normalized capital structure; and

- the resultant equity value is adjusted to reflect the difference between the assumed notional amount of debt and the actual amount of debt outstanding.

Therefore, the only differences between the equity value approach (levered) and the enterprise value approach (unlevered) are the ways in which outstanding debt and related interest expense are treated.

Although both approaches are theoretically acceptable, the calculations are simplified when the enterprise value approach is adopted. In the equity value approach, the notional debt adjustment becomes an iterative calculation based on changes in the assumed enterprise value. Furthermore, the equity value approach requires additional iterative calculations to rebalance the debt to equity ratio in each year of the forecast period (by adjusting for changes in debt principal) to ensure consistency in the levered cost of equity calculation. As a practical matter, corporate acquirers typically use the enterprise value approach.

However, in some cases the equity value approach can provide some additional insight for management. Specifically:

- incorporating debt servicing costs into the discretionary cash flow projections aids in the assessment of the ability of a company to service its debt obligations;

- where a business has non-capital losses for income tax purposes, it helps in assessing the likely timing of loss utilization, which is affected by interest expense; and

- it can make management more aware of the financial risk implications of using debt within the capital structure.

Importantly, assuming internal consistency in the application, the resultant equity value and enterprise value of the business should be the same under either the enterprise value approach or the equity value approach.

Take the example of L1 Limited, which has annual discretionary cash flow of $5 million, before consideration of debt servicing costs. Other relevant facts include the following:

- the nominal unlevered cost of equity for the company is 12%;

- an appropriate long-term growth rate is 2%, being the estimated rate of inflation (i.e., no real growth is assumed);

- L1 currently has $10 million of interest-bearing debt outstanding;

- the prevailing long-term interest rate for L1 is 6%;

- a normalized capital structure for the company is estimated at 40% debt to total capital;

- L1 pays income taxes at a rate of 25%;

- the present value of the tax shield on existing assets is nominal; and

- no adjustments are required for redundant assets, working capital or prospective one-time items.

Based on the foregoing, the WACC capitalization rate for L1 would be determined using Formula 7.6 (and deducting 2% for inflation) as follows:

$K_{UE} \times (1 - T \times D) - \text{inflation}$

$12\% \times (1 - 25\% \times 40\%) - 2\%$

$= 8.8\%$

Using the enterprise value approach, the resultant enterprise value and equity value for L1 are $56,818,000 and $46,818,000, respectively:

Exhibit 7R
L1 Limited
Capitalized Cash Flow
Enterprise Value Approach
($000)

Unlevered discretionary cash flow	5,000
Capitalization rate (real WACC)	8.8%
Equals: capitalized cash flow	56,818
Add: PV of tax shield on existing assets	nominal
Equals: enterprise value	56,818
Less: debt outstanding	(10,000)
Equals: equity value	46,818

However, where the equity value approach is adopted, the levered cost of equity is calculated using Formula 7.2 (and deducting 2% for inflation) as follows:

$$K_{UE} + (K_{UE} - K_D) \times (1- T) \times (D/E) - \text{inflation}$$

$$12\% + (12\% - 6\%) \times (1 - 25\%) \times (40/60) - 2\%$$

$$= 13.0\%$$

Using the equity value approach, the resultant enterprise value and equity value for L1 are the same as those determined pursuant to the enterprise value approach:

Exhibit 7S
L1 Limited
Capitalized Cash Flow
Equity Value Approach
($000)

Unlevered discretionary cash flow		5,000
Less: interest expense		
Notional debt	22,727	
Interest rate	6%	
Interest expense	1,364	
Tax shield thereon	(341)	
		(1,023)
Add: changes in debt principal outstanding		455
Equals: levered discretionary cash flow		4,432
Divided by: capitalization rate (real levered cost of equity)		13.0%
Equals: capitalized cash flow		34,091
Add: PV of tax shield on existing assets		nominal
Add: debt adjustment		12,727
Equals: equity value		46,818
Add: debt outstanding		10,000
Equals: enterprise value		56,818

Note that when following the equity value approach:

- interest is deducted based on the notional amount of debt outstanding. This is calculated as $22,727,000, which represents 40% of the enterprise value determined under the enterprise value approach (given the normalized capital structure of 40% debt to total capital);

- discretionary cash flows are increased by $455,000 per year, which represents 2% (the long-term growth rate) of the notional amount of debt outstanding. This adjustment is made to maintain the long-term capital structure of 40% debt, 60% equity; and

- a debt adjustment of $12,727,000 is made, which represents the difference between the notional amount of debt outstanding ($22,727,000) and the actual debt outstanding ($10 million).

Unless otherwise specified, the enterprise value approach (or unlevered approach) is used throughout this book.

The Capital Asset Pricing Model

The capital asset pricing model (CAPM) is a model commonly used by stock market analysts when estimating the required rate of return for a particular security. It is based on the concept that the required rate of return for a particular security is directly related to the riskiness of that security in comparison to other risky assets and the risk-free rate of return. Greater risk requires a higher expected rate of return. CAPM measures risk in terms of the volatility of the security price relative to a stock market index benchmark.

The capital market theory, of which the CAPM is a component, divides risk into two types:

- systematic risk, being the uncertainty of future returns because of the sensitivity of the return on the security to movements in the return for the market as a whole; and

- unsystematic risk, being related to the specific characteristics of the particular security.

The total risk to a business is the sum of its systematic and unsystematic risks. However, CAPM postulates that unsystematic risk can be eliminated by investors who hold a sufficiently diversified portfolio and accordingly, that the risk premium in CAPM relates solely to systematic risk.

The CAPM Methodology

The basic CAPM formula is expressed as follows:

Formula 7.8
CAPM Formula

$$R_E = R_F + B (R_M - R_F)$$

Where:

R_E is the rate of return on equity for a particular business;

R_F is the risk-free rate (normally taken as the yield to maturity on long-term government bonds);

B is Beta, a measure of relative risk (volatility); and

R_M is the long-term rate of return of the equity markets.

The CAPM formula is essentially a variation of the build-up methodology discussed previously where an equity risk premium is added to the risk-free rate. However, in the case of CAPM, industry risk factors are assumed to be incorporated through the use of the Beta factor and company-specific risk is assumed to be eliminated given the assumption of a fully diversified portfolio.

The equation $(R_M - R_F)$ is a measure of the equity risk premium, which is the additional return required over the risk-free rate for investing in the public equity market. It is calculated by subtracting the historic risk-free rate (normally expressed as the yield to maturity on long-term federal government bonds) from the historical return on common stocks. The return on common stocks is a long-term after-corporate-tax return based on increases in market indices such as the total return calculation for the S&P 500 index and reflects both reinvested dividends and capital appreciation. These statistics normally are obtained from publications such as *Stocks, Bonds, Bills, and Inflation* or the report on economic statistics prepared by the Canadian Institute of Actuaries, noted earlier in this chapter.

Beta is a measure of stock price volatility relative to the overall benchmark market index. Mathematically, Beta is equal to the covariance between the returns on a particular stock and those of the market viewed as a portfolio. An index such as the S&P 500 is usually taken as a proxy for the market as a whole. If a stock price varies directly with the movement of the index, it has a Beta of 1.0. If the price movements are greater, the stock price has a Beta greater than 1; if less, a Beta less than 1.

In CAPM theory, Beta is a measure of risk. A stock with a Beta of 1.5 is considered riskier than a stock with a Beta of 1.0.

The Beta for a particular company is estimated by using some average of the Beta factors for public companies believed to be comparable to the subject business, as contained in stock market services reports. This presumes that there are closely comparable public companies in the same line of business and that the shares of these companies have sufficient trading activity to permit a meaningful estimate of Beta. Where the equity risk premium is multiplied by Beta, the equity risk factor is adjusted for the price volatility of the comparable companies.

For example, if the risk-free rate is 4%, the long-term return on common stocks is 9% and the Beta factor is 1.2, then the return on equity derived using the CAPM methodology in Formula 7.8 is:

$$4\% + (9\% - 4\%) \times 1.2$$

$$= 10\%$$

Interpreting CAPM Results

Because public stock market data is used, CAPM-based rates of return represent those of freely tradable securities. Therefore, in the context of valuing a business *en bloc*, an adjustment may be required with respect to the reduced liquidity of an *en bloc* equity investment compared to a freely tradable and readily marketable security. Theoretically, CAPM rates of return have an embedded growth rate; an adjustment for that growth factor should be made to determine the discount rate. Unfortunately, the growth factor implied in CAPM rates of return is not readily identifiable, and an adjustment normally is not made.

CAPM rates of return represent a levered cost of equity. Therefore, CAPM-based rates of return should be applied to discretionary cash flows determined net of debt servicing costs. In addition, it should be recognized that the inherent leverage adjustment in the CAPM model is based on the comparables used in the derivation of the Beta factor. Therefore, to be consistent, the debt to equity ratio of the business being valued should be notionally adjusted to reflect the average debt to equity ratio of the group of companies adopted as comparable, thereby eliminating the need for any further adjustments for financial risk. Alternatively, the Betas of the comparable companies can be unlevered to derive an average unlevered Beta. A leverage factor can then be applied to the business being valued to determine levered equity. The formulas to derive unlevered and levered Beta are as follows:

Formula 7.9
Determination of Unlevered Beta and Levered Beta

Beta (unlevered) = Beta (levered) / [1 + (1-T) D/E]

and;

Beta (levered) = [1 + (1-T) D/E] × Beta (unlevered)

where:

$\quad$ T = marginal corporate tax rate; and

$\quad$ D/E = the market value of debt to equity.

For example, assume that the normalized capital structure for M1 Limited has a debt to equity ratio estimated at 30:70, and that the company is subject to a tax rate of 25%. Further assume that the average Beta for companies believed to be comparable to M1 is 1.4, based on an average debt to equity ratio of 40:60, and an average tax rate of 35%.

It follows that the Beta factor for M1 Limited would be determined by first calculating the unlevered Beta of the public company comparables as follows:

Beta (unlevered) = Beta (levered) / [1 + (1-T) D/E]

= 1.4 / [1 + (1 – 35%) × 40/60]

= 0.977

Then, the levered Beta for M1 would be calculated as follows:

Beta (levered) = [1 + (1-T) D/E] x Beta (unlevered)

= [1 + (1 – 25%) × (30/70)] × 0.977

= 1.291

Adjustments to the Basic CAPM Model

As previously noted, CAPM postulates that company-specific risk is irrelevant based on the assumption that it can be eliminated through a fully diversified portfolio. Where it is believed that this assumption is not valid, to account for the unique characteristics of a particular business, the CAPM formula can be modified as follows:

Formula 7.10
Modification of CAPM for Unsystematic Risk

$R_E = R_F + B (R_M – R_F) + R_C$

where R_C is company-specific (i.e., unsystematic) risk.

Company-specific risk factors represent additional risk not associated with comparable public companies. Such factors were addressed as internal company-specific risk adjustments as part of the rate of return build-up approach discussion earlier in this chapter. It is important to note that industry-specific adjustments are not required in the CAPM model because such influences are assumed to be addressed in the

Beta adjustment. Again, this approach to discount rate determination assumes that the comparable companies adopted are substantially similar to the business being valued, are closely comparable in so far as their respective business operations are concerned, and face largely similar market risks for their respective products and services.

Issues with CAPM

There are many issues surrounding the use of CAPM as a basis for determining appropriate discount and capitalization rates. In general terms:

- the identification of public companies that represent meaningful comparables to the subject business is a difficult and subjective task. As discussed in Chapter 4, true comparables seldom exist;

- CAPM postulates that investors are price-takers and by so doing eliminates the negotiating element in open market transactions;

- Beta is a measure of the relation between the price behaviour of shares of a particular company and a market viewed as a portfolio. Beta is influenced by returns both better and worse than market performance. However, corporate acquirers are more concerned with inadequate investment performance, and do not interpret excessive returns as risk;

- CAPM returns are implicitly based on a one-year hold period, which is different from the long-term investment assumptions associated with the determination of the value of a business *en bloc*;

- Beta figures for a given public company vary based on factors such as:
  - ✓ the market portfolio (i.e., the R_M component of CAPM) to which individual stock returns are compared. There are differences between the volatility of a particular equity market index adopted in computing Beta for a given business and the hypothetical market made up of all risky assets (which in theory is the relevant basis for measuring systematic risk). This is sometimes referred to as "benchmark error,"
  - ✓ the time period covered. Beta examines historical data and assumes the range of historical variability of the security, the market and the correlation between the two will persist. Where a company or its industry have undergone significant changes in recent years, Betas calculated based on historical data do not account for this, and
  - ✓ whether they are computed using daily, weekly or monthly data.

As a result, the Beta factor calculated for a particular company can vary with the source of data and the way in which it is calculated. In the end, Beta factors are unstable;

- empirical evidence indicates that actual returns do not match the theory of CAPM. Lower-Beta stocks have been found to generate higher than projected returns and vice versa;

- CAPM ignores the fact that stock market prices are based on factors other than Beta;

- Beta factors can be distorted for illiquid stocks, which may not move as much as the market, and could give the result of understated volatility; and

- as a practical matter, Canadian public equity markets lack the breadth and depth of the U.S markets and therefore the quantity of comparable companies is often insufficient for the purpose of using the CAPM methodology. Proponents of CAPM in Canada often advocate the use of U.S. data to generate a greater number of comparables. However, important differences between the two countries still exist (such as income tax rates and degree of market liquidity), which might have a significant impact on the application of U.S. data in Canada.

CAPM is commonly used by individual and institutional investors in public equity market security analysis and portfolio management, and the model lends itself reasonably well to that purpose. However, there are significant differences between these things and the valuation of a business *en bloc*. In particular:

- the basic CAPM model ignores company-specific risk. Although this may be acceptable to a portfolio manager or an adequately diversified individual investor, it is inconsistent with the basis upon which businesses are bought and sold *en bloc*;

- CAPM is based on public market data, which assumes liquidity. *En bloc* or controlling equity interests normally do not satisfy the strict definition of liquidity which generally assumes the ability to realize a known price quickly;

- acquirers of businesses *en bloc* typically have long-term investment objectives. Although individual and institutional investors may also intend to hold marketable securities for the long-term, the ability to liquidate their position quickly results in a reduced level of risk;

- individual and institutional investors rely primarily on publicly available information when making investment decisions. Conversely, where the *en bloc* equity value of a business is determined, the due diligence and acquisition process in an open market transaction is usually much longer, more detailed, and based on more information, including non-public information obtained under confidentiality agreements. It follows that in the latter case there is a larger base of information to assist in assessing the risks specific to a particular business. This difference in information availability is a fundamental difference between public equity market analysis and the acquisition of a business *en bloc*;

- individual and institutional investors can measure returns on public market investments almost immediately, and are able to do so continuously. Business owners typically measure returns on a monthly, quarterly or annual basis. This delay in return-measurement capability may increase the perceived risk associated with such investments;

- Beta is meant to indicate prospective risk based on historical results. As Beta changes, an individual investor or portfolio manager can readily alter their portfolio to compensate. However, most business owners cannot readily change the composition of their of business; and

- the risk of acquiring 100% or a controlling interest of a business is sometimes greater than the risk attached to acquiring a portfolio investment. The reason for this is that if the acquisition does not turn out as expected, the consequences can be significant for the buyer and the managers who recommended the deal. On the other hand, a bad stock pick can be absorbed by a diversified portfolio without significant loss of overall portfolio value.

As a practical matter, corporate acquirers tend to use pre-established threshold rates of return as opposed to short-term models such as CAPM. This is not to suggest that CAPM has no relevance whatsoever to a corporate acquirer. As noted earlier in this chapter, it is important to consider prevailing market rates of return when determining an appropriate discount rate or capitalization rate, and CAPM does accomplish that. Further, from the perspective of a public company acquirer, CAPM may be useful in measuring the minimum rate of return that buyer should seek at a given point in time. If the securities markets perceive an acquisition was completed at a rate of return below that suggested by CAPM, the acquirer's stock price may suffer following acquisition. Nevertheless, the appropriate rate of return to use when evaluating a target company may be greater than or less than that suggested by CAPM, depending on the specific circumstances of the subject business.

Common Errors in Determining Rates of Return

The determination of an appropriate rate of return is a subjective exercise that can be influenced by differences in judgment. However, it is important to ensure that the manner in which the rates of return are developed are both technically correct (based on the assumptions adopted) and internally consistent. In this regard, some of the more common errors made in the determination of rates of return are as follows:

- internal inconsistency. In some cases, the rates of return are not consistent with the cash flows against which they are applied. For example, where the forecast cash flows are in real dollars, the discount rate should exclude inflation; where the forecast cash flows are determined before debt servicing costs, the discount rate should reflect a WACC as opposed to a levered cost of equity;

- failure to account for financial leverage. In some cases, Formula 7.4 is used to determine the WACC. Where that is the case, the cost of equity must be expressed as a levered cost of equity, based on the assumed capital structure, and calculated in accordance with Formula 7.2. Using the simplified approach to calculating WACC (Formula 7.6) helps in avoiding this technical deficiency;

- double-counting risk factors. Where the forecast cash flows specifically account for a particular risk in the business, that risk should not again be included in the rate of return. Similarly, where industry-specific risk factors account for a particular risk, that same risk should not be used again as a component of company-specific risk;

- estimating a normalized capital structure. The capital structure estimate should reflect a long-term sustainable capital structure for the business, given the nature of its operations, the industry in which it operates and prevailing and anticipated economic conditions. In some cases, the capital structure is overestimated or underestimated because of anomalies in the business or the marketplace at the valuation date;

- long-term growth rate. When calculating the capitalization rate, a long-term growth rate is deducted from the discount rate. The long-term growth rate normally includes inflationary growth and may incorporate an element of real growth. The notion that a business can sustain a high rate of real growth over the long term usually is unrealistic, given that it implies the business can continuously generate a return on capital in excess of its cost of capital; and

- failure to objectively assess all of the factors (both positive and negative) that should be weighed in the determination of a reasonable rate of return.

Summary

A discount rate is the rate of return that converts a series of cash flows to present value. Where the discount rate is expressed as a weighted average cost of capital, its primary components are the unlevered cost of equity and a normalized capital structure. Following a build-up approach, the unlevered cost of equity is comprised of a risk-free rate, a public equity market risk premium, industry-specific risks, company-specific risks and possibly other adjustments. The normalized capital structure is the debt to enterprise value ratio that a business can sustain over the longer term based on consideration of its underlying assets, cash flow generation capabilities and qualitative factors. The WACC is applied to forecast unlevered cash flows (determined before consideration of debt servicing costs).

The capitalization rate is derived by deducting long-term growth from the nominal WACC discount rate. The long-term growth rate normally includes an inflation component and may include a modest rate of real growth. In addition, when used to calculate terminal value, the capitalization rate may be adjusted for a different risk profile beyond the forecast period.

While the CAPM is a popular tool for public market securities analysis, its application to the development of rates of return in the context of the valuation of a business *en bloc* is fraught with difficulties, most notably the determination of a Beta factor, which could materially distort the analysis.

Chapter 8

Controlling and Minority Interests

Introduction

Up to this point, the discussion and calculations in this book have assumed that 100% ownership of a business is being acquired, which provides the buyer with "absolute control". However, in many cases, what is being acquired is less than 100%.

A controlling shareholder is defined as one that owns, either directly or indirectly, more than 50% of the votes cast at a meeting of shareholders of a company (*de jure* control). A controlling shareholder is normally in a position to elect a majority of the board of directors and, through them, to directly influence the risk-reward relationship of that investment. A minority shareholder is one that owns 50% or less of the voting shares and therefore does not have *de jure* control. However, a minority shareholder might be in a position to exert considerable influence over the affairs of the company where they have effective control (*de facto* control). This can occur, for example, where a single shareholder holds a large block of shares and the remaining shares are widely held. However, *de facto* control can be overridden by *de jure* control.

The determination of the *en bloc* value of a business presumes the ability to both control its affairs pursuant to the election of the majority of the board of directors and to be unrestricted in its disposition. Where a given shareholding is viewed in isolation and the shareholder's power to control operations or deliver the shareholding free and clear of all encumbrances is fettered, a discount from a pro-rata portion of *en bloc* value may be warranted in order to reflect one or both of these.

The valuation of a minority interest requires an understanding of its important attributes in order to determine whether a discount from pro-rata value should apply and, if so, how much of a discount. In this regard, it is important to understand the relevant terms and provisions that might be included in the applicable incorporating statutes, articles of incorporation, any shareholder agreements or other relevant agreements that might exist, as well as any court decisions relating to the specific circumstances under review. It is also important to note that this book has been written in a Canadian context, and different considerations might be applicable for other jurisdictions.

The discussion of minority discounts is normally only applicable to privately held companies. In the case of public companies whose shares are widely held and highly liquid, it is generally accepted that a minority discount does not apply since the inability of an investor to control the business unilaterally is offset by a ready market for the equity interest. However, a discount from pro-rata value might be warranted in certain circumstances for small-cap and micro-cap public companies because of illiquidity concerns, particularly where a relatively large block of shares is held by a defined group and the shares are thinly traded.

Controlling vs. Minority Interests

Controlling Interests

En bloc value is the value of the equity ownership interest in a business viewed as a whole and includes the value associated with all the risks and rewards of control. In other words, *en bloc* value is equivalent to the value of a 100% controlling interest in the shares of a company. When *en bloc* value is divided by the number of shares outstanding, the resultant value is said to be the "ratable" or "pro-rata" portion. For example, if the value of a company's equity *en bloc* is $10 million and there are 1 million shares outstanding, then the pro-rata value is $10 per share.

A controlling shareholder (usually defined as one having in excess of 50% of the voting shares of a company) is in a position to:

- elect the majority of the board of directors, thereby effectively controlling decisions that influence the strategic direction of the business, including its level of operating risk and financial risk;

- determine the timing and quantum of dividend distributions, thereby influencing the return on investment;

- appoint themselves to a management position and thereby withdraw salaries and other forms of remuneration;

- determine the timing of the sale of control in the business and the acceptable form of consideration, thereby maximizing the selling price; and

- liquidate the business and distribute the proceeds, thereby mitigating continuing losses.

As a result, in a notional market context the per-share value of a controlling interest is expressed as a pro-rata portion of *en bloc* value. For example, assume the *en bloc* fair market value of the shares of M1 Limited is $10 million, and that there are 1 million shares outstanding. Further assume there are two shareholders, one owning 80% of the outstanding shares and the other 20%. The pro-rata value of each share in M1 is $10 per share. Although there may be circumstances where a controlling interest is valued at an amount less than pro-rata value, in most cases the notional fair market value of the interest held by the 80% shareholder of M1 would be estimated at $8 million.

Where the ability of a controlling shareholder to control the business is restricted, the issue arises as to whether or not there should be a discount from the pro-rata value of that controlling interest. A controlling shareholder's ability to control the business unilaterally might be impaired where:

- the controlling shareholder does not own a sufficient percentage to individually pass a special resolution, which usually requires a two-thirds majority (three-quarters in some jurisdictions). Special resolutions are required to approve certain fundamental changes in a business;

- decisions cannot be made unilaterally given the rights afforded to minority shareholders under certain legislation and case law;

- there are specific provisions in the articles of incorporation, by-laws or shareholder agreement (where one exists) that impair the degree of control. In particular, the rights granted to minority shareholders in respect of:

    ✓ a minimum percentage of votes (or unanimous agreement) being required for certain decisions, and/or

    ✓ the ability to block a sale of the controlling shareholder's interest either directly (by approval or acceptance) or by virtue of the absence of a mandatory sale provision in a shareholder agreement that would force the sale of 100% of the business to a prospective purchaser who would not execute a transaction in the absence of 100% ownership; and

- where the minority shareholding has "nuisance value" (discussed below), that could take away from the value of a controlling shareholder's interest otherwise determined.

As a practical matter, a discount from the pro-rata value of a controlling interest is seldom applied. Even though minority shareholders are afforded certain rights under governing legislation, shareholder agreements, and so on, these should not impair the control of the majority shareholder(s) acting reasonably. Further, in the case of a dissent and appraisal remedy (subsequently discussed), the courts generally have recognized that a balance must be struck between the rights of the minority and those of the majority. Therefore, a discount for non-control would likely only be applied to a majority ownership position in the unusual circumstance where control is restricted beyond the reasonable expectations of a prospective buyer.

In addition, any discount in the context of a controlling interest must take into account the fact that a majority shareholder might be viewed as benefiting from the fact that it enjoys a controlling position in a company without having to expend the financial resources to acquire 100% ownership. In some cases, the benefit of obtaining control of a company without having to finance the acquisition of all the shares may offset any limitations of control that arise by virtue of the rights afforded to the remaining minority shareholders.

Minority Interests

The determination of minority interest value is required in a number of different circumstances including:

- notional market circumstances where an actual negotiated transaction does not occur. Examples include minority shareholding values in privately held companies determined for estate planning, shareholder disputes, and income tax such as a deemed disposition. Such value determinations are infrequently tested by actual open market transactions;

- notional market circumstances where the value of minority shareholdings is determined by the courts. For example, judicial determinations of fair value for purposes of dissenting shareholder appraisal remedies or oppression remedies fall into this category. A family law dispute brought before the courts where the value of privately held company shareholdings is at issue is similar. In these circumstances, the litigation process generally promotes a detailed discussion of the issues that influence the value of minority shareholdings. Accordingly, prior case law dealing with the value of minority shareholdings tends to influence notional market value determinations;

- circumstances where actual transactions occur following negotiation or dispute resolution, but where a true open market test of value is not made. Such transactions arise between privately held company shareholders acting at arm's length, such as following a buyout on the death of a shareholder; and

- transactions where, following open market negotiation, a minority shareholding in a privately held company is acquired by a previously unrelated party. Usually this occurs in circumstances where new capital is received by the company in exchange for newly issued treasury shares, and in arm's length sales of existing minority shareholdings.

While there are general factors commonly considered, the value of a specific minority interest in the context of an actual transaction depends on the time-specific relevant facts and relative negotiating strengths of the parties to the transaction. In contrast, the valuation of minority shareholdings in a notional market context is usually based on a combination of fact and theory. In matters that are specifically related to income tax, notional market values are also influenced by the published policies and practices of the Canada Revenue Agency (CRA).

The valuation of minority interests (whether in a notional market context or in an open market transaction) must consider that minority shareholders typically do not enjoy the same rights and privileges as a controlling shareholder. Further detracting from the value of a minority interest is the fact that in most privately held companies (and some small-cap public companies) a less liquid market exists for a minority shareholding than for a controlling interest. As a result, a minority shareholder may be exposed to one or both of:

- a discount for the inability to unilaterally control the company (i.e., a discount for non-control); and

- a discount for the absence of a ready market in which to sell the minority interest (i.e., a discount for illiquidity).

In the example above, M1 Limited has an *en bloc* fair market value of $10 million, but the fair market value of the interest held by the 20% shareholder may not be its pro-rata value of $2 million. Rather, depending on the circumstances, the fair market value of that minority interest may be less, and possibly considerably less, than $2 million. Relevant factors to consider in determining the quantum of the discount include the relationship between the shareholders as well as provisions in the Articles of Incorporation, the prevailing shareholder agreement (if one exists) and other relevant contractual agreements and company-specific factors.

When arriving at the value of a particular shareholding, consideration must also be given to the restrictions, if any, placed on the transfer of shares in question. Such restrictions may be:

- contractual restrictions, typically found in the incorporating documents or shareholder agreement (if one exists);

- in the contractual form of escrowed public shares or some form of limitation placed on the transfer of a corporate interest. In the case of public companies, restrictions on transfer may be found in purchase agreements effected by a share exchange; and

- in the case of public company shareholdings, it may be in the form of practical restrictions having to do with the size of the minority shareholding vis-à-vis normal-sized trading blocks (i.e., liquidity issues).

Determinants of Control

It is not always apparent whether a particular shareholder has legal or, in particular, effective control of a company. The interpretation of whether or not control does exist may require the assistance of legal counsel.

Types of Control

In general terms, there are two types of control:

- legal control (or *de jure* control) as exercised by means of majority ownership of a company's issued voting shares, or by a contractual right; and

- effective control (or *de facto* control) which occurs where the economic or other circumstances in which a corporation is placed allow control to be exercised by someone holding only a minority of shares (i.e., 50% or less of the voting shares), or perhaps none at all (e.g., secured creditors where the company is in default of its loan agreements).

Effective control is a more elusive concept. While it may be as effective as any form of legal control, it can always be overridden by legal control. Control of either variety is no less real, even when it is infrequently exercised, since control is always available to the controlling shareholder whenever the shareholder chooses to use it.

De jure control exists when the shareholder holds shares which, taken together, carry more than 50% of the total votes that may be cast to elect directors at a shareholders' meeting. A shareholder with such voting power will usually be able to elect all or a majority of the board of directors and, through them, to govern the affairs of the business.

Although it is clear that legal control turns on ownership of voting shares, it is necessary to go further and examine the matters on which those shares may be voted. *De jure* control is key to a majority of the votes in the election of the board of directors. The power to elect directors is normally the most important criterion with which to assess the importance of voting power because, in the usual situation, directors are given broad authority to manage the corporation. Given this, the vesting of some specific and limited management authority elsewhere may not impair control.

The prominence of the power to elect directors will apply only when the directors have the usual powers of directors. Furthermore, consideration must be afforded to the circumstances where preferred shares and other company securities have the right to vote, as well as where different classes of common shares exist (e.g., voting, non-voting and multiple voting). As always, the facts of each case must be carefully considered.

Finally, control may be subject to the specific and general restraints on the freedom of a controlling shareholder such as minority shareholder rights legislation discussed later in this chapter. As a result, control comes in differing degrees. For example, a shareholder with 51% of the voting shares of a corporation may still be restricted in its ability to control the company because of its inability to independently pass a "special resolution" as permitted under the federal and provincial business corporations statutes. These provisions set out the voting requirement to pass a special resolution, which is usually either two-thirds or three-quarters, depending on the applicable business corporations statute. Special resolutions are required to enact a "fundamental change" in the business such as the sale of most of the underlying assets or a liquidation of the business. Specific requirements to abide by the terms of special resolution provisions may also be set out in a company's incorporation documents or by unanimous shareholder agreement.

If a shareholder owns 100% of the outstanding voting shares, it may be said to have absolute control subject only to fetters on that control that may be found in the governing corporations act, a shareholder agreement involving other classes of shares, or in the covenants of corporate financing agreements. Issues arise in circumstances where the securities of a corporation that do not possess the right to vote are given that right pursuant to corporate legislation. For example, in the *Canada Business Corporations Act* there are some matters in respect of which shares that ordinarily are non-voting can nevertheless vote. Where this is the case, a shareholder would have to own all the issued shares of all classes before it could be said to have absolute control.

A statute may define control in a particular way for the purposes of that statute, although there is often no statutory definition and the meaning of control must be found in the principles developed in case law. Most of the case law in Canada involving the issue of control has arisen under income tax legislation. A list of selected Canadian cases dealing with the issue of control is presented in Appendix A. Although these cases must be read with an awareness of the context in which the question of control arose, the principles laid out in those decisions are sufficiently general in their application to be useful for the purposes of determining whether control exists.

Means of Control

Control may not always be exercisable by a shareholder having direct ownership of a majority of the voting shares. Circumstances arise, for example, where control might be exercised through a casting vote or through intermediary corporations, nominees and trustees, voting agreements and the like. Each of these is addressed below. Importantly, where such provisions exist and the determination of value could be significantly influenced by whether or not a shareholder is deemed to have control, it may be advisable to seek the assistance of legal counsel.

Control Through a Casting Vote

In some cases, one shareholder has a casting vote that can be exercised in the event shareholders are evenly divided on some issue. However, it is not necessarily correct to say that a casting vote provides the shareholder possessing that right with legal control. For example, if there are two shareholders, a casting vote will not supervene to give one of them control where both shareholders are necessary to constitute a meeting. Casting vote provisions have also been characterized as techniques of *de facto* control not to be considered when determining *de jure* control.

Control Through Intermediate Corporations

It is well established that control may be exercised at one or more removed levels, or even indirectly in certain circumstances. Where, for example, the majority of a company's voting shares are held by another company, that other company's share register may be examined to discover the identity of those who control the first company through their control of the second company.

Control Through Trustees and Nominees

In the case of a corporate body owning shares, the question is not whether the voice of that corporate body is affected by some external control, but rather which voice is heard, since a company has no voice of its own. With respect to shares held in trust, it appears that:

- the courts have sometimes looked past a nominee shareholder or bare trustee (i.e., to find that control resides elsewhere) to find a shareholder who was prepared at all times to carry out the wishes and instructions of the person principally interested in the company;

- in those cases where the custodian trustee voted not with the voice of the management trustee(s) but with the voice of its own controlling shareholders, it was determined that control lay with the custodian trustee; and

- in the more complicated situation where there are joint trustees, it is the trustee or group of trustees directing the voting of the shares held in trust who are said to have control (assuming the joint trustees are not merely bare trustees).

The above summary simplifies the findings of several rather complex cases dealing with the issue of trustees and nominees. An in-depth discussion of this topic is, however, beyond the scope of this book. Moreover, there are several Canadian cases which contradict the findings summarized above. For example, there is a substantial number of cases in which registered shareholders, even after having been acknowledged to be nominees or solicitors for someone else, were said to be clothed with full and independent authority and the courts refused to look behind the share register to find the real controller. Further complicating this issue is the inclusion in some decisions of passages that imply that control includes *de facto* control.

Control Through Voting Agreements

The formation of shareholder agreements is expressly authorized in Section 146 of the *Canada Business Corporations Act*, and any such agreement may also be set out in the company's by-laws or its articles under subsections 103(1) and 6(2), respectively.

A unanimous shareholder agreement pertaining to voting rights (such as unanimous consent or that a certain percentage of votes is required for specific decisions) may influence whether or not a majority shareholder has control in certain circumstances.

Proxies and Powers of Attorney

Canadian courts have held that a vote cast under a proxy is a vote cast as agent for the owner of the share in question. That is, it is the principal who votes, not the agent. In any event, corporation law usually limits the life of a proxy, and both a proxy and a power of attorney may be revoked at any time. For these reasons it seems unlikely that a proxy-holder or an attorney could be said to have control of a corporation through such a temporary authority to vote shares in it.

Potential Control

A person is said to have potential or future control over a corporation if they are in a position to trigger some future event that would obtain a position having legal control of the company. Control of this kind may sometimes be deemed to be legal control under a particular provision of a statute, including certain provisions of the *Income Tax Act*. Without such statutory authority, however, potential control is no more than *de facto* control. Canadian courts have repeatedly concluded that the ability to obtain control through some course of conduct, in contrast to a presently existing means of controlling the corporation by voting power (e.g., the conversion of non-voting preference shares to common voting shares) will not be sufficient to give a person *de jure* control.

Group Control

When determining whether or not a particular shareholder controls a company, consideration should be given to the possibility that although the shareholder may not individually control the company, they might be part of a group which acts in concert to control the company. When no single person has legal control of a corporation it is sometimes necessary to investigate the circumstances in which two or more shareholders can be looked at collectively and treated as a group in control of the corporation.

Where shareholders are directly related, group control is often presumed to exist on the assumption that such shareholders will act in concert on important decisions involving the company and their respective interests. Circumstances may occur, however, where animosity arises among related shareholders and, as a consequence, the presumption of collaboration among family members (or any other normally cohesive group) may not be appropriate. This includes circumstances of marital dispute where the spouses collectively control a company.

Whether or not group control exists at a point in time clearly is a question of fact. If several minority shareholders act in concert to control a company (whether they have legally bound themselves to do so or not) a finding of group control may be appropriate. It is less certain whether facts suggesting that several persons are likely to act in concert are sufficient to establish control by these persons as a group. Even if such a group of persons has previously acted in concert, there is no assurance (in the absence of a *bona fide* agreement between them) that they will do so again. Further, while a number of individuals may be thought to constitute a group on the basis of the *de facto* relationship existing among them, the principle that control of a company can only be satisfied by legal considerations is not abrogated. A group may be established by factual circumstances but that group, once found, cannot, in law, control a company except through its power to vote a majority of the company's voting shares.

Most of the decisions in Canada regarding group control have been influenced heavily by the fact they arose in a tax-avoidance setting. Therefore, caution must be exercised in applying these rulings in a particular business valuation exercise.

The Canada Revenue Agency and Control

Where minority shareholder interests are valued for income tax purposes, the guidelines for group control and family control set out by the Canada Revenue Agency (CRA) should be considered. It must be remembered that these guidelines could change, and in any event may have little relevance in an open market context.

Family Control

When referring to the valuation of an individual minority shareholding in a corporation collectively controlled by individuals with a familial relationship, the term "family control" is often used. Family control, as group control, is a concept applied in connection with notional market valuation requirements for income tax purposes. The CRA takes the position that, barring family disputes, family members who collectively control may be presumed to act in concert over the economic direction and the liquidity of their investment. The argument supporting this position is that related shareholders who hold in the aggregate more than 50% of the voting shares can realize proceeds not less than the ratable value of their respective shareholdings by acting in concert to sell a control shareholding. CRA Information Circular 89-3 entitled "Policy Statement on Business Equity Valuations" also includes discussion of what to consider when assessing whether family control exists.

The wording of IC 89-3 seems to suggest that minority shareholders related to a family control group have the option of associating themselves with the family group. In other words, in those situations where such minority shareholders wish to establish a lower notional value for their shares, the CRA appears to offer the option of claiming or not claiming family control. Experience to date suggests the CRA looks primarily to consistent application of family control (or the lack thereof) at relevant valuation dates.

Group Control

Control may exist in a number of informal ways such as where no single person has *de jure* control, but two or more shareholders own, in the aggregate, more than 50% of the issued voting shares. According to the CRA, group control is deemed to lie with shareholders who, by voting shares aggregating more than

50% of the votes cast at a general meeting of shareholders, demonstrate a pattern of voting in concert, and are restricted in their right to sell and vote their shares independently.

To satisfy the CRA, such evidence could be contained in the Articles of Incorporation, the by-laws, or in a shareholder agreement. IC 89-3 includes a discussion as to the considerations to be made in assessing whether group control exists. A strict reading of IC 89-3 suggests that the CRA is offering taxpayers the option of claiming group control. Again, experience to date suggests that the CRA looks primarily for consistent application of group control (or the lack thereof) at relevant valuation dates.

Discounts and Premiums

Discounts for Non-Control and Illiquidity

Conceptually, there are two basic forms of discount that may be applicable for any given minority shareholding. These are discounts because of the inability of the minority shareholder to unilaterally:

- control the affairs of a business (e.g., its strategy, capital structure, dividend policy and other matters), referred to as a "discount for non-control"; and

- readily sell the equity investment free and clear of all encumbrances, referred to as a "discount for illiquidity".

Discounts for non-control relate to restrictions imposed by law, contract or that influence the risk and return parameters of the investment. Discounts for illiquidity relate to the inability of a shareholder to readily sell their investment at a known price. Discounts for non-control and illiquidity are inter-related, since a non-controlling equity position in a privately held company is less liquid than a controlling interest.

In theory and practice, an individual shareholder who has the power neither to control the affairs of a business nor to dictate the timing of the liquidity of the shareholding under the terms of a shareholder agreement or otherwise, may face a discount from pro-rata per-share value. In a notional market context, absent a specified discount in a shareholders' or other agreement, any discount from ratable value must be determined subjectively. In the case of an open market transaction, the price paid for a minority interest is established through negotiation.

Discounts for non-control and illiquidity in the context of individual shareholdings are relative concepts. Their quantification is dependent in the first instance on how *en bloc* value was determined. The factors that give rise to each of these discounts tend to be combined into one "minority discount" amount or percentage. That being said, discounts for non-control and illiquidity are distinct concepts. Control is a function of the relationship among the shareholders whereas liquidity is a function of the external demand for a particular shareholding with regard to all its attributes, including its degree of control over the business.

Over the years, many studies have been undertaken regarding the quantification of discounts for non-control and illiquidity (and minority discounts). These studies have found a significant range in the size of the discounts applied by the courts. Each case must therefore be assessed on its own evidence since the minority discounts accepted by the courts depend on the relevant time-specific facts. It is not possible to state unequivocally that minority shareholdings are consistently bought and sold at discounts from pro-rata value. It also is not possible to state unequivocally that discounts, where applied, always fall in a particular range.

Discounts for non-control and illiquidity are not all-or-nothing concepts. Rather, each moves along the following continuum dictated by fact and circumstance:

Exhibit 8A
Continuum of Discounts

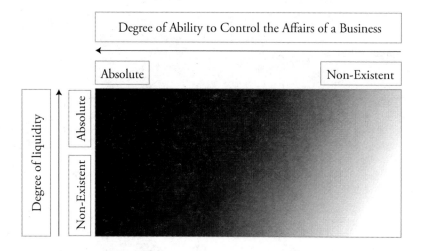

Absolute control and liquidity:

- control means the ability to do all those things normally associated with ownership. For example, the ownership of 100% of the common shares of a company typically allows the owner a free hand in establishing its strategy, capital structure and dividend policy, or selling or liquidating the company; and

- liquidity means the ability to convert an asset into a known amount of cash at any point in time, which in most cases involving a privately held company is influenced by the ability to control. In the case of a public company, liquidity is dictated by the trading volume of the securities and the size of the ownership block.

No control and illiquidity:

- the shareholder with no control has virtually no influence on the strategic direction of the company, its operations, dividend payments, and so on, and is severely restricted in their ability to readily divest their interest because of restrictions imposed by the circumstances or the other shareholders; and

- when shareholdings are illiquid the number of interested buyers is expected to be significantly reduced. In the case of a privately held company, the inability to control reduces liquidity .

Although the concepts of a discount for non-control and discount for illiquidity are distinct, the line between them is blurred. Indeed, the two have many factors in common. The sale of a particular shareholding at an attractive price (except where a company is sold *en bloc*) is contingent upon finding another party willing to be subjected to the impediments of non-control. Therefore, the separation of a discount for non-control and a discount for illiquidity is somewhat circular.

In circumstances where both discounts are warranted and are believed to be separately quantifiable, the calculation should be done by multiplication, and not by addition. For example, recall that M1 Limited has an *en bloc* fair market value of $10 million. If circumstances dictated that the 20% minority share-holder should be subjected to a 25% discount for non-control and a further 25% discount for illiquidity, the fair market value of the minority shareholder's interest would be $1,125,000, calculated as follows:

$10 million *en bloc* value × 20% ownership interest × (1-25% discount for non-control)
   × (1-25% discount for illiquidity).

   = $1,125,000

This represents a discount of $825,000 (or 41.25%) from the pro-rata value of the minority interest of $2 million.

Discounts for Non-Control

When a business is valued *en bloc*, the presumption is made that a single owner of that business has the ability to directly influence the risk-reward relationship of their investment as a result of:

- the election of the board of directors which provides control of the business strategy, capital structure (and by extension, level of financial risk) and dividend payments or other remuneration (which influ-ences the return on investment); and

- the ability to choose to discontinue their investment at any time through: (i) an *en bloc* sale to a third party; (ii) sale of a portion of the business (either directly or pursuant to an initial public offering or combined primary and secondary offering); or (iii) liquidating the business and distributing the net proceeds.

Control in this context does not presume that the business is not exposed to risk, but rather that the controlling shareholder can, within the constraints of normal business practices (e.g., creditors' rights, legislation, and so on) unilaterally modify the risk-reward relationship of the business.

Importantly, from a control standpoint, the ability to divest the business does not presume a market for the acquisition of that business exists. Rather it refers to circumstances where no internal restrictions pre-vent the business owner from choosing the timing and nature (i.e., shares or assets, form of consideration, and so on) of the sale. As subsequently discussed, whether or not a market for the business (or an interest in it) exists relates to the separate issue of comparative liquidity.

Where a shareholder owns 100% of all the issued and outstanding shares of a company, it is presumed they enjoy absolute control. Where an equity interest constitutes 50% or less ownership of the voting shares, a discount may be appropriate in recognition of impediments to control. In the absence of an agreement specifying otherwise, the application of a discount for non-control should be assessed in light of the degree of influence a shareholder enjoys relative to other shareholders in the company.

Discounts for non-control are typically associated with minority interests. However, they may be applied in some (unusual) circumstances to a controlling interest where there are impediments to control that a majority shareholder normally would enjoy. For example, where most operating decisions have to be agreed to by the minority shareholders, that fact would serve to impair the ability of the controlling share-holder to operate the business as they so choose.

Furthermore, a majority shareholder with 51% of the voting shares cannot unilaterally pass a special resolution requiring a two-thirds majority. Such a restriction may impair the controlling shareholder's ability to control business risk and financial risk, and to liquidate or sell the business *en bloc*. Where this is accompanied by restrictions on the ability to sell the majority interest under the terms of a shareholder agreement or other contractual arrangement, a discount for non-control may be appropriate.

Finally, circumstances should be considered where holders of other outstanding securities (e.g., preferred shares, warrants, convertible debentures, and other security) might erode the level of control based on some future events or in certain circumstances (such as voting rights accruing to shares that normally are non-voting). Prevailing shareholder agreements, articles of incorporation, by-laws and other agreements pertaining to any and all equity interests in the company and relevant corporate law provisions should be considered.

Discounts for Illiquidity

A discount for illiquidity (sometimes referred to as a "marketability discount") is a reduction in the pro-rata portion of *en bloc* value attributable to an equity interest caused by lack of an immediately available market in which it can be sold in the short term at a predictable price. It is the absence of an immediately available market for a particular shareholding that leads to a discount for illiquidity over and above that already reflected in the determination of *en bloc* value.

Liquidity may be defined as the ability to convert a non-cash asset into cash in a short period of time with relative certainty as to the net proceeds. In theory, a discount for illiquidity does not relate to the ability of the owner to choose whether or not to sell; that is an element of a discount for non-control. Rather, once the decision to sell has been made the discount for illiquidity pertains to:

- the time required to conclude a transaction (viewed in terms of when cash or other consideration is received); and

- the uncertainty surrounding the net proceeds that will ultimately be received.

Stated another way, a business interest (or any asset for that matter) that is not readily marketable may experience some level of discount resulting from having to:

- reduce the agreed-upon price from what might otherwise have been contemplated, in order to attract prospective buyers and to conclude a near-term sale; or

- expose the business interest or asset for sale in the open market for an unusually long period of time, thereby receiving lower proceeds in present value terms. Further, if it is necessary to expose a business interest or asset for sale over an unusually long period of time, its value may fluctuate as a result of changes in the business itself, the industry, and prevailing economic and credit market factors. This in turn results in uncertainty as to the ultimate net proceeds. Although the quantum of net proceeds might be greater than anticipated, finance theory equates uncertainty with risk.

Many of the factors that may give rise to a discount for non-control may also give rise to a discount for illiquidity. For example, (absent provisions in a shareholders' or other agreement to the contrary) a minority interest in a privately held company restricted as to its sale is often subject to a discount for non-control. In addition, the market for business interests with restrictions on control is usually not as liquid as the market for business interests where no such restrictions exist. Therefore, either separate discounts for each of non-control and illiquidity, or a combined minority discount to reflect both, might be warranted. As previously noted, when both a discount for non-control and a discount for illiquidity are applicable, and an attempt is made to quantify each separately, the calculation should be made by multiplication rather than by addition.

Premium for Control

The term "premium for control" is often cited in transactions involving the takeover of publicly traded companies. Historical studies have suggested that takeover prices often average 30% to 40% more than the market prices prior to the takeover announcement. However, the range of premiums varies significantly, from negative values to well in excess of 100%. These premiums for control most often arise because of synergies perceived by purchasers.

Some academics and practitioners submit that the quantification of minority discounts for shareholdings in privately held companies can be estimated based on the reciprocal of an average public market premium for control. According to this theory, if a 40% premium for control is taken as a rule of thumb then the minority discount is calculated to be approximately 29% (determined as: $1/(1 + 40\%)$). However, quantification of a minority discount in this manner may lead to an inappropriate conclusion, given that:

- where the shares of the acquired public company were actively traded on information widely disseminated prior to the bid, premiums to pre-bid prices typically relate to synergies perceived by the purchasers rather than to control per se;

- such a methodology presumes that the trading prices of shares of public companies incorporate a minority discount. This is not the consensus view which holds that the market prices of actively traded shares of widely held public companies do not incorporate a minority discount;

- for the shares of some public companies that are not widely traded, the premium likely, at least in part, reflects the elimination of a stock market discount for illiquidity;

- when a public company is "in play", competitive bidding for the acquisition sometimes occurs, which in turn may distort the premium;

- public company trading prices in some cases may advance on speculation of a takeover announcement and thus reduce the calculated premium in percentage terms;

- the premium for control is normally based on an average of the premiums of open market transactions. However, the actual premiums paid vary significantly, from negative amounts to well in excess of 100%. Further, published statistics summarizing the premiums paid over stock market prices in open market transactions may not reflect fact-specific control premiums because negative premiums that would serve to deflate the computed average may not be included. Furthermore, the statistics include both cash transactions and non-cash transactions (e.g., share-for-share-exchanges). The latter may include certain restrictions on behalf of the seller and therefore may not accurately reflect a cash-equivalent price;

- studies of takeover premiums are specific to point-in-time prices, and reflect only completed transactions, and do not include those merely contemplated but not pursued. Obviously, transactions are normally not pursued where economic analysis does not support the bid price. Statistics comparing average takeover premiums to market prices therefore reflect only completed takeovers and, as a result, represent a skewed sample of the population of all transactions both contemplated and completed. Because information with respect to transactions contemplated but abandoned generally is not available, takeover premiums to market statistics are incomplete and are not as meaningful as they are frequently represented to be; and

- takeovers of publicly traded companies may reflect circumstances where the buyer believes the target company's shares are trading at a bargain price. As a result, quoted premiums are likely, on average, to be greater than they otherwise might be.

Finally, the premium calculated in the course of a takeover transaction can be distorted based on the amount of debt in the target company. Consider the following example. The enterprise value of a business for takeover purposes is estimated at $100 million, compared to its enterprise value in the marketplace of $75 million. If the business has no debt, then the calculated share premium is 33%. However, if the business is financed by $25 million of debt and $50 million of equity, then the premium increases to 50%.

Exhibit 8B
Premiums for Control and Capital Structure
($000)

	No Debt	With Debt
Enterprise Value in Market	75,000	75,000
Comprised of		
Debt		25,000
Equity	75,000	50,000
Estimated enterprise value for takeover purposes	100,000	100,000
Allocation of purchase price		
Debt		25,000
Equity	100,000	75,000
Premium over share value	33%	50%

Therefore, where a minority discount is determined by taking the reciprocal of the rule of thumb for a so-called "premium for control", the quantum of discount may be distorted. It is important to take into account the specific facts of each situation in determining a minority discount. Furthermore, where practical, the segregation of that minority discount into its components of non-control and illiquidity (as discussed) may ultimately result in a more reasoned and supportable conclusion.

Block Premiums and Discounts

As previously discussed, it is generally accepted that shares of widely held public companies do not trade at prices that reflect an embedded minority discount, given that the inability of an individual investor to unilaterally control the affairs of the company is offset by their ability to readily sell their interest at the prevailing market price. However, in some cases, the shares of the public company in question are not actively traded, or the investor may hold a block of shares that is larger than the normal daily trading volume. In such cases, liquidity may be an issue. The rationale for a discount for illiquidity might be based on the fact that:

- a large block of shares sometimes creates an imbalance in the normal supply/demand equation. If supply is greater than demand, the price will likely decline; and

- it may take some time for the market to absorb a large share block if it is sold in *tranches*. The length of time needed to sell such a large shareholding has implications with respect to the time value of money and the risk of adverse price fluctuations.

On the other hand, the market price for the block could move to a premium if ownership is perceived as providing a greater degree of influence in company affairs than ownership of a normal-sized trading lots. If a premium is applicable, the quantum should be derived after considering such factors as:

- the size (both in relative and absolute terms) of the block of shares;

- whether the block of shares is sufficient for the shareholder to enjoy board representation and the impact of cumulative voting rights, if any;

- the level of interest in acquiring the block of shares by investors such as pension funds, private equity firms and other groups;

- whether other blocks of shares are held by related persons or unrelated persons; and

- whether and to what extent the public market prices are believed to incorporate a discount for illiquidity.

Factors to Consider When Quantifying Minority Discounts

Shareholders in most widely held public companies have access to a ready market for normal-sized trading lots that allows them to convert their interest into cash at a known price very quickly (sometimes within minutes). Such securities therefore are not subject to a discount for illiquidity. As noted above, while an individual shareholder cannot unilaterally influence the affairs of the company, that lack of control is offset by immediate liquidity. However, a discount for illiquidity for publicly held stocks might apply where the stock is thinly traded or where a disproportionately large trading block is being valued, as discussed under the caption "Block Premiums and Discounts", above.

Minority discounts are normally referenced in a privately held company context, however. The quantification of a minority discount is a subjective exercise. Regardless of whether discounts for non-control and illiquidity are quantified in isolation or combined into a minority discount, the following factors generally should be considered objectively in order to arrive at a plausible discounted value in the circumstances:

- the basis by which *en bloc* fair market value was determined;

- the provisions contained in an enforceable shareholder agreement;

- whether or not an organized market for the shares exists;

- the size of the particular equity interest, both in absolute and relative terms;

- the prevailing relationships between and among the shareholders;

- the shareholder's level of involvement in the business;

- the likelihood of an *en bloc* sale of the business or initial public offering;

- shareholder rights in the context of applicable corporate legislation and the likelihood of a statutory triggering event in the near term;

- the characteristics of the business itself; and

- whether the shareholding has, or may have, "nuisance value".

Where a shareholder agreement exists, its provisions normally have a significant bearing on whether a minority discount is applicable and its quantum. However, where a shareholder agreement (or other documentation with relevant provisions) does not exist, other factors such as any relationship among the other shareholders that impacts the minority shareholder's degree of influence in the affairs of the business will have a greater bearing on the existence and quantum of a minority discount.

Where a single shareholder controls a company and there is no shareholder agreement, the controlling shareholder's intent with respect to minority shareholdings is an important consideration. In such circumstances, the prior conduct of the controlling shareholder will often provide evidence as to how the minority shareholder(s) will be treated.

Finally, whether or not a minority discount applies also depends on the definition of value, be it fair market value, fair value, value to owner, and so on. As noted in Chapter 1, fair value is normally defined as being the ratable portion of *en bloc* fair market value without the application of a minority discount. Furthermore, certain shareholder agreements will specify that the fair market value of a minority interest in the business is to be determined without the application of a discount for non-control or illiquidity. However, absent these conditions, consideration should be given to whether, and to what extent, a minority discount should be applied in a given fact-specific situation.

The Basis of *En Bloc* Value Determination

Minority discounts cannot be meaningfully quantified without first understanding the way *en bloc* value is determined. In a notional market context, the *en bloc* value of a business can be determined based on different underlying assumptions. The principal assumptions are those surrounding:

- how the rates of return adopted when developing *en bloc* value were established, and the degree to which those rates assume a liquid investment;

- whether the business was valued as a stand-alone entity or post-acquisition synergies were considered. In this regard:

  ✓ unless the business operates in an industry where synergies are clearly evident and can be meaningfully quantified, a notional market *en bloc* value determination usually excludes consideration of synergies. Where, however, stand-alone value is adopted as the base of *en bloc* value, but there are buyers who perceive post-acquisition synergies to exist at the date of valuation, calculating a discount from stand-alone value may result in a double discount. Offsetting the perception of a double discount is the inability of a minority shareholder, in isolation, to realize the synergistic value that might crystallize only in an *en bloc* sale of the shares, and

✓ where synergistic value is reflected in *en bloc* value, consideration must be given to the likely inability of a minority shareholder to extract a pro-rata portion of that value given the minority shareholder's inability to conclude an *en bloc* open market transaction. This may lead to a higher discount than otherwise would be the case; and

- the assumptions regarding the capital structure and related financial risk of a business. A minority shareholder is normally unable to influence the capital structure meaningfully. To the extent that *en bloc* value was determined based on the assumption of a normalized capital structure, a discount from pro-rata value may be warranted where the company's actual capital structure is greater than or less than that amount.

Shareholder Agreements

Where a shareholder agreement exists, its specific provisions can have a significant impact on the quantum of discount, if any, for both non-control and illiquidity. Relevant provisions influencing control and liquidity might also be found in a company's articles of incorporation, by-laws, or other agreements. The following discussion summarizes the impact specific provisions within a shareholder agreement may have on the existence or quantum of a minority discount. A more in-depth discussion of shareholder agreements is set out later in this chapter.

Shareholder agreements can be categorized as either unanimous or ordinary. Unanimous agreements can override (to the extent allowed by corporate statutes) corporate by-laws and governance documents.

In some cases, a shareholder agreement will specify that a minority shareholder is to receive a ratable portion of *en bloc* value, or stipulate the quantum of discount (if any) to be applied. Further, where a shareholder agreement specifies that no minority discount is to be applied, such a condition may only apply in circumstances of certain specified triggering events.

When assessing the impact of a shareholder agreement on the value of a minority shareholding, it is important to determine whether a new shareholder will be subject to the existing agreement. Where this is not the case (which would be rare), and an external transaction is assumed, the provisions contained in the shareholder agreement may not be applicable. That factor should be considered in the valuation.

By definition, a minority shareholder does not have *de jure* control and hence cannot elect a majority of the board of directors. However, in some cases, a minority shareholder may enjoy *de facto* control. Further, the ability for a minority shareholder to exercise some degree of influence on the company as a whole may be provided for in a shareholder agreement. For example, a shareholder agreement might allow a minority shareholder the ability to exercise some influence over the direction of the business because of the requirement for unanimous shareholder approval (or a higher approval threshold than 51%) for certain significant corporate decisions or by way of representation on the company's board of directors. Accordingly, where a shareholder agreement exists, a minority shareholder might enjoy elements of "negative control" as a consequence of their power to block other shareholders from making certain changes to the business that would be undesirable from the other shareholders' perspective. Where such provisions exist, it is important they be carefully scrutinized to define the circumstances in which that influence can be exercised and the degree of influence possessed by individual shareholders.

Shareholder agreements (and articles of incorporation) often contain provisions regarding restrictions on the transfer of shares. Such restrictions might include the requirement for approval from other shareholders or the board of directors or a right of first refusal.

Restrictions on transfer often impair the ability of shareholder to control the risk-reward parameters of their investment since they cannot freely choose to divest themselves of that business interest. As a result, in the absence of the ability to control the risk and return of the company itself (which control is rare for a minority shareholder), a discount for non-control may be warranted. Again, the restrictions on transfer discussed in this context relate to control (i.e., the ability to sell at will) and not liquidity (i.e., the likely number of buyers and time required to conclude a sale). Whether or not a market exists for a particular minority shareholding is a separate issue.

In many cases, restrictions on transfer also impair the liquidity of an equity interest and a separate discount for illiquidity is required (or alternatively, a discount for illiquidity should be factored into the minority discount). In this regard:

- in an open market context a minority shareholding with restrictions on transfer has a limited number of eligible buyers (e.g., competitors typically would be excluded purchasers). In a notional market context, even though restrictions on transfer are considered to be lifted momentarily for the purpose of determining fair market value, the buyer is assumed to be subject to them. Accordingly, where restrictions on share transfer exist, they impair the liquidity of the equity interest. For example, where the sale of the shares requires approval from the board of directors or other shareholders, there is usually a requirement that such approval not be unreasonably withheld. However, a successful buyer will be subjected to the same restrictions on transfer. As a practical matter, a buyer may discount the price from what they otherwise might have been willing to pay, in recognition of the risk restrictions on transfer may impose;

- where there is a right of first refusal allowing existing shareholders the opportunity to match the price and terms offered by a third party, the liquidity of the selling shareholder's interest is often impaired. This is because few buyers are willing to invest the time and effort required to prepare an offer to purchase shares in circumstances where their offer will likely not be accepted. As a result, the number of prospective buyers willing to acquire the shares is often significantly reduced, thereby reducing the degree of liquidity for the seller;

- where the shareholder agreement contains a "coattail" (or "tag-along") provision to ensure that, in the event of a takeover bid, all shareholders are entitled to sell into the bid, such a provision may serve to reduce the degree of illiquidity that may normally exist;

- certain shareholder agreements afford minority shareholders a "put option", pursuant to which the shareholder has the right to sell their interest to the other shareholder(s) at a predetermined price or a price to be established. In most cases, the existence of a put option will serve to significantly reduce (or even eliminate) the illiquidity component of a minority interest, depending to the specific provisions regarding the determination of price and the terms of the sale; and

- in some cases, particularly where there are two shareholders with shareholdings of equal size, the shareholder agreement incorporates a buy-sell clause (or "shotgun" clause), which helps to ensure liquidity. In most cases, the existence of a shotgun clause serves to significantly reduce or even eliminate a minority discount, given that the inability of a particular shareholder to control the affairs of the business is substantially offset by the ability to liquidate the investment at a price known with reasonable certainty in a short time frame. That said, in some cases, the uncertainty caused by a shotgun (i.e., the fact that it could result in unexpected actions from the shareholder receiving the offer) and the terms on which it is executed (as set out in the shareholder agreement) may warrant some level of discount.

The Existence of an Organized Market

In some privately held companies, minority share transactions between employee-shareholders or other parties follow established procedures. For example, some companies have established an employee share ownership program (ESOP), pursuant to which employees are entitled to sell their shares back to the company at a specified price, or to sell their shares to other employee-shareholders.

Where such transactions occur, prices paid may be (but are not necessarily) a meaningful indicator of minority share values, particularly where the minority shareholding is of a size comparable to that normally traded. Where similar-sized minority shareholdings in the same company have been sold just prior to the valuation date, careful analysis of such transactions should be made before relying on them. It is necessary to have full knowledge of the circumstances surrounding such transactions, including:

- the dates on which the transactions were negotiated, and the indicated *en bloc* value of the outstanding shares of the company at each of those dates and at the valuation date. In some cases, an annual valuation is conducted and equity interests are bought and sold at that value during the following year;

- the reasons why the transactions took place. For example, some companies require departing employee-shareholders to divest themselves of their shares at the time of departure, a moment which may not give the employee the best share price;

- the knowledge of the business's opportunities, ongoing or prospective negotiations with respect to an *en bloc* sale, and other factors;

- the terms of any shareholder agreement or other agreements which may have dictated the transaction prices;

- the payments terms; and

- whether there was any familial or business relationship between buyer and seller that influenced the price, terms or conditions of the transaction.

Size of the Shareholding

Absent a shareholder agreement (or relevant provisions therein), the existence and quantum of a minority discount can be significantly impacted by the share ownership structure of the company and the relative degree of influence an individual shareholder has vis-à-vis the other existing shareholdings.

As a general rule, where no one shareholder has a controlling interest in the business, greater liquidity may attach to a particular minority shareholding, given the comparative size of the other shareholdings, than otherwise would be the case. Potential buyers of a minority interest in a privately held company may be less interested in going through with a transaction where one shareholder or a defined group of shareholders controls the company.

For example, the appropriate quantum of discount(s) for a shareholder with a 33 1/3% interest could be significantly different in circumstances where the remaining shares were held by a single shareholder (with 66 2/3%) or by two other shareholders each holding a 33 1/3% interest as well. In the former case, absent a shareholder agreement, in theory the minority shareholder is subject to the whims of the majority, and likely has little influence on the affairs of the company. Moreover, the market for a one-third interest where a single shareholder owns the remaining two-thirds is, in theory, likely limited where no provision for liquidity exists. Conversely, where a company is owned by three equal shareholders, generally two of the three are required to make significant business decisions. In theory, there is a natural market for any particular one-third equity interest since each of the other two shareholders would likely acquire their respective pro-rata share so as not to be disadvantaged.

In addition to the relative size of an individual equity interest, specific statutory rights pertain to various absolute sizes of shareholdings. As subsequently discussed in this chapter under the heading "Shareholder Rights and Remedies", the relevant incorporating statutes establish four significant shareholding percentage levels within a particular class of shares:

- 10% or less. In virtually all jurisdictions minority interests representing 10% or less of the issued shares of a particular class are subject to compulsory acquisition provisions. These provisions entitle a buyer, in the course of a takeover bid, of at least 90% of that class of shares which it did not previously own, to acquire the remaining shares of the class from those shareholders who did not tender their shares, at a price equal to that paid to the other shareholders. Although the shareholder owning 10% or less of the relevant class of shares cannot prevent a takeover, the opportunity to receive a pro-rata portion of *en bloc* value may reduce any disadvantage this might create;

- greater than 10% and up to 33 1/3% (25% in certain jurisdictions). A minority shareholder who is in a position to prevent the sale of their shares into a takeover bid (i.e., greater than 10% of the class) can prevent a takeover where a prospective buyer makes the acquisition of 100% a condition of its offer. As a result, that shareholder may positively influence the value of their shareholding at the time of the bid. However, the restrictions and limitations attaching to a minority shareholding can be severe where it represents less than 33 1/3% (25% in some jurisdictions) of the issued shares entitled to vote on a specific special resolution. In such circumstances the minority shareholder has no power to prevent the passing of such special resolution. Subject to statutory and common law limitations, a controlling shareholder owning more than 66 2/3% of the voting shares (75% in some jurisdictions) may amend the articles of incorporation. However, this disadvantage to a minority shareholder is tempered in most jurisdictions by dissent rights and related appraisal remedies available to minority shareholders. It is also tempered by voting privileges which accrue to all classes of shares directly affected by any such changes, regardless of whether they are ordinarily entitled to vote;

- greater than 33 1/3% (25% in some jurisdictions) and up to 50%. A minority shareholder who can unilaterally prevent the passing of a special resolution arguably is less disadvantaged than one who cannot. Accordingly, the value of such a shareholding may benefit from this power compared to the value of a smaller shareholding where such influence does not exist; and

- 50%. Where a shareholder owns a 50% voting interest, they are a minority shareholder from a legal standpoint, but may have effective control. This will largely depend upon the size and interrelationship of the other shareholdings in the company. Where each of two shareholders owns 50%, both are regarded as minority shareholders. However, in such circumstances the two shareholders often ensure each other's liquidity, although this is not always the case.

Shareholder Relationships

Personal and familial relationships between and among shareholders and shareholder groups who collectively control a business may affect the degree of influence and liquidity of their respective shareholdings, and therefore may affect the value of their equity interests at a particular point in time. Barring disputes, two or more shareholders often act in concert to exercise control over the economic direction and the liquidity of their investment. However, because interpersonal relationships can change over time, absent a written shareholder agreement, there is no assurance such "group control" or "family control" will continue indefinitely.

Where two shareholders are married to each other, their relationship as shareholders is commonly a direct reflection of their marital situation. A valuation issue that often arises in family law has to do with the determination of the value of a minority shareholding interest in a corporation controlled by the shareholder's estranged spouse. Where both spouses retain their shareholdings following a division of assets, and no shareholder agreement exists, the minority shareholder may have to resort to statutory oppression remedies in the event of unfair treatment by the majority.

Because value is specific to a point in time, the value of a minority interest in relation to *en bloc* value can be influenced by changes in relationships. Furthermore, if the minority interest were to be sold, the personal relationships would not attach to the equity interest. In a notional market context, the familial or other relationship among the shareholders is usually considered in the determination of the existence and quantum of a minority discount, presumably under the notion that the other shareholder(s) represent the most likely buyers for the minority interest.

Level of Involvement

The value of a particular equity interest might be affected by whether the shareholder in question is actively involved in the business. This involvement includes circumstances where the shareholder is:

- a senior manager or director of the corporation and can influence the affairs of the corporation through business decisions under their control;

- another corporation, and there is a supplier-customer relationship or some other form of dependence (such as a licensing or technology agreement); and

- also a key employee, possibly possessing personal and individual goodwill (as discussed in Chapter 1), particularly where a non-competition agreement is not in place. In that case, the shareholder might be able to influence the decisions of the majority by threatening to leave the company.

Alternatively, if a minority shareholder is not a key employee and other shareholders are, the non-active shareholder's interest may be subject to a higher discount.

An individual's position as an employee is usually not transferable upon the sale of their equity interest (except in circumstances where a board position is guaranteed to a new shareholder, either under the provisions of a shareholder agreement or for other reasons). Therefore, it could be argued that the fair market value of a particular equity interest should be established independent of the shareholder's personal involvement. The additional value that an employee-shareholder might enjoy as a result of their involvement in the company would be an element of "value to owner" (see Chapter 1).

Conversely, where a particular minority shareholder is not active in the business (or not acting in a key role) and other shareholders are actively involved in important management positions, the inactive shareholder may experience a higher discount because of the risk a third-party buyer might anticipate in future relations with the active shareholders.

The Likelihood of an *En Bloc* Sale or Initial Public Offering

A minority interest in a business may become liquid in the event the entire business is sold. Because a minority shareholder is not in a position to dictate whether a sale takes place, consideration must be given both to where such influence lies, and to the likely timing of such an event. With respect to the latter, it is necessary to assess whether either the controlling shareholder or control group (if either exists) is considering the possibility of offering the company for sale. Where there is evidence of activity leading toward such a sale, in both a notional market and open market context, where a discount for illiquidity is otherwise thought appropriate, this activity would tend to reduce (or possibly eliminate) any such discount.

In theory, absent other considerations, the value of a minority shareholding increases as the probability of a near-term *en bloc* sale of the business or an initial public offering increases. When assessing the likelihood and timing of an *en bloc* sale, consideration should be given to matters such as:

- the prevailing general economic conditions and market availability of funds. During good economic times, there is more disposable income available combined with an increase in the level of merger and acquisition activity across most industries;

- the prevailing conditions within the industry in which the company operates vis-à-vis evident buyer synergies, the number of recent transactions, trends in industry consolidation, and so on;

- the attractiveness of the business to potential buyers, in terms of its size, customer base, intellectual property and other factors;

- circumstances which might promote a sale. These can be external to the business such as a growing inability to compete effectively against larger competitors, or internal to the business such as a requirement for financing growth;

- whether the outstanding shares of the company have significantly increased in value during the period they have been owned by the current owners;

- the length of time the current controlling shareholder(s) have owned their investment and their stated or perceived interest with respect to their holding;

- the current profitability and future outlook for the business relative to other times during which the controlling shareholder(s) held their investment. In the absence of a distress situation, sellers of shares of both public and privately held companies time the sale of their interest to maximize the proceeds. In the case of privately held companies, the controlling shareholder(s) would be more likely to sell when the company is in an upward stage of its business cycle rather than during depressed times;

- where the controlling shareholder is an individual(s), the age(s) of the controlling shareholder(s), their health, their interest in selling in the near term, other relevant issues personal to them, and their other business interests; and

- whether the controlling shareholder(s) or the minority shareholder(s) as individuals contribute either personal or individual goodwill to the company, and the likelihood of such individuals continuing with the company long enough to transfer the individual goodwill accruing to them. In some instances, an *en bloc* sale may only be possible where the individual(s) agree to a management contract as part of the sale. Where a minority shareholder possesses individual goodwill, they may be able to enhance their negotiating position.

It is also important to consider whether a prospective buyer is likely to be interested only in purchasing the company *en bloc*, or is prepared to purchase only a controlling interest. In this regard it is important to consider:

- the provisions of a prevailing shareholder agreement, particularly to determine whether there are compulsory sale (or "drag-along") rights that force a minority shareholder to sell their shares to a prospective buyer on the same terms as a controlling shareholder;

- the size of the shareholding. As previously discussed, where a shareholder has more than 10% of the voting shares, absent compulsory sale provisions, they can prevent the acquisition of 100% of the shares of the company; and

- whether the shares have nuisance value (discussed below).

Liquidity may also be created by means of an initial public offering or joint initial public and secondary offering. However, the degree to which liquidity is created by such an event is dependent upon:

- whether it will be an initial public offering or joint initial and secondary offering. A minority shareholder might be able to achieve partial or entire liquidity through a secondary offering. Immediate liquidity may not be available pursuant to an initial public offering;

- the restrictions (if any) placed on trading the minority interest being valued. That is, where a shareholder is identified as an insider under securities legislation, some or all of those shares may be subject to trading restrictions for some period of time;

- whether a block premium or discount is applicable, as discussed above;

- the size of the offering, which will have a bearing on whether the shares, once publicly traded, are thinly traded or widely held. A large block of shares in a thinly traded company may face a (possibly significant) discount for illiquidity; and

- the conditions of the financial markets, including the number of IPOs coming to market, market volatility, and other factors that would affect valuation and the likelihood that an initial public offering will be fully subscribed.

Corporate Legislation and Shareholder Remedies

As discussed below, at any point in time a minority shareholder has legal entitlements established by federal and provincial business corporations statutes, and in common law relating to shareholder interests. It is important to know the jurisdiction in which a corporation was formed and the rights arising from the governing legislation. From a valuation standpoint, the impact of these rights is to reduce the minority discount from what it otherwise might have been. However, such rights in and of themselves do not eliminate altogether the appropriateness of a minority discount in a given situation.

As a general rule, absent consideration of other factors that influence the liquidity of a minority shareholding, the greater the opportunity for a minority shareholder to trigger a dissent or oppression remedy, the greater will be the liquidity of that shareholding. Accordingly, at a given point in time, the probability of triggering either a dissent remedy or an oppression remedy should be considered when determining the fair market value, or other value, of a minority shareholding.

A more in-depth discussion on shareholder rights and remedies is provided later in this chapter.

Characteristics of the Business Itself

As noted above, the characteristics of a business such as its size, customer base, intellectual property and other aspects, influence the degree to which it may be an attractive acquisition target and, by extension, the likelihood of an *en bloc* sale. In addition to these considerations, there are other factors within the business that can influence the quantum of minority discount for a particular equity interest. For example:

- historic and prospective dividend payments. A minority shareholder generally cannot dictate unilaterally the quantum or timing of dividend payments or other shareholder distributions. In reality, dividend yield seldom plays a significant part in privately held company share valuation because the (typically) close ownership of a privately held company permits broad discretion in the distribution of corporate funds to the shareholders. The personal requirements and motives of the controlling shareholders, combined with income tax planning and proposed or contemplated changes to the income tax laws, frequently dictate the timing and amount of dividend payments. Nevertheless, some privately held corporations have a history of regular dividend payments or payments of bonuses pro-rata to participating shareholders at comparable levels. These distributions provide a source of ongoing liquidity, which reduces what might otherwise be the applicable discount. However, in the absence of a contractual commitment, a minority shareholder usually cannot ensure the continuation of such policies;

- the composition of the underlying assets. Where the *en bloc* value of a business includes a large amount of excess cash or other redundant assets that can readily be liquidated, that fact normally gives rise to a lower minority discount. The other factor to consider is the likelihood that highly liquid redundant assets will be distributed among the shareholders as a dividend (or other form of return on investment) on a pro-rata basis; and

- the ability of a business to generate cash vs. its expected cash requirements. Where a business is a "cash cow" and has limited opportunities for investment, it may increase the likelihood that a dividend (or other form of return on investment) will be paid to shareholders.

Nuisance Value

The term nuisance is sometimes used in reference to a situation where the existence of one or more minority shareholdings forms an obstacle to the objectives or strategies of the controlling interest. These objectives or strategies often relate to the disposition of the controlling interest. However, they may also affect the management of the business. Where minority shareholdings are seen as a nuisance by the majority shareholder(s) at a point in time, they may be more valuable than they otherwise might be.

Nuisance value describes the incremental amount a buyer (often a controlling shareholder) would have to pay over what would otherwise be the value of a minority shareholding, in order to remove the minority from ownership of the company. Where it exists, it is but one component of the value of the particular minority shareholding. Nuisance value typically results from facts and circumstances that arise at a particular point in time. For example, a controlling shareholder may be prepared to pay a premium for nuisance value in order to remove a specific minority shareholder from future participation in the ownership of the company, either where:

- the minority shareholder is taking an absurd position. For example, a minority shareholder that misapplies or abuses the available statutory remedies can divert significant management time from the business and cause unnecessary expenses. In such circumstances, it may be desirable to remove the minority shareholder, even at a premium value;

- the minority shareholder is acting responsibly, but the continued ownership of their shareholding stands in the way of corporate reorganization or business changes contemplated by the controlling shareholder(s). The nuisance value arises from the special interests of the controlling shareholder(s) at the time. In some instances, it may also stem from conflicts in the personalities of the individual shareholders involved; or

- the minority shareholder is blocking the sale of the business pursuant to the buyer's stipulation of 100% ownership.

While nuisance value can sometimes occur in an open market context, it is not a factor that is considered in the notional valuation of minority shareholdings.

Shareholder Rights and Remedies

When valuing a controlling or minority interest, it is important to recognize the various factors that not only protect minority shareholders but may also place certain restraints on the ability of the majority shareholder to control the company. The value of either a controlling or minority interest in a corporation must be assessed in light of:

- the corporation's constitution, including its articles and by-laws;
- the statute under which it is incorporated; and
- relevant case law.

The provisions of the legislation under which the company is incorporated, and the related body of common law, establish the basic rights and protections available in that jurisdiction. Minority shareholders in publicly traded companies can also look to the provisions of current securities legislation in the jurisdictions where a market for the shares is made and the rules of the exchange(s) where the shares are traded. Further rights and/or restrictions that may affect the value of a shareholder's interest may be documented in the incorporating articles and by-laws of the specific company or in a shareholder agreement (if one exists).

It is the accumulation of facts discovered during the investigation of the above items (as they relate to each fact-specific valuation exercise) which provides the criteria necessary to assess the appropriate discount, if any, to be applied to the ratable portion of *en bloc* value when valuing a minority interest.

Business Corporation Legislation

Each of the federal and provincial business corporations statutes sets out various shareholder's rights and related matters which may potentially affect the value of a minority shareholding. Certain rights are accorded to both majority and minority shareholders by the provisions of the applicable corporations' legislation. The interpretation and application of these rights is guided by judicial interpretation. Absent other considerations, the extent to which these rights are available affects the value of minority shareholding interests in a particular jurisdiction. Shareholders' rights that are included in some, but not all, Acts include:

- distinguishing between public and privately held companies (also termed offering and non-offering companies), including restrictions and/or prohibitions on the offering of shares to the public by privately held companies;

- specification of the rights and entitlements of each authorized class of shares;

- conditions and restrictions for the transfer of issued and outstanding share capital;

- the availability of shareholders' pre-emptive rights. That is, the requirement that new issues of treasury share capital be offered first to existing shareholders holding shares of that class, in proportion to their holdings of the shares of that class, and on the same terms as any shares offered to others;

- shareholders' rights as to participation in corporate decisions, including:

  ✓ procedural requirements related to the conduct of shareholder meetings,

  ✓ specification of the types of transactions that require shareholder approval, either by simple or special majority. These include specific matters such as the issuance or alteration of share capital, alteration of share rights and restrictions, amendment of the corporate charter, amendment of the stated capital amount, amalgamation, dissolution and wind-up of the company, and fundamental changes to the principal business of the company. Unless specifically provided by the incorporating statute or incorporating documents, corporate decisions taken in general or special shareholder meetings are decided by majority vote. In the absence of cumulative voting, the votes of a simple majority will always be sufficient to elect the entire board of directors,

  ✓ provisions related to the requisitioning and content of extraordinary shareholders meetings, including the percentage of shareholder approval required to effect special resolutions (generally either two-thirds or three-quarters) and the availability of separate-class voting provisions,

  ✓ the right to enter into unanimous shareholder agreements, being written agreements among all the shareholders, or between all the shareholders and a person(s) who is not a shareholder, to restrict some or all of the powers of the board of directors to manage the affairs of the corporation. Unless specifically provided by statute, shareholders may not contract to restrain the discretion of the directors of the corporation, and

  ✓ entitlement to cumulative voting to determine the composition of the board of directors;

- related to the election of the board of directors and the powers conferred on the members of the board. This includes matters such as the number of directors to be elected, the number of directors constituting a quorum, the qualifications necessary for election, the powers of the directors and any restrictions, the duties and liabilities of the directors, and whether the chairman has a casting vote in the event of a tied vote;

- regarding access to specified corporate information such as financial statements, corporate records, and shareholder lists; and

- which arise in the event of a takeover bid for the shares of the company. In some jurisdictions, a "compulsory acquisition" provision gives an acquirer of at least 90% of the share capital of a corporation the right to acquire the remaining shares at the same price.

Further to the aforementioned shareholders' rights: the various corporation statutes may also provide other remedies, and hence protections, for minority shareholders in specific circumstances. Where provided, these may include:

- a right to dissent in certain prescribed circumstances. This right enables a shareholder to require the company to purchase their shares at fair value, if the company initiates certain "fundamental changes" from which they dissent. A further discussion on this topic is presented later in this chapter;

- the right of a minority shareholder (and sometimes other parties) to exercise an "oppression remedy" where the actions of the majority shareholder are viewed to be unfairly prejudicial to, or unfairly disregard the interests of, the minority. A further discussion on this topic is presented later in this chapter;

- the right to apply to a court for an order liquidating or dissolving the company if the affairs of the company have been conducted to the prejudice of the minority's interest;

- the right to bring a derivative action, being a suit by a person in the name of and on behalf of the corporation, to remedy a wrong done to the corporation. If the corporation has been wronged by the majority, a statutory derivative action allows the minority to seek leave (or permission) to prosecute or defend an action on behalf of the corporation;

- the right to apply to a court for an investigation order to collect evidence where corporate wrongdoing is suspected; and

- the right to apply to a court to compel the corporation to rectify its corporate register or records.

The availability in each Canadian jurisdiction of each of these remedies is summarized in the following exhibit. This information is provided for general purposes only. Any dissent or oppression claim or other shareholder dispute requires the involvement of experienced legal counsel.

Exhibit 8C
Shareholder Rights and Remedies

Legislation	Federal (CBCA) Alberta Manitoba New Brunswick Newfoundland Ontario Saskatchewan	British Columbia	Nova Scotia	Prince Edward Island	Quebec
Dissent Right Available	Yes	Yes	Yes	No	Yes
Correction of Corporate Records	Add or correct information	Correct information that was wrongly entered, retained, deleted or omitted	Correct registered name only	Add or correct name	Add or correct name
Investigation Order	Yes	Yes	Yes	No	Yes
Who Can Apply	Any shareholder except N.B. – must hold at least 10% of shares	Must hold at least 20% of the issued shares of the company	Must hold at least 10% of the shares in a corporation or be at least 1/5th of the members of an unincorporated entity		Must hold sufficient interest to satisfy Inspector General
Derivative Action Available	Yes	Yes	Yes	No	Yes
Oppression Remedy Available	Yes	Yes	Yes	No	Yes
Can Apply for Court Ordered Wind-Up	Yes	Yes	Yes	Yes	Yes

Further, the CBCA and various provincial business corporations statutes also give shareholders the authority to establish a unanimous shareholder agreement enabling them to agree upon and document their own interpretation of the division of authority granted to shareholders and directors.

Articles of Incorporation and By-Laws

A company's articles of incorporation, including any amendments, may include provisions that impact the value of an equity interest in that company. Relevant provisions in these articles might include:

- the maximum number of shares that may be issued;
- the existence of different classes of shares and their respective terms;
- the restrictions, if any, on the transfer of shares;
- the restrictions on the business or powers of the corporation;
- the restrictions on the corporation's right to purchase or redeem its shares; and
- any lien on the shares.

Special provisions may be included in the corporation's by-laws. If so, they will be subject to the statutory provisions regulating amendments to the articles and by-laws, subject again to any additional rules the shareholders may want to add.

Shareholder resolutions may also contain provisions impacting the rights and obligations of controlling and minority shareholders.

Dissent Remedy

Exercise of a dissent remedy enables minority shareholders to withdraw from the corporation rather than be subjected to fundamental changes proposed by the majority. At the same time, the majority is permitted to carry out such changes if it is willing to risk that minority shareholders will exercise their right of dissent. In other words, the dissent remedy protects minority shareholders from fundamental changes not to their liking, while it simultaneously preserves flexibility within the enterprise. As such, the dissent remedy is intended to represent a balancing of interests between the majority and minority shareholders.

A statutory dissent remedy is available in most jurisdictions. The triggering events specified in the federal legislation are set out in the *Canada Business Corporations Act*, section 190. The same criteria have been adopted in the other jurisdictions that provide a dissent remedy. In these jurisdictions, the circumstances which create a dissent and appraisal right are:

- the passage of an amendment to the articles to add, change, or remove any provisions restricting or constraining the issue, ownership, or transfer of shares or any restriction upon the business or businesses that the corporation may carry on;
- an amalgamation with a corporation other than its wholly owned subsidiary, its parent corporation if it is a wholly owned subsidiary, or its sister corporation, if both are wholly owned subsidiaries of the same corporation;
- the continuation of the corporation under the laws of another jurisdiction;
- a sale, lease, or exchange of all, or substantially all, of the corporation's property; and
- an amendment to the articles of incorporation which diminishes the rights or conditions attached to a class or series of shares, which amendment otherwise creates an entitlement to a class vote.

When a dissent remedy is activated, the business corporations statutes in Canada require the shares of the dissenting party to be purchased at their "fair value". As discussed in Chapter 1, the term fair value is not defined in the federal or any of the provincial business corporations statutes. Hence, the concept of fair value has been the subject of litigation both as to its interpretation as well as to its quantification. In dealing with dissent cases under the CBCA, Canadian courts have accepted the premise that it is the duty of the court to determine what fair value is.

A list of selected Canadian cases dealing with the term fair value can be found in Appendix A. Although these cases indicate some disparity in the interpretation of fair value, Canadian courts have found that:

- fair value and fair market value are not necessarily synonymous;
- the *en bloc* value of the outstanding shares of the subject company is to be determined on the assumption the company is a going concern, rather than on the assumption of a liquidation;
- whatever valuation method is used to determine *en bloc* value, no minority discount is applied when determining the fair value of a minority shareholding;
- the current or historical stock market price by itself may not be representative of fair value, particularly where trading is thin or sporadic;
- post-amalgamation benefits may be taken into account where the dissenting party was forced out, and not given the opportunity to participate as a shareholder. Conversely, participation in post-amalgamation benefits is less likely where the dissenting party had the opportunity to continue its participation but elected not to;
- a so-called "premium for forcible taking" has seldom been found to be applicable; and
- the specific facts underlying a given dissenting shareholder appraisal action may influence the interpretation of the meaning of fair value in the course of that action.

Oppression Remedy

Since a minority shareholder has no legal control over the affairs of a corporation, it is possible for the majority to act in a manner prejudicial to the interest of the minority. An oppression remedy permits an oppressed minority shareholder (and other specified parties) to request the courts to intervene (or remedy a demonstrated unfairness) in the affairs of the corporation to protect the complaining shareholder's interest.

Courts have broad discretion to make any interim or final order they see fit to deal with complaints, including ordering the corporation to purchase the minority shareholder's shares, and/or ordering the corporation to be wound up. Although the statutes do not specify the valuation method by which a minority shareholder's shares are to be repurchased, the courts appear to support the application of a fair value concept.

According to the CBCA, grounds for an oppression remedy application arise because:

- an act or omission of the corporation; or
- the manner in which the business or affairs of the corporation is carried on; or

- the manner in which the powers of the directors are exercised,

is oppressive, is unfairly prejudicial to, or unfairly disregards the interests of any security holder past or present, or any creditor, director or officer, former director or officer, or any other person who the court decides is a proper person to make an application.

The oppression remedy is a comprehensive protection designed to provide relief for most kinds of corporate unfairness. However, it is only available in situations involving corporate acts or conduct of directors, and not shareholders acting in their capacity as shareholders. Although the oppression remedy is available in a very broad range of situations, in general terms the courts have indicated that the oppression remedy is available where it is shown that:

- the actions of the majority excluded the minority from participation in the management of a privately held corporation;

- shares were issued for other than legitimate business reasons to the disadvantage of the minority;

- the majority treated the corporation as its own private company in a manner that unfairly disregarded the interests of the minority; and

- there was a denial of a legitimate expectation of the minority.

Where the court has determined that oppression has occurred, it has broad statutory scope in making an interim or final order. In the various Canadian jurisdictions, the courts generally have the power to make an order:

- restraining the conduct which gave rise to the complaint;

- appointing a receiver or receiver-manager;

- regulating a corporation's affairs by amending its articles or by-laws or creating or amending a unanimous shareholder agreement;

- directing an exchange of the securities held by the complainant;

- appointing directors in place of or in addition to all or any the directors then in office;

- directing a corporation, or any other person, to purchase securities of a security holder;

- directing a corporation, or any person, to pay a security holder any part of the monies paid by them for securities;

- varying or setting aside a transaction or contract to which a corporation is a party, and compensating the corporation or any other party to the transaction or contract;

- requiring a corporation to produce financial statements or an accounting in another form as specified by the court;

- compensating an aggrieved person;

- directing rectification of the registers or other records of a corporation;

- liquidating and dissolving the corporation;

- directing an investigation to be made; and

- requiring the trial of any issue.

Pursuant to minority shareholder oppression remedies, Canadian courts have determined fair value as a ratable portion of *en bloc* fair market value. However, the courts appear to have left open the possibility of awarding a discounted amount where the actions of the minority warrants such treatment.

Shareholder Agreements

A shareholder agreement, or other agreement related to the ownership of shares, defines the privileges, protections, and obligations of the shareholders who are party to it. In particular, such agreements frequently address the issues of, and sometimes ensure, minority shareholder involvement in decision making, liquidity and related valuation. The specific provisions of an enforceable shareholder agreement are usually a significant determinant of minority shareholding value. Absent an enforceable shareholder agreement, minority shareholders must rely on the rights and remedies afforded to them under corporate law.

A shareholder agreement attempts to define what is to occur in all subsequent transactions in a given company's shares. There are numerous (sometimes conflicting) elements that a shareholder agreement usually is designed to protect:

- provide a mechanism for liquidity in the event of certain circumstances such as death, change of control, termination or bankruptcy of a shareholder;

- provide continuing shareholders with control over outside parties becoming shareholders;

- ensure all shareholders that on any acquisition or disposition of shares among themselves, they pay or receive a fair price for their respective shareholdings, and that the agreement adequately documents their collective intent in this regard. A shareholder agreement can influence the fair market value of a minority shareholding by stipulating that "fair value" (i.e., a ratable portion of *en bloc* value of the shares, without the application of a minority discount) will be adopted, or by specifying in some other fashion the basis of value determination. The circumstances of a shareholder's departure can be a key determinant both of the price and of the terms of payment;

- ensure that if an offer is received for all the outstanding shares that is acceptable to shareholders who collectively own a prescribed number of shares (usually sufficient to constitute control), that all shareholders are obliged to tender to the offer pursuant to mandatory sale or "drag-along" provisions. Such provisions protect the liquidity of a controlling shareholder(s) where a buyer makes the acquisition of all outstanding shares a condition of the purchase offer; and

- ensure all shareholders of a "coattail" or "tag-along" ability in the event an offer for less than all the outstanding shares is received that is acceptable to shareholders who collectively own a prescribed number of shares (usually sufficient to constitute control). Such a provision protects the liquidity of all shareholders in the event of such an offer.

Shareholder agreements may also contain other provisions that may have an impact on value such as restrictions on competition after shares are sold and restrictions on share transfer.

It is incumbent upon persons entering into a shareholder agreement to ensure that it adequately documents their collective intent with respect to the terms and conditions of the transactions it provides for. As circumstances change over time, it is important to periodically review and modify, as necessary, the provisions of a shareholder agreement prior to such time as it becomes the basis for an actual transaction.

Types of Shareholder Agreements

An important distinction must be made between a unanimous shareholder agreement and an ordinary shareholder agreement. A unanimous shareholder agreement confers on the shareholders the rights, duties, obligations and liabilities of the corporation's directors as provided in the agreement. A unanimous shareholder agreement effectively transfers directors' responsibilities to the shareholders and may restrict in whole or in part the ability of the directors to manage the company. A unanimous shareholder agreement is a governing document that supersedes the by-laws, articles of incorporation and other corporate documents where there is a conflict between the unanimous shareholder agreement and these other documents, except where not permitted under corporate law. A unanimous shareholder agreement becomes part of a corporation's constitution and any purchaser of shares normally becomes subject to it.

Conversely, an ordinary shareholder agreement (i.e., one that is not a unanimous shareholder agreement) typically does not restrict the powers of the directors, but rather seeks to define the relationship and restrictions between shareholders in their role as owners of a corporation as opposed to its managers. An ordinary shareholder agreement may provide for such things as restrictions on share transfer, share purchase and sale provisions, the valuation of the share interests and so forth. Such provisions may also be found in a unanimous shareholder agreement.

In this book, unless otherwise specified, references to shareholder agreements should be taken to mean ordinary shareholder agreements as opposed to unanimous shareholder agreements.

Triggering Events

It is important for parties to a shareholder agreement to understand and distinguish the various potential future events that might affect their shareholding interests and to consider these events when structuring such an agreement. Further, shareholders must recognize the importance of ensuring the agreement clearly sets out their collective intent in dealing with any particular future circumstance.

Shareholder agreements contain provisions that either permit or require the sale of individual shareholdings in various circumstances. Such "triggering events" may include the:

- death of a shareholder or the wind-up or dissolution of a corporate shareholder;
- change of control of a corporate shareholder;
- permanent disability of an employee-shareholder;
- departure or termination of an employee-shareholder, where that individual was active in the business;
- marriage breakdown of an individual shareholder; and
- insolvency or bankruptcy of an individual or corporate shareholder.

In most of these cases, it is important that the shareholder agreement set out:

- whether the purchase or sale is mandatory or optional, and who has that obligation or option (i.e., the departing shareholder or the remaining shareholders);
- whether the other shareholders will purchase the selling shareholder's interest directly, or whether the shares will be purchased by the company for cancellation;
- the method of determining the value of the equity interest;
- the date at which value should be established;

- the terms of payment; and

- the remedies for non-compliance.

When determining the fair market value (or some other defined value) of the shares for the business as a whole, it is important to set out whether the value term adopted refers to the value of the shares on an intrinsic (i.e., stand-alone) basis, or whether special-interest purchasers should be taken into account. In addition, it is important to set out whether a minority interest should be valued at its ratable portion of the *en bloc* value (i.e., fair value) of the shares or on some other basis.

In some cases, different value terms may be ascribed to different events. For example, the death of a shareholder may not give rise to a minority discount, particularly where the purchase of the shares can be funded through life insurance proceeds. However, a discount and/or less attractive payment terms may be applied where a shareholder departs voluntarily, in order to act as a disincentive for departure, and to reduce the burden on the other shareholders or the company.

Where the shares of the selling shareholder are to be acquired by the company, it is also important to consider the implications of internal vs. external financing (see Chapter 10). As a practical matter, in open market transactions, the *en bloc* value of the shares of a business (and consequently the pro-rata value of any interest) may be affected depending on whether a transaction is financed using funds from inside or outside the company. That is, where the business must forego necessary operating expenditures or growth opportunities in favour of payments to the departing shareholder, the *en bloc* value of the shares may suffer as a result. However, the remaining shareholder(s) might subsequently benefit to a larger extent than would otherwise have been the case if a prospective buyer for the business can be found.

It is also important that careful consideration be given to the alternate income tax treatments that result from each of these triggering events. Shareholders and their advisors should continually monitor both amendments to income tax law and the significance of such amendments to the various buyout provisions set out in any given shareholder agreement. Relevant tax implications include such issues as capital gains reserves (where payment is made over time), the tax implications of earnout arrangements (where used) and the use of the lifetime capital gains exemption for individuals where the company in which the shares are held meets the definition of a qualified small business corporation. These tax issues are discussed in Chapter 9.

Death of a Shareholder

Shareholder agreements commonly include an obligatory purchase and sale provision effective in the event of a shareholder's death (wind-up or dissolution in the case of a corporate shareholder). Such purchase requirements are often funded by life insurance proceeds (in the case of an individual), thereby eliminating (or at least diminishing) what otherwise might prove to be directly or indirectly changed financial obligations for the continuing shareholders. The shareholder agreement must set out whether the corporation or the other shareholders will acquire the deceased's shares. It must also establish payment terms (including time period, applicable interest rate and security).

Where funding is provided all or in part by life insurance, the adequacy and availability of such insurance should be reviewed on a regular basis. Where life insurance is not used to fund such a purchase, the source and availability of funds to satisfy the buyout should be reviewed continually.

It also is important to specify whether the value of the shares should include or exclude the proceeds of corporate-owned life insurance. For example, if all the outstanding shares of a business with five equal shareholders have an *en bloc* value of $10 million, the pro-rata value of each shareholder's interest is $2 million. If one of the shareholders dies and the business receives non-taxable insurance proceeds of $2 million immediately following death, then the *en bloc* value of the shares increases to $12 million. The issue arises as to whether or not the deceased shareholder's estate should participate in the increase in *en bloc* equity value. If not, then technically the surviving shareholders have received a windfall benefit (in this case, a value premium of $500,000 per shareholder or 25%) as a result of one shareholder's death.

In addition, to avoid disputes, the shareholder agreement should specify how the proceeds of the life insurance are to be distributed to shareholders, since such proceeds flow through the capital dividend account of a privately held company and the distribution is usually tax-free. This has the effect of converting a taxable gain (i.e., a taxable capital gain that would result if the shares were sold to a third party) into non-taxable proceeds.

Change of Control

A change of control at a corporate shareholder often qualifies as a triggering event, in order to prevent an existing shareholder from unwillingly having a business partner they do not want. The question arises whether the remaining shareholders have the option of acquiring the shares that were subject to the change of control, or to cause the mandatory purchase of the shares from the corporate shareholder being acquired. Depending on materiality, a mandatory purchase provision can prove to be an impediment to sale for a shareholder looking to divest their interest.

Permanent Disability of an Employee-Shareholder

A shareholder agreement sometimes provides either for the optional or mandatory sale of a shareholding in the event an employee-shareholder suffers permanent disability. Where it does, the shareholder agreement should specify such details as:

- the circumstances that constitute permanent disability;

- how permanent disability is to be substantiated. This can require medical documentation or simply the passage of a specified period of time;

- whether a disabled shareholder is entitled to draw income from the company for a specified period of time. Individuals often acquire long-term disability insurance coverage as a means of providing cash while they are disabled. However, there may be a waiting period for a disability to be classified as permanent, during which time insurance benefits usually are not payable; and

- the timing of a transaction triggered by the disability.

Unlike a share purchase upon death, which is often funded by insurance proceeds, a purchase triggered by permanent disability typically is not. Therefore, the buyout may be a burden on the remaining shareholders. In addition, the issue of personal goodwill can sometimes arise where the company benefited from the unique abilities or contacts of the disabled shareholder. These factors can have an impact on valuation and the terms of a transaction.

Departure of an Employee-Shareholder

The departure of an employee-shareholder can be either voluntary or involuntary. It can arise for reasons such as retirement, inappropriate conduct, inadequate job performance or the individual's change of interests.

The retirement of an employee-shareholder is often addressed in a shareholder agreement. Specific matters that should be covered include:

- whether retirement is mandatory at a prescribed age;

- whether a change (rather than cessation) in employment (e.g., moving from full-time to part-time) constitutes retirement;

- conditions pursuant to which a shareholder may be forced to retire;

- restrictions on retirement. For example, shareholders may agree not to retire for a fixed number of years following execution of the shareholder agreement or before reaching a certain age;

- penalties or disincentives for early retirement. These are reflected either in the determination of the purchase price or in the terms of payment; and

- whether a retiring shareholder continues to draw remuneration, retain use of company assets or receive other benefits for a specified period of time following retirement.

In the case of all departing shareholders, the shareholder agreement should contain provisions with respect to non-disclosure of confidential information. In addition, consideration should be given to:

- non-solicitation of customers and employees. While active solicitation can be difficult to prove, the courts tend to enforce non-solicitation where inappropriate behaviour can be demonstrated (although enforceability is often still an issue); and

- in some circumstances, a requirement that departing shareholders execute non-competition agreements to ensure they do not re-enter the workforce in a manner that would be harmful to the business. In many circumstances, courts are reluctant to enforce non-competition covenants.

In the absence of a non-competition covenant in a shareholder agreement, a departing employee may, depending on factors such as health, financial ability and other factors, be able to compete with the business and impair its value as a result. From a valuation perspective the issue is whether that prospective diminution in value should be reflected in the *en bloc* value of the departing shareholders' interest. From a practical perspective, in the absence of clearly established and enforceable provisions, all shareholders may be able to negotiate an agreement whereby the departing shareholder receives a higher price for their shares in consideration for the non-competition covenant. Such an arrangement may enhance the enforceability of the non-competition provisions. If this is the case, then a portion of the purchase price may be allocated to the non-competition agreement for both the departing shareholder and the buyer (either the company or the remaining shareholders). The tax consequences of such an allocation should be carefully considered.

If the shareholder agreement contains provisions with respect to termination, it is appropriate to distinguish whether employment is terminated voluntarily. In the event of the termination of an employee-shareholder's employment, their shares should be acquired pursuant to prior agreement. Purchasing these shares becomes even more important as minority shareholder rights strengthen, because an adversarial minority shareholder may prove to be increasingly disruptive to ongoing business activities. In particular, a shareholder, at a minimum, is entitled to receive annual financial statements and be invited to attend the annual meeting of shareholders. The resultant external flow of what otherwise would be confidential information is undesirable.

Where an employee-shareholder is terminated, a further distinction should be made between termination without cause and termination with just cause. Employee-shareholders will want protection against the corporation terminating their employment without cause in poor economic times and buying their shares at a depressed price. When termination occurs with cause, the agreement should address the grounds that constitute just cause and, in specific situations, provide for advance notice of impending termination. Termination for cause often is difficult to establish.

If the employee-shareholder voluntarily resigns, the shareholder agreement might stipulate that a discount from the ratable value of their equity interest be applied, thereby preventing an employee-shareholder cashing out at a favourable price. In addition, the continuing business should be protected, where necessary, by appropriate non-disclosure, non-solicitation, and possibly non-competition agreements that become effective on voluntary termination.

Marriage Breakdown of a Shareholder

The marital situation of a privately held company shareholder can directly affect the interests of all the shareholders and the company itself. For example:

- in most provinces, shares in privately held corporations are potentially included among assets to be equalized on marriage breakdown;

- where corporate shares are included in the marital property pool, the non-titled spouse has the right upon marriage breakdown to obtain financial and other corporate information not usually made public;

- many jurisdictions give the courts the discretion to order the transfer of a spouse's assets to the other spouse; and

- the death of a spouse can be a triggering event for the equalization of assets in certain provinces.

Accordingly, consideration should be given to any provisions in shareholder agreements relating to marriage. Canadian family law provides little guidance on the extent to which a court is bound to consider the provisions of a shareholder agreement in the event of marriage breakdown if a spouse is not a signatory to the agreement. However, where a shareholder agreement is among unrelated parties, and has not been executed in contemplation of a marital dispute, it may provide persuasive evidence as to the value of a particular shareholding interest.

Where only one spouse is a shareholder in a privately held company, the following provisions may be included in a shareholder agreement:

- a requirement that all shareholders execute domestic contracts with their respective spouses excluding their shares from the marital asset pool for family law purposes. Alternatively, the shareholder agreement could include such a provision, and the non-shareholder spouses could be parties to it. The jurisdiction of residence will determine how such a provision is best documented;

- a requirement that each shareholder enter into an agreement with their respective spouse stipulating that any court order resulting from an adjudication under family law will not be satisfied all or in part by the transfer of shares of the company to the non-titled spouse. However, this agreement could be ignored by the court if a default in obligations to pay child support has occurred, or a default has occurred in fulfillment of a court order; and/or

- failing an agreement with respect to the two previous points, consideration should be given to providing for specific buyout and related valuation provisions to be applied in the event of a shareholder's marriage breakdown.

Where both spouses are shareholders in a company, a shareholder agreement might include the following provisions:

- where both spouses are active in the business, a right of first refusal between the spouses to purchase the other's shareholding in the event of death;

- where only one spouse is active in the business, a requirement that the non-active party also sell his or her shares upon the death or departure of the active spouse; and

- in the event of marital breakdown, a mandatory buy/sell provision between the spouses. Where only one spouse is active in the business, that individual would be the buyer. Where both spouses are active, the selection of the spouse who is to continue would require the concurrence of the other shareholders, if any.

Another issue that can arise in this context is the personal goodwill that may attach to one of the spouses, which may cause the company to be worth more to one spouse than the other. Recall from Chapter 1 that personal goodwill is an element of value to owner, but not fair market value (or fair value). Therefore, where value to owner exists, it may have to be considered in an equalization payment.

Shareholder Insolvency or Bankruptcy

When a shareholder (individual or corporation) becomes personally insolvent or bankrupt, a mandatory buyout of their interest may be desirable. Where the controlling shareholder is so affected, the control of the company could ultimately pass to a receiver or trustee in bankruptcy. This clearly would be an undesirable consequence. Similarly, the shareholder agreement may restrain the ability of a shareholder to pledge their interest in the company as security, in case it was called.

The shareholder agreement should specify the terms that constitute insolvency or bankruptcy and that the insolvent party's interest is to be acquired before transfer to a third party. In this regard, it is important that the terms by which value is established be perceived as fair so that the transaction is less likely to be contested.

Related Considerations in Triggering Events

In drafting the provisions of a shareholder agreement that pertain to triggering events, consideration should also be given to matters such as:

- the repayment of amounts owing to the company by the departing shareholder or members of their family, including credit card charges and similar current obligations;

- the repayment of amounts owing to the departing shareholder, including loans, outstanding bonuses, vacation pay, and other debts;

- the return or purchase by the departing shareholder of personal-use corporate assets (e.g., automobiles, cellular telephones, computer equipment and other assets);
- the release of a departing shareholder from any corporate guarantees; and
- the departing shareholder's resignation as an officer and/or director of the company.

Reciprocal Buy-Sell Provisions

A shareholder agreement may provide for reciprocal buy-sell provisions, often called "put-call", or "shotgun" clauses. Such clauses are most commonly found in situations involving two 50-50 shareholders. They provide that one party can offer to sell their shares to another shareholder at a price per share and on terms specified in the offer. The other shareholder is required to either accept the offer or to make an identical offer to the shareholder making the initial offer. Whichever course of action is adopted by the second shareholder, it results in a binding agreement of purchase and sale between the two. Assuming the shareholders are of relatively equal financial strength, have substantially equal knowledge of the business, and that neither shareholder enjoys personal or individual goodwill, a shotgun clause tends to ensure the liquidity of each shareholder's interest. Consequently, it establishes what the parties believe to be a fair price for the shares.

Issues may arise where both parties do not have an equal negotiating position. This might include circumstances where:

- one party is unable to obtain financing on reasonable terms and therefore might potentially be disadvantaged by having to sell at a low price;
- the parties have different proportional equity interests, thereby creating a greater financial burden for the shareholder with the smaller interest;
- only one of the parties is active in the business, and therefore is presumably more knowledgeable about the operations and the future prospects of the business; and
- the personal goodwill enjoyed by one of the shareholders results in the *en bloc* value of the shares being greater to one shareholder than the other(s). The same may be true where individual goodwill exists if the transaction is not accompanied by an enforceable non-competition agreement.

Right of First Refusal or First Offer

In privately held companies, agreements among shareholders often include provisions that enable the shareholders to have a pre-emptive right to acquire the shares of another shareholder that wants to divest. There are two distinct ways such rights can be drafted:

- in the first approach, usually referred to as a right of first refusal (ROFR), the shareholder wishing to sell solicits offers from third-party buyers. The shareholder holding the right of first refusal is then presented with the best third-party offer and is given the opportunity to purchase the selling shareholder's interest based on the price, terms and conditions of that offer. If the other shareholder elects not to purchase the shares within an agreed period of time, the seller can then sell their interest to the party making the offer (on those same terms); and
- in the second approach, usually referred to as a right of first offer (ROFO), the shareholder wishing to sell their interest establishes a price and terms of sale which is presented to the shareholder holding the

right of first offer. If the shareholder receiving the offer elects not to acquire the shares with the stated price and terms within an agreed time period, the prospective seller is free to sell their interest in the open market at a price equal to or higher, and on terms no less favourable than the price and terms offered to the shareholder holding the first offer right.

The right of first refusal is better from the point of view of the person holding the refusal right. Third-party buyers will often not spend a significant amount of time assessing a potential share acquisition in the face of an overriding right of first refusal. The right of first offer is better from the seller's perspective. Although it forces the prospective seller to be disciplined when establishing the initial price and terms offered to the shareholder holding the first offer right, in the event the shareholder to whom the shares are offered does not take them, the seller is able to deal with open market buyers unencumbered by a first refusal right.

Certain considerations should be kept in mind when drafting right of first refusal clauses. Where some of the terms and conditions of the consideration offered by a third party are specific to the offeror (e.g., shares of a offeror corporation), the remaining shareholder(s) should have the right to buy the shares on substantially similar terms and conditions and for consideration substantially equivalent to that set out in the third party's offer. Further, if the right of first refusal is not exercised, the right of a shareholder to sell their shares to the third party should remain open for a specified period of time.

The terms of a right of first refusal or right of first offer should specify that any third-party buyer must be one who deals at arm's length with the prospective seller. Further, it should include a clause stating that, if a sale to a third-party buyer is concluded, the buyer must become a party to the original shareholder agreement.

Drag-Along and Tag-Along Provisions

Both controlling and minority shareholders may want to ensure the delivery of all outstanding shares pursuant to mandatory sale (or "drag-along") provisions. Many buyers of privately held company shares will close a transaction only if 100% share ownership is delivered. In such circumstances, the controlling shareholder(s) will not want to have a transaction thwarted by the obstruction of one or more minority shareholders. Therefore, a shareholder agreement often provides that all minority shareholders must tender their shares on the same terms and conditions as a specified majority of shareholders are prepared to do.

At the same time, a shareholder agreement should ensure a minority shareholder the opportunity to sell into an offer at the same price, and on the same terms and conditions as accepted by the majority. These so-called "coattail" (or "tag-along") provisions protect the liquidity of a minority shareholder's interest in the event a third-party offer to acquire control of the company is received.

Restrictions on Share Transfer

In most shareholder agreements (and in most articles of incorporation), there are restrictions on the transfer of shares. Such provisions typically contain a requirement that approval be obtained from the board of directors or remaining shareholders and that such approval is not to be unreasonably withheld.

In a notional market context, the open and unrestricted market component of the definition of fair market value requires any restrictions on transfer contained in the shareholder agreement or the articles be temporarily set aside, but nonetheless considered by a buyer, when determining the final price. In an open market transaction, while there may be restrictions on transfer, it is sometimes the case that approval of the transfer cannot be unreasonably withheld.

As a general rule, in a notional market context share transfer restrictions are perceived to have a negative influence on the value of a specific minority shareholding. In actual transactions involving minority share-holdings, however, they tend to be of little practical consequence, since share transfers are approved as a condition of such transactions. Nonetheless, restrictions on transfer can have an impact on the liquidity of a particular equity interest, and hence its value.

Participation in a Subsequent Sale

In some cases, the interest of a particular shareholder is acquired and the entire business is later sold *en bloc* for a significantly higher value on a per share basis. This is particularly the case where:

- the transaction among shareholders was consummated based on the intrinsic value of the business and the subsequent sale was made to a strategic buyer that paid a price reflective of synergistic value; or
- the shares acquired in the transaction among shareholders were subject to a minority discount, but no such discount applied where the shares were sold *en bloc*.

In order to alleviate the perceived unfairness of this situation, a shareholder agreement will sometimes provide that the selling shareholder is eligible to participate in any gain from a subsequent sale for a period of time following the transaction among shareholders. This also prevents one particular shareholder from consolidating various minority positions at a discount and subsequently profiting by delivering 100% ownership to a strategic buyer.

The central issue to be addressed is the period of time the participation clause is in effect, given that business values change over time. Some (or all) of this change may be attributed to initiatives undertaken by the remaining shareholders following the initial transaction. Consequently, in some cases, the degree to which a departing shareholder is entitled to participate in the gain from a subsequent sale diminishes over time.

Value Terms in Shareholder Agreements

The implications of failing to adequately define value terms in shareholder agreements are sometimes misunderstood by those who advise on them and draft them, and by those who execute them. For example, shareholder agreements often state that an auditor or some other predetermined person or entity is to determine the fair market value of a given shareholding interest in a privately held company, but the agreement fails to clearly define what is meant by fair market value (i.e., intrinsic value, special-interest purchaser value or some other defined value). Accordingly, in such circumstances fair market value might be taken to mean either stand-alone value or an amount that includes a component of synergies (where they can be meaningfully quantified and are likely to be paid for).

The valuation provisions of shareholder agreements sometimes refer to book value, net book value, or adjusted net book value. These terms have generally accepted meanings. The use of such terms in shareholder agreements may or may not satisfy the intent of the parties to such an agreement.

Although not an exhaustive list, the definition of value in a shareholder agreement should clearly address whether:

- a minority interest should be subjected to a discount from ratable value if found to be applicable and, if so, whether the discount should be predetermined or subject to interpretation at the time of a transaction;

- special-interest purchasers are to be considered in determining *en bloc* value or whether the shares are to be valued on an intrinsic (or stand-alone) basis; and

- in the event of the death of a shareholder, the proceeds from a corporate-owned life insurance policy should be considered in the determination of value.

The shareholder agreement should also address which basis of value and payment terms are applicable given the event which triggered the need for a valuation. It may be the case that different definitions of value and different payment terms are applicable to different triggering events.

In summary, it is critical that the parties to a shareholder agreement ensure the value terms adopted in the agreement are carefully defined, and the definition(s) adopted reflect their collective intent. If relevant value terms are not addressed in the shareholder agreement, they are left to interpretation at the time a valuation is required. Depending on the situation, it may be beneficial for the valuator to request from the shareholders (separately, if each shareholder has a different bias with respect to the requested value) their reasoning as to which course of action they feel should be taken with respect to each of the afore-mentioned issues. In some cases, it may be appropriate to obtain a legal opinion as to the meaning of the wording in the agreement. The valuator can then consider all facts provided and subsequently make an informed decision.

Alternative Ways to Derive Value According to a Shareholder Agreement

The determination of value for the purpose of establishing a transaction price among shareholders may be dealt with in various ways. Shareholder agreements sometimes specify how fair market value (or some other definition of value) is to be determined. The most common are:

- value agreed to annually by the shareholders;

- value determined by formula;

- value determined by independent expert;

- value determined by mediation or arbitration; and

- a combination of the latter two where there is disagreement among experts.

Value Agreed to Annually by the Shareholders

As a general rule, the best approach is for the shareholders periodically to agree upon the value (or values) of specific shareholdings for various purposes, and to stipulate it (or them) in writing. Where this is done, it is important these values be updated on a regular basis, usually annually following receipt of year-end financial statements. In practice, however, the following difficulties are often encountered using this approach:

- shareholders lack knowledge as to the value options available to them and/or lack understanding of their importance or do not understand value;

- getting agreement among all shareholders, or the requisite majority if unanimity is not required;

- lack of discipline and diligence in systematically updating values, such that the values become stale-dated; and
- shareholders may be biased where they anticipate that a transaction will be consummated in the near term at the determined value.

These difficulties may be overcome by providing for an annual independent valuation as the basis for transactions in the ensuing year. In practice, this approach is best suited to situations where there is significant value, the company has many shareholders and frequent or periodic transactions are likely to occur.

Value Determined by Formula

In lieu of an annual value determination, shareholders sometimes set out a valuation formula in shareholder agreements. Formulas are often based on some predetermined multiple of historical accounting earnings (such as EBITDA) or book value. While attractive because of their simplicity, the use of predetermined formulas may result in inequities for at least the following reasons:

- given the various values shareholders may establish, or that may be required preceding or following different events contemplated in the agreement, any single formula will of necessity result in a compromise value that will satisfy each of the various required values to a greater or lesser degree at a given point in time;
- formulas, even if they do result in a reasonable value at a particular point in time to satisfy a particular purpose, will often not yield equitable results over a lengthy period. This occurs because value is influenced by factors both internal to and external to the business, which in turn can dramatically affect financial results. For example, a formula based on a multiple of EBITDA for a particular year may give rise to a higher or lower value than expected when based on the operating performance of the business over a relatively short time period;
- formulas that are based on a multiple of earnings are usually not adjusted appropriately for balance sheet items such as redundant assets or excess (deficient) working capital; and
- the formulaic approach may yield a price different from any objective value calculation, perhaps resulting in severe income tax or other implications.

Where a formulaic approach is adopted, there is sometimes a mechanism to contest the derived value if it is outside a reasonable range.

Value Determined by Independent Expert

A shareholder agreement will sometimes specify that an independent valuator is to determine the value of the company *en bloc* or an interest in it either periodically or when a triggering event occurs. Parties to a shareholder agreement should be satisfied the independent expert selected is knowledgeable about the business and that they will consider all relevant factors in determining value. Shareholder agreements sometimes contain a list of valuation firms or individuals from which the shareholders can select when required. The company's auditors are often precluded from acting in the role of independent valuation experts because of real or perceived conflicts of interest with one or more of the shareholders.

Often it is beneficial for the independent expert to produce a draft report and to allow the shareholders to respond to the draft in terms of factual errors or omissions prior to disclosing the value conclusion (i.e., a "blind draft"). This approach helps to ensure the parties commenting on the draft focus on ensuring the accuracy and completeness of all relevant facts contained in the report rather than becoming overly distracted and adversarial by the draft's conclusion. Once the independent valuator is satisfied all the relevant factors have been duly accounted for, they can then formulate a value conclusion.

Value Determined by Mediation or Arbitration

Another alternative to the determination of value according to a shareholder agreement is to provide for mediation or arbitration. Depending on the availability of appeal from such a value determination, this can be an expensive process. Further, it is often difficult for the different parties to come to a consensus regarding which valuator to use, although in many cases the valuation firm or list of acceptable firms is set out in the shareholder agreement.

Arbitration can be arranged such that:

- each party retains an expert who provides their respective opinions in a court-like environment to a single arbitrator or arbitration panel which reaches its own view based on the information presented to it; or

- each party retains an expert who provides their respective opinions to a single arbitrator or arbitration panel which, based on the information presented to it, selects one of the views presented to it without alteration (a so-called "baseball arbitration").

In some cases, an arbitrator's decision may be quashed where it can be shown that they did not consider all the relevant facts.

Common Issues with Minority Discounts

Minority discounts (or discounts for non-control and discounts for illiquidity) are subjective. The quantum of minority discounts (or even whether a minority discount should be applied at all) in any fact-specific situation is usually the subject of considerable debate.

In addition to their subjectivity, minority discounts sometimes contain technical or conceptual errors because of the following factors:

- a lack of understanding of the method by which *en bloc* fair market value was determined. Since discounts are relative concepts, it is important to consider the methodology and assumptions underlying the determination of *en bloc* fair market value in order to develop a meaningful discount from pro-rata value;

- inconsistent application of minority discounts at different points in time. A change in the quantum of discount of a particular shareholding should be supported by a demonstrable change in relevant factors affecting such a discount at different points in time (e.g., a change in the relationship among the shareholders);

- double-counting. Where a minority discount is derived based on a discount for non-control and a discount for illiquidity, the factors giving rise to each discount are sometimes double-counted, which may result in an overstatement of the combined minority discount;

- inadequate consideration of the specific facts that influence the magnitude or existence of a minority discount. In particular, the shareholder agreement (where one exists) must be carefully reviewed to understand the rights and privileges afforded to minority shareholders and majority shareholders; and

- developing a minority discount based on the inverse of control premiums observed in public market takeover transactions. In most cases, this approach is flawed. It assumes the premium paid in an open market transaction is entirely due to the elimination of an inherent minority discount embedded in the market price of the shares of the acquired public company prior to the transaction. It is generally accepted that shares of widely held public companies do not trade at prices that incorporate a minority discount. Rather, in most cases, some or all of a control premium is more likely attributable to post-acquisition synergies anticipated by the buyer, and/or the fact that the form of payment included non-cash terms (e.g., a share-for-share exchange), with a cash equivalent amount less than its face value. The existence of synergies or non-cash deal terms serves to inflate the premium paid to conclude the transaction, a value-determination method inconsistent with fair market value determined on an intrinsic basis.

Summary

A minority shareholder is defined as one that owns 50% or less of the outstanding voting shares of a company and, absent a shareholder agreement or other agreement, may have little influence on how the company is run. Accordingly, a discount from pro-rata *en bloc* value may be applied in the valuation of a minority interest. However, minority shareholders are afforded certain statutory rights that normally preclude the controlling shareholder from treating them unfairly.

Shareholders frequently enter into shareholder agreements that set out their privileges, protections and obligations as shareholders and define what is to occur when certain triggering events take place. Shareholder agreements also help protect the liquidity of minority shareholders in particular. When drafting shareholder agreements, it is important to ensure the value terms adopted are carefully defined to avoid issues that arise from differences in interpretation when various provisions calling for a determination of value are activated.

A minority discount can be thought of as made up of two related components: (i) a discount for non-control; and (ii) a discount for illiquidity. A discount for non-control recognizes the inability of a particular shareholder to elect a majority of the board of directors and, through them, to effectively influence the risk-return trade-off of a company, and to dictate the timing of an *en bloc* sale or liquidation of the business. A discount for illiquidity recognizes the absence of a ready market (i.e., a number of interested buyers) in which to sell a particular shareholding in the near term at a relatively predictable price. Discounts for non-control and illiquidity are typically associated with minority shareholdings, although in some circumstances, one or both of them may apply to a controlling interest. Further, while minority discounts are usually associated with privately held companies, a discount for illiquidity may apply to shares of public companies whose shares are thinly traded.

The quantification of discounts for non-control and illiquidity is a subjective exercise. The specific facts of each case must be carefully considered, including the terms of any existing shareholder agreement and the method by which *en bloc* value was determined. The factors giving rise to discounts for non-control and illiquidity overlap and are often combined into an all-inclusive minority discount.

Chapter 9

Special Topics

Introduction

This chapter deals with a variety of issues that commonly arise in valuation, including intangible assets, preferred shares and dilutive securities, holding companies, foreign entities and taxation.

The valuation of intangible assets has become a subject of major interest in recent years. While intangible value usually is determined in conjunction with the valuation of a business *en bloc*, there are many situations where the value of one or more specific intangible assets must be determined in isolation. These situations include open market transactions involving the purchase of an intangible asset such as a brand name, the determination of a reasonable royalty rate in respect of the use of proprietary technology, and purchase price allocation for financial accounting purposes.

The valuation of common shares is affected where a company has preferred shares outstanding. Where the preferred shares are redeemable or retractable, the value of the preferred shares normally is set at their redemption or retraction value. However, this can change depending on the attributes of the preferred shares, cross-ownership and other considerations. In addition, the value of common shares can be affected by dilutive securities, such as warrants, options, convertible debt and convertible preferreds, which may be outstanding at the valuation date.

The valuation of holding companies usually is based on the adjusted net book value methodology as discussed in Chapter 3, whereby the underlying equity investments normally are valued using a cash flow-based valuation methodology. However, there are certain issues that commonly arise with respect to holding company valuations that need to be addressed, particularly those pertaining to head office costs and taxation.

While this book has addressed valuation from the perspective of a Canadian business, the general principles can be broadly applied to virtually any entity in the world. However, when dealing with the valuation of foreign entities, additional considerations must be addressed, such as differences in taxation and specific economic and industry conditions. Further, the rate of return may require additional consideration and adjustments, particularly where the foreign entity is located in a higher-risk environment (inflation, political issues, repatriation of capital and other country-specific factors).

Finally, there are a variety of tax issues that arise in valuation, particularly in the context of privately held companies, which can influence valuation in a notional market context, as well as open market pricing and deal structuring.

Intangible Assets

Forms of Intangible Assets

Intangible assets can be found as a component of the equity value of a business or, in some cases, as a stand-alone asset. As illustrated in Exhibit 9A below, there are two broad categories of intangible assets: (i) identifiable intangible assets; and (ii) non-identifiable intangible assets.

Exhibit 9A
Breakdown of Equity Value

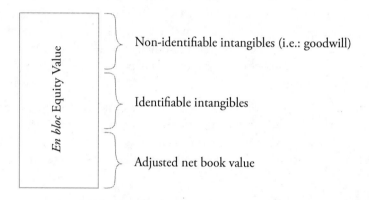

Identifiable intangible assets can then be segregated into three general subcategories:

- contractual rights;
- intellectual property; and
- business practices and relationships.

The discussion in this chapter pertains to intangible assets from the perspective of economic value. Intangible assets in the context of purchase price allocation is addressed in Chapter 10.

Non-Identifiable Intangible Assets (Goodwill)

Non-identifiable intangible assets are generally referred to as "goodwill". The value of goodwill is determined as the *en bloc* equity value of a business, typically determined by a cash flow-based valuation methodology, less the adjusted net book value of the business (which reflects the economic value of net tangible assets, as illustrated in Chapter 3), less the value of identifiable intangible assets.

Exhibit 9B
Determination of Non-Identifiable Intangible Assets

En bloc equity value

Less: adjusted net book value

Equals: intangible value

Less: identifiable intangible assets

Equals: non-identifiable intangible assets (goodwill)

As discussed in Chapter 1, goodwill may be commercial goodwill, individual goodwill or personal goodwill. Personal goodwill is non-transferable and therefore is not a component of fair market value. Where the goodwill is commercial in nature (and is not represented by an identifiable intangible asset) then it is not separable from the business itself.

Contractual Rights

Contractual rights are those that accrue to a business by way of a written or oral contract (where it can be enforced by law). A contract has distinct value where it affords the business a stream of cash flow for a period of time that is: (i) in excess of what the business could generate absent the contract; and / or (ii) at a lower level of risk than would be the case, absent the contract.

Examples of contractual rights include:

- a customer contract that secures the sale of products or services at an agreed price for a period of time (e.g., a take-or-pay contract);

- a supply agreement that secures a source of supply where the supply is in tight demand and alternative sources are not readily available;

- a franchise agreement that grants the business the right to use a certain brand name, know-how or other benefits for a specified period of time;

- a licence agreement that provides the business with the right to offer certain goods or services to its customers; and

- a premises lease at a rate below current market rental rates.

In some cases, there can be unfavourable contracts, such as a premises lease in excess of current market rates. Just as a favourable contract represents an asset to the business, an unfavourable contract represents a liability.

Intellectual Property

Intellectual property usually exists in the form of a patent, trademark or copyright that protects its owner against unauthorized exploitation by others for commercial gain. Intellectual property also includes proprietary technology, processes, information and know-how the owner elects not to protect at law in order to maintain secrecy. Distinct value accrues to intellectual property where one or more of the following occurs:

- the owner employs the intellectual property for economic advantage in the business in order to generate income or reduce costs in a manner that would not be commercially feasible absent the intellectual property;

- the employment of the intellectual property raises a barrier to entry in a particular market; or

- a third party is prepared to pay for the intellectual property in order to exploit the perceived economic advantages for their own benefit.

The value of intellectual property is influenced by the ability to protect it, either by law or by business practices (e.g., secrecy) so that it does not become generally available, thereby eroding the economic advantage.

Business Practices and Relationships

There are several types of business practices and relationships that a business can have that contribute to its intangible value. A common example is customer loyalty that can give rise to the expectation of future revenues and cash flows. However, it is often more difficult to isolate the incremental cash flow accruing to a business from its business practices and relationships than from other types of identifiable intangibles. For example, in the case of customer relationships, some may be attributable to the unique products or services offered by the business, or because of the personal connection between a key employee and the customer's management team. Therefore, intangible assets have to be considered collectively and not just individually. That said, certain types of business practices and relationships (e.g., customer lists) constitute "identifiable intangible assets" for financial reporting purposes, and in such cases are quantified in isolation (see Chapter 10).

Valuation of Identifiable Intangible Assets

In some cases, it is necessary to determine the value of an identifiable intangible asset such as a licence, patent, franchise, contract, brand name or customer list. Examples include purchase price allocation following an open market transaction (which is further discussed in Chapter 10), income tax determination where identifiable intangible assets with a finite life are assigned to eligible capital property for the purpose of calculating cumulative eligible capital (e.g., a franchise) and open market transactions where the identifiable intangibles will be sold separate from the business itself (e.g., the sale of an unused patent viewed as a redundant asset).

There are five approaches to establishing the value of an identifiable intangible asset: (i) the market approach; (ii) the cost approach; (iii) the incremental cash flow (or income) approach; (iv) the relief from royalty approach; and (v) the excess earnings approach.

The Market Approach

The market approach is similar to valuing real estate, as discussed in Chapter 3. It is premised on the assumption that two largely similar assets (houses or vacant land in real estate appraisals) should be worth approximately the same amount, subject to fact-specific considerations that support value differences. In theory, if the details of a transaction involving a reasonably comparable intangible asset are available, that transaction could be used as a basis to value the intangible asset that is the subject of valuation. In practice, however, there is usually a lack of truly comparable intangible asset transactions, let alone ones with meaningful data necessary for such a comparison available in the public domain. Even where detailed information is available, such transactions typically include other acquired assets. It is then difficult (and sometimes not possible) to segregate the value of the intangible asset meaningfully from the value of the other assets.

For example, sports team franchises are often valued with reference to recent comparable sales. However, the price paid for those franchises may be distorted by such things as a favourable lease agreement for access to the playing field or arena. Furthermore, the dynamics of each transaction, including prevailing market conditions, the negotiating positions of the parties and possible synergies, may distort any comparisons. That said, following an open market transaction where intangible assets were acquired, the notes to financial statements of the buyer will often provide some insight into the allocation of the purchase price among the tangible and intangible assets acquired and provide some assistance in making a comparison.

On occasion, reasonably comparative information can be found. In order for a comparable transaction to be used as a benchmark, there must be enough information available to assure the intangible asset was acquired at arm's length and is a meaningful comparable, in terms of the industry, related profitability levels, geographic location, remaining term of legal protection and other important parameters.

The Cost Approach

The cost approach is premised on the assumption that the value of an intangible asset is equal to its estimated replacement cost, as in the case of property or equipment discussed in Chapter 3. The inherent assumption is that the cost to acquire or internally recreate the intangible asset is equal to the economic benefit it provides. This assumption is often flawed because:

- in many cases, while significant cost and capital investment were required to develop the intangible asset, it may have limited or no commercial viability. In this case, the cost approach would cause the value conclusion to be overstated;

- existing commercially viable intangible assets may have depreciated in value since being created as a result of changed economic conditions, new competing intangibles introduced since inception and other factors. Again, the cost approach would cause the value conclusion to be overstated; and

- in some cases, the intangible asset represents a windfall, by providing the owner with economic benefits well beyond the cost incurred to produce the intangible. In this case, the cost approach would cause the value conclusion to be understated.

Another difficulty that arises with the cost approach is estimating the cost to recreate a given intangible. Many businesses do not keep detailed records of their employee's time and other expenses incurred to develop the intangible. The credibility of conclusions reached when applying the cost approach is a function of the quality of available cost data. A further difficulty arises when determining the proper definition of cost, (e.g., variable cost only, fully absorbed overheads, and so on).

As noted in Chapter 1, value looks to the future, while the cost approach focuses on historical results. In light of the foregoing issues, the cost approach is not frequently adopted as a basis for valuing intangible assets. That said, the cost approach is sometimes adopted in the context of purchase price allocation for financial accounting purposes where the cash flow attributable to an identifiable intangible asset cannot be readily segregated (and no meaningful comparable transactions exist).

The Incremental Cash Flow Approach

The incremental cash flow approach (sometimes referred to as the "with and without method") involves estimating the prospective incremental cash flows (or income) generated by a business as a result of owning a particular intangible asset. The prospective incremental cash flow is discounted to present value at an appropriate discount rate, in a way similar to the discounted cash flow methodology as illustrated in Chapter 6.

The issues that must be addressed using the incremental cash flow approach include:

- the current and prospective industry and economic conditions and related cycles. For example, when valuing the brand name of an automobile manufacturer, the cyclicality of the automotive industry should be considered;

- an assessment of current and prospective competitive threats (i.e., factors that might reasonably be expected to materialize that could reduce the economic benefits currently being derived by a business as a result of its intangible assets);

- incremental operating expenditures, capital expenditures and working capital required to generate the incremental revenues to be gained from using the intangible asset and to maintain compliance with any licensing or other associated requirements. For example, the continued use of a brand name that allows a product to be sold for a premium price may require additional expenditures and investment (e.g., advertising costs and higher accounts receivable); and

- the longevity or duration of the economic benefits associated with the intangible asset (e.g., the period of a licence agreement). Where the use of the intangible asset is available for an extended (or perpetual) duration, consideration should be given to the ability of the intangible asset to maintain its competitive advantage over that period.

As a practical matter, the separation of cash flows that would be generated by the business with the intangible asset and those that would be generated without it is a subjective task.

In addition to generating incremental cash flow, the identifiable intangible asset might impact the risk profile of the business. For example, a business that successfully negotiates the right to license a brand name might benefit by being able to command a higher price for its products and enjoy a lower risk profile because of the reduced volatility of sales volumes. In this case, the value of the intangible asset would be determined by valuing the business on a "with and without" basis (i.e., the enterprise value of the business with the licence vs. the enterprise value of the business without it). Like the incremental cash flow, the difference in risk profile would also be somewhat subjective.

Consider the following example. F1 Limited acquires a single-location restaurant that operates under a well-known fast food franchise. The restaurant generates revenues of $5 million per year and has operating costs of $3.5 million. In addition, the franchise agreement requires the franchisee to pay a royalty equal to 5% of revenues. The franchise agreement has 10 years remaining. The buyer estimates that, without the franchise, revenues would only be $3 million and annual operating costs would be $2 million. Because of its other business interests, F1 pays income tax at a rate of 28%. A discount rate of 18% is considered to be appropriate.

In the above example, the value of the franchise agreement would be calculated as follows:

Exhibit 9C
F1 Limited
Valuation of Franchise
Incremental Cash Flow Approach

	With Franchise	Without Franchise	Difference
Revenues	5,000,000	3,000,000	
Operating costs	3,500,000	2,000,000	
Royalties (5%)	250,000	n/a	
Pre-tax cash flow	1,250,000	1,000,000	
Income taxes at 28%	350,000	280,000	
Discretionary cash flow	900,000	720,000	180,000
Present value interest factor 18%, 10 years			4.494
Value of franchise			808,936

The difference in discretionary cash flow of $180,000 is discounted at 18% for 10 years (represented by a present value interest factor of 4.494) to derive the fair market value of the franchise of $808,936. The validity of this valuation estimate is premised on the reasonableness of the assumptions regarding what the business could generate without the franchise. The above example assumes that capital investment, working capital requirements and the risk profile of the business are the same under each of the two scenarios, which may not always be the case.

The Relief from Royalty Approach

The relief from royalty approach is premised on the estimated royalty that a business would pay to a third party, or vice versa, to commercially exploit the intangible asset. In this approach, a royalty rate is applied to the estimated revenues or cost savings generated by using the intangible asset.

The royalty rate adopted is often determined with reference to the royalty rates on somewhat comparable intangible assets, where meaningful information can be found. This in of itself can be problematic because the royalty rate paid under an arm's length agreement is influenced by a myriad of other factors, such as the duration of the agreement, whether minimum royalties apply, exclusivity provisions, and other terms, which might not be publicly disclosed. Royalty agreements are discussed later in this chapter. Furthermore, the current and prospective economic and industry conditions at the time the royalty agreement was struck are important to consider as well.

As an example of the relief from royalty approach, assume that G1 Limited is looking to value a newly developed proprietary technology. The technology is expected to result in revenues of $2 million in year one, $5 million in year two, $10 million in year three and grow at a rate of 3% per annum thereafter. The estimated useful life of the technology is 15 years. Assume that a royalty rate of 5%, and a discount rate of 20% are believed to be appropriate. Further assume that the applicable tax rate is 30%. Based on the foregoing, the fair market value of the technology would be estimated as follows:

Exhibit 9D
G1 Limited
Estimated Value of Technology
Relief from Royalty Approach
($000)

	Year 1	Year 2	Year 3	Thereafter
Revenues	2,000	5,000	10,000	10,300
Royalty at 5%	100	250	500	515
Less: taxes at 30%	(30)	(75)	(150)	(155)
After-tax cash flow	70	175	350	360
PVIFA, 17%, 12 years				4.988
Present value, years 4-15				1,798
Discounted at 20%	64	133	222	1,140
Fair market value	1,559			

Similar to the discounted cash flow methodology illustrated in Chapter 6, the royalty stream for the first three years is discounted at a rate of 20% (based on mid-year rates). The value of the royalty stream from years four through 15 is based on a present value interest factor of 4.988, which represents 17% for 12 years. The 17% rate adopted represents the nominal discount rate of 20%, less the long-term growth rate of 3%. The terminal value component of $1,798,000 is discounted for a period of 2.5 years and added to the discounted values from years one through three in order to derive the estimated fair market value of the proprietary technology of $1,559,000.

As with any valuation, the validity of the conclusion is subject to the reasonableness of the assumptions. In the case of technology, a common challenge is that revenues from its use may peak and then begin to decline. Where that is the case, annual cash flows for the duration of the technology's useful life should be estimated.

Excess Earnings Approach

The excess earnings approach is a derivative of the dual capitalization methodology presented in Chapter 5. According to this approach, a market-based rate of return is applied to the net tangible operating assets of the business in order to estimate the earnings that should be generated from the use of such assets. To the extent the earnings of the business exceed the earnings attributed to the net tangible operating assets, intangible value exists. Such excess earnings are divided by a capitalization rate that reflects the associated (normally higher) risk.

By way of example, assume that H1 Limited is a manufacturer of branded food products. Because of its recognized brand name, H1 is able to command a premium price. The company generates discretionary cash flow of $4 million on $25 million of net tangible operating assets (including net trade working capital and fixed assets). Management of H1 believes that a reasonable capitalization rate to apply against its net tangible operating assets is 10%, and a capitalization rate of 15% to the excess earnings (cash flows).

Based on these facts, the fair market value of H1's brand name would be estimated at $10 million, as illustrated in Exhibit 9E:

Exhibit 9E
H1 Limited
Estimated Fair Market Value of Brand Name
Excess Earnings Approach

Maintainable discretionary cash flow		4,000,000
Net tangible operating assets	25,000,000	
Return on net tangible operating assets	10%	
Discretionary cash flow attributable to net tangible operating assets		(2,500,000)
Excess cash flow		1,500,000
Rate of return attributable to excess cash flow		15%
Estimated fair market value of brand name		10,000,000

The excess earnings approach can also be conducted based on accounting earnings, although cash flow is a better measure of economic value.

Valuing Non-Competition Agreements

Non-competition agreements typically relate to the individual goodwill held by the business owner(s) given their relationship with customers and employees, operational knowledge and other factors that influence the value of the business.

In a notional market context, it is assumed a buyer and seller will strike a satisfactory non-competition agreement so the transaction can be concluded. In most open market transactions involving the purchase of a privately held company, the buyer requires the seller to exercise a non-competition agreement in order to preclude the seller from working with a competitor or establishing a new competitive business shortly after the closing of the transaction and thereby eroding the value of the target company.

In an open market transaction, buyers and sellers sometimes allocate a portion of the purchase price to a non-competition agreement. The courts have sometimes found that a non-competition agreement is more enforceable where the seller has received consideration attaching directly to such an agreement. Furthermore, the allocation of a portion of the purchase price to a non-competition agreement has become a more prevalent topic in recent years, given pending changes to the *Income Tax Act* (which remain in draft form at the time of writing [2012]) involving the tax treatment of payments under non-competition agreements. Consequently, in open market transactions, the portion of the purchase price allocated to a non-competition agreement (if any) can vary considerably depending on the negotiating positions of the buyer and seller and the structure of the deal for income tax purposes.

In some cases, the value of a non-competition agreement must be isolated in a notional market context. This includes purchase price allocation and fairness opinions, which are frequently required in the context of a proposed takeover transaction or related-party transaction (see Chapter 10). In these cases, the terms and provisions of the non-competition agreement provide guidance as to the portion of the aggregate purchase price that should be allocated to the non-competition agreement (see Chapter 10).

In other cases, where the provisions of a non-competition agreement are not established as part of the valuation exercise, it generally is not practical to hypothesize the terms and conditions that would be agreed between the seller and buyer. Accordingly, emphasis should be placed on determining that individual goodwill does exist, and the ability of the individual(s) in whom it resides to compete effectively with the business without a non-competition agreement.

Estimating the portion of value to attribute to a non-competition agreement is normally done by notionally determining the value of the acquired business without a non-competition agreement. The result then is compared with the value otherwise determined in a notional market context or the price paid in an open market transaction. In this regard, consideration should be given to:

- the individual business owner(s), their involvement in the business and personal characteristics. In general, the potential value attributed to a non-competition agreement increases where the business owner(s):
    - ✓ is relatively young and not expected to retire from daily business activity in the near term,
    - ✓ enjoys good physical health,
    - ✓ is expected to have a high level of interest in continuing the business or a similar business following the sale,
    - ✓ possesses valuable personal knowledge and good personal relationships with employees, suppliers and customers. These relationships are important to the prospective viability of the business, cannot be readily passed on, and will continue to reside with the business owner following the sale,
    - ✓ has the financial ability to compete following the sale, and
    - ✓ has in-depth knowledge of the near-term plans and long-term strategies of the business;
- characteristics of the business itself, such as the kind of product and service offerings and the degree of management depth. In general, the potential value attributed to a non-competition agreement increases where the business:
    - ✓ is relatively small in size,
    - ✓ sells non-proprietary products or services (particularly professional services), and
    - ✓ lacks depth in its management team beyond the individuals who are party to the non-competition agreement;
- the nature of the industry in which the business competes. In general, the potential value attributed to a non-competition agreement increases where the business in which the industry competes:
    - ✓ sells products in the earlier stages of the product life-cycle, and
    - ✓ is such that the business owner's options to compete would include a ready opportunity to start a new competitive business, enter into a joint venture or other participating equity relationship with an existing competitor or enter into an employment contract with a competitor,

> ✓   is subject to a comparatively weak competitive environment, and
>
> ✓   has the potential for, or would allow for, a comparatively rapid near-term expansion;

- the terms of payment in the transaction. For example, if a significant portion of the ultimate purchase price will be determined by an earnout type of arrangement, it is likely less value will be attributed to non-competition agreements than otherwise would be the case;

- the specific terms of the agreement itself, including the definition of the specific business(es) from which the seller is prohibited, and the geographic area in which, and length of time over which, competition is restricted. There should be a direct relationship between the compensation paid to a seller to not compete and the magnitude and scope of the competitive restrictions; and

- judicial interpretations with respect to non-competition agreements and non-competition itself. It is necessary to be aware of the case law affecting the enforceability of an assumed non-competition agreement. The greater the ability to legally enforce, the greater the potential value of an agreement to a buyer.

As a practical matter, many open market transactions would not be concluded if the buyer and seller did not agree to a mutually satisfactory non-competition agreement. Therefore, one might argue that all intangible value should be allocated to such an agreement. However, in most cases, it is a combination of the non-competition agreement and other intangible assets (e.g., customer relationships, proprietary technology, and other intangibles) that give rise to the aggregate intangible value in a business. Accordingly, it is typically the case that only a portion of the aggregate intangible value is allocated to the non-competition agreement.

Royalty Agreements

There are several circumstances where a royalty rate needs to be determined in the context of a notional valuation or open market transaction. Common cases include those where:

- the relief from royalty method is adopted in the valuation of an intangible asset; and

- a licence agreement is struck between a licensor and a licensee in respect of intellectual property, brand name or other intangible asset.

Royalty Structure

The most common bases for structuring royalty payments are either a fixed sum per unit sold or a percentage of revenues or profit (e.g., gross profit or operating profit) derived from the sale of licensed products or services.

Fixed-dollar royalty payments are often adopted where licensed products or services are sold as components of large systems and the price received may not be determinable in isolation. Where a fixed-dollar amount per unit sold is adopted, the dollar amount is usually adjusted for inflation although not always, particularly where a minimum royalty amount is specified.

One of the challenges to establishing royalties on a fixed-dollar basis is that there is typically no recognition of changing market conditions. Therefore, at any given point in time, or over time, fixed-dollar royalty arrangements may prove to be economically unfair to either the licensor or the licensee.

Royalties based on a percentage of the licensee's revenues or operating profit from the licensed products or services require the measurement base to be clearly defined. Where gross profit or operating profit is the measurement base, it is often determined by applying a pre-established profit percentage (or pre-established costs) to revenues generated from licensed products or services. The profit percentage is negotiated between licensor and licensee and normally reflects direct cost to manufacture the product or deliver the service, selling costs related to the licensed products or services, as well as a reasonable allocation of fixed overheads. The use of a predetermined percentage operating profit avoids any issues associated with accounting discrepancies. Where properly and equitably determined, profit-based royalty payments make the most economic sense to both the licensee and licensor. However, a percentage of revenue is frequently adopted because of the difficulty of agreeing on an operating profit percentage and for ease of administration.

Establishing Royalty Rates

Concurrent with the issue of royalty structure is the determination of royalty rates under a licensing agreement or other agreement (i.e., the dollar or percentage amount to be applied to the agreed measurement base). In any given transaction, royalty rates are negotiated between the licensor and licensee. Such rates (and the terms of the licence agreement) can vary widely depending on the relative negotiating abilities and negotiating positions of the parties.

The guiding principles of royalty rate determination are economic fairness to both the licensor and licensee, and the value received by the licensee from the licensor over the term of the licence agreement. The value conveyed from the licensor to the licensee is a function of specific factors relating to the licensed products or services, the terms of the licence agreement and the particular characteristics of the licensor.

In open market transactions, royalty rates are often gauged from a review of rates involving similar licensed property. Sources of such information include public company disclosures as well as subscription databases. However, as is the case with public company comparables in valuation, royalty rates taken from public records can vary widely depending on a variety of factors such as the relative negotiating positions of the parties involved, the terms and structure of the licence agreement and other provisions regarding the licence, that may not be disclosed.

Key considerations when reviewing licensing agreements believed to be comparable include:

- the degree of comparability with the property covered by the licence agreement, in terms of its competitive advantage, brand name strength, and other important parameters;

- the terms of the licence agreement (which may not be fully disclosed). Particular attention should be afforded to the length of the agreement, renewal provisions, the territory covered and whether or not exclusivity has been granted;

- whether there are any up-front payments, milestone payments or other forms of consideration that may influence the stated royalty rate; and

- the time frame during which the royalty rate was established, and important changes to industry and economic conditions during the interim period.

As a very general benchmark, subject to fact-specific adjustment, an amount equal to approximately 25% of the licensee's operating profit derived from the sale of licensed products or services is often viewed as an appropriate royalty payment where the licensor provides the licensee with significant value. Significant value generally implies all of the following: (i) products, services or other property with a long-term competitive advantage; (ii) licence terms favourable to the licensee; (iii) the licensor has critical mass and strongly supports its products or services and the licensee; and (iv) the licensee does not provide any significant non-cash value to the licensor. Where some or all of these criteria are not met, an appropriate royalty rate based on operating profit would be reduced.

It follows that, among the specific factors relating to the product, service or intangible asset that should be considered in establishing royalty rates, are:

- the uniqueness and competitive advantage of the licensed products, services or intangible asset, including the scope and remaining life of any patents. The importance of ongoing technology and product improvements to remain competitive, and the licensee's rights to those improvements, should also be considered;

- the markets in which the licensee will sell the licensed products, including market size, growth rates, extent of competition and recent developments. While the size of the territory should be specified in the licence agreement, the market dynamics within a licensed territory influences perceived profit potential and hence the level of interest among prospective licensees, which in turn is reflected in the royalty rate demanded by the licensor;

- the degree of complexity in the sale of licensed products or services, and the extent of customization in customer-specific applications. A greater level of sale complexity and licensee customization generally results in a reduction in the royalty rate;

- whether the licensee is afforded exclusivity within a defined territory. As a practical matter, where exclusivity is not granted, royalty rates tend to be significantly reduced;

- the length of the initial licence term and provisions for renewal. Where the provisions for renewal are favourable to the licensee, that fact would cause royalty rates to increase. Where a licensor does not intend to renew an existing licence agreement, it must develop a transition strategy to a new licensee or in-house resources. Depending on the nature of the licensed item and the territory, the licensor may find that it has substantive barriers to terminating an existing licence agreement;

- the provisions for termination. The conditions for unilateral licence termination (principally intended to protect the licensor) generally involve the licensee committing a material breach of the agreement and not rectifying it within a specified time period. In addition to licence termination, a party that commits a breach of contract may also be subject to damages for loss of existing or potential business, loss of reputation, and other claims;

- whether or not a minimum royalty exists;

- whether there are milestone payments or other fixed payments for the use of the licensed property;

- the licensee's ability to assign the licence to a third party, either directly or indirectly (i.e., through the purchase of a licensee's shares by a third-party buyer). To prevent the latter from occurring, licence agreements sometimes specify the licence can be terminated upon a change in control of the licensee;

- the licensor's presence within its own markets, its financial viability, and whether it has critical mass in terms of size, management depth and depth of technical knowledge. Licence arrangements are often pursued by licensors that are themselves small or medium-sized businesses and which may not be well financed, or which may be reliant on the strategic, selling, or technical abilities of one or only a few individuals. The greater the risk the licensor may not be able to support its licensed products or services, both financially and through ongoing technological improvements, the greater the risk to the licensee, and hence the greater the pressure to decrease royalty rates;

- the licensor's plans, strategies, and level of commitment relating to the licensed products and services. This should include committed R&D funding for improving licensed products and for developing new products or services that would form part of the existing licence agreement. A licensor with a well-developed strategy based on market analysis and research will be in a better negotiating position with respect to royalty rates. Ideally, the plans and strategies would be shared with the licensee to ensure consistency in objectives and to help promote a partnership atmosphere; and

- the extent and timeliness of support offered to the licensee, both in terms of technical product advice and assisting the licensee with sales and marketing efforts in its territory. This kind of support is especially important for technologically sophisticated products or services and applications, and for those products or services involving a complex selling process, particularly during the initial years of a licence arrangement where the licensee must go through a learning curve. Typically, the better the support offered to the licensee the greater should be the royalty rate, and vice versa.

While the licensee normally pays for the value received from the licensor in the form of cash royalties, the licensee may offer the licensor other things of value as well. The royalty rate will be influenced by the respective estimates of both licensor and licensee as to aggregate sales potential within the licensed territory, given the characteristics of the licensee. A licensee with a sound financial position and an established market presence may offer strong support and instant credibility for the licensed products. The licensee may also contribute value to the licensor in the form of product or service enhancements and new product or service developments. In some cases, the licensee may assist the licensor in the areas of strategic analysis, sales and marketing relating to the licensed products or services. Where the licensee provides the licensor with non-cash forms of value, this would normally reduce the cash royalty rate.

Other Considerations

The determination of an appropriate royalty rate becomes more complex where the licensee is required to purchase from the licensor certain components used in manufacturing or supplying the licensed products (e.g., mandatory supply arrangements). The licensor may argue that the arrangement is necessary to ensure the quality of manufactured or supplied products or to protect its proprietary know-how. In most cases, the mandatory supply arrangement results in an additional source of profit for the licensor (the quantum of which is seldom disclosed) and which therefore tends to decrease the royalty rate. Where the licensor and licensee are located in different countries, this arrangement may also subject the licensee to shipping delays and foreign exchange risk. Where a mandatory supply arrangement forms part of the licence agreement, the licensee should ensure the prices of the components in question are clearly established and there is an acceptable means of controlling price increases.

Finally, where royalties are earned in a currency other than the licensor's home currency, it is normally the licensor that bears the exchange risk. While it is sometimes possible to hedge exchange risk over a relatively short period (one to two years), practical limitations may make it impossible to hedge effectively over a longer term. Since the duration of licensing agreements typically extends beyond a short time frame, the licensor may be exposed to devaluation in its royalty earnings because of long-term structural economic factors in the licensed territory. The licensor should account for this risk when determining an acceptable royalty rate.

Royalty Rates in Notional Market Valuations

In some cases, an assumed royalty rate needs to be established for the valuation of an intangible asset in the context of a notional market valuation. In such cases, it is not possible to hypothesize the terms of the licensing agreement that may govern the use of the property. However, it is customary to assume the licensee has been granted an exclusive licence for an adequate period of time.

While the "25% of profit" rule, as noted above, may offer a general guideline in some circumstances, consideration should be given to important factors regarding the products or services to be licensed (as noted above) and the nature of the industry in which the licensee's business operates.

In some cases, royalty rates are determined by reference to comparable rates that have been disclosed. As is the case with comparable industry transactions (discussed in Chapter 4), comparable royalty rates must be carefully examined to determine whether or not a meaningful comparison can be drawn.

Preferred Shares

Where a corporation's capital structure includes preferred shares, the fair market value of the outstanding preferred shares must be deducted from aggregate *en bloc* equity value to derive *en bloc* common share value. For example, if the *en bloc* equity value of a company is $10 million and there are preferred shares outstanding with an aggregate fair market value of $2 million, the *en bloc* common share value would be $8 million. However, it is important to consider the characteristics of the preferred shares, including whether they are retractable, redeemable, convertible or possess other pertinent features. These factors could materially impact the valuation of the preferred shares, and by extension the common shares.

Retractable Preferred Shares

Where the preferred shares are retractable at any time at the option of the holder, they are normally valued at their retraction value plus any cumulative dividends in arrears, assuming a good covenant on the part of the issuer to retract them. Where the *en bloc* equity value is less than the aggregate retraction amount of the outstanding preferred shares, the value of such preferred shares is normally taken to be the *en bloc* equity value, thereby leaving no (or nominal) residual value to the common shares.

Where the retraction right vests only at a future date, a discount from the stated retraction price may be warranted, depending on the dividend yield during the interim period. However, the discounted amount should not be less than the value ascribed to the retractable preferred shares absent the retraction feature.

Redeemable Preferred Shares

Where preferred shares are redeemable at the issuer's option the redemption price plus cumulative dividends in arrears sets a ceiling on the value of the preferred shares. However, depending on their terms, conditions and attributes, the state of the issuer's covenant, and the timing and probability of redemption, their value may be less than their redemption price. Relevant considerations normally include:

- where the *en bloc* equity value of the company is less than the value of the redeemable preferred shares, that fact typically imposes a ceiling on the value of such preferred shares;

- cross-ownership of redeemable preferred and common voting shares. Where redeemable preference shares are held by the owner of a majority of the common voting shares, the likelihood of valuing the preference shares at their redemption value is greater than where the owner of the redeemable preferred shares does not control the issuer;

- whether the preferred shares enjoy voting rights at all times or only in special circumstances. The likelihood of a triggering event occurring that could give rise to voting rights must also be considered. Where the redeemable preferred shares impair the ability of the common shareholders to manage the company, the likelihood of their redemption (at their stated redemption value) is greater;

- the dividend yield on the preferred shares, including whether such dividends are fixed or variable in nature, and whether they are cumulative or non-cumulative. Where the dividends have an attractive yield (in comparison to similar investments and current interest rates) and where such dividends are cumulative, the preferred shares are more likely to be valued at their redemption amount. Conversely, preferred shares held by third parties that bear a below-market yield and/or are non-cumulative may be worth considerably less than their redemption value;

- the availability of funds to redeem the preferred shares;

- whether the redeemable preferred shares carry conversion rights that would cause a dilution in common share ownership. Depending on circumstances, the issuer may have an incentive to redeem the preferred shares when the redemption price is less than their post-conversion common share value;

- the quantum of premium, if any, to be paid to preferred shareholders on the dissolution of the company, and the likelihood of such dissolution occurring;

- where there is more than one class of preferred shares, their ranking in terms of dividend payments and proceeds on dissolution;

- whether and to what extent the preferred shares are participating (i.e., whether they share in the residual earnings available to all shareholders after payment of preferred dividends). The participation feature would serve to increase the value of the preferred shares; and

- restrictions on transfer found in corporate law and shareholder agreements. Such restrictions may serve to diminish the value of the preferred shares.

In any event, it would be unusual to value redeemable preferred shares in excess of their redemption value since an arm's length buyer of common shares would likely redeem the preferred shares at their redemption amount, thereby allowing the excess value to accrue to the common shares.

Convertible Preferred Shares

Where preferred shares are convertible into common shares, the provisions of the conversion feature must be considered.

Where the preferred shares are convertible at the option of the *holder*, they are valued at the greater of their conversion value or their value based on other features including redemption value, retraction value and dividend yield. Where the conversion value is higher, no reduction in the *en bloc* equity value is made for the convertible preferred shares. In these circumstances the convertible preferred shares are assumed to be converted and, assuming no other class of shares outstanding, the entire equity value accrues to the then notionally outstanding common shares. The pre-conversion ratable common share value declines as a result of conversion and the resultant dilution of the pre-conversion common shares. Conversely, where the value of the convertible preferred shares based on their features is less than conversion value, the value determined for the preferred shares is deducted from *en bloc* equity value and the pre-conversion common shares suffer no dilution.

For example, assume that M1 Limited has an *en bloc* equity value of $10 million with one million common shares outstanding. M1 has issued $2 million of redeemable preferred shares convertible into common shares at the option of the holder a rate of $5 per share. Given these facts, the value of the preferred shares and the common shares of M1 would be as follows:

Exhibit 9F
M1 Limited
Convertible Preferred Shares

	Before Conversion	After Conversion
En bloc equity value	10,000,000	10,000,000
Less: redemption value of preferred shares	(2,000,000)	n/a
En bloc value of common shares	8,000,000	10,000,000
Number of common shares outstanding		
Existing common shares	1,000,000	1,000,000
Conversion of preferred shares	n/a	400,000
Total	1,000,000	1,400,000
Value per common share	8.00	7.14
Share Values		
Existing common shares	8,000,000	7,142,857
Preferred shares	2,000,000	2,857,143
Total equity value	10,000,000	10,000,000

Prior to conversion, the preferred shares are valued at their redemption value of $2 million. Consequently, the one million existing common shares are worth $8 per share, or $8 million in total. However, the preferred shares could be converted into 400,000 common shares ($2 million divided by $5 per share), which would result in 1.4 million common shares outstanding post-conversion. The pro-rata value per common shares declines to $7.14. However, the preferred shareholders now hold 400,000 of these common shares, with an aggregate value of $2,857,143. The value of the one million existing common shares declines to $7,142,857. Consequently, the preferred shareholders would likely exercise the conversion option (at $5 per share) in order to maximize their value. Note that the aggregate *en bloc* equity value remains at $10 million. Only the allocation of value between the different classes of shareholders changes.

Where the preferred shares are convertible at any time at the option of the *issuer*, they are valued at the lower of their conversion value and their value based on other features. Where conversion value is lower, the convertible preferred shares are assumed to be converted. Assuming no other class of shares outstanding, the entire equity value accrues to the then notionally outstanding common shares. In these circumstances the pre-conversion ratable common share value increases as a result of conversion and resultant dilution of the pre-conversion common shares. Where the redemption value of preferred shares is less than conversion value, the redemption value of the preferred shares is deducted from aggregate *en bloc* equity value, with the remaining *en bloc* equity value accruing to the undiluted outstanding common shares.

Where the conversion right held by either the holder or the issuer of the preferred shares (or both) is deferred to a specific date, the value assigned to the conversion option should be discounted accordingly.

When estimating the value of convertible preferred shares, it is important to consider other features that might affect the conversion option. For example, where:

- the preferred shares are redeemable at the option of the issuer, the value of the conversion feature might be impaired where the shares can be redeemed prior to the time conversion rights vest; and

- conversion rights are triggered by an event such as non-payment of dividends, it is necessary to consider the probability of that event taking place, and the resultant value of the conversion feature.

In summary, when determining the value of preferred shares in relation to other equity share classes, their conversion feature as well as any other feature attaching to them must be considered in light of all of their characteristics and attributes.

Preferred Share Liquidation Premiums

In some cases, preferred shareholders are entitled to a premium over stated or par value on liquidation of the issuer. Where the issuer's business is valued as a going concern, such a premium typically would not be accounted for in the value of the preferred shares. Where the business is valued on a liquidation basis, any appropriate liquidation premium would be considered a component of preferred share value. However, where estimated after-tax proceeds on liquidation at the corporate level are less than the liquidation value of the preferred shares, a discount from the liquidation value of the preferred shares would be applied to reflect this.

Preferred Share Valuation Based on Dividend Yield

In simple terms, the annual dividend on a well-covenanted, non-retractable, non-redeemable cumulative preferred share is akin to an annuity where preferred share value normally can be determined using the formula:

Formula 9.1
Preferred Share Valuation Based on Dividend Yield

Annual Dividend Payment / Required Yield

For example, if a cumulative preferred share pays a quarterly dividend of $1 per share and an appropriate rate of return (yield) is estimated to be 8%, then the value of each preferred share would be $50 (calculated as $4 dividend per annum divided by 8% rate of return).

Dividend payments on preferred shares (be they cumulative or non-cumulative) can be either at fixed or variable rates (tied in the latter case to a benchmark such as the prime lending rate), but are known or are capable of estimation. Greater uncertainty is associated with the determination of an appropriate rate of return (yield) that requires consideration of:

- whether dividends are cumulative. Where cumulative, risk tends to be related to timing of payment rather than whether payment will be made;

- the financial stability of the issuer, including the size and operating risk of its business, and financial risk related to both dividend payments and preferred share redemption. In this context, operating risk relates to the issuer's operating activities, whereas financial risk relates to the fact that preferred shares are subordinated to senior debt and subordinated debt;

- whether preferred shares have voting rights, or voting rights triggered when dividends are in arrears or by some other event. Where preferred shares have voting rights or conditional voting rights, there may be (depending on the significance of the preferred share vote) an incentive for the board of directors to declare the preferred dividend;

- the issuer's preferred dividend payment history. Where regular dividend payments have been made, lower risk is implied than where dividend payments have been missed;

- the dividend yield paid by companies reasonably similar to the issuer, whose preferred shares are publicly traded and have like terms and conditions; and

- general economic and credit market conditions, in particular short-term and long-term interest rates, including prevailing risk-free rates of return.

Where dividends are cumulative and in arrears, and where the issuer's covenant ensures ultimate payment, unpaid cumulative dividends should be added to the value of the preferred shares otherwise determined. In circumstances where the company's *en bloc* equity value is less than the combined value of the preferred shares and cumulative dividends in arrears, a discount from that amount is warranted.

Participating Preferred Shares

Participating preferred shares are those entitled to receive incremental dividends beyond their stated dividend rate where dividends beyond prescribed dividend amounts per common share are paid. The valuation of participating preferred shares is an extension of the dividend yield valuation discussed above where the elements of the participation feature are appropriately incorporated. Factors to consider include:

- the history of participating preferred and common share dividend payments;

- operating projections of the issuer, including prospective cash reinvestment requirements and discretionary cash flows;

- participating preferred and common share ownership. Where the common shares and participating preferred shares are held by the same person(s), there is a greater likelihood of participating dividend payments; and

- other features attaching to the participating preferred shares, such as redemption, retraction and conversion rights that might encourage or discourage a company's board of directors from declaring common share dividends that give rise to participation rights.

In theory, the value of participating preferred shares is never less than their value without the participation feature. Accordingly, participating preferred shares can be valued as the sum of two components: (i) the value of the preferred shares absent the participation feature; and (ii) a premium over that value to account for the participation rights.

Different Classes of Common Shares

Where more than one class of common shares is outstanding, it may be necessary to apportion the *en bloc* value of the common equity among them. Such apportionment is a relative valuation that requires consideration of:

- the specific attributes of the common share classes, including:
  - ✓ voting rights (non-voting, voting or multiple voting),
  - ✓ the circumstances in which otherwise non-voting shares would become voting, and the likelihood of a triggering event occurring that would give rise to voting rights,
  - ✓ ranking of proceeds of distribution in the event of a wind-up, and
  - ✓ rights with respect to dividend distributions;
- the ownership structure of all classes of common shares. For example, where four shareholders each owns 25% of both outstanding voting and non-voting common shares, they normally would be expected to vote to protect their respective equity interests. Consequently, the non-voting common shares owned by each shareholder likely would be valued on a pro-rata basis with their respective voting common shares;
- whether an organized market for any or all of the common share classes exists;
- recent transactions involving any of the outstanding common shares, be they non-voting or voting; and
- the dividend history of all classes of common shares.

A list of selected Canadian court cases dealing with the apportionment of value among various common share classes is provided in Appendix A. When analyzing these cases it should be noted that most have arisen in an income tax context.

Dilutive Securities

Options and Warrants

Some companies offer stock options to their directors or employees as performance incentives. Warrants are normally offered in conjunction with the issue of debt or shares as an incentive to prospective investors, usually in exchange for a reduction in the interest rate or dividends that otherwise would be paid on those securities. In the context of business valuation, only outstanding treasury options and warrants are considered (i.e., those that, when exercised, require the issuer to issue new shares from its treasury). Trades in public company common share options represent contracts between parties external to the company, and hence are not relevant from a business valuation perspective, given that shares and proceeds are transferred between third parties and no change in the number of shares outstanding occurs.

The intrinsic value of a warrant or option is the amount, if any, by which the pro-rata valuation-date price per share exceeds the exercise price. Where an option or warrant has positive intrinsic value it is commonly referred to as being "in the money". A warrant or option issued by the company may trade for an amount in excess of its intrinsic value. Where the shares are publicly traded, placing a value on the warrant or option normally is done pursuant to an option pricing model, such as the Black-Scholes option pricing model.

According to the Black-Scholes model, the value of the options:

- increases, where the current share price increases;
- decreases, where the strike price increases, since the likelihood of the option being in the money declines;
- increases, as the length of time increases, since there is more time for the option to be in the money;
- increases, as the rate of volatility increases, since the likelihood of the option being in the money increases; and
- increases, as the risk-free rate increases, since the holder of the option benefits by placing their money in alternate investments until the time the option is exercised.

Given the complexity of the calculations, the Black-Scholes model is normally conducted by a computer program (which can be found online).

While Black-Scholes is sometimes applied in a private-company context, its application to shares of a privately held company becomes problematic given that a major variable (volatility) cannot be readily measured based on public market data. Furthermore, the volatility of publicly traded securities may be greater than the volatility of private company shares. This is particularly the case where the trading price of public securities is erratic, based on the market response to near-term public information (e.g., quarterly earnings announcements). By contrast, the valuation of a privately held company *en bloc* typically is based on non-public information that includes long-range plans and expectations. Consequently, quarterly earnings results and similar short-term developments tend to have less impact on the per-share value in the context of private company business valuation as contrasted with public market securities pricing.

The volatility assumption can have a significant impact on the value of an option. For example, assume that the shares of N1 Limited, a privately held business, are valued at $10 per share. N1 issues options to its directors with a strike price of $15 per share exercisable at any time within the next five years. Assuming a volatility factor of 50% and using Black-Scholes the options would be valued at $3.65 per share. If the volatility assumption were decreased to 25%, the value of each option would decrease to $1.47. If the volatility assumption were increased to 75%, the value of each option would be $5.56.

In addition, Black-Scholes not only assumes the price of the underlying security is readily available, it also assumes liquidity sufficient that, upon exercise of the option, the buyer of the security can immediately crystallize their gain by selling those shares in the open market. Such is not normally the case for shares of privately held companies. Therefore, use of Black-Scholes may overstate the economic value of an option for a privately held company due to its assumptions regarding volatility and liquidity.

Calculating the Dilutive Impact of Options and Warrants

When options or warrants are exercised in respect of common shares, the number of shares outstanding increases thereby reducing the pro-rata value of each common share. However, the exercise price paid to the issuer can be used either to reduce outstanding debt or be held as a redundant asset. It follows that the net exercise price (net proceeds received by the issuer) offsets the dilutive impact of an option or warrant.

In either a notional market valuation or an open market transaction the implications of options and warrants are as follows:

- where the options and warrants are "out of the money" (i.e., the exercise price exceeds the pro-rata value per share) there is no impact; and

- where the options and warrants are "in the money", (i.e., the pro-rata value per share exceeds the exercise price) then: (i) the *en bloc* value of the company's equity is increased by the proceeds of the exercise price; and (ii) the number of shares outstanding is increased. The net result is a decrease in the pro-rata value per share.

For example, assume the *en bloc* equity value of P1 Limited is $10 million and there are currently one million common shares outstanding. The pro-rata value per share is $10. P1 has issued 200,000 common share options to its senior managers at an exercise price of $5 per share. Consequently, the pro-rata value per common share following the exercise of the options is as follows:

Exhibit 9G
P1 Limited
Exercise of Options

En bloc equity value before exercise of options	10,000,000
Cash proceeds on exercise 200,000 shares at $5.00 per share	1,000,000
En bloc equity value after exercise of options	11,000,000
Number of common shares outstanding	
Existing common shares	1,000,000
Shares issued upon exercise of options	200,000
Total	1,200,000
Value per common share	
Before exercise of options	10.00
After exercise of options	9.17

Convertible Securities

When the capital structure of a business includes securities with a conversion feature (usually convertible debt or preferred shares), the potential impact on the *en bloc* value of the common shares must be addressed. The conversion feature is offered by the issuer in exchange for more favourable terms than otherwise would be available to it (e.g., a lower coupon rate on convertible debt).

In a business valuation context, convertible securities should be valued at the greater of their intrinsic value or their conversion value. An assessment can be made as to whether the conversion feature is "in the money" at the valuation date. An example was provided earlier in this chapter for M1 Limited, which illustrated the impact of convertible preferred shares where the conversion feature was "in the money". However, convertible securities are not always "in the money", particularly at the time of issuance and shortly thereafter. Furthermore, the conversion feature may be deferred.

Where convertible securities are valued on a stand-alone basis, the theoretical value of such securities is equal to their value without the conversion feature plus the value of the conversion feature. The value of the conversion feature is determined in a manner akin to that of a call option, which is usually done through an option pricing model, such as the Black-Scholes model discussed earlier in this chapter. As previously noted, while Black-Scholes and other models are widely used for publicly traded securities, their application to securities that are not publicly traded can be problematic.

Holding Companies

A holding company carries on no active business of its own; its principal activity is investing in various other assets. Alternatively, a company that operates two or more businesses as separately incorporated entities (which it might do for business management reasons or income tax purposes) might be referred to as a holding company. As such, the assets of holding companies may include:

- marketable securities including publicly traded shares and fixed-income securities;
- two or more distinct operating businesses;
- a controlling or minority interest in one or more privately held or public companies; and
- real estate assets, which might include income properties (e.g., office buildings, warehouses, etc.), vacant land or land under development.

Earnings generated by a holding company (in the form of rent or dividends, for example) are normally less significant from a value perspective than is the value of the underlying investments themselves. Accordingly, holding companies are typically valued using the adjusted net book value methodology (see Chapter 3) where each asset, investment, or division is valued separately on a market value or going concern basis as appropriate. As a result, holding companies are valued as a collection of individual assets such that no intangible value (or goodwill) exists within the holding company itself. However, the *en bloc* value of the outstanding shares of a holding company may indirectly incorporate intangible value where it exists in one or more of its investee companies.

Marketable Securities

In a holding company context, non-controlling marketable securities are valued in a manner similar to that adopted for redundant assets in an operating company (i.e., the gross value of marketable securities is based on the prevailing market price at the valuation date). From this amount, notional disposition costs (which, from a practical standpoint, are usually not significant) and income taxes on notional capital gains and losses are accounted for. Disposition costs and taxes may be discounted where the liquidation of the assets is not anticipated in the near term.

Normally a portfolio of marketable securities is considered as a whole; losses on individual securities serve to offset gains on others. Income tax recoveries related to capital losses are also recognized where offsetting capital gains from other sources (e.g., a business investment or real estate property) exist. Where capital losses exceed capital gains, value is rarely attributed to the excess, given that capital losses can only be applied against capital gains without carry-back.

An issue that sometimes arises in the calculation of income taxes on a notional disposition is the tax rate to adopt. As discussed later in this chapter, privately held companies pay a higher rate of taxes on investment income (including capital gains), because of additional refundable tax which, in turn, gives rise to refundable dividend tax on hand (RDTOH). At the time of writing (2012), the refundable tax component is 26.67% of the taxable component of capital gains. In most cases, the appropriate tax rate to adopt is the applicable rate excluding the refundable tax component, under the assumption that the refundable portion will be returned to the company upon the payment of dividends to its shareholders.

Where a holding company holds a significant block of shares of a public company, the issue arises as to whether the interest held should be valued at a ratable portion of the *en bloc* market capitalization of the public company. In some cases, it may be appropriate to apply a block premium or a block discount to the interest held. As discussed in Chapter 8, factors that should be considered in this regard include:

- the size of the share block, both in relative and absolute terms. Where the share block confers effective control on the holder, a premium to their ratable value may be appropriate;

- the degree of liquidity of the shares and normal trading volumes. Where the block of shares held by the holding company would be difficult to liquidate quickly, a discount to their ratable value may be appropriate;

- the existence of block trades in the securities and whether the holding company has received any interest in purchasing its block of shares;

- whether other blocks of shares are held by related persons or unrelated persons;

- whether and to what extent the daily trading prices of the company's shares are believed to incorporate a discount for illiquidity; and

- the likelihood and possible timing of a takeover of the public company or a combined primary-secondary public offering in which the block of shares could be liquidated.

Real Estate Assets

Income Properties

As discussed in Chapter 3, income properties (such as apartment buildings, shopping centres, hotels and office buildings) held by a holding company for investment purposes are usually valued using a cash flow-based methodology (e.g., capitalized cash flow) supplemented by asset-based methodologies and comparable transactions, where the latter methodologies are meaningful in the circumstances. Income taxes may be deducted depending on fact-specific circumstances including the number of income properties held, and whether other operating businesses are owned directly or indirectly.

Where income properties held for investment are not of material value in comparison to the holding company's interests in operating businesses, the income property likely would be valued as if redundant. In such circumstances, income tax is deducted at the corporate level based on the notional amount of recapture of capital cost allowance previously taken and tax on capital gains that would result on disposition. Disposition costs and income taxes may be discounted where there is uncertainty as to the timing of disposition.

Where the income property derives a significant portion of its rental revenues from a related business, it is important to segregate the value of the business from the value of the property. In this regard:

- where rental amounts do not reflect market rates they should be restated, with appropriate adjustments when valuing both the income property and the operating business; and

- whether the income property is viewed as a redundant asset depends on factors such as the extent to which the premises are occupied by arm's length third parties, whether the property is integral to the operating business and the likelihood the property can be sold independent of the business itself based on its physical characteristics, location and other attributes. These factors were addressed in Chapter 4.

Where income properties are valued on the assumption of an asset sale and represent the holding company's principal assets, an adjustment for income taxes is made to account for the capital cost allowance tax shield not available to a buyer of shares (see Chapter 4). However, income taxes are normally not deducted on the notional disposition of the property(ies) as a whole.

Where a holding company owns a portfolio of investment properties, consideration should be given to whether they should be sold individually or as a group. Where the portfolio of assets is diverse (either due to the nature of the operations or geographic location) a buyer may be interested in only one or a subset of the properties. Where this is the case, consideration should be given to income taxes that would be incurred as the result of a sale of the investment properties to different buyers. Specifically:

- if one or more of the underlying income properties is sold, recapture and capital gains or losses might result; or

- if one or more of the income properties is spun off on a tax-deferred basis to a newly incorporated subsidiary of the holding company, then the value of the shares of the newly formed subsidiary would have to reflect the flow-through of the existing tax base of said property(ies). Furthermore, a capital gain may result on the disposition of the shares of the newly formed subsidiary.

The income tax liability otherwise determined following the sale of a diverse portfolio of properties would normally be discounted to reflect the uncertainty of the timing of the disposition of the properties and other tax planning opportunities where available. The quantification of this discount, if any, will vary depending on the fact-specific circumstances.

Vacant Land

Where a holding company owns vacant land, the market value of the land usually is estimated based on benchmarks such as recent sales and listings of similar properties, adjusted for the unique characteristics of the particular parcel(s) of land held. In a holding company context, vacant land is viewed as a redundant asset. As such, disposition costs and income taxes (at the corporate level) are calculated and deducted as for marketable securities. Where specific development plans exist, the amount of income tax deducted on any imputed capital gain should consider this.

Investments in Operating Companies or Divisions

Where a holding company owns a controlling interest in one or more operating companies, those investments should be valued using a going concern valuation methodology (such as the capitalized cash flow methodology or the discounted cash flow methodology). This is also the case where a holding company owns a minority interest in a privately held company, although fact-specific circumstances may dictate otherwise. In the case of minority interests, a minority discount may be appropriate (see Chapter 8). Where the operating entities are unincorporated divisions (as opposed to incorporated entities), then whether each division is valued as a separate entity depends on the uniqueness of its operations, underlying business risks and the likelihood that it could be readily segregated from other divisions.

When the estimated value of the underlying business interests held by the holding company exceeds the tax cost base, a notional capital gain results. Whether or not income taxes are deducted depends on the prevailing circumstances. As a general rule, where a holding company owns 90% or more of the outstanding common shares of an operating business, income taxes are not deducted since a holding company is able to wind up the subsidiary operating company on a tax-deferred basis, and is subsequently able to operate the business as an unincorporated division of the parent company. However, whether an indefinite tax deferral is assumed is fact specific and dependent on:

- whether the holding company is expected to operate "as is" for the foreseeable future;

- the other assets and liabilities owned by the holding company. Where these are immaterial, a wind-up into the holding company may be practical;

- whether the holding company or operating company has litigation outstanding that upon wind-up of the subsidiary into the holding company would expose other assets to litigation risk; and

- the practicality of wind-up, given factors such as minority shareholder appraisal and oppression rights (see Chapter 8).

Where a holding company owns a minority interest in one or more operating companies, or where a tax-free wind-up of an operating business owned 90% or more is not practical, income taxes are deducted on any notional capital gain amount. Income taxes payable are frequently discounted having regard to:

- the uncertainty as to the timing of the disposition of the underlying operating businesses, which reduces the present value of the income tax burden;

- the amount of "safe income" available from the operating business to the holding company. As explained later in this chapter, safe income can serve to defer a gain on the sale of a subsidiary by payment of a tax-deferred dividend to the holding company up to the amount of the subsidiary's safe income thereby reducing the subsequent sale price of the operating business; and

- other tax planning opportunities, such as unused capital losses at the holding company level.

Multi-Divisional Businesses

A multi-divisional business is defined as a business with two or more distinct operating segments of material size. The legal structure of the business might include a corporate entity with segregated unincorporated divisions, parent-subsidiary relationships, or a holding company that owns a controlling interest in two or more subsidiaries. When valuing a multi-divisional business where the nature of each of those businesses, the industries in which they operate, and appropriate rates of return and other valuation factors are distinct, it may be appropriate to separately value one or more divisions (or subsidiaries). When valuing a multi-divisional business, issues that often arise include the treatment of: (i) head office costs; and (ii) income taxes, in circumstances where the disposition of one or more divisions is assumed.

Head Office Costs

In many multi-divisional businesses, the operating businesses are centrally managed. Combined with support staff and general administrative expenses involved in business management, such costs are often referred to as head office costs. Often it is impossible or impractical to allocate head office costs to specific divisions or operating entities in a meaningful way. Accordingly, where a multi-divisional business is being valued *en bloc*, the usual treatment of head office costs is to capitalize the annual normalized net head office expenses and to deduct that amount from the sum of the values determined for the divisions. Net expenses would be those head office costs, including sustaining capital expenditures, net of income taxes.

The capitalization rate and income tax rate adopted should be the blended weighted average rates applied to the divisions overseen by head office personnel. Finally, one-time costs (net of income taxes) prospectively to be incurred at the head office level should be separately deducted.

For example, assume that Q1 Limited has three distinct operating divisions, designated A, B and C. The valuation of each of these divisions and adjustment for head office costs is as follows:

Exhibit 9H
Q1 Limited
Adjustment for Head Office Costs
($000)

Division	Capitalization Rate	*En bloc* Fair Market Value
A	13%	20,000
B	11%	90,000
C	15%	50,000
		160,000

Head office costs		
Annual expense (after tax)	2,000	
Capitalization rate	12.5%	
Capitalized value		16,000
Net value		144,000

Q1 has a head office administrative staff that oversees all operations at a cost of $2 million per annum after income taxes. Adopting a blended rate of return, the capitalized amount of these head office costs would be determined as $2 million / 12.5% = $16 million. The 12.5% capitalization rate is the blended weighted average capitalization rate of the operating divisions. Therefore, the *en bloc* fair market value of Q1 (before consideration of income taxes, discussed below) would be $144 million ($160 million *en bloc* fair market value less $16 million in capitalized head office costs).

Where it becomes necessary to determine the value of a particular operating division(s) or subsidiary(s) on a stand-alone basis, an allocation of head office costs may be required. Such an allocation typically should be made in consideration of head office management time spent by division, gauged through discussions with management and based on factors such as the complexity, size and strategic importance of the division relative to the company as a whole.

Due to administrative economies of scale that a multi-divisional business may enjoy, head office costs so allocated might be less than would actually be incurred on a stand-alone basis. Where this is the case, the amount of normalized head office costs included in each division should consider:

- the nature, size and complexity of the division; and

- the amount of administrative costs incurred in businesses of a similar nature, both in absolute terms and expressed as a percentage of sales.

Income Taxes

Buyers may only be interested in purchasing specific divisions or subsidiaries. In such circumstances, in order to maximize net proceeds on sale, a multi-divisional business might have to:

- sell each underlying operating division/subsidiary to different buyers who perceive the greatest ability to generate post-acquisition synergies; or

- dispose of all of the operating businesses *en bloc* to one buyer who would then divest those operating businesses it did not wish to retain. Since disposal costs and income taxes would be incurred on the subsequent divestiture, the buyer would seek to be compensated by a reduced *en bloc* purchase price for the collective operating companies.

It follows that for a multi-divisional business, it may be appropriate in some circumstances to deduct an amount in respect of income taxes and other disposition costs. Such an adjustment is sometimes referred to as a "portfolio discount". Where it is deemed appropriate to reflect all or part of the income taxes and other costs that would arise on the sale of the underlying net assets or shares of divisions/subsidiaries (respectively), such taxes and costs are usually discounted having regard to the:

- amount of "safe income" available (see discussion later in this chapter);

- basis of determining the fair market value of the operating entities, specifically the extent to which special-interest purchasers are reflected (see Chapter 11);

- degree to which the divisions are operationally integrated;

- plausibility of combining one or more operating divisions to reduce the number of dispositions;

- extent to which income tax planning opportunities are perceived to exist that could reduce the overall tax liability; and

- expected timing as to when, if ever, the underlying operating businesses would be sold.

Foreign Entities

Up to this point the discussion has assumed the business being valued is Canadian. However, in some cases the Canadian entity has a subsidiary or an equity investment in a business located outside Canada. While the valuation methodologies for a foreign entity are the same (i.e., adjusted net book value, multiple of EBITDA, capitalized cash flow or discounted cash flow), there are certain differences in their application, as discussed below.

Foreign Exchange Considerations

The foreign entity will operate in a currency other than Canadian dollars. Where a cash flow-based valuation is adopted, the cash flow should be expressed in the operating currency of the foreign entity (e.g., a U.S.-based subsidiary should be valued in U.S. dollars). The valuation result should then be converted to Canadian dollars at the exchange rate at the valuation date.

An issue that arises frequently is foreign exchange risk. The Canadian entity is subject to exchange rate fluctuations for its foreign investment. Theoretically, whether a company sells its products and services into another country directly or through a foreign subsidiary, the valuation should effectively be the same (subject to tax considerations). Factors that should be considered when assessing foreign exchange risk include the following:

- the ability to hedge foreign exchange risk through financing. For example, if a Canadian business has a subsidiary in Germany, it may borrow funds in euros in order to finance that operation and mitigate the foreign exchange risk. Note that the duration of the hedge is important to consider. While forward contracts and futures contracts can reduce foreign exchange risk over the short term, long-term hedging normally requires the ability to offset the operating value of the business with a long-term financial instrument such as a long-term foreign-denominated bond;

- inter-corporate transactions. Where the Canadian parent company sells products or services to, or buys products or services from, its foreign subsidiary or affiliate, that serves to reduce the foreign exchange exposure since the exchange gains or losses in one entity will somewhat offset the gains or losses in the other; and

- historical and prospective foreign exchange rates. Where exchange rates have been highly volatile, that risk should be factored into the valuation, either in the cash flows or the rate of return.

Rates of Return

Where the foreign entity is being valued using a cash flow-based methodology, the rates of return or the valuation multiple adopted may need to be adjusted to reflect the additional operating risks of conducting business in a foreign country. These risks may include:

- political risk. The political risk of the foreign country may be significantly greater than that experienced in Canada, particularly in the case of developing countries. Various reporting services provide an indication of the estimated premium on account of political risk. This normally includes the risk of unfavourable political developments, which may include expropriation of corporate assets, political instability and difficulties in repatriating profits;

- regulatory environment. The regulatory environment of a foreign country may be significantly different from that in Canada. This could have an impact on the required rate of return. However, no adjustment to the rate of return is required where the impact of the regulatory environment is incorporated in the cash flow projections;

- inflation expectations. Many countries, particularly developing nations, have an inflation rate significantly higher than Canada. Where long-term government bonds of the foreign country are adopted as the risk-free rate, that may effectively incorporate the diverging inflationary expectations; and

- cultural considerations. Where cultural differences can lead to performance issues, labour disruptions or other potential issues, those factors should be reflected in the rate of return.

As noted in Chapter 7, there must be internal consistency between the rate of return and the cash flow against which it is applied.

Taxation

When determining the prospective discretionary cash flow of the foreign entity (using a capitalized cash flow or discounted cash flow methodology), it is important to reflect the tax rate and tax laws applicable in the foreign country. In addition, when determining the rate of return, it is important to ensure internal consistency with respect to tax rates and interest deductibility.

Another issue with respect to taxation involves the repatriation of earnings to Canada. In some cases, the applicable foreign country has a tax treaty with Canada that significantly reduces or eliminates the impact of double taxation. However, where such a treaty does not exist, the issue arises as to whether incremental Canadian taxes should be taken into account. This generally depends on the assumption regarding whether the profits can be reinvested in the foreign country over the longer term thereby deferring the incremental tax impact. Similar to the taxes that would be incurred on a deferred sale of a redundant asset, incremental taxes will be incurred upon the ultimate repatriation of the profits. Accordingly, it is appropriate to apply a probability or discount factor to the incremental taxes that will be incurred based on the expected timing of when they will have to be paid.

Tax Issues in Valuation

The tax rate applicable to a particular business can have a significant impact on its value. Some of the more common tax issues encountered in business valuation were addressed in Chapter 4. These include the application of the small business deduction, scientific research and experimental development (SRED) tax credits, and tax losses.

Taxation and Fair Market Value

The term "fair market value", although undefined in the *Income Tax Act* is nevertheless used throughout the Act. Many types of transactions are deemed to occur on the basis of fair market value and there are usually adverse tax consequences if such transactions are completed on any basis other than at fair market value.

Section 69 of the *Act* prevents a taxpayer in certain circumstances from recognizing consideration in excess of fair market value paid to persons with whom the taxpayer is not dealing at arm's length, or from failing to account for the full value of anything disposed of in similar circumstances. The meaning of "arm's length" is defined in section 251 of the *Act* and the administrative position of the Canada Revenue Agency (CRA) is discussed in the current version of Interpretation Bulletin IT-419R2. In general, individuals connected by blood relationship, marriage, or adoption do not deal with each other at arm's length, nor do a corporation and the individual who controls that corporation. If non-arm's length transactions are carried out on a basis other than at fair market value, there is potential for double taxation.

There are numerous circumstances where a business valuation might be required for tax purposes (e.g., on the death of a taxpayer or in a capital reorganization). In such cases, there are potential adverse consequences of effecting transactions on any basis other than at fair market value. Occasionally, even where a *bona fide* attempt is made to arrive at fair market value, the CRA may not agree with the conclusion, particularly where the parties are not acting at arm's length. Price adjustment clauses can be inserted into agreements in such situations to protect the parties involved.

Valuations are often done at a non-current date and the provisions of the *Act* in force at those dates should be considered. A detailed discussion of changes to income tax legislation over the past decades is beyond the scope of this book; accordingly, when conducting a notional market valuation, it is important to consider current and prospective tax rates, and regulations at the valuation date.

Acquisition of Property

Except in special circumstances, a taxpayer who acquires anything from a non-arm's length person for a consideration greater than the fair market value will be deemed to have acquired it at fair market value (paragraph 69(1)(a) of the *Act*). For example, assume that Individuals A and B do not deal with each other at arm's length and that A owns 100 shares of R1 Limited. On June 1, 2011, A sells these shares to B for cash consideration of $2 million. However, the fair market value of the shares at that date is $1 million. The cost to A of those shares is $500,000.

In this situation, paragraph 69(1)(a) will deem B to have acquired the shares for $1 million despite the fact that $2 million was paid for them. If B subsequently sold these shares in an arm's length transaction for $1.5 million, B would have a capital gain of $500,000 ($1,500,000 less the deemed adjusted cost base of the shares of $1 million). Individual A, in computing the capital gain on the sale, will still have deemed proceeds equal to the actual proceeds of $2 million for a capital gain of $1,500,000 ($2 million less the adjusted cost base of the shares of $500,000). Individual B has effectively lost $1 million of cost base (which will be subject to tax). Double taxation results because the proceeds to the seller are greater than the adjusted cost base of the buyer and the difference between these two amounts is effectively taxed twice—once in the hands of the seller and once in the hands of the buyer.

Except in special circumstances, a taxpayer who has acquired property by way of gift, bequest, or inheritance is deemed to have acquired such property at its fair market value at the time of acquisition (paragraph 69(1)(c)). There is no distinction between arm's length and non-arm's length parties to transactions covered by this section of the *Act*.

Disposition of Property

Except in special circumstances, a taxpayer who disposes of anything for no proceeds or for proceeds less than fair market value to a non-arm's length person, or by way of an *inter vivos* gift whether at arm's length or not, is deemed to have received proceeds equal to its fair market value (paragraph 69(1)(b)). However, the provisions of section 69(1)(b) do not apply to dispositions and acquisitions on death.

For example, assume that Individuals C and D do not deal with each other at arm's length and that C owns 100 shares of R2 Limited. On June 1, 2011 C sells these shares to D for a cash consideration of $750,000. However, the fair market value of the shares is $1 million. The cost to C of those shares (acquired in an arm's length transaction in 1995) is $500,000.

In this situation, paragraph 69(1)(b) will deem C to have received proceeds of $1 million despite the fact that only $750,000 was actually received, resulting in a capital gain of $500,000 ($1 million less the deemed adjusted cost base of the shares of $500,000). Individual D will have a cost base for the shares of $750,000. Individual C will effectively have to pay tax on $250,000 of capital gains which was not received. Again double taxation will eventually result because the cost base of the shares to the buyer is not equal to the deemed proceeds on the sale of the shares to the seller.

Subsection 70(5) of the *Act* deems a person to have disposed of certain assets immediately before death including capital property, depreciable property, eligible capital property, resource property and land inventory. The fair market value of such assets must be determined in order to calculate any resulting tax liability. Court decisions suggest the words "immediately before his death" do not make it necessary to take into account the imminence of death in valuing assets though subsection 70(5.3) provides a specific exception with regard to property whose value is attributable in part to a life insurance policy. Subsection 70(6) and subsection 73(1) provide rollovers that permit recognition of a gain (or loss) to be deferred in certain circumstances when property is transferred either upon the death of a taxpayer, or during the taxpayer's lifetime, to a resident spouse or spousal trust.

Certain trusts, on the twenty-first anniversary of their creation, are deemed to have disposed of each capital property, resource property or land included in the inventory of a business of the trust for proceeds equal to their fair market value and to have immediately re-acquired them at a cost equal to that amount. This deemed disposition at fair market value is then repeated on each twenty-first anniversary of the first deemed disposition.

Each capital property owned by the taxpayer is deemed to be disposed of immediately before death for an amount equal to its fair market value (subparagraph 70(5)(a)), which will result in a capital gain or loss or, in the case of depreciable property, recaptured capital cost allowance or a terminal loss, to the deceased taxpayer. When the capital cost to the deceased taxpayer of the depreciable property exceeds the property's fair market value immediately before death, the transferee inherits the deceased taxpayer's capital cost and the excess is deemed to have been allowed to the transferee as capital cost allowance (paragraph 70(5) (c)). Special rules in subsection 13(21.1) apply where the depreciable property is a building disposed of together with the land on which it is located.

Subsection 69(5) deals with situations in which property of a corporation has been appropriated by or for the benefit of a shareholder on a wind-up of the corporation. In such cases the corporation will be deemed to have sold the property immediately before the wind-up and to have received proceeds equal to the fair market value of the property at that time. There is no restriction on the recognition of a loss created as a result of the deemed disposition.

Eligible Capital Property

Where a taxpayer has died, and by reason of the death, another person has acquired a particular eligible capital property of the taxpayer in respect of a business carried on by the taxpayer, the taxpayer is deemed to have disposed of the eligible capital property immediately before death for proceeds of disposition equal to four thirds of the cumulative eligible capital to the taxpayer in respect of that business. The effect of this rule is that the deemed proceeds will be offset by the deceased's undeducted eligible capital expenditures and no amount is added to the deceased's income in the year of death.

The person who has acquired the particular eligible capital property is deemed to have acquired a capital property at the time of the taxpayer's death at a cost equal to the deceased's deemed proceeds of disposition. If, however, the transferee continues to carry on the business previously carried on by the taxpayer, the transferee is deemed to have acquired an eligible capital property and to have made an eligible capital expenditure at a cost equal to the proceeds. The net effect of these rules is that, if the business is carried on by the transferee, the deceased's cumulative eligible capital in respect of the business will become the transferee's cumulative eligible capital in respect of the business and the transferee can continue to deduct such cumulative eligible capital on a declining balance basis of 7% annually. If the business is not carried on by the transferee, the transferee will have a capital property which cannot be written off on any basis and when the property is sold the beneficiary will have a capital gain or a capital loss. Subsection 24(2) of the *Act* provides special rules where an individual has ceased to carry on a business and thereafter the spouse, or a corporation controlled by the deceased, carries on the business.

Becoming or Ceasing to Be a Resident of Canada

Section 128.1 of the *Act* contains rules which apply when a taxpayer becomes, or ceases to be, a resident of Canada. In general, they are designed to ensure gains that accrue on property while a person (individual, trust or corporation) is a resident of Canada are subject to Canadian tax. A taxpayer who becomes a resident of Canada is therefore deemed to acquire each property at a cost equal to its fair market value at that time and, on ceasing to be a resident of Canada, is deemed to dispose of each property for proceeds equal to its fair market value at that time. Among the items excluded from the deemed disposition upon emigration are real property situated in Canada, inventory, eligible capital property in respect of, and other capital property used in, a business carried on by the taxpayer through a Canadian permanent establishment, and property in respect of which the taxpayer had elected not to realize the deemed disposition on an earlier emigration from Canada.

Corporate Restructuring

Transfers to a Corporation

Subsection 85(1) provides for a tax-deferred rollover in respect of a transfer of certain types of property (including capital property, depreciable property, eligible capital property and inventory) by a taxpayer to a taxable Canadian corporation. The rollover provisions of 85(1) are often used in a business valuation context where:

- an estate freeze is being executed following a notional market valuation of an equity interest;

- redundant assets are removed from a corporation prior to an open market transaction; and

- a corporation reorganizes into two or more separate entities in contemplation of a divestiture of one or more of the new entities.

A joint election must be made by the taxpayer and the corporation and the consideration received for the transfer must include shares in the capital stock of the corporation. Similar provisions are contained for rollovers by partnerships in subsection 85(2). The amount which may be elected on the transfer is limited by the following rules:

- the elected amount cannot be less than the value of any non-share consideration received;

- the elected amount cannot be greater than the fair market value of the property transferred;

- depreciable property cannot be transferred at less than the least of: (i) its cost; (ii) its fair market value; and (iii) the undepreciated capital cost to the taxpayer of all the property of the same class;

- inventory, non-depreciable capital property and securities or debt obligations used in an insurance or money-lending business cannot be transferred at less than the lesser of: (i) their cost amount; and (ii) fair market value; and

- eligible capital property in respect of a business of the transferor cannot be transferred at less than the least of: (i) its cost; (ii) fair market value; and (iii) four thirds of the transferor's cumulative eligible capital in respect of the business immediately prior to the transfer.

The elected transfer price is important because it serves as the proceeds of disposition to the transferor, the cost of the property to the corporation and is relevant in determining the cost of shares taken by the transferor from the corporation in return for the assets transferred to the corporation. The taxpayer is deemed to have acquired any non-share consideration at a cost equal to its fair market value. Preferred shares are deemed to be acquired at the lesser of their fair market value and the amount by which the elected amount exceeds the value of the non-share consideration (subject to apportionment according to fair market values if there is more than one class of preferred shares issued to the taxpayer). The common shares are deemed to be acquired at a cost equal to the difference between the elected amount and the total of the value of non-share consideration plus the cost of the preferred shares (subject to the same apportionment if there is more than one class of common shares issued).

In addition to fair market value considerations, further care must be exercised in using section 85 as there are a number of anti-avoidance provisions in the *Act* (including subsection 84.1 and subsections 55(2) to (5)) which can result in adverse consequences to the taxpayer, as discussed later in this chapter.

Where a subsection 85(1) election is made and where immediately before it is transferred to the corporation, the fair market value of the property exceeds the greater of the fair market value immediately after the transfer of all consideration received by the corporation and the elected amount, and it is reasonable to consider the excess to be a benefit conferred on a related person, the amount of such benefit may be converted into an immediate capital gain to the seller by paragraph 85(1)(e.2). Accordingly, care must be taken to ensure that property (particularly shares) received on a subsection 85(1) are valued appropriately. Where there are shareholders in the transferee corporation other than the transferor, it is usual to use preferred shares for this purpose, redeemable at the option of the shareholder (i.e., retractable) with a redemption amount equal to the desired fair market value.

Share Capital Reorganizations

Section 86 of the *Act* provides for a tax-deferred rollover on the disposition by a taxpayer of shares that represent capital property to the taxpayer in the course of a reorganization of the capital of a corporation. The rollover applies where the taxpayer has disposed of all of the shares of a particular class and where new shares of the same corporation, with or without non-share consideration, are received. The provisions of section 86 of the *Act* are commonly used in estate freezes where the common shares of a parent might be converted into preference shares and new common shares would be issued to children in whom equity growth was to vest.

As with the other forms of corporate reorganizations, there are fair market value considerations. The taxpayer is deemed to have acquired the new shares at a cost equal to the adjusted cost base of its old shares, less the fair market value of any non-share consideration receivable in the reorganization, and is deemed to have disposed of its old shares for proceeds of disposition equal to the cost of the new shares and the fair market value of any non-share consideration received (subject to apportionment according to fair market values if there is more than one class of new shares received). Generally, no immediate tax liability will result from the application of section 86 as long as the paid-up capital of any shares received by the shareholder in the course of the reorganization is no greater than the paid-up capital of the shares which the taxpayer turned over to the corporation, the non-share consideration does not exceed the adjusted cost base of the shares disposed of and there is no indirect gift conferred on a related party to the taxpayer as a result of the transaction. An indirect gift can result if the fair market value of the shares disposed of by the taxpayer exceeds the fair market value of non-share consideration (such as debt) and the fair market value of the new shares acquired. The amount of the indirect gift is added to the adjusted cost base of the shares exchanged and the deemed proceeds will result in an immediate capital gain.

Price Adjustment Clauses

There are several situations in which it may be appropriate to insert a price adjustment clause into a sale agreement to avoid adverse tax consequences resulting from the CRA assessing a different fair market value than that arrived at by the parties to the agreement, including non-arm's length transactions and the situation where parties to a sale agreement make an election under subsection 85(1) of the *Act* in respect of the sale (as discussed below) and the CRA determines that the fair market value of the property sold is greater than the value of the consideration paid.

Interpretation Bulletin IT-169 sets out the CRA's position that price adjustment clauses will be accepted if a *bona fide* effort was made to arrive at fair market value, both seller and buyer inform the CRA of the clause and both are willing to accept the CRA's valuation as binding. Although there have been no court cases dealing with such clauses since IT-169 was issued, the previous decisions suggest that price adjustment clauses will be accepted by a court of law as long as a *bona fide* attempt is made by the parties to effect the sale at fair market value, notwithstanding that the CRA's requirements as contained in IT-169 have not been fully complied with. This usually means that the taxpayer has commissioned a formal valuation report (either an estimate valuation report or a comprehensive valuation report) from an independent valuation professional (see Chapter 10).

The leading Canadian income tax decision dealing with a price adjustment clause is *Guilder News Co. v MNR*. The taxpayers entered into a transaction and included a price adjustment clause in the sale agreement. The court found that the transaction price indicated that no reasonable attempt was made to estimate fair market value and therefore the price adjustment clause was not recognized. It would therefore appear that a court will recognize a price adjustment clause as long as the parties to the sale, reasonably and in good faith, attempt to transact at a sale price that approximates fair market value. It also appears a court would find it unacceptable to artificially lower the price until an adjustment is required by the CRA.

Amalgamation

Amalgamations are commonly used in leveraged buyouts and in going-private transactions. A business combination can be effected by the use of the appropriate corporate law provisions and by relying on the section 87 statutory amalgamation provisions. This will, in general, result in the following:

- all the properties and liabilities of the predecessor corporations become those of the amalgamated company;
- all the shareholders, except predecessor corporations, become shareholders of the amalgamated company;
- all tax bases are rolled over from the predecessor corporations to the amalgamated corporation; and
- all loss carry-forward balances of predecessor corporations become loss carry-forward balances of the amalgamated corporation, subject only to the change in control rules.

There are, however, numerous detailed rules in section 87 and care must be taken to review thoroughly any proposed amalgamation.

Fair market value is an issue when there is more than one class of shares acquired in the amalgamated corporation or where an indirect benefit has been conferred. Where shares of more than one class of the amalgamated corporation are acquired, the cost of the old shares is prorated among the classes in proportion to their respective fair market values. Indirect benefit provisions, similar to those described in the previous section on share capital reorganizations, apply if the fair market value of the shares of a shareholder in a predecessor corporation exceeds the fair market value of the shares received in the amalgamated corporation. It is reasonable to regard any portion of the excess as a benefit which the taxpayer desired to confer on a related person.

Wind-Up of a 90% Subsidiary

Section 88(1) of the *Act* provides for a tax-deferred rollover on the wind-up of a subsidiary corporation in which the parent corporation owns at least 90% of the shares of each class. Both corporations must be taxable Canadian corporations and shares of the subsidiary not owned by the parent must be owned by persons dealing at arm's length with the parent. Section 88(1) wind-ups are most commonly used in corporate restructuring and where a subsidiary is determined to no longer be a going concern, as discussed in Chapter 3.

As illustrated in Chapter 11 under the heading "Assets vs. Shares", one of the disadvantages of buying shares of a corporation is that the buyer is left with the historic tax values of the target corporation's assets. Some relief is available through the use of a paragraph 88(1)(d) "bump". In general, upon the wind-up of the subsidiary, the parent can increase the adjusted cost base of any of the subsidiary's non-depreciable capital property. However, the amount of the increase is restricted to the lesser of: (i) the fair market value of the property at the time the parent last acquired control, minus the subsidiary's cost for tax purposes of the property at the time of winding up; and (ii) the amount by which the parent's adjusted cost base of the shares in the subsidiary exceeds the net value for tax purposes of the subsidiary's net assets immediately prior to the wind-up, plus any dividends paid by the subsidiary to the parent or a person who is not dealing at arm's length with the parent. Special rules limit the bump with respect to property transferred to the corporation by a parent corporation or other non-arm's length person or in so-called "butterfly" transactions.

Fair market value is a consideration if property is distributed to minority shareholders as part of the transaction. Subsection 69(5) deems such property to have been sold by the subsidiary for proceeds equal to fair market value and acquired by the shareholder at a cost equal to that amount.

Section 88(2) Wind-Up

Section 88(2) of the *Act* applies to the wind-up of a Canadian corporation in circumstances where the rules in section 88(1) do not apply. Where section 88(2) applies, the corporation is deemed to have disposed of each property distributed by it on the wind-up for proceeds equal to its fair market value so that any accrued gains or losses are realized at that time. To the extent the value of the property distributed by the corporation on the wind-up exceeds the paid-up capital of its shares, section 84(2) deems the corporation to have paid a dividend at the time equal to the excess. This wind-up dividend is deemed to be paid first out of the capital dividend account as a tax-free capital dividend and, to the extent of the corporation's pre-1972 capital surplus on hand (CSOH), is deemed not to be a dividend. This allows these amounts to be removed from the corporation free of tax. Any remaining portion of the wind-up dividend is deemed to be a separate taxable dividend received ratably by the shareholders of the corporation at that time. The effect of a wind-up under section 88(2) is illustrated in Chapter 3.

Share Exchanges

Where, in an open market transaction, the buyer's shares are used as its currency in lieu of cash, a rollover may be available under section 85.1 of the *Act* where a shareholder sells shares of a corporation to another corporation and receives treasury shares of the purchasing corporation as consideration. For a section 85.1 rollover to apply, the purchasing corporation must be a Canadian corporation and the shareholder must hold the shares as capital property. If those considerations are met, the capital gain or loss to the selling shareholder is deferred automatically unless the taxpayer specifically chooses not to have the provisions of this section of the *Act* apply (i.e., no election is required to be filed for the rollover to apply).

Fair market value is a consideration to the buyer corporation as the cost of the shares acquired are generally deemed to be the lesser of their fair market value and their paid-up capital. In most situations, the paid-up capital of shares would be less than their fair market value. Where it is not, it may be preferable to use subsection 85(1) to transfer the shares rather than section 85.1 because the buyer can elect the adjusted cost base of the seller as its cost base. Share exchanges are further addressed as part of open market transactions in Chapter 11.

Tax Issues in Privately Held Corporations

In notional valuations and open market transactions, consideration must be given to the income tax impact of the capital dividend account (CDA) which is available to a privately held corporation, and to the refundable dividend tax on hand account (RDTOH) which is available to a Canadian controlled private corporation (CCPC). It should be noted that the benefits associated with these accounts will be lost if control of the private corporation is acquired by a public corporation or by non-residents of Canada such that private corporation or CCPC status is lost.

The CDA and RDTOH tax accounts are the mechanism for the integration of the taxation of investment income of CCPC's with that of their individual shareholders. This integration system is designed to ensure investment income earned by an individual through such a corporation will be taxed in approximately the same manner as if it had been earned by the individual directly.

Capital Dividend Account (CDA)

The CDA operates by allowing a corporation to distribute on a tax-free basis the non-taxable portion of capital gains. The CDA involves complex calculations; however, it is essentially composed of the following amounts:

- the portion of net capital gains not recognized in computing income, which was:
  - ✓ 50% before 1988,
  - ✓ 33% after 1987 but before 1990,
  - ✓ 25% after 1989 but before March 2000,
  - ✓ 33% after February 2000 but before 2001, and

   ✓   50% in 2001 and thereafter;

- capital dividends received;

- the portion of proceeds not recognized on the disposition of eligible capital property (i.e., the sale of goodwill pursuant to an asset sale); and

- life insurance proceeds received upon the death of the insured to the extent they exceed original cost.

Dividends deemed to have been paid from the CDA (on making an appropriate election pursuant to sub-section 83(2)) are received tax free by the taxpayer. It is often prudent to pay out capital dividends prior to the sale of a corporation because the ability to do so may subsequently be lost on a change of control. Furthermore, the seller usually wants to receive income on a tax-free basis. However, anti-avoidance provisions may disallow the capital dividend and declare it a taxable dividend if the sole purpose of the sale transaction is for the buyer to acquire the right to the capital dividend.

On the sale of a corporation, if a corporation has a balance in its CDA and also accrued but as yet unrealized capital losses, it may be good planning to distribute the capital dividend account and then realize the capital losses. By doing so, the capital dividend account will not be reduced on realization of the capital losses.

While the CDA does not impact the value of a business from a notional valuation perspective (since the value of a business is not impacted by personal income tax considerations), it does become an important consideration when structuring an open market transaction.

Refundable Dividend Tax on Hand (RDTOH)

The RDTOH account operates to allow an eligible corporation a refund of a portion of its tax paid on investment income upon the payment of sufficient dividends to the shareholder. If the shareholder is another privately held corporation, the refunded tax will be paid by the recipient corporation. If the recipient is an individual shareholder, the corporation receives the refund and the individual includes the income in computing their income in the normal manner. The availability of the dividend tax credit for an individual will then adjust the amount of tax paid at the individual level to integrate the overall taxation.

A CCPC pays corporate income tax on investment income at ordinary corporate tax rates plus a 6 2/3% tax on investment income under section 123.3. An amount equal to 26 2/3% of investment income is added to the corporation's RDTOH. For every $3 of dividends paid, $1 of taxes is refunded from this account. On the sale of a CCPC consideration should also be given to paying dividends prior to the sale in order to trigger refundable taxes from RDTOH. Attention must be paid to the timing of the sale of shares to ensure that CCPCs receive the full benefit of refundable dividends from RDTOH.

In the context of a notional valuation, where a company has an RDTOH balance, it is assumed that the company will reap the benefit of that prospective refund by the payment of a sufficient taxable dividend to the shareholders. Therefore, the RDTOH balance is added to *en bloc* equity value otherwise determined. Where the business does not have sufficient funds to pay out a dividend immediately that would give rise to the refund, it is usually assumed the company would borrow the necessary funds in order to do so. Therefore, in notional market valuations the refundable tax payable is normally not taken into account when determining fair market value, on the assumption the company will receive a full refund of the additional refundable taxes in the near term following payment of a taxable dividend to its shareholders.

Tax Avoidance Provisions

Arm's Length Disposition to Obtain Tax Benefits

Subsection 69(11) of the *Act* contains an anti-avoidance rule which applies where a taxpayer disposes of property at arm's length (as part of a series of transactions) for proceeds of disposition less than fair market value and it may reasonably be considered that one of the main purposes of the transactions was to obtain the benefit of the tax deductions or entitlements of a person not affiliated with the taxpayer, or the tax exemptions available to any person on a subsequent disposition of the property. The definition of "affiliated persons" is contained in section 251.1 of the *Act* and generally is similar to, but somewhat more restricted than, the concept of "related persons" contained in subsection 251(2) of the *Act*.

The provision is intended to address the situation where a taxpayer transfers property with an accrued gain to an unrelated party on a tax-free rollover basis so that, on a subsequent disposition of the property, the transferor may offset the accrued profit with losses or other available deductions such as unclaimed undepreciated capital cost, unutilized scientific research and development (SRED) credits or balances in resource expenditure pools. When subsection 69(11) applies, the taxpayer is deemed to have disposed of the property for proceeds of disposition equal to its fair market value at the time. For the purposes of determining whether subsection 69(11) applies to a merger or amalgamation of corporations, subsection 69(13) deems each corporation to have disposed of Canadian and foreign resource properties for nil proceeds and any other property for proceeds equal to its cost amount.

Dividend Stripping

Section 84.1 of the *Act* applies to a transferor who is a Canadian resident individual or trust and deals with so-called "dividend stripping". The provisions of this section of the *Act* are best demonstrated by way of example. Assume that Individual E owns 100% of the shares of an operating company (R3 Limited) that have a paid-up capital and an adjusted cost base of $100,000, and fair market value of $1 million. Individual E sets up a holding company (Holdco) and transfers his shares of R3 to Holdco using the provisions of section 85, taking as consideration on the transfer $100,000 cash and shares of Holdco with a fair market value and paid-up capital of $900,000. Holdco could then borrow $900,000 and pay it to Individual E as a tax-free reduction of paid-up capital.

The net result (absent section 84.1) would be that E would strip out his accrued gain of $900,000. Section 84.1 operates to reduce the paid up capital of the shares issued by Holdco to the adjusted cost base of the transferred shares, resulting in a deemed dividend to Individual E of $900,000. The paid-up capital of the Holdco shares issued to Individual E and the fair market value of any non-share consideration is compared with the greater of the paid-up capital of the shares transferred to Holdco and the adjusted cost base of such shares. Where the former exceeds the latter, section 84.1 operates to effect a reduction in the paid-up capital of the shares of Holdco and, depending on the circumstances, a deemed dividend to the transferor. Special rules determine the adjusted cost base where the shares were held before 1972 or acquired after 1971 in a non-arm's length transaction. Note that 1971 is relevant in many cases, as December 31, 1971, represents the date at which capital gains became taxable in Canada.

Section 212.1 applies to non-resident transferors and contains rules similar to section 84.1, except that under section 212.1 only the paid-up capital of the shares transferred is taken into account in determining any deemed dividend or reduction in paid-up capital of shares of the holding corporation.

Generally, to avoid the application of sections 84.1 and 212.1, only shares should be taken back as consideration and their paid-up capital should be limited to the paid-up capital of the shares transferred (or, if section 84.1 applies, the adjusted cost base of the shares transferred determined under the rules in section 84.1). Where neither sections 84.1 nor 212.1 apply (e.g., an intercorporate transfer), subsection 85(2.1) will apply to reduce the paid-up capital of the shares to the amount by which the increase in the paid-up capital of the shares issued as a result of the transfer exceeds the cost to the corporation of the property less the fair market value of any non-share consideration.

Capital Gains Strips

Section 55 of the *Act* prevents a Canadian resident corporate shareholder from converting a capital gain on the disposition of shares held in another corporation into a dividend that would not be taxable under the *Act*. For example, assume Individual A owns shares of Holdco, which in turn owns shares of operating company R4 Limited. Further assume that Individual A wishes to dispose of their R4 shares, which have an adjusted cost base of $100,000 and a fair market value of $1 million. One method to accomplish such a disposition would be for A to arrange for R4 to pay Holdco a $900,000 dividend and then sell the R4 shares for $100,000, (i.e., the remaining fair market value of the shares). If not for subsection 55(2), there would be no immediate tax consequence because Holdco would receive the dividend on the shares tax free and there would be no capital gain on the disposition of the shares of R4 because the adjusted cost base of the shares would be equal to the proceeds. But under subsection 55(2), to the extent the dividend of $900,000 is deemed to have been paid from anything other than the after-tax earnings of the corporation after 1971, the amount of the dividend paid to Holdco will be added to the proceeds of disposition on the sale of the R4 shares, thereby resulting in a deemed capital gain.

Another way in which the capital gain can be stripped is to have Holdco transfer its shares of R4 to a buyer corporation in return for treasury shares of the buyer issued at a fair market value of $1 million and paid up capital of $100,000. The buyer could then redeem the shares issued to Holdco for $1 million, which would result in a $900,000 deemed dividend to Holdco which would be received tax free (the transaction would be designed so as to make Holdco and the buyer "connected" by definition of the *Act*). Again, subsection 55(2) of the *Act* may deem the seller's dividend to be a taxable gain to the extent such dividend is deemed to have been paid from anything other than after-tax earnings of R4 after 1971.

Safe Income

The after-tax undistributed earnings of a corporation earned after 1971 are commonly referred to as "safe income". Where the amount of an actual or deemed dividend paid to Holdco exceeds safe income, the entire dividend may become tainted for the purposes of subsection 55(2). A special designation can be filed under paragraph 55(5)(f) whereby the taxpayer can designate the appropriate portion of the dividend as being paid out of safe income so as not to taint the entire amount of the dividend.

Safe income is not a defined term in the *Act*, but is the term generally used to describe the dividend which can be safely paid without triggering tax. In general, safe income is the after-tax undistributed income of a corporation calculated in respect of a particular share from the time the share was acquired by its current owner. The calculation of safe income is governed to a significant extent by complex CRA administrative rules and any calculation of safe income requires a careful review of those rules. The ability of a corporation to pay a safe income dividend which will reduce the capital gain realized on the disposition of the shares of the corporation may be a significant factor in determining the structure for the sale of a business.

General Anti-Avoidance Rule (GAAR)

In addition to specific anti-avoidance provisions contained in the *Act*, there are general anti-avoidance rules (GAAR). For the GAAR not to apply, a taxpayer must establish that a transaction was undertaken or arranged primarily for a *bona fide* purpose other than to obtain a tax benefit. If this cannot be established, the GAAR will apply if the Minister of National Revenue can establish that the transaction results in a misuse or abuse of the provisions of the *Act* taken as a whole. Information Circular 88-2 and supplements discuss how the CRA would apply the GAAR in specific situations. There have been a handful Supreme Court of Canada decisions issued since 2005 on the GAAR (see Appendix A) which have provided significant clarity on how the GAAR applies and when. However, many commentators still believe the GAAR comes down to a judicial "smell test". The possible application of the GAAR should be considered in any business restructuring exercise.

Other Taxation Issues

Transfer Pricing

Section 247 of the *Act* contains transfer pricing rules which were enacted to ensure that cross-border non-arm's length transactions in goods and services are accounted for as if they had occurred at arm's length which, by definition, is at fair market value prices. Section 247 does not contain any definition of fair market value but is intended to provide a statutory base for application of the transaction-based methods of determining arm's length prices approved by the Organisation for Economic Co-operation and Development (OECD). The OECD's views and the CRA's related administrative policy are described in Information Circular 87-2R, dated September 27, 1999.

The transfer pricing rules in section 247 apply to transactions between a person resident in Canada or carrying on business in Canada (or a partnership of which such a person is a member) or any non-arm's length non-resident. If any of the terms or conditions in the transactions are different from those that would have been made between arm's length persons or the transaction would not have been entered into by arm's length persons and was not entered into primarily for a *bona fide* purpose other than to obtain a tax benefit, the results of the transaction for Canadian tax purposes may be adjusted or re-characterized.

"Tax benefit" is defined in the same manner as for the general anti-avoidance rule under section 245 of the *Act*, as a reduction, avoidance or deferral of tax or income or a refund. The adjustments will be made so that the results of the transaction reflect the terms and conditions which would have been made had the transaction been at arm's length. If the transaction would not have been entered into by arm's length persons, the results are re-characterized on the basis of the hypothetical transaction that would have been entered into by arm's length persons.

There is no protection for taxpayers who fail to establish that transactions do not constitute an abuse of the *Act*. The provisions of section 247 override the more general provisions of subsections 69(1) and 69(1.2). The rules apply not only to transfers of goods and services but also to transfers of depreciable and non-depreciable capital property and extend to cross-border guarantees. Section 247 contains provision for substantial penalties for failure to respect the transfer pricing rules by not making reasonable efforts to determine arm's length prices or allocations. The taxpayer is deemed not to have made such reasonable efforts if detailed and extensive documentation of transactions is not made by the taxpayer.

Corporate Owned Life Insurance

As previously noted, on the death of a taxpayer there is a deemed disposition of shares owned at the time of his death at fair market value. Sometimes the corporation in which the deceased taxpayer owned shares may own life insurance policies on the life of the deceased taxpayer. The determination of the fair market value of the shares is made on the basis that the fair market value of the life insurance policy is its cash surrender value at the time immediately before the taxpayer's death (subsection 70(5.3)).

The cash surrender value of life insurance policies is computed without regard to policy loans or policy dividends (other than paid-up additions) payable under the policy or interest payable on such dividends. Subsection 70(5.3) probably does not apply where the deceased owned shares of a holding corporation and the beneficiary of the policy was an operating corporation owned by the holding corporation. This subsection of the *Act* applies to deaths occurring after December 1, 1982, and reflects the decision of the Federal Court of Appeal in *R. v. Mastronardi Estate.*

In the *Mastronardi* case, a deceased taxpayer was a major shareholder in a corporation that owned a policy on his life. Upon the taxpayer's death, the corporation received the proceeds from the policy. The Minister of National Revenue argued that the phrase "immediately before death" was the equivalent to the instant of death and that, accordingly, the proceeds of the life insurance policy should be considered in the valuation of the deceased taxpayer's shares due to the imminence of death. The court rejected the Minister's arguments and held that the amount of the insurance proceeds did not have to be taken into account in valuing the shares of the corporation for determining capital gains of the deceased taxpayer.

Where death occurred prior to December 2, 1982, the CRA has taken the position (Interpretation Bulletin IT-416R3) that the *Mastronardi* decision is limited to the situation where the death of a taxpayer was sudden or unexpected. In the situation where it was known that the taxpayer had a terminal illness or was critically injured and would not recover, the amount of insurance proceeds might properly be taken into account in valuing shares.

Interest Deductibility

In general, interest expense on money borrowed to purchase shares of a corporation or in connection with the purchase of assets of a business is deductible under paragraph 20(1)(c) of the *Act*. The use of the borrowed funds is the key determinant as to whether interest will be deductible.

The CRA's policies on the issue of interest deductibility, reflected in Interpretation Bulletin IT-533, have undergone a significant change in the last decade, largely due to court decisions that have significantly expanded the circumstances in which an interest deduction will be available. With regard to the deductibility of interest on money borrowed to purchase shares, the Supreme Court of Canada in *Ludco Enterprises Ltd. v. Canada*, [2001] 2 S.C.R. 1082 SCC 62 has confirmed that interest may be deductible if the shares acquired can pay dividends, even if the amount of dividends expected is low and dividends need not be the primary purpose of the investment. The CRA, commenting on Ludco, has stated that where an investment (e.g., interest-bearing instrument or preferred shares) carries a stated interest or dividend rate, the purpose of the earning income test will be met "absent a sham or window dressing or similar vitiating circumstances". Further, assuming all of the other requisite tests are met, interest will neither be denied in full nor restricted to the amount of income from the investment where the income does not exceed the interest expense.

Where an investment does not carry a stated interest or dividend rate such as some common shares do, the determination of the reasonable expectation of income at the time the investment is made is less clear. Normally, however, the CRA considers interest costs in respect of funds borrowed to purchase common shares to be deductible on the grounds that there is a reasonable expectation, at the time the shares are acquired, that the common shareholder will receive dividends. Nonetheless, each situation must be dealt with on the basis of the particular facts involved.

The Department of Finance released for public comment draft proposals regarding the deductibility of interest and other expenses for income tax purposes in 2003, but no Bill has yet been put forward in Parliament and the whole matter now appears to be on hold indefinitely.

Summary

The valuation of intangible assets has become an increasingly pertinent topic in recent years, particularly with new requirements for purchase price allocation among identifiable intangible assets. Common methods of valuing intangibles include the market approach, the cost approach, the incremental cash flow approach, the relief from royalty approach and the excess earnings approach.

The determination of royalty rates, whether pursuant to the relief from royalty approach or an open market transaction regarding tangible or intangible property, is a subjective exercise. The rate can vary dramatically depending on the nature of the property and the structure of the agreement, including provisions dealing with exclusivity, territory, renewal rights, minimum royalty payments and other terms.

The value of preferred shares is normally taken to be their redemption or retraction value. However, their value can vary depending on their characteristics, including voting rights and other rights attached thereto. Dilutive securities can also have an impact on common share value, where such securities are "in the money" at the valuation date.

Holding companies are normally valued using the adjusted net book value methodology. Additional considerations include the treatment of income taxes and head office costs, where the holding company is comprised of several divergent assets or business divisions.

Foreign entities can be valued using the same methodologies as presented in this book. However, additional consideration should be given to issues such as taxation, foreign exchange fluctuations and economic and political risks.

The *Income Tax Act* normally specifies that fair market value is the value definition to be adopted when dealing with issues that require arm's length equivalent value to be established. In an open market transaction the tax treatment of special tax accounts of privately held companies and corporate restructuring possibilities all ultimately may affect the price that is paid and received. The income tax considerations of each valuation exercise are unique, and professional advice should be obtained where necessary.

Chapter 10

Notional Market Valuations

Introduction

Notional market valuations attempt to reflect what would reasonably be expected in an open market transaction, assuming a cash deal. Common reasons for commissioning a formal valuation report include transactions among the existing shareholder of a company, shareholder disputes (including dissent and oppression remedies), income tax-related matters (e.g., estate freezes, restructuring, income tax disputes), matrimonial purposes and employee share ownership plans. In most of these cases, fair market value is determined on an intrinsic basis due to the uncertainty relating to the quantification and realization of post-acquisition synergies. However, there may be circumstances where it is appropriate to incorporate expected post-acquisition synergies, where such synergies are likely to be paid for and can be meaningfully quantified.

The Canadian Institute of Chartered Business Valuators (CICBV) establishes standards for different types of valuation reports. This includes a comprehensive valuation report, an estimate valuation report and a calculation valuation report. The types of reports differ mainly in the scope of review and the level of assurance afforded, with the comprehensive valuation report providing the highest level of assurance and a calculation valuation report providing the lowest. The type of valuation report required in a specific circumstance depends on the nature of the mandate and the level of assurance required.

Valuations are also required in connection with actual or proposed open market transactions. Where a buyer acquires the shares or assets of another company, the purchase price must be allocated among the assets and liabilities acquired. In this regard, both Generally Accepted Accounting Principles (GAAP) and International Financial Reporting Standards (IFRSs) require the allocation of the purchase price be made among net tangible assets, identifiable intangible assets and non-identifiable intangible assets (or goodwill). Identifiable intangible assets are amortized into income over their estimated economic lives, whereas goodwill is not, but rather is tested for impairment on a periodic (usually annual) basis.

In many cases where a company is faced with a proposed transaction such as a takeover bid, its board of directors will commission a fairness opinion from an independent financial expert (normally either a valuator or investment banker). The fairness opinion will assess whether the proposed transaction is fair from a financial point of view to a certain group of shareholders (or all shareholders) or other stakeholders of the company. Assessing fairness requires the financial expert to determine whether the consideration received is greater than the consideration given up. Such an assessment can become more complex where the consideration received includes non-cash components, such as illiquid shares of the buyer, promissory notes, earnout arrangements and other forms of consideration. The fairness opinion should also take into account the expected synergies to be realized as well as other factors, where applicable.

Value in a Notional Market Context

When determining fair market value, fair value or some other definition of value in a notional market context, it is necessary to address the question of possible open market prices that might be paid by buyers who perceive they can generate post-acquisition synergies by combining the acquired business with their existing operations. Unless qualified to the contrary, fair market value by definition incorporates the possibility of special-interest purchasers as part of the "highest price available" component. Court cases dealing with the issue of special-interest purchasers in a notional market context have concluded that where such buyers can be readily identified and the price they may pay reasonably determinable, post-acquisition synergies should be considered in the determination of fair market value. Appendix A contains a list of selected court cases dealing with this issue.

In most cases, a notional market valuation is prepared where arm's length negotiations have not taken place. As a result it is often difficult to identify possible buyers who might be interested in acquiring a given business at a given point in time. Further, where such possible buyers are identified, it is difficult to determine which of them should be considered qualified buyers with the financial capability to effect a purchase. Moreover, if and when qualified buyers can be identified it is often very difficult, if not impossible, to identify and meaningfully quantify post-acquisition synergies each might enjoy. The buyer is in a better position to identify and quantify what it perceives to be post-acquisition synergies. Importantly, the quantum of such benefits can vary significantly from one buyer to the next. Finally, even if post-acquisition synergies can be identified and meaningfully quantified, it is still difficult to ascertain the degree to which buyers will negotiate to pay for some or all of those post-acquisition benefits. This usually depends on the relative negotiating positions of the parties involved and the structure of the deal.

It follows that in a notional market context there are four distinct scenarios where one or more potential buyers who might enjoy post-acquisition synergies can:

- not be specifically identified, and it is believed that no such buyers exist;
- not be specifically identified, but it is believed one or more such buyers may exist;
- be identified, but the value of synergies to each prospective buyer cannot be meaningfully quantified; and
- be identified, and the value of synergies to each prospective buyer can be meaningfully quantified.

In the first three instances, it is usual to state the parameters of the analysis undertaken and the conclusions reached. In the third instance, it is usual to state that, while certain special-interest purchasers have been identified, the value of post-acquisition synergies cannot be meaningfully quantified and the reasons why this is so. In each of the first three instances, notional market value determinations are based on intrinsic (or stand-alone) value, and are qualified to reflect the fact that an open market price might be different (and presumably higher) than the value determination. In these circumstances, reports expressing notional value opinions are often qualified in respect of the inability to reasonably quantify post-acquisition synergies, if any exist at all.

In the fourth instance, it is usual to attempt to quantify value inclusive of the post-acquisition synergies that have been identified. In such cases, the value for a particular business sometimes is divided between the value component expressing the intrinsic value and the value component expressing the estimated post-acquisition synergies, with the latter usually being somewhat qualified. Further, the value of synergies is often discounted to reflect the uncertainty that a buyer could be negotiated into paying for some or all of such synergies in the form of cash or equivalent at closing.

Valuation Reports and Standards

In Canada, the CICBV is the pre-eminent professional body for business valuation. The CICBV has established standards for the scope of review, documentation and reporting. The discussion below summarizes the valuation standards at the time of writing (2012). It is not intended to be a substitute for the full standards, as published on the CICBV's website (www.cicbv.ca). Furthermore, since valuation standards and practices are continuously evolving, the valuation expert should ensure they are aware of the prevailing valuation standards.

Types of Reports

Valuation Reports

According to CICBV Standard #110 (2), a valuation report is defined as "any written communication containing a conclusion as to the value of shares, assets or an interest in a business prepared by a valuator acting independently". This definition assumes the valuator has been retained as an independent expert and not as an advocate.

Formal valuation reports fall into three broad categories: (i) calculation valuation reports; (ii) estimate valuation reports; and (iii) comprehensive valuation reports. The types of reports are distinguished by the valuator's scope of review and the amount of disclosure provided, as well as the level of assurance being provided in the conclusion. In this regard:

- a calculation valuation report contains a conclusion based on minimal review and analysis and little or no corroboration of relevant information. A calculation valuation report provides the lowest level of assurance;

- an estimate valuation report contains a conclusion based on limited review, analysis and corroboration of relevant information; and

- a comprehensive valuation report contains a conclusion based on a comprehensive review and analysis of the business, its industry and all other relevant factors, adequately corroborated. A comprehensive valuation report provides the highest level of assurance.

The type of valuation report required in a particular engagement should be discussed and agreed between the valuator and the client, and then reflected in the terms of the engagement. In this regard, the valuator and the client should consider the purpose for which the valuation report is being prepared, the availability of information on which to base a conclusion, and the client's need for assurance. The valuator should also consider whether the type of valuation report will be credible for the purpose intended and ensure any conclusions will not be misleading to a reader and not dependent on any assumptions known by the valuator to be false.

In practice, a calculation valuation report tends to be used to provide a preliminary indication of value. An estimate valuation report tends to be associated with smaller and/or non-litigious situations such as an estate freeze involving a small or mid-sized privately held company. However, where the matter is litigious or involves a significant monetary transaction, the additional rigour of a comprehensive valuation report is often appropriate.

Advisory Reports

According to CICBV Standard #210 (2.a), an advisory report contains a conclusion as to the value of shares, assets, a business interest or the quantum of financial gain or loss, or comments on a report containing a conclusion on such matters, but the valuator has not been engaged to act independently. Therefore, the advisory report must clearly state that the valuator has acted in an advisory capacity and has not been engaged to prepare an independent valuation report.

Apart from the role of the valuator, the disclosure standards of an advisory report are the same as those of a valuation report.

Expert Reports

According to CICBV Standard #310 (2), an expert report is defined as "any written communication other than a valuation report, containing a conclusion as to the quantum of financial gain/loss, or any conclusion of a financial nature in the context of litigation or a dispute, prepared by an expert, acting independently."

While expert reports are not valuation reports per se, they can address the issue of valuation in such contexts as the loss of value from business disruption, breach of contract, patent infringement and similar issues.

Limited Critique Reports

According to CICBV Standard #410 (2), a limited critique report is defined as "any written communication containing comments on a report that was prepared by a (CICBV) member or non-member containing a conclusion as to the value of shares, assets or an interest in a business, or a conclusion as to the quantum of financial gain/loss or any conclusion of a financial nature in the context of litigation or a dispute (the "original report"), prepared by a valuator (the "reviewer") that does not itself contain a valuation conclusion or conclusion as to the quantum of financial gain/loss, or any conclusion of a financial nature in the context of litigation or dispute."

A limited critique report typically is prepared in the context of a litigious matter, where a valuation expert believes that the valuation report put forth by the opposing expert is not reasonable in terms of its conclusions or other content for reasons such as:

- technical errors in the calculations;
- inappropriate valuation methodology, or the misapplication of the valuation methodology adopted;
- failure to consider certain pertinent facts;
- failure to prepare a valuation or expert report in accordance with applicable standards;
- internal inconsistency in the assumptions, calculations or other aspects of the report; and
- significant differences in judgment.

The valuator preparing the limited critique report may also be asked to prepare an independent valuation report, setting out their valuation conclusions.

The valuator whose valuation report is critiqued often will be asked to prepare a rebuttal report, setting out the reasons why they disagree with the points raised in the limited critique report.

In the context of being an independent expert, the valuator preparing the limited critique report is expected to raise issues that may be contrary to the interest of their client as well as points in favour of their client. Likewise, the rebuttal report should acknowledge errors and issues that are properly identified in the limited critique report, where they exist.

Fairness Opinions

According to CICBV Standard #510 (2), a fairness opinion is defined as "any written communication containing a conclusion as to the fairness of a proposed transaction to security holders (or a group of security holders), from a financial point of view."

A company's board of directors (particularly of public companies) will often ask for a fairness opinion to satisfy their fiduciary duties or duty of care to the company that is the subject to a proposed transaction. Examples include takeover bids, related-party transactions and going-private transactions. A fairness opinion (or a summary) is often provided to the stakeholders as part of the proxy materials relating to the proposed transaction.

In recent years, the courts have become increasingly mindful of the potential conflict of interest in fairness opinions, both in fact and appearance. For example, fairness opinions are often rendered by an investment bank that stands to earn a significant contingency fee in the event that the proposed transaction does proceed. Consequently, there is a trend to retain an independent valuation expert to render the fairness opinion in order for the board of directors to better discharge their fiduciary or other duties.

The particular facts of a proposed transaction may affect the degree to which the proposed transaction will be perceived as fair (or not fair) from a financial point of view (e.g., terms of the proposed transaction, the degree to which alternative proposals were sought etc.). Fairness opinions are discussed in greater detail below.

Valuation Report Contents

The specific contents of a valuation report will vary widely, depending on the nature of the engagement, the type of report and other factors. However, CICBV Standard #110 requires the items set out below be disclosed as a minimum:

Introduction Section:

- to whom the valuation report is being provided;
- a description of the shares, assets or interest in a business being valued;
- the effective date of the valuation (i.e., the valuation date);
- the date of the valuation report;
- the purpose for which the valuation report is being prepared;
- the name of the firm responsible for preparing the valuation report, as well as the name of the valuator(s) when the valuation report is prepared for litigation purposes;

- the type of valuation report being provided (i.e., comprehensive, estimate or calculation valuation report);

- a statement that the valuation report was prepared by the valuator acting independently and objectively;

- a statement that the valuator's compensation is not contingent on an action or event resulting from the use of the valuation report; and

- a statement that that valuation report has been prepared in conformity with the practice standards of the CICBV.

Report Definitions:

- the valuation report shall contain definitions for the terms of value used, such as "fair market value", "market value", "fair value" or "adjusted net asset value"; and

- with respect to the definition of fair market value, the valuation report should indicate the extent to which special purchasers were considered and the reasons why.

Scope of Review:

- the valuation report shall contain a scope of review that clearly identifies the specific information on which the valuator relied to arrive at a conclusion;

- for estimate and calculation valuation reports, the valuator shall disclose that the scope of review is limited by the type of valuation report being provided, and that the conclusion expressed may have been different had a comprehensive valuation report been provided; and

- where the conclusion is qualified by a scope limitation, regardless of the type of valuation report being provided, the limitation shall be explained by setting out the reasons for the limitation.

Report Disclosure:

- the valuation report shall provide sufficient information to allow the reader to understand how the valuator arrived at the conclusion expressed;

- at a minimum, all valuation reports shall include the following information:

  ✓ the basis of the valuation as well as the approach and methods used,

  ✓ a statement of the key assumptions made in arriving at the valuation conclusion;

- in addition to the minimum information required for all valuation reports as noted above, comprehensive and estimate valuation reports shall also include the following information:

  ✓ a description of the valuation calculations,

  ✓ where relevant to the valuation assignment, a full description of the classes of shares and any attached rights, where interests other than common shares have to be valued either directly or as part of the overall valuation,

  ✓ a summary of relevant financial information,

✓ a description of the business being valued, sufficient for the reader to understand the valuation basis and approach adopted, as well as the various earnings/cash flow risk factors present,

✓ a reference to trading volumes and price ranges, in the case of publicly traded securities; and

- in addition to the above, a comprehensive valuation report shall include a description of the economic context and industry outlook bearing on the shares, assets or interest in a business being valued.

Report Restrictions and Qualifications:

- all valuation reports shall disclose any restrictions that affect the valuator's conclusions, as noted below:

  ✓ a statement restricting the use of the valuation report to the persons for whom the report was prepared and for only the purpose stated,

  ✓ a statement denying responsibility for losses resulting from any unauthorized or improper use of the valuation report,

  ✓ a statement giving the valuator the right to make revisions and/or to further support the conclusion under specified circumstances such as when facts existing at the valuation date become apparent to the valuator only after the valuation report is issued; and

- comprehensive and estimate valuation reports shall disclose any qualifications that affect the valuator's conclusions.

Conclusion:

The valuation report shall contain a conclusion as to the value of the shares, assets or interest in a business being valued.

Other Disclosure Requirements:

Additional disclosure standards are provided for valuation reports prepared for:

- the purposes of securities legislation, regulations or policies in the context of non-arm's length transactions;

- financial reporting purposes (e.g., goodwill impairment testing); or

- a labour sponsored or venture capital fund, to perform an independent review to assess whether the value of the venture investments or the net asset value of the fund, as determined by the manager of the fund or another party, is reasonable.

In addition, advisory reports, expert reports and limited critique reports also have specific disclosure requirements that must be observed.

Scope of Work

This section summarizes CICBV Standard #120, dealing with the scope of work standards and recommendations for valuation reports. These elements should be considered in the context of conducting an analysis of the business, as set out in Chapter 2.

Other standards may apply to different types of reports (e.g., expert reports). As is the case above, the CICBV website (www.cicbv.ca) should be consulted for a more holistic discussion of the prevailing scope of work standards.

General Standards

The general standards apply to all types of valuation reports (i.e., comprehensive, estimate and calculation valuation reports) are set out below:

- the valuator should obtain clear instructions from the person requesting the valuation, including the type of valuation report required;

- the work shall be performed by a person or persons having adequate technical training and proficiency in financial analysis and/or business valuation concepts, principles and techniques, with due care and with an objective state of mind;

- the work shall be adequately planned and properly executed. If assistants are employed, they shall be properly supervised;

- sufficient evidence shall be gathered by such means as inspection, inquiry, computation and analysis to ensure the valuation report and its conclusion are properly supported. When determining the extent of evidence necessary to support the valuation report, valuators shall exercise professional judgment considering the nature of the valuation, the type of valuation report being provided (i.e., comprehensive, estimate or calculation valuation report) and the use to which the valuation report will be put;

- the valuator shall perform the work in accordance with the practice standards and the code of ethics of the CICBV; and

- when access to essential information is denied by the client or some other party, or the information is otherwise unavailable to the valuator, any conclusion expressed by the valuation in respect of such valuation shall be qualified and the limitation(s) on the scope of work clearly set out in the valuation report.

Specific Standards

The following specific standards apply to comprehensive and estimate valuation reports (and should be considered in the context of a calculation valuation report):

- when planning the scope of work for a particular engagement, the valuator shall obtain:
  - ✓ sufficient understanding of the subject of the valuation,
  - ✓ sufficient understanding of the underlying business operations,
  - ✓ sufficient financial information relating to past results, future prospects and present financial position,
  - ✓ sufficient understanding of the relevant industry(ies) in which the underlying business operates,
  - ✓ sufficient information relating to the general economic conditions affecting the underlying business operations;

- in performing the business valuation, the valuator shall determine the appropriate valuation basis and approach to be employed;

- the valuator shall consider key valuation components and assumptions;

- the valuator shall consider the necessity of relying on the work of a specialist; and

- the valuator shall determine the necessity of obtaining client representations in writing and, if possible, representations from management or other representatives of the underlying business.

Specific Applications

There are a variety of reasons that formal valuation reports (comprehensive, estimate or calculation) may be prepared. Some valuation mandates are inherently litigious (e.g., shareholder and tax disputes), while others are less so (e.g., employee share ownership plans and purchase price allocations). However, any valuation mandate has the potential to become litigious if the conclusions are challenged.

This section addresses various applications that often give rise to the need for a formal valuation report and the challenges valuators commonly face in the preparation of such reports. The discussion here is general in nature; the specific facts of a particular valuation may dictate further considerations or other approaches.

Transactions Among Shareholders

Transactions among shareholders refer to the buyout of one existing shareholder by the other existing shareholder(s) of a privately held company, upon death, retirement, termination, or other circumstances that gives rise to an optional or mandatory purchase and sale. The terms of the buyout are usually governed by the provisions of a shareholder agreement, that may establish:

- the basis by which value is to be determined and, specifically, whether a minority discount is to be applied;

- the procedures for establishing value (e.g., whether a single valuator is appointed by both parties or whether each party retains its own);

- the valuation date; and

- the terms of payment.

Where the shareholder agreement is silent or vague on these issues, they can become significant matters of contention. In particular, whether a minority discount should apply is a central issue. In some cases, the shareholder agreement specifies the departing shareholder is entitled to receive "fair value" for their interest, which is most often interpreted to mean a pro-rata portion of *en bloc* fair market value, without the application of a minority discount. However, in other cases, the shareholder agreement is unclear. In such cases, whether a minority discount should apply is often a legal issue. Factors influencing the quantum of a minority discount, where applicable, were addressed in Chapter 8.

Shareholder buyouts are sometimes conducted in the context of intergenerational transfers, such as where a younger generation acquires the equity interests of an older generation. This can give rise to taxation issues if the CRA finds that the transaction was not concluded at fair market value (see Chapter 9). In addition, where the younger generation includes individuals who will not participate in the buyout, those individuals may contest the valuation on the grounds it favours the buyer (e.g., siblings, cousins, etc.) to the detriment of the sellers (e.g., the parents) and consequently could diminish the potential inheritance that the non-shareholder might hope to enjoy.

In other cases, shareholder buyouts are prepared in connection with a "shotgun" clause as set out in a shareholder agreement. Recall from Chapter 8 that a shotgun clause will specify the procedures to be followed, including the length of time the shareholder receiving the offer has to respond. Shotgun clauses can provide the appearance of fairness, given that the shareholder preparing the offer must carefully consider the offer amount. However, the application of a shotgun clause can be problematic, given that the offer can be influenced by a multitude of factors such as where the shareholders have:

- a preference for being a buyer or a seller;
- differing abilities to finance the buyout because of personal resources or access to external financing;
- differing knowledge of the business, including its risk profile and growth prospects because of the level or nature of their involvement; and
- personal goodwill, which causes the business to be worth more to one shareholder than the other.

Consequently, in many cases, the parties work to circumvent the strict application of the shotgun clause in favour of a negotiated agreement.

Funding the Shareholder Buyout

Where the buyout of an existing shareholder is required because of their death, the funds for such a buyout are often provided through life insurance. This helps to ensure the buyout does not unduly burden the company or the surviving shareholders. As noted in Chapter 8, an issue might arise with respect to whether the value of the business is to be determined on a basis that includes or excludes the life insurance proceeds. In effect, the receipt of life insurance proceeds could result in a windfall for the surviving shareholders.

In other situations, the funding for the shareholder buyout must be provided by the business (at least in part). An issue that sometimes arises in that context is that of "internal vs. external financing", which is discussed later in this chapter. Recall from Chapter 1 the fundamental valuation principle that the value of a business is independent of how it is financed. However, as a practical matter, where a business must forgo necessary operating expenses or capital expenditures in favour of funding the shareholder buyer, it can have an impact on the value of the business in an open market context. Alternatively, where significant amounts of bank financing are used, such financing sometimes comes with restrictive covenants that impair the ability of the remaining shareholders to operate the business as they choose. This restriction, in turn may impact the growth prospects of the business.

The departing shareholder will object to the notion that the value of their interest is diminished because of the inability to secure adequate financing from external sources (e.g., a new equity partner) to prevent the value of the business from being affected. However, finding a new equity partner may be difficult or impractical, depending on the nature of the business and the preferences of the remaining shareholders.

In light of these factors, while a formal valuation report may provide a conclusion as to the value of a particular equity interest for a departing shareholder, the terms of payment are sometimes negotiated so as not to overly burden the company and the remaining shareholders. The issue from the departing shareholder's perspective is to ensure that any deferred portion of the purchase price is adequately secured.

Engagement Approach

The parties involved in a shareholder buyout may or may not be on amicable terms. Whichever is the case, each party will want to maximize its position. Therefore, the departing shareholder will want to receive the highest price for their equity interest, while the remaining shareholders will want to pay the lowest price. Therefore, the conclusions set out in the valuation report are likely to be contested by one or both parties.

There are various approaches that can be used to establish the value of the departing shareholders' interest, which may or may not be set out in the shareholder agreement. The first approach is for one party to retain an independent valuation expert to render a conclusion that is shared with the other party. Where the conclusions reached by the valuator are not agreed to by the other party (which is often the case), that other party retains its own valuation expert. The differences between the two valuation conclusions may be settled in a variety of ways, including: (i) mutual agreement; (ii) mediation or arbitration; (iii) the courts; or (iv) the retention of a third valuation expert (as agreed to by both parties) who either prepares an independent report or selects one of the two valuation conclusions presented (so-called "baseball arbitration").

The other approach is for both parties to jointly retain an independent valuation expert who delivers a valuation conclusion that is (usually) binding on the parties. In this regard, it is common for the valuation expert to prepare a "blind draft" valuation report that is circulated to the parties for comment. The blind draft report contains the pertinent facts and methodology supporting the valuation, but does not contain a value conclusion. Each party is provided a specified period of time to comment on the draft report with respect to errors, omissions and discrepancies. In light of these submissions, the valuator may seek additional information. Once the valuator is satisfied the necessary facts are complete and correct and the assumptions are reasonable, the valuator can then finalize their value conclusion. The benefit of the blind-draft approach is that it allows the parties to focus on ensuring the facts underlying the valuation are correct and complete and the assumptions reasonable and internally consistent, rather than becoming immediately distracted with the value conclusion.

Shareholder Disputes

Recall from Chapter 8 that business corporation legislation provides shareholders of privately held companies and public companies with a dissent remedy and an oppression remedy in certain circumstances. Whether or not such a claim has merit in a particular situation is a legal issue.

The dissent remedy gives the dissenting shareholder the right to receive fair value for their shares upon the occurrence of certain events. As discussed in Chapter 8, these events include:

- the passage of an amendment to the articles of incorporation to add, change, or remove any provisions restricting or constraining the issue, ownership, or transfer of shares or any restriction upon the business or businesses that the corporation may carry on;

- an amalgamation with a corporation other than its wholly owned subsidiary, its parent corporation (if it is a wholly owned subsidiary), or its sister corporation, if both are wholly owned subsidiaries of the same corporation;

- the continuation of the corporation under the laws of another jurisdiction;

- a sale, lease, or exchange of all, or substantially all, the corporation's property; and

- an amendment to the articles of incorporation which diminishes the rights or conditions attached to a class or series of shares, which amendment otherwise creates an entitlement to a class vote.

The oppression remedy may be available where a minority shareholder can demonstrate that they have been treated in a manner that is oppressive, unfairly prejudicial, or is in unfair disregard of their interests. While the courts have a broad range of remedies available to rectify the oppressive conduct, the one common resolution is to require that the oppressed shareholder's interest be acquired for fair value.

Recall from Chapter 1 that fair value is normally defined as a pro-rata portion of *en bloc* fair market value, without the application of a minority discount. However, in the context of a dissent or oppression remedy, there are other issues that can arise, including: (i) the extent to which special-interest purchasers should be considered; and (ii) whether a "premium for forcible taking" should be considered.

These are legal issues that have been addressed in several decisions by the courts (see Appendix A). As a general statement, consideration of special-interest purchasers may be appropriate where such purchasers can be identified and the premium they would be willing to pay can be meaningfully quantified. A premium for forcible taking has rarely been awarded by the courts, but may be applicable where the departing shareholder was being forced out, instead of electing to dispose of their equity interest.

Shareholder disputes are inherently litigious and the parties providing information for valuation reports have a strong bias. The valuator needs to be aware of these biases and to seek corroborating evidence to support the information provided by the parties, where appropriate.

In the context of a privately held company, the determination of fair market value, fair value or other definition of value may be governed by a shareholder agreement. Where the shareholder agreement is ambiguous or silent on certain key matters, such as the application of a minority discount, then legal advice or assumptions may be necessary. Such advice or assumptions are also necessary in the context of public company dissent and oppression remedies.

Another issue that sometimes arises in the context of shareholder disputes is the determination of the valuation date. Again, this is a legal issue. The fair market value of a business can fluctuate significantly over time based on factors such as prevailing economic and industry conditions and the outlook for a given business at a particular point in time. It is generally accepted that hindsight is not admissible in the determination of the value of a particular business at a given point in time. However, the use of hindsight has sometimes been allowed for the limited purpose of assessing the reasonableness of certain assumptions made at a particular valuation date (see Appendix A). Where significant events occur shortly after the valuation date, the valuator must assess the degree to which the event could be foreseen at the valuation date.

Income Tax Valuations

Recall from Chapter 9 that the Canada Revenue Agency (CRA) requires transactions among related parties to be conducted at fair market value. Failure to do so can result in adverse tax consequences to the buyer, the seller or (in some cases) both. Common income tax valuations include estate freezes, corporate reorganizations, deemed dispositions on death or upon becoming a non-resident of Canada, transactions with foreign entities and the determination of asset values (e.g., software and eligible capital property) for capital cost allowance purposes.

For income tax purposes the fair market value of a business is normally determined on an intrinsic (or stand-alone) basis, without consideration of the synergies, economies of scale, or other advantages that might be perceived to exist by one or more special-interest purchasers. This is because, in the absence of an open market transaction, it is difficult to quantify the additional value that might be perceived by a particular (often hypothetical) buyer of a given business. Furthermore, even if such additional value can be meaningfully quantified, it is speculative as to whether a buyer can be negotiated into a position of paying for some or all of that premium.

Historically, the CRA has accepted valuations prepared on an intrinsic basis. That said, there might be circumstances where special-interest purchasers should be considered and where sufficient information is available to meaningfully quantify a special purchaser premium. For example, in certain industries, obvious synergistic buyers do exist, and the disclosure surrounding recent open market transactions in those industries is sufficient to permit a meaningful analysis of the synergistic component of the purchase price. Unless qualified to the contrary, the definition of fair market value in Canada may include a premium created by the existence of special-interest purchasers.

It is important to determine the appropriate valuation date because it establishes the information base to be considered when determining fair market value. One challenge sometimes encountered by valuators in notional market valuations for income tax purposes arises when the value of a business or asset must be determined at a date already several years in the past. Often in such cases, individuals having detailed knowledge of the business' operations at the valuation date are no longer accessible, or they simply cannot recall what they knew and expected at that time. In addition, many companies do not retain all their documentation for long periods of time (e.g., detailed forecasts of previous years). In some cases, the valuation conclusions are qualified where the valuator believes all the necessary information could not be obtained. Such qualifications sometimes impair the usefulness of the valuation report and the credibility of its conclusions.

Estate Freezes

Recall from Chapter 9 that an estate freeze is a mechanism commonly used to transfer wealth between generations on a tax-deferred basis. In most cases involving intergenerational estate freezes, there is a bias toward establishing a low value in order to increase the benefit to the younger generation. This is achieved when fair market value is determined on an intrinsic basis.

That being said, the CRA requires that a "reasonable attempt" be made to establish fair market value, failing which the CRA may disallow the use of the price adjustment clause. A price adjustment clause is normally included in estate freeze transactions in order to protect the parties to the transaction against immediate tax consequences as a result of being successfully contested by the tax authorities.

Minority Discounts in Tax Valuations

When determining the value of minority shareholdings for Canadian income tax purposes, the CRA's attitudes and practices must be considered. This includes the CRA's interpretation bulletins on family and group control, as discussed in Chapter 8.

The CRA imposes a general requirement of consistency in reviewing notional market values of privately held company shares. In most circumstances, share values for income tax purposes are determined to measure capital gains or losses. As a result, values at two different dates are commonly compared to measure the base on which any applicable income tax will be calculated. Unless there have been demonstrable changes between the two measurement dates, the CRA will usually insist that comparable valuation principles be applied, particularly with respect to matters such as group or family control.

While the relatively few Canadian court decisions dealing with minority-interest values for income tax purposes limits analysis, they have usually held that in a notional market context, minority shareholdings in privately held companies for income tax purposes have a fair market value somewhat lower than their ratable value.

Historically, the CRA has combined the concepts of non-control and illiquidity into an all-encompassing minority discount. With respect to the quantum of minority discounts, in the absence of an enforceable shareholder agreement, the CRA has tended to accept discounts from ratable value as follows:

- where there are two 50% shareholdings, discounts in the range of 10% to 20%; and

- where a shareholding is less than 50% of the outstanding voting shares, discounts in the range of 20% to 40%.

However, as noted in Chapter 8, minority discounts can vary significantly depending on specific facts and circumstances.

Goodwill

Another issue that commonly arises in the context of income tax valuations is the nature of goodwill. This is particularly the case for smaller businesses, especially those businesses that rely on the continued active involvement of the owner. Recall from Chapter 1 that there are three types of goodwill: (i) commercial goodwill; (ii) individual goodwill; and (iii) personal goodwill.

Commercial goodwill includes such things as a business's brand names, market presence, favourable location, and similar attributes. These are things that a buyer normally expects to inherit when it acquires a business. Therefore, a buyer normally is prepared to pay for the commercial goodwill of a particular business. Hence, commercial goodwill forms part of fair market value.

Individual goodwill is due to the personal contacts, knowledge or other unique characteristics of the individual (generally the business owner) that would be lost if the person departed the business and competed with it. In the context of an open market transaction, a prudent buyer will only pay for individual goodwill where that component of value will remain with the business following the transaction. This is normally accomplished through deal structuring, whereby the buyer requires the individual seller(s) possessing individual goodwill characteristics to enter into a non-competition agreement and/or a management contract concurrent with the transaction. In addition, a buyer will often structure a portion of the purchase price such that payment is contingent upon the achievement of certain prospective operating results of the acquired business (e.g., an earnout arrangement). Hence, in open market transactions, individual goodwill often forms part of the price paid.

It follows that when determining the fair market value of a business for income tax purposes, individual goodwill should be included, consistent with the "highest price available" component of fair market value. Stated differently, reasonable commercial terms should be assumed in a fair market value determination. Therefore, in the context of determining fair market value in a notional market context, the usual assumption is that the business owner possessing the individual goodwill will enter into an enforceable non-competition agreement thereby realizing the value of the business. Hence, individual goodwill typically forms part of fair market value.

However, a notional market valuation must consider that the definition of fair market value assumes a cash transaction (where the seller assumes no risk), whereas the form(s) of consideration used to pay for individual goodwill often transfers some or all of the risk from the buyer to the seller. As such, the cash-equivalent value of the individual goodwill component of the purchase price would be less than its face value. In the context of a notional market valuation, the risk associated with payment for individual goodwill is normally recognized by adjusting (increasing) the required rate of return. Any such "individual goodwill risk premium" factored into the rate of return is subjective.

Personal goodwill is also attributed to an individual's knowledge, abilities, reputation, and other personal characteristics. However, unlike individual goodwill, the value of personal goodwill is lost to a business as soon as the individual possessing personal goodwill departs the business for any reason (including death, retirement, and other reasons). In an open market transaction a buyer will not pay for the personal good-will component of value. Hence, personal goodwill is excluded from fair market value. The courts have confirmed this view.

The distinction between individual goodwill and personal goodwill is a grey area. In many companies that rely on the reputation and abilities of their owner(s), some customers will depart when the owner is no longer involved, whereas other customers may remain with the business so long as their needs can be satisfied by other individuals within the company. Therefore, in a notional market valuation, the valuator should perform adequate analysis to determine what portion of goodwill should form part of fair market value. Such analysis is subjective.

Related to the issue of individual goodwill (and personal goodwill) is the issue of assigning a portion of the purchase price of a business to a non-competition agreement for income tax purposes. This issue was addressed in Chapter 9.

Matrimonial Disputes

In Canada, divorce is federally legislated. Related matters, such as custody of children and support payments, may be adjudicated either federally or provincially. Property rights fall under provincial jurisdiction. Accordingly, each province has its own legislation governing the division of assets upon the termination of marriage. In all provinces except Quebec, individuals retain their respective property ownership rights throughout the marriage. On the occurrence of a specified triggering event such as divorce, annulment, separation, or death of one spouse, a spouse may acquire a right to an interest in the property of the other spouse generally evidenced by what is referred to as an "equalization payment".

When structuring their affairs, business owners should consider the potential impact of family law on their business in the event of marriage breakdown. Not only does the possibility of marriage breakdown become a factor, but, since several provinces have extended the availability of equalization rights to the death of a spouse in priority to will provisions, family law can also affect estate plans and other business succession arrangements. Business assets receive different treatment in the various provinces, ranging from specific exclusion from division, to availability for sharing at the discretion of the courts, to mandatory equal division. Further, family legislation varies by jurisdiction as to what events trigger rights of property division, the relevant valuation date, and the basis of valuation. In Quebec, property rights are determined pursuant to the Civil Code. The Civil Code provides for full community of property. That is, all property acquired during a marriage is deemed to be held jointly by both spouses. Each province specifies various assets excluded from division.

A province-by-province comparison of the legislative treatment of various key family law matters is provided in Exhibit 10A. This exhibit is provided for reference only; legal advice should be sought for any fact-specific situation.

Exhibit 10A
Overview of Property Rights for Family Law Purposes

Legislation	Alberta	British Columbia	Manitoba	New Brunswick	Nfld.	Nova Scotia	Ontario	P.E.I.	Quebec	Sask.
Property Rights Triggered by										
Separation	Yes	Yes	No	Yes	Yes	Yes	Yes	Yes	Yes	No
Divorce	Yes	Yes	No	Yes	Yes	Yes	Yes	Yes	Yes	No
Dissipation of Property	Yes	No	No	No	No	No	Yes	No	No	No
Nullity	No	Yes	No	Yes	Yes	Yes	Yes	Yes	Yes	No
Death of spouse	Yes	No	No	No	Yes	Yes	Yes	No	Yes	Yes
Upon Application	No	No	Yes	No	No	No	No	No	No	Yes
Value Basis	Not Stated	Not Stated	Fair Market Value	Not Stated	Not Stated	Not Stated	Value	Not Stated	Not Stated	Fair Market Value
Valuation Date	Not Stated	Not Stated	Date of Last Cohabitation	Not Stated	Not Stated	Not Stated	Earliest of Triggering Events	Not Stated	Earliest of Triggering Events	Date of Application or Adjudication
Property Specifically Exempted										
Business assets	No	Yes	No	Yes	Yes	Yes	No	Yes	No	No
Pre-marriage assets	Yes	No	Yes	No	No	No	Yes*	No	No	Yes
Post-separation assets	No	No	Yes	No	Yes	Yes	Yes	No	Yes	Yes
Gifts and inheritances	No	Yes	Yes	Yes	Yes	Yes	Yes*	Yes	No	Yes
Gifts made by spouse	Yes	No	No	Yes	No	No	No	No	No	No
Personal injury awards	Yes	Yes	Yes	No	Yes	No	Yes	Yes	No	Yes
Insurance proceeds	Yes	Yes	Yes	No	No	No	Yes	Yes	No	Yes
Property traceable from exempt property	Yes	No	No	No	No	No	Yes	No	No	No
Family heirlooms	No	No	No	No	Yes	No	Yes	No	No	No
Personal effects	No	No	No	No	Yes	Yes	No	No	No	No

*except matrimonial home

In the context of matrimonial disputes, the business assets at issue are usually transacted between the separating spouses in a notional market context (i.e., they are seldom sold in the open market). As a result, notwithstanding the lack of uniformity in provincial matrimonial property legislation, certain issues regularly surface to complicate the process of dividing property on marriage breakdown.

The Definition of Value

Most provincial legislation does not specifically define value. Presumably this follows from the general intent to provide in law for the orderly and perceived equitable settlement of the affairs of the spouses. Where value is not specifically defined, an assessment must be made as to what value term (fair market value, fair value, value to owner, etc.) is appropriate in each fact-specific circumstance.

Of particular importance in those jurisdictions which do not define the term "value" is the concept of whether personal goodwill should form part of the definition of value. Recall from the discussion above (and in Chapter 1) that personal goodwill is not paid for in an open market context, and therefore does not form part of fair market value. However, one spouse may be able to generate considerable business income as a result of his or her personal knowledge, abilities, reputation and business contacts. As a result, the business may be worth much more to the spouse who is active in the business (i.e., "value to owner") than would be generated if the business were sold in an arm's length transaction.

Where value is required for transactions under family law, the following factors may be significant to its determination:

- "value to owner" usually has no commercial value nor does it form a component of fair market value in family law matters;

- in those jurisdictions where fair market value is not specifically prescribed as the basis of valuation, there may be opportunity to consider alternate value concepts in the interest of achieving an equitable outcome;

- if a court believes an equalization payment based on agreed or adjudicated asset values does not result in an equitable final settlement between spouses, it may make adjustments it deems appropriate by dictating ongoing spousal support payments;

- unless the sale of a business seems imminent, buyers who perceive post-acquisition synergies are likely to materialize and the quantum of premium inherent in the prices such buyers might pay can be estimated with reasonable certainty, intrinsic value tends to be taken as the basis by which value is determined;

- consideration should be given to whether a notional transaction would be consummated by way of financial resources internal or external to the business being valued (see "Internal vs. External Financing", below); and

- where spouses together own all the outstanding shares of a corporation, or where spouses together control a corporation, their respective ownership interests should be dealt with on a ratable (i.e., non-discounted) basis for equalization purposes, provided that equal liquidity is ensured to both spouses in the context of the final asset equalization agreement.

Valuation Date

Some provinces specify the relevant date(s) value must be determined (in some instances even specifying the appropriate time of day) while others are silent. Several provinces have extended the availability of division or equalization rights upon the death of a spouse, in which case the death of a spouse is considered to be a triggering event for purposes of dividing marital assets.

Equalization payments are based on the increase in wealth generated during the term of the marriage. Therefore, an issue that sometimes arises pertains to the value of the business at the date of marriage, which may now be in the distant past. As in the discussion regarding taxation above, in many cases the individuals involved in the business are no longer accessible (or their recollections may be vague) and certain information may no longer be available. This complicates the valuation engagement.

Minority Discounts

Where spouses collectively control a corporation and have a continuing marriage, it is logical to expect they will share a common pool of wealth and income and act in their mutual best interest. As a result, so long as a marriage is intact, when valuing minority interests held by spouses that collectively comprise either all the outstanding shares or a control shareholding, as a practical matter, a discount from a ratable portion of *en bloc* value is seldom applied.

Upon the breakdown of marriage, the shareholding relationship all too often changes to a less cordial one. Should one spouse retain a minority interest after the equalization, as a continuing minority shareholder they would have available the protection of the appraisal and oppression remedies of the applicable corporations statute. Nevertheless, assuming the overall objective of family law is to achieve an equitable distribution of assets, the acquisition of the minority interest by the majority, or a separation of equity interests as a result of a corporate reorganization, should be a priority in settlement.

Financing the Equalization Payment or Spousal Buyout

When addressing value in a matrimonial context as in shareholder disputes, a determination must be made as to how the payment (whether an equalization payment, a buyout, or a combination of the two) is to be financed. The specific issue that must be addressed is whether:

- the required funds are available external to any operating business assets; or
- it will be necessary to look to operating business assets within the familial asset pool for all or part of the required funds.

In many family situations, shareholding interests in a privately held company may represent the only asset of any significance other than the matrimonial home. As a result, where the spouses own all the outstanding shares or a control shareholding, equalization payments often must be, and are, funded through those businesses. As discussed under the section "Internal vs. External Financing" below, where the spouse acquiring the business must rely on the cash flow generated from the business to finance the buyout, it can result in the business having to forgo other required expenditures, and hence diminish the value of the business. Alternatively, excessive borrowing to fund the buyout can lead to banking covenants that impair the growth potential or economic stability of the business.

Where the equalization payment amount is based on stand-alone value and is financed directly or indirectly by the business, undue financial hardship may be placed on the business. This eventually could force a sale of the business or cause its insolvency, which in turn would affect the:

- spouse whose shares were re-organized or sold in circumstances where the equalization payment was not fully paid;
- spouse who continued as a shareholder; and
- all other non-spouse shareholders of the business.

In the end, financing the equalization payment from the business might threaten the jobs of employees and expose suppliers and other stakeholders to losses.

As a result, in order to achieve equity in a family dispute, it may be necessary to look to all of the assets comprising each spouse's net family property and determine the extent to which internal financing of the equalization payment might be required. This analysis should then consider whether *en bloc* value should be established on a stand-alone basis, under an assumption of internal financing, or on some other assumption.

Extended and favourable equalization payment terms may aid in reducing hardship where intrinsic value is used as the basis of determining *en bloc* value. Where the price that could be obtained pursuant to an open market transaction is taken as value, it may be that an arm's length sale of the shares owned by the spouse(s) is the only means of effecting the equalization payment without unduly impairing the underlying and future value of the business. As a forced sale is undesirable from the standpoint of equitable treatment and otherwise, extended and favourable payment terms may provide the only means of avoiding this.

Income Taxes and Disposition Costs

Most provincial legislation is silent with respect to the treatment of tax costs and other expenses that should be accounted for where specific assets notionally are disposed of pursuant to equalization determination. This then becomes an extension of the question regarding the appropriate definition of value. Where equity interests are sold, typically disposition costs as well as underlying tax liabilities are incurred. The magnitude of underlying contingent disposition costs and, in particular, income tax liabilities can be significant in the case of business assets. Where income tax treatment is not legislatively specified, in family law matters Canadian courts have accepted taxes on notional disposition as either:

- full disposal and income tax costs;
- no disposal or income tax costs; or
- some discounted amount representing the deferral and/or uncertainty associated with the existing contingent disposal costs and income tax liabilities.

When determining the treatment and quantum of income taxes and disposition costs on notional disposition in family law matters, at least the following factors should be considered:

- the appropriate assumption(s) as to business continuity following the equalization payment, including consideration of the plans for the business vis-à-vis expansion, diversification, succession planning, and other initiatives;

- the basis on which value was determined and the likely timing of sale. Where, based on current market conditions, a premium that a special-interest purchaser might pay has been incorporated in the value conclusion, the likely only means of extracting that additional value may be as the result of a near-term sale;

- the age, health and personal interests of the majority shareholder(s);

- income tax planning opportunities known or likely to exist; and

- where the business requires additional capital, the ability of the owner(s) to provide same from personal resources.

Finally, no guidance is provided in provincial family law legislation as to the appropriate treatment of personal guarantees (e.g., bank guarantees and lease guarantees) that are often inherent in business ownership.

Value Impairment

Notional market valuations are sometimes conducted for the purpose of determining the impairment in the value of a business or an intangible asset pursuant to litigation. Examples include the loss of value due to:

- business interruption (e.g., a natural catastrophe, riot, or other event, that may lead to an insurance claim);

- patent infringement; and

- the termination of a distribution agreement, supply contract, franchise agreement or other contractual right.

A value impairment claim involves comparing the estimated value of the business under the prevailing circumstances, compared to the estimated value of the business assuming no impairment in value. Essential to the derivation of a meaningful loss of value conclusion are the assumptions of how the business would have performed absent the alleged action(s) giving rise to the claim. The impact of mitigation may also need to be taken into account.

Another issue is taxation, and whether an award for financial loss would be taxable to the recipient and/or tax deductible to the payer. Where taxable to the recipient, the amount of loss should be grossed-up so that the injured party is put in the same financial position they would have enjoyed had there been no loss.

The determination of liability is a legal issue. The valuator's role is to assist the court in quantifying the losses, assuming liability does exist. As with other valuations involving litigation, there is a bias as to the impact the alleged activity had on the business or the asset. The determination of a loss in value is usually expressed in an expert report as opposed to a valuation report. As noted above, while there are substantial commonalities between the two types of reports, the prevailing standards on expert reports as published by the CICBV should be consulted to ensure that they are adhered to.

Employee Share Ownership Plans

Some privately held companies have introduced (or are considering) an employee share ownership plan (ESOP) as a means of attracting, retaining and motivating their employees. ESOPs can also be a means of raising equity capital among existing employees, but this tends to be a secondary objective since the amounts invested are usually relatively small.

In essence, an ESOP is an arrangement whereby certain employees of a company can become shareholders if they meet the specified criteria. Qualifying employees are either granted shares or an option to buy shares in the company at a specified price. The acquired shares are usually held until the employee leaves the company or a liquidity event occurs, such as a sale of the company to a strategic buyer or an initial public offering.

There is a considerable amount of flexibility in how an ESOP is designed in terms of criteria for participation, the size of the ESOP pool, and whether the ESOP will take the form of shares or options that can be exercised for shares. A related question is whether shares will be gifted to employees or employees must acquire them at their prevailing fair market value.

In some cases, the shares issued under an ESOP have different rights and privileges from those held by existing shareholders. For example, ESOP shares may be non-voting or have limited voting rights.

Finally, the provisions and restrictions governing the liquidity of the ESOP shares must be clearly established. In most cases, the shares cannot be freely traded, and employees must wait for a "liquidity event" in order to receive the value of their shares. Where the liquidity event involves a sale of the company to a strategic buyer or an initial public offering, then payment for the ESOP shares is a non-issue, since external financing is available. However, liquidity events are more problematic when the company must finance the purchase of its own ESOP shares such as when an employee resigns or is terminated (most privately held companies do not want former employees holding shares). In this regard, many ESOPs are designed such that, in the event of a voluntary departure from the company, the redemption price is subject to a minority discount and/or deferred payment terms. This serves as a type of penalty to an employee who leaves the company and wants to cash out.

Valuation and Related Issues

The rules governing the valuation of ESOP shares should be clearly established in a properly structured shareholder agreement. In this regard, it is important to consider the following aspects:

- whether *en bloc* value should be calculated on an intrinsic basis. While this is the usual case, there may be some circumstances where the premium that might be available upon the sale of the company or initial public offering should be considered, particularly if a liquidity event is anticipated in the near term;

- whether, and to what extent, a minority discount should be applied. ESOP shares are often non-voting. Furthermore, an individual holder of ESOP shares does not have a sufficient ownership interest in the company to meaningfully influence decision making at the board level. Where the quantum of a minority discount is pre-established in the shareholder agreement, it can help in avoiding disputes over valuation. Furthermore, it can serve as a disincentive for employees to leave prior to the occurrence of a liquidity event. However, a fixed minority discount may not reflect the pertinent facts at a point in time;

- provisions relating to restrictions on the transfer of the ESOP shares. In particular, it should be clear whether the ESOP shares can be acquired by other eligible employees, or whether they need to be redeemed by the company;

- the frequency of conducting a valuation that will establish the price of the ESOP shares. In this regard, there is a trade-off between the cost of conducting an annual valuation, and the risk the business or industry may have significantly changed since the date of the last valuation, thereby causing the prior valuation to be unduly overstated or understated; and

- the terms of payment for an ESOP shareholder who chooses to (or is required to) dispose of their interest. In this regard, the terms of payment sometimes differ, depending on the reason for the sale. For example, payment in full may be applicable in the event of the death of an ESOP shareholder, whereas deferred payment terms may be applicable where an ESOP shareholder voluntarily leaves, as a form of disincentive and to not overly burden the company.

Management Buyouts

Formal valuation reports are sometimes prepared in connection with a contemplated management buyout (MBO), whereby members of a company's existing management team look to acquire the business from its existing shareholders. Where the MBO involves a mid-sized or larger business, it is common for the management team to align with one or more financial investors (e.g., banks and private equity firms) that help to facilitate the transaction. Where that is the case, the price and terms ultimately paid in the MBO transaction will be subject to the views of the financial investors involved and the structure of the deal. Furthermore, in some cases, a portion of the financing raised is invested into the business to help generate incremental growth. Where this is the case, the value implications of primary offerings vs. secondary offerings need to be considered (see Chapter 1).

An MBO can represent an attractive exit strategy alternative for business owners, as well as for larger privately held companies or public companies looking to spin off a segment of their business. However, they can be fraught with challenges. Most notably:

- management will have a bias to reducing the value of the business. Directors may require a fairness opinion in order to discharge their fiduciary duties;

- where a private equity firm becomes involved, and/or where the existing shareholders retain a residual interest, the terms of a shareholder agreement become paramount (see Chapter 8);

- the management team usually has limited financial resources of their own. Therefore, where adequate external financing cannot be secured (which is sometimes the case for smaller MBO transactions), the price management can afford to pay is often based on the cash flow generating ability of the business following the transaction. This has a downward influence on price and/or a negative impact on the terms of sale (see "Internal vs. External Financing" later in this chapter); and

- MBOs are often effected with greater amounts of financial leverage than would normally be used to fund the operations of the business. Therefore, consideration must be given to the ability of the business to service its debt as well as its banking covenants that might unduly limit management's flexibility.

Management Purposes

Valuations are sometimes commissioned by the owners or management group in order to gauge a company's current value for internal planning purposes. This may be for the sake of benchmarking, performance measurement or to identify opportunities for enhancing shareholder value. As such, the valuation report may incorporate additional analysis comparing the business with public companies or industry statistics believed to be meaningful. In some cases, management compensation is based in part on the change in value. Therefore, the valuator must be aware of any real or perceived bias.

Where the valuation is for estimating the price the business might sell for in the open market, it may be appropriate to consider special-interest purchasers. This is normally done by identifying and analyzing comparable transactions. However, the valuation report should include a caveat as to the risk of realizing a premium, and that the terms of the transaction may be substantially different from the "cash on closing" outcome contemplated in the definition of fair market value.

A valuation for management purposes may also identify areas for potential value enhancement, or help in the business planning process. This is particularly the case where a detailed long-term forecast is prepared that forces management to consider key assumptions and business strategies.

Internal vs. External Financing

In a notional market context, the means by which a transaction is financed should not have an impact on its value, given the principle that the value of a business is independent of how it is financed. However, in an open market transaction, the price that a buyer is willing or able to pay is dependent on the funding sources available to the buyer. Depending on the reason why a value determination is necessary, one important aspect of this financing issue has to do with whether the buyer has access to funds external to the business being acquired in order to complete the transaction, or whether they must utilize what would otherwise be all or a portion of the post-acquisition cash flow to pay for it.

A transaction where the buyer does not require any part of the purchase price to be funded from the post-acquisition cash flow is referred to as an "externally financed" transaction. Conversely, a transaction where the buyer requires all or part of the purchase price to be funded from the post-acquisition cash flow is referred to as an "internally financed" transaction.

In an internally financed transaction the purchase price may be funded by:

- incremental funds borrowed at arm's length by the acquired business at or following closing; or
- post-acquisition cash flows of the acquired business that are paid to the seller over an agreed period of time.

The distinction between internally and externally financed transactions normally arises where:

- privately held businesses are sold to employees in a management buyout;
- privately held company shareholdings are bought and sold among existing shareholders for reasons such as termination, retirement, disability or death. The terms and valuation guidelines for such transactions are normally set out in a shareholder agreement. In the case of death, insurance funding is often used to avoid the necessity of utilizing the post-acquisition cash flow to acquire the deceased's equity interest. Insurance will also keep the new owners from having to sell the business because funding the purchase from internally generated cash flow has created too much financial risk for the company;
- the value of a privately held business interest must be determined while the parties are in dispute. An open market sale will not likely occur, but the value determination will influence the quantum and terms of any financial arrangement between the parties. Examples arise in litigation, including the quantification of payments to equalize the value of net assets accumulated by separating spouses as

required by family law, and in shareholder disputes (including minority shareholder appraisal and oppression remedy actions); and

- in open market transactions involving a high utilization of debt, such as leveraged buyouts.

In transactions among shareholders, fairness may be viewed as a notional value or transaction price according to which no individual stakeholder is better or worse off relative to the intrinsic value of the ownership interest of each before and after such transaction. For example, assume the intrinsic value of S1 Limited is $2 million and that there are four equal shareholders. It follows that the pro-rata value of each shareholder's interest is $500,000. Further assume that one of the four shareholders retires and the remaining three shareholders agree to purchase the one-quarter interest held by the retiring shareholder at its ratable value. If this transaction was to be financed internally, this might be accomplished by:

- S1 borrowing $500,000 and paying it to the departing shareholder;

- paying the departing shareholder over time (at commercial rates of interest) from what otherwise would be the discretionary cash flows of S1; or

- paying the departing shareholder a sum of $500,000 from redundant cash or cash equivalents held by S1.

In each case, in theory, the *en bloc* value of S1's equity would decline from $2 million to $1.5 million. However, the remaining shareholders would now have a one-third interest with a ratable value of $500,000. Accordingly, the value of each of their economic interests has not changed relative to the intrinsic value of S1's equity. As a result, fairness, defined in terms of pro-rata value, is preserved. However, in practice this does not always result.

In the case of a going concern, the value of a business is largely a function of prospective discretionary cash flows that accrue to it and the risk attached to those discretionary cash flows. Accordingly, an internally financed transaction based on intrinsic value may be less for any particular shareholding than the intrinsic value determined based on an assumption of an externally financed transaction since, in order to finance the payout required pursuant to an internally financed transaction, the business may have to:

- forgo necessary expenditures to maintain its operations at present levels;

- forgo anticipated growth opportunities; or

- obtain incremental financing and thereby be subject to bank covenants that may restrict the operation of the business in a manner that impairs its value.

As a result, internal financing may cause the post-acquisition *en bloc* intrinsic value of the business to decline by more than the pre-acquisition ratable intrinsic value of the equity interest being acquired. In such circumstances the post-acquisition pro-rata equity interest held by each remaining shareholder declines. Further, as a practical matter in an open market transaction, the fact that internal funds are required to finance an acquisition often enters into negotiations and places downward pressure on the departing shareholder with respect to price.

To the extent that buyers perceiving synergies would push an open market sale price above *en bloc* intrinsic value, the remaining shareholders following an internally financed transaction could benefit from what would be their comparative equity interest in any incremental open market price over intrinsic value. This may somewhat offset the risk associated with the remaining shareholders assuming additional risk associated with the internally financed transaction. Such perceived inequity is sometimes addressed by allowing the departing shareholder to participate in any premium paid over intrinsic value, if the company is sold to a third party within an agreed-upon period of time (e.g., pursuant to a "participation in a subsequent sale" provision of a shareholder agreement).

Purchase Price Allocation

Following an open market transaction, for Generally Accepted Accounting Principles (GAAP) and International Financial Reporting Standards (IFRSs), a buyer is required to allocate the purchase price among the assets acquired. In this regard, there are three broad categories of assets: (i) tangible assets; (ii) identifiable intangible assets; and (iii) non-identifiable intangible assets.

The allocation of a portion of the purchase price to tangible assets and financial liabilities is generally based on:

- their net book value, for current assets and liabilities;
- depreciated replacement cost for equipment;
- market value for real property assets; and
- the present value of future obligations for long-term liabilities.

The approach to the valuation of tangible assets and financial liabilities was discussed in Chapter 3, during the derivation of adjusted net book value. The amount by which the purchase price exceeds adjusted net book value represents total intangible value, which is divided into identifiable intangible assets and non-identifiable intangible assets.

Purchase price allocation is a zero-sum game. Consequently, it is important for the valuator, working in conjunction with company management and the company's auditor, to identify all the tangible and intangible assets and allocate reasonable value among them.

Where the transaction was concluded following an acquisition of assets, the buyer and seller need to agree on the allocation of the purchase price for income tax purposes. This can provide important insight into purchase price allocation for accounting purposes. However, there may be circumstances where the price allocation for income tax purposes is different than for financial reporting purposes. This is particularly the case for goodwill. For income tax purposes, the buyer and seller will agree on the amount allocated to goodwill, which the buyer recognizes as eligible capital property and is entitled to claim a cumulative eligible capital deduction on 75% of it at a rate of 7% per annum on a declining-balance basis (see Chapter 11). However, for accounting purposes, that goodwill may need to be separated into identifiable intangible assets (such as brand names, customer lists, and other qualifying intangibles), which categorization is irrelevant from an income tax perspective.

The following discussion summarizes the purchase price accounting standards prevailing at the time of writing (2012) under GAAP and IFRSs. This summary is not meant to be a substitute for these standards. Furthermore, given that accounting standards evolve over time, the applicable standards at any valuation date should be carefully reviewed.

Generally Accepted Accounting Principles

Section 1582 "Business Combinations" of the *CICA Handbook - Accounting* addresses the issue of purchase price allocation. As noted above, the purchase price must be allocated among tangible assets, identifiable intangible assets and non-identifiable intangible assets (i.e., goodwill).

According to section 1582, an intangible asset is defined as an identifiable non-monetary asset without physical substance. The section further defines an asset as identifiable if it either:

- is separable (i.e., capable of being separated or divided from the entity and sold, transferred, licensed, rented or exchanged, either individually or together with a related contract, identifiable asset or liability, regardless of whether the entity intends to do so); or

- arises from contractual or legal rights, regardless of whether those rights are transferable or separable from the entity or from other rights and obligations.

The identification of intangible assets is fact-specific to each business acquisition. Section 1582 specifies that certain intangibles such as an assembled workforce or potential contracts, do not meet the criteria of being an identifiable intangible asset. Therefore, the value of such intangible assets is subsumed into goodwill.

Once identified, the fair value of the intangible assets (and assumed liabilities) needs to be established. Section 3064 "Goodwill and Intangible Assets" provides some guidance in this regard by defining fair value as the amount of the consideration that would be agreed upon in an arm's length transaction between knowledgeable, willing parties who are under no obligation to transact.

An intangible asset is recognized if:

- it is probable that the expected future economic benefits attributable to the asset will flow to the entity; and

- the cost of the asset can be measured reliably.

The three basic approaches that can be applied to determine the fair value of an identifiable intangible asset or an assumed liability are the:

- income method, such as a capitalized cash flow or discounted cash flow methodology. In this regard, the cash flows applicable to the intangible asset to be capitalized or discounted may be based on the:

    ✓ royalties that would be applicable to the intangible asset (i.e., the relief from royalty approach set out in Chapter 9), or

    ✓ earnings (or cash flow) generated from the use of the intangible, in excess of a reasonable return on the underlying net tangible asset (similar to the excess earnings approach or the incremental cash flow approach, as set out in Chapter 9);

- market method, based on a comparison to similar intangible assets acquired in recent years. In most cases, the application of the market method is problematic because of the limited number of cases where sufficient information regarding the price paid for a similar intangible asset has been disclosed, the unique terms of each transaction, and other factors as set out in Chapter 4; and

- cost method, where the cost that would be incurred to replace or replicate the intangible can be reasonably estimated (e.g., software). However, the cost approach may be misleading because it does not address the future cash flows that can be generated from the use of the intangible asset.

Intangible assets are amortized over their estimated economic lives. The estimate of the useful life of an intangible asset should be based on analysis of pertinent factors and can be subjective, particularly for assets such as brand names and customer lists that do not have a legally defined term. Intangible assets considered to have indefinite lives are not subject to amortization. Goodwill is not amortized under GAAP, but rather is subject to a periodic (normally annual) impairment review.

International Financial Reporting Standards

Purchase price allocation under IFRSs is covered by IFRS 3. IFRSs broaden the GAAP definition of intangible assets. IFRSs provide examples of items that meet the definition of an intangible asset where acquired in a business acquisition. These intangible assets are recognized separately from goodwill where their fair values can be measured in a reliable manner.

To meet the definition of an intangible, a non-monetary asset without physical substance must be identifiable (i.e., it must arise from contractual or other legal rights, or be separable from the business). An intangible is separable if it is capable of being separated or divided from the entity and sold, transferred, licensed, rented or exchanged, either individually or together with a related contract, identifiable asset or liability, regardless of whether the entity intends to do so. An acquired intangible meets the separability criterion if there is evidence of exchange transactions for that type of asset or an asset of a similar type, even if those transactions are infrequent and regardless of whether the acquirer is involved in them. An intangible asset that is not individually separable from the acquirer or combined entity meets the separability criterion if it is separable in combination with a related contract, identifiable asset or liability.

An intangible that arises from contractual or other legal rights is identifiable regardless of whether those rights are transferable or separable from the acquirer or from other rights and obligations.

IFRS 3 identifies five categories of intangible assets:

- marketing-related intangible assets, which are used primarily in the marketing or promotion of products or services. Examples of marketing-related intangibles are trademarks, trade dress (e.g., unique colour, shape or package design), Internet domain names and non-competition agreements;

- customer-related intangible assets, such as customer lists, order backlogs, customer contracts and non-contractual customer relationships;

- artistic-related intangible assets, such as plays, books, magazines, musical works, photographs and movies. In many cases, these intangibles are protected by copyright;

- contract-based intangible assets, which represent the value of rights that arise from contractual arrangements. Examples of contract-based intangible assets include licensing, royalty and standstill agreements, advertising, construction, management, service or supply contracts, lease agreements (where the acquiree is the lessee or the lessor), construction permits, franchise agreements and employment contracts). If the terms of a contract give rise to a liability, (e.g., a lease with terms that are less favourable than market), then the acquirer recognizes it as a liability assumed in the business combination; and

- technology-related intangible assets, such as patented technology, computer software, unpatented technology, databases and trade secrets.

The identification of intangible assets is fact-specific to each business acquisition. Once identified, the value of the intangible assets needs to be established. While IFRS 3 does not provide extensive guidance on valuation, the three basic valuation approaches discussed above would apply (i.e., the income approach, market approach and cost approach).

Intangible assets are amortized over their estimated economic lives. Those intangible assets that are considered to have indefinite lives are not subject to amortization. Goodwill is not amortized under IFRSs, but rather is subject to an annual impairment review. It is also noteworthy that IFRS 3 permits the revaluation of intangible assets that have an active market.

Fairness Opinions

Where a company is contemplating a major transaction, such as a takeover bid, going-private transaction, or significant related-party transaction, its board of directors may seek to obtain a fairness opinion from an independent financial expert or firm, such as a Chartered Business Valuator or an investment banker. A fairness opinion can assist the board of directors in discharging its fiduciary or other duties to the company. While fairness opinions traditionally have been commissioned in the context of transactions involving public companies, they are increasingly being used in privately held companies, crown corporations and large not-for-profit organizations.

A fairness opinion is a letter report from a financial advisor that provides an opinion on the fairness from a financial point of view of a proposed transaction, from the perspective of the shareholders of the company or a set of shareholders (e.g., those that are not insiders). Fairness from a financial point of view is not formally defined, but is usually taken to mean the shareholders (or subset thereof) will be in an economic position following the transaction equal to or better than their economic position prior to the transaction. Therefore, a fairness opinion requires that a comparison be made of the consideration given up and the consideration received in a proposed transaction. This is not an assurance that the shareholders are receiving the best value for their equity interests, but rather that the value being received is at least equal to, or greater than, the value given up.

Fairness opinions typically are in the form of a fairly short letter (generally a few pages). As noted earlier in this chapter, the CICBV has issued standards with respect to fairness opinions, which should be consulted where applicable. Standards with respect to fairness opinions are also issued by the Investment Industry Regulatory Organization of Canada (IIROC). In both cases, the standards require the opinion provider to disclose the reasons or basis for their conclusions. A fairness opinion does not contain a conclusion as to the value of the shares of the company. However, a formal valuation is often prepared in connection with a fairness opinion, in order to support the conclusions as to fairness. In addition, a formal valuation is sometimes required under securities legislation for issuer bids, insider bids, business combinations and related party transactions.

In most cases, the board of directors strikes a special committee to interact with the financial expert providing the fairness opinion. Both the special committee and the board should satisfy themselves that the expert has discharged their responsibilities in a professional and independent manner and that their conclusion makes sense in light of all the relevant facts. In this regard, the board and the special committee must carefully consider the qualifications and independence of the financial expert. In some cases, the investment banker who negotiated the transaction is engaged to provide the fairness opinion. This can be problematic, as it can lead to a question of independence, both in fact and in appearance, given that the investment banker typically stands to earn a significant contingency fee if the proposed transaction proceeds. The courts have also questioned the independence of advisors preparing a fairness opinion where they have an interest in the proposed transaction.

Consideration Given Up

In most cases, the consideration given up consists of shares of either a privately held company or public company. Factors that should normally be considered include the following:

- the current stock price, historical prices and volatility, where the subject business is a public company. In this regard, where the company's shares are thinly traded, consideration should be given to whether or not the prevailing and historical trading prices reflect fair market value;

- net book value, adjusted net book value and tangible net worth;

- fair market value, based on a discounted cash flow methodology, capitalized cash flow methodology, multiple of EBITDA or other valuation methodology. In the context of determining fair market value, the financial expert will have access to non-public information, including budgets and projections, detailed records and in-depth management discussions. The non-public information may provide a basis for concluding that the prevailing stock price does not reflect fair market value;

- industry transactions, where meaningful comparators can be identified and relevant information disclosed;

- valuation multiples of meaningfully comparable public companies; and

- other offers received for the shares or assets of the subject company, including their terms.

In the case of a privately held company, a valuation is normally required in order to assess the fair market value of the business or the equity interest in question.

Consideration Received

Where the seller is a public company, securities legislation may limit the form of consideration to cash, freely traded securities of the buyer or a combination thereof. Hence, the only issue is whether the fair market value of the freely traded shares of the buyer are equivalent to their face value. A difference can sometimes arise where the shares of the buyer are thinly traded. However, a significantly broader range of forms of consideration can be involved where the seller is a privately held company.

Where the consideration received is in a form other than cash at closing, it is necessary to determine the fair market value of that non-cash consideration. For example, where:

- shares of the buyer are received, an assessment must be made as to whether those shares have a fair market value equal to their face value. This may not be the case where the market capitalization of the buyer is relatively small (e.g., a small-cap public company) and/or its shares are thinly traded. Furthermore, where the shares received as consideration are subject to restrictions on trading for a period of time, the financial expert must consider whether a discount should be applied for illiquidity, given the risk of adverse developments during the restriction period;

- promissory notes are received, an assessment must be made of the time value of money as well as the likelihood of collection, given the terms and conditions of the note, the amount and quality of security, and the buyer's covenant; and

- a portion of the consideration will be received in the form of an earnout or similar arrangement, an assessment must be made of the likelihood the performance target(s) will be achieved, as well as the time value of money and the likelihood of collection, given the security provided over earnout payments (if any) and the covenant of the buyer. An example of the valuation of an earnout was provided in Chapter 4.

Synergy Considerations

In most open market transactions where the buyer is an operating company (and sometimes in the case of a financial buyer with similar operating companies in its portfolio), the buyer anticipates that it will realize synergies as a result of the transaction. While in many notional market valuations, fair market value is determined exclusive of synergies (unless they can be meaningfully quantified and likely will be paid for) such is not the case for fairness opinions. This is because the buyer, price and terms of the proposed transaction are known. Therefore, in the determination of fair market value, and in the assessment of fairness, the financial expert should normally take synergies into account. Consideration should be afforded to the:

- nature of the synergies expected (e.g., cost reductions, incremental revenues, lower cost of capital, operating risk reduction, tax loss utilization, and other post-transaction benefits);

- timing of synergy realization;

- costs involved to realize the synergies (e.g., severance, moving costs, and other expenses); and

- likelihood that the synergies will be realized.

Synergies are discussed in more depth as part of open market transactions in Chapter 11.

Other Considerations

When considering whether or not the proposed transaction is fair from a financial point of view, the financial expert should normally consider other factors as well, both quantitative and qualitative. These might include:

- the divestiture process. Where the seller's intermediary conducted an active search for buyers, then any other offers received can be assessed to determine whether or not the selected proposal is fair. In addition, a formal divestiture process may provide some level of comfort that all (or most) of the qualified buyers have been solicited;

- offers or expressions of interest received in previous years. Such offers should be assessed in the context of the business, industry and economic conditions prevailing at those dates; and

- the level of market activity. An active market for transactions in the industry where the subject business operates might suggest a greater level of liquidity, and therefore generally higher valuations for all companies in that industry than might otherwise be the case.

Common Issues with Notional Market Valuations

Some of the more common issues that arise in the preparation of a formal valuation report include the following:

- the type of report prepared (comprehensive, estimate or calculation) does not suffice for the purpose for which it was intended. In particular, litigation (e.g., shareholder disputes) and valuations that may lead to a transaction involving a large monetary amount (e.g., following a buyout among existing shareholders) normally require the rigour found only in a comprehensive valuation report;

- when preparing a comprehensive valuation report or an estimate valuation report, it is important that the valuator obtain an understanding of all the material facts that might influence the value conclusion. In this regard, valuators sometimes fail to speak with key individuals who have an understanding of the business's operations. In the context of a shareholder dispute, shareholder transaction or other activity involving parties with opposing interests in the value conclusion, it is usually appropriate for the valuator to solicit input from both sides and to assess it objectively;

- clients and users of valuation reports sometimes impose constraints on the valuator with respect to cost and time for report preparation. Such constraints should not compromise the work of the valuator nor compliance with applicable standards. Where such constraints limit the scope of work conducted, that fact should be disclosed in the valuation report. In circumstances where limitations are imposed that severely restrict the scope of work, they may force the valuator to decline the engagement;

- valuations prepared in a notional market context are subjective, and subject to various assumptions. In some cases, the assumptions are not internally consistent and/or they do not reflect current market conditions. A credible valuation conclusion requires internally consistent assumptions that are plausible in light of prevailing industry, economic and business conditions; and

- valuation conclusions are sometimes skewed by hindsight. As noted in Chapter 1, hindsight is inadmissible in a notional market context, except in limited circumstances for the purpose of testing the plausibility of assumptions made at the valuation date. Accordingly, valuators must be careful only to rely on the specific facts, assumptions and market conditions existing at the valuation date.

Summary

Notional market valuations are inherently subjective. The derivation of a reasonable valuation conclusion requires an objective consideration of the relevant material facts existing at the valuation date, including those relating to the business itself, the industry in which the business operates and current and prospective economic conditions.

The Canadian Institute of Chartered Business Valuators (CICBV) establishes standards for valuation reports, in terms of the various types of reports (comprehensive, estimate and calculation), applicable disclosure requirements, scope of work and documentation. The appropriate type of report depends on the level of assurance warranted, given the nature of the engagement and other fact-specific circumstances.

Formal valuation reports are required in a variety of different situations, including transactions among existing shareholders, shareholder disputes, income tax matters, matrimonial disputes, employee share ownership plans, management buyouts and for other purposes.

Purchase price allocations rules require the aggregate purchase price be allocated among net tangible assets, identifiable intangible assets and non-identifiable intangibles (or goodwill). Purchase price allocation rules are governed by Generally Accepted Accounting Principles and International Financial Reporting Standards.

Fairness opinions occur in the context of a proposed transaction and are subject to the standards established by the CICBV and the Investment Industry Regulatory Organization of Canada. Fairness opinions require the financial expert to determine whether the proposed transaction is fair from a financial point of view from the standpoint of certain shareholders (or all shareholders) or another group. A fairness opinion may be accompanied by a formal valuation where applicable. The assessment of fairness becomes more complex where the consideration received is in a form other than cash such as shares of the buyer that cannot readily be sold in the open market, promissory notes, earnout arrangements and so on. Fairness from a financial point of view should also take into account other pertinent factors, such as the synergies expected from the transaction, the divestiture process, and other relevant considerations.

Chapter 11

Open Market Transactions

Introduction

There can be, and often is a significant difference between fair market value determined in a notional market context and the price paid for a business, as negotiated in an open market transaction. There are many reasons for this, including the buyer's perception of post-acquisition synergies, expected integration costs, the structure of the deal, the buyer's ability to finance the transaction, and the differing negotiating positions of the buyer and seller.

In most open market transactions where the buyer is a corporation, the buyer anticipates that the value of an acquisition, defined in terms of the present value of its discretionary cash flows, extends beyond the intrinsic value of the target company. Fact-specific benefits accruing to each potential buyer beyond intrinsic value might include anticipated incremental revenues, cost reductions, entry into a strategically important market, and other benefits.

Offsetting the potential benefit of synergies are the integration costs and risks that inevitably arise in a transaction involving two corporate entities. These can include the costs of realizing synergies (e.g., severance), the potential loss of key employees or major customers, as well as other general costs associated with the integration of information systems, changes in employee benefit plans, and so on.

The structure of the deal includes whether the shares or assets of the target company are acquired and the forms of consideration that set out how, when and the conditions under which the seller is paid. Apart from cash on closing, other common forms of consideration include holdbacks, promissory notes, shares of the buyer's corporation and earnouts. In addition, in the case of a privately held corporation, the individual sellers often enter into a management contract for a period of time in order to facilitate the transition.

The financing of the transaction also has a bearing on the price that a buyer is able to pay. In some cases, the buyer is able to defer a portion of the purchase price through deal structuring with the seller. However, the portion that needs to be financed at closing may be funded through the buyer's existing resources, raising new debt or new equity.

Ultimately, the price paid in any open market transaction is influenced by the relative negotiating positions and negotiating skills of the buyer, the seller and their respective advisors. A detailed discussion of negotiating strategies and tactics is beyond the scope of this book. However, readers who are interested in learning more about negotiating strategies and open market transactions in general might refer to:

- Johnson, Howard E., *Selling Your Private Company* (Canadian Institute of Chartered Accountants, 2005); and

- Johnson, Howard E., *The Acquisition Value Cycle*™ (Carswell, 2009).

Notional Market Valuations vs. Open Market Transactions

Fair Market Value vs. Price

As discussed in Chapter 1, fair market value is defined as the highest price available in an open and un-restricted market between informed and prudent parties acting at arm's length under no compulsion to act, expressed in terms of cash. In an open market transaction, however, there are inevitably departures from this theoretical definition that influence the price paid. For example:

- the "highest price available" assumes that all potential qualified buyers have been solicited. This can-not be known with certainty in most open market transactions. Further, it is not always the case that a logical buyer is able to, or wishes to, submit an offer for the company (e.g., due to timing issues or financial constraints);

- in reality, markets are not "open and unrestricted". There may be external restrictions, such as govern-ment regulations (e.g., the *Competition Act*) or internal restrictions such as those imposed by a com-pany's board of directors or that exist under the terms of shareholder agreements;

- parties to open market transactions seldom are fully "informed". Specifically, prospective buyers, even following a thorough due diligence exercise, cannot expect to uncover all details about a prospective acquisition. Accordingly, they typically seek protection from material misrepresentations through seller warranties and indemnities included in the purchase agreement. The seller, on the other hand, is usually not aware of the details of a prospective buyer's financial position nor the specific post-acquisition synergies and quantification the buyer expects to realize from the acquisition;

- parties to open market transactions are not always "prudent". The level of due diligence undertaken var-ies considerably between buyers and, as a result, important factors which might have a material impact on price are sometimes missed;

- parties do not always act at "arm's length";

- the seller (and sometimes the buyer) in an open market transaction may be "compelled to act". For example, a seller may need to sell quickly in light of the deteriorating health of an owner-manager or as a result of financial pressure. Alternatively, the buyer might feel compelled to transact to prevent the target company from being acquired by a competitor; and

- the price may not always be "in terms of cash". Other forms of consideration are often used in an acqui-sition such as promissory notes, an earnout or a share exchange. The conversion of non-cash considera-tion to a cash-equivalent value is subject to estimates and interpretation.

The Inclusion of Post-Acquisition Synergies

There are two possible components in the valuation of a business:

- a component reflecting the value of all the outstanding shares or assets viewed on an intrinsic basis (i.e., the value of the business assuming the business will continue to operate as is, absent a combination or consolidation of the business with that of a buyer or merger partner). This value component is referred to as intrinsic (or stand-alone) value; and

- a value added to intrinsic value for the synergies that a buyer anticipates will be realized following the acquisition. The quantification of this added value is unique to each potential buyer.

In most open market transactions involving the purchase of a business of a meaningful size, some level of synergies is perceived to exist by one or more corporate buyers and possibly financial buyers (i.e., special-interest purchasers). However, the extent to which these benefits are paid for varies significantly depending on the negotiating abilities of the parties involved and the structure of the transaction. Where not paid for, post-acquisition synergies act as a buffer against unexpected costs incurred as part of the acquisition.

Small owner-managed businesses are generally less attractive to large corporate buyers who believe it is not economical to invest the time and effort required to consummate a transaction. Conversely, small businesses sometimes are of interest to one or more individuals who may undertake the acquisition for reasons such as:

- to act in the role of owner-manager of the business, thereby securing personal employment and realizing a return on both physical and invested capital in the form of salary, bonuses, dividends and other benefits; or

- as a personal investment with the objective of generating a return on capital through dividends or the eventual sale of the investment at a gain.

Where individual buyers are involved, there are seldom buyer-perceived post-acquisition synergies except to the extent that the prospective individual buyer believes he or she can operate the target business more efficiently or use their personal contacts to generate incremental revenues. Even if such opportunities do exist, they typically are not paid for. As a result, the basis for determining the value of a small owner-managed business is normally intrinsic value. In addition, the buyer of a small owner-managed business must be aware of the consequences of personal and individual goodwill that might exist in the seller and which might not be transferable to the buyer (see Chapter 1).

In the end, no matter what the seller's motivation for selling, it is buyer-perceived opportunity that usually dictates the final negotiated price. Buyers assess an acquisition candidate in light of the target company's own operations on a stand-alone basis, combined with its perception of post-acquisition synergies that might be available as a result of a business combination. Each potential buyer brings unique opportunities to a combination of its own business and the one offered for sale. Accordingly, each such buyer will perceive different opportunities and hence will presume itself capable of generating different degrees of post-acquisition synergies from the same acquisition opportunity. It follows that each buyer can afford to, and likely will, pay a different price than every other buyer for a particular pool of assets. Assuming disciplined buyers, this price will be their "walk away" price. It defines the upper end of each buyer's price range.

In theory, the buyer who expects to realize the greatest level of post-acquisition synergies will pay the highest price for a particular business. However, in any given circumstance it may not be possible for a seller to negotiate a potential corporate buyer into paying more (or significantly more) than intrinsic value for the target company for at least the following reasons:

- a specific corporate buyer may not be able to realize significant post-acquisition synergies, net of associated costs of realizing those synergies and other costs associated with the integration of the two entities;

- some post-acquisition synergies cannot be readily identified or quantified. For example, entry into a new market may be highly valued by a prospective buyer not presently in that market, but the value of entry may be unknown or not quantifiable from the seller's perspective. Inevitably, the buyer and seller will differ in their perception of the post-acquisition synergies to be realized in any given transaction;

- the seller may not have the negotiating strength necessary to extract a price reflecting some or all of the buyer's perceived post-acquisition synergy expectations;

- all prospective buyers may not have been solicited, or may not be able or interested in making an acquisition at anything other than a bargain price. For example, the target business may be outside a prospective buyer's size requirements, management of the buyer may prefer to go the route of internal growth, or the prospective buyer may not have the financial resources to pay in full for synergies; and

- the buyer does not want to pay in full for prospective synergies that might not be realized and to retain that portion of value for its own benefit. Some companies may be willing to pay close to 100% for synergies whereas others may be willing to pay for few or none. The amount that a buyer is willing to pay for post-acquisition synergies is dependent on the buyer's perception of the importance of those synergies, the risks of achieving their benefits and the buyer's perception of the level of competition for the business being sold (which influences negotiations).

The likelihood and quantum of post-acquisition synergies being paid for increase when:

- several prospective buyers have expressed an interest in the business. This increases the likelihood one or more buyers has the ability to realize considerable synergies. The presence of these potential buyers substantially improves the negotiating position of the seller. Conversely, by limiting market exposure and dealing only with one or a few buyers, a seller's ability to maximize price through negotiation is reduced, often materially. Theoretically, in both an open market transaction and a notional market context (absent middle market speculators), where only one special-interest purchaser exists, that buyer may pay only a nominal amount more than intrinsic value. However, as a practical matter a single special-interest purchaser's desire to complete a particular transaction, combined with the buyer's likely incomplete knowledge of the existence of other possible buyers, may result in such a buyer being willing to pay a much higher price than intrinsic value;

- the target business has a unique competitive advantage that is attractive to and can be readily transferred to a corporate acquirer. This could include circumstances where the target business is of strategic importance because of brand name recognition, market coverage, proprietary technology, customer contracts, and so on;

- economies of scale are evident in the industry (e.g., the elimination of back-office operations in industries with a comparatively high administrative component);

- the industry is going through a consolidation phase. This normally increases the number of active buyers. Corporate acquirers may be actively competing for acquisition candidates;

- the relative and absolute size of the business in relation to its competitors. A larger business is more likely to realize a premium for strategic benefits than a smaller business because of its better competitive position, market clout, and general level of buyer interest; and

- the structure of the transaction. Where a portion of the purchase price (including synergies) is made by way of contingent consideration (e.g., an earnout), a buyer is more likely to agree to pay for the synergies than where the terms of the deal are cash at closing.

Even where a seller has specific information with respect to the post-acquisition synergies perceived by one or more potential buyers, it is only through the active marketing of a business and negotiations with specific buyers that a seller can do other than speculate as to the value of these perceived synergies to such buyers. Only when these things have been identified and quantified in economic terms by the seller does the seller have any opportunity to reflect them in a sale price. The buyer has greater knowledge of its own business and the way it plans to integrate the acquisition than does the seller. Hence the potential buyer is in a far better position to quantify the value of the post-acquisition synergies it perceives than is the seller. Nevertheless, the most meaningful open market pricing exercise from a prospective seller's point of view should involve the best possible assessment of buyer-perceived post-acquisition synergies.

The more that is known by the buyer and the seller about the various elements that comprise buyer-perceived post-acquisition synergies, the better each will be able to quantify them. In turn, because each of the elements has yet to be proven at the date of transaction closing, the greater the value attributed to such things in relation to the aggregate purchase price, the greater is the acquisition risk.

The Parties to a Transaction

Buyers

There are at least five identifiable categories of buyers. Within each category each buyer has its, or their individual motivations and investment philosophies. The five buyer categories are: (i) individuals; (ii) privately held companies; (iii) public companies; (iv) financial buyers; and (v) company management.

Individuals

Many individuals look to buy a business for various reasons, including self employment, economic gain, lifestyle and prestige. However, most individuals lack the financial resources required to consummate a sizable transaction. Consequently, transactions involving individuals tend to be smaller in size and are often financed to a large degree by the post-acquisition cash flow of the target company. Therefore, the structure of the transaction often includes a significant non-cash component such as a promissory note to the seller. Accordingly, the value implications as described in Chapter 10, under the caption "Internal vs. External Financing", often come into play. In some cases, an individual is able to secure financing from one or more financial investors who can provide more meaningful amounts of capital to facilitate the transaction.

Privately Held Companies

Privately held companies purchase primarily other privately held businesses but may also acquire public companies or divisions. In the case of the acquisition of a public company:

- the privately held acquirer can use the acquiree as a vehicle to become public itself. Such transactions are completed through share exchanges and are referred to as "reverse takeovers"; or

- where 100% of the outstanding shares are not purchased in the first instance, the acquiree may be taken private, in which case any remaining minority shareholders are bought out; or

- where minority shareholders remain, the acquiree continues as a publicly traded company.

Management of privately held acquirers is accountable to no one but the lending institutions they deal with and to their own, typically close-knit, shareholder group. Frequently the owners are the management group. While they must be aware of the motivations of other potential buyers, privately held companies tend to look to rates of return that combine consideration of both their long-term financing costs and the risks they perceive associated with the business of an acquisition candidate. They tend to be less concerned with near-term accretive earnings per share than with near-term and long-term accretive discretionary cash flows. Privately held companies usually look at acquisitions as long-term investments that will generate post-acquisition synergies.

Public Companies

Public companies typically have access to larger amounts of capital (and a lower cost of capital) than do privately held companies. Moreover, in some circumstances and at their option, public company buyers are able to use their own stock as currency in a transaction. Management of a public company answer to its board of directors, its lending institutions, and (frequently) a widely based shareholder group.

Management of public companies perceive synergies as coming from a combination of their existing business operations and those of acquisition candidates. Public companies tend to be long-term investors who intend to integrate the acquired business with little or no intent of re-selling it. When analyzing potential acquisitions they normally focus on:

- how the operations of the target company will advance their long-term corporate strategy;

- the motivations of other potential buyers (i.e., competitors for the acquisition);

- rates of return on investment that consider long-term financing costs, the risks associated with the operations of the acquisition candidate, and the multiples of EBITDA, EBIT, discretionary cash flow and after-tax earnings implied in their purchase offer;

- the expected reaction from the investment community, including stock market analysts, bankers, and other groups; and

- the amount of intangible value implied in the final purchase price and its amortization period. Applicable accounting standards will dictate whether the buyer will experience near-term post-acquisition dilution in consolidated earnings per share and, if so, how long it will take before the acquisition is expected to have an accretive affect on post-acquisition consolidated earnings per share.

There is a motivation to acquire businesses at prices that result in little or no near-term post-acquisition dilution but rather in a near-term positive (accretive) contribution to consolidated earnings per share. Accordingly, public company rate of return objectives in acquisitions typically are higher than the rates of return implied by prevailing stock market prices for their own shares. Stated differently, as a general rule public companies set multiples of prospective (including from expected post-acquisition synergies) incremental discretionary cash flows and after-tax earnings criteria for target acquisitions that are no higher than the prevailing and prospective multiples paid by stock market participants for normal-lot shareholdings in the acquirer company.

Financial Buyers

Financial buyers are buyers who view acquisitions of businesses essentially as financial transactions. These buyers tend to be financially sophisticated, rely on professional managers, and do not necessarily purchase businesses to hold for the long term. Financial buyers usually have a stated investment horizon within which they want to resell the acquired company for a gain and to realize a target rate of return.

Financial buyers usually have a stated set of investment criteria, which may include:

- company-specific attributes, such as size, industry segment, geographic location, and life cycle stage (e.g., start-ups vs. mature companies);
- whether the investor wants a controlling or only a minority interest; and
- reasons for the transaction (e.g., a management buyout, spin-off of a division, growth capital, etc.).

Financial buyers tend to have an appetite for post-acquisition debt in relation to underlying assets and equity that sometimes results in "leveraged buyouts". Often the price they are willing to pay is strongly influenced, and in some cases dictated by, the amount, terms, and conditions of capital available from credit sources. Post-acquisition synergies are not available to financial buyers, except where synergies can be generated through one or more of their other existing portfolio companies or through better access to financing than the target company.

Company Management

Where the management team of a company acquires most or all of the shares from the existing owner, it is commonly known as a management buyout (MBO). Management generally is more informed as to the operations of the business that is acquired than are other categories of buyers, although they may suffer from a narrower outlook relative to external business influences.

Management buyouts are often supported by financial buyers, particularly in the case of larger transactions. As such, management buyouts tend to involve the use of more debt than with transactions involving a privately held company or public company buyers. Where the management team has limited or no external financing available, these transactions tend to be internally financed, and are frequently influenced by circumstances peculiar to the management group and the business itself.

Management buyouts by themselves usually result in no significant post-acquisition synergies. The price paid is often strongly influenced by the amount, terms and conditions of capital available from credit sources, and tends to be lower than that which a strategic buyer might pay.

Sellers

Sellers generally can be categorized as:

- the shareholders of a privately held company selling all (or a majority) of their shares or net assets of the company;

- unincorporated businesses (e.g., sole proprietorships or partnerships) selling all or substantially all their net assets;

- a public company selling all (or a majority) of its shares or assets; or

- a business (partnership, privately held company or public company) selling a portion of its operations.

Privately Held Companies

In the case of privately held companies, reasons for divestments of all (or a majority) of the shares or assets of the business may include one or more of the following:

- the age or health of the owner/manager;

- a reduction in, or loss of, interest in the business on the part of the owner/manager that is either emotionally driven, or driven by changed personal or business interests or circumstances;

- familial or partner pressure to sell based on dissention among owners;

- a desire to reduce the risk resulting from having a disproportion of one's personal wealth in a single asset;

- opportunistic, such as where the shareholders receive an unsolicited offer that they perceive as attractive;

- a desire to be released from continued exposure to risk of personal guarantees;

- the inability to exploit growth opportunities due to limited access to capital; and

- lack of management depth or succession, and an inability to change management readily.

The reasons for divestiture will often dictate the need and the desire of the seller to transact, which in turn can influence their negotiating position and the forms of consideration the seller is prepared to accept. For example, where a divestiture is motivated by health issues, there is a greater need to transact than is the case with opportunistic motivations. In addition, where the seller is willing to remain with the business following the transaction, they usually are more amenable to receiving a portion of the proceeds in the form of contingent consideration, as contrasted with a seller that plans to exit the business shortly after closing.

Unincorporated Businesses

The reasons for the sale of an unincorporated business are similar to those of a privately held company, except that the assets are being sold (as opposed to having a choice between assets and shares). The unincorporated entity is typically dissolved shortly after the closing date. In some cases, the seller will transfer the assets of an unincorporated entity into a corporation prior to the sale, in order to benefit from the lifetime capital gains exemption (see Chapter 9).

Public Companies

The divestiture of a public company may be initiated by its board of directors as a result of:

- an unsolicited takeover bid (friendly or hostile). As a practical matter, hostile takeovers are relatively rare, except for larger, widely held companies;

- pressure from shareholders, where the stock price has remained below expectations for a prolonged period of time;

- financial difficulties stemming from poor operating performance or excessive financial leverage; and

- the inability to capitalize on growth opportunities because of resource limitations. This is more common for small-cap and mid-cap public companies that may not be able to raise adequate capital (despite being public) or which may suffer from lack of management depth.

In most cases involving the sale of a public company, in order to comply with securities laws, the transaction must be fully financed at the closing date, either in the form of cash or freely tradable shares of the buyer corporation.

Divestiture of a Business Segment

Generally, the reasons a seller divests only a portion of its operations are economic, contractually or legislatively driven. These reasons may include one or more of the following:

- the business segment to be sold is not generating a sufficient return on investment, and is not expected to do so in the foreseeable future;

- the business segment to be sold is not integral to the seller's long-range strategy;

- the seller is in financial difficulty and looks to sale proceeds as a total or partial remedy;

- the seller is required to sell because of a new statute, court order or government direction;

- the seller perceives prospective negative changes in the market position for the products or services of the business segment, or significant capital expenditure requirements, often related to technological change issues; and

- in the case of a public company seller, a public market perception that the business segment to be sold is a negative influence on the public company's current share price and would be more valuable to shareholders as a spin-off.

A challenge in the divestiture of a business segment arises where the segment was integrated with the operations of the entire company in terms of management, information systems, facilities and other aspects. This can add complexity to the valuation exercise since a buyer may or may not require these things and the physical segregation of the business segment may give rise to unanticipated costs or other issues.

Intermediaries

Most transactions involving the purchase and sale of a business are completed with the assistance of external advisors, including intermediaries (e.g., investment bankers or business brokers), lawyers, accountants and other advisors. Intermediaries do not take a neutral role in the transaction process, and as a result play either a constructive or destructive role. They frequently influence open market price—sometimes to a significant degree. Of particular importance in this regard are the:

- understanding and execution by each intermediary of its role in the negotiation process leading to the structure of the transaction and the final price;
- understanding and execution by each intermediary of its role in the process leading to the final documentation of the transaction;
- intermediary's level of understanding of the respective motivations and objectives of the buyer and seller;
- ability of the intermediary to set the tone in negotiations and to assist in crucial decisions;
- experience, ability, and negotiating skill of each intermediary; and
- basis of remuneration of each intermediary and the related degree of possible intermediary vested interest and lack of objectivity in pushing the transaction to close.

Essentially, intermediaries fall into one of three categories:

- financial intermediaries (e.g., investment bankers, business brokers and merger/acquisition specialists);
- legal advisors; and
- income tax advisors (usually either lawyers or professional accountants).

Financial Intermediaries

In Canada, the low end of the transactions market for privately held companies is served principally by business brokers (and real estate brokers where real property is significant compared to business operations). Transactions involving public companies and the middle and high-end market (measured by business size) for privately held companies is served by intermediaries such as investment bankers with widely diverse backgrounds, business experience and knowledge, abilities, resources, and negotiating skills. As a result, different intermediaries contribute varying amounts of either value added or negative value to a given open market transaction.

Financial intermediaries provide a full range of services to both buyers and sellers. Their remuneration is usually all or in part contingent upon the successful completion of the transaction and the way it is structured (particularly where the intermediary is acting on behalf of the seller). In such circumstances, depending upon the terms and conditions of the fee arrangement, the intermediary is to some degree a direct participant in the transaction. It is important to note that financial intermediaries acting in the purchase or sale of a business frequently have a vested interest in a transaction closing. In such circumstances they are in a conflict of interest, albeit one their client presumably finds acceptable. Thoughtful structuring of the financial intermediary's fee arrangement can assist in mitigating this negative influence.

The role played by a financial intermediary in any given transaction can include:

- assisting in the identification of possible buyers or sellers;
- co-ordinating the preparation and circulation of a confidential information memorandum and other information with respect to the business of a seller;
- researching and ranking possible buyers or sellers as to fit, and the resultant possible synergies perceived to accrue to each;
- making initial contact with possible buyers or sellers;
- co-ordinating the collection and analysis of information required to assess the possible transaction, including hosting a data room for the seller;
- arranging and co-ordinating meetings between the buyer and seller;
- acting as a sounding board for ideas of the buyer or seller and reviewing the analysis of each;
- acting to deflect and resolve conflict between buyer and seller where it arises;
- functioning as part of the acquisition or divestiture team, thereby providing transaction planning and analysis expertise not otherwise available to seller or buyer;
- assisting in the negotiation and structuring of the transaction;
- arranging or assisting in the arrangement of financing for the transaction;
- assisting the buyer in conducting due diligence reviews prior to closing; and
- reviewing the transaction documentation, in conjunction with legal counsel, tax advisors and other advisors.

It is often the ability of the financial intermediary to bring creative solutions to bear on seemingly irreconcilable positions that determines the ultimate success of the purchase and sale of a business. However, not all financial intermediaries bring the same experience, capability and objectivity to a transaction. For this reason, the highest open market price may not be achieved in the sale of a given business. However, careful selection of a financial intermediary, including an assessment of personality fit between the intermediary and its client, can assist in the maximization of sale proceeds to a seller or price minimization to a buyer.

Legal and Income Tax Advisors

It is common practice for lawyers to participate actively in the negotiation process, in particular to deal with the finalization of the purchase and sale agreement, corporate law issues that relate to transaction structuring and with issues surrounding representations and warranties that survive the closing of the transaction. Likewise, it is common practice for income tax advisors to participate actively in the negotiation process (albeit indirectly), in particular to deal with income tax issues relating to transaction structuring.

As is the case with financial intermediaries, individual lawyers and income tax advisors bring different levels of experience, business knowledge and judgment, ability, and negotiating skills to the bargaining table. However, their respective fees are usually not contingent on whether or not a transaction is completed.

The Acquisition and Divestiture Process

The acquisition and divestiture process can vary considerably depending on the needs, circumstances and preferences of the buyer and the seller. Each acts initially in isolation in terms of pre-transaction planning (i.e., prior to the seller contacting the buyer, or vice versa). Once contact has been made between the buyer and the seller, the two parties increasingly interact until a transaction is concluded (or the parties decide not to transact). This process is illustrated in Exhibit 11A.

Exhibit 11A
The Purchase and Sale Process

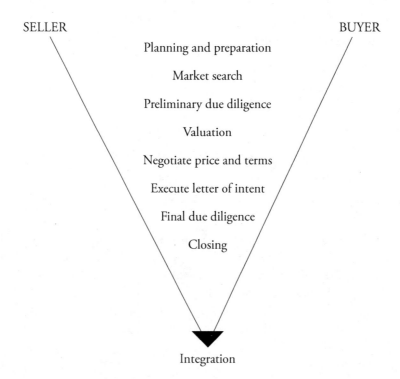

SELLER   BUYER

Planning and preparation

Market search

Preliminary due diligence

Valuation

Negotiate price and terms

Execute letter of intent

Final due diligence

Closing

Integration

While the acquisition and divestiture process tends to follow the sequence noted above, it is important to note that it is not so in every case. Certain steps may be bypassed, combined or changed, depending on a variety of factors. In addition, the steps can be rather fluid and extend over a large portion of the process. For example, while the buyer normally prepares an initial valuation of the seller's business at an early stage, that valuation is updated as more information becomes available throughout the acquisition process.

It is essential for both the buyer and seller to recognize the significant time commitment and costs involved in any transaction. In most cases the acquisition or divestiture of a business will take between six to 12 months to complete (after the planning and preparation stage), and perhaps even longer. Accordingly, both parties must be prepared to commit adequate resources to the process.

In most cases, the seller has more control over the timing of the process up to the execution of a letter of intent. Following the execution of a letter of intent, the buyer has more control through to the closing of the transaction.

That said, the parties to a transaction and their advisors should approach the acquisition and divestiture process with flexibility in order to ensure they can react to issues and opportunities as they arise.

Planning and Preparation

Buyer's Perspective

Before embarking on an acquisition program, buyers should have a clearly defined business strategy and establish how prospective acquisitions will help them to achieve their strategic objectives. The buyer should establish clear acquisition criteria in terms of product and service offerings, target company size, geographic region and other relevant parameters.

Buyers must also objectively assess the resources they are capable of, and willing to, dedicate to the search for acquisition opportunities. This includes existing financial resources, external financing capabilities, in-house personnel and external advisors. Regardless of the extent to which external advisors are used, it is important for the buyer to appoint an individual within its organization to oversee the acquisition process.

Seller's Perspective

From the seller's perspective, pre-transaction planning and preparation normally involve:

- deciding on the timing of the sale;
- preparing the business for sale;
- tax and estate planning;
- the engagement of intermediaries; and
- an initial valuation.

There are many factors that influence the timing of the sale. These include:

- for privately held companies, the personal characteristics of the business owners, including their age, health, interest levels and other factors;
- an unsolicited approach from a prospective buyer;
- the historical and prospective operating results and financial position of the business. Where the business is overburdened with debt, a sale may be necessary. Alternatively, the inability of the business to raise significant amounts of capital on reasonable terms may influence the need for a sale; and
- current and forecast industry and economic conditions, which can influence the number of prospective buyers at any given time, as well as the ability for buyers to raise capital in order to consummate the deal.

Preparing the business for sale involves undertaking initiatives that make the business more attractive to prospective buyers and that will ultimately serve to maximize shareholder value. These include:

- ensuring a strong management team is in place. Particularly for privately held companies, buyers are wary of acquiring a business where there is not a strong management team (apart from the business owners), that possesses the customer relationships, technical knowledge and other attributes to ensure the continuation of the goodwill of the business following the closing date;

- solidifying customer relationships (ideally through contractual arrangements). The ability of a seller to demonstrate predictability in revenues reduces risk and, by extension, increases shareholder value;

- managing the balance sheet. Buyers prefer to acquire businesses with clean balance sheets (e.g., one that does not have redundant assets but has adequate levels of working capital). In this regard, sellers can sometimes realize incremental value by managing working capital and capital expenditures in the years prior to entertaining a possible transaction; and

- various operational initiatives such as liquidating old inventory, ensuring the website is up to date and other measures that can portray the business as a more attractive acquisition target.

For shareholders of privately held companies, tax and estate planning prior to the transaction is important in order to minimize or defer the tax burden upon the sale. Such initiatives may include structuring their personal and corporate affairs in order to multiply the lifetime capital gains exemption, taking advantage of "safe income" within the corporation and other measures, many of which were addressed in Chapter 9.

During the planning and preparation period, the seller should retain the advisors who will assist in the transaction. These include intermediaries (e.g., investment bankers or business brokers), lawyers, tax advisors and other advisors (where required) that will assist the seller in finalizing the transaction, minimizing the tax burden and maximizing shareholder value.

As part of presale planning and preparation, most sellers engage a valuator or investment banker to estimate the value of their business and the price they might expect to receive in the open market. This may come in the form of a formal valuation report (e.g., an advisory report, as discussed in Chapter 10) or simply an oral estimate given in conversation with an advisor. However, as noted above, for a variety of reasons the estimate of fair market value can be significantly different from the price that is ultimately received. However, an independent valuation can assist in identifying possible buyers as well as opportunities for increasing shareholder value prior to the time the business is exposed to the market. Valuations conducted in the context of presale planning also tend to place greater emphasis on industry transactions as a benchmark for price expectations, subject, of course, to the caveats of relying on such measures, as noted in Chapter 4.

Ideally, sellers should begin planning for the sale at least two years (or more) prior to the time their company is expected to be exposed to the market, as some of the planning initiatives will take time to execute and/or vest. Even where a sale of the business is not anticipated in the near future, business owners and executives are well advised to prepare for a sale nonetheless in the event they receive an unsolicited offer or circumstances change suddenly and force a sale.

Market Search

Buyer's Perspective

Buyers must establish whether they will conduct a passive or active search for acquisition targets. Passive buyers wait to be solicited by would-be sellers, and then decide whether to pursue the opportunity based on the fit with their established acquisition criteria.

Active buyers conduct market research to identify possible candidates. This may include a review of trade journals, participation in industry associations, Internet searches, public company information and other sources. Active buyers then initiate contact with possible sellers, normally in an effort to avoid an auction process.

In either case, an analysis of industry transactions that have taken place in recent years can be helpful in assessing the likely level of interest in a particular acquisition opportunity on the part of other possible buyers, and in estimating what might be competitive bids for the target company. This can influence the relative negotiating positions of the buyer and the seller.

Seller's Perspective

Where the seller initiates the divestiture process, it or its intermediary conduct industry research to identify prospective buyers to contact. These may include:

- competitors as well as customers, suppliers and businesses with complementary product and service offerings;

- a review of industry associations, trade journals and similar resources;

- Internet and database searches. In this regard, many intermediaries subscribe to databases containing details of public and privately held companies, transaction activity and other information that helps in identifying prospective buyers;

- a review of public company information, including annual reports, management discussion and analysis and other disclosures;

- an analysis of recent industry transactions. This not only helps in identifying possible buyers, but also the multiples paid (subject to the caveats regarding industry transactions as noted in Chapter 4); and

- financial buyers, such as private equity firms.

The seller should also consider whether a management buyout presents an alternative. As noted above, for transactions of a meaningful size, the management team is normally supported by one or more financial investors. In this regard, the seller should be wary of the possible conflict of interest created where the management team becomes a possible buyer. In the context of a public company, a transaction involving the management team may necessitate the board of directors obtaining a fairness opinion in order to discharge their fiduciary duties, as noted in Chapter 10.

A fundamental decision that the seller must make at an early stage is how the sale process will be structured. This involves considerations such as:

- the number of possible buyers to be approached, and whether certain parties should *not* be approached;

- whether parties should be approached simultaneously or sequentially; and

- whether specified deadlines should be established for key events such as the submission of expressions of interest, letters of intent and other milestones.

A broad search may uncover a possible buyer that was not immediately obvious, or a buyer that was believed to be less interested. This sometimes occurs where buyers are in different industry verticals and may perceive an acquisition opportunity as a means of entry into a new industry segment. However, a broad search increases the risk the market will become aware that a company is for sale, which could raise problems when dealing with employees and customers.

In the case of a small business, where the likely buyer is an individual, the search can be difficult. In many cases, the seller needs to identify an individual who has access to capital and who wants to take an active role in the company.

Preliminary Due Diligence

The purpose of preliminary due diligence from a buyer's perspective is to develop the business case for the prospective acquisition. In the course of preliminary due diligence, a buyer should focus on the following:

- assessing whether the target company represents a fit with its acquisition criteria and business strategy;

- identifying key areas where further investigation is required;

- understanding the underlying economic drivers of the target company, including its customer base, selling proposition, cost structure, key employees and other important value drivers;

- developing a preliminary range of value, having regard to the prospective cash flow and risk profile of the target company;

- identifying possible synergies that might be generated through the acquisition. In this regard, the buyer should consider both the risks and costs associated with synergy realization; and

- assessing the likelihood of successful integration. In this regard, potential issues should be identified and work on an integration plan should begin at an early stage. If effective integration is expected to be extremely challenging or unlikely, the buyer should reconsider whether to pursue the acquisition opportunity.

Prior to disclosing any non-public information about their company, sellers will normally insist that buyers execute some form of confidentiality or non-disclosure agreement.

The first document the seller provides to the buyer in the course of preliminary due diligence is the confidential information memorandum (CIM). The CIM normally contains limited information about the target company, including an overview of its product and service offerings, operations, employees and financial performance. The seller normally uses the CIM to position the company in a way that creates a positive perception and engages buyer interest. The CIM also sets out the agenda for the sale process.

In addition to reviewing the CIM, buyers should conduct their own research on the target company and the industry in which it operates (while respecting the terms of the confidentiality agreement). Such research normally includes reviewing publicly available information about the acquisition target (including its website) as well as information regarding comparable companies and recent transactions that have taken place within the industry.

Following a review of the CIM, interested buyers will seek to arrange a meeting with the seller. Initial meetings normally consist of a management presentation (which provides detail additional to what was disclosed in the CIM) and general discussions regarding the target company and the industry in which it operates. The main purpose of the initial meetings is for both the buyer and the seller to establish whether or not there is a fit between their respective organizations and the basis for further discussions. It also provides the seller the opportunity to better understand the buyer's objectives, motivations, business strategy and acquisition approval process. This knowledge can assist the seller in estimating the synergies a buyer might perceive and the likelihood these synergies will be paid for.

In most cases, arrangements are made for the buyer to have a tour of the seller's operating facilities. In some cases tours are conducted outside normal hours in order to help maintain confidentiality.

Buyers will also look for additional information such as financial statements, customer and supplier data, information regarding employees, the facilities and other aspects of the seller's operations. Such information should be sufficient for the buyer to conduct its business analysis, as discussed in Chapter 2. In most cases, much of this information is provided via an electronic data room. Sellers are often hesitant to provide such information for reasons of confidentiality. Therefore, the information may be provided in a cryptic form whereby the real names of customers, suppliers and employees are not disclosed.

Valuation

Seller's Perspective

As noted above, sellers will often commission an estimate of value prior to exposing their business to the marketplace. However, the seller and its advisors will revise and update that initial estimate throughout the course of the divestiture process for:

- changes in the business, including actual financial results and other changes such as winning or losing a major contract or other significant developments;

- the synergies that might be anticipated from specific buyers that have expressed an interest in the business. While the value of synergies is less clear to the seller than to the buyer, and there is no assurance the buyer will pay for synergies in any event, the quantification of synergies can be helpful to the seller in negotiating the deal.

In order to make an informed decision and to assist in understanding their negotiating position, the seller should: (i) establish the economic value of its business on an intrinsic basis; (ii) estimate the synergies each prospective buyer might realize; and (iii) evaluate the impact of deal structuring and financing.

Buyer's Perspective

From the buyer's perspective, the valuation of the target company is an evolving process. In most cases, the buyer is initially provided with limited information such as historical and budgeted revenue and normalized EBITDA figures. Therefore, the buyer may only be able to derive a very preliminary estimate of value based on a multiple of EBITDA methodology, which conclusions will be based on numerous assumptions.

As more financial and operational information regarding the target company is made available, the buyer is able to revise its value conclusions. Most sophisticated buyers and financial investors will develop valuation conclusions based on a discounted cash flow methodology. The underlying projections for the DCF methodology are normally provided by the seller (or developed by the buyer based on discussions with the seller). The buyer's DCF model will then take into account other factors such as the synergies the buyer expects to realize, integration costs and financing of the transaction.

The valuation is also influenced by the terms of the deal, including whether assets or shares are acquired, the forms of consideration and the terms of any management contracts with the seller. These factors are addressed later in this chapter.

While valuation in the context of an open market transaction can take into account synergies, integration costs and financing, the price ultimately paid and the terms of the deal are, in the end, influenced by other non-economic variables, most notably the negotiating abilities and relative negotiating positions of the buyer and seller. Therefore, buyers often approach valuation in the context of an open market transaction as a range, with:

- the lower end of the range approximating the value of the target company on an intrinsic basis, given the cash flows that the target company expects to generate as a stand-alone entity and a rate of return that reflects the risks and growth prospects inherent in the target company; and

- the higher end of the range accounting for the synergies expected as part of prospective cash flows (net of integration costs), the buyer's cost of capital and possible further adjustments for the perceived strategic value of the target company. The buyer may also take into account the impact of deal structuring and financing.

While the buyer would like to negotiate a deal near the lower end of the range, it should develop and keep in mind the maximum amount it may be willing to pay. In addition, public company buyers also consider the impact of earnings dilution or accretion based on different price points and the resultant intangible value and related amortization.

Most buyers use more than one approach to valuation in order to test their conclusions. While the discounted cash flow methodology is usually preferred, the conclusions can then be tested by one or more of the multiple of EBITDA methodology, multiple of EBIT, capitalized cash flow, adjusted net book value or other approaches discussed in Chapters 3, 4 and 5.

Negotiating Price and Terms

In a notional market context both the buyer and seller are assumed to enjoy equal negotiating positions and abilities. However, a key determinant of the ultimate price paid in an open market transaction is the comparative negotiating positions and abilities of the buyer, the seller, and their respective advisors. As a general rule, the important things to consider when negotiating price in an open market context from the seller's perspective are:

- the degree to which the seller is willing, anxious, or required to sell;

- the seller's ability to identify potential buyers of the business;

- the number of interested, financially capable buyers for a given business at any particular point in time. This availability of potential buyers, commonly referred to as liquidity, usually has a significant influence on the price and terms ultimately negotiated in an open market transaction;

- the seller's depth of knowledge of the businesses of each potential buyer and the reasons motivating each to buy. In particular, the seller's awareness of the possible post-acquisition synergies that each potential buyer perceives is important;
- the uniqueness or lack thereof of the seller's business operations, product and service offerings, technology and other aspects; and
- the level of flexibility the seller displays in terms of the buyer's financing of the transaction. Sometimes the seller requires an all-cash deal, that may restrict the ability or interest of some prospective buyers. Conversely, where the seller will accept a promissory note, share exchange, or some other form of consideration, a higher price might be attainable.

From the buyer's perspective, key considerations include:

- the ability to quantify the synergies potentially created from the acquisition. In this regard, each buyer's synergy perceptions are different and change over time;
- the reliance of the buyer on non-cash forms of consideration. Where a buyer has the ability to finance an acquisition entirely by cash, it is in a better negotiating position than is a buyer that requires significant non-cash forms of consideration, such as promissory notes or earnouts;
- the buyer's depth of knowledge with respect to both the target business and the reasons motivating the seller to sell;
- the buyer's perception of likely competitive bids for the target business, including the number of potential bidders and estimated post-acquisition synergies each might enjoy;
- other opportunities or alternatives available to the buyer in order to attain its objectives such as internal growth or the acquisition of another business; and
- the buyer's cost of capital and its flexibility with respect to the required rate of return from the transaction.

In the end, the buyer should consider the price it is willing to pay for an existing business compared to creating a similar operation on its own. The decision whether to buy or build requires analyzing and balancing the benefit of acquiring a business opportunity immediately against the time required to create comparable capability and value using existing internal resources. In the case of an acquisition, the buyer also benefits from a reduction in competition that would otherwise exist. Further, the acquisition of another business may provide the buyer with access to patents, licences and other intangible value, which cannot be readily recreated.

Executing the Letter of Intent

Following negotiations, the buyer will prepare a letter of intent (LOI), setting out the terms of its proposal. LOIs can come in varying levels of detail, depending on the amount of information provided to the buyer, the relative negotiating positions of the parties and other circumstances. In most cases, the LOI contains all major aspects of the deal, including:

- the price (or price range);
- whether the assets or shares are being acquired;

- the forms of payment, including when, how and under what conditions the purchase price will (or will not) be paid;

- whether the offer is conditional upon financing or other factors; and

- the exclusivity period, which normally ranges from 30 days to 120 days, depending on the size and complexity of the transaction.

The LOI is not a binding document with respect to a transaction, given that it is subject to the buyer's due diligence, the execution of a purchase and sale agreement and other conditions before closing. However, once accepted by the seller, the LOI is binding in terms of confidentiality and the exclusivity period granted to the buyer to complete its due diligence and complete the deal.

From the seller's perspective it is advisable to obtain a comprehensive LOI that clearly addresses all the important aspects of the deal. This helps to reduce the risk that a buyer will negotiate key points following its final due diligence based on terms in the LOI that were ambiguous or not addressed at all. Conversely, the buyer will normally seek a loosely worded LOI in order to maintain its negotiating flexibility through closing.

Final Due Diligence

The purpose of final due diligence is to allow the buyer the opportunity to verify the accuracy and completeness of key facts and assumptions surrounding the target company and to ensure that it fully understands the business risks involved in the acquisition. During this stage, buyers generally focus on:

- satisfying themselves that the prospective cash flows they anticipated from the target company are realistic;

- ensuring that all significant operating risks of the target company have been identified;

- determining how to capitalize on growth opportunities;

- identifying, quantifying and assessing the risks related to synergies; and

- identifying and formulating a plan to deal with potential integration issues.

The final due diligence phase involves the buyer conducting a comprehensive review of all aspects of the target company. These generally include a detailed review of:

- historical financial statements, supporting schedules and budgets. In this regard, buyers tend to place their emphasis on identifying possible overvalued assets, underaccrued (or unrecorded) liabilities and poor financial controls;

- contracts, commitments, and other agreements. Buyers generally focus on obligations that change the risk profile of the target company or that diminish their ability to realize synergies (e.g., lease commitments);

- operational matters, including the age and condition of facilities and fixed assets, production capabilities, etc.;

- sales and marketing plans and strategies. While buyers normally consider synergy opportunities from initiatives such as consolidating distribution channels, they also assess differing pricing and promotional strategies that may lead to perceived inconsistencies (and issues) with the buyer's existing suite of products and services;

- personnel, including interviews with key employees. Buyers are concerned with key employees who might leave the target company following a transaction, or cultural issues that will complicate integration efforts. The terms of any non-competition or non-solicitation agreements and management contracts should be finalized at this stage;

- information systems and technology, including identifying possible technology integration issues that may arise;

- customers and suppliers. Buyers sometimes request they be allowed to contact some of these parties. This can sometimes be an issue from the seller's standpoint. How and when customers and suppliers are approached is a matter that needs to be discussed and agreed between the buyer and seller; and

- other aspects of the target company that allow the buyer to satisfy itself the facts and assumptions regarding the business are accurate and complete.

The more comprehensive the buyer's final due diligence the greater the likelihood it will identify issues with the target company that must be addressed prior to finalizing the transaction. If major issues are identified during final due diligence that were not previously known or fully understood, the proposed terms of the deal set out in the letter of intent may have to be modified or, in some cases, the new information may cause the buyer to withdraw from the transaction.

Closing

The closing of the transaction involves executing a purchase and sale agreement and the exchange of cash, shares and other consideration. The purchase and sale agreement represents the legal binding agreement to acquire the shares or assets of the target company. It is usually drafted by the buyer's legal representatives and submitted to the seller's legal counsel for review. The purchase and sale agreement is drafted concurrently with the buyer's final due diligence in order to expedite the closing process.

The purchase and sale agreement contains all the terms and conditions of the deal, including the seller's and buyer's indemnifications, representations and warranties. These components of the agreement can be the subject of significant negotiations, given the magnitude of the implications to each party. The nature and extent of representations and warranties will vary depending on the size of the transaction, the nature of the company, whether assets or shares are being acquired and whether the target company is privately held or public. In the case of a privately held company, the buyer has greater opportunity for recourse against the individual shareholders. Such recourse is not usually available where the acquisition target is a public company. Therefore, the buyer is exposed to greater risk for such things as legal claims, understated liabilities, overstated assets and other risks.

The formal closing of the transaction normally takes place at a lawyer's office, usually within 30 days of signing the purchase and sale agreement, or concurrent with the signing (where no further approvals are required and no further issues are outstanding). At closing, the shares or assets of the target company are exchanged for cash and other consideration (as applicable) and the transaction is complete. In some cases there are last-minute negotiations, but ideally these issues are kept to a minimum.

Post-Closing Price Adjustments

Where the target company is privately held, the purchase and sale agreement usually contains a mechanism for purchase price adjustments for things such as working capital levels, debt levels, legal claims and hidden liabilities that come to light following the transaction. In this regard, it is common in the purchase of privately held companies for the buyer and seller to agree that a portion of the purchase price be placed in escrow as a holdback, pending an audit or review of the target company's financial statements and the outcome of other issues (e.g., legal claims). As noted above, holdback mechanisms are usually not possible where the target company is publicly traded; the buyer assumes the risk of adverse post-closing developments.

Integration

The integration of the target company with the buyer's existing operations can be fraught with challenges. Poor integration is cited as one of the most common reasons for deal failure. Common integration issues include the loss of key employees, the loss of major customers, higher than anticipated costs for severance, difficulties integrating information systems and other issues.

A well-conceived integration plan is critical to ensuring the transaction meets the buyer's expectations. Preparation of the integration plan should begin well before the deal is closed. Significant integration issues should be identified as soon as possible since they will impact the price and terms of the deal (and even whether the acquisition makes sense). The integration plan should be detailed and set clear milestones for defined objectives.

While a detailed discussion of acquisition integration is beyond the scope of this book, buyers should not underestimate the time and effort involved to ensure they fully realize the expected benefits from the acquisition.

Post-Acquisition Synergies

Synergies often form a core component of the investment thesis for buyers. Cost savings, incremental revenues and other benefits are anticipated from such things as access to new customers, expansion into new markets, operating efficiencies, access to proprietary technology and other benefits.

The nature and quantum of synergies available from an acquisition are unique to every buyer, and the buyer invariably is in the best position to determine their value. That said, sellers should attempt to identify strategic buyers and to quantify the synergies that each might realize as part of their negotiating strategy. Even in a notional market context, it is often necessary to consider whether strategic buyers exist and to attempt to quantify the value of synergies (where this can be done in a meaningful way).

Identifying Strategic Buyers

Generally, it is only through well-researched, well-executed market exposure that a determination can be made as to whether there are in fact potential buyers who:

- perceive potential economies of scale and/or strategic advantages;
- can identify and reasonably quantify the potential synergies;

- are understood by the seller to perceive such post-acquisition advantages to the degree they can be meaningfully quantified; and

- most importantly, can be negotiated into paying for some or all of that value-added component.

Where fair market value is not so qualified as to exclude special-interest purchasers, in a notional market valuation, without careful consideration, the issue of special-interest purchasers and the premium they might pay should not be readily dismissed or assumed not to be quantifiable.

In an open market context, a primary objective of the seller is maximization of the selling price and, hence, after-tax proceeds of sale (taking into consideration forms of payment). Accordingly, the seller should attempt to identify those buyers with the greatest apparent potential economic benefit and the best possible strategic fit with the operations of the seller's business. The more buyers that believe they are not alone in being able to achieve post-acquisition economies of scale and strategic advantages, the greater the likelihood that one or more of them will be prepared to pay for the post-acquisition synergies. Therefore, market liquidity (defined in terms of the number of potential buyers in the market at any given time) usually plays a significant role in determining the price a seller can expect to receive. This is consistent with the principles of valuation discussed in Chapter 1.

The process of identifying the buyers most likely to realize post-acquisition synergies includes:

- discussions with shareholders, management and industry analysts as to who they expect the most logical buyers might be. In this regard, shareholders and management may be aware of previous solicitations by potential buyers;

- review and analysis of competitors, suppliers and customers. Most open market transactions involve companies buying other businesses in the same or similar industry such as a competitor, or a business that enables the buyer to move into a new geographic market or integrates a supplier. Some industries are characterized by a few major players who commonly acquire smaller competitors; and

- a review of news releases, databases and other sources of information that contain details of recent transactions involving similar businesses.

Identifying Post-Acquisition Synergies

The buyer is in a better position to identify and quantify post-acquisition synergies than is the seller, who can only speculate on them. Post-acquisition synergies encompass all those things that increase the value of the combined business beyond its intrinsic value and result from:

- increases in the quantum of the combined prospective cash flows of the buyer and the seller;

- reducing the risk of either the buyer or the seller or both of achieving prospective cash flows; and

- creating growth opportunities and strategic advantage not otherwise available to either the buyer or the seller.

These benefits may accrue to the buyer, the acquired business or a combination of the two.

Some post-acquisition synergies are more readily quantifiable than are others. Nonetheless, a critical step from the perspective of a buyer or seller in an open market transaction is the identification of likely post-acquisition benefits. From the seller's perspective, this will assist in ascertaining which potential buyers to canvass and the estimated price that each might pay. From the buyer's standpoint, the identification of post-acquisition synergies is important from the perspective of determining all potential value components of the acquisition candidate and in estimating the price other possible buyers might pay.

Examples of post-acquisition synergies commonly anticipated are listed below. Although these benefits have been categorized as marketing, operating, financial and strategic, it is important to recognize that these classifications often overlap.

Marketing

- leveraging brand names and corporate reputation through a broader base of product and service offerings;

- benefits associated with increased market share. Increased market share often lends itself to efficiencies in terms of general marketing expenses (advertising and promotion), administration and various other fixed costs. In addition, increased market share can help a buyer in terms of the credibility associated with greater market presence and corporate awareness;

- the elimination of a competitor, thereby reducing price competition and the threat of new products or services being introduced by that competitor;

- improved market coverage resulting from the integration of product lines or service offerings. This benefit most commonly occurs where complementary products or services are acquired;

- gaining new customers to whom other products and services in the buyer's portfolio can be sold. Incremental revenue opportunities may also arise from cross-selling to existing customers or offering a more competitive basket of products or services by combining those of the acquired business and the buyer; and

- improved distribution of products resulting from better utilization of the marketing organization and distribution channels of the combined entities, and more efficient marketing and sales cost per unit sold. There may also be an overall reduction in the number of sales staff or the consolidation of distribution facilities.

Operating

- the ability to immediately transfer technology from the buyer's business to the seller's business and vice versa, thereby increasing profitability and eliminating the time and cost the buyer or seller would otherwise require to develop the same capabilities internally;

- the ability to offset the seasonal/cyclical nature of the buyer's existing operations. This might lead to operating efficiencies where facilities have been underutilized for part of the year or industry cycle. Counter-cyclical products may also lead to a reduction in the risk related to the volatility of prospective cash flows;

- the benefits of improved capacity utilization. Where excess capacity exists there may be an opportunity for incremental throughput, utilization of engineering and design services, and improved overall operating efficiencies;

- increased purchasing power. Where the buyer significantly increases its size as a result of an acquisition, it often can realize post-acquisition purchasing efficiencies;

- access to key management talent or employees with valuable technical skills and knowledge. This benefit is particularly important where such employees are in short supply or where the training period for new employees is lengthy; and

- headcount reductions. Reducing the total number of personnel is among the most common benefits anticipated following an acquisition, particularly where the buyer is a competitor. Headcount reductions often include managerial and administrative functions, although reductions in sales and operations employees are also frequently expected.

Financial

- accelerated growth potential for the seller's business through access to lower-cost financing and greater financial resources. In most cases where the buyer is a larger company than the seller, the buyer enjoys a lower cost of capital (particularly where the buyer is a public company and the seller is a privately held company);

- better utilization of capital structure. For example, enhanced financing capabilities for the buyer by virtue of the underlying assets and cash flow generation capability of the acquired business; and

- in the case of public companies, an increase in the share price due to greater analyst coverage and financial market expectations, thereby reducing the buyer's cost of equity.

Strategic

- potential risk reduction resulting from upstream and downstream integration opportunities;

- entry into a new strategically important market, from either a product/service or geographic standpoint; and

- a reduction in risk through greater diversification of products and service offerings, customer base or geographic markets.

All the foregoing may affect the perceived value of the target company to the extent the buyer believes the potential benefits are realizable and is prepared pay for some or all of them. The benefits may be in the form of increased revenues, reduced costs, and a reduction of the risk from that which otherwise would exist. For example, the elimination of competition through acquisition may result in monetary benefits such as improved facilities utilization, staff reductions, and better market penetration. It may also reduce price competition. To the extent such benefits are realized, the cash flow volatility of the buyer, and hence the risk associated with the acquisition, may be reduced. The valuation of a business in an open market context requires a careful examination of all such factors and a reasoned assessment of their likely realization and timing.

Quantifying Synergies

As noted above, where the valuation of a target company incorporates synergies, then the quantification of such synergies should be a separate and distinct component within the buyer's valuation model. Accordingly, the intrinsic value of the target business should be estimated as the base value and the value of synergies should be added to that base. This segregation of values not only assists in evaluating the reasonableness of the value components, but in an open market transaction also enables the buyer to consider separately the portion of the anticipated synergies it wants to pay for in its negotiations. Where a buyer does not pay for expected synergies, these serve to compensate for shortfalls from expected post-acquisition cash flows. No acquisition review can be so complete as to eliminate all post-acquisition surprises. In many instances, a lower level of post-acquisition benefits and a higher level of costs materialize following acquisition than were anticipated during negotiations. Consequently, if the synergies component is fully paid for, the buyer has eliminated all downside protection and the likelihood of acquisition success is reduced.

A proper quantification of synergies requires a balanced, realistic assessment of the potential benefits to be derived from the acquisition, as well as an assessment of the likely incremental costs to be incurred in their realization.

From the standpoint of the seller, the quantification of possible synergies in a given transaction requires at least the following:

- identification of the most logical buyer(s);

- an understanding of the motivations of each potential buyer;

- a review of public information with respect to potential buyers; and

- a determination of whether the acquisition falls within each potential buyer's corporate strategy and whether each recently has been an active or interested buyer of other relevant businesses.

From the standpoint of the buyer, the quantification of possible synergies in a given transaction generally requires:

- estimating incremental cash flows expected to be realized beyond those expected to be generated by the target company on a stand-alone basis;

- assessing the risks related to achieving these estimated incremental cash flows;

- assessing the expected timing of receipt of the perceived post-acquisition incremental cash flows;

- estimating the costs associated with achieving the perceived post-acquisition incremental cash flows; and

- assessing the likely level of competition for the acquisition, combined with the seller's complacency or anxiety with respect to the transaction and the buyer's level of interest with respect to completing the acquisition.

In most open market transactions involving mid-sized and large-sized businesses, one or more buyers anticipate post-acquisition synergies. It is unusual for a seller to be paid fully for all of the synergies a buyer perceives. However, the valuation of a business for open market purposes should incorporate an effort to quantify the value-added potentially created by a transaction. Uncertainty as to the amount and likely realization of the value-added component should not prevent this.

Although buyers will estimate the value of synergies, they typically do not want to pay for them because most buyers perceive the synergies as "theirs", and because most buyers perceive risks in realizing some or all of the synergistic component. Ultimately, whether and to what extent synergies are paid for is a function of the relative negotiating strengths of the buyer and the seller and the structure of the deal.

To increase the likelihood of getting paid for an element of synergies the seller should consider what specific synergies a particular buyer might realize, and how existing operations can be structured to maximize the ease and depth of post-transaction integration. The greater the quantum of synergies and the lower the perceived risk in achieving them, the greater the likelihood the buyer will extend an offer that incorporates at least a portion of the synergistic value.

The quantification of post-acquisition synergies can be divided into three categories:

- tangible operating synergies (i.e., those that can be isolated and quantified in terms of incremental prospective cash flows). Tangible operating synergies typically relate to specific incremental revenue opportunities and cost reductions;

- intangible operating synergies (i.e., those that cannot be readily segregated and analyzed on an individual basis). Intangible operating synergies typically relate to incremental growth opportunities or a reduction in business risk that has not been quantified as part of prospective cash flows; and

- financial synergies, (i.e., those related to a more efficient capital structure and lower cost financing). Financial synergies are normally reflected in the rates of return or valuation multiple adopted in the buyer's valuation model.

Quantifying Tangible Operating Synergies

The quantification of tangible operating synergies involves:

- determining the increase in EBITDA from incremental revenue opportunities, net of associated costs, or from cost savings;

- determining the costs of implementing and realizing the expected synergies. This should include both initial and ongoing costs and may include incremental operating expenses, capital expenditures and increased working capital requirements; and

- income tax effecting the expected net synergies.

The net incremental discretionary cash flows should be discounted (or capitalized) at a rate of return that reflects the risk of achieving the expected net synergies. In theory, in order to reflect incremental risk related to uncertainty of achievement, this should be a higher discount (capitalization) rate than is adopted when estimating the intrinsic value of the target company. In addition, there may be circumstances where it is appropriate to apply a different discount (or capitalization) rate to different sources of synergies (e.g., cost reductions vs. incremental revenues) to properly reflect the different levels of risk of achieving each.

Alternatively, the net synergies can be expressed net of a probability factor related to the added risk of their realization. Where this is done, the expected net synergies would be discounted at more moderate, market-driven rates of return, commonly the discount (capitalization) rate used in estimating the value of the target company on an intrinsic basis. This latter approach is more commonly adopted in practice.

The discounted cash flow methodology is the preferred approach to quantifying the value of synergies. The discounted cash flow model explicitly considers all costs of realizing the expected net synergies, including the impact on working capital, any capital expenditure additions and the timing of income tax loss utilization. Importantly, the discounted cash flow methodology should be used where significant up-front costs are anticipated or where post-acquisition synergies are expected to emerge over time. This may be the case where:

- initial costs such as severance, lease termination, systems integration and so on, are required in order to obtain cost reductions;

- incremental spending is required for new equipment, working capital, start-up costs and other expenses in order to generate incremental revenue opportunities; and

- the benefits are expected to phase in over time. This is particularly the case where the post-acquisition synergies relate to incremental revenue opportunities.

As an example of the quantification of tangible operating synergies, consider T1 Limited, which expects to achieve two sources of synergies through its acquisition of Targetco:

- incremental revenues from cross-selling T1 Limited's product and service offerings to Targetco's existing customer base. The incremental revenues will start at $1 million in the first year and increase by $1 million per year to $5 million in the fifth year following the transaction. T1 generates a contribution margin of 20% on its revenues. As a consequence of excess operating capacity, T1 will not have to incur any up-front costs in order to generate the additional revenues. However, incremental working capital requirements are estimated at 10% of revenues; and

- headcount reductions, which will lead to salary reductions of $500,000 in Year 1, increasing by the long-term growth rate of 3% per annum. Severance costs are estimated at $250,000.

T1 Limited believes probability factors of 50% should be applied to the incremental revenues and 75% to the headcount reductions. Targetco's income tax rate is 27%. T1 adopted a discount rate of 15% and a long-term growth rate of 3% (and, by extension, a capitalization rate of 12%) in its valuation analysis.

Based on the foregoing, the value of the tangible operating synergies would be estimated as follows:

Exhibit 11B
T1 Limited
Estimated Value of Tangible Operating Synergies

	Year 1	Year 2	Year 3	Year 4	Year 5	Thereafter
Cross-Selling Opportunities						
Incremental revenues	1,000,000	2,000,000	3,000,000	4,000,000	5,000,000	5,150,000
Contribution at 20%	200,000	400,000	600,000	800,000	1,000,000	1,030,000
Less: income taxes at 27%	(54,000)	(108,000)	(162,000)	(216,000)	(270,000)	(278,100)
Less: incremental working cap	(100,000)	(100,000)	(100,000)	(100,000)	(100,000)	(15,000)
Equals: incremental cash flow	46,000	192,000	338,000	484,000	630,000	736,900
Probability factor of 50% (A)	23,000	96,000	169,000	242,000	315,000	368,450
Headcount Reductions						
Salary savings	500,000	515,000	530,000	546,000	562,000	579,000
Less: severance costs	(250,000)					
Pre-tax savings	250,000	515,000	530,000	546,000	562,000	579,000
Less: income taxes at 27%	(67,500)	(139,050)	(143,100)	(147,420)	(151,740)	(156,330)
Equals: incremental cash flow	182,500	375,950	386,900	398,580	410,260	422,670
Probability factor of 75% (B)	136,875	281,963	290,175	298,935	307,695	317,003
Total probable cash flow (A+B)	159,875	377,963	459,175	540,935	622,695	685,453
Capitalized at						12%
Terminal value						5,712,104
Discounted at 15% (mid-year)	149,084	306,480	323,768	331,667	331,998	3,045,481
Value of synergies	4,488,477					

In the example above, the normalized discount rate and capitalization rate were adopted, given that the risk of synergy realization was reflected in the probability factors applied.

Quantifying Intangible Operating Synergies

Intangible operating synergies normally relate to one or both of:

- a reduced level of risk in achieving the prospective operating results, for example, the reduction in the risk of a critical manufacturing input through the acquisition of a supplier; and

- enhanced long-term growth prospects or strategic advantages not separately quantified, for example, the anticipated benefits related to the acquisition of new leading-edge technology.

Although the value of these post-acquisition synergies is often difficult to isolate, their quantification can be achieved through the application of a lower discount rate or capitalization rate to the prospective intrinsic discretionary cash flows of the target company than would otherwise be applied. In some cases, it may be appropriate to increase the value of tangible operating synergies otherwise quantified for such intangible factors as well. However, it is important to ensure that post-acquisition synergies are not double-counted.

In theory, the quantification of intangible operating synergies involves calculating the difference between:

- the value of the target company on an intrinsic basis; and

- the higher value of the target company based on the same cash flows, but with lower rates of return that incorporate intangible operating synergies.

The difference between the two resulting value determinations represents the value of intangible operating synergies. Again, it may be appropriate to apply a probability factor to that incremental value in recognition of the risks inherent in its realization. As a practical matter, buyers often adjust their price upward in recognition of strategic importance and other intangible operating synergies. However, in many cases the quantification of such benefits is more influenced by a buyer's qualitative assessment of the level of importance and amount of competition for a target company than it is by any mathematical exercise.

In theory, a downward adjustment to the discount (capitalization) rate resulting from the perceived reduction in the risk of realizing the projected post-acquisition unlevered discretionary cash flows should be made by reducing the unlevered cost of equity before adjusting for financial leverage. In practice however, where the rate of return is adjusted downward to account for intangible operating synergies (both risk reduction and incremental growth opportunities), the reduction is directly applied to the discount (capitalization) rate itself, being either a weighted average cost of capital (the more common approach) or levered cost of equity.

By way of example, assume that an acquisition target, U1 Limited, is expected to generate discretionary cash flows (on an intrinsic basis) of $5 million in Year 1, increasing by $1 million annually to $9 million by Year 5, and growing at a perpetual rate of 3% per annum thereafter. On an intrinsic value basis, the appropriate discount rate for U1 is 15%, and the appropriate capitalization rate is 12%, resulting in an intrinsic value of $65,364,000.

The buyer believes it would be highly synergistic to acquire U1 Limited because it would provide geographic diversification, even though tangible operating synergies would be negligible. Therefore, the buyer estimates the synergistic value of U1 by reducing the discount rate and the capitalization rate to 13% and 10%, respectively. The resultant synergistic value of U1 is $78,748,000.

The difference between the synergistic value and the intrinsic value of U1 of $13,394,000 represents the value of the intangible operating synergies. However, the buyer elects to assign a 50% probability factor to this amount, in order to reflect the risk of its realization and as part of its pricing strategy. The resultant probable value of the intangible operating synergies is $6,697,000, as illustrated in Exhibit 11C, below.

Exhibit 11C
U1 Limited
Estimated Value of Intangible Operating Synergies
($000)

	Year 1	Year 2	Year 3	Year 4	Year 5	Thereafter	Total Value
Discretionary Cash Flow	5,000	6,000	7,000	8,000	9,000	9,270	
Intrinsic Value Basis							
Capitalized at						12%	
Terminal Value						77,250	
Discounted at 15% (mid-year)	4,663	4,865	4,936	4,905	4,798	41,187	65,354
Synergistic Value Basis							
Capitalized at						10%	
Terminal Value						92,700	
Discounted at 13% (mid-year)	4,704	4,995	5,157	5,216	5,193	53,484	78,748
Value of intangible operating synergies							13,394
Probability Factor							50%
Probable Amount							6,697

While this approach to quantifying intangible operating synergies is not commonly applied in practice, it can help in assessing the reasonableness of making an adjustment for strategic factors, which is a subjective exercise.

Quantifying Financial Synergies

Financial synergies are those related to the ability of the buyer to obtain lower-cost financing or to employ a more efficient capital structure than the target company could accomplish on its own, or as a result of combining the two entities. Financial synergies may arise from:

- benefits related to the larger size of the combined entity, where the increased asset base provides greater security to debt and equity holders. The ability of larger organizations to attract a greater number of interested lenders and prospective investors can also lead to reduced financing costs;

- existing lending and investor relationships the buyer enjoys which can be extended to the target company to create a more efficient capital structure or obtain lower-cost financing than might otherwise be available to the target company. In many cases, the buyer has a lower cost of capital than the seller because the buyer typically is a larger organization. Alternatively, where the buyer is a public company, it may enjoy a lower cost of capital than an acquisition target that is a privately held company;

- where both the seller and the buyer are privately held companies and neither is of sufficient size to justify an initial public offering, but where the combined entity could offer its shares to the public and achieve a reduction in their respective costs of capital; and

- the ability to use more financial leverage in the capital structure of the combined entity because of greater stability of prospective cash flows or an enhanced degree of lender interest.

As discussed in Chapter 7, the discount (capitalization) rate normally should first be derived as an unlevered cost of equity. Subsequently, the impact of financial leverage should be considered to express the discount or capitalization rate as a weighted average cost of capital (in some cases, as a levered cost of equity). Accordingly, in theory the value of financial synergies can be quantified by calculating the value of the target company using a capital structure and rates of return that incorporate financial synergies, compared to the value of the target company absent the benefits associated with those financial synergies. Once again, it may be appropriate to apply a probability factor to the value of financial synergies to reflect the risk in their ultimate realization.

For example, assume the outstanding shares of V1 Limited (which has no interest-bearing debt or redundant assets) are valued on a stand-alone basis at $25 million, based on:

- $3 million of expected maintainable discretionary cash flow; and

- a capitalization rate of 12%, comprised of a nominal unlevered cost of equity of 15%, a normalized debt to total capitalization ratio of 20%, an income tax rate of 30% and long-term growth of 2%. As illustrated in Chapter 7, the calculation of the capitalization rate is as follows:

Weighted Average Cost of Capital (Formula 7.6):

15% x (1 – 30% x 20%) = 14% (rounded)

And:

14% WACC less 2% growth = 12% capitalization rate

Management of Buyco is contemplating acquiring the V1's outstanding shares. It believes, based on Buyco's better access to debt financing, that it could reasonably increase V1's debt to total capital ratio from 20% to 40%. Ignoring other possible sources of synergies, the benefit from that more efficient capital structure would be to reduce V1's capitalization rate to 11%, as follows:

Weighted Average Cost of Capital (Formula 7.6):

15% x (1 − 30% x 40%) = 13% (rounded)

And:

13% WACC less 2% growth = 11% capitalization rate

The resultant difference in the capitalized value of V1 Limited is $2,273,000. Assigning a probability factor of 50% results in a probable value of the financial synergies of $1,136,000.

Exhibit 11D
V1 Limited
Quantification of Financial Synergies
($000)

	Without Financial Synergies	With Financial Synergies	Difference
Discretionary Cash Flow	3,000	3,000	
Capitalization Rate	12%	11%	
Capitalized Value	25,000	27,273	2,273
Probability Factor			50%
Probable Value of Financial Synergies			1,136

Where it is believed that financial synergies will accrue to the buyer's existing operations following the transaction, an estimate should be made of the increase in the *en bloc* value of the buyer's business following the transaction as a result of the lower cost of capital. As is the case with intangible operating synergies, in practice the value of anticipated financial synergies is often quantified more by way of a subjective estimate than a purely mathematical exercise.

Where the buyer discounts the intrinsic discretionary cash flow of the target company using the buyer's cost of capital, the impact of financial synergies may be fully captured in the resultant valuation, and no further adjustment on account of financial synergies may be necessary.

Transaction and Integration Costs

The quantification of potential benefits expected to accrue from an acquisition is frequently emphasized. Often adequate consideration is not given to the costs of integration, the capital expenditures required to meet post-acquisition growth expectations, the timing of the anticipated benefits and the risks related to the ultimate realization of the perceived benefits. In fact, post-acquisition costs often exceed buyer expectations, thus reducing the synergies from what had been anticipated. If transaction benefits have also been overstated, the resultant cash flow shortfall from projections made by the buyer when assessing price could be significant.

The buyer incurs costs prior to, during and after the finalization of a transaction. Costs incurred up to and including the acquisition date often include:

- legal and advisory fees. These costs can vary significantly depending on the nature and size of the target company, and whether internal or external resources are used to fulfill these functions;

- management time. The successful purchase and integration of any acquired company involves a considerable amount of management time and effort. Larger companies will often employ one or more individuals whose primary function is corporate acquisitions; and

- incidental costs such as travel and accommodation, telephone expenses, and so on.

These costs are incurred as a normal part of the acquisition process, which includes bid preparation, due diligence and finalization of the purchase and sale documentation. As a result, most of these expenses are incurred regardless of whether a transaction closes. In most open market transactions such "sunk costs" are not factored into the price. In notional market valuations, such costs are not deducted from the value otherwise determined.

After transaction closing, the buyer will incur additional costs (either directly or through the acquired business) that should be considered and quantified when establishing the price for the target company. These costs are associated with the post-acquisition integration of the target business. The necessary expenses to realize post-acquisition synergies commonly include:

- severance costs associated with headcount reductions. These can represent a significant expense and can be complicated if management and union contracts specify terms and conditions related to terminations and layoffs. Although anticipated headcount reductions may be achieved through attrition and working notice periods, severance payment quantification may require legal advice;

- system integration costs. In many acquisitions, there is a need to integrate the accounting and reporting systems so that reliable and timely financial and other information can be generated. Frequently the systems are not compatible and considerable time and expense must be incurred to convert the acquired business's systems;

- employee training costs. These may include formal employee programs regarding the use of different technology, or training in the use of reporting formats, procedures, and other aspects of the buyer's business. The cost of informal training may be difficult to quantify;

- lease termination payments and facilities disposition costs. Where economies of scale include the reduction of duplicate facilities, the costs of terminating the occupation of existing premises must be determined. Where the premises are leased, lease termination payments may be required. Alternatively, if the acquired business owns the facilities to be disposed of, then that property should likely be regarded as a redundant asset. Disposition costs, including income taxes at the corporate level, should be calculated. Relocation expenses should also be considered;

- general integration and monitoring costs. Where the operations of the target company are to be integrated with that of the buyer, numerous integration costs arise. These may include expenses related to the implementation of policies and procedures, internal controls, administrative guidelines (e.g., forms and reports), changing signage, letterhead, and so on;

- quality standards. The product quality standards and operating standards of the buyer may be considerably different (usually more rigorous) than those of the acquired business. A detailed analysis of product quality, product standards, quality control, production systems, and so on must be undertaken by the buyer in order to assess the changes that will likely be required subsequent to acquisition;

- income tax consequences. In virtually all cases, a corporate buyer acquiring a privately held company does not have access to the small business deduction. Therefore, the intrinsic value of such a privately held company where it qualifies as a Canadian Controlled Private Corporation may be greater than the value to such a buyer before consideration of synergies. Other income tax consequences must also be considered, including the potential impact on the utilization of income tax losses, the impact on scientific research and experimental development (SRED) tax credits, and other tax incentives;

- management depth. In many businesses, particularly those that are small and privately held, the management team is dominated by a single person or only a few people. Where management personnel have not been groomed to provide for business continuity, buyers often find it necessary to supplement management of the acquired business following acquisition;

- employee benefit and incentive plans. Where the employees of an acquired business have significantly different benefits and incentives compared with the employees of the buyer, the transitional costs to deal with the differences must be considered. Where employees of the acquired business have a less favourable compensation package, it may be necessary to increase their compensation, particularly if the two companies will be highly integrated. Conversely, if the employees at the acquired business enjoy a significantly better compensation package than is offered by the buyer, changes to the plans covering those employees may have to be made. For example, employees of the acquired business may be offered a one-time cash payment in exchange for a reduced compensation plan to ensure consistency between the seller's compensation plan and that of the buyer;

- key personnel turnover. One of the consequences of acquisitions is that key employees may leave the acquired business due to uncertainty, differing management philosophies, or to seek other career opportunities. Where such employees perform a function that must be replaced, incidental costs may be incurred for hiring and training replacements. In addition, where the employees leaving possess important knowledge, abilities or customer contacts that cannot be readily replaced, the prospective discretionary cash flows of the acquired business may be at risk;

- deferred costs. Prior to sale, management of the target business may have deferred expenses in order to improve the business's reported financial results. Common items of this kind include deferred equipment maintenance, a moratorium on new hires, reduced advertising and research expenditures, and other expenses where the benefits may not be immediately realized. During the pre-acquisition review, the buyer must critically assess whether certain costs have been deferred and if so, what the short-term and long-term impact on the acquired business will be; and

- penalties for breaching minimum purchase or other commitments. Alternatively, if those commitments are fulfilled, the buyer may incur an incremental cost.

The buyer should attempt to quantify transaction and integration costs where it is able to do so, and factor those costs into its valuation model. However, certain costs cannot be readily quantified in isolation, such as the risk of losing major customers or key employees following the transaction. This is sometimes referred to "transition risk". Rather, the quantification of transition risk is normally done by increasing the required rates of return. As a result, the quantification of transition risk tends to be made by increasing the discount or capitalization rate.

Deal Structuring

Assets vs. Shares

A fundamental decision to be made in connection with the purchase and sale of an incorporated business is whether the shares or the assets should be acquired. For unincorporated entities (e.g., partnerships, sole proprietorships and unincorporated joint ventures) the assets of the business are acquired by default.

In the case of public companies, the transaction is typically structured as a sale of shares. In cases where the assets of a public company are sold, the net proceeds are distributed to the shareholders, then the company is wound up.

For privately held companies, sellers usually prefer to sell shares because of the income tax savings available through such a structure. In Canada, capital gains (which arise on the sale of shares) are taxed at more favourable rates than other forms of income (e.g., ordinary income and dividend income). In addition, individuals (Canadian residents) who sell shares of a company that meets the definition of a "Qualified Small Business Corporation" for income tax purposes can qualify for the lifetime capital gains exemption, which exempts an individual from taxation on the first $750,000 of capital gain income ($500,000 prior to 2007). Furthermore, the lifetime capital gains exemption can be multiplied among family members where a trust is properly established. To qualify for the lifetime capital gains exemption, the shares sold must be of a "small business corporation". This is a corporation which is a:

- Canadian controlled private corporation as defined in the *Income Tax Act*; and

- 90% of the fair market value of the assets of which: (i) are used principally in carrying on an active business in Canada; or (ii) consist of shares or debt of one or more connected small business corporations.

In general, a shareholder must have held the shares for at least 24 months and a complex definition is used to prevent the "stacking" of corporations to avoid the asset test described above.

The *Income Tax Act* contains a number of specific anti-avoidance provisions relating to the capital gains exemption and a careful review is required in any case to ensure the exemption is available. Because the exemption is only available to individuals, consideration must be given to the form of a transaction for the sale of a business if access to the exemption is desired.

Conversely, buyers usually prefer to acquire the assets of a privately held company. This is primarily because of the:

- reduced liability assumed by the buyer of assets as opposed to shares. Buyers of assets are only accountable for the specific liabilities they agree to assume from the target company. This limitation reduces the buyer's exposure to hidden liabilities, such as unidentified lawsuits, underaccrued liabilities, etc.; and

- step-up in tax base on depreciable assets, which allows the buyer to claim higher levels of capital cost allowance and incur less tax following the transaction. In addition, where goodwill is acquired pursuant to an asset transaction, 75% of the goodwill acquired is added to the buyer's cumulative eligible capital pool for Canadian tax purposes, and deducted at a rate of 7% per annum on a declining balance basis. By contrast, a buyer of shares assumes the existing tax base of the acquired company's assets, and is not permitted to increase the cumulative eligible capital balance because of goodwill acquired in the transaction.

As a result of these benefits, motivated buyers will sometimes pay more for assets than for shares. Where the assets of a company are sold, the seller can then distribute the net proceeds, which are subject to dividend tax. However, many sellers retain the net proceeds within the shell company following the transaction in order to defer personal income taxes.

Whenever the assets of a business are purchased, section 68 of the *Income Tax Act* requires the total purchase price to be allocated among the assets purchased on a reasonable basis. The amount so allocated to each asset is then deemed to be the proceeds of disposition of the property to the seller and the cost of the property to the buyer. Often this allocation is included in the purchase agreement and is a result of genuine bargaining on the part of the buyer and seller acting at arm's length. Where this is not the case, and the allocation is grossly at variance with the fair market value of the assets, an allocation will be made on some reasonable basis which is frequently the fair market value of the various assets.

This allocation causes an issue between the buyer and seller. The buyer typically wants to allocate the highest justifiable amount of proceeds to assets that can be depreciated rapidly in order to minimize income taxes (e.g., software and production equipment). However, to the extent that the allocation to depreciable assets is greater than their tax base (UCC), the target company is subject to tax on recaptured depreciation. By contrast, the portion of the purchase price allocated to goodwill for Canadian income tax purposes receives favourable tax treatment from the seller's perspective because 50% of the amount received on account of goodwill is attributed to the capital dividend account, which can be paid to the shareholders tax-free (see Chapter 9). The remaining 50% of goodwill is subject to corporate tax at regular business rates.

Example

Assume that a buyer is looking to acquire W1 Limited, a Canadian controlled private corporation. The parties have agreed that the enterprise value of W1 is $8 million determined as a multiple of 4x normalized EBITDA of $2 million. Since the company has $2 million of debt outstanding the agreed equity value of W1 is therefore $6 million. A comparison of the book value and fair market value of W1's assets and liabilities is as follows:

Exhibit 11E
W1 Limited
Allocation of Purchase Price

	Book Value	Fair Market Value
Accounts receivable	3,000,000	3,000,000
Other current assets	500,000	500,000
Total current assets	3,500,000	3,500,000
Software	250,000	1,000,000
Office equipment	1,250,000	1,500,000
Goodwill	0	3,200,000
Total assets	5,000,000	9,200,000
Bank loan	500,000	500,000
Accounts payable	1,100,000	1,100,000
Other current liabilities	100,000	100,000
Total current liabilities	1,700,000	1,700,000
Long-term debt	1,500,000	1,500,000
Total liabilities	3,200,000	3,200,000
Common shares	100,000	6,000,000
Retained earnings	1,700,000	
	1,800,000	6,000,000
Total liabilities and equity	5,000,000	9,200,000

Other relevant facts include:

- the original cost of the software was $800,000. The remaining UCC balance is $100,000, which is deductible at a CCA rate of 100% (subject to the half year rule);

- the original cost of the office equipment is $2 million. Its UCC balance is $1 million, which is subject to a CCA rate of 20% on a declining balance basis;

- the buyer's income tax rate is 30% and the applicable cost of capital (WACC) for this acquisition is 15%;

- because of common ownership with another Canadian corporation, W1 pays income taxes at a rate of 27% on its active business income and is not eligible for the small business deduction. Investment income is taxed at a rate of 46.67%, including the refundable tax component of 26.67%. The transaction takes place on the first day of W1's taxation year; and

- the sole shareholder of W1, Mr. West, has not yet used his lifetime capital gains exemption of $750,000. His tax rate is 46% on the taxable portion of capital gains and 28% on eligible dividend income. The paid up capital of the common shares is $10,000, and their cost base is $100,000.

The parties are still negotiating whether the transaction will be finalized as a sale of shares or a sale of assets.

Buyer's Perspective

Estimating the enterprise value of a business based on a multiple of EBITDA (as is the case in this example) assumes a share-based purchase. From the perspective of the buyer, a purchase of shares would entail a capital outlay of $6 million for the shares and the assumption of $2 million of debt (consisting of the bank loan for $500,000 and the long-term debt of $1.5 million). The existing UCC balances of the software and office equipment would carry over. While goodwill of $3.2 million would be acquired for accounting purposes, it would not give rise to a tax deduction. (As an aside, the goodwill would be allocated among identifiable intangible assets and non-identifiable intangible assets for purchase price accounting purposes, as discussed in Chapter 10).

Conversely, if the buyer acquired the assets of W1, then the amount the buyer should be willing to pay is in excess of $8.5 million, as illustrated below.

Exhibit 11F
Value of W1 Limited
Based on Asset Purchase

Enterprise value based on share purchase			8,000,000
Deduct: CCA not available on the purchase of shares			
Software: $100,000 x 100% CCA rate x 27% tax rate			(27,000)
Office Equipment:	$1,000,000 \times 20\% \times 27\%$		(154,286)
(Formula 3.3)	$(15\% + 20\%)$		
Add: CCA based on stepped-up value of assets			
Software	$1,000,000 \times 100\% \times 30\%$	$\times (1 + .5 \times 15\%)$	243,856
(Formula 3.2)	$(15\% + 100\%)$	$(1 + 15\%)$	
Office Equipment	$1,500,000 \times 20\% \times 30\%$	$\times (1 + .5 \times 15\%)$	240,373
(Formula 3.2)	$(15\% + 20\%)$	$(1 + 15\%)$	
Goodwill	$75\% \times \$3,200,000 \times 7\% \times 30\%$		229,091
(Formula 5.5)	$(15\% + 7\%)$		
Enterprise Value based on asset purchase			8,532,034

In this calculation (see also Chapter 5 – "Assets vs. Shares"), the buyer of assets is not entitled to claim CCA using the existing tax base of the assets (software and office equipment in this case, based on the seller's tax rate of 27%). However, the buyer is entitled to claim CCA on the stepped-up value of the software and the office equipment, subject to the half year rule, and based on the buyer's tax rate of 30%. Using Formula 3.2, the present value of the CCA tax shield on these assets is calculated at $243,856 and $240,373, respectively. In addition, 75% of the goodwill acquired in an asset deal is deductible at a rate of 7% per annum, on a declining balance basis. Goodwill (eligible capital property) is not subject to the half year rule. Therefore, the present value of the tax shield on goodwill is calculated based on Formula 5.5.

While the buyer should calculate the value of the target company based on the stepped-up value of the assets, whether or not that incremental value is paid for is a function of the relative negotiating positions of the parties and the structure of the deal.

Seller's Perspective

From the perspective of Mr. West, the sole shareholder of W1 Limited, a sale of shares would give rise to a capital gain, and allow Mr. West to use his lifetime capital gains exemption. The net proceeds pursuant to a sale of shares would therefore be $4,815,500 as illustrated in Exhibit 11G:

Exhibit 11G
Proceeds to Mr. West on the Sale of W1 Limited Shares

Selling price of the shares (A)	6,000,000
Less: cost base of the shares	(100,000)
Equals: capital gain	5,900,000
Less: lifetime capital gains exemption	(750,000)
Capital gain net of exemption	5,150,000
50% taxable	2,575,000
Personal taxes at 46% (B)	1,184,500
Net proceeds (A - B)	4,815,500

However, if the assets of W1 Limited are sold for $8 million (enterprise value), then the net proceeds to Mr. West are calculated in a two step process, which entails:

- first calculating the after-tax proceeds that would be retained in W1; then
- calculating the after-tax proceeds retained by Mr. West.

The net proceeds that would be retained by W1 are $5,264,830, as illustrated in Exhibit 11H. According to this calculation:

- the sale of software for $1 million gives rise to business income (recapture) of $700,000, the difference between the original cost of $800,000 and the UCC of $100,000. In addition, there is a capital gain of

$200,000 (of which $100,000 is taxable) based on the difference between the proceeds of $1 million and the original cost of $800,000;

- the sale of office equipment for $1.5 million gives rise to business income (recapture) of $250,000, being the excess over the UCC balance of $1,250,000. There is no capital gain on the office equipment, given that the proceeds are less than the cost base;

- the sale of goodwill for $3.2 million is 50% taxable as ordinary business income (i.e., $1.6 million);

- taxes on business income (including recapture and the taxable portion of goodwill) are based on a rate of 27%; and

- taxes on the taxable portion of the capital gain on the sale of software ($100,000) are calculated at 46.67%, which includes the refundable tax component.

The capital dividend account for W1 would be increased by $1.7 million because of the non-taxable portion of the capital gain on the software ($100,000) and the non-taxable portion of the gain on goodwill ($1.6 million).

Exhibit 11H
Net Proceeds to W1 Limited on Sale of Assets

	Proceeds	Cost Base	UCC	Business Income	Taxable Capital Gain
Accounts receivable	3,000,000	3,000,000			
Other current assets	500,000	500,000			
Software	1,000,000	800,000	100,000	700,000	100,000
Office equipment	1,500,000	2,000,000	1,250,000	250,000	
Goodwill	3,200,000			1,600,000	
Total assets acquired	9,200,000				
Bank loan	500,000	500,000			
Accounts payable	1,100,000	1,100,000			
Other current liabilities	100,000	100,000			
Long-term debt	1,500,000	1,500,000			
Total liabilities assumed or settled	3,200,000				
Proceeds before taxes	6,000,000				
Total income				2,550,000	100,000
Taxes on active business income at 27%	688,500				
Taxes on taxable capital gain at 46.67%	46,670		(includes refundable taxes of 26,700)		
Proceeds after taxes	5,264,830				

Next, the proceeds retained by Mr. West are determined by deducting taxes on the dividend and the capital gain (loss) created by the wind-up of W1 Limited. In this regard:

- the proceeds available for distribution include the refundable taxes paid by Company W1, which are refunded at a rate of $1 for every $3 of taxable dividends paid;

- Mr. West can receive the capital dividend of $1.7 million on a tax-free basis;

- the deemed dividend (an "eligible dividend") is taxed at an effective rate of 28%; and

- a capital loss is created to the extent that the paid-up capital is less than the adjusted cost base of the shares. Capital losses can only be offset against capital gains.

Exhibit 11I
Net Proceeds to Mr. West on Wind-Up of W1 Limited

Total proceeds of distribution	5,264,830
Add: refundable taxes	26,700
Total proceeds of distribution (A)	5,291,530
Less: paid-up capital	10,000
Equals: deemed dividend on wind-up	5,281,530
Less: capital dividend account	1,700,000
Equals: deemed taxable dividend	3,581,530
Taxes on eligible dividends at 28% (B)	1,002,828
Net proceeds (A-B)	4,288,702

It follows that Mr. West would prefer to sell the shares of W1 rather than the assets, or at least to negotiate a higher price from the buyer in order to reduce or eliminate the difference. That said, Mr. West can defer the taxes on the deemed dividend by retaining the net proceeds within the company.

In this example, it was assumed that the dividends distributed to Mr. West were taxed as eligible dividends, given that W1 paid income tax at the full corporate rate of 27%. To the extent that a corporation enjoys the benefits of the small business rate, the dividends paid from such after-tax profits are treated as ineligible dividends and subject to a higher personal income tax rate than eligible dividends. This helps to ensure integration between corporate tax rates and personal tax rates within the Canadian income tax system.

Forms of Consideration

The forms of consideration represent when, how and under what conditions the purchase price is (or is not) paid. Price and form of consideration are interdependent. In a notional market context, fair market value is determined on a cash or cash-equivalent basis. In open market transactions, other forms of consideration (termed "transaction structuring") are frequently used.

The ability to undertake transaction structuring involving non-cash forms of consideration depends on whether the target company is public or private. In the case of a public company, because of securities legislation, the acquisition typically has to be structured either as cash or freely tradable shares of the buyer at closing. Therefore, the buyer assumes the risk of adverse developments following the closing of the transaction. However, in the case of a privately held company acquisition (or where a public company is divesting of a portion of its operations) considerably more flexibility is available.

The forms of consideration in an open market transaction are a function of the negotiating positions of the buyer and seller, each party's respective interests and motivations, and the resources available to the buyer. For obvious reasons sellers prefer to receive as much cash on closing as possible, whereas buyers tend to prefer payments over time and, ideally, conditional upon the attainment of satisfactory operating results following the transaction.

While non-cash forms of consideration can vary widely, the most common include holdbacks, promissory notes, share exchanges and earnouts. Where a transaction involves a non-cash component, both the buyer and seller should attempt to determine the implied cash-equivalent value to provide a basis for comparison.

Holdbacks

Holdbacks are very common in private company transactions. Holdbacks are normally used to protect the buyer against:

- inadequate working capital. As discussed in Chapter 4, the enterprise value of a business assumes a normalized level of working capital, which has been negotiated as part of the transaction. Where the working capital delivered at the closing date is less than the agreed target, there is usually a downward adjustment to the purchase price;

- overpaying for the shares (following a share deal) because the debt levels of the target company at the closing date are higher than anticipated;

- hidden liabilities, such as underaccrued warranties, vacation pay, and so on; and

- contingent liabilities, such as a lawsuit, environmental claim or other issue.

While the amount of the holdback is negotiated in each transaction, it is not unusual for a holdback to represent between 5% and 15% of the purchase price, for a period ranging from six months to two years. In many cases, the holdback is placed into an escrow account to reduce the risk of non-collection to the seller, assuming that all of the conditions attached to the holdback are satisfied.

Promissory Notes

Promissory notes (sometimes referred to as "vendor take-backs") are used where the seller agrees to receive some (or all) of the purchase price over a period of time. In some cases, redeemable preferred shares are used rather than a promissory note.

Promissory notes provide a form of financing to the buyer. They typically rank as unsecured (subordinated) debt, behind bank debt and other creditors, and therefore they expose the seller to the risk of non-collection. The terms of the note, including the length of time and applicable interest rate, are negotiated in each case. Where the rate of return on the promissory note is below (or above) market rates compared to financial instruments of similar risk, the difference can be attributed to a price discount or premium as the case may be.

Promissory notes are sometimes structured with performance conditions of the target company as well, thereby incorporating an element of a holdback or earnout (discussed below).

From the seller's perspective, if full payment for the sale of shares is not received in the year of sale and part of the purchase price is to be deferred (e.g., according to the terms of a promissory note or earnout, discussed below), the seller is entitled to deduct a reasonable reserve in computing its capital gain. Generally, the maximum deferral period of capital gains using reserves is five years; a minimum of 20% of the total gain must be recognized in the first year after the transaction, 40% in the second year, 60% in the third year, and so on.

Share Exchanges

A buyer may offer its shares as currency to finance a transaction leaving the seller with an interest in the combined company after the transaction has taken place.

Where a public company is acquired in a share exchange for the shares of another public company, benchmarks exist by which to measure both the value received and the value given up. In these cases, the principal issue is often the extent to which anticipated post-acquisition synergies are shared between buyer and seller. Synergies likely will be perceived to exist by both buyer and seller as well as by market analysts and the investing public.

Where the seller is a privately held company and the buyer is a public company, the seller can often assess the value received if the shares taken in exchange are freely tradable. However, the valuation exercise becomes more complex where the seller is restricted from selling the shares for some period of time and/or the public company buyer has a relatively small market capitalization, thereby causing the block of shares held by the seller following the transaction to be somewhat illiquid.

Determining a cash-equivalent price in a share exchange is particularly complicated where the buyer is not a public company. In effect, it becomes a relative valuation exercise between the buyer and seller. Further complications arise after the seller exchanges a controlling interest in a privately held company for a minority interest position in a (likely larger) privately held company. As discussed in Chapter 8, absent a shareholder agreement or some other agreement that dictates otherwise, a minority position in a privately held company may be worth less than its pro-rata portion of *en bloc* value. Therefore, in a share exchange involving privately held companies, the provisions of such post-transaction agreements become critical.

As a practical matter, sellers are not normally interested in receiving shares of privately held companies as consideration unless there is some assurance of liquidity. Liquidity may come in the form of a put option or from the expectation (contractual or otherwise) the buyer will float an initial public offering or the business will be sold *en bloc* to a third party in the near future.

Where the buyer's shares are used as currency in lieu of cash, a rollover may be available under section 85.1 of the *Income Tax Act* where a shareholder sells shares of a corporation to another corporation and receives treasury shares of the purchasing corporation as consideration (see Chapter 9). For a section 85.1 rollover to apply, the purchasing corporation must be a Canadian corporation and the shareholder must hold the shares as capital property. If those considerations are met, the capital gain or loss to the selling shareholder is deferred automatically unless the taxpayer specifically chooses not to have the provisions of this section of the *Income Tax Act* apply (i.e., a joint election is not required by both the seller and the buyer of the shares). This makes share exchanges attractive from a tax perspective. However, the tax advantages are sometimes outweighed by the absence of liquidity. In some cases, the seller is restricted from disposing of the acquired shares for a period of time following the transaction, which subjects the seller to the risk of adverse changes in the share price. In addition, where the shares of the buyer are thinly traded and the seller holds a significant interest following the transaction, the acquired shares may be subject to a block discount (see Chapter 8). Alternatively, the acquired shares may have to be sold into the market over a prolonged period, placing downward pressure on the share price and again exposing the seller to the risk of adverse price changes over that period.

Share exchanges are also commonly used in the context of an amalgamation. Section 87 of the *Income Tax Act* allows two or more Canadian organizations to transfer their respective shares into a newly formed corporation on a tax-deferred basis. In order to effect an income tax deferral, all shares of each predecessor company must be transferred to the amalgamated company with the only consideration received being shares of the amalgamated company.

In an amalgamation, one of the predecessor parties might control the combined entity. Where one party emerges as the controlling shareholder, in many ways an amalgamation is not dissimilar to a share acquisition. Both privately held and public companies may be involved. However, as a practical matter, amalgamations tend to take place among companies that are not too dissimilar in size, whereas acquisitions tend to be take place where a larger company acquires the outstanding shares or assets of a smaller company.

Amalgamations are sometimes used to squeeze out minority shareholders by issuing them redeemable preferred shares for their common share interest and subsequently redeeming the preferred shares. As discussed in Chapter 8, amalgamations may give rise to a dissent remedy available to minority shareholders in most jurisdictions.

Where amalgamating entities are not dissimilar in size, there is normally the expectation of post-amalgamation synergies. Therefore, the valuation issues that arise include not only the relative value of the amalgamating entities on a stand-alone basis, but also how the post-amalgamation synergies will be divided. As a practical matter, smaller businesses sometimes enjoy a relatively greater portion of the overall synergies by combining with a larger business because of the relative increase in the value of the interest held by the shareholders of the smaller company subsequent to the amalgamation. That being said, merger transactions are often facilitated where both parties agree that the interest held by each shareholder in the newly formed corporation will be a function of the relative intrinsic values of the companies prior to the transaction. The justification for this is that, if the amalgamation does not proceed, the post-amalgamation synergies will not materialize. Whether or not parties agree in advance to put aside post-amalgamation synergies for the purposes of amalgamation discussions depends on several factors, including:

- the alternatives available to each party in terms of other prospective buyers who would purchase the outstanding shares or assets of the target company *en bloc*;

- the quantum of perceived synergies. Where post-amalgamation synergies are expected to be significant, the parties will recognize the value of their respective businesses might be significantly enhanced regardless of what reasonable share ownership percentage they obtain in the combined entity; and

- other matters agreed on by the parties in respect of the combined entity including management responsibility and the provisions of a post-merger shareholder agreement or other agreements.

Earnouts

In some cases, a portion of the purchase price is based on the prospective revenues, earnings, or some other measure related to the post-acquisition results of the acquired business. An earnout is commonly used to bridge a pricing gap between buyer and seller where the two disagree on the future prospects of the target company. An earnout effectively shifts the risk from buyer to seller because, if prospective results are not realized, the purchase price is reduced.

The key considerations to be addressed when negotiating an earnout include:

- the duration of the earnout. In this regard, a period of one to five years is not uncommon. However, longer earnout periods entail greater risk for the seller;

- the performance metrics adopted. Sellers generally prefer high-level criteria such as revenues, whereas buyers generally prefer measures such as gross profit or pre-tax income. The performance criteria selected will depend to some extent on the level of involvement and influence the seller will have on the operations of the acquired company following the transaction;

- whether there are minimum and/or maximum earnout levels established. Most earnouts are structured as a "cliff" such that if performance falls below an amount that is close to the target, no earnout is paid. In addition, most earnouts have a stated maximum amount that can be earned; and

- whether the earnout measures are cumulative. That is, whether underperformance or overperformance in a given year carries over to the following year.

Earnouts can be highly complex and often become problematic because of unanticipated developments or changing business conditions in the years following the transaction closing date. Consequently, determining the cash-equivalent value of an earnout can be a subjective task. It requires a realistic assessment of the likelihood the performance measures will be met, the time value of money and the likelihood of collection from the buyer (see Chapter 4).

In addition, earnouts need to be properly structured to ensure that they can be treated as proceeds of disposition to the seller and hence qualify for capital gains treatment. In this regard, earnouts are commonly structured as "reverse earnouts", whereby the seller sets the purchase price at a reasonable maximum, subject to reduction if the performance guidelines set out in the earnout arrangement are not met. The seller then uses the "cost recovery" method to account for the proceeds of sale. In this method, the seller claims the maximum amount of the earnout to be received at the closing date and takes a reserve against amounts not yet received. The *Income Tax Act* allows a seller to claim a reserve against amounts not received, which must be taken into income over a five-year period following the transaction closing at a rate of 20% per year. Therefore, caution must be used to ensure the amount of eligible reserve is sufficient to offset earnout payments not yet received.

Failure to properly structure an earnout for tax purposes could result in the entire purchase price being treated as ordinary income. This problem can occur where the purchase price is set at a minimum amount and subject to increase by the formula in the earnout arrangement. Therefore, any sale based in whole or in part on an earnout should be structured as a reverse earn-out, and the cost recovery method should be utilized. The cost recovery method can be used if:

- the buyer and seller act at arm's length;

- the shares are capital property of the seller;

- it is reasonable to assume the earnout relates to the value of goodwill, which cannot be easily valued at the time of sale;

- the earnout period does not exceed five years; and

- the seller undertakes to follow the cost recovery procedure.

If the earnout arrangement is in accordance with these conditions, the proceeds of disposition will be first considered to reduce the adjusted cost base of the shares. Only when total proceeds exceed such adjusted cost base will any gains be recognized. No capital losses may be realized until the ultimate proceeds are determined.

Partial Buyouts

As an alternative to an earnout, the buyer and seller sometimes strike an agreement whereby the buyer acquires a majority interest in the target company and the seller retains the residual (minority) interest. The shareholder agreement normally contains put-call provisions that either entitle or require the buyer to acquire the seller's residual interest at or after a specific point in time.

Partial buyouts can be an attractive deal structuring mechanism because they can create an alignment of interests between the buyer and seller. Specifically, such an alignment benefits the buyer by incentivizing the seller to increase the earnings and value of the target company after the closing date, and rewards the seller for doing so. In addition, the buyer is able to acquire control of the target company without having to finance 100% of the purchase price up front.

However, partial buyouts can become more complex because of the presence of minority shareholder rights that require the buyer holding the controlling interest to be accountable to the seller holding the minority interest. Furthermore, the existence of a minority shareholder can impede the buyer's efforts to integrate the operations of the target company with its existing operations.

Where the seller retains a minority interest, the provisions of a shareholder agreement and related valuation provisions are particularly important (see Chapter 8). In this regard, the put-call provisions are sometimes established with reference to a pre-determined formula, which can be problematic and result in unintended consequences for either the buyer or the seller, because of changing business, economic and industry conditions.

Management Contracts

In transactions involving the purchase of a privately held company where the owner was actively involved in the operations, it is common for the buyer to strike a management agreement or consulting agreement with the seller in order to ensure the seller remains active in the acquired business for an agreed period of time following the transaction. The owner/seller can help to ensure the successful transition of the target company's customers, employees and other parties, as well as bring over any technical knowledge or other know-how. Management contracts are commonly of one-to-three years' duration and vary considerably in terms of responsibility, authority and remuneration.

There is a trade-off between the price paid for a business and the remuneration package afforded to the seller pursuant to a management contract or consulting agreement. From an economic perspective, sellers generally prefer to receive a higher price for their company rather than a compensation adjustment because of the different tax treatment of these income sources. Remuneration paid under a management or consulting contract is fully taxable to the seller (and tax deductible for the buyer), whereas higher proceeds of sale for the shares of a company would give rise to more favourable capital gains treatment to the seller (but be non-deductible for the buyer).

Alternatively, buyers will prefer higher remuneration arrangements because of the more favourable tax treatment from their perspective and because lucrative management or consulting contracts help the buyer to ensure the seller is motivated to facilitate the transition of the acquired business.

Non-Competition Agreements

Non-competition agreements are a condition precedent to the acquisition of a privately held business, particularly where a selling shareholder is active in the operations of the target company and is believed by the buyer, absent such an agreement, to be in a position to negatively affect the acquired business following the transaction. Non-competition agreements specify the parameters of agreed non-competition, which normally include the:

- geographic area where the seller is prohibited from competing. This is usually determined by the existing or prospective geographic coverage of the acquired company;

- nature of non-permissible activities (e.g., management or shareholder role in a business whose operations are similar to the acquired business or the buyer's business); and

- term of the non-competition provisions (typically two to five years).

Historically in Canada, a portion of the aggregate purchase price has seldom been allocated to the non-competition agreement during the negotiation process. However, this has changed in recent years. The current view is that if specific compensation is given for not competing, that non-competition may prove to be more enforceable than it otherwise would be. In addition, pending changes to tax legislation would require that a portion of the purchase price be allocated to a non-competition agreement. The valuation of non-competition agreements was discussed in Chapter 10. The portion of the purchase price allocated to a non-competition agreement becomes eligible capital property to the buyer and ordinary income for the seller.

Non-Solicitation Agreements

In addition to non-competition agreements (or sometimes in lieu of), the buyer and seller enter into a separate non-solicitation agreement whereby the seller is prohibited from soliciting the customers and employees of the acquired business for a specified period following the transaction. Such provisions are normally incorporated into a non-competition agreement where one exists.

Non-solicitation agreements typically afford less protection to the buyer, because it is usually more difficult to prove the seller enticed customers and employees away from the acquired business, as distinct from those parties leaving of their own volition. However, where active solicitation is proven, it tends to be enforced by the courts.

While it is rare for a buyer and seller to assign a particular value to the non-solicitation agreement as part of the purchase and sale agreement, a portion of the purchase price may be attributed to the non-solicitation agreement for financial accounting purposes. However, since such agreements provide less protection to the buyer as contrasted with a non-competition agreement, the value attributable to a non-solicitation agreement is typically less.

Other Factors Influencing Price in Open Market Transactions

Public vs. Privately Held Companies

There are important differences between public and privately held companies that can impact the price paid in the open market. These include:

- the level of awareness surrounding a divestiture. Unlike the public stock markets, or other organized regulated exchanges, the market for privately held businesses is not regulated, nor is it organized in any formal way. As a result, particularly where privately held businesses are not widely marketed, transactions involving privately held businesses are characterized by prices being struck where:
  - ✓ there is no widespread knowledge of the transaction prior to its closing,
  - ✓ sellers can never be certain that all possible buyers have been canvassed and, hence, that they have achieved the highest possible price,
  - ✓ potential buyers may only hear about a transaction after closing, and
  - ✓ as a rule, buyers can never be certain during the negotiation process whether there is an alternate bidder for a given acquisition, or what price that other bidder(s) might be willing or able to pay.

By contrast, a bid for all the shares, a controlling interest, or a significant minority interest in a public company is characterized by media coverage. In many cases, such publicity brings forth prospective buyers who only express an interest when they learn that the outstanding shares of a company are "in play". This in turn may place upward pressure on the transaction price;

- the fact that recent trading in a public company's shares can create a benchmark price whereas privately held companies have no such benchmark. The shareholders and board of directors of the target public company typically review any price offered at least in part in relation to those trading prices; and

- the fact that in public company takeovers, there is an overriding emphasis on economic interests (i.e., shareholders are focused on short-term capital gain maximization). Conversely, sellers of privately held businesses may be acting out of both economic and non-economic interests, including satisfaction of personal income tax planning objectives, continuity of corporate culture, paternalistic sentiment toward both family and employees, and personal employment continuity after the transaction.

Availability of Financing

In theory, the enterprise value of a business is independent of how it is financed. In practice however, the price a buyer is willing to pay is usually influenced, at least to some degree, by the financing resources the buyer has available. In the acquisition of a privately held company, the buyer might be able to source a portion of the financing through transaction structuring, including promissory notes and earnouts. Where the buyer is a relatively small public company, shares are often used as currency instead of cash. However, these alternate forms of consideration sometimes place the buyer at a disadvantage in the negotiations where other prospective buyers can close a transaction entirely (or primarily) in cash.

Where cash is necessary or desirable to finalize a deal, and where the buyer does not have cash on hand, it becomes necessary to raise additional capital. Even where the buyer does have cash on hand, it may want to use the acquisition as a reason for raising new capital in order to preserve existing cash for other purposes.

The various forms of capital raising a buyer will normally consider are:

- senior debt secured against the assets of the acquired entity, and possibly by a guarantee from the buyer. Senior debt is attractive because of its low cost, although the related covenants must be carefully considered;

- subordinated debt, where sufficient senior debt capacity does not exist. While subordinated debt is considerably more costly than senior debt, it is cheaper than equity financing and usually has less stringent covenants and greater flexibility; and

- equity. In this regard, public company buyers may go to the market for a public offering or a private placement. Equity financing becomes more problematic for privately held companies, unless the owners are prepared to inject new equity capital personally or they are prepared to entertain a private equity firm or other third-party investor.

The higher the cost of capital to the buyer, the less it can realistically afford to pay for the target company. The amount and type of capital to raise is part of the company's capital structure decision, which was discussed in Chapter 7.

Earnings Dilution

When determining value, the cash flow the target company is expected to generate is of primary importance. After-tax earnings determined pursuant to Generally Accepted Accounting Principles or International Financial Reporting Standards are less important, although forecast post-acquisition consolidated after-tax earnings do play an important role in acquisitions by public companies (and to a lesser extent by some privately held companies).

Public company buyers estimate post-acquisition consolidated earnings per share to determine whether the acquisition is expected to be accretive or dilutive to their reported earnings per share in the near term following closing.

Estimating the degree of prospective earnings accretion or dilution is further complicated due to the fact the allocation of intangible value among identifiable intangible assets and non-identifiable intangible assets (goodwill), and consequently the prospective amortization charges, are usually not known for certain until sometime after closing. Purchase price allocation was discussed in Chapter 10.

By way of example, assume that public company X1 Limited has 60 million shares outstanding, and the current market price is $3 per share. X1 generates net income of $15 million per year, and therefore its earnings per share are $0.25. The implied price/earnings multiple is 12x.

X1 Limited acquires Targetco for $30 million by issuing 10 million treasury shares of X1 in exchange for all the outstanding shares of Targetco, which generates net income of $4 million per year.

The market value of Targetco's net assets approximates their book value of $15 million. Therefore, intangible value of $15 million has been acquired in this transaction. A purchase price allocation for the intangible value establishes the following:

- $3 million to a non-competition agreement, which is amortized evenly over its three-year life;

- $10 million to the customer base, which is amortized over the estimated average customer life of 10 years; and

- $2 million to goodwill, which is not amortized for accounting purposes, but rather periodically tested for impairment.

Assuming that accounting earnings for each of X1 and Targetco are expected to remain stable in the year following acquisition, and assuming that no synergies are generated in that year, the post-acquisition consolidated earnings per share of X1 Limited in the year following acquisition would be as follows:

Exhibit 11J
X1 Limited
Calculation of Pro-forma Earnings Per Share

Net income on a stand-alone basis	
X1 Limited	15,000,000
Targetco	4,000,000
	19,000,000
Deduct: amortization of intangibles	
Non-competition agreement	(1,000,000)
Customer relationships	(1,000,000)
Pro-forma net income (A)	17,000,000
Shares outstanding	
Original	60,000,000
Issued on acquisition	10,000,000
Total (B)	70,000,000
Pro-forma EPS (A/B)	0.24
Price-earnings multiple	12.0x
Pro-forma share price	2.88

The post-acquisition consolidated earnings per share of X1 have decreased from $0.25 to $0.24. If stock market participants continue to value X1 at a price-earnings multiple of 12x, the price of X1 shares would decline to $2.88 from $3.00.

Common Issues in Open Market Transactions

Both buyers and sellers frequently make errors when concluding open market transactions. These errors can have a material impact on the value received by the buyer or the seller, as the case may be. Some of the more common issues are as follows:

- while the economics of any transaction are important, buyers and sellers sometimes underestimate how much the dynamics of negotiations and deal structuring determine whether a transaction will be concluded, and at what price and terms;

- buyers frequently overestimate the synergies expected from a transaction, and understate the costs and risks associated with realizing those synergies;

- both buyers and sellers underestimate the amount of time and effort required to conclude a transaction. Buyers need to be prepared to expend the time and resources required to conduct adequate due diligence. Sellers need to ensure management time is available to produce the documentation requested from the buyer and to correspond with legal counsel and other advisors when reviewing the transaction documentation;

- sellers in particular often do not place sufficient emphasis on the importance of a letter of intent. While the letter of intent is non-binding, once it is accepted by the seller, it affords the buyer a period of exclusivity in order to negotiate the purchase and sale agreement and close the deal. The seller must ensure that the letter of intent fully reflects all of the important considerations in the transaction. Anything that is not addressed or that is ambiguous in the letter of intent is subject to negotiation during the exclusivity period, when the buyer typically has a negotiating advantage; and

- buyers often do not adequately plan and prepare for the integration of the target company prior to concluding an acquisition. Poor integration is repeatedly cited as one of the principal reasons for deal failure. Prudent buyers consider potential integration issues at an early stage in the acquisition process and have a well-developed acquisition plan prior to the closing of a transaction.

Summary

The price paid for a business in an open market transaction can be materially different from the fair market value of the business, as estimated in a notional market context. The reasons for this include the consideration of synergies, the relative negotiating positions of the parties and the terms of the deal.

In most cases, notional fair market value is determined on an intrinsic basis, given that it is usually difficult to quantify the synergies that might be perceived by a particular buyer, and to determine the likelihood that such synergies would be paid for. However, in an open market context, synergies become a key consideration where negotiations are taking place with a particular buyer. Synergies can be classified as tangible operating synergies, intangible operating synergies and financial synergies. The quantification of synergies should take into account the associated costs and risk in their realization. However, whether, and to what extent, synergies are paid for depends on the negotiating positions of the parties and the terms of the deal.

The terms of the deal include whether the assets or shares of the target company are acquired, the forms of consideration and, in the case of a privately held company, the provisions of a management contract. Apart from cash at closing, other common forms of consideration include holdbacks, promissory notes, share exchanges and earnout arrangements. In the case of a public company takeover, forms of consideration are usually restricted to cash or freely tradable shares of the buyer. However, considerably more flexibility exists in the case of private company acquisitions.

The seller should consider the tax implications of deal structuring and the risk of not receiving the portion of the purchase price that is deferred or conditional upon the attainment of post-acquisition operating results. The buyer should consider the tax structure of the transaction, the availability of financing, the impact on pro-forma earnings per share (for public companies), and potential integration issues that may ultimately dictate whether or not the transaction was considered successful.

List of Selected Court Cases

Overview

This appendix consists of a list of selected Canadian court cases involving valuation-related matters. It is provided by way of reference only and is not intended to be exhaustive. The facts and findings in each of these cases should be carefully reviewed to assess whether they are pertinent to a specific valuation issue. Legal advice should be obtained as necessary.

Appraisal Remedy

Arthur v. Signum Communications Ltd., [1993] O.J. No. 1928

Baniuk v. Carpenter (1990), 1 B.L.R. (2d) 300

Smeenk v. Dexleigh Corp. (1990), 49 B.L.R. 1

Fraser Inc. v. Aitken (1988), 41 B.L.R. 87

Goguen v. Metro Oil Co. (1989), 42 B.L.R. 30

Hermitage v. Kruger Inc., [1995] A.Q No. 294, [1993] Q.J. No. 600

Jakobson v. Aggasiz Enterprises Ltd. (1987), 49 Man. R. (2d) 270

Lajoie v. Lajoie Bros. Contracting Ltd. (1989), 45 B.L.R. 113

Les Investissements Mont-Soleil Inc. v. National Drug Ltd. (1982), 22 B.L.R. 139

LoCicero v. BACM Industries Ltd. (1984), 31 Man. R. (2d) 208; (1986) 25 D.L.R. (4th) 269, 38 Man. R. (2d) 134 (Man. C.A.), [1988] 1 S.C.R. 399, [1988] 4 W.W.R. 671, 49 D.L.R. (4th) 159

Manning v. Harris Steel Group Inc., [1987] 1 W.W.R. 86, [1990] 1 W.W.R. 346 (C.A.)

Mica Management Centre Inc. v. Lockett (1986), 37 B.L.R. 209

New Quebec Raglan Mines Ltd. v. Blok-Andersen (1993), 9 B.L.R. (2d) 93

Nunachiaq Inc. v. Chow (1993), 8 B.L.R. (2d) 109 (B.C.S.C.); affd [1994] B.C.J. No. 608

Brant Investments Ltd. v. KeepRite Inc. (1987), 60 O.R. (2d) 737

Domglas Inc. v. Jarislowsky (1980), 13 B.L.R. 135; affd (1982), 138 D.L.R. (3d) 521

Safarik v. Ocean Fisheries Ltd. (1996), Vancouver registry No. CA17791/CA018274/CA018007; [1995] B.C.J. No. 76; (1993) 10 B.L.R. (2d) 246

Second Shirley Rubin Family Trust (Trustee of) v. Revenue Properties Co., [1992] O.J. No. 1028

Ultramar Canada Inc. v. Montreal Pipe Line Ltd. (1990), 49 B.L.R. 279

Westfair Foods Ltd. v. Watt (1992), 5 B.L.R. (2d) 179

Arbitrator

Arenson v. Arenson, [1973] 2 All E.R. 235, [1973] Ch 346

Arenson v. Casson Beckman Rutley & Co, [1975] 2 All E.R. 901

Bottomly v. Ambler (1877), 38 L.T. 545

Finnegan v. Allen, [1943] 1 All E.R. 493

Muskoka & Parry Sound Telephone Co. v. Ontario Telephone Development Corp. (1984), 32 L.C.R. 154 (O.M.B.); (1985) 32 L.C.R. 238 (O.M.B.)

Parrot v. Shellard (1868), 15 W.R. 928

Hopper (Re) (1867), L.R. 2 Q.B. 367

Portnoy (Re), [1949] 3 D.L.R. 449

Taylor v. Yielding (1912), 56 Sol. Jo. 253

Turner v. Goulden (1873), L.R. 9 C.P. 57

Buy-Sell Agreements

Irwin v. D.W. Coates Enterprises Ltd., [1985] 3 W.W.R. 765

Capitalization Rates

Footitt v. Gleason, [1995] O.J. No. 2662, Commercial List No. B177/95

Ivesleigh Holdings Inc. v. M.N.R., 78 D.T.C. 1716

R.G. Mersereau v. M.N.R., [1977] C.T.C. 2412

Seto Holdings Ltd. v. M.N.R., 75 D.T.C. 1

Cash Consideration

R. v. Mastronardi, 77 D.T.C. 5217, [1976] C.T.C. 355

Henfrey Samson Belair Ltd. v. Wedgewood Village Estates Ltd. (1986), 59 C.B.R. 38 (B.C.S.C.); (1987) 14 B.C.L.R. (2d) 1 (B.C.C.A.)

J.C. Adam v. M.N.R., [1952] C.T.C. 400, 53 D.T.C. 1001

Schroder Estate v. M.N.R., [1955] C.T.C. 290, 55 D.T.C. 1128

Charitable Donations

Aikman v. Canada, 2000 D.T.C. 1874 (T.C.C.)

Maréchaux v. Canada (2009), Docket: 2006-410(IT)G (T.C.C.)

Klotz v. Canada, 2004 D.T.C. 2236 (T.C.C.), 2005 D.T.C. 5279 (F.C.A.)

Malette v. Canada, 2003 TCC 542

Marechel v. Canada, 2004 D.T.C. 3227 (T.C.C.), 2005 D.T.C. 5223 (F.C.A.)

Canada v. Zelinski, 96 D.T.C. 1594 (T.C.C.), [2000] 1 C.T.C. 329 (F.C.A.)

Compulsion to Act

Crane Estate v. F.C. of T., 75 A.T.C. 4001

Findlay's Trustees v. I.R.C. (1938), 22 A.T.C. 437

Village of South Orange v. Alden Corp., 365 A.2d 469

Control

Barclays Bank Ltd. v. I.R.C., [1961] A.C. 509, [1960] 2 All. E.R. 817

Fairgreen Investments Ltd. v. M.N.R., [1972] C.T.C. 2446, 72 D.T.C. 1374

I.R.C. v. Harten Coal Co., [1960] 3 All E.R. 48

New Hamburg Mills Ltd. v. M.N.R. (1965), 40 Tax A.B.C. 89, 66 D.T.C. 53

Sheldon's Engineering Ltd. v. M.N.R., 55 D.T.C. 1110, 54 D.T.C. 1106, 53 D.T.C. 11

Vineland Quarries and Crushed Stone Ltd. v. M.N.R., [1966] Ex. C.R. 417, [1966] C.T.C. 69, 66 D.T.C. 5092; affd without written reasons 67 D.T.C. 5283 (S.C.C.)

Control Premium

Dean v. Prince, [1953] 1 Ch. 590

Gold Coast Section Trust Ltd. v. Humphrey, [1948] 2 All E.R. 379 (H.L.), affd in part [1946] 2 All E.R. 742 (C.A.)

Magna International Inc. (Re) (Ont. S.C.J., August 2010)

British Columbia (Minister of Finance) v. Mann, [1972] 5 W.W.R. 23 at 27 (B.S.C.S.); affd [1973] C.T.C. 561 (B.C.C.A.); affd [1974] C.T.C. 222 (S.C.C.)

Domglas Inc. v. Jarislowsky (1980), 13 B.L.R. 135; affd (1982), 138 D.L.R. (3d) 521

Short v. Treasury Commissioners, [1948] A.C. 534, [1948] 2 All E.R. 509

Winram Estate v. M.N.R., [1972] F.C. 463, [1972] C.T.C. 193, 72 D.T.C. 6187

Control Through Casting Vote

Allied Business Supervisions Ltd. v. M.N.R., [1967] 1 Ex. C.R. 21, [1966] C.T.C. 330, 66 D.T.C. 5244

Alpine Drywall & Decorating Ltd. v. M.N.R., [1966] Ex. C.R. 1148, [1966] C.T.C. 359, 66 D.T.C. 5263

B.W. Noble Ltd. v. I.R.C. (1926), 12 T.C. 911

Bert Robbins Excavating Ltd. v. M.N.R., [1966] Ex. C.R. 1160, [1966] C.T.C. 371, 66 D.T.C. 5269

CJOY Ltd. v. M.N.R. (1966), 42 Tax A.B.C. 364, 67 D.T.C. 6

Dealers Acceptance Corp. Ltd. v. M.N.R. (1964), 37 Tax A.B.C. 33, 64 D.T.C. 771

Dominion Fibre Drum Corp. v. M.N.R. (1965), 40 Tax A.B.C. 79, 66 D.T.C. 46

I.R.C. v. Monnick Ltd. (1949), 29 T.C. 379

M.N.R. v. Dworkin Furs (Pembroke) Ltd., [1967] S.C.R. 223, [1967] C.T.C. 50, 67 D.T.C. 5035

Pender Enterprises Ltd. v. M.N.R., [1965] Ex. C.R. 180, [1965] C.T.C. 343, 65 D.T.C. 5202

Control Through Intermediate Corporations

Bert Robbins Excavating Ltd. v. M.N.R., [1966] Ex. C.R. 1160, [1966] C.T.C. 371, 66 D.T.C. 5269

British American Tobacco Ltd. v. I.R.C., [1943] A.C. 335, [1943] 1 All E.R. 13

Glaspie v. M.N.R. (1963), 33 Tax A.B.C. 274, 63 D.T.C. 828

I.R.C. v. F.A. Clark & Sons Ltd., [1941] 2 K.B. 270, 29 T.C. 49

Vancouver Towing Co. v. M.N.R., [1946] Ex. C.R. 623, [1947] C.T.C. 18, 2 D.T.C. 706

Vineland Quarries and Crushed Stone Ltd. v. M.N.R., [1966] Ex. C.R. 417, [1966] C.T.C. 69, 66 D.T.C. 5092; affd without written reasons 67 D.T.C. 5283 (S.C.C.)

R. v. Yarmouth Industrial Leasing Ltd., 85 D.T.C. 5401 (F.C.T.D.)

Control Through Trustees and Nominees

Anglo-B.C. Distributors Ltd. v. M.N.R., [1970] C.T.C. 138, 70 D.T.C. 6105

Barclays Bank Ltd. v. I.R.C., [1961] A.C. 509, [1960] 2 All E.R. 817

Benaby Realties Ltd. v. M.N.R. (1961), 28 Tax A.B.C. 176, 61 D.T.C. 3

Berendsen Ltd. v. I.R.C., [1958] 1 Ch. 1, [1957] 2 All E.R. 612

C.A. de Fehr & Sons Ltd. v. M.N.R. (1954), 11 Tax A.B.C. 190, 54 D.T.C. 390

Career Girl Store Ltd. v. M.N.R., [1967] 1 Ex. C.R. 21, [1966] C.T.C. 330, 66 D.T.C. 5244

Deshaies & Raymond Inc. v. M.N.R., [1970] Tax A.B.C. 725, 70 D.T.C. 1466

Edison Wholesale Ltd. v. M.N.R. (1963), 32 Tax A.B.C. 307, 63 D.T.C. 583

Finley v. M.N.R., 84 D.T.C. 1536 (T.C.C.)

H.A. Fawcett & Sons Ltd. v. Canada, 80 D.T.C. 6195 (F.C.A.)

I.R.C. v. J. Bibby and Sons Ltd., [1945] 1 All E.R. 667, 29 T.C. 167

I.R.C. v. Silverts Ltd., [1951] 1 Ch. 521, [1951] 1 All E.R. 703, 29 T.C. 491

John Shields & Co. (Perth) Ltd. v. I.R.C., [1950] S.C. 441, 29 T.C. 475

M.N.R. v. Consolidated Holdings Co., [1972] C.T.C. 18, 72 D.T.C. 6007 (S.C.C.)

M.N.R. v. Dworkin Furs (Pembroke) Ltd., [1967] S.C.R. 223, [1967] C.T.C. 50, 67 D.T.C. 5035

M.N.R. v. Kirby Maurice Co., [1958] Ex. C.R. 77, [1958] C.T.C. 41, 58 D.T.C. 1033

M.N.R. v. Sheldon Engineering Ltd., [1955] S.C.R. 637, [1955] C.T.C. 174, 55 D.T.C. 1110

R. v. Ans, [1983] C.T.C. 8, 83 D.T.C. 5038 (F.C.T.D.)

R. M. Ballantyne Co. v. M.N.R. (1952), 6 Tax A.B.C. 71, 52 D.T.C. 115

R. Truax Son & Co. v. M.N.R. (1954), 12 Tax A.B.C. 12, 54 D.T.C. 562

Rolka v. M.N.R., [1963] Ex. C.R. 138, [1962] C.T.C. 637, 62 D.T.C. 1394

Rubenstein v. M.N.R. (1965), 39 Tax A.B.C. 7, 65 D.T.C. 494

R. v. Scandia Plate Ltd., [1983] 1 F.C. 51, [1982] C.T.C. 431, 83 D.T.C. 5009 (T.D.)

Special Risks Holdings Inc. v. Canada, [1984] C.T.C. 553, 84 D.T.C. 6505 (F.C.T.D.); affd [1986] C.T.C. 201, 86 D.T.C. 6035, 63 N.R. 390 (F.C.A.)

Taylor Lumber Co. and Matheson Lumber Ltd. v. M.N.R., [1967] Tax A.B.C. 875, 67 D.T.C. 593

R. v. Canada Trust Company, [1981] C.T.C. 319, 81 D.T.C. 5248 (F.C.T.D.)

R. v. Ann-Gus Holdings Ltd., 84 D.T.C. 6363 (F.C.A.)

R. v. Lusita Holdings Ltd., 84 D.T.C. 6346

W. Ralston & Co. (Canada) Ltd. v. M.N.R., [1982] C.T.C. 2108, 82 D.T.C. 1128 (T.R.B.)

Wynndel Logging Co. v. M.N.R., [1980] C.T.C. 2141, 80 D.T.C. 1125 (T.R.B.)

Control Through Voting Agreements

Aaron's Ladies Apparel Ltd. v. M.N.R., [1967] 1 Ex. C.R. 21, [1966] C.T.C. 330, 66 D.T.C. 5244, [1967] S.C.R. 223, [1967] C.T.C. 50, 67 D.T.C. 5035

Credit La Verendrye Ltee v. M.N.R., [1972] C.T.C. 2404, 72 D.T.C. 1344

International Iron & Metal Co. v. M.N.R., [1969] C.T.C. 668, 69 D.T.C. 5445; affd [1974] S.C.R. 898, 27 D.L.R. (3d) 1, [1972] C.T.C. 242, 72 D.T.C. 6205

I.R.C. v. James Hodgkinson (Salford) Ltd. (1949), 29 T.C. 395

Lou's Service (Sault) Ltd. v. M.N.R., [1967] C.T.C. 315, 67 D.T.C. 5201

Rubenstein v. M.N.R. (1965), 39 Tax A.B.C. 7, 65 D.T.C. 494

De Facto Control

Buckerfield's Ltd. v. M.N.R., [1965] 1 Ex. C.R. 299, [1964] C.T.C. 504, 64 D.T.C. 5301

M.N.R. v. Dworkin Furs (Pembroke) Ltd., [1967] S.C.R. 223, [1967] C.T.C. 50, 67 D.T.C. 5035

Vina-Rug (Canada) Ltd. v. M.N.R., [1968] S.C.R. 193, [1968] C.T.C. 1

De Jure Control

B.W. Noble Ltd. v. I.R.C. (1926), 12 T.C. 911

British American Tobacco Ltd. v. I.R.C., [1943] A.C. 335, [1943] 1 All E.R. 13

Buckerfield's Ltd. v. M.N.R., [1965] 1 Ex. C.R. 299, [1964] C.T.C. 504, 64 D.T.C. 5301

Donald Applicators Ltd. v. M.N.R., [1969] C.T.C. 98, 69 D.T.C. 5122; affd [1971] C.T.C. 402, 71 D.T.C. 5202

Glasgow Expanded Metal Co. v. I.R.C., [1923] S.C. 365, 12 T.C. 573

Dworkin Furs (Pembroke) Ltd. v. M.N.R., [1967] S.C.R. 223, [1967] C.T.C. 50, 67 D.T.C. 5035

M.N.R. v. Wrights' Canadian Ropes Ltd., [1947] A.C. 109, [1947] C.T.C. 1, 2 D.T.C. 927

Oakfield Developments (Toronto) Ltd. v. M.N.R., [1971] S.C.R. 1032, [1971] C.T.C. 283, 71 D.T.C. 5175

R. v. Imperial General Properties Ltd., [1985] 2 S.C.R. 288, 85 D.T.C. 5500, [1985] 2 C.T.C. 299

Vancouver Towing Co. v. M.N.R., [1946] Ex. C.R. 623, [1947] C.T.C. 18, 2 D.T.C. 706

Degree of Care and Skill

Jenkins v. Betham (1855), 15 C.B. 168, 139 E.R. 384

Directors' Powers

Donald Applicators Ltd. v. M.N.R., [1969] C.T.C. 98, 69 D.T.C. 5122; affd [1971] C.T.C. 402, 71 D.T.C. 5202

Dividends

Winram v. M.N.R., [1972] F.C. 463, [1972] C.T.C. 193, 72 D.T.C. 6187

Employment Contract

Crutchfield v. Crutchfield (1987), 10 R.F.L. (3d) 247 (Ont. H.C.J.)

Expert Evidence

McCoy v. Canada, 2003 TCC 332

CIT Financial Ltd. v. Canada, 2003 D.T.C. 1138 (T.C.C.), 2004 D.T.C. 6573 (F.C.A.)

De Gobeo v. De Gobeo, 2003 MBQB 274

Debora v. Debora (2004), 2004 CarswellONt 4987, 8 R.F.L. (6th) 32 (Ont. S.C.J.)

Footitt v. Gleason, [1995] O.J. No. 2662, Commercial List No. B177/95

Friedman v. M.N.R., [1978] C.T.C. 2809, 78 D.T.C. 1599 (T.R.B.)

Fraser Inc. v. Aitken (1988), 41 B.L.R. 87

Trepanier v. M.N.R., 79 D.T.C. 924

Garron Family Trust v. Canada, 2009 TCC 450

Love v. Acuity Investment Management Inc., 2009 CarswellOnt 3138, 74 C.C.E.L. (3d) 272; 2011 CarswellOnt 1060, 2011 ONCA 130, 89 C.C.E.L. (3d) 157, 2011 C.L.L.C. 210-024, 277 O.A.C. 15, Docket: CA C50725 (Ont. C.A., February 16, 2011)

Hallatt v. Canada, 2001 D.T.C. 128 (T.C.C.)

Mathew v. Canada, [2001] T.C.J. No. 491 (T.C.C.)

Morley v. Canada, 2004 D.T.C. 2604 (T.C.C.)

Poirier v. Poirier (2005), 19 R.F.L. (6th) 197, [2006] W.D.F.L. 79, [2006] W.D.F.L. 108

Brant Investments Ltd. v. KeepRite Inc. (1987), 60 O.R. (2d) 737

Schaefer Brothers Inc. v. M.N.R., 79 D.T.C. 288

Fair Market Value

McCoy v. Canada, 2003 TCC 332

CIT Financial Ltd. v. Canada, 2003 D.T.C. 1138 (T.C.C.), 2004 D.T.C. 6573 (F.C.A.)

Deer Creek Energy Ltd. v. Paulson & Co. (2008), 49 B.L.R. (4th) 1 (Alta. Q.B.)

Dibbley v. Dibbley (1986), 5 R.F.L. (3d) 381

Enterprise Payment Solutions Inc. v. Soft Tracks Enterprises Ltd., [2005] B.C.J. No. 847 (B.C.S.C.)

Garron Family Trust v. Canada, 2009 TCC 450

Heon v. Heon (1989), 22 R.F.L. (3d) 273 (Ont. H.C.J.)

Jackh v. Jackh, 22 B.C.L.R. 182 (B.C.S.C.)

Hallatt v. Canada, 2001 D.T.C. 128 (T.C.C.)

Menage v. Hedges (1987), 8 R.F.L. (3d) 225

British Columbia (Minister of Finance) v. Mann, [1972] 5 W.W.R. 23 at 27 (B.S.C.S.); affd [1973] C.T.C. 561 (B.C.C.A.); affd [1974] C.T.C. 222 (S.C.C.)

Morley v. Canada, 2004 D.T.C. 2604 (T.C.C.)

Muscillo v. Bulk Transfer Systems Inc., 2010 ONSC 490 (Ont. S.C.J. (Comm. List), January 2010)

Petro-Canada v. Canada (2002) (T.C.C.)

Brant Investments Ltd. v. KeepRite Inc. (1987), 60 O.R. (2d) 737

Domglas Inc. v. Jarislowsky (1980), 13 B.L.R. 135; affd (1982), 138 D.L.R. (3d) 521

Wall & Redekop Corp. (Re) (1974), 50 D.L.R. (3d) 733 (B.C.S.C.)

Teranet Inc. v. Canarab Marketing Corp. (2008) (Ont. S.C.J. (Comm. List))

Winter v. Canada (1989) (F.C.T.D.), Court File No. T-1711-86

Fair Value

Baniuk v. Carpenter (1990), 1 B.L.R. (2d) 300

Canadian Gas & Energy Fund Ltd. v. Sceptre Resources Ltd., 1985 CarswellAlta 101, 38 Alta. L.R. (2d) 223, 29 B.L.R. 178, [1985] 5 W.W.R. 43, 61 A.R. 67, Docket: Calgary No. 8201-17100 (Alta. Q.B., May 17, 1985)

Calmont Leasing Ltd. v. Kredl, [1996] A.J. No. 283

Cyprus Anvil Mining Corp. v. Dickson (1982), 20 B.L.R. 21, 40 B.C.L.R. 180; (1986), 8 B.C.L.R. (2d) 145

Diligenti v. RWMD Operations Kelowna Ltd. (1977), 4 B.C.L.R. 134

Footitt v. Gleason, [1995] O.J. No. 2662, Commercial List No. B177/95

Ford Motor Co. of Canada Ltd. v. Ontario Municipal Employees Retirement Board (2004), 41 B.L.R. (3d) 74 (Ont. S.C.J.)

Smeenk v. Dexleigh Corp. (1990), 49 B.L.R. 1

Fraser Inc. v. Aitken (1988), 41 B.L.R. 87

Hermitage v. Kruger Inc., [1995] A.Q No. 294, [1993] Q.J. No. 600

Anthem Works Ltd. (Re), 2005 BCSC 766

Jakobson v. Aggasiz Enterprises Ltd. (1987), 49 Man. R. (2d) 270

Jepson v. Canadian Salt Co., [1979] A.J. No. 481, 7 B.L.R. 181 (Alta. S.C.)

Lajoie v. Lajoie Brothers Contracting (1989), 45 B.L.R. 113

Les Investissements Mont-Soleil Inc. v. National Drug Ltd. (1982), 22 B.L.R. 139

LoCicero v. BACM Industries Ltd. (1984), 31 Man. R. (2d) 208; (1986) 25 D.L.R. (4th) 269, 38 Man. R. (2d) 134 (Man. C.A.), [1988] 1 S.C.R. 399, [1988] 4 W.W.R. 671, 49 D.L.R. (4th) 159

Lough v. Canadian Natural Resources Ltd. (1983), 45 B.C.L.R. 335

Manning v. Harris Steel Group Inc., [1987] 1 W.W.R. 86, [1990] 1 W.W.R. 346 (C.A.)

Montgomery v. Shell Canada Ltd. (1980), 5 W.W.R. 543, 111 D.L.R. (3d) 116

Morrison v. United Westburne Industries Ltd. (1988), Toronto RE 1926/87 (April 15, 1988)

Neonex International Ltd. v. Kolasa (1978), 84 D.L.R. (3d) 446, [1978] 2 W.W.R. 593, 3 B.L.R. 1, [1978] B.C.J. No. 19 (B.C.S.C.)

New Quebec Raglan Mines Ltd. v. Blok-Andersen (1993), 9 B.L.R. (2d) 93

Nunachiaq Inc. v. Chow (1993), 8 B.L.R. (2d) 109 (B.C.S.C.); affd [1994] B.C.J. No. 608

Brant Investments Ltd. v. KeepRite Inc. (1987), 60 O.R. (2d) 737

Domglas Inc. v. Jarislowsky (1980), 13 B.L.R. 135; affd (1982), 138 D.L.R. (3d) 521

VCS Holdings v. Helliwell (1978), 5 B.L.R. 265

Wall & Redekop Corp. (Re) (1974), 50 D.L.R. (3d) 733 (B.C.S.C.)

Hudson Bay Mining and Smelting Co. v. Lueck (1980), 10 B.L.R. 113

Robertson v. Canadian Canners Ltd. (1978), 4 B.L.R. 290

Safarik v. Ocean Fisheries Ltd. (1996), Vancouver registry No. CA17791/CA018274/CA018007; [1995] B.C.J. No. 76; (1993) 10 B.L.R. (2d) 246

Second Shirley Rubin Family Trust (Trustee of) v. Revenue Properties Co., [1992] O.J. No. 1028

Silber v. BGR Precious Metals Inc., 1998 CarswellOnt 2994 (Ont. Ct. (Gen. Div.))

Ultramar Canada Inc. v. Montreal Pipe Line Ltd. (1990), 49 B.L.R. 279

Westfair Foods Ltd. v. Watt (1992), 5 B.L.R. (2d) 179

Fiduciary Responsibility

Bell v. Source Data Control Ltd. (1988), 29 OAC 134; (1986) 14581/81

Dusik v. Newton (1983), 50 B.C.L.R. 321

Magna International Inc. (Re) (Ont. S.C.J., August 2010)

Percival v. Wright, [1902] 2 Ch. 421

Sterling Centrecorp Inc. (Re) (2007) (Ont. S.C.J.)

Trimac Ltd. v. C.I.L. Inc. (1989), 69 Alta. L.R. (2d) 113, [1990] 1 W.W.R. 133

Forcing Out Premium

Fraser Inc. v. Aitken (1988), 41 B.L.R. 87

Jakobson v. Aggasiz Enterprises Ltd. (1987), 49 Man. R. (2d) 270

Les Investissements Mont-Soleil Inc. v. National Drug Ltd. (1982), 22 B.L.R. 139

LoCicero v. BACM Industries Ltd. (1984), 31 Man. R. (2d) 208; (1986) 25 D.L.R. (4th) 269, 38 Man. R. (2d) 134 (Man. C.A.), [1988] 1 S.C.R. 399, [1988] 4 W.W.R. 671, 49 D.L.R. (4th) 159

Manning v. Harris Steel Group Inc., [1987] 1 W.W.R. 86, [1990] 1 W.W.R. 346 (C.A.)

New Quebec Raglan Mines Ltd. v. Blok-Andersen (1993), 9 B.L.R. (2d) 93

Brant Investments Ltd. v. KeepRite Inc. (1987), 60 O.R. (2d) 737

Domglas Inc. v. Jarislowsky (1980), 13 B.L.R. 135; affd (1982), 138 D.L.R. (3d) 521

Second Shirley Rubin Family Trust (Trustee of) v. Revenue Properties Co., [1992] O.J. No. 1028

Westfair Foods Ltd. v. Watt (1992), 5 B.L.R. (2d) 179

Xerox Canada Inc. v. Ontario Municipal Employees Retirement Board (1991), 3 B.L.R. (2d) 68

General Anti Avoidance Rule (GAAR)

R. v. Canada Trustco Mortgage Co., [2005] 2 S.C.R. 602

Mathew v. Canada, [2005] 2 S.C.R. 643

Lipson v. Canada, [2009] 1 S.C.R. 3

Copthorne Holdings Ltd. v. Canada, 2011 SCC 63

Going-Concern Value and Fair Value

Diligenti v. RWMD Operations Kelowna Ltd. (1977), 4 B.C.L.R. 134

VCS Holdings v. Helliwell (1978), 5 B.L.R. 265

Wall & Redekop Corp. (Re) (1974), 50 D.L.R. (3d) 733 (B.C.S.C.)

Goodwill – Valuation

Transalta Corp. v. Canada, 2010 TCC 375

U.S.M. Canada Ltd. v. Canada, [1996] 2 C.T.C. 2289

Group Control

Adelaide Motors Ltd. v. F.C.T. (1942), 66 C.L.R. 436, 7 A.T.D. 147

Ancaster Development Co. v. M.N.R., [1961] Ex. C.R. 201, [1961] C.T.C. 9, 61 D.T.C. 1047

Atomic Truck Cartage v. Canada, [1985] 2 C.T.C. 21, 85 D.T.C. 5427 (F.C.T.D.)

Buckerfield's Ltd. v. M.N.R., [1965] 1 Ex. C.R. 299, [1964] C.T.C. 504, 64 D.T.C. 5301

Cholakis v. Cholakis, 2010 MBQB 116, 72 B.L.R. (4th) 120 (May 7, 2010)

Commissioner of Income Tax v. Bjordal, [1955] A.C. 309, [1955] 1 All E.R. 401 (P.C.)

Dad's Cookie Co. (Ontario) Ltd. v. M.N.R. (1965), 39 Tax A.B.C. 73, 65 D.T.C. 535

Express Cable Television Ltd. v. M.N.R., [1982] C.T.C. 2447, 82 D.T.C. 1431 (T.R.B.)

F. v. V., [2002] O.J. No. 3900 (Ont. S.C.J.)

F.C.T. v. West Australian Tanners & Fellmongers Ltd. (1945), 70 C.L.R. 623, 8 A.T.D. 25

Golden Arrow Sprayers Ltd. v. M.N.R., [1961] Ex. C.R. 432, [1961] C.T.C. 318, 61 D.T.C. 1185

Jacob Mayer & Sons Ltd. v. M.N.R., [1954] Ex. C.R. 310, [1954] C.T.C. 141, 54 D.T.C. 1075

King George Hotels Ltd. v. M.N.R., [1968] Tax A.B.C. 785, 68 D.T.C. 635

Les Messageries de Presse Periodique Ltee v. M.N.R., [1968] Tax A.B.C. 881

LeVan v. LeVan, 2006 CarswellOnt 7334, 82 O.R. (3d) 1 at 76, 32 R.F.L. (6th) 359, [2007] W.D.F.L. 675, [2007] W.D.F.L. 676, [2007] W.D.F.L. 686, [2007] W.D.F.L. 705, [2007] W.D.F.L. 681, [2007] W.D.F.L. 677, [2007] W.D.F.L. 778, [2007] W.D.F.L. 784, [2007] W.D.F.L. 803, [2007] W.D.F.L. 802, [2007] W.D.F.L. 758, Docket: 03-ST-36181 (Ont. S.C.J., September 28, 2006)

Lundberg Explorations Ltd. v. M.N.R. (1958), 19 Tax A.B.C. 208, 58 D.T.C. 291

Maurice J. Walsh Ltd. v. M.N.R. (1955), 14 Tax A.B.C. 69, 55 D.T.C. 593

McMillan Hotel Co. v. M.N.R. (1953), 8 Tax A.B.C. 334, 53 D.T.C. 231

Miron & Freres Ltd. v. M.N.R., [1955] S.C.R. 679, [1955] C.T.C. 182, 55 D.T.C. 1109

M.N.R. v. Consolidated Holdings Co., [1972] C.T.C. 18, 72 D.T.C. 6007 (S.C.C.)

New Hamburg Mills Ltd. v. M.N.R. (1965), 40 Tax A.B.C. 89, 66 D.T.C. 53

No. 264 v. M.N.R. (1955), 13 Tax A.B.C. 46, 55 D.T.C. 300

No. 324 v. M.N.R. (1956), 14 Tax A.B.C. 391, 56 D.T.C. 133

No. 60 v. M.N.R. (1952), 6 Tax A.B.C. 412, 52 D.T.C. 268

Wellport Broadcasting Ltd. v. M.N.R., [1969] Tax A.B.C. 565, 69 D.T.C. 420

Ronda Holdings Ltd. v. M.N.R., [1984] C.T.C. 2357, 84 D.T.C. 1331 (T.C.C.)

S. Madill Ltd. v. M.N.R., [1972] C.T.C. 47, 72 D.T.C. 6027

Southside Car Market Ltd. v. Canada, [1982] 2 F.C. 755, [1982] C.T.C. 214, 82 D.T.C. 6179 at 6186 (T.D.)

R. v. B.B. Fast & Sons Distributors Ltd. (1986), 64 N.R. 297, 1 C.T.C. 299, 86 D.T.C. 6106 (F.C.A.)

Baxter v. Biotech Electronics Ltd., District of Montreal, No. 500-05-003585-856 (February 15, 1990)

Vina-Rug (Canada) Ltd. v. M.N.R., [1968] S.C.R. 193, [1968] C.T.C. 1

Yardley Plastics of Canada Ltd. v. M.N.R., [1966] Ex. C.R. 102n, [1966] C.T.C. 215, 66 D.T.C. 5183

Highest Price

I.R.C. v. Clay, [1914] 3 K.B. 466 (C.A.)

Hindsight

Cyprus Anvil Mining Corp. v. Dickson (1982), 20 B.L.R. 21, 40 B.C.L.R. 180; (1986), 8 B.C.L.R. (2d) 145

Diligenti v. RWMD Operations Kelowna Ltd. (1977), 4 B.C.L.R. 134

F. v. V., [2002] O.J. No. 3900 (Ont. S.C.J.)

Fischer v. Fischer (1993), 109 D.L.R. (4th) 189

Fitzpatrick v. Fitzpatrick, [2004] O.J. No. 2695 (Ont. S.C.J.)

Smeenk v. Dexleigh Corp. (1990), 49 B.L.R. 1

Ganson v. Ganson (1996), 66 A.C.W.S. (3d) 706

Taylor Estate v. M.N.R., [1990] 2 C.T.C. 2304

Holt v. I.R.C., [1953] 2 All E.R. 1499

Carr v. M.N.R., [1993] 2 C.T.C. 3018

Joseph Simard & Cie, Ltee v. M.N.R., [1964] C.T.C. 461, 64 D.T.C. 5289

Manning v. Harris Steel Group Inc., [1987] 1 W.W.R. 86, [1990] 1 W.W.R. 346 (C.A.)

McClintock v. Canada, 2003 CarswellNat 1160, 2003 TCC 259, 2003 D.T.C. 576, [2003] 3 C.T.C. 2839

National System of Baking of Alberta Ltd. v. M.N.R., [1978] C.T.C. 30, 78 D.T.C. 6018; affd [1980] C.T.C. 237, 80 D.T.C. 6178

New Quebec Raglan Mines Ltd. v. Blok-Andersen (1993), 9 B.L.R. (2d) 93

Nunachiaq Inc. v. Chow (1993), 8 B.L.R. (2d) 109 (B.C.S.C.); affd [1994] B.C.J. No. 608

Produits LDG Products Inc. v. Canada, [1973] C.T.C. 273, 73 D.T.C. 5222 (F.C.T.D.)

Domglas Inc. v. Jarislowsky (1980), 13 B.L.R. 135; affd (1982), 138 D.L.R. (3d) 521

Lohn Estate (Re), [1997] B.C.J. No. 1367

S.G. & S. Investments (1972) Ltd. v. Golden Boy Foods Inc. (1991), 3 B.L.R. (2d) 80

Taylor Estate v. M.N.R., [1967] Tax A.B.C. 555, 67 D.T.C. 405

Crandall v. M.N.R., [1974] C.T.C. 2289, 74 D.T.C. 1204

Brunelle v. M.N.R., [1977] C.T.C. 2506, 77 D.T.C. 326

Woeller v. Woeller (1988), 15 R.F.L. (3d) 120

Industry Knowledge

Fraser Inc. v. Aitken (1988), 41 B.L.R. 87

Information Disclosure

Holt v. I.R.C., [1953] 2 All E.R. 1499

National System of Baking of Alberta Ltd. v. M.N.R., [1978] C.T.C. 30, 78 D.T.C. 6018; affd [1980] C.T.C. 237, 80 D.T.C. 6178

No. 179 v. M.N.R. (1954), 11 Tax A.B.C. 78, 54 D.T.C. 336

Lynall (Re), [1969] 3 All E.R. 984 at 990 (C.A.)

Insider Knowledge

National System of Baking of Alberta Ltd. v. M.N.R., [1978] C.T.C. 30, 78 D.T.C. 6018; affd [1980] C.T.C. 237, 80 D.T.C. 6178

Insurance – Life

R. v. Mastronardi Estate, 77 D.T.C. 5217, [1977] C.T.C. 355

Interest Deductibility

Canada v. Bronfman Trust, 87 D.T.C. 5059

Entreprises Ludco Ltee v. Canada, [2001] 2 S.C.R. 1082

Minority Discount

Baniuk v. Carpenter (1990), 1 B.L.R. (2d) 300

Bogoch v. Bogoch Estate, [2002] M.J. No. 83 (Man. Q.B.)

Calmont Leasing Ltd. v. Kredl, [1996] A.J. No. 283

Cholakis v. Cholakis, 2010 MBQB 116, 72 B.L.R. (4th) 120 (May 7, 2010)

Derdall v. Derdall Irrigation Farms Ltd., 2010 SKCA 104, [2010] 11 W.W.R. 607 (September 2, 2010)

Diligenti v. RWMD Operations Kelowna Ltd. (1977), 4 B.C.L.R. 134

F. v. V., [2002] O.J. No. 3900 (Ont. S.C.J.)

Henfrey Samson Belair Ltd. v. Wedgewood Village Estates Ltd. (1986), 59 C.B.R. 38 (B.C.S.C.); (1987) 14 B.C.L.R. (2d) 1 (B.C.C.A.)

Hermitage v. Kruger Inc., [1995] A.Q No. 294, [1993] Q.J. No. 600

Irwin v. D.W. Coates Enterprises Ltd., [1985] 3 W.W.R. 765

Khoury v. Khoury (1991), 122 N.B.R. (2d) 150, 306 A.P.R. 150 (N.B.Q.B.)

Les Investissements Mont-Soleil Inc. v. National Drug Ltd. (1982), 22 B.L.R. 139

LeVan v. LeVan, 2006 CarswellOnt 7334, 82 O.R. (3d) 1 at 76, 32 R.F.L. (6th) 359, [2007] W.D.F.L. 675, [2007] W.D.F.L. 676, [2007] W.D.F.L. 686, [2007] W.D.F.L. 705, [2007] W.D.F.L. 681, [2007] W.D.F.L. 677, [2007] W.D.F.L. 778, [2007] W.D.F.L. 784, [2007] W.D.F.L. 803, [2007] W.D.F.L. 802, [2007] W.D.F.L. 758, Docket: 03-ST-36181 (Ont. S.C.J., September 28, 2006)

Allred v. M.N.R. (1986), 86 D.T.C. 1479, 83-886(IT)

Mathers v. Mathers (1992), 113 N.S.R. (2d) 284, 309 A.P.R. 284 (N.S.S.C.T.D.); (1993) 123 N.S.R. (2d) 14, 340 A.P.R. 14 (N.S.C.A.)

Naneff v. Con-Crete Holdings Ltd. (1995), 23 O.R. (3d) 481

Nunachiaq Inc. v. Chow (1993), 8 B.L.R. (2d) 109 (B.C.S.C.); affd [1994] B.C.J. No. 608

O'Conner v. Winchester Oil & Gas Inc. (1986), 69 B.C.L.R. 330, [1986] 2 W.W.R. 737

Domglas Inc. v. Jarislowsky (1980), 13 B.L.R. 135; affd (1982), 138 D.L.R. (3d) 521

Roberts v. Pelling (1981), 16 B.L.R. 150 (B.C.S.C.)

Rosenau v. Rosenau (2004), 132 A.C.W.S. (3d) 80 (Sask. Q.B.)

Safarik v. Ocean Fisheries Ltd. (1996), Vancouver registry No. CA17791/CA018274/CA018007; [1995] B.C.J. No. 76; (1993) 10 B.L.R. (2d) 246

Krafve v. M.N.R., 84 D.T.C. 1002

Steen v. Canada, 86 D.T.C. 6498

Minority Shareholdings

Yager v. Canada, [1985] 1 C.T.C. 89

Johansen v. M.N.R., 72 D.T.C. 1528

New v. M.N.R., [1971] Tax A.B.C. 583, 71 D.T.C. 359

Carruthers v. Canada, 82 D.T.C. 6009; 79 D.T.C. 906

Lawson v. Proirier Estate, [1998] N.B.J. No. 154

Meszaros v. M.N.R., [1982] C.T.C. 2509

No. 179 v. M.N.R. (1954), 11 Tax A.B.C. 78, 54 D.T.C. 336

No. 513 v. M.N.R., [1958] 19 Tax A.B.C. 243, 58 D.T.C. 301

Taylor Estate v. M.N.R., [1967] Tax A.B.C. 555, 67 D.T.C. 405

Moynihan v. M.N.R., [1962] 28 Tax A.B.C. 293, 62 D.T.C. 64

Non-Arm's Length Transaction

Corner Brook Pulp and Paper Ltd. v. Canada, 2006 D.T.C. 2329 (T.C.C.)

Ford Motor Co. of Canada Ltd. v. Ontario Municipal Employees Retirement Board (2004), 41 B.L.R. (3d) 74 (Ont. S.C.J.)

Glaxosmithkline Inc. v. Canada, 2008 CarswellNat 1666, 2008 TCC 324, 2008 D.T.C. 3957 (Eng.)

O'Neill v. O'Neill (2007), 39 R.F.L. (6th) 72 (Ont. S.C.J.)

Non-Competition Agreements

Annabelle Candy Co. v. Commissioner, 314 F. 2d 1, 7-8 (9th Cir 1962)

Better Beverages Inc. v. U.S., 80-2 USTC Para. 9516

Bogoch v. Bogoch Estate, [2002] M.J. No. 83 (Man. Q.B.)

Crutchfield v. Crutchfield (1987), 10 R.F.L. (3d) 247 (Ont. H.C.J.)

Deguire v. Deguire (1997), 34 R.F.L. (4th) 164

Forward Communications Corp. v. U.S., 78-2 USTC Para. 9542 (Ct. Cl. Trial Div. 1978); affd in part and revd in part, 608 F. 2d 485 (Ct. Cl. 1979)

General Insurance Agency Inc. v. Commissioner, 17 B.T.A. 1213 (1929)

Golden State Towel and Linen Service v. U.S., 67-1 USTC Para. 9302, 179 Ct. Cl. 300, 373 F. 2d 938 (1967)

Katz v. Katz (June 27, 1989, Ontario U.F.C.) (unreported)

Michaels v. Commissioner, 12 T.C. 17, 19 (1949)

Morrison v. Rathmell, 650 S.W. 2d 145

Manrell v. Canada, 2003 D.T.C. 5225 (F.C.A.)

Visador Co. v. Commissioner, T.C. Memo 1973-173

Oppression Remedy

Arthur v. Signum Communications Ltd., [1993] O.J. No. 1928

Bloom v. Grynwald (2002) (Que. S.C.)

Camroux v. Armstrong (1992), 47 B.L.R. 302

Cholakis v. Cholakis, 2010 MBQB 116, 72 B.L.R. (4th) 120 (May 7, 2010)

Derdall v. Derdall Irrigation Farms Ltd., 2010 SKCA 104, [2010] 11 W.W.R. 607 (September 2, 2010)

Diligenti v. RWMD Operations Kelowna Ltd. (1977), 4 B.C.L.R. 134

Discovery Enterprises Inc. v. Ebco Industries Ltd., 2002 BCSC 1236

Envirodrive Inc. v. 836442 Alberta Ltd. (2005) (446, Alta. Q.B.)

Ford Motor Co. of Canada Ltd. v. Ontario Municipal Employees Retirement Board (2004), 41 B.L.R. (3d) 74 (Ont. S.C.J.)

Mason v. Intercity Properties Ltd. (1987), 59 O.R. (2d) 631 (Ont. C.A.)

Fulmer v. Peter D. Fulmer Holdings Inc., [1997] O.J. No. 4121

Johnston v. West Fraser Timber Co. (1982), 17 B.L.R. 16 (B.C.S.C.); 19 B.L.R. 193 (B.C.C.A.)

Mathers v. Mathers (1992), 113 N.S.R. (2d) 284, 309 A.P.R. 284 (N.S.S.C.T.D.); (1993) 123 N.S.R. (2d) 14, 340 A.P.R. 14 (N.S.C.A.)

Michalak v. Biotech Electronics Ltd. (1986), 35 B.L.R. 1

Naneff v. Con-Crete Holdings Ltd. (1995), 23 O.R. (3d) 481

O'Conner v. Winchester Oil & Gas Inc. (1986), 69 B.C.L.R. 330, [1986] 2 W.W.R. 737

Oakly v. McDouball (No. 2) (1987), 37 B.L.R. 47

Abraham v. Inter Wide Investments Ltd. (1985), 51 O.R. (2d) 460

Ferguson v. Imax Systems Corp. (1983), 43 O.R. (2d) 128 (Ont. C.A.), leave to appeal to S.C.C. refused 52 N.R. 317n

Gandalman Investments Inc. v. Fogle (1985), 52 O.R. (2d) 614

Trimac Ltd. v. C.I.L. Inc. (1989), 69 Alta. L.R. (2d) 113, [1990] 1 W.W.R. 133

Vedova v. Garden House Inn Ltd. (1985), 29 B.L.R. 236

Xerox Canada Inc. v. Ontario Municipal Employees Retirement Board (1991), 3 B.L.R. (2d) 68

Partnerships (General and Limited)

McCoy v. Canada, 2003 TCC 332

Mathew v. Canada, [2001] T.C.J. No. 491 (T.C.C.)

Personal Goodwill

1860-3043 Quebec Inc. v. Canada, [1995] 1 C.T.C. 2793

A & N Robitaille Inc. v. M.N.R. (1994), 96 C.T.C. 2141

Adair v. M.N.R. (1962), 29 Tax A.B.C. 324, 62 D.T.C. 356

Beaubien v. Campbell, [2003] S.J. No. 301, 33 B.L.R. (3d) 33 (Sask. Q.B.)

Croteau v. M.N.R. (1964), 36 Tax A.B.C. 299, 65 D.T.C. 643

G-H Couture v. M.N.R., 78 D.T.C. 1511

Greither v. Greither (2005), 22 R.F.L. (6th) 10 (B.C.C.A.)

Hawboldt v. Hawboldt, 2007 BCSC 1613

Lecompte v. M.N.R., [1976] C.T.C. 2127, 76 D.T.C. 1104

Losey v. M.N.R., [1957] C.T.C. 146, 57 D.T.C. 1098

Majean Investments Co. v. Canada, [1994] 1 C.T.C. 2578

Marentette v. M.N.R., [1977] C.T.C. 2147, 77 D.T.C. 97

Nail v. Nail (1972), 477 S.W. (2d) 395

Rabow v. M.N.R., 26 Tax A.B.C. 445

Samila v. Samila (1988), 32 B.C.L.R. (2d) 25

Thomas v. M.N.R., 75 D.T.C. 37

Crandall v. M.N.R., [1974] C.T.C. 2289, 74 D.T.C. 1204

Legere v. M.N.R. [1980] C.T.C. 2202, 80 D.T.C. 1171

Young v. M.N.R. (1965), 38 Tax A.B.C. 73, 65 D.T.C. 242

Point in Time

Dominion Metal & Refining Works Ltd. v. M.N.R., [1983] C.T.C. 2386

Lakehouse Enterprises Ltd. v. M.N.R., [1983] C.T.C. 2431

Potential Control

Arctic Geophysical Ltd. v. M.N.R., [1967] C.T.C. 571, 68 D.T.C. 5013

Fritz Werner Ltd. v. M.N.R., [1971] Tax A.B.C. 209, 71 D.T.C. 189

Himley Estates Ltd. and Humble Investments Ltd. v. I.R.C., [1933] 1 K.B. 472, 17 T.C. 367

John Shields & Co. (Perth) Ltd. v. I.R.C., [1950] S.C. 441, 29 T.C. 475

M.F.C.T. v. Sidney Williams (Holdings) Ltd., [1957] 100 C.L.R. 95, 11 A.T.D. 368

Renown Steel & Service Ltd. v. M.N.R., [1969] Tax A.B.C. 678, 69 D.T.C. 497

Rous & Mann Press Ltd. v. M.N.R. (1953), 9 Tax A.B.C. 56, 53 D.T.C. 326

R. v. Ann-Gus Holdings Ltd., 84 D.T.C. 6363 (F.C.A.)

R. v. Lusita Holdings Ltd., 84 D.T.C. 6346

W.P. Leigherly Proprietary Ltd. v. F.C.T., [1957] 100 C.L.R. 66, 11 A.T.D. 359

Prescribed Price

J.J. West Estate v. Minister of Finance (B.C.), [1976] C.T.C. 313

Lomb v. Sugden, [1936] 82 F. 2d 166

Price Adjustment Clause

Guilder News Co. (1963) Ltd. v. M.N.R., [1973] C.T.C. 1, 73 D.T.C. 5048 (F.C.T.D.)

Price Based on Shareholder Agreement

Irwin v. D.W. Coates Enterprises Ltd., [1983] B.C.J. No. 2026, 49 B.C.L.R. 383 (B.C.S.C.); affd [1985] B.C.J. No. 8, [1985] 3 W.W.R. 765 (B.C.C.A.)

Harmer v. McNeely Engineering Consultants Ltd., [1997] O.J. No. 4272, 44 B.L.R. (2d) 254 (Ont. Ct. (Gen. Div.))

Heeg v. Hitech Piping (HTP) Ltd., [2009] Q.J. No. 8968, 68 B.L.R. (4th) 276 (Que. S.C.)

Dashney v. McKinlay, [1996] O.J. No. 2037, 30 B.L.R. (2d) 211 (Ont. Ct. (Gen. Div.))

Property in Control

Farnham v. Fingold, [1973] 2 O.R. 132 (Ont. C.A.)

Jones v. H.F. Ahmanson & Co., [1969] 1 Cal. 3d 93, 460 P. 2d 464 (1969)

Perlman v. Feldman, 219 F. 2d 173, cert. denied 349 U.S. 952 (1955), 154 F. Sup. 436 (1957)

Brant Investments Ltd. v. KeepRite Inc. (1987), 60 O.R. (2d) 737

R.J. Jowsey Mining Co. (Re), [1969] 2 O.R. 549, 6 D.L.R. (3d) 97

Short v. Treasury Commissioners, [1948] A.C. 534, [1948] 2 All E.R. 509

Purchase Price Allocation

Canada v. Demco Management Ltd., [1986] 1 C.T.C. 92

Franciss Enderes and IEM Management Ltd. v. M.N.R. (1980), 80 D.T.C. 1523

J.J. West Estate v. Minister of Finance (B.C.), [1976] C.T.C. 313

Salomon v. Commissioners of Customs and Excise, [1966] 3 W.L.R. 36

Rateable Value

Diligenti v. RWMD Operations Kelowna Ltd. (1977), 4 B.C.L.R. 134

Neonex International Ltd. v. Kolasa (1978), 84 D.L.R. (3d) 446, [1978] 2 W.W.R. 593, 3 B.L.R. 1, [1978] B.C.J. No. 19 (B.C.S.C.)

Whitehorse Copper Mines Ltd. (Re), Hudson Bay Mining and Smelting Co. v. Lueck (1980), 10 B.L.R. 113

Restrictions on Shares

Attorney General for Ireland v. Jameson, [1904] 2 I.R. 644 (upheld on appeal [1905] 2 I.R. 218)

Beament v. M.N.R., [1970] S.C.R. 680

Groupe D' Investissement Savoie, Lavoie Inc. v. M.N.R., [1992] 1 C.T.C. 2355

Connor v. Canada, [1978] C.T.C. 669; affd [1979] C.T.C. 365

I.R.C. v. Crossman, [1937] A.C. 26 at 34 (H.L.); [1936] All E.R. 762 (H.L.)

J.J. West Estate v. Minister of Finance (B.C.), [1976] C.T.C. 313

Salvesen's Trustees v. I.R.C., [1930] S.L.T. 387

Trimac Ltd. v. C.I.L. Inc. (1989), 69 Alta. L.R. (2d) 113, [1990] 1 W.W.R. 133

Shareholder Remedies

Foss v. Harbottle (1843), 2 Hare 461, 67 E.R. 189

Special-Interest Purchaser

Cyprus Anvil Mining Corp. v. Dickson (1982), 20 B.L.R. 21, 40 B.C.L.R. 180; (1986), 8 B.C.L.R. (2d) 145

Littler v. M.N.R., [1976] C.T.C. 379; affd [1978] C.T.C. 235

Glass v. I.R.C., [1915] 52 Sc. L.R. 414

Holt v. I.R.C., [1953] 2 All E.R. 1499

R. v. Hugh Waddell Ltd., [1982] C.T.C. 24

I.R.C. v. Clay, [1914] 3 K.B. 466 (C.A.)

I.R.C. v. Crossman, [1937] A.C. 26 at 34 (H.L.); [1936] All E.R. 762 (H.L.)

Levitt v. M.N.R., [1976] C.T.C. 2307, 76 D.T.C. 1047

Milne v. Canada, [1994] 2 C.T.C. 2190

New Quebec Raglan Mines Ltd. v. Blok-Andersen (1993), 9 B.L.R. (2d) 93

Lynall (Re), [1969] 3 All E.R. 984 at 990 (C.A.)

Second Shirley Rubin Family Trust (Trustee of) v. Revenue Properties Co., [1992] O.J. No. 1028

Untermyer Estate v. Attorney General (B.C.), [1929] S.C.R. 84

Verdun v. Verdun (1994), 9 R.F.L. (4th) 54

Westfair Foods Ltd. v. Watt (1992), 5 B.L.R. (2d) 179

Special-Purpose Software

McCoy v. Canada, 2003 TCC 332

Brown v. Canada (2001), 97-3264(IT)G

CIT Financial Ltd. v. Canada, 2003 D.T.C. 1138 (T.C.C.), 2004 D.T.C. 6573 (F.C.A.)

Mathew v. Canada, [2001] T.C.J. No. 491 (T.C.C.)

Morley v. Canada, 2004 D.T.C. 2604 (T.C.C.)

Sherman v. Canada, 2008 TCC 186; affd 2009 FCA 9

Stock Market Data

Clarke v. Commissioner (1976), 35 T.C.M. 1482

Ivesleigh Holdings Inc. v. M.N.R., 78 D.T.C. 1716

Re Libby, McNeill & Libby, 406 A. 2d 54 (Maine); revd August 16, 1979

Tallichet v. Commissioner (1974), 33 T.C.M. 1133

Stock Market Price and Fair Value/Fair Market Value

Dairy Queen Canada Inc. v. Canada [1995] 2 C.T.C. 2543

Deer Creek Energy Ltd. v. Paulson & Co. (2008), 49 B.L.R. (4th) 1 (Alta. Q.B.)

Henderson Estate v. M.N.R., 75 D.T.C. 5332, 73 D.T.C. 5471

Smeenk v. Dexleigh Corp. (1990), 49 B.L.R. 1

Fraser Inc. v. Aitken (1988), 41 B.L.R. 87

LeVan v. LeVan, 2006 CarswellOnt 7334, 82 O.R. (3d) 1 at 76, 32 R.F.L. (6th) 359, [2007] W.D.F.L. 675, [2007] W.D.F.L. 676, [2007] W.D.F.L. 686, [2007] W.D.F.L. 705, [2007] W.D.F.L. 681, [2007] W.D.F.L. 677, [2007] W.D.F.L. 778, [2007] W.D.F.L. 784, [2007] W.D.F.L. 803, [2007] W.D.F.L. 802, [2007] W.D.F.L. 758, Docket: 03-ST-36181 (Ont. S.C.J., September 28, 2006)

Lough v. Canadian Natural Resources Ltd. (1983), 45 B.C.L.R. 335

Manning v. Harris Steel Group Inc., [1987] 1 W.W.R. 86, [1990] 1 W.W.R. 346 (C.A.)

McClintock v. Canada, 2003 CarswellNat 1160, 2003 TCC 259, 2003 D.T.C. 576, [2003] 3 C.T.C. 2839

Montgomery v. Shell Canada Ltd. (1980), 5 W.W.R. 543, 111 D.L.R. (3d) 116

Morrison v. United Westburne Industries Ltd. (1988), Toronto RE 1926/87 (April 15, 1988)

Neonex International Ltd. v. Kolasa (1978), 84 D.L.R. (3d) 446, [1978] 2 W.W.R. 593, 3 B.L.R. 1, [1978] B.C.J. No. 19 (B.C.S.C.)

New Quebec Raglan Mines Ltd. v. Blok-Andersen (1993), 9 B.L.R. (2d) 93

Nunachiaq Inc. v. Chow (1993), 8 B.L.R. (2d) 109 (B.C.S.C.); affd [1994] B.C.J. No. 608

Domglas Inc. v. Jarislowsky (1980), 13 B.L.R. 135; affd (1982), 138 D.L.R. (3d) 521

Wall & Redekop Corp. (Re) (1974), 50 D.L.R. (3d) 733 (B.C.S.C.)

Silber v. BGR Precious Metals Inc., 1998 CarswellOnt 2994 (Ont. Ct. (Gen. Div.))

Westfair Foods Ltd. v. Watt (1992), 5 B.L.R. (2d) 179

Xerox Canada Inc. v. Ontario Municipal Employees Retirement Board (1991), 3 B.L.R. (2d) 68

Tax and Disposition Costs

85956 Holdings Lt. v. Fayerman Brothers Ltd. (1987), 57 Sask. 141; [1986] 2 W.W.R. 754

Derdall v. Derdall Irrigation Farms Ltd., 2010 SKCA 104, [2010] 11 W.W.R. 607 (September 2, 2010)

F. v. V., [2002] O.J. No. 3900 (Ont. S.C.J.)

Ganson v. Ganson (1996), 66 A.C.W.S. (3d) 706

Goodfield v. Goodfield (1989), 71 O.R. (2d) 457

Heon v. Heon (1989), 22 R.F.L. (3d) 273 (Ont. H.C.J.)

Kelly v. Kelly (1986), 50 R.F.L. (2d) 360

Khoury v. Khoury (1991), 122 N.B.R. (2d) 150, 306 A.P.R. 150 (N.B.Q.B.)

LeVan v. LeVan, 2006 CarswellOnt 7334, 82 O.R. (3d) 1 at 76, 32 R.F.L. (6th) 359, [2007] W.D.F.L. 675, [2007] W.D.F.L. 676, [2007] W.D.F.L. 686, [2007] W.D.F.L. 705, [2007] W.D.F.L. 681, [2007] W.D.F.L. 677, [2007] W.D.F.L. 778, [2007] W.D.F.L. 784, [2007] W.D.F.L. 803, [2007] W.D.F.L. 802, [2007] W.D.F.L. 758, Docket: 03-ST-36181 (Ont. S.C.J., September 28, 2006)

McPherson v. McPherson (1988), 48 D.L.R. (4th) 577

Nixon v. Trace, 2010 BCSC 175 (February 9, 2010)

Sengmueller v. Sengmueller (1994), 17 O.R. (3d) 208 (Ont. C.A.)

Thinly Traded Shares

Domglas Inc. v. Jarislowsky (1980), 13 B.L.R. 135; affd (1982), 138 D.L.R. (3d) 521

Grandison v. NovaGold Resources Inc., [2007] B.C.J. No. 2639, 43 B.L.R. (4th) 251 (B.C.S.C.)

Manning v. Haris Steel Group Inc., [1986] B.C.J. No. 816, 7 B.C.L.R. (2d) 69 (B.C.S.C.)

Neonex International Ltd. v. Kolasa (1978), 84 D.L.R. (3d) 446, [1978] 2 W.W.R. 593, 3 B.L.R. 1, [1978] B.C.J. No. 19 (B.C.S.C.)

Wall & Redekop Corp. (Re), [1974] B.C.J. No. 924, 50 D.L.R. (3d) 733 (B.C.S.C.); affd [1975] B.C.J. No. 1 (B.C.C.A.)

Hudson Bay Mining & Smelting Co. v. Lueck, 1980 CarswellBC 453, 10 B.L.R. 113, Docket: Vancouver No. A782426 (B.C.S.C., June 3, 1980)

Transaction Causing Dissent

Deer Creek Energy Ltd. v. Paulson & Co. (2008), 49 B.L.R. (4th) 1 (Alta. Q.B.)

Fraser Inc. v. Aitken (1988), 41 B.L.R. 87

Anthem Works Ltd. (Re), 2005 BCSC 766

Les Investissements Mont-Soleil Inc. v. National Drug Ltd. (1982), 22 B.L.R. 139

Magna International Inc. (Re) (Ont. S.C.J., August 2010)

Brant Investments Ltd. v. KeepRite Inc. (1987), 60 O.R. (2d) 737

Ripley International Ltd. (Re) (1977), 1 B.L.R. 269

Sterling Centrecorp Inc. (Re) (2007) (Ont. S.C.J.)

Valuation Approach/Methodology

Baniuk v. Carpenter (1990), 1 B.L.R. (2d) 300

Brant Investments Ltd. v. KeepRite Inc. (1987), 60 O.R. (2d) 737

British Columbia v. MacMillan Bloedel Ltd. (1995), 127 D.L.R. (4th) 629

Cholakis v. Cholakis, 2010 MBQB 116, 72 B.L.R. (4th) 120 (May 7, 2010)

Cyprus Anvil Mining Corp. v. Dickson (1982), 20 B.L.R. 21, 40 B.C.L.R. 180; (1986), 8 B.C.L.R. (2d) 145

Smeenk v. Dexleigh Corp. (1990), 49 B.L.R. 1

Stanfield v. M.N.R., 79 D.T.C. 128

Gilvesy Enterprises Inc. v. Canada, [1997] 1 C.T.C. 2410

Glenex Industries Inc. v. Canada, [1997] 3 C.T.C. 2217

Gregoric v. Gregoric (1990), 4 O.R. (3d) 588

Taylor Estate v. M.N.R., [1990] 2 C.T.C. 2304

Jakobson v. Aggasiz Enterprises Ltd. (1987), 49 Man. R. (2d) 270

Kelvin Energy Ltd. v. Bahan (1987), 52 Alta. L.R. (2d) 71

Khoury v. Khoury (1991), 122 N.B.R. (2d) 150, 306 A.P.R. 150 (N.B.Q.B.)

Lessany v. Lessany (1988), 17 R.F.L. (3d) 433

LoCicero v. BACM Industries Ltd. (1984), 31 Man. R. (2d) 208; (1986) 25 D.L.R. (4th) 269, 38 Man. R. (2d) 134 (Man. C.A.), [1988] 1 S.C.R. 399, [1988] 4 W.W.R. 671, 49 D.L.R. (4th) 159

Manning v. Harris Steel Group Inc., [1987] 1 W.W.R. 86, [1990] 1 W.W.R. 346 (C.A.)

Mica Management Centre Inc. v. Lockett (1986), 37 B.L.R. 209

Moase Produce Ltd. v. Royal Bank of Canada (1987), 64 C.B.R. (N.S.) 191

Muskoka & Parry Sound Telephone Co. v. Ontario Telephone Development Corp. (1984), 32 L.C.R. 154 (O.M.B.); (1985) 32 L.C.R. 238 (O.M.B.)

Nunachiaq Inc. v. Chow (1993), 8 B.L.R. (2d) 109 (B.C.S.C.); affd [1994] B.C.J. No. 608

Pocklington Foods Inc. v. Alberta (Provincial Treasurer), [1998] A.J. No. 364

Domglas Inc. v. Jarislowsky (1980), 13 B.L.R. 135; affd (1982), 138 D.L.R. (3d) 521

S.G. & S. Investments (1972) Ltd. v. Golden Boy Foods Inc. (1991), 3 B.L.R. (2d) 80

R. v. Shepp, 1999 Carswell Nat 72

Samila v. Samila (1988), 32 B.C.L.R. (2d) 25

R. v. Stan Steevs & Sons Ltd., [1996] 1 C.T.C. 2818

Starkman v. Starkman (1990), 75 O.R. (2d) 19

Westfair Foods Ltd. v. Watt (1992), 5 B.L.R. (2d) 179

Value

Caratun v. Caratun (1992), 42 R.F.L. (3d) 113

Dibbley v. Dibbley (1986), 5 R.F.L. (3d) 381

Heon v. Heon (1989), 22 R.F.L. (3d) 273 (Ont. H.C.J.)

Jackh v. Jackh, 22 B.C.L.R. 182 (B.C.S.C.)

Menage v. Hedges (1987), 8 R.F.L. (3d) 225

Montague v. Montague (1992), 37 A.C.W.S. (3d) 520 (Ont. Ct. (Gen. Div.)); affd (1996), 23 R.F.L. (4th) 62 (Ont. C.A.)

Pocklington Foods Inc. v. Alberta (Provincial Treasurer), [1998] A.J. No. 364

Rawluk v. Rawluk (1986) 55 O.R. (2d) 704, 3 R.F.L. (3d) 113 (Ont. H.C.J.); affd 10 R.F.L. (3d) 113 (Ont. C.A.); (S.C.C., January 25, 1990)

Corless v. Corless (1987), 58 O.R. (2d) 19

Sartori v. Sartori (1993), 13 O.R. (3d) 710

Value Based on Prospects

Cyprus Anvil Mining Corp. v. Dickson (1982), 20 B.L.R. 21, 40 B.C.L.R. 180; (1986), 8 B.C.L.R. (2d) 145

Value to Owner

Brinkos v. Brinkos (1986), 4 R.F.L. (3d) 381; revd (1989) 20 R.F.L. (3d) 445 (Ont. C.A.)

LoCicero v. BACM Industries Ltd. (1984), 31 Man. R. (2d) 208; (1986) 25 D.L.R. (4th) 269, 38 Man. R. (2d) 134 (Man. C.A.), [1988] 1 S.C.R. 399, [1988] 4 W.W.R. 671, 49 D.L.R. (4th) 159

Montague v. Montague (1992), 37 A.C.W.S. (3d) 520 (Ont. Ct. (Gen. Div.)); affd (1996), 23 R.F.L. (4th) 62 (Ont. C.A.)

Wind-Up – Court Ordered

Mason v. Intercity Properties Ltd. (1987), 59 O.R. (2d) 631 (Ont. C.A.)

Index

A

D

E

F

G

H

I

L

M

N

Q

R

T

U

V